Learning the Language of

ADDICTION
COUNSELING

Learning the Language of
ADDICTION COUNSELING

Fourth Edition

GERI MILLER

WILEY

Library of Congress Cataloging-in-Publication Data:

Miller, Geraldine A., 1955–
  Learning the language of addiction counseling/Geri Miller. — Fourth edition.
    pages cm
  Includes bibliographical references and index.
  ISBN 978-1-118-72177-3 (pbk.: acid-free paper); ISBN 978-1-118-72169-8 (ebk);
  ISBN 978-1-118- 72145-2 (ebk)
  1. Drug abuse counseling. 2. Substance abuse—Patients—Counseling of. 3. Drug addicts—Counseling of.
I. Title.
  RC564.M536 2014
  362.29'186—dc23

                                                                                                      2014007138

This book is dedicated to:

Ron Hood, my husband and friend, who is there through it all. Gale, Abby, and Jason Miller; and Tom, Laura, Natalie, and Kate Prow—my family.

The women, my "sisters," who were with me from the beginning: Pat Mitchell Anderson, Kathleen Kasprick, and Judy Retterath; and Betty Gridley and Angela Wagner, who joined my journey along the way.

The addicted clients and their loved ones whom I had the honor of counseling and the counselors who remain committed to this important work.

CONTENTS

PREFACE

Learning the Language of Addiction Counseling emerged from a desire to summarize the clinical, theoretical, and research work in the addiction counseling field from a practitioner's point of view. The fourth edition of this book involves substantial changes that need to be highlighted at the onset. First, in order to present my views of addiction counseling that have evolved after working in the addiction counseling field for more than 30 years, teaching undergraduate and graduate students in addiction counseling for more than 20 years, and training mental health and addiction professionals for more than 20 years, I have updated the "Personal Reflections" section at the beginning of each chapter.

Second, all of the chapters have been updated, with some having significant revisions, including sections with additional components to reflect changes in the field and sections being moved to more appropriate chapters. Third, additional case studies and exercises and suggested readings/resources/websites sections have been expanded and updated at the end of each chapter.

Finally, for instructors, instructor resources have been updated, including PowerPoint slides and test bank questions, for each revised chapter. Additionally, six short video clips have been included to assist the reader in understanding some of the concepts presented in the text. These clips include: Overall Philosophy, General Counseling Suggestions (Chapter 5), Relapse Prevention (Chapter 7), Self-Help Groups (Chapter 8), and Self-Care (Chapter 11; 2 video clips-1 has audio included and 1 is a silent video demonstration). These changes have been made because counselors and educators are increasingly being asked to "hit the ground running" when they begin their work. Syllabi for classes I have taught in the addictions area are included to also assist counselors and educators. It is hoped that this book will assist counselors and educators in more readily being able to do their work.

I have been blessed in my life to have been trained by numerous addiction counseling professionals who are deeply committed to the field, to helping people who are caught in a destructive cycle of addiction and who face horrific odds in life. Throughout my years of work in the addictions field, I have watched these professionals respect and care for individuals who have experienced, at a piercing level, a lack of respect and love both within themselves and from others. The compassion of these professionals—for the suffering of both addicts and their loved ones and their hope for the healing of addiction recovery for all addicts and their loved ones—led me to this field and has kept me in it all of these years.

This book provides a summary of addiction counseling based on practical application of both theory and research. It serves as a reference that can be used by two groups: (1) undergraduate and graduate students who are training to be direct service workers with addicted individuals and (2) clinicians who are new to the field of addiction counseling or who would like to review the state of the art of addiction counseling.

Although the book discusses techniques and approaches that are grounded in research, this book is focused on the practitioner. Throughout the text, interactive exercises, such as case studies and discussion exercises, are provided to assist the reader in applying the information and to assist the teacher in integrating the material into the classroom discussion. Because of the different approaches in the addictions field, there are often controversies regarding theory and practice. This book does not reconcile these differences, but it does fuse theoretical and practical concerns into a pragmatic counseling framework, resulting in a helpful manual for counselors who work with addicts. *Learning the Language of Addiction Counseling* is a text that a practitioner can turn to for fundamental, practical, and clinical guidelines.

Brief Summaries of Each Chapter in the Book

Chapter 1, "Introduction," is a brief overview of addiction counseling that examines past and current influences on addiction counseling and models used to explain addiction.

Chapter 2, "Theories of Counseling Applied to Addiction Treatment," explores theories of counseling as they apply to counseling addicted individuals.

Chapter 3, "Assessment and Diagnosis of Addiction," examines the assessment process with clients. Interviews, behavioral observations, physiological instruments, and psychometric instruments are discussed. Additional sections on diagnosis and the stages-of-change model are also presented. *DSM-5* criteria are referenced in this chapter.

Chapter 4, "Co-Occurring Disorders and Behavioral Addictions," provides an overview of co-occurring disorders with general assessment and treatment suggestions as well as an overview on behavioral addictions. Again, *DSM-5* criteria are referenced.

Chapter 5, "The Core Treatment Process for Addictions," provides an overview of four specific forms of addiction counseling: crisis intervention, individual, group, and family— with an initial review of the philosophies of harm reduction and recovery movement that can impact these treatment processes.

Chapter 6, "Treatment-Related Issues and Counseling Approaches," explores issues that may arise in relation to addiction counseling: sexual issues, HIV/AIDS, intimate partner violence, and homelessness. Recommendations for counseling in these related areas are provided. Specific counseling approaches, dialectical behavior therapy (DBT), Seeking Safety, and grief counseling, which may be used in addressing these issues are discussed in this chapter. Also, because many clients have legal issues, there is a special section on drug court.

Chapter 7, "Relapse Prevention," provides an overview of relapse prevention issues. Counselor approaches, models, and techniques are explored. Dual diagnosis issues are also discussed.

Chapter 8, "Self-Help Groups," addresses the national, abstinence-based self-help groups in the United States in terms of their historical development, basic concepts, use in counseling, and strengths and limitations. Information is also provided on how to assist clients in finding an appropriate group and sponsor/mentor and special issues related to self-help groups.

Chapter 9, "Elaboration on Specific Therapies and Techniques Relevant to Addiction Counseling," explores one core concept of counseling (client resilience), four therapy approaches and techniques (positive psychology, the stages-of-change model, motivational interviewing, and brief therapy) as well as evidence-based practices.

Chapter 10, "Culturally Sensitive Addiction Counseling," examines issues that have an impact on addiction counseling. This chapter provides an overall perspective on multicultural counseling and techniques. In addition, it presents assessment, treatment, and aftercare issues as they relate to gender, ethnicity, sexual orientation, disability, and age (adolescents, the elderly).

Chapter 11, "Chronic Pain Assessment and Treatment," discusses the overlapping areas of substance abuse and pain management with suggestions of specific approaches and techniques that can be used to explore chronic pain in the substance-abusing client.

Chapter 12, "Incorporating Spirituality into Addiction Counseling," explores four areas related to the incorporation of spiritual perspectives in the addiction counseling field: the history; barriers and bridges; spiritual identity development; and counseling resources and techniques.

Chapter 13, "Personal and Professional Development of the Counselor," opens with a brief discussion of some concerns of technology's impact on counseling and suggestions on how to address these concerns. It then explores general topic areas that impact the personal and professional development of the counselor (ethical issues, testifying in court, working in difficult systems, working with addicts, and self-care).

Chapter 14, "Obtaining Addiction Professional Credentials," presents the different types of credentials, credentialing process stages, and helpful strategics to assist the reader in the credentialing process.

ACKNOWLEDGMENTS

I cannot name all of the excellent professional role models I have encountered in the field, but I do acknowledge every one of you. You know who you are. You spent time explaining basic concepts of working in this field to me, you challenged me to be the best therapist, researcher, teacher, and person I could be, and you never settled for less in me or gave up on me. Thank you from the core of my being.

I also gratefully acknowledge the addicted clients I have worked with and their loved ones, who taught me through their amazing life stories about the destructive nature of addiction and the incredible capacity of the human spirit to survive and change. I thank these many people for showing me how to work in this field and how to live in this world. The courage and integrity of watching individuals struggle to break out of the pain of the addictive cycle is a powerful experience. To these people, I simply say, thank you.

I also want to thank the many addiction professionals and graduate and undergraduate students I have trained over the years. You have taught me so much about the addictions field and have helped encourage my passion and commitment to this important work through your passion and commitment to it. Such wonderful times we have had together.

Additionally, I want to thank the people who believed I could write such a book and supported me on the journey. Marquita Flemming, my editor at John Wiley & Sons, supported and assisted me throughout the writing of the book. She showered me with enthusiasm and encouragement in the writing of this book that stayed me on the discouraging days; she believed in me and the importance of this book. I also want to acknowledge the other Wiley employees who worked so hard with me on this book: Judi Knott and Heather Dunphy in marketing, Linda Indig as production editor, and Sherry Wasserman as editorial program coordinator. Thank you also to the reviewers obtained by Wiley—you enhanced the quality of this book with your careful, thorough, thoughtful comments and suggestions.

George Dennis, my computer teacher, helped me with my computer struggles, spending hours with me patiently wading through the technological advances that have occurred since the third edition was published and creatively developing with me the diagrams and figures throughout this book. George is one of the kindest, smartest, most patient individuals I have ever known.

The University of North Carolina–Charlotte counseling department doctoral students— Regina Moro, Bailey MacLeod, Astra Czerny, and Leigh Zick Dongre—worked hard, efficiently, and reliably on literature reviews to make sure the book was solidly anchored in current research and resources. Kate Hoffman also worked carefully and thoroughly on various chapters to make sure that information was accurate and current.

Kyndy Boyle, Craig Cashwell, Danny Graves, Bruce Kaplan, Dale Kirkley, Paul Nagy, Kathy Norins, and Laura Veach, all busy professionals in the addictions/helping professionals fields, took time to comment carefully and thoroughly on specific sections of the manuscript based on their expertise in the addictions field or in areas related to the addictions field; such kindness and generosity each of you showed me. A special acknowledgment goes to Dr. Betty Gridley, my statistics teacher and mentor, who assisted in the development of test questions for the second time during her retirement.

To Charles Duke, Linda Foulsham, Alice Krueger, Laurie Percival Oates, Joyce Reese and her wonderful family, Rod and Marilou Steinmetz, who hold special places in my heart for their kindness, compassion, and amazing ability to create a safe space for others in the world, including me, for providing support through the writing of this book.

To my buddies who have left this world: Ken Schmidt and Judy Retterath. To Ken, who left during the third edition: "I still miss you, and I thank you for believing in me and teaching me how to work in a 'man's world.'" To Judy, who left in 2013, a pioneer in the addictions field who cared for and helped innumerable addicted people and their families: "I thank you, I love you, and I will miss you until I too leave this world." To Howie Meier, who worked with me as a tech in "Edna's detox" with Judy as our nursing supervisor: "I couldn't have done it without you."

I also thank "my" Boone, North Carolina coffee shops that provided me with support (and coffee) to help me write: Conrad's Coffee Company (Conrad, Jody, Chris (Sir Christopher Poe), Travis, Josh, and Tyler Poe) and Higher Ground Coffee Shoppe (Matt and Gloria Scott). I also appreciate the support from my Saturday-morning coffee-drinking buddies, who held me steadfast on this journey. I thank each of you.

To the employees of the Paul H. Broyhill Wellness Center—Jodi Cash (director), Paul Moore (assistant director), Michael Darling (personal trainer and friend), Amy Genberg and Klaire Roberson (muses), and all the rest of my buddies (including those early morning women's locker room buddies—Glenna Hollar, Jeanne Keasey, and Peri Moretz), who encouraged and supported me every day with their friendship and laughter—"Thank you." A special thank you to these individuals who helped create the videos that accompany this book: Michael Darling (senior audiovisual consultant); Steven Peterson (assistant audiovisual consultant); George Dennis (computer consultant); Dr. Susan Gilbert (makeup consultant/set decorator); Samantha Mahoney (stage manager); and Martin Hubner (muse); with special thanks to Jodi Cash and Ron Hood—it was great fun being a part of a modern-day Cinderella story with you.

Finally, to Ron Hood, my husband and my best friend, who demonstrated his love and support by painstakingly reading every word written in every draft of this book and previous editions: "Thank you, Ron, for being with me on this life path. I love you. You're the best buddy ever." Also, a thank-you to our Appalachian Mountain coon dog, Maggie, a force of nature that keeps Ron and me young in spirit through her love for us.

CHAPTER 1

INTRODUCTION

PERSONAL REFLECTIONS

As we approach addiction counseling, it is important, as clinicians, that we have as clear an understanding as possible of who we are both personally and professionally in relation to addiction. We need to be brave enough to examine our own experiences with addictive tendencies within ourselves and our loved ones as well as our professional experiences with addicts. These experiences color and shape our work with our addicted clients. If we engage in a thorough self-exploration, we can enter encounters with addicts using a clear, balanced approach and avoid being thrown off balance by the intense force of addiction as it has expressed and expresses itself in our client's life.

I also need to comment on the terminology I have chosen to use throughout the text to describe those clients who struggle with addiction. I use the term *addicts* or *addicted clients* even though some readers may prefer the terms *person with addiction* or *people with substance use disorders* in order to emphasize the "personhood" of the client. I have chosen these terms because, in my experience of addiction counseling, experienced therapists tend to use the terms I have chosen as well as the clients. By no means is the term meant to be disrespectful to the client. For example, in clinical meetings, I always insist that the person's name be used before their disorder is discussed because, as I tell my students, "They were a person before they developed the disorder and their name is important. They are not their disorder." My hope is that I do not offend the reader with my choice of terminology, but rather, I encourage the reader to choose a term to discuss the addicted client that they believe is most respectful to their population. I believe that what is important, so critical, so necessary, is that we find terminology and an approach that powerfully invites our clients and their loved ones to heal from the destructive force of addiction.

OBJECTIVES

1. To learn the main models of addiction counseling.
2. To understand the history of three influences on addiction counseling.
3. To explore how one's own models of addiction and understanding of influences impact the view of the addicted client, the cause of addiction, and treatment approaches.

Current statistics support the concern for alcohol and drug use in America. The 2011 National Survey on Drug Use and Health (Substance Abuse and Mental Health Services Administration [SAMHSA]) found that about 133.4 million Americans (51.8% of the total population over age 12) drank alcohol, with 22.6% (one quarter; 58.3 million people) having a binge drinking experience at least once in the previous month and 6.2% reporting being heavy drinkers (15.9 million). The survey also found that approximately 22.5 million Americans (8.7% of the total population over age 12) had used an illicit drug during the month before being interviewed.

Marijuana was the most common illicit drug used. One area of alarming concern is prescription painkiller medication. The number and percentage of persons aged 12 or older, who were current nonmedical users of pain relievers in 2011, was 4.5 million or 1.7%. The Centers for Disease Control and Prevention (2013) reported that in 2010, the amount of prescribed painkiller medication could result in every American being medicated through an entire day for one month; while they were prescribed for medical reasons, they were misused or abused by others. Overdoses of the prescription painkillers (opioid or narcotic) have tripled in the past 20 years in the United States (SAMSHA, 2010, 2011). Their abuse/misuse has doubled in emergency room visits (SAMSHA, 2010) and teens and adults use them to experience a "high" or use them for other nonmedical reasons (SAMSHA, 2011).

These statistics underscore the importance of understanding the dynamics of alcohol and drug abuse and addiction. The high number of individuals using alcohol and drugs in the United States also supports the need for counselors to understand the dynamics of addiction: It is highly likely that a counselor will work with individuals who are abusing alcohol or drugs in any counseling setting. Understanding the dynamics of addiction can help the mental health professional more effectively meet the needs of the client.

Working with the substance-abusing population, however, can be difficult. Mental health workers, both historically and currently, have not always liked working with alcoholics and addicts for at least two reasons: (1) the difficulty in treating them because of factors such as relapses, poor impulse control, emotional reactivity, and/or lying to protect their addiction; and (2) the lack of knowledge (techniques) on how best to treat them.

However, openness to treating addicts grew as information on how to treat addicts emerged and as additional funding for treatment became available. For example, because addicts commonly deny the consequences of their usage to themselves and others (Levinthal, 1996), it became

easier for counselors to deal with denial when the technique of intervention was introduced (Fields, 1995).

Counselors also have potential issues with countertransference. Many helping professionals have negative personal as well as professional experiences working with addicted individuals. This may cause them to avoid or hesitate to work with this population. When working with addicts, they may be caught in familiar patterns of enabling or judging the addicted individual and their loved ones based on their own personal or professional experiences. Also, professionals can have concern they are being conned by addicts to enable their addiction and, as a result, may approach the addicted person in a manner that invites anger and manipulation from the client (Compton, 1999).

Changes in public policy also affected the work of counselors. In 1970, the National Institute on Alcohol Abuse and Alcoholism (NIAAA) was established to provide funding for alcoholism treatment and research, and in the 1970s, insurance companies began to reimburse agencies for providing addiction treatment (O'Dwyer, 1993). The Hughes Act (PL 91-616) established the NIAAA, funded states that established alcoholism divisions, and started alcohol treatment programs for federal employees (Fisher & Harrison, 1997). This policy change expanded the field of addiction counseling. As a result, states started to create credentialing and licensing bodies to ensure quality addiction counseling (O'Dwyer, 1993); being a recovering addict no longer meant immediate entry into the addiction counseling field. Instead, addiction professionals needed to document a combination of credentials regarding both counseling experience and training. Up to the present day, different mental health professional groups have increasingly developed certification and licensure processes for addiction counselors. A general approach to certification and licensure is presented in Chapter 14.

This general expansion of the addiction field (effective treatment, research, certification/licensure) now allows for many routes of entry into addiction counseling. A professional may enter the field initially through research, a certification/licensure process, or additionally through a grass-roots network experience of their own addiction recovery. As a result of various starting points of interest and involvement, there are numerous disagreements in the field of addictions on applicable models and effective treatment approaches. For example, some addiction experts emphasize the strengths of the disease model of addiction and Alcoholics Anonymous (AA; Gragg, 1991), whereas other experts point out the weaknesses of the disease model and AA (G. A. Marlatt, 1985b). The influences on and models of addiction counseling are explored in the remainder of this chapter.

This chapter is intended to set the tone for the entire book and is divided into two sections. In the first section of this chapter, three addiction counseling influences that have and continue to shape the addiction counseling field are explored. These are the disease model of treatment, addiction research, and managed care. This exploration is meant to expose the reader to the different forces that have shaped and continue to shape the field of addiction counseling.

The second section presents a view of models used in understanding addiction; these models shape the view of the alcoholic, the cause of addiction, and the focus of treatment. The model is like the foundation of the house, the theory (theories) makes up the structure of the house, and the different rooms in the house are the treatment intervention techniques.

ADDICTION COUNSELING INFLUENCES

Currently, there are at least three main influences in addiction counseling:

1. The traditional addiction counseling *disease model approach* that asks: Is this approach healing for the addict within the scope of the disease model of addiction?

2. The *addiction research approach* that presents counselors with the question: Which addiction counseling approaches are supported in research findings?

3. The *managed care approach* that confronts counselors with the question: What counseling approaches provide the greatest benefit for the least cost?

Each of these influences has an important impact on addiction counseling and because of their different orientations, there may be confusing messages sent to addiction counselors. For example, disease model counselors may advocate use of the term *codependency* for the partners and family members of addicts, but the research community may respond by stating that there is not enough research to warrant the use of such a diagnostic term, and the managed care organizations may not be willing to pay for codependency treatment because of the disagreement among professionals. To facilitate working within these influences, it is important to understand the historical influences of the disease model of addiction treatment, addiction research, and managed care. Such understanding can enhance the treatment strategies of the counselor. Note that the section on managed care is longer due to the stressful impact of this influence on the addiction counselor and its potentially negative impact on the client.

Disease Model Approach

Influence on Counseling: Is this approach healing for the addict within the scope of the disease model of addiction?

The addiction counseling field has two main root systems: a grassroots addiction recovery network and a research community base. Lay therapy with this population began in 1913, when Courtenay Baylor was hired by the clinic of Boston's Emmanual Church (that began in 1906) after receiving treatment there. Many lay counselors became sober before AA or without affiliation with it once it emerged in 1935 (W. L. White, 1999). AA looked at alcoholics as having an allergy to alcohol, which results in a craving and a loss of control (AA, 1939). Other than Thomas Trotter and Benjamin Rush—who, at the end of the 18th century, viewed alcoholism as a disease—alcoholism was typically viewed as a moral weakness (O'Dwyer, 1993). AA's view of alcoholism as an allergic reaction helped shift alcoholism from a moral problem to a physical or medical problem: The alcoholic was no longer blamed for developing the addiction (G. A. Marlatt, 1985b).

The AA view of alcoholism as an allergic reaction affected treatment in a number of ways. First, defining addiction as a physical reaction (allergy, craving) allowed the addicted individual to feel less like a "bad person" and more like a "sick person," which preserved or restored self-esteem and self-respect. Second, viewing addicts as having an allergic reaction to mood-altering substances provided a simple, straightforward definition of their struggle that most people can readily grasp. Third, this grassroots model encouraged the use of self-help groups, thereby helping addicts develop a sense of community.

W. L. White (1999) describes the evolution of the professional addiction counselor role. With the birth of AA, members of AA began to be employed at treatment facilities. In the 1940s, boundaries between AA members and employers were clarified. The Minnesota model of treatment emerged from three programs in Minnesota that operated with an AA philosophy (Pioneer House established in 1948; Hazelden established in 1949; Willmar State Hospital established in 1950). In 1954, the Minnesota Civil Service Commission provided a title, Counselor on Alcoholism, that created a professional role for the addiction counselor.

Addiction Research Approach

Influence on Counseling: Which addiction counseling approaches are supported in research findings?

While the self-help group movement was growing, so was the research on addiction. About the same time as AA's development, the federal government began two drug treatment programs for prisoners, which facilitated research opportunities on addictions (O'Dwyer, 1993). Through his alcoholism research and the creation of the Yale School of Alcohol Studies in 1942, Jellinek developed the disease model of alcoholism (Bowman & Jellinek, 1941; Gragg, 1995; Jellinek, 1960). The disease model of alcoholism fit well with AA's model of an allergy, and a significant bridge developed between the self-help group movement and the research community. In 1956, the American Medical Association (AMA) agreed that alcoholism was a disease (G. A. Marlatt, 1985b). Through the development of the disease model of alcoholism, both the self-help group movement and the research community guided mental health professionals in their work with addicts (Gragg, 1995).

In a manner similar to AA's view of addiction as an allergy, the disease model of addiction had an impact on treatment. The addict's self-esteem and respect is preserved or restored, because the problem is framed as physically, not morally, based. Also, the disease model provided information about the stages of the disease's development, thereby enhancing the diagnostic process. Finally, the model provided counselors with a framework and terminology to provide clients with information about the current and eventual progression of the disease.

Managed Care Approach

Influence on Counseling: What counseling approaches provide the greatest benefit for the least cost?

Austad and Berman (1991) describe the history of managed care development in the United States. Managed care systems came with two emphases: to provide quality care and to reduce costs. HMOs began in the 1900s as alternative forms of health care for poor people, laborers, and farmers who might be obliterated financially by intense, sudden medical costs. Initially, HMOs were opposed by medical professionals; however, acceptability for the concept of "prepaid care" (health care is provided by specific individuals or groups for a specific fee predetermined in a contract) grew by the 1970s, as evidenced in the passing of the 1973 HMO Act, which decreased legal restrictions on these organizations and provided loans and grants. In terms of mental health services, this same 1973 act required HMOs to provide mental health services if they wanted federal assistance. In the 1980s, less money, growing costs, and increased counseling demands by consumers resulted in an interest in more efficient and less costly counseling.

Although significant concerns abound in the addiction counseling field about this third influence, the managed care orientation is currently fused with service delivery. Whether one works at an agency or in a private practice, each treatment funding source increasingly asks for monitoring throughout treatment and has its own standards regarding treatment limits, accountability, audits, and reviews. Such momentous accountability is frustrating and overwhelming for addiction counselors. Also, there may be additional stress due to a behavioral focus, a sense of having to "do more with less" (G. Miller, 2001), and generally feeling dehumanized throughout the process (Sachs, 1996). Although counselors may experience negative reactions to the treatment control of managed care, they have no choice but to work with the economic realities of the managed care philosophy (Hood & Miller, 1997).

The logic of managed care is to make sure services provided are necessary and that monies are used thoughtfully (Kinney, 2003). However, Margolis and Zweben (1998) point out that research over the past 30 years shows that people improve the longer they are in treatment, yet managed care plans emphasize less intense and shorter treatment duration (they may not cover individual sessions or focus on outpatient treatment). Also, managed care plans may measure

successful outcomes by "no immediate problems or complaints," which is a different treatment success measure than that used by an addiction counseling professional. Van Wormer and Davis (2008) state that managed care is more of a management of costs than care and has significantly limited substance abuse treatment in terms of type of treatments, shorter length of outpatient treatment, and emphasis on medication rather than individual therapy.

Because counselors simply have less time to work with clients and need to practice under managed care directions (Whittinghill, Whittinghill, & Loesch, 2000), this reality raises concerns in areas such as confidentiality, reimbursement, and treatment needs that can impact the relationship between the counselor and the client (Hood & Miller, 1997). The counselor working in the area of addictions needs to find a balance between addressing the financial realities of managed care with the ethical commitment to client welfare.

The responsibility of ethics falls to the counselor. The SAMHSA (1998b) makes five recommendations:

1. Be aware of a commitment to both client and society.

2. Use the most effective and cost-effective treatment.

3. Promote the greatest good for the greatest number.

4. Use resources carefully.

5. Advocate for clients in terms of benefits in their best interest with the managed care company or through professional associations, noting that such advocacy involves a risk.

With regard to living within the realistic restraints of managed care, the counselor in this situation may feel like a worker at a fast-food franchise: Every burger gets the same ingredients no matter what. A three-pronged approach of self-care, professional organization involvement, and a compassionate, collaborative approach toward managed care providers can truly enhance the counselor's practice and client welfare. First, in terms of *self-care*, the counselor needs people or places to vent the frustration in working with such organizations so that the client does not hear such negative views from the therapist or experience negative consequences about reimbursement as a result of the conflict between the counselor and the managed care representative. Second, the counselor can become involved in state and national *professional groups* that advocate against the negative impact of managed health care (Pipal, 1995). Third, the counselor can use a *compassionate approach* with the managed care professional: Attempt to understand that individual's role and responsibilities with regard to providing services to the client in order to encourage collaboration to provide for the client's best interests (Hood & Miller, 1997). The practice of self-care, involvement in professional organizations, and a compassionate approach to managed care personnel can help the counselor decide what can and cannot be done to help each client. Providing clients with such information in a professional manner can be a powerful role model for clients on dealing with life's realities: do what we can and let go of the rest.

This text's response to the increasing emphasis of cost containment where time-limited interventions are preferred over long-term counseling is: Chapter 7 focuses on relapse prevention, Chapter 8 focuses on self-help groups that are free and community-based, and Chapter 9 focuses on therapy approaches that may be a good match to this orientation. (See Case Study 1.1.)

MODELS OF ADDICTION

As stated in the personal reflections section, the model of addiction can have a strong influence on the counselor's approach to addiction counseling in terms of view of the addict, cause of addiction, and treatment—it can be considered the foundation of the counseling. These models have changed and expanded over time; however, each currently exists in various counseling contexts. Some models may be more popular in one geographical area, or one counselor training approach, etc. than another. A counselor working with addicted individuals should find and become familiar with a model he or she is comfortable using for the assessment and treatment process. The models are the underpinnings of the views and policies of the counselor's employer, the client's funding organization, and the state's addiction credentialing and licensing board and legislature, to name a few, and the models indirectly or directly impact the counselor's employment, the client's treatment, and the counselor's liability, especially in court testimony.

Models, as stated in the personal reflections section of this chapter, are different than theories. A historical four-part framework (moral, psychological, sociocultural, and medical), developed by McHugh, Beckman, and Frieze (1979) is presented here with the biopsychosocial model added because of its widespread acceptance in the field for its incorporation of different models. Although each of the five models includes a view of alcoholism, cause of alcoholism, and form of treatment, each one

CASE STUDY 1.1

You are an experienced counselor with a specialty in addictions counseling. You are approached by a counselor in your agency—who is new to addiction counseling—for advice on working with the managed care aspects of your organization. What suggestions would you make to this counselor to enhance his or her survival in the managed care world?

emphasizes different addiction components. Four components are (Leigh, 1985):

1. *Cultural factors*, which influence how a person decides to take a drug, attitudes toward taking the drug, the practices of a group/subculture, and the drug's availability.

2. *Environmental factors*, which include conditioning and reinforcement principles (drugs are taken to experience pleasure and reduce discomfort), learning factors (modeling, imitation, identification, etc.), and life events.

3. *Interpersonal factors*, which include social influences (lifestyle choice, peer pressure, expectations of drug use, etc.) and family factors (system maintenance, genetic influences, etc.).

4. *Intrapersonal factors*, which include human development, personality, affect/cognition, and sex differences.

The models are summarized in Table 1.1. Those aspects of models that are usable in addiction treatment are noted both in the table and at the end of the section describing that model.

Moral Model

The moral model views the alcoholic as a degenerate and sees alcoholism as a moral weakness (M. Keller, 1976). Punishment is preferred over treatment, because a cure is not envisioned (McHugh et al., 1979).

Psychological Models

There are three main psychological models: psychodynamic, personality trait, and behavior learning. Although each views the specific cause of alcoholism differently, they all share a similar outlook: The causal factors must be changed in order for treatment to be effective.

The psychodynamic model focuses on the personal pathology of alcoholics. The goal in treatment is to uncover the unconscious conflicts. Because the conflicts are seen as fairly unchanging, treatment is not viewed as very effective. An example of such a conflict is parental rejection that results in dependency needs that cannot be met in reality (Zimberg, 1985).

The focus in the personality trait model is on changing the personality traits of the alcoholic (e.g., treating high anxiety) (Barry, 1974).

Table 1.1 Theoretical Models

Model	View of Alcoholic/ Addict	Cause of Addiction	Treatment
Moral	Degenerate	Moral weakness	Punishment (ineffective)
Psychological/ psychodynamic	Personal pathology	Unconscious conflicts	Conflicts do not change (ineffective)
Psychological/ personality trait	Personality trait problems	Personality traits	Personality traits do not change much (ineffective)
Psychological/ behavior learning	Learning problem	Alcohol/drug and environmental reinforcers of usage	Change reinforcers
Sociocultural	Situation problem	Social forces and context	Change environmental context
Medical/disease	Patient/client	Physiological dysfunction/loss of control, progressive	No specific treatment/treat body, mind, spirit
Biopsychosocial	Client and environment factors	Biological/psychological/social factors (interacting)	Treat interacting factors (individualized)

However, treatment is not very effective because of the stability of personality traits (McHugh et al., 1979). Although the personality of an addicted person has been examined, a clear or firm definition of such a personality does not exist (DiClemente, 2003).

The behavior-learning model emphasizes the changing of reinforcements, because alcohol is reinforcing for alcoholics. For instance, a change in reinforcers may occur by changing environments (J. Wallace, 1985). This model is the most treatment-friendly of the three psychological models because reinforcers can be readily changed. The counselor can develop a plan with the client that examines how the client is specifically reinforced by abusing alcohol/drugs. For example, if a client is psychologically addicted to marijuana because it reduces stress, the counselor can use this information to help the client develop a treatment and recovery maintenance plan that includes relaxation coping skills.

Sociocultural Models

The sociocultural model emphasizes social forces and contexts that give birth to and feed alcoholism. These include: cultural attitudes (G. A. Marlatt, 1985a), family structure (Bowen, 1978), crisis times (Bratter, 1985) as well as peer pressure, social policies, availability, and family influences of genetics and system dynamics (DiClemente, 2003). In this model, treatment focuses on changing the environmental contexts for the alcoholic.

One example of a sociocultural model is Cushman's (1990) empty self theory. In this model, industrialization, urbanization, and secularism are societal aspects that have resulted in the increasing loss of family, community, and tradition—those things that offer people shared meaning in their lives. The loss of these aspects results in an empty self, who views psychological boundaries as specific ("My mental health depends on me"), a locus of control as internal ("I am in charge of my life"), and a wish to manipulate the external world for personal ends ("I will be happy if I manage well"). Cushman (1990) believes that the active addict is using drugs to fight off feelings of alienation, fragmentation, worthlessness, and confusion (particularly around values). This theory can be readily applied in addiction counseling by assisting the client in recovering a lifestyle that involves a sense of family, community, and tradition, all supporting the addiction recovery.

Medical Model

The medical model looks at specific physiological dysfunctions such as endocrine dysfunction (Gross, 1945). Although theories in the medical model may assist in defining and describing alcoholism, they fail to promote any specific treatments. The disease model of alcoholism is related to this category because of its basis in physiology (i.e., genetic predisposition, allergic reaction); however, it has a slightly different twist to it because of the individual's responsibility for future behavior and the need for spiritual help in recovery. Addiction is seen as the primary disease that is caused by a loss of control, and denial of having the disease and treatment requires abstinence (Denning, 2005).

The disease model views alcoholism as a progressive disease with symptoms. The two key elements in this model are loss of control over drinking and the progression of the disease, which ends in death. This view, a shift from the moral view, is more compassionate and open to treatment and insurance coverage (S. Goodman & Levy, 2003). This view is partially accepted by AA (McHugh et al., 1979): Alcoholism is an illness that is physical, mental, and spiritual in nature, and the alcoholic is not responsible for the development of the addiction but is responsible for future behavior. The alcoholic enters into recovery from addiction by admitting powerlessness over alcohol, as well as wrongs done to others, and receiving the help of a Higher Power—what might be called a spiritual solution.

This theory of addiction, according to AA, has been implemented in the Minnesota Model of treatment: Professional services are combined with the 12 steps of AA, using counselors who are often in addiction recovery themselves (O'Dwyer, 1993). This model involves the components of education, fellowship, and therapy (Schulz, Williams, & Galligan, 2009). It was developed at Minnesota's Hazelden guesthouse program for alcoholic men that had five simple expectations: (1) be responsible, (2) go to AA 12-step lectures, (3) interact with other clients, (4) make one's own bed, and (5) stay sober (Shaw, Ritvo, & Irvine, 2005).

It shifted the treatment of alcoholics from custodial care to one based on dignity and respect of the alcoholic with an emphasis on peer assistance, particularly in the sharing of personal stories (Shaw et al., 2005). This model, which was very strong in the 1960s and 1970s, encourages the treatment of the whole individual in terms of body, mind, and spirit (S. Goodman & Levy, 2003). Gragg (1995) highlights the benefits of using the disease model of alcoholism/addiction within an HMO framework: It reduces the client's guilt over the addiction, and it encourages community involvement to supplement managed care therapy.

Biopsychosocial Model

More recently, models of addiction have been presented as biopsychosocial (Perkinson, 1997). In this type of model, biogenetic traits and psychosocial factors are combined when addressing addiction in an attempt to provide an integrated, comprehensive model.

Ray and Ksir (2004) discuss the disease model argument as follows: While psychiatrists had viewed alcoholism as a secondary problem and focused on treating the primary mental health

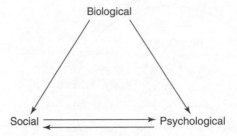

Figure 1.1 Biopsychosocial Model.

disorder (telling their patients to use alcohol less), AA viewed alcoholism as the main problem that required direct treatment. Allegiance to the disease model is based on this commitment to alcoholism being the primary problem that needs to be treated. The debate about alcoholism being a disease continues to the present day.

Some argue that alcoholism does not meet the criteria of being a disease because we cannot find the cause, directly treat it, or even know if there is a disease present. These critics also warn that the definition of the disease can be watered down by the view of seeing all excessive behaviors from this perspective. Some say it may be most appropriate to view the disease concept as a metaphor (G. A. Marlatt & Fromme, 1988). The biopsychosocial model of addiction may be a bridge across these conflicts. The biopsychosocial model (Figure 1.1) is holistic in that it views biological aspects impacting psychological aspects impacting social aspects of the individual in an ongoing, interactive manner (G. W. Lawson, Lawson, & Rivers, 2001). It looks at causality in a complicated way with regard to how the person becomes involved in addictive behavior, stays involved in addictive behavior, and stops the addictive behavior (DiClemente, 2003).

Kumpfer, Trunnell, and Whiteside (2003) describe the components of these three areas as follows: Biological includes genetic inheritance, in utero damage, and temperament or physiological differences. Psychological and social factors are combined into psychosocial, which

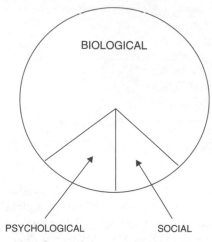

PSYCHOLOGICAL   SOCIAL

Figure 1.2 Contributing Factors of Addiction: Example 1.

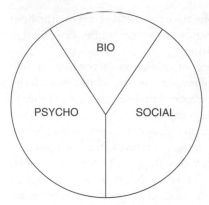

Figure 1.3 Contributing Factors of Addiction: Example 2.

includes an interaction between the individual and family, community, school, work, peer, and social factors.

There are some benefits to this perspective. First, it accounts for the complicating, contributing factors of addiction. This perspective encourages an individual assessment of the alcoholic or addict that accounts for causes in varying amounts like pieces of a pie. For example, some alcoholics/addicts may have a significant biological component without much in the other two areas (Figure 1.2) while other alcoholics/addicts have a small biological component (Figure 1.3). The model encourages a complex yet individualized understanding of one's cause of addiction. Figures 1.2 and 1.3 demonstrate these differences.

This broad assessment perspective also encourages a broader treatment perspective. As G. W. Lawson et al. (2001) report, treatment may then involve addressing more than one problem at a time. An example of this is when a woman in a domestic violence situation has a drinking/drug problem and needs to address both issues simultaneously because they impact each other. She can best protect herself if she is sober, and the experience of being battered may

encourage or trigger her alcohol or drug usage. The model is one of the best practices, where the counselor looks for the best fit between the client's need and the available treatment (Addictions Foundation of Manitoba, 2000). Yet, as DiClemente (2003) outlines, the drawbacks to the use of this model are threefold: (1) typically an emphasis is placed on one aspect of the model without a solid integration of the three aspects; (2) it is difficult to provide interventions on all aspects at the same time; and (3) some factors, such as risk and protective factors, cannot be changed.

Although DiClemente's concerns are important to consider, the use of the biopsychosocial model in the treatment of addiction remains valid because of its emphasis on complicating factors interacting in order for an addiction to be born and live in an individual. Treatment and aftercare from this perspective invite a holistic, personalized approach. It provides humanistic care to the individual (Smith, Fortin, Dwamena, & Frankel, 2013). Also note that some authors have advocated that different aspects be added to this model, i.e. spiritual (Amodia, Cano, & Eliason, 2005) to enhance the holistic view of the client. (See Case Study 1.2.)

CASE STUDY 1.2

Jacob is a 30-year-old male who came to your agency for an addiction assessment. At his first session, he was diagnosed as addicted to cocaine, his drug of choice. Jacob's HMO insurance coverage is limited to 5 days of inpatient treatment and 10 outpatient sessions with you. This is his first treatment for addiction. He tells you that all of his friends use cocaine and that his roommate started him on it. He says he likes cocaine because he does not feel depressed when he takes it. He also states that he feels like a failure because he became a drug addict like his father.

1. How would you use behavioral theories in terms of Jacob's recovery?
2. How would his culture be important to his recovery process?
3. What aspect of the disease model might be helpful to him?

SUMMARY

Models of addiction play a critical part in the assessment and treatment process for the client. The counselor working with addicted clients needs to be aware of the biases of his or her model orientation to determine exactly what aspects will be addressed as well as overlooked by the model's approach. An awareness of one's model at this level can result in a holistic therapeutic approach that incorporates a respectful view of the addicted client, the cause of addiction, and the treatment approaches and interventions.

This chapter establishes a baseline for examining addiction by addressing different models in the field. Table 1.1 is a summary of the models discussed in this chapter.

Finally, three excellent resources for the addiction counselor are: the National Institute on Alcohol Abuse and Alcoholism [NIAAA]; the National Institute on Drug Abuse [NIDA]; and the Substance Abuse and Mental Health Services Administration [SAMHSA]. These organizations provide reliable, current, research-based information—including treatment approaches—regarding the field of addictions. These groups provide a variety of information both online and in hard copy that can be mailed to the reader.

The remaining chapters focus on counseling theories, assessment and diagnosis, treatment, special issues in treatment, relapse prevention, self-help groups, therapies, incorporation of spirituality, pain management, personal and professional development of the counselor, and certification and licensure preparation.

QUESTIONS

1. What are the main models of addiction?

2. What are three main influences on addiction counseling?

3. How have these models and influences affected your view of addicted individuals, the cause of addiction, and addiction treatment approaches?

EXERCISES

Exercise 1.1

Discuss with a peer the various models of addiction (moral, psychological, sociocultural, medical [disease], biopsychosocial) in terms of:

1. Which one you feel most *comfortable* using in addiction counseling and why.

2. Which one you feel most *uncomfortable* using in addiction counseling and why.

Exercise 1.2

With a peer, discuss any concerns you have working with the managed care orientation with these statements/questions in mind:

1. My worst experience (or anticipated experience) in working with managed care was:

2. My best experience (or anticipated experience) in working with managed care was:

3. I can take action with regard to managed care by:

READINGS/RESOURCES/WEBSITES

SUGGESTED READINGS

Coombs, R. H., & Howatt, W. A. (2005). *The addiction counselor's desk reference*. Hoboken, NJ: Wiley.

This book is divided into eight sections: substances, conceptual tools, assessment and treatment, clinical skills and resources, treatment resources, professional management, career enhancement resources, and information resources.

Shaw, B. F., Ritvo, P., & Irvine, J. (2005). *Addiction and recovery for dummies*. Hoboken, NJ: Wiley.

This book has five sections: overview of addiction, assessment, treatment, recovery, and resources. It is written in layperson's terms and yet is based on sound clinical information.

WEBSITES

Addiction Information Resources

National Institute on Alcohol Abuse and Alcoholism (NIAAA)
(301) 443-3860
E-mail: niaaweb-r@exchange.nih.gov
www.niaaa.nih.gov

NIAAA conducts and funds alcohol research. Most publications are free (fact sheets, journals, videos, classroom resources, and clinical guides).

National Institute on Drug Abuse (NIDA)
(301) 443-1124
www.drugabuse.gov

NIDA utilizes science to research the effects of drug abuse and addiction on health and provides its findings on the website through podcasts, publications, e-newsletters, and public education projects.

Substance Abuse and Mental Health Services Administration (SAMHSA)
(877) 726-4727; TYY (800) 487-4889
(240) 276-2420 Prevention; (240) 276-1660 Treatment
www.samhsa.gov

SAMHSA works to minimize the impact of substance abuse and mental illness on society. Free publications and reports of research are accessible through the website (printed materials are charged shipping).

CHAPTER *2*

THEORIES OF COUNSELING APPLIED TO ADDICTION TREATMENT

PERSONAL REFLECTIONS

Our view of counseling is a reflection of our personal views, our professional training, and the client populations with which we have worked. Each of us needs to find a theoretical framework that clearly reflects our approach to counseling. It is easy to be swayed by charismatic "teachers" and "fads" that come and go, but our clients deserve better than this. They deserve to know and experience our counseling approach shortly after they meet us. They deserve, whatever the theoretical framework, to be treated with respect and care for their dignity and their humanity as they are invited to heal from the addiction with which they struggle and the scars from it that they carry and have caused in others.

My biggest difficulty in this area of theories and techniques has been in the translation of them into addiction counseling work. Note that not everyone in the counseling field respects addiction counseling as a specialty area. I myself have been told by influential professionals that "anyone, anywhere, anytime, can teach anything on addictions." I believe that is a potentially dangerous philosophy that speaks to a lack of awareness of the unique dynamics of addiction counseling.

Instead we need to take the general counseling theories and techniques and apply them to the addicted client in a way that is healing for the client, not being in denial of or enabling their addiction. In the revision of this chapter, I emphasize the application of these theories and techniques as they relate specifically to the addicted client. As I propose such approaches, I encourage the reader to remember to only use these applied techniques if they are helpful to the client. As I tell my students, "If you go to use a technique and it does not seem to be working, just stop it because both you and the client know it is not being effective."

OBJECTIVES

1. To be able to facilitate the development of our theoretical framework of addiction counseling.
2. To develop an understanding of the dangers in developing a theoretical framework and how to avoid them.
3. To apply these theories of counseling to our clinical work with the addictive process.

In counseling, we may be legitimately asked by clients, colleagues, and/or supervisors: "What is your view of counseling?" This question may not be asked directly; it can be embedded in other questions, such as when a client asks, "What is wrong with me?" or when a client, colleague, or supervisor says, "What is causing this problem?"

In Chapter 1 there was a discussion of how theoretical models of addiction may impact the client's treatment. Once a counselor selects a model (with or without awareness), that model impacts the selection of theories and techniques used in treating the addiction. As counselors, we must remember that our theoretical perspective significantly shapes how our client, our client's problem, and our client's life are viewed by us, our clients, and others. Those views shape the treatment of the client's addiction. That is why it is necessary for us to have an awareness of the addiction model we choose as well as our theoretical framework and techniques.

One way of viewing the impact of your theoretical framework on your clients is to watch their story being discussed in an agency staff meeting. Your recounting of a client's story and the counselors hearing it shape their interpretations by consciously or unconsciously emphasizing or deemphasizing certain aspects of the client's narrative. These professionals make selections based on their theoretical frameworks and areas of training. For example, a counselor focused on family system dynamics may emphasize relational dynamics of a client's story. Counselors, through their storytelling, as well as through their story-listening, punctuate the story by their theoretical frameworks.

Varying theories become obvious in questions asked of the storyteller and in disagreements among the professionals. Intense debates can be educational in learning about different counselors' theoretical orientations. Recommendations for treatment can vary substantially as a result of these varying frameworks.

DEVELOPMENT OF A THEORETICAL FRAMEWORK FOR ADDICTION COUNSELING

Johnson (2004) states that theory consists of ideas and explanations that the counselor bears the responsibility for proving; that no one theory explains everything about human behavior. Rarely does any counselor adhere to only one theoretical framework. Most counselors understand that they

need a large repertoire of counseling techniques to meet clients' needs. These techniques evolve from your understanding of the theory and research. For example, using the Gestalt technique of role playing without understanding the Gestalt treatment philosophy of wholeness or the interconnectedness of an individual in terms of thoughts, feelings, and behaviors may limit the effectiveness of the technique. Treatment effectiveness and ethical principles for different schools of thought require that you understand and communicate an understanding of core counseling theories.

In addition, it is critical that you recognize how your theoretical framework shapes clinical work in terms of assessment, treatment, and aftercare. Understanding your theoretical counseling framework and its impact on counseling is as necessary in the addiction counseling field as it is in any area of counseling. The framework provides a foundation for you to manage the information you receive about a client's situation. Early treatment planning requires the ability to discern when there is enough information from the client's story to develop a treatment plan; this strategy prevents an assessment from either being too long or too short.

Also, it is important to adhere to one main theory while integrating other theories with that main theory. Being too eclectic can result in a counselor confusing both oneself and one's clients (Johnson, 2004). The theory serves as a guide for both counselor and client throughout the treatment process.

A theoretical framework can be viewed metaphorically as a tree: The trunk is the core theory of how people heal in counseling. The branches of the tree are related theories that naturally connect with and evolve from the core theory. The smaller branches and twigs are those specific techniques that emerge from your theoretical framework. This tree metaphor can assist in the development of a professional balance that prevents you from being overwhelmed by the numerous theoretical perspectives and subsequent treatment choices required by each of these theories and techniques. This balance assists you in effectively and

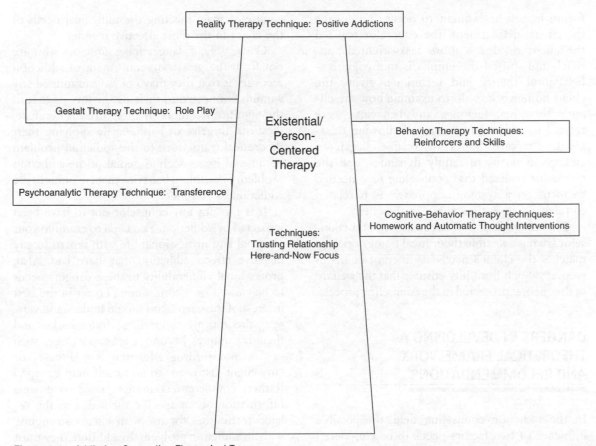

Figure 2.1 Addiction Counseling Theoretical Tree.

efficiently assessing and treating clients by matching client treatment need with the appropriate theory and techniques and by facilitating referrals for emerging needs. An example of the author's theoretical tree, as it relates to addiction counseling, is Figure 2.1.

To conduct effective counseling, you must have a grounding theoretical framework as well as flexibility in the use of such a framework. This allows for the unique needs of a client. For example, a counselor who mainly uses a client-centered theoretical approach in counseling may have a client who needs therapy to be more task-oriented for certain problems or during different phases of treatment. The counselor may want to rely more on a cognitive-behavioral theoretical framework

that engages the client in a more task-oriented counseling process.

Flexibility with your theoretical framework is important for the preservation of an ethical counseling process. Match the theoretical aspect of the framework with what fits the client's needs in terms of assessment, treatment, and aftercare. Theoretical perspectives and techniques may vary as the client changes his or her inner world or contextual world. Changes in either or both pose different dilemmas for the client and the counselor in the treatment planning.

As an example of treatment planning, assume that the counselor described earlier used client-centered therapy to help establish a trusting relationship with the addicted client in order for an honest assessment to occur. To engage the client in treatment, the counselor realized the client needed a more task-oriented approach and shifted the emphasis to a cognitive-behavioral theory and technique, giving the client homework to do to examine how the client's thoughts, feelings, and behaviors were related to addiction recovery. Following treatment, aftercare issues of relapse began to emerge in terms of family dynamics, and the counselor realized that counseling now needed to focus on a systemic approach as it related to relapse-prevention needs in the client.

This example shows the necessity of a counselor having a flexible theoretical framework that matches the client's needs at different points in recovery. Such flexibility ensures that the welfare of the client is protected in the counseling process.

DANGERS IN DEVELOPING A THEORETICAL FRAMEWORK AND RECOMMENDATIONS

In the addiction counseling field, the possible influence of two factors needs to be considered in the application of theories of counseling: the grassroots history of the addictions field as discussed in Chapter 1 and the closed system dynamics sometimes present in the field. Both factors can influence the perspective and behavior of addiction and mental health counselors.

Counselors who work in the addiction counseling field enter it from a variety of avenues and experiences. Those who come from the grassroots history—for example, they are recovering addicts or they are recovering from the impact of a significant other's addiction on their lives—may be wedded to their own view of recovery. This frame of reference may limit their theoretical perspective or cause them to believe there is no need to understand other theories of counseling. This is one danger for counselors who are intimately acquainted with their own wounds from addiction; such a narrow focus can prevent a

counselor from meeting the individual needs of the client in the most effective manner.

Conversely, a danger for counselors who are not from the grassroots movement of addiction recovery is that they may not have examined any wounds connected to their use history or that of the significant others in their lives. Therefore, they run the risk of haphazardly applying their theoretical framework to the addiction problem because of issues such as denial of the addiction problem or enabling behavior that encourages the addiction to continue.

It is rare for any counselor not to have been impacted by addiction. You need to examine your personal and professional life with regard to any negative effects addiction may have had. Also, professional vulnerability to these dangers needs to be viewed on a continuum. To act in the best interest of the client, you should understand various theoretical counseling frameworks and their techniques beyond a grassroots one, such as "alcoholism/drug addiction is a disease" or "my client just needs to go to self-help groups." Rather, competent counselors need to possess information about specific theories and the related techniques for use with clients struggling with an addiction problem. In addition, they must be able to explain and demonstrate how these theories and techniques are appropriate with a particular client.

The addiction counseling field, at times, appears to be a closed system to mental health counselors outside of the field. These outsiders may view addiction counselors as closed to feedback or suggestions from counselors who are not designated experts in the addiction counseling field. When asking questions of, or giving feedback to, addiction counselors regarding a client case, they may have found the addiction counselors to be unwilling to hear different theoretical perspectives in terms of assessment and treatment. This closed system attitude may stem from various sources. First, the addiction counselor may feel threatened or inadequate in comparison to the educational level of the mental health counselor and be unwilling to admit to such feelings.

Second, the addiction counselor may have observed well-intentioned mental health counselors err in treating addiction problems, who encouraged the addiction through denial or enabling behavior. Experiencing these responses may convey a hardheadedness to counselors outside of the addictions field.

The grassroots addiction counselor needs to recognize the need to have a broadly based theoretical framework to help the client. The counselor also needs to be open to various perspectives, because the focus of counseling is to act in the best interests of the client, not to protect the ego needs of the counselor.

Mental health counselors need to be wary of intimidating addiction counselors with their extensive credentials and educational levels, understanding and respecting that addiction counseling is a specialty area of counseling. Educating an addiction counselor colleague on different theoretical approaches and techniques must be done thoughtfully and respectfully. Additionally, the mental health counselor needs to make a commitment to develop a "sniffer for addiction."

A sniffer for addiction allows a counselor to hear a client's story and, like a dog, intuitively pick up the scent of addiction. This scent needs to be explored as a tentative hypothesis by asking questions related to aspects of the client's life. The personal reflections section of this chapter has some specific personal suggestions on development of an addictions sniffer.

An addiction sniffer can be developed by:

1. Obtaining information and education on the dynamics of addiction.

2. Exploring your own use of alcohol/drugs and the impact of significant others' use of alcohol/drugs on your life.

3. Engaging in ongoing dialogue with addiction professionals about client cases.

4. Being mentored into the field by an experienced addiction counseling professional.

These four tasks fuse to form an effective systematic framework of addiction counseling. This framework assists you in developing a way of thinking that enhances the effectiveness of addiction assessment and treatment by integrating theory, techniques, and research.

The same four-part framework can help addiction counselors develop a mental health sniffer to assist in the assessment and treatment of mental health problems. These mental health problems may coexist with the addiction problem or be solely present in the client (alcohol/drug use masks the real problem, which is a mental health diagnosis). These four aspects are slightly altered as follows:

1. Obtain information and education on general, common mental health diagnoses, particularly those that frequently coexist with an addiction problem.

2. Explore your own biases with regard to mental health problems as they relate to addiction.

3. Engage in ongoing dialogue with mental health professionals about client cases.

4. Be mentored into the mental health counseling field by an experienced mental health professional.

The addiction counselor who develops a mental health sniffer then has an effective systematic framework that enhances the assessment and treatment of the mental health needs of the client.

There are some cautions for counselors who want to develop a sniffer as it relates to these four aspects. Overall, both addiction and mental health counselors need to take into account realistic, personal limits with regard to time, energy, and money that impact their professional development choices. They need to approach developing a sniffer carefully, as if they are a critical consumer. Interested counselors can turn to state counselor licensure or certification boards for information on training that has received board approval. They can also check informally with counselors whom they respect in the unknown field for insider information on who is an effective trainer. Trainers need to be carefully chosen. There is a continuum in terms of quality trainers in the addictions field and one needs to be a careful consumer—never assume the credentials are enough. Even when someone is declared as knowledgeable in the field or they have the "right" credentials, that does not mean that they know how or can effectively teach someone how to work with addicted clients. These individuals may have "head" knowledge of addiction, but they would be hard pressed to sit with an addicted client and establish an effective treatment relationship— even though they talk as though they can. One can appreciate the information they can glean from this type of trainer as well as understand the limits of what they are learning.

As to your personal use history, you may want to instigate a formal assessment of your alcohol/ drug use by a certified/licensed addiction counselor, particularly if there is any history of abusive use and/or negative consequences related to your alcohol and drug usage. This assessor needs to be chosen carefully so a dual relationship is avoided and an accurate, neutral assessment is done of your use. In addition, if your experiences involve a significant other (i.e., parent or intimate partner), you need to have the resulting wounds assessed by a professional to determine if therapy, self-help groups, or information would be helpful. This healing is necessary for the counselor to be effective.

Biases about mental health problems also need to be explored. As stated previously, you need to recognize that a client may appear to be actively addicted, when in fact the usage is masking a mental health problem that, once treated, naturally results in nonproblematic alcohol/drug use. This is an extremely sensitive assessment and treatment issue, because the client may have developed an addiction problem in addition to the mental health problem. However, if you are willing and able to assess this situation competently, without bias, you can more effectively treat clients.

In terms of dialogue with colleagues, create opportunities in agency staff meetings or informal gatherings with counselors in the respective field for mutually safe, respectful discussions of client cases. Discussions can also occur spontaneously at training, workshops, or conferences that focus on that particular field of counseling.

Finally, having a mentor in the respective field can assist in the development of a sniffer. Watching an experienced, licensed/certified counselor review cases with a focus on a specialty area can help you learn the factors/dynamics of this area at a deeper level. This mentor, however, needs to be someone you trust, someone with whom you feel safe to not know and, as stated in the personal reflection section of this chapter, someone who has a "spirit of recovery." "Spirit of recovery" means those professionals who have an "ease of being" in living and communicate a genuineness, honesty, and authenticity in their relationships that their clients and others sense. They keep clinical work in addictions genuine, honest, and authentic. One way to spot them is that they tend to have a good sense of humor and a flexible approach to living—they are easy to be around like an old, trusted friend. (See Case Study 2.1.)

CASE STUDY 2.1

A mental health counselor is in a staff meeting where an addiction counselor is presenting the case of a client. The addiction counselor asks for feedback on possible interventions because of a recent relapse to alcohol/drugs by the client. The counselor views the addiction counselor as becoming increasingly defensive as the other mental health counselors make suggestions. The mental health counselor believes that the counselor is too wedded to the disease model of addiction and unwilling to examine the impact of family-of-origin dynamics on the client's recovery.

1. What can this counselor do to intervene?
2. What suggestions would you make to the counselor on how to approach the addiction counselor?
3. How could this counselor assist the addiction counselor both inside and outside of staff meetings in expanding his or her theoretical framework?
4. Now flip the roles. Have a mental health counselor tell the client story. The addiction counselor perceives that the mental health counselor is missing an aspect of addiction in the client's story. Answer the same three questions from this perspective.

Theoretical Choice for Case Presentations

A case presentation may occur before a board of examiners. In this section, a few points related to the integration of a theoretical framework are addressed. For more complete overall suggestions on preparing for licensure and certification in the addiction counseling field, see Chapter 14. The suggestions that follow are broad, and you need to work with the material in a flexible manner, because licensure and certification requirements for addiction specialists vary from state to state and for different mental health professions.

First, choose theories that are considered standard in the field of counseling. When presenting a case, the issue of time constraints is always a reality. There is not time to educate the evaluators on a particular counseling theory. Therefore, choosing standard theories such as those discussed later in this chapter increases your efficiency in the presentation. Choosing a standard theory provides you and the evaluators with a common language, making it more likely that the evaluators will understand the main concepts and techniques discussed in the case. Second, by choosing a standard theory and related techniques, you are choosing a *proven* effective form of therapy, thereby enhancing the ethics of applying the theory to your clinical case. Should you choose to work with a theory that is not standard, be prepared to provide a succinct summary of the theory and evidence of the effectiveness of related therapeutic techniques.

Do not attempt to dazzle the evaluators with a fancy, complicated theoretical framework of addiction counseling. Rather, show competence by having a core theory, with a few related theories, and an explanation for how these theories and techniques assisted your client in addressing an addiction problem. Finally, make sure to choose a theory that matches your clinical work. It may help to use the "tree metaphor" presented earlier in this chapter as a guide in making choices.

GENERAL COUNSELING THEORIES APPLIED TO ADDICTION TREATMENT

Addiction specialists or mental health specialists may not adhere to these specific theories rigorously. However, it is important for you, no matter what the specialty in counseling, to be able to communicate with other professionals in these theoretical languages to facilitate cross talk between professions. Through the use of a common language, general counseling theories provide professionals with a bridge across their differences.

There are many excellent books that review counseling theories in general (see Corey, 2013). The eight theories addressed here are: psychoanalytic/Adlerian, existential/person-centered/Gestalt, reality, behavior, and cognitive-behavior. Because most counselors have been exposed to general counseling theories as a result of their training, only a brief overview of the theory's main points are given followed by ideas of how they can be applied to addiction counseling. While suggestions are made on how they can be applied to addiction counseling, the reader is encouraged to explore the publications related to their theory (theories) of choice that are explicitly designed for work with addicted individuals. For example, one of my texts discussed in Chapter 5, *Group Exercises for Addiction Counseling* (2012), takes group theory and related techniques and applies them to addiction counseling. Another example is at the end of Chapter 9 when different resource books related to specific theories are cited.

Psychoanalytic/Adlerian

Five main points of psychoanalytic theory are separately addressed here: developmental stages, personality structure, defense mechanisms, transference/countertransference, and object relations theory. Following the description of each point, its application to addiction counseling is presented.

Main Point #1: Developmental Stages

In psychoanalytic theory, the core philosophy is that clients' early experiences shape them in terms of their personalities. The psychosexual development stages (oral [0 to 1 years], anal [1 to 3 years], phallic [3 to 6 years], latency [6 to 12 years], and genital [12 to 18 years]) need to be resolved for a person to have proper personality development. Problems in the personality are considered a result of being stuck at a developmental stage (Corey, 2013). Typically, this model has viewed alcoholics and addicts as stuck at the oral stage of development (McHugh, Beckman, & Frieze, 1979).

Application to Addiction Counseling Applying this model to clinical work with addicts can pose a problem, because many addiction counselors will not work from a pure psychoanalytic model. For example, a client's addiction is seen

as the result of conflicts and motives that are unconsciously expressed. Therapy is an attempt to make the unconscious conscious, by helping clients work through their conflicts and relive early childhood experiences. In therapy, the therapist uses transference and countertransference with the client to discover any unconscious dynamics.

With the reality of financial constraints and the practical emphasis on helping clients get and stay sober, addiction counselors may be tempted to avoid the use of this theory. However, some authors provide excellent suggestions on merging psychoanalytic theory with addiction work. For example, S. Goodman and Levy (2003) describe core psychological vulnerabilities (ego deficits), defensive structures, and the secondary gain from a psychodynamic perspective within the context of addiction counseling work. Some specific aspects of the psychodynamic model can be used in clinical work with addicted clients—personality structure, defense mechanisms, and transference/countertransference.

Main Point #2: Personality Structure

Personality structure is made up of the id (biological), ego (psychological), and superego (social). The id is based on instincts and operates on the pleasure principle. It wants to avoid pain and have the person experience reduced tension. The ego is thought of as the aspect of personality that regulates it; it is the mediator between the instincts and the environment. The rational aspect of self operates in the reality principle. The superego is the part of ourselves that judges what we do (Corey, 2013). Anxiety comes from conflict among these three areas.

Application to Addiction Counseling In terms of personality structure, the addicted client may have an overactive id, that is, a tendency toward poor impulse control and a drive for pleasure. The client may also have an overactive superego, where criticism and judgment are too harsh. You can assist the client in developing a stronger ego by helping the client become aware of what is realistic. A referral to self-help groups may assist in the development of what is realistic for the client, thereby complementing therapy work.

Main Point #3: Defense Mechanisms

Defense mechanisms help repress anxiety so the ego can function. Corey (2013) outlines these defense mechanisms as repression (unaware of experiences), denial (do not see what is real), reaction formation (express the opposite of the impulse we experience that threatens us), projection (put desires onto others), displacement (express impulses in a safer place), rationalization (use of reasons to justify our behavior), sublimation (put energy into socially acceptable arenas), regression (go back to old behavior we had outgrown), introjection (taking in others' values), identification (identify with others in order to feel better about self), and compensation (hide weaknesses or develop traits so weaknesses are not seen).

Application to Addiction Counseling Helping the client determine how defense mechanisms can be used in detrimental ways can lead to recovery. For example, it is typical for someone to deny an alcohol or drug problem or to have repressed memories of trauma. Helping a client determine a favored type of defense mechanism can help you and your client develop a clinical focus and a treatment intervention plan. Both of you can then discern how the defense mechanism is inhibiting recovery.

Main Point #4: Transference/Countertransference

Transference is what the client projects onto the counselor. By being aware of the impact of your gender on counseling, for instance, you may be able to understand and work more effectively with the projections of the client in terms of issues with his or her mother or father. In terms of counter-transference, be aware of your own personal issues the client raises so that you can work with any projections as a part of the process.

Application to Addiction Counseling The addiction counselor can be aware of the projections of the client on him or her and use these projections to increase the client's awareness of self and how these projections can impact the client's relationships with authority. For example, a male client may have an actively alcoholic father who was abusive. A male counselor working with the client who is aware of those experiences of the client with his father can sensitively point out to the client the projections of mistrust when they emerge in counseling sessions as well as raising them when the client relates stories of interactions with males in authority. Such awareness can assist the client in making choices about interactions rather than responding automatically based on previous experiences.

Regarding countertransference, the importance of the counselor being aware of his or her projections on the addicted client based on personal and professional experiences with addicted individuals has been discussed in Chapter 1, this chapter, and will be discussed throughout the remainder of the text. An example of counter-transference operating is as follows. A female counselor's alcoholic father died of alcoholism when she was a teenager and she never addressed her grief issues adequately. Because she loved her father deeply, when she works with chronic alcoholics she has a tendency to enable their addiction (rescue them, not give them or let others give them consequences for their behavior). This counselor needs to be aware of her counter-transference tendency and explore them, as well as her grief, in her own personal counseling.

Main Point #5: Object Relations Theory

Object relations theory is probably one of the most current psychoanalytic models helpful in understanding addiction. Several theories on object relations exist (St. Clair, 2000). Here the object is the "being" that meets one's needs: "the significant person or thing that is the object or target of another's feelings or drives" (p. 1).

Application to Addiction Counseling The relationships that the addicted client has in the present are reflective as leftovers of past relationships. Because this theory emphasizes the relationship the client has with childhood objects in the present, both you and the client can become aware of projections made onto the world in terms of people and events, so that the client has choices about how to act rather than being driven into automatic responses based on projections. For example, the heterosexual, addicted, male client may project on to women that they will rescue him from his sense of aloneness based on the unmet needs of a narcissistic mother. If the client can be aware of these tendencies and work with the urges associated with them, the client will be less likely to become involved in relationships with women who cannot meet his needs either because of their limitations or the extensiveness of his needs. (See Case Study 2.2.)

they can develop goals that are helpful to society. In therapy, you and the client work together. Three techniques from this theory may be especially beneficial: confrontation, family constellations, and early recollections.

Application to Addiction Counseling Addicted clients may have some views about the past that strongly weigh them down in the present. For example, early abusive relationships with parents may result in clients seeing themselves negatively, and life choices are made out of that perspective: "My parents always thought I was a failure, so I will be one. What is the point of trying to change?" The cycle of alcohol/drug addiction may also have caused the client to develop a

CASE STUDY 2.2

The client is a bright, well-educated individual who does not believe he has an alcohol/drug problem but is in treatment because of a DWI. He reports having a highly critical, alcoholic father who is retired from the military. His mother is described as a very passive individual who simply followed her husband's wishes. Think of this case in terms of five questions:

1. What are your hunches about the client's personality development issues as they relate to id, ego, and superego?
2. What defense mechanisms do you think he might use?
3. How might your gender play out in terms of transference with this client?
4. What countertransference issues may you have with him?
5. What tentative clinical interventions would you make based on the information you have written in response to the four previous questions?

Adlerian

Main Points

Adler emphasized a more positive view of human nature from the psychoanalytic perspective: While the past influenced a client, he believed that how the person viewed the past was what influenced current behavior (Corey, 2013). In their lives, people make choices motivated by social interest and obtainable goals. Therapy becomes a place where clients can have their views challenged about themselves and their lives, and

very narrow, self-centered life perspective resulting in self-centered choices and behaviors. This reduces social interest with an emphasis on narcissistic goals.

You can work collaboratively with the client by confronting his or her negative perspectives on self, others, and the world and by developing goals that are meaningful to the client and beneficial to society. One way to heighten self-awareness and clarify necessary intervention strategies is to have the client draw out a family constellation or discuss early childhood recollections. Such an exercise can challenge the client's awareness of self and clarify how this self-perspective, in combination with other perspectives, is controlling the client's choice to use alcohol/drugs and act in a self-destructive manner. This confrontation may lead to a discussion of early recollections for the client that feed this self-perception and lifestyle. With increased awareness, the counselor can help the client find goals that are meaningful to self and others. Some self-help groups, such as Alcoholics Anonymous (AA), have this emphasis. For example, in Chapter 8, the 12th step of AA discusses reaching out to others who still suffer from alcoholism. By addressing his or her own addiction, the client may choose to help others recover, a goal that provides meaning to the client's life.

Referring to the previous case study, answer the questions:

1. Which Adlerian technique (confrontation, family constellation, early recollection) might you use with this client?

2. With the techniques chosen, what would be your rationale for each in terms of addressing the addiction problem?

3. How would you use social interest and personal goals to help motivate this client with regard to addiction recovery?

Existential/Person–Centered/Gestalt

Main Points

These three theoretical frameworks are grouped together because of some common philosophical perspectives, namely, the belief that becoming more aware of self, others, and the world allows a person to make more mindful choices for which he or she can be responsible. This increased awareness occurs by focusing on experiencing feelings in the moment. The differences among the three theories are primarily in emphasis. *Existential therapy* responds to the human condition of anxiety being a part of living by encouraging self-awareness and experiencing of our common struggles of existence (being alone, meaninglessness, and death). *Person-centered therapy* also encourages clients to become more aware so that their potential is enhanced, that is, there is less difference between what a person is and what he or she wants to be. *Gestalt therapy* encourages the client to integrate thoughts, feelings, and behaviors so that the client is more whole. All three theories emphasize the importance of the therapeutic relationship. In the existential approach, the counselor is attempting to be authentic and human. In the client-centered approach, the counselor uses genuineness, empathy, and positive regard to facilitate the relationship. In the Gestalt approach, the counselor helps the client experience feelings more intensely in order to integrate them.

Application to Addiction Counseling

To assist a client in becoming sober, a strong therapeutic alliance must be developed. Setting up this alliance is discussed in Chapter 5, including the necessary components for working with an addicted client, such as honesty, genuineness, and collaboration. Therefore, one critical therapeutic technique from these theories is establishing a trusting relationship with a client by being very human, authentic, genuine, empathic, and respectful. By exposing the client to such a relationship, you can assist the client in developing a taste for this type of relationship so the client can begin to recognize these healing dynamics in relationships outside the clinical setting.

Another core technique that can be very effective in addiction counseling is the focus in all three therapies on being in the present moment. For example, when a client looks at sobering up, it can be an overwhelming perspective. You can help with that sense of being overwhelmed by focusing the client on the present. Staying sober for the rest of your life can be broken into more reasonable time segments of a moment, an hour, or a day. Also, staying in the present can help the client manage staying sober in the face of difficult memories from the past, stress of the present, or fear of the future.

Working in the present moment can also be helpful with emotional intensity. Many alcoholics and addicts report high sensitivity and intense emotional reactions to situations.

By focusing on the present, you help the addicted person learn how to cope with such

vulnerable through the process of a role play where the client talks with the abusive parent. This can be adapted so that the client talks with the abusive parent in the empty chair or switches chairs and exchanges a dialogue between the self and the absent parent. (See Case Study 2.3.)

CASE STUDY 2.3

The client is in her fourth treatment for alcohol and drug abuse. She is a former prostitute who was severely traumatized as a child. She has little trust or faith in treatment or treatment counselors. Answer three questions:

1. How might you establish a rapport with this client?
2. How would you work with her in terms of the present moment?
3. Which Gestalt techniques might be most helpful and why?

sensitivity and intense emotional reactions. Within the context of a nonjudgmental relationship, being aware of intense emotions and learning to experience them without acting on them can assist the client in developing heightened self-awareness, thereby increasing a sense of choice and tools of self-control that can be very effective in terms of addiction recovery.

Specific Gestalt techniques that may be helpful with addicted clients are confrontation, role playing, and experiencing feelings (in an exaggerated manner). These can assist the client in developing increased self-awareness and self-control tools through an awareness of their polarities (extremes in personality that need to be balanced). An example of this theoretical application to addicted clients is Ramey's (1998) three interventions for use with an alcoholic's resistance to treatment. These are the double chair experiment (play out the ambivalence around recovery), exploring polarities through sentence fragments ("If I continue to drink/choose not drink . . ."), and homework (list reasons to not quit and be ready to explain them in session).

Another example is with the client who presents a tough persona; you can help the client learn about the polar opposite in self that is so very

Control Theory/Reality Therapy

Main Points
Control theory/reality therapy (CT/RT) is similar to the three previous theories of existential/person-centered/Gestalt in that it focuses on the clients' perception of how the world influences their behavior in terms of freedom, choices, and responsibility (Corey, 2013). However, it is different because of the emphasis on total behavior: Clients are responsible for doing, thinking, feeling, and physical reactions (physiology). Like existential and person-centered, this theory advocates a supportive relationship with the counselor so the client feels comfortable evaluating his or her lifestyle. The focus is on helping people evaluate what they are doing and decide if the choices they are making meet their needs.

In this approach, you must be very active and direct, focusing on what needs are not being met and establishing a plan and a commitment to realistically meet those needs through different choices. Use any techniques that assist the client in seeing discrepancies between what is needed and what is currently happening. There is also an emphasis on helping the person form a success identity (view self as significant and powerful, having self-worth, able to meet own needs, and able to exchange love). This helps them be strong and thereby develop greater satisfaction with their life.

The counselor can use the WDEP acronym (Glasser & Wubbolding, 1995; Wubbolding, 1991, 1994) to guide their clinical work. **W** stands for Wants ("What do you want?"), **D** is for Direction/Doing ("What are you doing?"), **E** means Evaluation ("Is what you are doing getting you what you want?"), and **P** is for Planning ("What can you do now to start a chain reaction of change in your life?"). Note that the P section can be easily paired with motivational interviewing approaches discussed in Chapter 9.

Application to Addiction Counseling Because the general approach in addiction counseling is often a very practical one focused on an individual stopping the use of alcohol/drugs, CT/RT is often a good match. The counselor can use the WDEP model to help the client assess the impact of alcohol/drug usage on his or her life. You can

making a commitment to recovery and to important life goals. You can also assist the client in forming a success identity that will help make him or her stronger in the recovery process. Providing the client with opportunities in counseling to feel empowered and loved, as well as respecting the impact of the usage on the client's life and a commitment to a new lifestyle, can facilitate the positive choices in the client's world outside of counseling. Also, encourage the client to develop positive addictions that provide the client with a sense of strength such as self-help group attendance, physical exercise, meditation, spiritual beliefs, and so on. The counselor might use the concept of positive addiction as it applies to the client's drug of choice. For example, your client uses drugs to help relax; you can help the client learn some relaxation techniques that the client becomes "addicted" to, and thereby have a replacement to the drugs, reducing the chance of relapse. Finally, the counselor can use the WDEP model to help the client assess the impact of the alcohol/drug use. (See Case Study 2.4.)

CASE STUDY 2.4

The client is an adolescent who has come to treatment because of pressure from his parents and the legal system. The client is very angry, rebellious, and has made it clear that he is not interested in treatment. Answer four questions with regard to this scenario:

1. How might it be beneficial to teach the client to be aware of the four reactions (doing, thinking, feeling, and physical reactions) in terms of chemical use?
2. How would you phrase the WDEP questions to fit this client and situation?
3. How would you work with the concept of a success identity with this client?
4. How might you encourage positive addictions with this client?

help clients become aware of what they are doing, thinking, feeling, and experiencing in terms of physical reactions. Clients can become aware of choices they make that lead them to using or sobriety as well as general life choices. Examining these choices within a supportive therapeutic relationship enhances the chances of a client

Behavior Therapy

Main Points
Behavior therapy's focus is the impact of learning on a person's behavior. Based on learning theory, it views normal behavior as a result of a person experiencing reinforcement for his or

her behavior and imitating others' behavior (Corey, 2013). Clients are encouraged to get rid of their problem behaviors and learn and practice more adaptive behaviors through treatment goals and plans.

In this approach, counselors and clients work as a team to establish goals and plans for change as well as to evaluate the treatment process and outcome. The counselor is quite active in the counseling process, although the relationship is not emphasized in the same humanistic orientation as in some of the theories previously dis-

for staying sober, new individuals (e.g., sponsor) to imitate (model), and new skills that increase the chances of recovery, such as relaxation, assertiveness, and social skills. You can also employ the use of behavioral contracts and homework assignments with the client to enhance active participation in making the necessary life changes. Some additional examples are cue exposure (being exposed to cues to use, but not using, resulting in an extinction of use behavior), and counterconditioning (giving negative consequences for using behavior). (See Case Study 2.5.)

CASE STUDY 2.5

The client grew up in an alcoholic home where she had to focus on simply surviving. She basically raised herself physically and psychologically. Answer two questions:

1. Based on this short description, what dynamics of learning theory (reinforcers, role models, skill deficits) do you believe might be present for this client?

2. What types of reinforcers, role models, and skills would you incorporate into her recovery process?

cussed. Techniques that can be used with addicted clients are relaxation, reinforcement, modeling, assertiveness and social-skills training, contracts, and homework assignments.

Application to Addiction Counseling This theory of counseling is very amenable to addiction counseling. Because an addiction is behavioral in nature, the concepts of learning and reinforcement are critical in the development of an addiction and the recovery process. You help the client learn what reinforces the addictive behavior, who the client has been imitating in this process, and what faulty learning has occurred in the development of the addiction. Gather this information through the assessment, treatment, and aftercare process as the client continues to learn about his or her addiction. These same areas (reinforcement, imitation, learning) can be applied to the recovery process. You help the client find new reinforcers

Cognitive–Behavior Therapy

Main Points

This form of therapy focuses on the client's faulty thinking, which impacts feelings and behaviors negatively. Here the client is encouraged to examine his or her thinking and learn to respond to negative thoughts and assumptions. One form of this therapy is rational emotive behavior therapy (REBT), previously called *rational emotive therapy* (RET), where you teach the client in a very active and directive manner. This form uses an ABC model to intervene on the client's cognitive distortions that result in upset feelings and maladaptive behaviors: **A** is the activating event, **B** is the belief, **C** is the emotional and behavioral consequence, and **D** is the disputing intervention that results in **E** (effect) and **F** (new feeling). B is seen as primarily causing the reactions in the individual. Focus on the beliefs of the individual to determine the cause of the individual's problems and therein the solution for the problem. Examining irrational beliefs, doing homework, keeping a record of thoughts and behaviors, and role playing are some techniques used in this approach.

Another approach in this therapy is cognitive therapy (CT). Although similarities exist

You can readily use homework, record keeping, and role playing to help the client learn to identify negative thoughts and respond to them differently. Assisting clients in identifying their commonly held irrational beliefs or distortions and identifying their defense mechanisms helps identify a clinical focus and treatment intervention plan. (See Case Study 2.6.)

CASE STUDY 2.6

The client is a very negative person who might be described as someone who would describe a glass as half empty and the water as dirty, too. This negativity is strongly evidenced in how the client talks about himself, others, and his general perception of the world. These beliefs are consistent, whether the client talks about the past, present, or future. Based on this information, answer the following questions:

1. How might you use this theory to address the client's negativity in terms of:
   • The ABC model?
   • Irrational beliefs?
   • Cognitive distortions?
2. Are there any specific homework assignments you might give the client that could be helpful treatment interventions?

between RET and CT, this approach emphasizes the concept of automatic thoughts and assisting the individual in learning how to identify these negative automatic thoughts, gather evidence as if their existence can be supported, and respond to them in a rational manner. Cognitive distortions (arbitrary inferences, selective abstractions, over-generalizations, magnification/minimization, personalization, labeling/mislabeling, polarized thinking) need to be identified and addressed. The counselor can help the client by assigning homework that may include keeping a record of the experiences.

Application to Addiction Counseling This theory of counseling also fits well with the addiction field, because many clients deal with negative thinking in terms of themselves and their recovery process.

Stages-of-Change Transtheoretical Model

This model is described more extensively in Chapter 9. The transtheoretical model is mentioned in this chapter because the counselor approaches therapy with a client from a specific theoretical perspective. This theoretical perspective influences the techniques chosen to implement a treatment plan for behavior change in the client. The change in the client hinges on the client's motivation; therefore, the counselor needs to accurately assess the client's motivation level for change and match it to the client's treatment plan to invite a change in behavior (Coombs & Howatt, 2005). The six levels of motivation to change sound like their labels: Precontemplation, Contemplation, Preparation, Action, Maintenance, and Termination. These stages are described in more detail for the reader in Chapter 9. Counselors are encouraged to assess the level of motivation in the client before implementing a treatment plan and possibly as early as in the selection of a theoretical framework. (See Case Study 2.7.)

> ## CASE STUDY 2.7
>
> Your client comes in for a DWI assessment and states openly that he does not view himself as having any problem with alcohol, except that the police seem to "have it in" for him. He said he will do whatever you tell him to do, but he really has no desire to change his alcohol usage.
>
> 1. What stage of change do you see him at?
> 2. What theoretical approach would you find most helpful in working with him?
> 3. Which techniques do you think would be most effective given his intention to change?

SUMMARY

This chapter explores the process of developing an addiction counseling theoretical framework with an elaboration on ways to avoid the pitfalls in the development of such a framework. Also, the main points of eight theories of counseling, and their related techniques, are presented with some suggestions as to how they can be applied specifically to addiction counseling. A knowledgeable counselor can find the best theoretical fit for the counselor, client, and problem, thus developing an assessment approach and treatment plan that truly operates in the best interest of the client. Blending these theories and techniques in a balanced manner allows the counselor to operate therapeutically out of a flexible framework that is readily adjustable to the client's needs and problems. A brief summary of the stages-of-change transtheoretical model is also provided to encourage counselors to assess the client's motivational level for change that may impact the counselor's choice of theory and techniques in working with a client.

QUESTIONS

1. What is the purpose of a theoretical framework for counseling?

2. What are some dangers in developing an addiction counseling framework? What are accompanying recommendations?

3. How can you develop a sniffer for addiction? For mental health problems?

4. How do some of the main concepts for these theories fit in addiction counseling?

   • Psychoanalytic/Adlerian

   • Existential/person-centered/Gestalt

   • Control theory/reality therapy

   • Behavior therapy

   • Cognitive-behavior therapy

EXERCISES

EXERCISE 2.1

Discuss your theoretical framework of counseling with a colleague in answer to this question: "What helps someone heal from addiction?" Ask your colleague to assist you in determining your answer to this question regarding:

1. Your core theory of counseling
2. Related theories of counseling and how they connect to your core theory
3. Techniques you use in addiction counseling and how they are connected to the theory from which they evolve

EXERCISE 2.2

With this theoretical framework in mind, think of a case with an addicted person with whom you used this theoretical framework. Pretend that you are presenting your theory of addiction counseling within this framework and answer three questions:

1. What theory/theories most influenced your work?
2. Which techniques did you use and why?
3. How did you find these theories and techniques helpful in addressing the problem with addiction?

EXERCISE 2.3

Rate yourself in terms of developing an effective addiction sniffer.

	Yes	No
I have received training in the addictive process.	—	—
I continue to receive ongoing training in the addictions field.	—	—
I have carefully examined my own alcohol/drug use and that of significant others in my life.	—	—
I engage in ongoing dialogue with addiction professionals about cases.	—	—
I have been mentored into the addiction counseling field by an experienced professional.	—	—

Use this checklist to determine if you want or need to expand your addiction sniffer. Examine barriers of time, money, or energy that inhibit your development of a sniffer and how you may work around these barriers.

EXERCISE 2.4

In terms of the stages-of-change transtheoretical model, which theoretical techniques are you most comfortable using at the different stages (precontemplation, contemplation, preparation, action, maintenance, and termination)?

READINGS/RESOURCES/WEBSITES

SUGGESTED READINGS

Corey, G. (2013). *Theories and practice of counseling and psychotherapy* (9th ed.). Belmont, CA: Brooks/Cole.

This book provides a thorough, excellent overview of general counseling theories.

Howett, W. A. (2005). Classical counseling models. In R. H. Coombs (Ed.), *Addiction counseling review* (pp. 319–336). Mahwah, NJ: Erlbaum.

This chapter provides an overview of theory, therapy, and techniques as they relate to person-centered, existential, Jungian, and Adlerian counseling and provides a helpful table comparing the different theories.

Howett, W. A. (2005). Cognitive-behavioral models. In R. H. Coombs (Ed.), *Addiction counseling review* (pp. 337–356). Mahwah, NJ: Erlbaum.

This chapter reviews three cognitive-behavioral theories—choice theory and reality therapy; rational emotive behavior therapy (REBT); and cognitive-behavioral therapy (CBT)—in terms of theory, therapy, and techniques. It also presents theory and therapy overviews of classical conditioning, operant conditioning, and social cognitive learning strategy. Finally, it presents 10 behavioral counseling strategies and a table comparing the different theories.

Walters, S. T., & Rotgers, F. (Ed.). (2011). *Treating substance abuse: Theory and technique* (3rd ed.). New York, NY: Guilford Press.

This book has chapters on the theories of 12-step–oriented treatment, psychoanalytic, family therapy, cognitive-behavioral, behavioral, and motivational interviewing with accompanying chapters on techniques.

CHAPTER 3

ASSESSMENT AND DIAGNOSIS OF ADDICTION

PERSONAL REFLECTIONS

Addiction assessment can be overwhelming for the counselor. First, there are numerous assessment instruments available, which can be confusing to the counselor. Most counselors I have trained address this concern by using one broad screening instrument and one specific instrument that addresses the issues of many clients with whom they work. That way they are familiar and comfortable with the instrument they administer. Sometimes, after using a broad instrument, they will refer the client to another counselor who specializes in the assessment of addiction. Second, the alcohol/drug use history itself can be extensive, chaotic, and elusive. Clients may intentionally provide an inaccurate use history in order to protect themselves and/or may unintentionally do so because of simply not keeping track of usage. Significant others may not be able to accurately corroborate the use history because the addict hid it from them or they are trying to protect the addict by lying about the addict's use (significant others who are also using addicts lie to protect the addicted person). Here counselors need to practice patience in the data collection from self-reports of addicts with the understanding and expectation that the addicts will lie to them about their drug use (maximize, minimize). In anticipation of this tendency to lie, as a part of the disorder, the counselor needs to respond by obtaining as much information from as many outside sources as possible and by staying steady, calm, and firm through the assessment process. The third area is the counselor's concern for placing the diagnostic label on the client. The diagnosis of addiction will remain with clients all of their lives and is a significant life-changing diagnosis that carries discrimination with it. I encourage counselors who are concerned about this responsibility to seek assessment training and appropriate certification and licensure and to consult with colleagues, supervisors, and mentors regarding ways to handle such concerns.

OBJECTIVES

1. To learn a general chemical dependency assessment approach.
2. To become familiar with both broad and specific assessment instruments.
3. To learn an approach of integrating the various sources of information in an assessment process.

Assessment of alcohol/drug use requires a counselor to be thorough in terms of both depth and breadth. Stauffer, Capuzzi, and Tanigoshi (2008) describe the philosophy of a substance abuse assessment. Both counselor and client need to be hopeful collaborators, and there needs to be an emphasis on client strengths as well as problems and an examination of the whole person, including intrinsic motivators for change. Assessment is where the counselor gathers and uses information at some point in the treatment process to develop appropriate treatment plans

(Connors, DiClemente, Velasquez, & Donovan, 2013). It needs to be careful and accurate, looking for problems with substances, co-occurring disorders, leading to treatment that is appropriate, and encouraging to clients to change (Greenfield & Hennessy, 2008). It needs to be "timely, thorough, and continuous" (Johnson, 2004).

J. L. Johnson (2004) encourages counselors to follow eight principles in the assessment of substance abuse:

1. Remember the uniqueness of each client and his or her story.

2. Engage the client in the assessment process.

3. Ask about use and abuse of substances with every client and take appropriate action.

4. Understand the differences between use, abuse, and dependency.

5. Know that not everyone who uses or abuses substances becomes dependent.

6. Remember that no one chemical dependency theory fits every client.

7. Develop an approach that is flexible in the treatment of the unique client needs.

8. Be aware of one's own projections on people who use.

These principles can assist the counselor in being anchored in an assessment process that acts in the best interests of the client. Another assessment anchoring point is the *Diagnostic and Statistical Manual of Mental Disorders* (*DSM-5*; American Psychiatric Association [APA], 2013). This manual can provide a common "language" for discussion of addiction by various professionals. Due to recent revisions of the *DSM-5*, the changes in the area of substance use diagnoses are reviewed briefly here. The reader is referred to the resource section of this chapter for additional reading that may assist in understanding the new diagnostic criteria.

Overall the *DSM-5* has been changed with the intent to enhance clinical utility (Neimeyer, 2013). The *DSM-5* now classifies mood-altering substances into nine classes: alcohol; caffeine; cannabis; hallucinogens (including PCP, LSD, and MDMA); inhalants; opioids; sedatives, hypnotics, and anxiolytics; stimulants (including amphetamine and cocaine); and tobacco (APA, 2013; Nussbaum, 2013; Reichenberg, 2014). It also included gambling disorder because all of these impact the brain's reward system even though they have different effects (APA, 2013; Nussbaum, 2013; Reichenberg, 2014). However, in this updated manual, there is no longer a distinction between substance abuse and dependence (APA, 2013; Nussbaum, 2013; Reichenberg, 2014). Instead, substance use is viewed on a continuum of symptoms that range from mild to severe (Reichenberg, 2014; Rollins, 2013). The hope is that this version will more accurately capture the intent of the client's use (Nussbaum, 2013). For example, clinicians need to note if physiological dependence is present. Therefore, intentionally it can be noted about physiological dependence: is it a result of taking a prescribed maintenance dose of methadone and benzodiazepines or abusing such substances (Nussbaum, 2013)?

The current manual has categories for use, intoxication, and withdrawal, as well as substance-induced categories of mental disorders, following the pattern for alcohol (Nussbaum, 2013). A substance use disorder is a "maladaptive pattern leading to clinically significant impairment or distress for at least 12 months" (Paris, 2013, p. 131) with features that meet 2 of the 11 criteria with severity specifiers hinging on how many of the criteria are met. There are also course specifiers regarding remission (early full, early partial, sustained full, sustained partial on agonist therapy in a controlled environment) (APA, 2013). The word "*dependence* is used for the symptoms of tolerance and/or withdrawal (Paris, 2013).

Paris (2013) summarizes some of the current controversy with the revisions of the *DSM*. One of the concerns is that because many definitions for disorders have been expanded (life is pathologized), overtreatment may result. The author encourages practitioners, then, to use the criteria, but avoid applying them rigidly when application does not make sense. These cautions are also applicable to substance use disorder diagnoses with the concern that assessing impairment may be clear with severe cases, but not so with common or milder client usage (Paris, 2013; Reichenberg, 2014).

Shaffer and Kauffman (1985) suggest using many different sources in order to make a quality assessment. These sources, which are discussed in the following section, include interviews with clients (along with case histories) and significant others, behavioral observations, physiological instruments, and psychometric instruments.

Two case studies and two exercises are provided throughout the chapter to facilitate the application of the information provided.

INTERVIEWS

The clinical interview is a core component of the assessment process. The clinical interview with two populations, an addiction assessment involving the client and the client's significant others, are explored here.

Interviewing Clients

As Straussner (1993, 2004) indicates, the first priority of an assessment is to refrain from stereotyping the individual who is being assessed. Margolis and Zweben (1998, 2011) state that the core of the assessment process is the diagnostic interview where the counselor is nonjudgmental and empathic. The authors stress the importance of this approach because these clients are often shamed and told they are failures or bad people. To accomplish this openness, the counselor must be able to hear the individual's story as well as obtain verification that the client's story is accurate. Hearing the individual's story means that the clinician must establish an atmosphere where the client feels invited to tell his or her story of alcohol/drug usage. Treating clients with respect can facilitate any evaluation, including those of clients who are involuntarily present for an assessment. The concepts of motivational interviewing and the stages-of-change model discussed in Chapter 9 are very appropriate for use in the assessment process.

Because individuals who are addicted may use defense mechanisms (e.g., denial) when asked about their usage (Griffin, 1991), a counselor may be drawn to using a confrontational approach in the interview process. However, the style of the interview (i.e., focusing on labeling the problem and insisting the client accept this label) may encourage resistance and defensiveness in the client (Lewis, Dana, & Blevins, 1994). The counselor walks a fine line between a commitment to obtaining accurate information in order to maintain a quality assessment and being aware that individuals who are addicted may distort their usage to prevent their addiction from being discovered by the counselor or, in the case of some populations such as adolescents as discussed in Chapter 10, being aware that clients may exaggerate their usage. Margolis and Zweben (2011) state that adolescents may be stating the truth about their use as they recall it, but they may lack problem insight due to being developmentally delayed and having social and emotional impairments due to their drug usage. Freimuth (2002) also notes that clients who appear in denial simply may not have connected their problems with their use. Sometimes educational brochures that combine information with personal exploration questions are useful. One such brochure, such as *Rethinking Drinking: Alcohol and Your Health*, is available at the National Institute on Alcohol Abuse and Alcoholism (NIAAA) website (www .niaaa.nih.gov).

One way to approach an assessment process fairly is to tell the client that information will be drawn from numerous sources and that a pattern of behaviors will be looked for throughout the assessment process. The client will have awareness from the beginning, then, that not only will his or her story be a source of information, but also other avenues of information will be sought.

Initially, a counselor may want to use a broad general screening instrument discussed in the Psychometric Instruments section of this chapter. The use of one of these instruments may determine whether additional evaluation is required. Often, addiction professionals incorporate some broad assessment instrument into their initial interview. If a counselor does not elect to do so, a simple question on an intake form where the client can mark yes or no may elicit a story that could indicate a problem with alcohol/drugs (e.g., "Have you ever had any unplanned use of alcohol/drugs?"). This question followed up in the interview with a statement such as "Give me your most recent example of unplanned use" can serve as a broad screening device to detect a problem with alcohol/drugs. This type of question captures the loss of control where individuals cannot predict control when they use alcohol, rather than the concept that they lose control every time they use (Margolis & Zweben, 1998). This question is similar to the TICS, which is a two-question screening instrument used in medical situations where a positive response to either question encourages further assessment (R. L. Brown, Leonard, Saunders, & Papasouliotis, 2001):

1. In the past year, have you ever drunk or used drugs more than you meant to?

2. Have you felt you want or need to cut down on your drinking or drug use in the past year?

Finally, NIAAA has developed a single-question screening test that may assist in early detection of alcohol problems in a primary care setting (Harvard Mental Health Letter, 2009). This question is: "How many times in the past year have you had X or more drinks in a day?" ($X = 5$ for men and 4 for women). An answer of more than once in the past year may indicate unhealthy alcohol use.

In the interview process, the counselor needs to ask the client what the client sees as the presenting problem. Although this answer may be different from the answer of the referral source (if the referral source is different from the client), it may assist the counselor in determining the client's level of concern with his or her alcohol/drug use. In addition, gathering information about the client's family of origin, particularly around history of addiction, may be beneficial to the assessment process. Finally, knowledge of the client's living situation may underscore some environmental factors (e.g., roommate's usage) that are influencing client use and may be possible sources for relapse if it is determined that the client has an alcohol/drug problem.

As to chemical use history, a counselor should find out the date of the client's last use, drug of choice, drugs that have been used, prior treatments for abuse and addiction problems, and any consequences for using drugs (legal; family, significant others, friends; job, school, military; medical; financial; etc.). Senay (1997) suggests that the counselor ask about frequency and amount with regard to alcohol, cannabis, central nervous system (CNS) depressants (barbiturates, benzodiazepines), CNS stimulants (amphetamines, crack, cocaine), opioids, hallucinogens, PCP, inhalants, nicotine, caffeine, and over-the-counter drugs. The date of the client's last chemical usage is important in determining the presence of a life-threatening process of withdrawal. Alcohol, barbiturates, and benzodiazepines can have life-threatening withdrawals (Margolis & Zweben, 2011). For example, seizures can happen 2 weeks after stopping usage with the benzodiazepines. Also, the reported date of last use can provide the counselor with helpful baseline information for possible confrontation later in the interview. For example, the client may say he drinks only a couple of beers once a week on Fridays, yet he may say he had four mixed drinks on Tuesday.

The assessment may reveal that the client may or may not have a drug of choice (i.e., the drug the client most frequently uses or prefers). If there is a drug of choice, it is important to determine the pattern of usage with this drug, why the client likes the drug, and the life consequences that it has brought the client. Information on the drug of choice can help the counselor in developing a treatment recommendation for the client whether the client is abusing or addicted. Understanding the reason for using a particular drug can help the counselor recommend an appropriate harm-reduction approach for the client that may help prevent the development of an addiction, or a treatment plan can be developed that may help prevent a relapse.

For example, a client may use marijuana to help relax. If the client is not assessed as addicted or even if the client is addicted, the counselor can recommend some alternative ways to cope with stress that can help prevent addiction or relapse. Discussion of life consequences may also assist with the client's denial process to again help prevent the development of an addiction or a relapse. If the client can follow the self-help adage, "Follow the (*drink*) through," the client may be able to not use by anticipating the possible consequences of use. Also, discussion of use consequences may help break the client's denial of a substance use problem. For example, a client may realize there is a problem with the drug of choice but be able to rationalize the usage of other drugs.

When taking drug history information, the counselor should note the age of the client's first use and the age of last use for each drug reported. Then, for each drug, the counselor should examine the typical use pattern and the most recent typical use pattern (including how much, how often, use setting, and administration route). For example, a woman may have increased her marijuana usage to daily at the time of a divorce for about 2 years, even though she had been smoking marijuana once a week for 10 years, and in the past year (3 years since her divorce) she has smoked it only once a month. This provides an indication that she probably used the marijuana as a way to cope with the stress of her divorce.

It may be frustrating for a client to be asked such specific questions about each drug ever used. Prefacing and restating throughout the information-gathering process that the client is making the best guess about dates will help alleviate this problem. Throughout the assessment, the client may need to be reminded that accurate information requires very specific questioning, and the counselor is not intending to upset him or her by asking such detailed questions. In reality, most people probably do not keep track of the amount of alcohol/drugs that they use. This can be expected with people who have a history of alcohol/drug abuse when they are drunk or high, making it even more difficult to keep track of their usage. The counselor must balance the need for accurate information on use history with the need to develop a therapeutic alliance with the client and not frustrate or alienate him or her in the assessment process.

A part of the assessment process is finding out the administration route used by the client. When assessing the administration route, Hart and Ksir (2012) summarize the routes of drug administration to consider:

- *Oral.* Most common and easiest but the most complicated in terms of bloodstream entry.

- *Insufflation.* Snorting or sniffing drugs through the nose.

- *Injection:* There are three types of usage with a hypodermic syringe:

  1. *Intravenous (IV).* Quickest entry into the bloodstream, making drug action felt quickly.

  2. *Subcutaneous.* Injection under the skin, called *skin popping* by narcotic users.

  3. *Intramuscular.* Injection into the muscle; quicker in terms of effects than subcutaneous.

- *Inhalation.* Quickest way to feel the effects of psychoactive drugs.

- *Topical.* Not commonly used because the skin does not absorb most drugs well.

During the assessment process, asking how the person takes in the drug may help the counselor understand some of the issues facing the client in terms of either a harm-reduction or abstinence-based approach. For example, a client who likes to shoot up substances may like it because of a need for intense, quick sensations. Awareness of this tendency can help the person build such experiences into his or her recovery so that need is met sober.

Also during the assessment process, it is helpful to find out the types of drugs a person has used to understand his or her reasons for using them. What benefit does that drug provide the individual? Why be committed to using the drug despite harmful consequences? Reference material is an essential tool to enrich the assessment process. Hart and Ksir (2012) provide information on the specific drug actions of different drugs. A more extensive reference book is *Buzzed* (Kuhn, Swartzwelder, & Wilson, 2008), and a helpful booklet is *The Brain's Response to Drugs: Teacher's Guide* (NIDA, 2000), which summarizes specific drug actions in a simple manner. The National Institute on Drug Abuse (NIDA) also has available online (www.drugabuse.gov) a chart of commonly abused drugs in terms of categories/names, examples of commercial and street names, Drug Enforcement Agency schedule/administration routes, and intoxication effects and consequences. (See Table 3.1.)

In learning the specific impact of drugs on the body, it can help to know a general rule about drugs: What a drug does going into the body will be the opposite of what happens to the body as the drug leaves. For example, alcohol is a depressant, so when it enters the body, it has a depressing, slowing down effect on the body. That means that someone withdrawing from alcohol will experience agitation as it leaves his or her system. Although this is a tendency, it may be helpful to the assessing counselor to be aware of how drugs generally interact with the body.

A general understanding of the impact dynamics of psychoactive drugs is also helpful in assessment. The psychoactive drug enters the bloodstream and crosses the blood-brain barrier, allowing for an impact on the brain and, thereby, impact on the brain's electrical-chemical communication system. The electrical and chemical system works in concert with the communication system of the brain. The different categories of drugs (stimulants, depressants, etc.) result in different effects on a person (chemically, neurologically, thoughts/feelings/behaviors) because of different interactions with the brain's neurotransmitters, the brain's chemicals used to transmit information. The neurotransmitters are the body's natural chemicals, and psychoactive drugs impact how available they are "by increasing or decreasing the transmitter chemical's rate of synthesis, metabolism, release from storage vesicles, or reuptake into the releasing neuron" (Ray & Ksir, 2004, p. 158). This process is explained more both generally and specifically in the texts mentioned previously.

Such information can help the client understand that drugs cannot do anything to the body that the body's natural chemicals, neurotransmitters, do. Therefore, addicts can look for ways to produce a similar high naturally in recovery that they formerly obtained with drugs, or individuals who are open to reducing their drug intake can find alternative highs.

Asking the client about prior treatment for substance abuse or dependency is important for several reasons. First, previous treatment is indicative of an abuse problem with alcohol/drugs. Second, previous treatment means that records can be obtained, with the client's consent, for corroborating information. Third, previous treatment experiences may affect the view of the client in terms of his or her approach to this assessment. Fourth, previous treatment information may be used to guide the treatment planning to make it more effective for the client. A client may have relapsed, for example, because of an untreated trauma, which was mentioned in the interview with the counselor, but not in the treatment records.

The counselor should also know of any consequences experienced due to the use of alcohol/drugs. Specific areas to examine include legal; family, significant others, and friends; job, school, and military; medical; and financial. One way to

Table 3.1 National Institute on Drug Abuse (NIDA) Commonly Abused Drugs

COMMONLY ABUSED DRUGS
Visit NIDA at www.drugabuse.gov

NIDA
NATIONAL INSTITUTE
ON DRUG ABUSE

Substances: Category and Name	Examples of Commercial and Street Names	DEA Schedule*/ How Administered**	Intoxication Effects/Potential Health Consequences
Cannabinoids			euphoria; slowed thinking and reaction time; confusion; impaired balance and coordination/cough; frequent respiratory infections; impaired memory and learning; increased heart rate, anxiety, panic attacks; tolerance; addiction
hashish	boom, chronic, gangster, hash, hash oil, hemp	I/swallowed, smoked	
marijuana	blunt, dope, ganja, grass, herb, joints, Mary Jane, pot, reefer, sinsemilla, skunk, weed	I/swallowed, smoked	
Depressants			reduced anxiety; feeling of well-being; lowered inhibitions; slowed pulse and breathing; lowered blood pressure; poor concentration/fatigue; confusion; impaired coordination, memory, judgment; addiction; respiratory depression and arrest, death
barbiturates	Amytal, Nembutal, Seconal, Phenobarbital: barbs, reds, red birds, phennies, tooies, yellows, yellow jackets	II, III, IV/injected, swallowed	Also, for barbiturates—sedation, drowsiness/depression, unusual excitement, fever, irritability, poor judgment, slurred speech, dizziness, life-threatening withdrawal
benzodiazepines (other than flunitrazepam)	Ativan, Halcion, Librium, Valium, Xanax: candy, downers, sleeping pills, tranks	IV/swallowed, injected	for benzodiazepines—sedation, drowsiness/dizziness
flunitrazepam***	Rohypnol: forget-me pill, Mexican Valium, R2, Roche, roofies, roofinol, rope, rophies	IV/swallowed, snorted	for flunitrazepam—visual and gastrointestinal disturbances, urinary retention, memory loss for the time under the drug's effects
GHB***	gamma-hydroxybutyrate: G, Georgia home boy, grievous bodily harm, liquid ecstasy	I/swallowed	for GHB—drowsiness, nausea/vomiting, headache, loss of consciousness, loss of reflexes, seizures, coma, death
methaqualone	Quaalude, Sopor, Parest: ludes, mandrex, quad, quay	I/injected, swallowed	for methaqualone—euphoria/depression, poor reflexes, slurred speech, coma
Dissociative Anesthetics			increased heart rate and blood pressure, impaired motor function/memory loss; numbness; nausea/vomiting
ketamine	Ketalar SV: cat Valiums, K, Special K, vitamin K	III/injected, snorted, smoked	Also, for ketamine—at high doses, delirium, depression, respiratory depression and arrest
PCP and analogs	phencyclidine: angel dust, boat, hog, love boat, peace pill	I, II/injected, swallowed, smoked	for PCP and analogs—possible decrease in blood pressure and heart rate, panic, aggression, violence/loss of appetite, depression
Hallucinogens			altered states of perception and feeling; nausea; persisting perception disorder (flashbacks)
LSD	lysergic acid diethylamide: acid, blotter, boomers, cubes, microdot, yellow sunshines	I/swallowed, absorbed through mouth tissues	Also, for LSD and mescaline—increased body temperature, heart rate, blood pressure; loss of appetite, sleeplessness, numbness, weakness, tremors
mescaline	buttons, cactus, mesc, peyote	I/swallowed, smoked	for LSD—persistent mental disorders
psilocybin	magic mushroom, purple passion, shrooms	I/swallowed	for psilocybin—nervousness, paranoia
Opioids and Morphine Derivatives			pain relief, euphoria, drowsiness/nausea, constipation, confusion, sedation, respiratory depression and arrest, tolerance, addiction, unconsciousness, coma, death
codeine	Empirin with Codeine, Fiorinal with Codeine, Robitussin A-C, Tylenol with Codeine: Captain Cody, Cody, schoolboy; (with glutethimide) doors & fours, loads, pancakes and syrup	II, III, IV, V/injected, swallowed	Also, for codeine—less analgesia, sedation, and respiratory depression than morphine
fentanyl and fentanyl analogs	Actiq, Duragesic, Sublimaze: Apache, China girl, China white, dance fever, friend, goodfella, jackpot, murder 8, TNT, Tango and Cash	I, II/injected, smoked, snorted	for heroin—staggering gait
heroin	diacetylmorphine: brown sugar, dope, H, horse, junk, skag, skunk, smack, white horse	I/injected, smoked, snorted	
morphine	Roxanol, Duramorph: M, Miss Emma, monkey, white stuff	II, III/injected, swallowed, smoked	
opium	laudanum, paregoric: big O, black stuff, block, gum, hop	II, III, V/swallowed, smoked	
oxycodone HCL	OxyContin: Oxy, O.C., killer	II/swallowed, snorted, injected	
hydrocodone bitartrate, acetaminophen	Vicodin: vike, Watson-387	II/swallowed	
Stimulants			increased heart rate, blood pressure, metabolism; feelings of exhilaration, energy, increased mental alertness/rapid or irregular heart beat; reduced appetite, weight loss, heart failure, nervousness, insomnia
amphetamine	Biphetamine, Dexedrine: bennies, black beauties, crosses, hearts, LA turnaround, speed, truck drivers, uppers	II/injected, swallowed, smoked, snorted	Also, for amphetamine—rapid breathing/tremor, loss of coordination; irritability, anxiousness, restlessness, delirium, panic, paranoia, impulsive behavior, aggressiveness, tolerance, addiction, psychosis
cocaine	Cocaine hydrochloride: blow, bump, C, candy, Charlie, coke, crack, flake, rock, snow, toot	II/injected, smoked, snorted	for cocaine—increased temperature/chest pain, respiratory failure, nausea, abdominal pain, strokes, seizures, headaches, malnutrition, panic attacks

*Schedule I and II drugs have a high potential for abuse. They require greater storage security and have a quota on manufacturing, among other restrictions. Schedule I drugs are available for research only and have no approved medical use. Schedule II drugs are available only by prescription (unrefillable) and require a form for ordering. Schedule III and IV drugs are available by prescription, may have five refills in 6 months, and may be ordered orally. Most Schedule V drugs are available over the counter.
**Taking drugs by injection can increase the risk of infection through needle contamination with staphylococci, HIV, hepatitis, and other organisms.
***Associated with sexual assaults.

5/05

Substances: Category and Name	Examples of Commercial and Street Names	DEA Schedule*/ How Administered**	Intoxication Effects/Potential Health Consequences
Stimulants (continued)			
MDMA (methylenedioxymethamphetamine)	Adam, clarity, ecstasy, Eve, lover's speed, peace, STP, X, XTC	I/swallowed	for MDMA—mild hallucinogenic effects, increased tactile sensitivity, empathic feelings/impaired memory and learning, hyperthermia, cardiac toxicity, renal failure, liver toxicity
methamphetamine	Desoxyn: chalk, crank, crystal, fire, glass, go fast, ice, meth, speed	II/injected, swallowed, smoked, snorted	for methamphetamine—aggression, violence, psychotic behavior/memory loss, cardiac and neurological damage; impaired memory and learning, tolerance, addiction
methylphenidate (safe and effective for treatment of ADHD)	Ritalin: JIF, MPH, R-ball, Skippy, the smart drug, vitamin R	II/injected, swallowed, snorted	for nicotine—additional effects attributable to tobacco exposure: adverse pregnancy outcomes; chronic lung disease, cardiovascular disease, stroke, cancer; tolerance, addiction
nicotine	cigarettes, cigars, smokeless tobacco, snuff, spit tobacco, bidis, chew	not scheduled/smoked, snorted, taken in snuff and spit tobacco	
Other Compounds			
anabolic steroids	Anadrol, Oxandrin, Durabolin, Depo-Testosterone, Equipoise: roids, juice	III/injected, swallowed, applied to skin	no intoxication effects/hypertension, blood clotting and cholesterol changes, liver cysts and cancer, kidney cancer, hostility and aggression, acne; in adolescents, premature stoppage of growth; in males, prostate cancer, reduced sperm production, shrunken testicles, breast enlargement; in females, menstrual irregularities, development of beard and other masculine characteristics
inhalants	Solvents (paint thinners, gasoline, glues), gases (butane, propane, aerosol propellants, nitrous oxide), nitrites (isoamyl, isobutyl, cyclohexyl): laughing gas, poppers, snappers, whippets	not scheduled/inhaled through nose or mouth	stimulation, loss of inhibition; headache; nausea or vomiting; slurred speech, loss of motor coordination; wheezing/unconsciousness, cramps, weight loss, muscle weakness, depression, memory impairment, damage to cardiovascular and nervous systems, sudden death

Principles of Drug Addiction Treatment

Nearly three decades of scientific research have yielded 13 fundamental principles that characterize effective drug abuse treatment. These principles are detailed in NIDA's *Principles of Drug Addiction Treatment: A Research-Based Guide*.

1. No single treatment is appropriate for all individuals. Matching treatment settings, interventions, and services to each patient's problems and needs is critical.

2. Treatment needs to be readily available. Treatment applicants can be lost if treatment is not immediately available or readily accessible.

3. Effective treatment attends to multiple needs of the individual, not just his or her drug use. Treatment must address the individual's drug use and associated medical, psychological, social, vocational, and legal problems.

4. At different times during treatment, a patient may develop a need for medical services, family therapy, vocational rehabilitation, and social and legal services.

5. Remaining in treatment for an adequate period of time is critical for treatment effectiveness. The time depends on an individual's needs. For most patients, the threshold of significant improvement is reached at about 3 months in treatment. Additional treatment can produce further progress. Programs should include strategies to prevent patients from leaving treatment prematurely.

6. Individual and/or group counseling and other behavioral therapies are critical components of effective treatment for addiction. In therapy, patients address motivation, build skills to resist drug use, replace drug using activities with constructive and rewarding nondrug-using activities, and improve problem-solving abilities. Behavioral therapy also facilitates interpersonal relationships.

7. Medications are an important element of treatment for many patients, especially when combined with counseling and other behavioral therapies. Buprenorphine, methadone, and levo-alpha-acetylmethadol (LAAM) help persons addicted to opiates stabilize their lives and reduce their drug use. Naltrexone is effective for some opiate addicts and some patients with co-occurring alcohol dependence. Nicotine patches or gum, or an oral medication, such as bupropion, can help persons addicted to nicotine.

8. Addicted or drug-abusing individuals with coexisting mental disorders should have both disorders treated in an integrated way.

9. Medical detoxification is only the first stage of addiction treatment and by itself does little to change long-term drug use. Medical detoxification manages the acute physical symptoms of withdrawal. For some individuals it is a precursor to effective drug addiction treatment.

10. Treatment does not need to be voluntary to be effective. Sanctions or enticements in the family, employment setting, or criminal justice system can significantly increase treatment entry, retention, and success.

11. Possible drug use during treatment must be monitored continuously. Monitoring a patient's drug and alcohol use during treatment, such as through urinalysis, can help the patient withstand urges to use drugs. Such monitoring also can provide early evidence of drug use so that treatment can be adjusted.

12. Treatment programs should provide assessment for HIV/AIDS, hepatitis B and C, tuberculosis and other infectious diseases, and counseling to help patients modify or change behaviors that place them or others at risk of infection. Counseling can help patients avoid high-risk behavior and help people who are already infected manage their illness.

13. Recovery from drug addiction can be a long-term process and frequently requires multiple episodes of treatment. As with other chronic illnesses, relapses to drug use can occur during or after successful treatment episodes. Participation in self-help support programs during and following treatment often helps maintain abstinence.

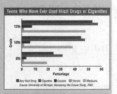

Teens Who Have Ever Used Illicit Drugs or Cigarettes

Percentage of U.S. Population (Aged 12 and Over) Who Have Ever Used Drugs of Abuse

Order NIDA publications from NCADI:
1-800-729-6686
or TDD: 1-800-487-4889

inquire about consequences is to ask the client whether there have ever been any problems in these areas where alcohol/drugs have been involved. Asking the question in such a manner does not imply causality but does get at the overlap of using alcohol/drugs and behavior. It can also show the client's level of denial (e.g., "I had that many DUIs because the cops are after me"). The consequences are an important source of corroborating information by the counselor. If the client agrees, releases of information can be obtained for each area that seems pertinent in order to receive information about the level of the alcohol/drug problem. If the client does not agree to signing releases of information, the counselor needs to document on the chart that the assessment is limited in scope and possibly in terms of accuracy because the client refused to allow information to be gathered from specific, relevant sources. This refusal also needs to be shared with any referral agent for the client's evaluation.

Ten sample questions that may be used in an interview process follow:

1. What has happened in your life now that caused you to come in for an assessment of your alcohol/drug usage?

2. Is there any history of addiction (chemical or other) in your family of origin?

3. Where do you currently live? Whom do you currently live with? What is that person's (persons') use of alcohol/drugs like? Do you use with this person(s)? What is your pattern of use like with that person(s)?

4. When is the last time you used alcohol or drugs?

5. What is your favorite drug and how do you like to take it (smoking, inhaling, injecting, ingesting)?

6. Tell me all the drugs you have ever tried.

7. (For each drug reported.) When did you first take this drug? When did you last take this drug? What was your typical use pattern with this drug? Within the past few months (or years, depending on the person's length of use history), how have you typically used this drug? Have you ever quit the drug you are currently using and, if so, why and for how long?

8. Have you been treated previously for addiction? If so, where, when, how long, and what type of treatment (detox, inpatient, outpatient)? How long did your stay sober after each treatment and what helped you stay sober that long?

9. (If the client had previous treatment.) What was most helpful to you in that treatment? What was least helpful to you? Also, who was most helpful/least helpful to you?

10. Have you ever experienced any problems in this area connected with your alcohol and drug use? (Insert one area each time this question is asked: legal; family, significant others, friends; job, school, military; medical; financial.)

Finally, the counselor needs to use a mental status examination throughout the interview process. Perkinson (2008) provides an excellent example of a mental status exam in the Appendix section of his book. G. Buelow and Buelow (1998) suggest that the exam cover the client's functioning in terms of appearance, orientation, behavior, speech, cooperation, mood, perception, thinking process, intellectual abilities, and insight/judgment. In the area of *appearance*, the counselor should look at how clients are sitting, at how they are dressed, and at their hygiene. As to *orientation*, are they oriented to person, place, and time? As to their *behavior*, how active are they; do they have tremors; what are their mannerisms, facial expressions, and eye contact like? As to *speech*, what does their voice sound like, what words do they use as well as the rate and rhythm, and how *cooperative* are they in the session? What kind of *mood* are they in—how labile, appropriate, and intense is it? As to *perception, thinking process, intellectual abilities,* and *insight/judgment,* look at how alert they are; do they have delusions, hallucinations, anxiety, phobias, obsessions/compulsions, suicidal or violent tendencies, problems with immediate, short-term, or long-term memory; can they concentrate? In summary, Nussbaum (2013) adds the importance of assessing additional components in terms of: *behavior* (stereotypes-repetitive and nongoal-directed behavior that is abnormal; posturing—striking a pose and maintaining it, waxy flexibility—limbs being resistive to passive motion, catalepsy—maintaining a position, agitation, psychomotor retardation, extrapyramidal symptoms, and tardive dyskinesia); *speech* (volume, quality, presence of latency); and *emotion* (quality, range).

DWI/DUI/OWI/OUI Assessments

Counselors may conduct specific assessments for clients who have been charged with a DWI (driving while intoxicated), DUI (driving under the influence), OWI (operating while intoxicated), or OUI (operating under the influence). Although these terms vary, they all mean the same thing: The client was operating a motor vehicle while under the effects of alcohol or drugs. In the United States, many states have an educational intervention for these clients, and some require an assessment of the client's alcohol and drug use (although they may vary in terms of when and how the assessment is given). Counselors who anticipate conducting these types of assessments need to contact their appropriate state agency that oversees this charge for information about the specific interventions and assessments required for this population. In the instrument section of this chapter are two instruments specifically designed for this population: (1) the Driver Risk Inventory–II (DRI-11), and (2) the Behaviors & Attitudes Drinking & Driving Scale (BADDS) that may be especially useful in prevention programs for measuring behaviors before and after the experience. Counselors who work specifically with this population may find *A Guide to Sentencing DWI*

Offenders (2nd ed., 2005), which was developed by the National Highway Traffic Safety Administration (NHTSA) and NIAAA, to be a helpful resource. The guide can be accessed at www.nhtsa.dot.gov

Interviewing Significant Others

Interviews with significant others are similar to those with the client. Significant others include those individuals who are close to the client and know the client well (e.g., parents, children, intimate partner, and coworkers). When interviewing significant others, it is necessary for the counselor to remember that the significant other may have a hidden agenda (e.g., pent-up anger) that slants the significant other's viewpoint, or may have denial about the alcohol/drug problem, or may be unable to tell the truth about concerns because of some dynamics of the relationship (e.g., a domestic violence situation). Keeping in mind these possible limitations, the counselor can begin to obtain information from the significant other. The client needs to sign a release that allows the counselor to talk with the significant other. The significant other needs to understand that the client is aware of and has agreed to a discussion of the alcohol/drug-taking behavior.

Once the parameters of the situation are understood, the counselor needs to obtain a brief history of the relationship between the client and the significant other. This will provide the counselor with a context for understanding the information given before obtaining the information without causing unnecessary harm to the client or significant other. In some situations, it may be best to interview the significant other in the presence of the client, so the client can hear all the information being told to the counselor, thereby reducing the secrecy and denial around the addiction. In other situations, it may be best to interview the significant other alone to try to prevent abuse from happening to the significant other due to information disclosed in the interview. It is also important for the counselor to determine whether the significant other may also have a drinking/drug problem by asking questions such as: Do you often use with (client)? How often and how much do the two of you use in a week? Even though the significant other is not being evaluated for a drinking/drug problem, the counselor needs to know whether there is a possibility of such a problem in the significant other, because it could affect the assessment and, if appropriate, treatment and aftercare process.

The significant other needs to be asked questions about the client's alcohol/drug usage similar to the questions the client was asked. Finding out what the significant other views as the presenting problem may provide the counselor with valuable information. In addition, hearing from the significant other about the client's family of origin, living situation, drug of choice, drug use history, previous treatment, and consequences of his or her usage may provide additional, clarifying information that can be used in the assessment process. The significant other may involve more than one individual. For example, the counselor may want to talk with an entire family about the client's use. Once again, the counselor needs to remember that individuals may differ in their perceptions, but what is being sought are patterns of behavior that emerge in different areas of the client's life.

Also, in the interview with the significant others, the counselor can assess the level of support that may be available to the client during the treatment and recovery process (Margolis & Zweben, 2011).

BEHAVIORAL OBSERVATIONS

Involving the client in observing his or her own alcohol/drug-using behavior can work to educate the client and the counselor about the client's usage. One example of such a behavioral observation is to have the client agree to a limited-use contract. In this type of contract, the counselor asks the client to set a limit on his or her usage with one drug (and not using other drugs at all), preferably the client's drug of choice or most frequently used drug. This limit is set for less than the typical amount used and for a specific time. For instance, the client may normally drink six beers three times a week and use small amounts of marijuana and speed. The contract may read that the client will not drink more than three beers at a sitting for 1 month (and will not use marijuana, speed, or any other drug at all). The counselor would ask the client to keep a log of use. If the amount is exceeded, the counselor would then ask the client to note the situation and why the amount was exceeded. The client needs to understand that an inability to follow the agreed-on limit indicates a problem with alcohol/drugs.

The client may be in denial and return to the counselor with notations made as to when the agreement was violated and why. This is an excellent opportunity for the counselor to confront the client about the possible drug problem. The client also may not tell the counselor the truth about usage. Even if the information about breaking the limit does not get back to the session, that does not mean that the client did not learn from the experience. The client may have learned that there is an alcohol/drug problem because of the inability to limit usage. If the client was able to follow the use limit, this information can also be used in the diagnostic process as an indication of control over chemical use. The limited-use contract needs to be used carefully and thoughtfully by the counselor. The counselor needs to avoid the appearance of encouraging use and be aware that some usage of specific drugs is simply dangerous to the client (e.g., inhalants).

Other behavioral observations may occur more formally or informally. That information can be supplied through chart notations made at institutions and through conversations with individuals in different aspects of the client's life. These behavioral observations need to be relayed back to the client in order to intervene effectively on the alcohol/drug use program (e.g., break denial) and develop the therapeutic alliance by avoiding secrets.

PHYSIOLOGICAL INSTRUMENTS

One way to obtain information about a client's chemical usage is through medical examinations and diagnostic tests. Physicians may be able to document the irrefutable impact of alcohol/drugs on the client's body. Also, when high or in withdrawal, an addicted client may appear to have physical or psychiatric problems that are present only because of their relationship with the drug(s) (Vereby & Buchan, 1997). Therefore, a summary of medical history and concerns may assist the assessing counselor in determining whether a problem is present by providing factual information about the client's body that can be readily linked to problems with alcohol/drugs.

Another avenue for determining whether a client has been free of alcohol/drugs is through drug testing. Inaba and Cohen (1989) report that numerous forms of drug testing can be done with samples of tissue, hair, blood, saliva, and urine. Van Wormer and Davis (2008) add that if urinalysis testing needs to be done, drug and sweat patches are an option: There is an adhesive that collects sweat over a period of time (weeks, months) or a product called Macroduct that creates sweat and is very helpful in detecting opiates and cocaine. There is also a Quick-strip or instant in-house STAT urine test that reduces the urinalysis results wait time. Portable breathalyzers and IV blood alcohol levels are additional ways to test for drugs. If a counselor uses a form of drug testing, the counselor needs to receive informed consent from the client, carefully choose the laboratory that will do the testing, and know both the limitations and strengths of the methods used (G. Miller & Kaplan, 1996). For overall information on drug testing in the schools, NIH has a short brochure, *Frequently Asked Questions About Drug Testing in the Schools*, through its website (www.nih.gov).

An obvious drawback to such an approach in an assessment process is that it may cause the client to feel mistrusted by the counselor in terms of the client's self-report. Using drug testing in the assessment process needs to be carefully weighed by the counselor in terms of this potential mistrust. The counselor may decrease the anxiety and/or defensiveness of the client by reframing the purpose of the drug testing. For example, it may help clients to be reminded that people who are addicted tend to have a sense of denial about their addiction and that during their assessment and treatment process, they may need to have some validation of their sobriety by taking a test. This process does not need to occur throughout their recovery, but sometimes, especially early in the process, it may prevent the client and counselor from conflicting views around usage by having an outside, objective view (test results) incorporated into the counseling. In addition, a matter-of-fact attitude by the counselor can communicate this testing as a routine process done with clients so the client does not take the requirement as personal to his or her situation, but rather as a standard approach.

The same approaches can be used when the client is court-ordered for testing. In this context, the counselor needs to talk openly with the client about the requirement for the testing and the impact of this testing on the counseling relationship.

PSYCHOMETRIC INSTRUMENTS

It is a legitimate question to ask: Why even learn about and/or use psychometric instruments when a counselor can obtain information from other sources? There are a number of reasons for their use. First, the counselor can use the results of the instrument as another source of information that can assist clients and their significant others in understanding the depth of the substance use disorder, i.e. break their denial about the addiction. Second, some settings use the instruments as a typical part of the assessment process. Third, some funding sources will require the use of psychometric instruments as a part of the assessment. Fourth, because increasingly counselors come into the substance abuse field with variation of training, the counselor may not have specific training on assessment instruments and a psychometric instrument can anchor the results of the assessment. Finally, a psychometric instrument can protect the counselor both legally and ethically as a standard measure of the substance use disorder.

A counselor needs to carefully choose psychometric instruments. The National Institute on Alcohol Abuse and Alcoholism (NIAAA; 1995a) lists nine factors that a counselor needs to consider when selecting an assessment instrument:

1. The use of the instrument.

2. The alcohol use time frame that is specifically being assessed.

3. The population for which the instrument was developed.

4. The groups used in determining the evaluative capacity of the instrument.

5. The comparison norms available.

6. The options for administration.

7. The administration training required.

8. The availability of computerized scoring.

9. The cost.

In addition to this list, the counselor needs to carefully consider matching the instrument to the client. Use of an instrument with which the client feels comfortable will increase their willingness to talk about their alcohol/drug use (Tuunanen, Aalto, & Seppa, 2013). Also, the counselor may need to consider cost and availability of instruments (e.g., copyright versus public domain). The book *Assessing Common Mental Health and Addiction Issues with Free-Access Instruments*, which is referenced at the end of this chapter, may assist the counselor in making an instrument choice that is free of charge.

Regarding the texts reviewed in this section, the counselor may: (1) have limited or no access to the tests, (2) find some instruments more comfortable to use than others, and/or (3) find the number of assessment instruments available to be overwhelming. Therefore, the beginning addiction professional may want to choose one or two from each section (broad/overview, adult, adolescent) based on the criteria outlined above. Addiction professionals may also find it helpful to develop competency with instruments that assess adolescents and adults. Sometimes they choose two instruments covering the age span that are developed by the same company, because familiarity with one age group test (e.g., adolescents) will result in familiarity with a similar instrument for the other age group (e.g., adults). Also, the professional may choose to use one instrument that covers the broad age range with whom he or she normally works. The counselor may then become familiar with the instrument he or she anticipates using most often through readings, trainings, and workshops. The NIAAA (1995a) provides a thorough review of alcohol assessment instruments. The following review is a select one, emphasizing a few instruments that may be used in a broad fashion and more extensive assessment instruments that may be used with adults and adolescents.

In general, a counselor needs to have some understanding of the statistical properties of a test to make a good choice in the use and proper interpretation of the test. When choosing and administering tests, the counselor should be familiar with the reliability and validity of the tests. *Reliability* reflects the consistency of the instrument (the stability of the instrument), and *validity* reflects whether the test meets its intended purpose (it measures what it intends to measure). There are different types of reliability (test-retest, alternate form, internal consistency, Kuder-Richardson formula 20 coefficient, and Cronbach's coefficient alpha) and validity (content, construct, criterion-related, and predictive; Sattler, 1992). Typically, reliability coefficients of .80 or greater reflect adequate reliability (80% of the score is true and 20% is due to error). The *validity* of the instrument will address whether the instrument has been tested with the population to which the client belongs (e.g., is it a valid test to use with this client?).

In addition, tests select targeted populations by establishing a cutoff score. A test with high *sensitivity* has few false negatives. This means: "This is the test's 'hit rate' out of only those who are diagnosed with the disorder (i.e., the proportion of people with depression the test would identify)" (Erford, 2013, p. 159). A test with high *specificity* has few false positives. This means: "This is the test's 'hit rate' out of only those who are not diagnosed with the disorder (i.e., the proportion of people without depression the test would identify as not having depression)" (Erford, 2013, p. 159).

Broad Screening Instruments

Regarding broad screening instruments, in 2003, SAMHSA launched the initiative Screening for Substance Use, Brief Intervention and/or Referral to Treatment (SBIRT) in seven states to integrate substance use services into the medical mainstream (Gonzales et al., 2012). The effectiveness of brief interventions in medical settings has been supported in the research (Gonzales et al., 2012). The guidelines for SBIRT can be found at the SAMHSA website (www.samhsa.gov). A summary of one medical setting brief intervention that counselors may be able to use in their setting can be found at http://www.niaaa.nih.gov/research/niaaa-research-highlights/screening-and-brief-interventions-performed-er-staff-can-reduce

The following instruments can be used by a clinician to obtain a general overview of the client's alcohol/drug usage. There are two main sections: broad screening instruments (adults, adolescents, elderly) and specific screening instruments (adults, adolescents). Note that some of the adult broad screening instruments can also be used with adolescents. Positive broad screening instrument indicators of an alcohol/drug problem can be more extensively evaluated through the use

of specific screening instruments. Descriptions of specific instruments follow the broad screening instruments section.

Broad Screening Instruments (Adults)

Broad screening instruments that can be used with adults are described in this section. Some of these, as noted earlier, can also be used with an adolescent population.

Alcohol, Smoking, and Substance Involvement Screening Test (ASSIST)

The World Health Organization developed the ASSIST, an adult and adolescent screening tool that is available online (www.who.int/substance_abuse/activities/assist_test/en/index.html). It is a questionnaire that is directed by an interviewer. It has eight questions and takes 15 to 20 minutes to administer. Scoring procedures are included in the website link. The instrument shows adequate reliability and validity (K. M. Sandberg et al., 2013).

Alcohol Use Disorders Identification Test (AUDIT) (and Related Tests)

The *Alcohol Use Disorders Identification Test* (AUDIT; Saunders, Aasland, Babor, de la Fuente, & Grant, 1993) came out of a study in six nations. It came from the World Health Organization's interest in developing a tool that could be used in different cultural settings. It has 10 Likert-type items: alcohol consumption (three questions), dependence symptoms (four questions), and alcohol-related problems (three questions). The questions can be answered as part of an interview or responded to by paper and pencil. It takes about 2 minutes, and there are multiple language translations. A score of 8 indicates at-risk drinking (see Table 3.2). It has test-retest reliability of .86 and internal consistency of .75 to .94. It has shown construct, discriminant, and criteria-related validity.

Another question that can distinguish risky drinkers is the *AUDIT: Frequency of Drunkenness*

Table 3.2   Audit

Please circle the answer that is correct for you.

1. How often do you have a drink containing alcohol?

   Never   Monthly or less   Two to four times a month   Two to three times a week   Four or more times a week

2. How many drinks containing alcohol do you have on a typical day when you are drinking?

   1 or 2   3 or 4   5 or 6   7 to 9   10 or more

3. How often do you have six or more drinks on one occasion?

   Never   Less than monthly   Monthly   Weekly   Daily or almost daily

4. How often during the last year have you found that you were not able to stop drinking once you had started?

   Never   Less than monthly   Monthly   Weekly   Daily or almost daily

5. How often during the last year have you failed to do what was normally expected from you because of drinking?

   Never   Less than monthly   Monthly   Weekly   Daily or almost daily

6. How often during the last year have you needed a first drink in the morning to get yourself going after a heavy drinking session?

   Never   Less than monthly   Monthly   Weekly   Daily or almost daily

7. How often during the last year have you had a feeling of guilt or remorse after drinking?

   Never   Less than monthly   Monthly   Weekly   Daily or almost daily

8. How often during the last year have you been unable to remember what happened the night before because you had been drinking?

   Never   Less than monthly   Monthly   Weekly   Daily or almost daily

9. Have you or someone else been injured as a result of your drinking?

   No   Yes, but not in the last year   Yes, during the last year

10. Has a relative or friend, or a doctor or other health worker been concerned about your drinking or suggested you cut down?

    No   Yes, but not in the last year   Yes, during the last year

Note: Questions 1–8 are scored 0, 1, 2, 3, or 4 ("Never" to "4 or more times per week" respectively). Questions 9 and 10 are scored 0, 2, or 4 respectively.

Source: AUDIT: Guidelines for Use in Primary Care, 2nd edition, by T. F. Babor, J. C. Higgins Biddle, J. B. Saunders, and M. G. Monteiro, 2002. Reprinted with permission. Copyright permission has been granted by Dr. Vladmir Poznyak (poznyakv@who.ch), Department of Mental Health and Substance Dependence, World Health Organization, CH-1211 Geneva 27, Switzerland. Reprinted with permission of John Wiley & Sons, Inc.

Question: "In a typical week, how many days do you get drunk?" (drunk defined as dizzy, unsteady, or sick to your stomach) (O'Brien, Reboussin, Veach, & Miller, 2012).

The *AUDIT-C* (C = Consumption) is a broad screening instrument for adolescents. It consists of the first three items of the AUDIT, a cutoff score of 5, and has been shown to have acceptable levels of reliability and validity (Rumpf, Wohlert, Freyer-Adams, Grothues, & Bischoff, 2013; Sandberg, Richards, & Erford, 2013).

There is also the 10-item *CUDIT* (Adamson & Sellman, 2003) that directly modified the AUDIT to assess for clients using cannabis in harmful ways within the previous 6 months. Again it appears to have acceptable levels of reliability and validity (Adamson et al., 2010; Guillem et al., 2011). The *CUDIT-R* is an eight-item instrument that has four items from the original CUDIT and four additional items; it also appears to have acceptable levels of reliability and validity (Adamson et al., 2010).

Behaviors & Attitudes Drinking & Driving Scale (BADDS)

The BADDS (Jewel & Hupp, 2005) was developed with a college student population and has been expanded to adult DUI and traffic offenders (Jewel, Hupp, & Segrist, 2008). It has been shown to have internal reliability, test-retest reliability and validity (concurrent criterion, construct, predictive criterion, discriminant) (Jewel et al., 2008). This instrument may be especially useful in prevention programs to track behaviors before and after the program experience (Jewel et al., 2008).

In this author's opinion, this instrument may also be useful as a screening instrument with adults in that it may point out behaviors and attitudes about drinking and driving that raise a counselor's concern. Such concern would warrant further investigation of a potential substance use problem through one of the broad screening instruments for substance abuse discussed in this section.

CAGE

The CAGE (Ewing, 1984) has been used to determine whether a client has a problem with alcohol. It can be given verbally or in a paper-and-pencil format. It takes about 1 minute to administer. The first letter of each of the capitalized phrases spells out the acronym. The instrument can be used with individuals age 16 or older and appears to have internal consistency reliability and criterion validity (NIAAA, 1995a). Fleming (2003) recommends that it be used with questions that explore the client's quantity and frequency of use as well as binge drinking. A cutoff score of 2 is typically used. Internal consistency reliability is .89 (for a score of 2) with a sensitivity of 74% and specificity of 91%.

T-ACE

The T-ACE (Sokol, Martier, & Ager, 1989), also similar to the CAGE, was developed for pregnant women. It is a four-item questionnaire that requires about 1 minute to administer (see Table 3.3). If it takes more than two drinks to make her high, a woman receives two points for tolerance; each of the other items receive one point if answered positively. A total score of more than 2 indicates at-risk drinking. It has a sensitivity of 69% and a specificity of 89%.

Table 3.3   T-ACE

1. How many drinks does it take to make you feel high (TOLERANCE)?
2. Have people ANNOYED you by criticizing your drinking?
3. Have you felt you ought to CUT DOWN on your drinking?
4. Have you ever had a drink first thing in the morning to steady your nerves or get rid of a hangover (EYE OPENER)?

Source: "The T-ACE Questions: Practical Prenatal Detection of Risk Drinking," by R. J. Sokol, S. S. Martier, and J. W. Ager, 1989, *American Journal of Obstetrics and Gynecology, 160,* pp. 863–870.

TWEAK

The TWEAK (M. Russell, Martier, & Sokol, 1991), a five-item scale, was based on the CAGE and was developed for pregnant women. It also can be given verbally or in a paper-and-pencil format. It requires less than 2 minutes to take (see Table 3.4). It has a sensitivity of 79% and a specificity of 83%.

Table 3.4   TWEAK

TWEAK is a five-item scale developed originally to screen for risk drinking during pregnancy. It is an acronym for the following questions:

T—Tolerance: "How many drinks can you hold?"

W—Worried: "Have close friends or relatives Worried or complained about your drinking in the past year?"

E—Eye-openers: "Do you sometimes take a drink in the morning when you first get up?"

A—Amnesia (blackouts): "Has a friend or family member ever told you about things you said or did while you were drinking that you could not remember?"

K(C)—Cut Down: "Do you sometimes feel the need to Cut Down on your drinking?"

Source: From "Screening for Pregnancy Risk-Drinking: Tweaking the Tests," by M. Russell, S. S. Martier, and R. J. Sokol, 1991, *Alcoholism: Clinical and Experimental Research, 15*(2), p. 368.

To score the test, a 7-point scale is used. The tolerance question scores 2 points if a woman reports she can hold more than five drinks without passing out, and a positive response to the worry question scores 2 points. Each of the last three questions scores 1 point for positive responses. A total score of 3 or more points indicates the woman is likely to be a heavy/problem drinker (NIAAA, 1995a, p. 545). With a 3-point cutoff, the sensitivity ranges from 70% to 90% and specificity from 75% to 80%.

MacAndrew Alcoholism Scale (MAC) and MacAndrew Alcoholism Scale–Revised (MAC- R)

The MacAndrew Alcoholism Scale (MAC) and the MacAndrew Alcoholism Scale–Revised (MAC-R) are also measurements of alcohol/drug use (J. Duckworth & Anderson, 1986; J. R. Graham, 1990). The MAC consists of 49 objective true/false statements included in the 566-item Minnesota Multiphasic Personality Inventory (MMPI), which was developed in the 1930s and 1940s. The MAC-R was created in the MMPI-2 (1989; 567 items) by deleting 4 objectionable items from the MAC and adding four additional items, resulting in the same number of true/false statements (49). Both the MAC and the MAC-R are self-administered tests, work as well for drugs as alcohol, and are easily scored by clerical personnel. It takes approximately 90 minutes to administer the tests, and it takes about 2 to 3 minutes each to score by hand, although typically the instrument is computer scored. Both the MAC and the MAC-R measure the *potential* for addiction to alcohol/drugs. Both have adequate test-retest reliability (MAC-R has .82 for males and .75 for females over a 6-week interval). Because they measure more than one dimension, the construct validity is questionable. Graham (1990) recommends no clinical decisions be based on the MAC or the MAC-R scores alone because of problems with the accuracy of classification.

Michigan Alcohol Screening Test (MAST)

The purpose of the Michigan Alcohol Screening Test (MAST; Selzer, 1971) is to detect the

Table 3.5 The Short Michigan Alcoholism Screening Test (SMAST)

1. Do you feel you are a normal drinker? (By *normal* we mean you drink less than or as much as most other people?) (No)
2. Does your wife, husband, a parent, or other near relative ever worry or complain about your drinking? (Yes)
3. Do you ever feel guilty about your drinking? (Yes)
4. Do friends or relatives think you are a normal drinker? (No)
5. Are you able to stop drinking when you want to? (No)
6. Have you ever attended a meeting of Alcoholics Anonymous? (Yes)
7. Has drinking ever created problems between you and your wife, husband, a parent, or other near relative? (Yes)
8. Have you ever gotten into trouble at work because of your drinking? (Yes)
9. Have you ever neglected your obligations, your family, or your work for two or more days in a row because you were drinking? (Yes)
10. Have you ever gone to anyone for help about your drinking? (Yes)
11. Have you ever been in a hospital because of drinking? (Yes)
12. Have you ever been arrested for drunken driving, driving while intoxicated, or driving under the influence of alcoholic beverages? (Yes)
13. Have you ever been arrested, even for a few hours, because of other drunken behavior? (Yes)

Note. Answers related to alcoholism are given in parentheses after each question. Three or more of these answers indicate probable alcoholism; two answers indicate the possibility of alcoholism; less than two answers indicate that alcoholism is not likely.

Source: Reprinted with permission from *Journal of Studies on Alcohol, 36,* 1975, pp. 117–126. Copyright *Journal of Studies on Alcohol,* Rutgers Center of Alcohol Studies, Piscataway, NJ 08854.

presence and extent of drinking in adults. This paper-and-pencil test (see Table 3.5) is a convenient, efficient screening (not diagnostic) measure of drinking problems. It uses a yes/no format and has 25 items. It can be completed in approximately 10 minutes. The most popular scoring procedure assigns scores of 2 or 1 for each of the questions (0 if the response is nondrinking), except item number 7, which does not receive a score. Because item 7 ("Do you ever try to limit your drinking to certain times of the day or to certain places?") does not receive a score of 1 or 2, this item is sometimes eliminated in the test taking (Selzer, 1985).

To control for clients who appear to have alcohol problems when they actually do not, the counselor may need to gather more clinical information or modify the scoring system to make it more stringent. (The more conservative scoring system makes a score of 5 indicative of alcoholism.) The instrument appears valid; a number of studies show high agreement between MAST scores and previous alcohol-related problems. Studies report high internal consistency reliabilities of .83 to .95, and test-retest reliability over 1 to 3 days is .86 (Connors & Tarbox, 1985).

A shortened version of the MAST is called the SMAST (Short MAST; Selzer, Vinokur, & van-Rooijen, 1975), shown in Table 3.5. Using stepwise multiple regression, 13 MAST items (1, 3, 5, 6, 8, 9, 11, 14, 16, 20, 21, 24, 25) were retained, because they distinguished especially well between alcoholics and nonalcoholics, and one MAST item (24) was expanded to alcohol-related arrests. All items are scored one point if the answer indicates alcoholism. A total of three or more points means that alcoholism is probable, 2 or more points means it is possible, and less than 2 points means it is unlikely. With pregnant women, it has a risk-drinking sensitivity of 11.4% and a specificity of 95.9%.

In addition, the Brief Michigan Alcoholism Screening Test (Brief MAST; Pokorny, Miller, & Kaplan, 1972) has 10 items (see Table 3.5). The Brief MAST has an overall sensitivity of 30% to 78% and a specificity of 80% to 99%.

Finally, the Michigan Alcoholism Screening Test for Alcohol and Drugs (MAST/AD) examines drug abuse and dependence beyond alcohol.

It has 24 items from the MAST, but it also has reference to drug use.

Broad Screening Instruments (Adolescents)

NIAAA developed an alcohol screening and brief intervention for ages 9 to 18 in collaboration with the AAP. Its publication, *Alcohol Screening and Brief Intervention for Youth: A Practitioner's Guide*, can be obtained at the NIAAA website (http://pubs.niaaa.nih.gov/publications/Practitioner/YouthGuide/YouthGuide.pdf). The screening instrument consists of two questions that are focused on: the client's friends' drinking (a predictor of future drinking) and the client's drinking frequency (the best predictor of current risk). The questions vary slightly as they are applied to elementary, middle, and high school students as well as the ordering of the questions. In 2011, the American Academy of Pediatrics (AAP) recommended that pediatricians use the SBIRT guidelines developed by SAMHSA with all adolescents (NIDA, 2011). SAMHSA (1999b) also developed a manual for working with adolescents, *Screening and Assessing Adolescents for Substance Use Disorders*, which is an update of its first manual on adolescent assessment. It provides excellent suggestions for assessment and a thorough summary of assessment instruments that can be used with adolescents.

Alcohol, Smoking, and Substance Involvement Screening Test (ASSIST)

The ASSIST is described in the adult section earlier.

Alcohol Use Disorders Identification Test–Consumption (AUDIT-C)

The AUDIT-C is described in the section of the AUDIT earlier.

CAGE

The CAGE is described in the adult section earlier.

CRAFFT[1]

The CRAFFT (Knight, Sherritt, Shrier, Harris, & Chang, 2002) acronym stands for car, relax, alone, forget, family/friends, and trouble. The CRAFFT is a screener developed specifically for adolescents (ages 14–18) that is available online through the Boston Children's Hospital Center for Adolescent Substance Abuse Research (CeASAR)(http://ceasar.org/CRAFFT/index.php). The website provides instructions on the administration of the instrument.

The six questions are:

C—Have you ever ridden in a CAR driven by someone (including yourself) who was "high" or had been using alcohol or drugs?

R—Do you ever use alcohol or drugs to RELAX, feel better about yourself, or fit in?

A—Do you ever use alcohol/drugs while you are by yourself, ALONE?

F—Do you ever FORGET things you did while using alcohol or drugs?

F—Do your family or FRIENDS ever tell you that you should cut down on your drinking or drug use?

T—Have you ever gotten in TROUBLE while you were using alcohol or drugs?

These six questions are preceded by three opening questions asking whether any alcohol, marijuana, or other drugs were used in the past 12 months. If no alcohol or drugs were used, only the "C" or Car question is asked. If there was any use, then all six questions are asked. It can be self-administered (paper-pencil or on the computer) or orally administered (it can be accessed online by clinicians and clients). Items are scored 0 or 1 (1 = Yes) with cutoff scores of 2 indicating a possible problem (Rumpf et al., 2013; Sandberg et al., 2013). The instrument shows adequate reliability and validity (Rumpf et al., 2013; Sandberg et al., 2013). It is helpful in determining risky use (sensitivity .76 and specificity .94) and dependence (sensitivity .92 and specificity .80) (Pilowsky & Wu, 2013).

Rutgers Alcohol Problem Index (RAPI)

The RAPI was designed and validated specifically to assess problem drinking in adolescents (White & Labouvie, 1989). It is one of the most frequently used alcohol problem assessment instruments with adolescents and college students (Neal, Corbin, & Fromme, 2006). Its internal consistency is .92 and it has strong validity (White & Labouvie, 1989). It has 23 items and is a self-administered instrument. It takes about 10 minutes and can be read at the 12-year-old level. No administration training is required and items can be read to the respondent if there are reading difficulties. The instruction is: "How many times did the following things happen while you were drinking or because of your alcohol use during the *past 3 months*?" It measures the frequency of alcohol-related consequences that have occurred in the past year with a range of 0 (never) to 5 (more than 10 times) (Cohn, Hagman, Graff, & Noel, 2011; Light et al., 2011; White & Labouvie, 1989). The standard score is based on the sum of the 23 items and allows for problem drinking scores to be compared across groups. There is also an 18-item version that has a .99 correlation with the longer version (White & Labouvie, 2000). The RAPI is available from H. White, Center of Alcohol Studies, Rutgers University, Piscataway, NJ, 08854–0989 and can be downloaded from http://research.alcohol-studies.rutgers.edu/rapi. It is free and there is no copyright.

Broad Screening Instruments (Elderly)

The CAGE, the MAST, and the AUDIT have all been used as screening instruments with the

---

[1] © John R. Knight, MD, Boston Children's Hospital, 2014. All rights reserved. Reproduced with permission. For more information, contact ceasar@childrens.harvard.edu.

elderly. The MAST-G is a version specifically designed for the elderly (Blow et al., 1992), as is the SMAST-G, which has 10 items. In addition, SAMHSA (1998c) developed a manual, *Substance Abuse Among Older Adults*, that has an excellent section on identification, screening, and assessment issues in older adults.

Specific Screening Instruments (Adults)

The following instruments can be used for a more in-depth evaluation of adults if there are positive indicators of an alcohol/drug problem based on broad overview instrument results or otherwise obtained client information.

Addiction Severity Index (ASI) and the ASI Multimedia Version

The Addiction Severity Index (ASI; McLellan, Luborsky, O'Brien, & Woody, 1980) is a semistructured interview to be used with adults. It has 200 items divided into seven subscales (employment/support, use of drugs, use of alcohol, status of medical, legal, family/social, and psychiatric in nature). The amount of use and impairment of use are assessed on a 10-point scale from 0 to 9 for each of the seven areas. It takes about an hour to administer, with about 5 minutes to determine severity (which determines client need of treatment), and composite scores are calculated by computer. The ASI was normed on various alcohol/drug treatment groups and subject groups (e.g., homeless and gamblers). It has shown reliability (test-retest, split-half, internal consistency) and validity (content, criterion, construct). Computerized versions showed .68 to .95 (composite scores) and .62 to .84 (severity ratings) in terms of test-retest reliability. Internal consistency of composite scores range from .48 to .88. The ASI-MV is a multimedia version of the ASI, where the client self-administers the instrument in a video or audio format, resulting in a paper-and-pencil self-report or a computerized report.

Alcohol Use Inventory (AUI)

The Alcohol Use Inventory (AUI; Horn, Wanberg, & Foster, 1987) has 228 items and

24 subscales and takes about 35 to 60 minutes to self-administer, 3 to 5 minutes for scoring, and 10 minutes to interpret (without computer). It can be used with adults and adolescents over 16. It has shown good reliability (test-retest, internal consistency) and validity (content, criterion, construct). Most primary scale coefficients range from .65 to .80. It examines perceived benefits and consequences of drinking and thoughts about addressing drinking problems.

Driver Risk Inventory (DRI)

The Driver Risk Inventory (DRI; Behavior Data Systems, 1987) is a self-report test that has 140 items and takes about 25 to 30 minutes to administer and score. It results in risk-level classifications and recommendations based on those classifications. The test uses six behavioral pattern scales (truthfulness, alcohol, drugs, substance dependency/abuse in accordance with *DSM-IV-TR* [American Psychiatric Association, 2000] criteria, driver risk, and stress coping ability), test booklets are in English and Spanish, and it can be given in either a paper-and-pencil or computer format. The DRI was researched and normed on a driving while intoxicated (DWI) population. It was validated in comparison with screener and evaluator ratings, and its internal consistency reliabilities for the five scales range from .83 to .93.

Global Appraisal of Individual Needs (GAIN)

The GAIN is evidence-based and has been used with both adults and adolescents. It consists of eight sections: Background, Substance Use, Physical Health, Risk Behaviors and Disease Prevention, Mental and Emotional Health, Environment and Living Situation, Legal, and Vocational. Each area examines problem recency, symptom breadth, and recent prevalence, as well as utilization concerns (lifetime service, recency, and frequency of recency). It is available in both hardcopy and electronic forms so it can be administered by paper and pencil or computer. There are six versions of the GAIN:

1. GAIN–Short Screener (GAIN-SS): 5-minute administration, two-page instrument used for broad screening.

2. GAIN–Quick (GAIN-Q): 15- to 20-minute administration, 11- to 19-page instrument used to determine appropriate referral agency and/or support motivational interviewing.

3. GAIN–Initial (GAIN-I): 60- to 120-minute administration, 77- to 113-page instrument used as a biopsychosocial assessment instrument for clients entering a substance abuse treatment.

4. GAIN Treatment Satisfaction Index (GAIN-TxSI): 3-minute administration, one page to assess working alliance.

5. GAIN–Monitoring 90-Day (GAIN-M90): The quarterly follow-up of the GAIN-I to look at change over time.

6. GAIN–Quick Monitoring (GAIN-QM): Another quarterly follow-up of the GAIN-Q that looks at change over time and is four pages.

The GAIN has good test-retest reliability on days of use and symptom counts ($r = .7$ to $.8$) and diagnosis (kappa of $.5$ to $.7$). Self-reports are consistent (kappa in $.5$ to $.8$ range) regarding parental reports, on-site urine and saliva testing, and urine testing (laboratory-based EMIT and GC.MS).

Substance Abuse Life Circumstances Evaluation (SALCE)

The Substance Abuse Life Circumstances Evaluation (SALCE; ADE, 1991) has 98 items, takes about 20 minutes to administer, and is computer based. It evaluates alcohol and drug use and locates the current stressors in the client's life. It has construct validity with professional interviews (94%) and a 1-month interval test-retest reliability of .91.

Substance Abuse Subtle Screening Inventory (SASSI)

The Substance Abuse Subtle Screening Inventory (SASSI; G. A. Miller, 1985) consists of 67 items in a true/false format (adult). It can be used with ages 12 to adult. There are eight subscales: a true/false measure of the substance misuse symptoms (SYM), six subtle substance use–related scales—Obvious Attributes Scale (OAT; openness to admit to problems), Subtle Attributes Scale (SAT; chemical dependency predisposition), Defensiveness (DEF; defensiveness in test taking), Supplemental Addiction Measure (SAM), Family versus Controls (FAM), Correctional (COR)—and Random Answering Pattern (RAP). This paper-and-pencil test takes about 5 to 10 minutes to complete and 1 to 2 minutes to score, unless combined with the Face Valid Alcohol and Face Valid Other Drugs scales, which increase the completion and scoring time to 10 to 15 minutes. Validation studies found 85% to 90% accuracy in differentiating residential abusers from nonabusers. It has been found to have good test-retest reliability (.92 to 1.00 for 1- to 2-week intervals) and criterion-related validity (clinical diagnosis). The Adult SASSI-3 has an accuracy of .93 with regard to substance dependence.

Specific Screening Instruments (Adolescents)

The following adolescent assessment instruments can further evaluate the presence of an alcohol/drug problem, as evidenced in the results of a broad overview assessment instrument or other sources of clinical information.

Alcohol Use Inventory (AUI)

This instrument is described under the adult specific screening instruments section.

Global Appraisal of Individual Needs (GAIN)

See description earlier under the adult specific screening instruments section.

Juvenile Automated Substance Abuse Evaluation (JASAE)

The Juvenile Automated Substance Abuse Evaluation (JASAE; ADE, 1988) has a format and administration procedure similar to the SALCE instruments for adults; however, it has been normed with adolescents. It examines the individual (use of alcohol and drugs based on *DSM-IV-TR* and American Society of Addiction Medicine [ASAM] guidelines, attitudes, and life stresses) and provides recommendations for interventions. The computer-based JASAE has 107 items and is designed for 12- to 18-year-olds. It takes about 20 minutes to administer and process. There is construct validity with professional interview results of 85%, and the 1-month interval test-retest reliability is .93.

Personal Experience Screen Questionnaire (PESQ)

The Personal Experience Screen Questionnaire (PESQ; Winters, 1991) has 40 items and is designed for 12- to 18-year-olds. The paper-and-pencil test takes about 10 minutes and is written at a fourth-grade reading level. It is a screening instrument that examines the severity of the problem with alcohol/drugs (psychological and behavioral involvement), the psychological risks (personal and environmental problems) related to substance abuse, and drug use history (beginning use, frequency of use of 12 substances over 12 months). There are also two validity scales that help determine whether the client is lying in his or her responses. Problem severity has construct validity with treatment history, treatment referral decisions, diagnosis, and group status, and alpha reliability coefficients range from .90 to .95.

Substance Abuse Subtle Screening Inventory (SASSI)

Because the SASSI can be used with individuals ranging in age from 12 to adult, it was reviewed under the adults section. It has 72 items in the adolescent form. In addition to the OAT, SAT, DEF, SAM, and COR scales, it has a measure for family substance misuse (FRISK), an alcohol/drug attitudes and beliefs scale (ATT), and items measuring substance abuse symptoms (SYM), a validity check scale (VAL), and Secondary Classification Scale (SCS) that distinguishes between abuse and dependence. The Adolescent SASSI-A2 has an accuracy of .94 with identification of substance use disorders. Coefficients for the subscales range from .81 to .92. Coefficient alpha for the overall inventory is .75. Test-retest (2-week interval) has a coefficient of .89. (See Case Study 3.1.)

CASE STUDY 3.1

Your client is a 17-year-old female who has been referred for an assessment of her alcohol and drug usage by her high school counselor. Her parents come with her to the assessment, but refuse to talk with you during the session about any of their concerns. They seem embarrassed about their daughter's behavior and say they simply want "all of this put behind them" so she can resume plans for college.

1. How would you set up the session in terms of the parents and your client being present (i.e., everyone present in the room all the time; only the parents and/or daughter present at different times; alternate them all being together with the parents and/or daughter being present)?

2. How would you approach the parents and your client in order to establish a trusting relationship?

3. Who would be additional sources of information about the young woman's chemical usage that you would plan to contact?

4. Would you use a psychometric instrument and, if so, which one?

EXERCISE 3.1

Answer the following questions based on NIAAA's nine criteria:

If you have not used an assessment instrument:

1. Which broad assessment instrument would you use? Why?
2. Which adult assessment instrument would you use? Why?
3. Which adolescent assessment instrument would you use? Why?

If you have used assessment instruments:

1. Which ones have you used for the broad, adult, and assessment processes? Why?
2. Do these instruments adequately fit your population?
3. Are there any populations you may miss in using these instruments?

DIAGNOSIS

The diagnosis of use, abuse, and addiction to alcohol/drugs is both an art and a science. Working with addicted individuals and problem drinkers over time provides a counselor with a sixth sense of the type of problem that is being presented, or a sniffer for addiction. Nonetheless, both experienced and novice counselors in the addictions field need to have their senses supported by clinical data. Such a grounding of assessment will assist the counselor in situations such as testifying in court (G. Miller & Kaplan, 1996). The counselor assessing addiction level needs to have as much information as possible from as many sources as possible.

A thorough addiction assessment requires time, energy, and a commitment to thoroughness by the counselor. The counselor needs to look for a pattern of problems related to alcohol/drug usage that does not seem to respond significantly to environmental changes. This pattern is strengthened if it appears in more than one area of consequences (legal; family, significant other, friends; job, school, military; medical; financial) and occurs in different contexts over time. The pattern is stronger if it is broader and longer in terms of its consequences. Data from numerous

sources can indicate conflictual areas where more information is needed to make a diagnosis as well as provide support for clinical decisions.

This chapter began with a discussion of the *DSM-5*. The counselor assessing the level of usage of a client needs to be familiar with these different substance use disorder categories. Awareness of the different categories will facilitate a continuum of care, the referral process, treatment planning, outcome measures, and work with other professionals to ensure client change. For a counselor who is new to the addictions field, it is important to have supervision with a qualified professional in the addictions field when initially giving diagnoses based on the *DSM-5* criteria.

When the client has been diagnosed as being addicted, matching a client to an appropriate treatment program should be based on the results of the thorough assessment process that summarizes the unique needs of the client. Then the client's needs must be matched with the client's resources (e.g., financial) and community resources (e.g., treatment availability). SAMHSA's 1995 *The Role and Current Status of Patient Placement Criteria in the Treatment of Substance Use Disorders* provides a summary of patient placement criteria based on the biopsychosocial model of addiction. This manual does not contain uniform patient placement criteria, but it attempts to lay groundwork for the development of criteria to assess how severe a client's problems are medically, psychologically, and socially, so that the client is placed in the most appropriate treatment level.

One formal matching process is the widely used ASAM patient placement criteria (ASAM, 2013). As discussed in Chapter 5, it provides comprehensive guidelines for working with addiction disordered clients (adolescents, adults) with regard to their treatment placement, continued stay, and discharge. These criteria were developed in an attempt to have more consistency in treatment levels for addiction and to have the client in the most appropriate, least intensive, safest, and most cost-effective treatment. The ASAM handbook was revised in 2013 and is an excellent reference for counselors. Because these criteria are being increasingly used in treatment programs throughout the United States (Shulman, 1997), counselors would be well advised to obtain a manual for reference in the assessment and treatment process.

Some counselors work in settings where ASAM criteria are used to place a client in treatment. For counselors working closely with these criteria, workshop training or supervised on-the-job training in the use of these criteria is beneficial.

Finally, when providing the client with the diagnosis regarding alcohol/drug usage, it is important to do so with the utmost respect of the individual, particularly when the diagnosis is one of addiction. No one ever sets out to achieve alcohol/drug addiction as a life goal. Clients who are diagnosed as addicted need to be given the diagnosis with compassion. Clients who are diagnosed as abusing alcohol/drugs need to be given the diagnosis with a warning of what further abuse of these chemicals may do to their lives. Such respect in the communication with a client can enhance the client's motivation to follow treatment recommendations. Even if the client does not want to comply with the recommendations at the time they are made, the client may remember the respectful treatment and return to the counselor at another time for assistance. As Margolis and Zweben (1998, 2011) state, it is very

important that the counselor communicate hope for change to the client. Therefore, each counselor needs to find a way to welcome a client to therapy and instill a sense of hope.

STAGES OF CHANGE

The stages-of-change model was created to show how a client's attitudes, intentions, and behaviors are connected with changing their problem behaviors (Connors, DiClemente, Velasquez, & Donovan, 2013). The stages-of-change transtheoretical model is mentioned in Chapter 2 and described extensively in Chapter 9. It is included in this assessment chapter because assessments are especially helpful in giving feedback to clients at the precontemplation and contemplation stages (where there is denial about the problem or ambivalence about changing the problem behavior) (Connors, Donovan, & DiClemente, 2001). Also, the model can assist in developing hypotheses that explain the factors that are contributing to the client's use (Connors et al., 2001). For example, if the counselor finds the client to be at the precontemplation stage, the counselor may find in the assessment process that the client spends most or all of his or her time with others that use alcohol/drugs heavily and that environment contributes significantly to the client's use and denial. Finally, if a counselor determines that the client's substance use is a problem that needs to be addressed, then the counselor needs to determine the client's stage of change so that an appropriate intervention is made based on the assessment.

Some specific instruments classifying and identifying the dominant stage of the client (precontemplation, contemplation, preparation, action, maintenance) are reviewed briefly here and more extensively in Connors et al., 2013.

Classification of the client can be done through the *staging algorithm* that uses five questions about the current behavior problem, if the client is considering quitting (in 6 months, in 30 days), if the client has stopped smoking for 24 hours in the past year, and the length of time the client has quit (Prochaska & DiClemente, 1992). Additional scales that can be used for classification of the client in the stage include the *University of Rhode Island Change Assessment Scale* (URICA; McConnaughy, DiClemente, Prochaska, & Velicer, 1989; McConnaughy, Prochaska, & Velicer, 1983); the *Stages of Change Readiness and Treatment Eagerness Scale* (SOCRATES; Miller & Tonigan, 1996), where the focus is on drinking; and the *Readiness to Change Questionnaire* (RCQ), which also focuses on drinking (Rollnick, Heather, Gold, & Hall, 1992).

SUMMARY

This chapter reviews the types of interviews, behavioral observations, physiological instruments, and psychometric instruments that may be used in the assessment process, as well as how they may be used by the counselor. Specific instruments that are used to assess the client's readiness to change (stages-of-change model) are also discussed. The diagnostic process is presented with specific suggestions for clinical use.

QUESTIONS

1. How can a counselor obtain accurate information yet also be respectful of clients?

2. Which instruments are helpful in a broad, general screening of alcohol/drug use?

3. What aspects of a chemical use history are important for a counselor to know?

4. How may it be helpful, clinically, to know about a client's previous treatments?

5. What areas of life need to be examined for consequences of alcohol/drug use?

6. Why is interviewing significant others important?

7. What is a limited-use contract, and how is it helpful to an assessment?

8. How might physiological instruments help an assessment?

9. What are some examples of psychometric instruments that can be used for adults? Adolescents? Drinking/drug-related driving charges?

10. How is the *DSM-5* used in the assessment and diagnosis process?

CASE STUDY 3.2

Jay is a 45-year-old male who has been referred for an assessment of his alcohol/drug usage. He recently received his first DUI charge. He divorced in the past year and reports that he has had a difficult time adjusting to living away from his ex-wife and their three children, which is why he is drinking more than normal. He says his ex-wife left him because of his drinking, but he also said she has a "history of mental problems and always exaggerates everything."

He denies any job or social problems related to his alcohol use. He says he mostly uses alcohol, although he has "tried a few other things along the way."

1. Does Jay have any significant others you would want to interview? If so, who?

2. Would you use a limited-use contract or any physiological instruments in the assessment? Why or why not?

3. Which broad overview psychometric instrument would you use? Why did you choose that one?

4. Which adult psychometric instrument would you use if you discovered Jay was positive for alcohol abuse on the broad overview psychometric instrument? Why?

5. If you discovered this client was alcoholic, how would you tell him his diagnosis?

6. If you determined this client was not alcoholic, what warnings might you give him about his usage?

7. What stage of change would you tentatively place him at?

8. Which stage-of-change assessment instrument might you use to clarify your initial assessment of his stage of change?

EXERCISE 3.2

Discuss your views about assessment with a peer by answering five questions:

1. What do you believe would be your strengths in an assessment?

2. What do you believe would be areas of concern for you in doing an assessment?

3. In conducting an interview (with clients and significant others), are some areas more comfortable for you than others?

4. Are there some populations you feel more adequate in assessing than others?

5. What concerns do you have regarding making and giving a diagnosis to a client?

READINGS/RESOURCES/WEBSITES

SUGGESTED READINGS

DSM-5

American Psychiatric Association. (2013). *Diagnostic and statistical manual of mental disorders* (5th ed.). Arlington, VA: American Psychiatric Publishing.

This is the manual for the *DSM-5* diagnostic criteria.

Nussbaum, A. M. (2013). *The pocket guide to the DSM-5 diagnostic exam* (5th ed.). Washington, DC: Author.

This book is a helpful brief overview that focuses on the diagnostic interview in three areas that are divided into 13 sections.

Paris, J. (2013). *The intelligent clinician's guide to the DSM-5*. New York, NY: Oxford University Press.

This book is divided into three areas that consist of 15 chapters. It provides information on diagnostic principles, specific diagnoses, and an overview.

Reichenberg, L. W. (2014). *DSM-5 essentials: The savvy clinician's guide to changes in the criteria*. Hoboken, NJ: Wiley.

This book presents the diagnostic changes from the *DSM IV-TR* to the *DSM-5* with discussion of the implications of the changes on choosing evidence-based treatment.

General

Donovan, D. M., & Marlatt, G. A. (2005). *Assessment of addictive behaviors* (2nd ed.). New York, NY: Guilford Press.

This book has 13 chapters that cover assessment. The topics are relapse prevention, ethnic-minority cultures, alcohol, smoking, cocaine, amphetamine, opioid, cannabis, club drug/hallucinogen/inhalant/steroid, eating disorder/obesity, gambling, sexual offenders, and sexually risky behavior.

Hart, C. L., & Ksir, C. (2012). *Drugs, society, and human behavior* (15th ed.). Boston, MA: McGraw-Hill.

This book has excellent chapters on the nervous system and the action of drugs.

Kuhn, C., Swartzwelder, S., & Wilson, W. (2008). *Buzzed: The straight facts about the most used and abused drugs from alcohol to ecstasy* (3rd ed.). New York, NY: Norton.

This book concisely, yet thoroughly, describes the impact of drugs on the body. The specific drugs discussed are alcohol, caffeine, entactogens (e.g., ecstasy), hallucinogens, herbal drugs, inhalants, marijuana, nicotine, opiates, sedatives, steroids, and stimulants.

Mee-Lee, D. (Ed.). (2013). *The ASAM criteria: Treatment criteria for addictive, substance-related, and co-occurring conditions*. Chevy Chase, MD: American Society of Addiction Medicine.

This book provides an overall summary of the placement criteria.

National Institute on Alcohol Abuse and Alcoholism. (1995). *Assessing alcohol problems: A guide for clinicians and researchers* (NIH Publication No. 95–3745). Bethesda, MD: Author.

This text discusses screening, diagnosis, assessment, treatment, and outcome issues as they relate to substance abuse. Its appendix has 415 pages of instruments (description, instrument itself, scoring).

Sandberg, K. M., Richards, T. E., & Erford, B. T. (2013). *Assessing common mental health and addiction issues with free-access instruments*. New York, NY: Routledge.

This book is designed to provide counselors with efficient free-access instruments that assess common diagnostic categories. Seven of the eight chapters focus on specific disorders: anxiety; mood; addiction and related; AD/HD, disruptive, impulse control, obsessive compulsive, and related; autistic and schizophrenic spectrums; eating; and trauma and stressor-related.

Substance Abuse and Mental Health Services Administration. (1995). *The role and current status of patient placement criteria in the treatment of substance use disorders* (DHHS Publication No. 95–3021). Rockville, MD: Author.

Although this booklet does not provide patient placement criteria, it reviews criteria available and presents a perspective on the need for and ways to implement criteria in substance abuse treatment.

Substance Abuse and Mental Health Services Administration. (1998). *Substance abuse among older adults* (DHHS Publication No. 98–3179). Rockville, MD: Author.

This booklet provides information on alcohol, prescription drug, and over-the-counter drug use with this population. It also discusses screening, assessment, and treatment issues as they relate to this population.

Substance Abuse and Mental Health Services Administration. (1999). *Screening and assessing adolescents for substance use disorders* (DHHS Publication No. 99–3282). Rockville, MD: Author.

This booklet describes screening assessment issues as they relate to adolescents. There is also discussion of legal issues and assessment in juvenile justice settings. It has numerous screening, assessment, and measurement instruments.

Workbooks

Quinn, S. C., & Scaffa, M. E. (2000). *Making choices: A personal look at alcohol & drug use* (2nd ed.). New York, NY: McGraw-Hill.

This workbook is directed to college students to encourage their exploration of their knowledge, attitudes, and behaviors regarding alcohol and drug use. It has five sections that examine personal use, the influence of others on use, the influence of community on use, a summary section, and an answer/scoring section. There are both questionnaires and exercises that can be used to enhance awareness of personal chemical use. It has numerous exercises that can be used in conjunction with a drug education class.

CHAPTER 4

CO-OCCURRING DISORDERS AND BEHAVIORAL ADDICTIONS

PERSONAL REFLECTIONS

As we work with this population, we, as counselors, and our clients can become frustrated with the complicated overlapping of at least two co-occurring disorders. It is crucial that we stay hopeful and encouraging to our clients. They may have few people they interact with both personally and professionally who have an understanding and compassion for the complication of their struggle. We may be an oasis for them in a desert of support; we can provide them in our contacts with them with hope and encouragement to continue on their journey of finding a way to live with at least two disorders. We can also work hard with them at finding supportive individuals and systems outside of counseling who can provide them with hope and encouragement for change on a daily basis. Our belief in their ability to live with their disorders may sustain them when nothing else does as they face barriers with regards to one or both of their disorders. By simply staying with them on their recovery journey and supporting, but not enabling them, we can be a part of miracles happening in their lives.

OBJECTIVES

1. To develop an understanding of the various types of co-occurring disorders and behavioral addictions.
2. To learn some of the general issues in assessing co-occurring disorders and behavioral addictions.
3. To learn a general approach for treating co-occurring disorders and behavioral addictions.

This chapter provides an overview of some common co-occurring disorders. By no means can the reader assume it is all inclusive. Rather, the author has chosen those disorders that seem to occur readily in clients who struggle with substance abuse issues. The reader is encouraged to use this chapter as one anchoring point in addiction counseling and to supplement this information with other information on co-occurring disorders that frequently appear in one's clinical work.

The chapter is divided into two sections: *co-occurring disorders* (depression, anxiety, PTSD, eating, violence, gambling, and personality) as listed in order by their diagnoses in the *DSM-5* manual (American Psychiatric Association, 2013) and *behavioral addictions*. The first section provides an overview of co-occurring disorders with general assessment and treatment suggestions; each diagnostic topic area in this section also includes an overview with assessment and treatment suggestions, concluding with two case studies and two exercises. The second section provides an overview and a case study and exercise.

CO-OCCURRING DISORDERS

The Center for Substance Abuse Treatment (CSAT) refers to substance abuse/dependence and mental health disorders as *co-occurring disorders* (COD). The 2011 National Survey on Drug Use and Health found Serious Mental Illness (SMI) associated with substance dependence or abuse: 22.6% of the 11.5 million adults with SMI had substance abuse dependence or abuse in the past year. In the past, this population has been labeled different terms: *dual diagnosis* (Evans & Sullivan, 2001; Zimberg, 1993), *coexisting disorders* (van Wormer & Davis, 2008); *mental illness, chemical abuse, and addictions* (MICAA), later changed to *mentally ill chemically addicted* (MICA), to diagnose clients with severe, persistent mental illness (Axis I disorder in *DSM*) with an accompanying abuse/addiction problem (van Wormer & Davis, 2008); *chemically addicted mentally ill* (CAMI; Shollar, 1993) to diagnose those with an addiction problem accompanied by other mental illness (often Axis II personality disorders in *DSM*); and *persons in dual recovery—co-occurring psychiatric and addictive disorders*. This chapter uses the term *co-occurring disorders* and discussion is limited to clients who are *addicted* and have a psychiatric problem.

Since the 1980s, there has been awareness that co-occurring disorders exist and that they are common (Biegel, Kola, Ronis, & Kruszynski, 2013). Yet, while they are common, they are also complex (SAMHSA, 2002a); their issues have been described as complicated and reciprocal (DiClemente, 2003) or complex and heterogeneous (Drake & Green, 2013). For example, it is difficult to obtain an accurate reading on the frequency of co-occurring diagnosis because: Diagnostic procedures are not standard, gender

and socioeconomic status have an impact, and personnel in treatment centers have biases (Watkins, Lewellen, & Barrett, 2001). In spite of these difficulties, it is important to review what we currently know about these clients.

Research studies show a high percentage of psychiatric patients have substance abuse disorders (Greenfield & Hennessey, 2008)—a higher rate than the general population (Ross, 2008). Almost half of people addicted to opiates struggled with depression, and 80% of them had a psychiatric disorder at minimum (Harvard Mental Health Letter, 2003a): "1/3 to 2/3 of all drug-dependent people have at least one co-occurring psychiatric disorder" (Blume, 2005, p. 22) and often use drugs to self-medicate their psychiatric problems (Blume, 2005). Co-occurring diagnosis is common among the homeless, incarcerated, and mental hospital populations (Dual Diagnosis, 2003a). An example of this is in the criminal justice system, where 75% of the population is estimated to struggle with both issues in a system that often has a lack of these services (NIDA, 2008).

The strong relationship between substance abuse and mental health problems may be caused by several factors (Dual Diagnosis, 2003a). First, there may be common biological, psychological, or social causal factors (childhood abuse, limited social support, heredity). Second, alcohol/drug abuse may cause psychiatric symptoms (alcoholic/heroin addicts may experience depression in early abstinence, whereas cocaine addicts may look as though they are struggling with panic or compulsivity). Third, symptoms may be related to the impact of the drug, or symptoms might be related to the person's lifestyle. Fourth, psychiatric-disordered clients may develop a substance abuse problem as a result of impaired judgment or self-medication (such as schizophrenia, anxiety, sleeplessness, depression). Finally, both problems (drug abuse, mental health) are caused by overlapping factors (e.g., "underlying brain deficits, genetic vulnerabilities, and/or early exposure to stress or trauma" [NIDA, 2008, p. 3]; NIDA, 2010).

Some of the general tendencies in the co-occurring diagnosis population (as a group), as compared with other psychiatric patients, are that they tend to be more suicidal/homicidal/impulsive, more intelligent, more likely to use in a binge style, and more manipulative; they are less likely to focus on total abstinence; and although they have less severe psychotic problems, they have more difficulty being sober (Doweiko, 2002). In a summary of the research, Biegel et al. (2013) state that in comparison with clients who only have one diagnosis, clients with co-occurring disorders have higher rates of: relapse, hospitalization, violence, incarceration, homelessness, and HIV/AIDS and hepatitis. The authors also state this population is involved in riskier sexual (unprotected) and drug taking (i.e., needle sharing) behaviors and those that are bipolar have an intensity of symptoms and treatment complications (i.e., early, frequent hospitalizations). They also state these clients may have difficulty developing and staying with treatment plans and have precarious social support networks.

Although awareness of the relationship between mental health problems and substance abuse problems expanded in the late 1980s and 1990s, the impact of substance abuse on mental health problems was not understood, and substance abuse treatment's tendency to use techniques—such as strong confrontation—did not fit this population. Both the separateness of the treatment systems (mental health and substance abuse) and the stigma of both disorders keep this population from being treated effectively (SAMHSA, 2002a). Therefore, there are problems in receiving assistance that are both external and internal for the co-occurring disordered client (Biegel et al., 2013). Van Wormer and Davis (2008) summarize the current collaboration between the two fields as having improved by an increase in special programs, yet cite evidence that many individuals do not receive integrated care; services for both problems either don't exist or they are fragmented (Biegel et al., 2013). The resources needed to treat this clientele (including financial) may simply not be available (Burnett, Porter, & Stallings, 2011). Clients may find themselves needed to straddle two separate systems that may offer them conflicting advice (Edward & Robins, 2012). Because these clients have two problems that tend to be treated separately, they are the *most likely* clients to not have their needs met by the system and end up living on the streets (G. Buelow & Buelow, 1998).

In an attempt to enhance the assessment and treatment effectiveness for this client population, this chapter section begins with a summary of the struggles between the mental health and substance abuse fields and suggestions for collaboration followed by some general assessment and treatment recommendations.

COLLABORATION BETWEEN THE MENTAL HEALTH AND SUBSTANCE ABUSE FIELDS

Co-occurring diagnosis clients, because of the nature of their problems, require an exceptional amount of teamwork among professionals in both the mental health and addictions fields. A dually diagnosed client needs to have a psychiatrist, addictions counselor, and mental health counselor who can work collaboratively and flexibly together to ensure that the client's needs are met. For example, at one point in the client's recovery, the psychiatric problem may be top priority, and at another point, the chemical dependency problem may need to be the top priority. Such flexibility by counselors requires a great amount of honest communication, trust, and cooperation.

One of the main problems in working with co-occurring disorders is the separateness of mental health and addiction counselor training (Dual Diagnosis, 2003b; NIDA, 2008; van Wormer & Davis, 2008). Often, counselors who have been trained in mental health have little or no experience in diagnosing or working in the addictions field. Also, counselors who have been trained in addictions counseling often have little or no experience in diagnosing or working in the mental health field. A lack of training in both areas may result in the counselor missing the disorder in the area in which he or she is least familiar (Dual Diagnosis, 2003b; Mericle, Martin, Carise, & Love, 2012).

Furthermore, there continues to be suspiciousness between the two fields (as well as disagreements) concerning the quality and integrity of the counselors in each field. Mental health counselors may believe that if the underlying problems were addressed, the addiction would diminish, whereas addiction counselors may not see the psychiatric problems as being severe and may not believe in the need for medication (K. Evans & Sullivan, 2001). Yet, as Burton (1998) states, treating one alone will not help the other. In addition, there is disagreement in the field as to whether psychiatric problems should be treated only after people have been sober a while or whether they should be treated simultaneously when there is family history or personal history with psychiatric problems (especially when someone has been sober or the problems are unchanging in fluctuating use; Biegel et al., 2013; Dual Diagnosis, 2003b).

Another issue between the two fields is territorial (van Wormer & Davis, 2008). Because the dual-disordered client needs assistance from counselors in both fields, counselors need to share information openly with one another. Yet, counselors in each field may hesitate to share information about their perceptions of the client for fear that they may be ridiculed, ignored, or misunderstood. They also may be hesitant to share information out of concern that the other counselors may not be open to suggestions; therefore, they may have a sense of "Why bother?" Clients may also be resistant while in one treatment program to admit to the other problem, and if they are referred between programs, the different

information they receive may cause them to leave treatment (Dual Diagnosis, 2003b; Edward & Robins, 2012).

Part of the problem between the fields is historical. Initially, when mental health workers did not know how to assist addicted individuals and found them, as a whole, to be difficult clients (i.e., they would lie, relapse, struggle with those in authority), addicted clients mainly had to rely on themselves, whereby the self-help organizations, such as Alcoholics Anonymous (AA), developed. The addictions field, then, became much more of a grassroots movement, with its early professional counselors eventually evolving out of that context. The mental health field had a more professional development separate from a grassroots movement.

These early developmental differences laid the group work for another difficulty between the areas, which is in the framework and language used by each field. One example of this is Gold's (1995) outline of different viewpoints between the self-help focus and the psychiatric focus. In terms of the self-help focus, groups such as AA may be viewed as lifesavers for the addict, whereas psychiatry may view them as possibly missing psychiatric problems in the individuals who attend them. Another difference is in the area of medication. Here, the self-help focus may view taking medication as potentially harmful to the addict, whereas psychiatry may view it as helpful. Note that this bias may also exist in addiction treatment centers (NIDA, 2008). The self-help focus may see psychological problems as resulting from the alcohol/drug use (therefore, such problems will stop when the person sobers up), whereas psychiatry may be concerned that problems were present before the alcohol/drug use. The differences between these two areas indicate the potential struggles when addiction counselors and mental health counselors begin to work together.

Evans and Sullivan (2001) describe these differences between the two fields in terms of models. They describe the *recovery model* as one where the client is always recovering, needs to abstain from alcohol/drug use, needs to develop various coping skills, and typically needs to attend self-help meetings, obtain a sponsor, and work the steps of recovery. The *mental health model* for recovery looks more at physiological problems, developing systems that reinforce certain behaviors, and developing coping skills in the client, which includes an awareness in the client of his or her thoughts, feelings, and behaviors. Burton (1998) states that treatment teams tend to have one perspective or the other, resulting in a rigid approach that does not allow for the flexible treatment approach required to work with the dually diagnosed. These differing perspectives can lead to difficulties in communication and trust between the counselors in the addictions and mental health fields. One way of avoiding or minimizing these conflicts is for professionals to work hard at communication and collaboration. Increased awareness of co-occurring disorders may enhance communication and collaboration.

Finally, a treatment barrier for the development of co-occurring diagnosis treatment programs is the inaccurate view that they are difficult to develop and expensive to maintain (Burton, 1998). Although this population has shown to be difficult to treat, have high relapse rates, and have high treatment costs (Kendall, 2004), the development of these much-needed programs has been too slow, too simplified, and has had a tendency to employ people who have not been adequately trained to treat clients in both areas (Burton, 1998). Barriers to these combined programs result in clients who have multiple needs not receiving the services they need (Jerrell, Wilson, & Hiller, 2000). Yet, as Jerrell et al. (2000) recommend, for such programs to be successful, they need to make decisions collaboratively about staffing, operating, and funding; all staff need to be both trained and committed to collaboration on both issues; there needs to be administrative support; and treatment needs to be flexible to meet the changing needs of consumers. Mueser, Noordsy, Drake, and Fox (2003) provide an excellent chapter on principles of integrated treatment.

Both mental health and substance abuse counseling systems need to examine how they approach their work with the co-occurring disordered population. SAMHSA's Co-Occurring Center for Excellence (2007) suggests 12 principles to guide systems in addressing their needs:

1. Expect COD in all behavioral health settings.

2. Have an integrated system to serve the best interest of all individuals and systems involved.

3. Be accessible from multiple entry points and be caring and accepting.

4. Avoid being limited to one approach.

5. Reflect the connection between science and service and the use of evidence-based and consensus-based practices.

6. Collaborate with other professionals in the best interest of the client.

7. Expect these issues in the evaluation of all clients.

8. Consider both issues primary.

9. Have empathy and respect for the client and belief in the ability to change.

10. Individualize treatment to fit client needs, goals, and culture in terms of their level of stage of change.

11. Recognize the needs of children and adolescents.

12. Integrate community contributions to the recovery process and the individual contributions to the community.

Figure 4.1 may assist the reader in understanding how to incorporate SAMHSA's 12 suggestions into the assessment and treatment process as well as guide the reader in the general assessment and treatment suggestions made for working with this population.

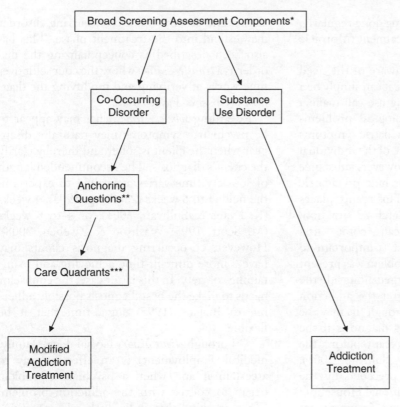

Figure 4.1 Co-Occurring Disorder Decision Tree for Clients with Substance Use Disorders.

The diagram shows:

Broad Screening Assessment Components*

Co-Occurring Disorder → Substance Use Disorder

Co-Occurring Disorder → Anchoring Questions**

Anchoring Questions** → Care Quadrants***

Care Quadrants*** → Modified Addiction Treatment

Substance Use Disorder → Addiction Treatment

* = Flexible diagnosing ("transfer station")
Sobriety time
Client history
Typical Client Population
Treatment

** = Which problem occurred first?
Which is primary?
Which needs to be treated first?

*** = Care Quadrants:

		Mental Disorder Severity	
		Less	More
Substance Disorder Severity	Less		
	More		

ASSESSMENT

Counselors in both settings (substance abuse, mental health) may not detect, diagnosis, and, thereby, inadequately treat clients with co-occurring disorders (Morojele, Saban, & Seedat, 2012; Staiger et al., 2011). Clients entering substance abuse treatment may not have their mental health problems detected by counselors because of their counselors' lack of training, supervision, or support to identify the problem(s) and assist them in obtaining care (Mericle et al., 2012). It is critical, whichever setting in which a counselor works, for screening of both disorders being done regularly, thoroughly, and as a part of treatment (Morojele et al., 2012).

Even when a counselor is aware of the need for assessing for both problems, it can simply be a difficult task. Alcohol and drug use can make a client appear to have psychological problems (Zimberg, 1993); apparent psychiatric symptoms may disappear as the abstinence of the individual increases (M. Scott, 1995). However, substance abuse can initiate, enhance, or hide psychiatric problems (Schneider, 2005). This reality places the assessing counselor in a Catch-22 situation. Because either problem can come first (Capuzzi & Stauffer, 2008), it is important to determine if the psychiatric problem was present before the addiction, if it emerged alongside the addiction, or if it emerged after the addiction began (Zimberg, 1993). Although it may be easier to make a co-occurring diagnosis if the psychiatric problems were present before the addiction problems (Evans & Sullivan, 2001), and typically drug abuse is preceded by the psychiatric problems (2002 National Household Survey on Drug Abuse) in some circumstances (e.g., depression in men), the psychiatric problem follows the alcoholism (Dual Diagnosis, 2003a). In summary, the relationship between the two is complicated in that alcohol and drug use and withdrawal (1) can cause symptoms that are psychotic and mimic such disorders; (2) can cause these disorders to occur, reoccur, or worsen; (3) can hide these symptoms and disorders; (4) can coexist; and (5) psychiatric behaviors can look like drug-related behaviors (NIDA, 2010; SAMHSA, 1994).

There are five broad screening assessment components that may assist the counselor in conducting a broad screening of all clients. These are: flexible diagnosing, sobriety time, client history, typical client population, and treatment setting.

Flexible diagnosing (Inaba, 1995) means the use of a provisional diagnosis until the clinician has enough information to make an established diagnosis. This suggestion can be helpful because the assessment process for a co-occurring disorder may extend into the treatment phase. This has also been described as conceptualizing the disorder as a *transfer station* where the counselor over time works at verifying and modifying the diagnoses (Cosci & Fava, 2010).

Regarding *sobriety time*, what may appear to be psychiatric symptoms may naturally disappear when the client is sober and thereby clarify the client's diagnosis. The recommended length of sobriety time varies according to experts in the field: 3 to 6 weeks (Zimberg, 1993), 4 weeks (K. Evans & Sullivan, 2001), or 4 to 8 weeks (M. Scott, 1995; Washton & Zweben, 2008). However, co-occurring diagnosis clients may have a more difficult time achieving and maintaining sobriety. In this latter case, the counselor needs to make the best diagnosis possibly adhering to Inaba's (1995) suggestion that it be flexible.

A thorough *client history* (social, legal, family, medical, employment) is an effective way to ascertain if and when a psychiatric problem began to coexist with the addiction problem. [Keep in mind that individuals with cognitive impairments, such as poor attention and memory problems, may not be able to give accurate self-reports about substance use history (Mueser et al., 2003).] In addition to the client history of mental health problems, the counselor also should ask about a history of mental health problems in the family to help determine a possible genetic predisposition to mental health problems; the same is true when approaching co-occurring assessment from a mental counseling perspective (ask about personal and family substance abuse). The mental health status exam and substance abuse assessment instruments discussed in Chapter 3 are also helpful in determining if a client has a co-occurring diagnosis. Additionally, there may be *historical clues* for a possible co-occurring diagnosis: history of sexual abuse, persisting symptoms during abstinence, using alcohol/drugs to change how you feel, difficulty staying sober, later onset of substance abuse (over age 20), and use of four or more different substances (M. Scott, 1995). A final notation, as discussed in Chapter 3, it is important for the counselor to obtain information from significant others as well as the addicted individual to be assured of obtaining accurate information.

The counselor needs to note behaviors outside of those expected of the *typical client population* with whom he or she works (mental health, substance abuse). This includes differences in how the client interacts with others and how the client responds to treatment. Extremes in thoughts, feelings, and behaviors, or unusual aspects in these three areas, can alert a counselor to the possible presence of a co-occurring diagnosis. Although this terminology is vague, seasoned counselors, in both the mental health and addictions fields, develop a sense of what are normal behaviors and problems for the populations with which they work. Neophyte counselors need to rely on supervision to determine if a client's behavior is unusual.

Included in this is the client's treatment recovery process. If in the addiction treatment process the client is unable to remain sober, there may be an accompanying mental health problem: the client may be self-medicating by relapsing. In addition, if, as part of the treatment process, a client routinely takes psychological tests, the counselor can use these tests to determine if psychological problems are diminishing as the client receives more treatment and has a longer period of time in recovery. The same is true for the mental health client. If the mental health client is not responding typically to treatment, the counselor may want to examine his or her substance use. Finally, if a client responds to psychiatric medication, a co-occurring diagnosis is present (K. Evans & Sullivan, 2001).

The *treatment setting* may also be used as a way to enhance the assessment of the co-occurring disordered client. Overall, some behavioral characteristics may occur across different drug treatment settings that will alert a clinician to the possible presence of a dual disorder. One of those characteristics, which commonly occurs across

settings, is that the client does not calm down during the treatment process. Rather, the clinician finds that the client becomes more agitated the longer the client is in treatment. Another common characteristic is that such clients will become more troublesome—they simply are more difficult to work with than other clientele. A final clue, in a group or inpatient setting, is that they may become scapegoated by others in the setting because their behaviors are different and bothersome. The treatment setting will be viewed from an addiction counseling perspective followed by a mental health setting perspective based on Fayne's work (1993).

Regarding addiction treatment, during the detoxification process, clients may be quite needy but have a difficult time relating to others, particularly in a group setting. Depression in these clients may not be picked up by the staff because of their irritating behaviors.

In the inpatient rehabilitation process, the difficulty relating to others in a group may again pose a problem. In addition, such clients may have trouble being close with others emotionally and experiencing confrontation. As a result of these problems, they may either withdraw or become more agitated in the setting. Similarly, in the outpatient setting, there may be problems in group counseling: Clients may either withdraw from others or be ostracized by them because they are different. There is also a tendency for these clients either to split off from emotions or become explosive. Finally, these clients may have difficulty staying sober.

On an inpatient psychiatric unit, specific behaviors may indicate a substance abuse problem. In the substance-abusing client, these include physiological problems (e.g., neurological difficulties or withdrawal syndromes, medication-seeking behaviors), as well as comparatively better social skills with an alternating threatening manner.

In an outpatient psychiatric clinic, the behaviors of the substance-abusing client include: numerous treatment failures, medication noncompliance, absenteeism, inconsistent behavior, superficial sessions, consequences that could be the result of alcohol/drug use, and the therapist's clinical sense that something is not right about the treatment.

These five assessment components can guide the counselor in the determination of the existence of a co-occurring disorder. If it is determined that there is only a substance use disorder, addiction treatment, without modifications, can follow. If the client has co-occurring disorders, then addiction treatment modifications can be determined.

To obtain the goal of an appropriately modified addiction treatment for the client, the counselor may want to anchor him/herself in three questions: which problem occurred first, which is primary, and which needs to be treated first (Capuzzi & Stauffer, 2008). CSAT's four care quadrants (2005, p. xviii) may assist the counselor in prioritizing the diagnoses and the resulting treatment plan: (1) less severe mental disorder/less severe substance disorder; (2) more severe mental disorder/less severe substance disorder; (3) less severe mental disorder/more severe substance disorder; and (4) more severe mental disorder/more severe substance disorder. This process may need to be repeated throughout the client's addiction treatment as new information is gathered. (See Case Study 4.1.)

CASE STUDY 4.1

Jane is a 50-year-old woman with a 12-year history of severe alcoholism with four hospital detoxifications and four chemical dependency treatments, none of which had any significant impact on her drinking. She was court-ordered to treatment for her third DUI (driving under the influence). After 2 weeks in the treatment center, the staff noted that Jane rarely was seen sleeping. At night, she would walk up and down the halls of the treatment center. She was also becoming more agitated in group therapy. In group therapy, she alternated between being very quiet yet agitated (unable to sit still) and very hostile when confronted or probed for information about herself by the counselor or other clients. She was the topic of most staff meetings, as counselors complained about how frustrating it was to work with her. There was discussion in the meetings of discharging her. The other clients increasingly refused to associate with her because of her highly critical manner and her tendency to be emotionally explosive.

1. What aspects of this situation indicate that Jane may be struggling with a dual disorder?
2. How would you initially intervene in the situation with Jane?
3. How would you approach the staff about the situation with Jane? The clients?

EXERCISE 4.1

Imagine that you work in a mental health setting. If you were to choose a broad-based assessment instrument from Chapter 3, which one would you choose? Why?

Now imagine you work in a substance abuse setting. How would you screen for mental health problems?

TREATMENT

SAMHSA (1994) states that treatment needs to engage these clients by providing them with social services, eliminating barriers to treatment, and connecting them with additional services, such as job skills training, and by helping them cope with problems that arise. Second, they recommend integrated and comprehensive treatment for these clients so they do not fall between the cracks. Barriers to treatment include clients not knowing about services available, the referral process being broken, and systems delaying in their response and being inflexible (Staiger et al., 2011). Treatment needs to be multifaceted with severity of disorder matching treatment intensity (Kelly, Daley, & Douaihy, 2012).

Orlin and Davis (1993) indicate some similarities in addiction and psychiatric treatment that may facilitate the counselor's attempt to treat the client who has problems in both areas. Both treatment styles are attempting to educate clients and provide supportive counseling, group and family counseling, case management, crisis intervention, and relapse-prevention approaches. Approaches such as CBT, DBT, group therapy, family therapy, case management, and residential treatment may be effective with this clientele (Burnett et al., 2011). These treatment similarities can assure the counselor of a general approach to take with clients who have co-occurring disorders, keeping in mind that some modifications need to occur. Also, because of the heterogeneity of the clientele, we may need to develop more general approaches to co-occurring disorders in order to facilitate their integration into treatment (Drake & Green, 2013).

Zweben (1995) suggests that counselors can enhance the treatment process by joining dual-disordered clients in their pain, avoiding punishment of their ambivalence about recovery, and encouraging them to try a period of abstinence. One possible source of bibliotherapy for clients is the *Dual Diagnosis Series* of brochures published by Hazelden (K. Evans & Sullivan, 1991a, 1991b,

1991c; Fields & Vandenbelt, 1992a, 1992b; N. J., 1992). These pamphlets discuss both diagnoses in layperson's terms, the overlap between the diagnoses, and recovery suggestions. Another resource is *Co-Occurring Addiction and Mental Health Disorders: A Handbook for Recovery* that is specifically written for the client. This resource is described at the end of this chapter.

Burton (1998) recommends that treatment centers be established for co-occurring diagnosis clients because (1) substance abuse and mental health problems coexist and both require treatment; (2) there is common group treatment in both areas; and (3) these programs can be developed in 6 to 12 months. Integrated approaches are viewed as more effective than traditional treatments (Biegel et al., 2013; Burnett et al., 2011; Palmieri & Accordino, 2004) and services need to cover all the areas of the client's daily living with a sensitivity to the unique needs of the client (Biegel et al., 2013; Burnett et al., 2011). Further, recommendations are: all staff (beyond clinical) should be cross-trained; both disorders should be viewed as primary; treatment needs to be integrated—a cohesive, united approach is needed thereby placing the responsibility for effective treatment on the center, not the client; and the decision making needs to be shared and collaborative between the counselor (system) and client (Biegel et al., 2013). It is recommended that overall treatment incorporate enhancing motivation, use of behavioral techniques that encourage treatment engagement, and the teaching of coping and relapse prevention skills (Biegel et al., 2013) as well as being long term and involving outreach (Burnett et al., 2011).

In the previous assessment section, the impact of cognitive limitations and reading abilities were discussed. Regarding treatment, those with cognitive impairments, which are chronic in nature, may appear uninterested in the treatment or may be viewed as defiant. In reality, they have difficulty in sustaining attention and concentration, controlling their emotions and being empathetic toward others, as well as being logical and engaging in a self-awareness process. Counselors working with these clients may need to watch for cues of problems with memory, empathy, logic, and self-awareness. Counselors may consider a referral for psychiatric assessment of their limitations, which could be incorporated into their treatment plans. For those of low intelligence, the counselor should develop their treatment plans in a tangible, concrete manner (Perkinson, 2004). For those clients who can read, determine how well they can read and match their reading level to appropriate materials, and for those who cannot read, the oral forms of providing information and treatment plans need to be individualized, along with additional support in group therapy (Perkinson, 2004).

As a result of complications that occur when the two problems interface and it being more difficult to treat them (K. Evans & Sullivan, 2001), modifications to the treatment process need to be discussed. Six modifications to the treatment process for co-occurring disordered clients are: abstinence time, medication, psychiatric support, counseling/confrontational style, screening for use, and self-help groups.

Co-occurring diagnosis clients may require a *longer time frame to achieve abstinence* (Orlin & Davis, 1993) and may relapse more often (Zimberg, 1993). Zimberg also recommends that treatment be more frequent for this type of client (i.e., two to three times weekly). Orlin and Davis suggest a brief psychiatric hospitalization, followed by rehabilitation treatment for 6 to 12 months, followed by a combination of outpatient psychiatric care and self-help groups. In addition, they suggest that although abstinence is a goal for treatment, a relapse should not be used as a reason for discharge from treatment.

Psychotropic medication will sometimes assist the recovery process of dual-diagnosed patients (Orlin & Davis, 1993; Washton & Zweben, 2008). Yet, Mueser et al. (2003) state that doctors may hesitate to use psychotropic medication, because they are concerned about how substances and medicine may interact, and they may think that mental illness follows substance abuse and that prescribed medication may encourage

substance abuse. However, the authors state that some clients simply need to be stabilized on medicine so the substance abuse problems can be addressed adequately. They recommend that agencies train their staff about how pharmacology can be helpful with this population, be open to consultation with doctors trained in addiction medicine, and include drug interaction information and educate clients about following prescriptions.

K. Evans and Sullivan (2001) suggest the use of non-mood-altering medications when possible. Inaba (1995) also suggests avoiding the use of reinforcing drugs for this population. For example, K. Evans and Sullivan (1991c) recommend that PTSD survivors use medications such as antidepressants, beta-blocker antihypertensives, and antipsychotics, when appropriate, while avoiding tranquilizers, sedative-hypnotics, and painkillers.

Zimberg (1993) suggests that the symptoms for both diagnoses be stabilized and treated simultaneously in order to be effective with this clientele. Addiction counselors need to work closely with *psychiatric support* to facilitate the client's recovery (Orlin & Davis, 1993). M. Scott (1995) supports this approach by encouraging the counselor not to work alone with these clients. Zimberg suggests that one counselor be the primary counselor for the client, and, if more than one counselor is involved in the client's treatment, they should talk frequently. Orlin and Davis (1993) view a team approach as critical for effective treatment with this population.

In terms of *counseling/confrontational style*, specific suggestions can be made. M. Scott (1995) recommends that counselors working with this population be flexible in their work, especially in terms of confrontational style. The clientele may require a less confrontive style of counseling (Orlin & Davis, 1993) for treatment to be effective. SAMHSA (1994) states that counseling style needs to be modified to fit the client's mental health fragility. Zimberg (1993) cautions counselors that dual-disordered clients may stir more transference and countertransference issues and that treatment should be less rigid and confrontational, in particular in giving up the use of alcohol/drugs.

The counselor walks a thin line when working with co-occurring diagnosis clients on giving up alcohol/drugs. Although it is important for the counselor to be aware that these clients may have more difficulty initially achieving and maintaining sobriety, the counselor needs to be careful that an enabling pattern is not set up with the client. It is also important for the counselor to believe in the client's capacity to become sober, regardless of the client's diagnosis. This hope and belief in the client can facilitate treatment for clients who live in the difficult life circumstances of having a co-occurring diagnosis. Counselors need to remember that co-occurring diagnosis is treatable (Inaba, 1995). Clients tend to become abstinent through more of a gradual harm-reduction approach than through immediate abstinence (Mueser et al., 2003).

Co-occurring diagnosis clients are often reluctant clients (Dual Diagnosis, 2003b) who show their reluctance by not coming, not staying for an entire session, and not following medication regimes. They may also be late for sessions, fail to work on their treatment goals or assignments, drop out of treatment, and miss self-help meetings (Daley & Zuckoff, 1999). Such noncompliance can have negative effects on the client, the client's family/significant others, the counselor, and the treatment program (Daley & Zuckoff, 1999).

Understanding where the client is in terms of readiness to change (precontemplation, contemplation, determination, action, maintenance, and relapse prevention) can help the counselor to determine appropriate intervention strategies. Finnell (2003) found these clients required support and interventions throughout the change process. Motivational interviewing approaches can facilitate the client's moving through the stages of change and, especially with co-occurring diagnosis clients, engage them in treatment and enhance the therapy success by the development of the therapeutic alliance (Dual Diagnosis, 2003b; Kelly, Daley, &

Douaihy, 2012). Research on the effectiveness of motivational interviewing with this population has shown increased treatment engagement and reduction of substance use and hospitalizations (Biegel et al., 2013). The motivational interviewing and stages-of-change model are discussed at length in Chapter 9.

Watkins et al. (2001) state that because motivational interviewing is nonconfrontational and emphasizes self-efficacy and self-esteem, it may be an excellent match with this population. They also state that it is important to remember that the client may be at a different stage level with the two disorders. These authors outline approaches for each stage of change that can be used with this population. Mueser et al. (2003) also provide specific intervention strategies for working with this population regarding their readiness for change and enhancing motivation, focusing one entire chapter of their book on motivational interviewing. Kavanagh, Mueser, and Tidsskrift (2007) state that motivational interventions help engage these clients in the treatment process. DelGiudice and Kutinsky (2007) recommend the use of motivational interviewing in treating clients who have substance abuse disorders and sexual compulsivity problems. The authors recommend specific techniques (reflective listening, affirmations, rolling with resistance, establishing alliance early) and provide case studies. Motivational interviewing also appears to work well with juvenile justice populations (Feldstein & Ginsburg, 2006).

One way to ensure that co-occurring diagnosis clients are being truthful about their abstinence is *screening for* use: using screening devices to validate their sobriety. Urine monitoring and breathalyzers may be necessary to facilitate recovery for the dual-disordered client to stay sober (Orlin & Davis, 1993). Such screening devices, however, need to be used in a respectful manner, which involves informed consent of the client. It is most beneficial if the screening approaches are discussed early in the treatment process, the client is aware that it is a standard procedure for someone who has a dual disorder, and it is introduced as a tool to assist in recovery rather than as a punishment for relapse. As discussed in Chapter 3, having screening procedures as a common practice and then explaining those procedures as common practice to a client can facilitate the development of the therapeutic alliance. Mueser et al. (2003) recommend that agency policies state the purpose and method of screening, as well as client confidentiality guidelines. The importance of relapse prevention is discussed extensively in Chapter 7.

As discussed in Chapter 8, a helpful addition to treatment is *self-help groups*. Zimberg (1993) indicates that effective treatment for co-occurring diagnosis clients cannot be limited to attendance at self-help groups such as AA, yet these groups can be an important resource. A review of the literature shows general benefit for these clients in attending 12-step groups (Aase, Jason, & Robinson, 2008; Biegel et al., 2013; Bogenschutz, Geppert, & George, 2006; Woodhead, Hindash, & Tinko, 2013). As discussed in Chapter 8, self-help groups can be an important, cost-free resource for addicted clients. They can also pose some problems for those people with co-occurring diagnosis. One place of difficulty for clients may be the 12 steps of AA (or other programs based on the 12 steps). As Thiesse (1984) states, AA generally encourages its members to be free of chemicals. However, the co-occurring diagnosis client may interpret this suggestion to mean he or she should not be on any psychotropic medication, which could be hazardous for recovery from both problems.

The counselor needs to forewarn clients who attend self-help meetings that advocate total abstinence that this suggestion does not include psychotropic medication (Washton & Zweben, 2006). Other possible difficulties with 12-step programs may be the very steps of recovery (Thiesse, 1984). In the first step, there is an emphasis on acknowledging powerlessness; however, the dual-disordered client needs to have a sense of power in addressing his or her mental health problems. In the second and third steps, a Higher Power is reportedly going to restore the client to sanity. The difficulty with these steps for the dual-disordered client is that this concept may fuel mental health delusions of the past.

The fourth and fifth steps, which address taking a moral inventory of oneself, may be difficult for the dual-disordered client because of low ego strength and high vulnerability. Finally, the eighth and ninth steps involve making amends to other individuals. Again, low ego strength and difficulty in personal relationships due to social skill deficiency may make these steps difficult for the dual-disordered client. Mueser et al. (2003) outlined six additional struggles:

1. Unwillingness to be abstinent initially.

2. Uncomfortable feeling in meetings due to group size.

3. Trouble connecting with other people in the group.

4. Struggling with spiritual orientation.

5. Difficulty identifying with losses such as marriages and jobs because they have not had these in their lives.

6. Trouble fitting in because they look different.

Three groups that may be better matches for this population are: *Dual Diagnosis Anonymous*; *Double Trouble in Recovery*; and *Dual Recovery Anonymous* (T. Hamilton & Samples, 1994). All three provide information on living with mental health problems within the 12-step model, thereby providing clients with helpful social support (Mueser et al., 2003). Contact information on these groups is available in the resource section at the end of this chapter.

Dual Diagnosis Anonymous (DDA) has an additional 5 steps added to their version of the 12 steps of recovery. DDA blends the social recovery model philosophy with the medical model clinical philosophy.

Double Trouble in Recovery (DTR) groups are for those individuals who have both mental health and addiction problems (Zaslav, 1993). Their steps are a revised version of the 12 steps of Alcoholics Anonymous. The concerns expressed by Thiesse (1984) about the first three steps (a sense of powerlessness and a Higher Power restoration to sanity) are not present for this program. The emphasis in the revised first three steps is on personal control. The fifth step changes the word *wrongs* to *problems*, which may eliminate some of the sense of morality from this step.

Dual Recovery Anonymous (DRA) is a national self-help program based on the 12 steps of Alcoholics Anonymous. DRA began in Kansas City in 1989. It focuses on illnesses in an attempt to avoid relapse to alcohol/drug use and a return of emotional/psychiatric symptoms. Roberts (2004) suggests tips to clients to help themselves (e.g., self-education about co-occurring diagnosis, discussions with their doctor about feelings

Whatever self-help group to which the counselor refers the dual-disordered client, spots of difficulty, such as those just stated, need to be anticipated through an acquaintance of the steps or guidelines for the program. For example, some excellent samples of modified 12-step work for schizophrenic/organic mental-disordered, manic-depressive, borderline, and antisocial clients are provided by K. Evans and Sullivan (2001). Mueser et al. (2003) recommend enhancing the client's success in self-help meetings by helping them understand the group purpose and what they can expect in group meetings, role-playing a meeting, and teaching the clients social skills. In addition, the counselor needs to check with dual-disordered individuals to determine how they are being received at the meetings and what they are learning about the process of recovery, which may have a negative or positive impact on their mental health problems. (See Case Study 4.2.)

CASE STUDY 4.2

Continue to work with Case Study 4.1 but now answer these two questions from a treatment perspective:

1. What form of therapy (individual or group) would you recommend for Jane?
2. How would you work with Jane in individual therapy? In group therapy?

EXERCISE 4.2

Refer to the motivational interviewing and stages of change section in this chapter and Chapter 9. Describe to someone else how you could use these approaches with a co-occurring diagnosis client whom you might encounter in your work setting.

and symptoms, medication adherence, location of an effective treatment program, remembering that others are dual diagnosed, to be patient, and to reach out to family, friends, and self-help groups).

Types of Co-Occurring Disorders: Diagnostic Topics Listed in the *DSM-5*

Because the changes in the *DSM-5* (APA, 2013) related to diagnoses are discussed at more length in Chapter 3, this section focuses on some of the co-occurring disorders that an addictions counselor may see in a clinical setting. As stated at the beginning of this chapter, this review is not meant to be exhaustive, but only to highlight some of the common co-occurring disorders found in substance abusing clients. Also, as stated earlier, the reader needs to be especially sensitive to common co-occurring disorders that have a tendency to appear in one's typical clinical population and seek out additional training, collaboration, and supervision in order to be prepared for addressing these typical co-occurring disorders with one's primary clinical population. Note that training may increase a counselor's confidence in both the assessment and treatment process (Thomas, Staiger, & McCabe, 2012). Each area focuses on assessment (including pertinent *DSM-5* information) and treatment, concluding with two case studies and two exercises.

Depression

There is a strong relationship between depressive disorders and substance abuse disorders (Diaz, Green, & Horton, 2009). For example, approximately 25% to 30% of those with a major depressive disorder also have a substance use disorder (Davis et al., 2012).

The 2011 SAMHSA National Survey on Drug Use and Health found that 16.2% of adults (18 or older) with a major depressive episode (MDE in the past year) were abusing or dependent on substances in the past year. Adults with MDE were more likely to be abusing or dependent on substances than those who did not have MDE in the past year (20% versus 7.3%). This survey also found that 21.4% of adolescents (12- to 17-year-olds) who had an MDE in the past year were abusing or dependent on substances; those with MDE were more liking to be abusing or dependent on substances than those who did not have MDE in the past year (18.2% versus 5.8%).

Assessment The symptoms of depression are common both in clients who are intoxicated

with and in withdrawal from substances (APA, 2013). A depressive disorder induced by substances needs to be diagnosed when the symptoms are severe enough to draw independent clinical attention (APA, 2013)—the symptoms are beyond what is typically seen related to the substance use. For example, depression is a common symptom of withdrawal from alcohol, which begins several hours after the last drink and can continue for up to 48 hours (Solomon, 1993). Therefore, it is helpful if the client has been sober for a period of time to determine if the depression is drug related.

For counselors who work with adolescents, this co-occurrence is frequently reported (Rao, 2006).

Treatment It is also important to note that because depression appears to be connected to alcohol/drug relapse (Loosen, Dew, & Prange, 1990), it is critical that it be addressed as a part of the client's recovery. First and Gladis (1993) indicate that one of the first things to consider for the client who is both depressed and addicted is psychotropic medications. They suggest antidepressants for the client whose depression is the primary diagnosis, but possibly a medication such as Antabuse for the client whose primary diagnosis is addiction. In the past, there has been a hesitancy to give antidepressant medication to a client who has a substance use disorder because they may be ineffective or there was the hope that abstinence would resolve the depression (Davis et al., 2012).

An excellent resource for working with this co-occurring population is the SAMHSA CSAT TIP Manual 48, *Managing Depressive Symptoms in Substance Abuse Clients During Early Recovery*, reviewed at the end of this chapter. As discussed in Chapter 9, Motivational Interviewing (MI) added to treatment seems to enhance treatment engagement and clinical outcomes with this population (Westra, Aviram, & Doell, 2011). Also, dialectical behavior therapy (DBT) can be used with this population, as well as best practices cognitive-behavioral techniques (CBT), which are discussed, respectively, in Chapters 6 and 9.

Anxiety

Clients who struggle with an anxiety disorder are twice as likely to struggle with substance abuse or dependence, and women have higher rates of anxiety disorders in general than men (NIDA, 2010; NIDA, 2011). Some anxiety disorders that are closely affiliated with specific drug use, such as social anxiety and alcohol, are prevalent co-occurring disorders (Schneier et al., 2010). The counselor needs to determine if the anxiety diagnosis is a result of the substance abuse disorder or if it coexists as a separate disorder from the substance abuse.

Assessment Some type of laboratory evaluation (urine or blood screen) may assist the assessment process for drugs that are being used recreationally or that are not prescribed (APA, 2013). In the presence of recent or prolonged substance use, withdrawal from the substance needs to be considered in terms of causing the anxiety (APA, 2013). For example, anxiety is a common withdrawal symptom in the early stages (several hours up to 48 hours) of alcohol withdrawal (Solomon, 1993).

Because anxiety can be a natural part of the withdrawal process, the counselor needs to allow for a period of sober time in order to accurately diagnose an anxiety disorder. According to the *DSM-5* (APA, 2013), anxiety symptoms occurring within 4 weeks of intoxication or withdrawal may indicate a substance/medication-induced anxiety disorder—this depends on the type, duration, and amount of the substance used by the client. Anxiety present after 30 days should be assessed for a coexisting anxiety disorder (van Wormer & Davis, 2008).

Treatment Self-help groups can be a helpful adjunct to treatment even with those clients who struggle with social anxiety (Timko, Cronkite, McKellar, Zemore, & Moos, 2013). To facilitate the benefits of self-help groups for the client struggling with social anxiety, the counselor may need to assist the client in learning ways to manage his or her social anxiety when

attending these groups (Timko et al., 2013). Again, as discussed in the previous section on depression, MI, DBT, and CBT may be effective in working with this co-occurring disorder of anxiety.

Posttraumatic Stress Disorder (PTSD)

PTSD is strongly connected to alcohol use disorders and is twice as common in women as men (Sannibale et al., 2013). At least some of this increased risk may be due to an increased risk of interpersonal violence experienced by women (APA, 2013). Clients who have PTSD are 80% more likely to have another mental health disorder, i.e. substance use disorder, than those who are not diagnosed with PTSD (APA, 2013).

Assessment Because of the frequency of this co-occurring disorder, it is critical that counselors assess for the occurrence of PTSD in the substance abusing client. It is also important to assess for PTSD because it can increase the severity of problems in many aspects of the client's life and thereby negatively impact treatment (McGovern et al., 2009).

Treatment In the past there has sometimes been a hesitancy of addressing PTSD issues out of concern for jeopardizing the client's sobriety (McGovern et al., 2009). However, as discussed in Chapter 6, the counselor can work effectively with both issues simultaneously if the emphasis is on the client staying sober. It would be appropriate to stabilize the substance abuse recovery process and then return to PTSD-oriented treatment. Nace (1992) recommends that individuals who have PTSD and an addiction problem be treated for the addiction first. Following that treatment and an attainment of sobriety, the traumatic experience(s) can be explored gradually, so the experience is slowly integrated into the individual.

Working with trauma is discussed at greater length in Chapter 6 both in terms of common types of trauma experienced by addicted clients and effective trauma treatments. For example, CBT has been shown to be highly effective with this population (Sannibale et al., 2013) as well as Seeking Safety (Boden et al., 2011).

Evans and Sullivan (2001) warn that PTSD clients often invite counselors to become involved in some part of the Karpman Triangle, where one person is the rescuer, another is the victim, and the third is the persecutor. They suggest that counselors work at staying out of the triangle by resisting the role of rescuer, victim, or persecutor and instead work from a point of strength and balance. When a counselor experiences the anger of a PTSD survivor, it may be helpful to determine what the client fears. Peer groups mean a lot to these individuals and can be utilized as a resource in the treatment of survivors (Evans & Sullivan, 1995).

Evans and Sullivan (1991c) suggest that clients emphasize that they are survivors rather than victims and that they are actively involved in their recovery for both disorders: obtain support from other individuals, practice self-care, work through their trauma, and possibly obtain psychiatric medication. Van Wormer and Davis (2008) recommend integrated treatment rather than substance abuse treatment alone, as well as monitoring the need for anxiety medication and a plan for safety. Integrated psychosocial treatments, such as Seeking Safety, which is discussed in Chapter 6, has helped in reducing symptom problems for both PTSD and substance use disorders (Back, Waldrop, Brady, & Hien, 2006). If PTSD is not treated, substance abuse treatment can be negatively impacted (Ford, Russo, & Mallon, 2007). In general, the order of treatment is an ongoing treatment planning process.

Eating

Substance use disorders and eating disorders frequently co-occur and eating disorders occur more frequently in women (SAMHSA, 2011). Vastag (2001) summarizes some of the crossover between eating disorders and substance abuse: both problems are typically long term, involve relapses, can be life-threatening, and seem to involve the brain's reward system. Eating disorders, framed as addictive in nature by some theorists, have similarities with other addictions (D. Scott, 1983; Zweben, 1987). L. Buchanan and Buchanan (1992) outline some of the similarities and differences between eating disorders and other addictions. One of these similarities is the compulsive behavior that is combined with a sense of powerlessness and a preoccupation with food. Another similarity is avoidance of feeling and attaining a sense of relief by abusing food. A main difference, however, is that food, unlike alcohol and drugs, cannot be given up totally, so the client with an eating disorder needs to learn to manage the food differently.

Assessment SAMHSA (2011) suggests that assessment for eating disorders be regularly done with substance abusing clients in order to effectively identify them, make referrals, and help them understand the interactions between the two disorders in order to enhance their treatment and recovery process. Screening for eating disorders, then, is recommended as a common practice for both men and women in substance abuse treatment, with a tendency to treat the substance abuse problem first (Vastag, 2001). The *DSM-5* (APA, 2013) has three categorizations of eating disorders: anorexia nervosa, bulimia nervosa, and binge-eating disorders.

The *DSM-5* (APA, 2013) makes specific notations regarding substance abuse in relation to these disorders. *Anorexia nervosa* has a 10-to-1 female-to-male ratio. Some substance use disorder clients may have low weight (a result of their nutritional intake), but these clients, who do not have this eating disorder, are not afraid of gaining weight nor do they have a disturbed body image. Those substance use disorder clients who need to be evaluated for co-occurrence of this disorder are those clients who are abusing substances that reduce appetite and who are afraid of weight gain. Those clients with *bulimia nervosa* have a lifetime prevalence of substance abuse (especially with alcohol or stimulants) of at least 30%. Note that stimulant use with this disorder usually begins because of an attempt to control one's appetite and weight. There is also relationship between substance use disorders and *binge-eating*.

In addition to crossovers between substance abuse and eating disorders, there may be a crossover between eating disorders and sexual abuse (K. MacDonald, Lambie, & Simmonds, 1995). There is disagreement as to whether child sexual abuse predisposes women to developing eating disorders (Rorty & Yager, 1996). It does appear that bulimics report more trauma than anorexics (Vanderlinden & Vandereycken, 1996). Nonetheless, a direct causal relationship cannot be drawn between sexual abuse and eating disorders; however, M. F. Schwartz and Cohn (1996) argue that counselors who work with trauma need to have a familiarity with eating disorders. Thompson, Heinberg, Altabe, and Tantleff-Dunn (1999) state that these experiences do impact how people view their body and expand the definition of abuse to covert forms (i.e., sexual harassment, appearance harassment, and inappropriate sexualization).

It appears necessary, then, for addiction counselors who frequently work with traumatized clients to be prepared to assess for eating disorders in both their male and female clientele. An avoidance of examining such concerns could facilitate a relapse in either the eating disorder or the substance abuse/dependency, which could facilitate a relapse in the other disorder. For example, the recovering addict who has an eating disorder relapse may drink in response to the guilt and shame experienced from the eating disorder relapse.

Treatment If both problems are present for a client, but only one is addressed, chemical dependency treatment may not be effective (Vastag, 2001). Treatment for eating disorders requires an examination for each individual about how sociocultural, personal, and demographic factors interact within that person's life, so that treatment of the eating disorder is specifically designed to meet that person's needs. Yet there are few

programs on integrated treatment (even though this is typically recommended) and there is no research on the best ways to simultaneously treat them (SAMHSA, 2011).

L. Buchanan and Buchanan (1992) recommend a three-stage treatment model: (1) developing a relationship and educating the client about the eating disorder; (2) reducing symptoms by using cognitive-behavioral approaches, such as confronting irrational beliefs and learning positive self-talk; and (3) experiencing interpersonal therapy that is dynamic (i.e., using the therapeutic relationship to understand interpersonal dynamics and assisting the client in developing a support system). Cognitive-behavioral approaches appear effective in working with anorexics to change eating patterns. Additionally, mindfulness treatment approaches may be helpful in addressing binge eating (Courbasson, Nishikawa, & Shapira, 2011) and MI added to treatment seems to enhance treatment engagement and clinical outcomes for eating disorders as it does anxiety and depression (Westra et al., 2011). Further treatment suggestions based on various theories of eating disorders (societal/social, interpersonal, feminist, behavioral, cognitive, and integrative) are provided by Thompson et al. (1999).

As with any compulsive behavior, an awareness of the compulsion, along with specific coping skills, can assist a client in breaking free of the eating disorder. A 12-step program, such as Overeaters Anonymous, may be helpful to the client, but as with any self-help group, the group must be monitored for its health and its helpfulness to the client. This support group contact information is listed in the resource section at the end of this chapter.

Violence

A tendency toward violence may accompany a diagnosis of addiction. Mueser et al. (2003) state that clients who are severely mentally ill have a higher risk to be violent and that the best predictor of violence is a history of violent behavior. Nuckols (1995) states that addicted individuals may exhibit violence for different reasons.

One reason may be organic. For example, some alcoholics have had closed head injuries that have resulted in their having violent tendencies. Another cause may be psychosis. A third cause may be characterological problems related to personality disorders (e.g., antisocial, borderline, or PTSD survivors who may use anger as a protective mechanism).

Assessment The *DSM-5* (APA, 2013) has different diagnoses that may fit under this category. Some of these that may coexist with substance use disorders are oppositional defiant, intermittent explosive, and conduct disorder. With intermittent explosive disorders, this diagnosis should not be given when the outbursts occur almost always when the client is intoxicated or in withdrawal. However, when this is not the case, the counselor needs to carefully assess for the presence of the intermittent explosive disorder.

Counselors need to assess for past and future violence risk factors, such as substance abuse, and give attentiveness to both disorder so a decrease in substance abuse could result in a decrease in violence (Mueser et al., 2003). A careful, overall assessment of the cause of the violence (organic, psychotic, characterological) needs to be done in order to determine the effective treatment approach. For example, awareness that alcohol and high levels of benzodiazepines can trigger violent crimes should be taken into consideration by the counselor in the assessment, treatment, and relapse prevention for clients who have a substance use disorder and have committed a violent crime (Lundholm, Haggard, Moeller, Hallqvist, & Thiblin, 2013). Assessing can be a complex problem because the counselor needs to assess critical areas: the type of violence, the circumstances under which it occurred or may occur, and who might be a possible victim.

Treatment As stated above, a careful assessment of the cause of the violence can guide the treatment plan. If organic, it can be determined how to address the cause medically as well as behaviorally

with the client. If psychotic, antipsychotic medication can be helpful. If characterological, evidence-based treatments (EBTs) that have been demonstrated as helpful with this population can be used.

If counselors are doing outreach to such clients, it is recommended that "double staffing, cell phones, and personal emergency alarms" (p. 43) be used (Mueser et al., 2003). If the legal system is involved in the client's situation, it is recommended that counselors work closely and collaboratively with them (Mueser et al., 2003). Also, some violent clients may prey on other clients in treatment, so counselors need to monitor and limit the violent client's behavior, including a shift in treatment to one that is home-based (Mueser et al., 2003).

Nuckols (1995) reports that clients who hurt deeply may feel that retaliation toward others is a right. Nuckols's suggestions for counselors include their working with the anger as grief work by establishing rapport, drawing out the emotional pain, and controlling countertransference with regard to violence. Verbal management of these clients includes the counselor's being calm, appearing in control, speaking softly, listening to the client, and showing concern for his or her own safety in the situation; and, if possible, both counselor and client should be sitting. Finally, the counselor should assess the level of violence and know his or her own personal reactions to anger, violence, and the client (Nuckols, 1995).

Gambling

Inaba and Cohen (2000) describe four categories of gamblers: recreational/social, business (professional gamblers), antisocial (steal to gamble), and pathological (obsessed with it). Approximately 80% to 90% of people gamble—most for entertainment, with 1% to 2% as compulsive gamblers (Martin, Weinberg, & Bealer, 2007). Gamblers in treatment show 5 times greater prevalence of alcohol/drug addiction than the general population (Arseneault, Ladouceur, & Vitaro, 2001). Women tend to like forms such as slots and bingo, whereas men tend to like table casino games and roulette (Harvard Medical School Special Health Report, 2008). Yip and Potenza (2009) state the disorder usually starts in adolescence/young adulthood and has a telescopic effect in women (it takes them less time to develop the disorder). Buck and Sales (2000) describe the experience of gambling addiction that includes a rush while gaming and consequences that are financial, legal, medical, and psychological (i.e., depression, suicide).

Gambling is widespread, with most states allowing it and some using it financially through state lotteries (Hayes, 1999; Martin et al., 2007). In addition to the typical forms of gambling with which most of us are familiar, such as casino and lottery, there is also electronic gambling, which includes video poker and the Internet (Hayes, 1999). In the past 10 years, online casinos have facilitated gambling because people can use their credit cards and gamble anytime at home (Martin et al., 2007).

The growing concern about gambling is apparent in the establishment in 1996 of the National Center for Responsible Gaming (NCRG; www .ncrg.org), which encourages research on gambling disorders that is rigorous and reviewed by peers. There is also the National Council on Problem Gambling (NCPG; www.ncpgam bling.org), which focuses on increasing awareness, providing information, and encouraging research on gambling.

Assessment The *DSM-5* (APA, 2013) has expanded the substance-related disorders chapter to include gambling disorder because it activates the brain reward system in a similar way to drugs and its symptoms are similar to substance use disorders. Gamblers look at money as both causing and solving their problems (APA, 2013). Martin et al. (2007) frame it as a disease where there is tolerance, dependence, and withdrawal.

Those with gambling disorders have high co-occurrence with substance use, depressive, anxiety, and personality disorders (APA, 2013). They may especially occur prior to substance use and anxiety disorders (APA, 2013). Therefore, the counselor may want to screen for gambling disorder when working with an addicted client.

Treatment The first formal treatment for gambling was established in 1971 at the Veterans Affairs Hospital in Brecksville, Ohio (Martin et al., 2007). Buck and Sales (2000) make some specific treatment recommendations. Treatment requires looking at money differently, developing a financial plan (maybe including restitution), having daily structure, and working on cognitions when compulsive urges are experienced. Basic treatment recommendations include cognitive restructuring, relaxation training, covert sensitization (associating negative emotional and physical states with stimuli related to gambling), alternate activities, and relapse prevention. Petry (2002) suggests that treatment for older pathological gamblers may need to be individualized to address the specific issues they face. This may also be true for adolescents, as Ste-Marie, Gupta, and Derevensky (2006) found high state and trait anxiety scores with this population and women, for whom gender differences in demographics, behavior, and consequences and treatment have been found (Wenzel & Dahl, 2009).

Clients may use Gamblers Anonymous (www .gamblersanonymous.org) or Debtors Anonymous (www.debtorsanonymous.org), both based on a 12-step framework for support. Debtors Anonymous (DA) has a book of 38 DA recovery stories, *A Currency of Hope*. There is also Gam-Anon for family members (www.gam-anon.org). Both clients and counselors can contact the National Council on Problem Gambling (www .ncpgambling.org) for treatment information. SAMHSA also has a Problem Gambling Toolkit that contains advice for family members, which can be accessed at www.samhsa.gov

Personality

The *Harvard Mental Health Letter* (Dual Diagnosis, 2003a) states that substance abuse is common with personality disorders, such as antisocial and borderline, that involve struggles with being responsible, controlling impulses, and learning from experience. Antisocial and borderline personality disorders are examined in this section, because addicted clients often show these symptoms (Gianoli, Serrita, O'Brien, & Ralevski, 2012; Mueser et al., 2012; NIDA, 2011; Solomon, 1993; Zuckerman, 2012). Van Wormer and Davis (2008) caution that these diagnoses may reflect counselor bias that is culturally, ethnically, or personally based. They recommend that treatment focus on working with these clients on goals that have meaning for them in small steps.

Assessment Regarding *antisocial personality disorder*, when parents of both adopted and biological children have an antisocial personality disorder, the children have a greater chance of developing an antisocial personality disorder, a substance use disorder, and a somatic symptom disorder (APA, 2013). In an adult who has a substance related disorder and shows signs of antisocial behavior, the diagnosis of antisocial personality disorder is not given unless these antisocial behaviors were present from childhood into adulthood (APA, 2013). If both were present throughout, the diagnoses for both are given even if some of their antisocial behavior is a result of their drug use. However, if both are not present throughout, the counselor needs to carefully make the assessment of a co-occurring disorder because addicted individuals may commit antisocial acts in conjunction with their addiction.

In the assessment process for *borderline personality disorder*, individuals who have this disorder may show impulsivity in abusing substances (APA, 2013). The counselor needs to carefully assess the presence of substance use disorder symptoms as well as the presence of the personality disorder features in order to determine if one or both are present due to the potentially significant overlap.

Treatment Criminal justice agencies are often involved in the referral of these clients to treatment. When working with *antisocial personality disorder* clients, a therapeutic alliance may not be possible (Shollar, 1993). Confrontation about substance abuse may then be required. When referring these clients to self-help groups for support, the counselor needs to help the client examine dysfunctional behavior at meetings to help the client change (Zaslav, 1993).

There are few treatments that treat both *borderline personality* and substance use disorders (Gianoli et al., 2012). Some treatment suggestions follow. Fayne (1993) indicates that borderline personality-disordered clientele may react with intense anger to limits set with them or when they experience emotions and may be involved in community struggles. Zaslav (1993) suggests referring these clients to supportive self-help groups, which are very tolerant of individuals' idiosyncrasies. Finally, dialectical behavior therapy (DBT), described in Chapter 6, has been demonstrated to be effective with this population. (See Case Studies 4.3 and 4.4.)

CASE STUDY 4.3

Maryanne is a 28-year-old female who has come to counseling for the first time. She is the oldest of three children and reports that her parents are still married. She was referred to treatment by a physician who was concerned about her weight fluctuations and her admission to him of amphetamine use. She entered a combination inpatient/outpatient treatment and completed it about three weeks ago. She has not attended any self-help groups in her community, even though she was given referrals, because she did not want to bring further shame to her family. In her intake session, Maryanne reports a pattern of immersing herself in different addictive behaviors during her life. For example, for a time, she was involved with alcohol, then sex, then religion, then drugs, each in an addictive manner that appeared serial in nature. During the session, Maryanne brings food in with her: chips, cookies, candy, sugared soda, and the like. She eats these rapidly during the session and then midway through the session she says she needs to use the bathroom. When she returns, she appears slightly pale.

1. What do you say to Maryanne about her behavior when she returns from using the bathroom?
2. How do you need to work with other professionals to be helpful to this client?
3. What type of treatment plan would you develop for Maryanne?

CASE STUDY 4.4

Now work with a revised version of Case Study 4.3.

Maryanne is a 28-year-old female who has come to counseling for the first time. She is the oldest of three children and reports that her parents are still married. She was referred to treatment by a physician who was concerned about her use of amphetamines. She entered a combination inpatient/outpatient treatment and completed it about three weeks ago. She has not attended any self-help groups in her community, even though she was given referrals, because she did not want to bring further shame to her family. In her intake session, Maryanne reports a pattern of immersing herself in different addictive behaviors during her life. For example, for a time, she was involved with alcohol, then sex, then religion, then drugs, each in an addictive manner that appeared serial in nature.

Process in small groups two questions:

1. How would you work with other professionals if in addition to her substance abuse, you believed she was struggling with depression? Anxiety? PTSD? Violent tendencies? Gambling? Personality Disorder?
2. How would your treatment plan shift for her if you found she was struggling with depression? Anxiety? PTSD? Violent tendencies? Gambling? Personality Disorder?

EXERCISE 4.3

Of those disorders listed in this chapter from the *DSM-5* (depression, anxiety, PTSD, eating, violence, gambling, personality) place them on a continuum that ranges from highest to lowest in terms of your comfort level in addressing them. Process with another person what makes you more comfortable in working with some areas more than others and how might you become more comfortable working in those areas at the lower end of the continuum.

EXERCISE 4.4

For a few minutes:

1. Write down all of the negative comments you have heard from a client (or if you have not counseled, make it someone you know personally—it may be you) about their mental health struggles.

2. Group these comments into common themes of others "voices": family, friends, professionals, acquaintances.

3. Choose three common negative themes that emerge across these different "voices."

4. Now brainstorm ways you may counter these negative messages in terms of thoughts or behaviors.

5. Finally, examine how addiction may complicate this process in terms of discrimination, recovery, and relapse.

BEHAVIORAL ADDICTIONS

Behavioral addictions have been defined as "human drives gone awry" (Martin et al., 2007, p. 139). Some experts have called these behaviors (compulsive gambling, eating disorders, sexual addiction, compulsive buying, workaholism) "process addiction," where it is viewed as a disease and treatment fits the disease model of addiction (psychosocial counseling, 12-step groups, medication) (Smith & Seymour, 2001). They have also been called "impulse control disorders" and "impulsive-compulsive behaviors" (Karim & Chaudhri, 2012). The term *behavioral addiction* is used in this chapter, because the author agrees with the experts who use this term that the natural drive is abnormal because of the compulsivity of behavior; it is complex (different components make up the addiction); it results from different contributing factors over time; and it appears differently in different people (Martin et al., 2007). In a behavioral addiction there is:

• An increased need to be involved in the activity.

• Use of the activity to numb emotions.

• Evidence of increased vulnerability in the person as a result of emotional problems (depression, anxiety, etc.), social factors (family dynamics, peer pressure), and lack of alternative activities (Martin et al., 2007).

There is disagreement between experts on inclusion criteria in this classification. Some organize the criteria as the "3 Cs" (craving, loss of control, continued use despite adverse consequences) (Harvard Medical School Special Health Report, 2008), whereas others (Yip & Potenza, 2009) add items such as "compulsive engagement" to this list of three items. It has been described as compulsive behavior that one cannot stop (Fong, Reid, & Parhami, 2012).

There is disagreement about inclusion of behavioral activities. For example, the Harvard Medical School Special Health Report (2008) lists four addictions (eating, sexual activity, shopping, and computer/Internet use), whereas Yip and Potenza (2009) list eight areas (binge eating, compulsive sexual behavior, compulsive buying disorder, problematic Internet use, kleptomania [uncontrollable stealing], trichotillomania [pulling out of hair], skin picking, and intermittent explosive disorder).

This chapter navigates through the professional disagreement in this area by using the term *behavioral addiction* and the criteria of the "3 Cs." When working in this area, addiction counselors need to keep in mind:

- There is little known about how quickly behavioral addictions develop and how severe they can become.

- Behavioral addictions are strongly impacted by availability.

- Also, a person can switch from one behavioral addiction to another.

- Behavioral addictions can occur simultaneously and trigger each other (Martin et al., 2007).

This means the addiction counselor needs to assess the client's ease of accessibility to the behavioral addiction and the interplay between addictive behaviors (sequential or simultaneous). An example of this could be a client who is addicted to alcohol/drugs with intertwined behavioral addictions of sexual activity on the Internet. When this client enters alcohol/drug addiction recovery, triggers for relapse into compulsive sexual activity and/or alcohol/drugs may occur when the client uses a computer.

Three behavioral addictions are explored in this section in alphabetical order: Internet/video game, sexual, and shopping. Counselors need to be sensitive in the assessment of these behaviors because clients may experience extreme feelings of shame, guilt, and embarrassment with regard to them (Fong, Reid, & Parhami, 2012).

Internet/Video Game

In the past, computer/Internet behavioral addiction has been defined as "nonchemical or behavioral addictions which involve human-machine interactions" (Liu & Potenza, 2007, p. 138). It appears to be a conduit for sexual and shopping behavioral addictions (Harvard Medical School Special Health Report, 2008).

The focus here is on *Internet/video game behavioral addiction* that has been called: Internet gaming disorder, Internet use disorder, Internet addiction, and gaming addiction (APA, 2013). The remainder of this section is a summary from the *DSM-5*. The *DSM-5* has Internet gaming disorder included in its section on "Conditions for Further Study" that includes proposed criteria sets for conditions for which they want to encourage research (APA, 2013). The manual states there is a substantial amount of literature on compulsive Internet game playing and there are similarities to gambling and substance use disorders, but there lacks a standard definition. It is defined in the manual as "a pattern of excessive and prolonged Internet gaming that results in a cluster of cognitive and behavioral symptoms, including progressive loss of control over gaming, tolerance, and withdrawal symptoms, analogous to the symptoms of substance use disorders." (APA, 2013, p. 796). The main feature of it is persistently playing games (usually group ones) for hours.

It seems highest in Asian countries and in male adolescents (12 to 20) with possible influences of Asian environments and/or genetic background. Using the Internet excessively in other ways (social media—Facebook, pornography viewing) is not considered the same as Internet gaming disorder and excessive online gambling may be a separate diagnosis of gambling disorder in a future manual. Griffiths (2003) reports that numerous factors impact the rise of Internet gambling, such as its accessibility, affordability, convenience, anonymity, escapism, disinhibition, and antisocial nature. It may be difficult to identify this condition, because the person may be embarrassed or may not see it as a disorder (Yip & Potenza, 2009). An efficient free-access instrument to assess Internet addiction is the Online Cognition Scale (OCS). It is one of the first instruments developed to assess this addiction and it has been translated into Turkish and Chinese (Sandberg, Richards, & Erford, 2013). An overall review of this instrument is available in the book, *Assessing Common Mental Health and Addiction Issues with Free-Access Instrument* (Sandberg et al., 2013).

Young (2011) outlines a cognitive-behavioral therapy for Internet addiction (CBT-IA) that uses CBT in conjunction with harm reduction therapy. A 3-phase approach is described that involves behavior modification, addressing denial, and exploring and treating coexisting issues.

Sexual

Margolis and Zweben (1998) describe compulsive sexual behavior that is "repetitive, compelling or driven quality that persists despite adverse consequences" (p. 289). It is difficult to obtain accurate numbers on it because of its secrecy (Harvard Medical School Special Health Report, 2008). Margolis and Zweben (1998) summarize Travin's (1995) four models of compulsive sexual behavior that may overlap:

1. Obsessive-compulsive

2. Compulsive sexual behaviors (affective disorder–related, such as depression)

3. Sexual addiction

4. Sexual impulsivity

This section focuses on the area of sexual addiction, although the addiction professional may want to generally explore a client's sexual history for the presence of the other three models, because any of these four behaviors could be a potential relapse trigger for substance-abusing clients. Note that this area has also been called *hypersexual disorder* (Fong et al., 2012; Karim & Chaudhri, 2012). It has been argued to be an addictive disorder (Garcia & Thibaut, 2010) as well as stated that more research is needed before it can be classified as an addiction (Kor, Fogel, Reid, & Potenza, 2013).

Sexual addiction, as defined by A. Goodman (1997), is when sexual behavior results in pleasure and a decrease in pain, where the client repeatedly cannot control the behavior and continues it despite harmful consequences. The majority of people who experience this addiction are men, although Martin et al. (2007) report that women hide it more. The addiction seems to begin before age 18, and the behavior is at its height between ages 20 and 30 (A. Goodman, 1997). Counselors need to be cognizant of the use of cybersex on the Internet, which includes "pornographic sites, virtual reality, and sexual chat rooms" (Buck & Sales, 2000, p. 7). Martin et al. (2007) define computer pornography as the "cocaine of sexual addiction" (p. 142) because of its availability and its tendency to speed up the addictive process.

Carnes (1995) presents 10 different types of sexual addiction that may co-occur with an alcohol/drug addiction:

1. Fantasy sex (masturbating compulsively, stalking others)

2. Seductive role sex (focusing on conquest and power)

3. Voyeuristic sex (accessing information through one primary sensory mode such as visual; e.g., "peeping Toms")

4. Exhibitionism (exposing oneself to others, which can take different forms)

5. Trading sex (replicating fearful childhood sexual experiences, only this time having the sense of being in control)

6. Paying for sex (paying another for sexual acts)

7. Intrusive sex (using violation to experience eroticism, which was paired with boundary violations as a child)

8. Anonymous sex (seeking instant gratification)

9. Pain exchange (experiencing arousal when hurt is repetition of early trauma and may include objects as part of the violence experienced)

10. Exploitive sex (seeking a vulnerable individual to exploit)

Kafka (2010) adds pornography, cybersex, telephone sex, and strip clubs to this list and describes the list as a hypersexual disorder. Buck and Sales (2000) state that sexual addiction is strongly shamed; therefore, addicts tend to be highly secretive because of puritanical cultural views and possibly religious beliefs. They recommend that counselors be careful to avoid language that can trigger shame in a client. Carnes (1995) states that these individuals share a common core of pain with alcohol/drug addiction. He suggests that these sexual addicts are trying to appease their pain through alcohol/drugs and sex. Treatment for these dual-disordered clients needs to address the common source of pain they are responding to through their alcohol/drug addiction and their sexual addiction. Treatment has included pharmacology and various therapies (cognitive-behavioral, group, couples, family, psychodynamic; A. Goodman, 1997). Buck and Sales (2000) recommend helping clients identify internal and external triggers, reducing shame, and finding group support with this addiction.

One such group is Sex Addicts Anonymous. This group was founded in 1977 by men who wanted more anonymity than they received from other 12-step programs designed for sex addicts. Another group is Sexaholics Anonymous (SA), which is also based on the 12 steps of Alcoholics Anonymous and views the condition as a disease. Contact information for these groups is listed at the end of this chapter in the resource section. Another resource is the Society for the Advancement of Sexual Health (SASH; www.sash.net). This nonprofit organization provides information on the promotion of sexual health and the overcoming of problematic sexual behaviors. It has annual membership fees with different membership levels.

Shopping

This has been called *oniomania* ("buying mania" [Karim & Chaudhri, 2012]. Although it has been acknowledged as a problem for almost a century, little is known about compulsive buying disorder (Yip & Potenza, 2009). The numerous terms used for this behavioral addiction speak to the lack of consensus regarding the disorder (compulsive shopping, oniomania, shopaholism, compulsive spending, compulsive buying, and shopping addiction) (Fong et al., 2012). The same dynamics of the "3 Cs" (craving, loss of control, continued use despite adverse consequences) need to be examined in the assessment process. It involves compulsive thoughts or impulses to buy unneeded or large quantities of items even though negative consequences result from the behavior" (Karim & Chaudhri, 2012). The client anticipates, prepares, shops, and spends—these are considered the four phases of the addiction (Black, Monihan, Schlosser, & Repertinger, 2001). Hartston (2012) argues that it needs to be considered an addictive behavior.

It has been described as having similarities to substance use disorders and can occur along with substance use disorders (Fong et al., 2012). Therefore, counselors need to be aware that this condition can exist for their clients and assess and address this issue as a part of treatment if necessary.

One treatment program that has recently emerged is the Stopping Overshopping Group Treatment Program (Benson & Eisenach, 2013). This program draws from different therapies (psychodynamic, CBT, DBT, MI, mindfulness, and acceptance and commitment therapy). Counselors may find it helpful to refer their clients who struggle with this behavioral addiction to the self-help group Debtors Anonymous, whose contact information is listed at the end of this chapter. Because little is currently known about this behavioral addiction, the reader is encouraged to continue to monitor the theoretical and research developments in this area to learn how to accurately assess and treat this behavioral addiction. (See Case Study 4.5.)

CASE STUDY 4.5

Franklin is a 30-year-old male who has successfully completed alcohol and drug treatment. He has been able to stay sober for 4 years. However, he has come to you as a counselor because he has never been able to maintain an ongoing intimate relationship. He says his last partner told him he needed to look at how much time he spent on the Internet as the partner was breaking up with him. As you complete your intake on Franklin, you begin to suspect he has some behavioral addictions that are connected with his Internet use.

1. Which behavioral addictions would you need to be sure to ask him about?
2. How would you approach him in your questions given the sensitive nature of some of the behavioral addictions?
3. What would be your concerns professionally about addressing such issues?
4. Which behavioral addictions do you believe you would be competent in addressing with him and which ones do you believe you would need to refer out?

EXERCISE 4.5

Discuss in a dyad or a small group your views on behavioral addictions. In particular, discuss your views regarding if you believe they are addictions and why. Also discuss those that would be comfortable for you to address in counseling and those you believe would be a stretch for you given your knowledge base, experience, and views. If any are a stretch for you, how would you address that through supervision, consultation, or a referral?

SUMMARY

Working with co-occurring diagnosis clients requires the clinician to exhibit sensitivity in assessment, treatment, and aftercare in mental health issues as well as substance abuse issues. In addition, the chemical dependency counselor needs to work closely and collaboratively with other mental health professionals to ensure that the client obtains the best possible care. Counselors need to practice within their area of competence and consult with and/or refer to other professionals as necessary. Providing treatment that effectively meets the needs of both problems is critical for addiction recovery.

QUESTIONS

1. What are some definitions of *co-occurring diagnosis*?

2. What are some of the historical struggles between the two fields of chemical

dependency and mental health counseling?

3. How can clients with co-occurring disorders be recognized in addiction treatment? In mental health treatment?

4. What are common problems in diagnosing clients with co-occurring disorders?

5. What are general treatment guidelines for working with clients who have co-occurring disorders?

6. What treatment modifications may need to be made for clients with dual disorders in terms of time, medication, confrontation,

psychiatric support, self-help groups, and use screening?

7. What are some general assessment and treatment approaches when working with the different co-occurring disorders (depression, anxiety, PTSD, eating, violence, gambling, personality)?

8. What are behavioral addictions?

9. How might behavioral addictions overlap or interact with alcohol/drug addictions?

10. How may these issues complicate the treatment and recovery process in relation to addiction?

READINGS, RESOURCES, WEBSITES

SUGGESTED READINGS

Substance Abuse

Center for Substance Abuse Treatment (CSAT). (2005). *Substance abuse treatment for persons with co-occurring disorders*. Treatment Improvement Protocol (TIP) Series, No. 42. DHHS Publication No. (SMA) 05–3922. Rockville, MD: Substance Abuse and Mental Health Services Administration.

The manual provides a general overall of treatment with these disorders.

Daley, D. C., & Moss, H. B. (2002). *Dual disorders: Counseling clients with chemical dependency and mental illness*. Center City, MN: Hazelden.

This book has 15 chapters that provide an overview of treatment and recovery issues including family involvement, relapse prevention, and group treatment.

Daley, D. C., & Zuckoff, A. (1999). *Improving treatment compliance: Counseling & systems strategies for substance abuse & dual disorders*. Center City, MN: Hazelden.

This book is divided into three sections: an overview, strategies, and motivational strategies of clinical applications.

Hamilton, T., & Samples, P. (1994). *The twelve steps and dual disorders*. Center City, MN: Hazelden.

This book describes how the 12 steps can be effectively used with this population.

Hazelden (1993). *The dual disorders recovery book: A twelve step program for those of us with addiction and an emotional or psychiatric illness*. Center City, MN: Hazelden.

This book focuses on the 12-step program of dual disorders (Dual Recovery Anonymous) through the stories of individuals.

Klott, J. (2013). *Integrated treatment for co-occurring disorders*. Hoboken, NJ: Wiley.

This book has seven chapters that provide treatment principles, formulation of treatment plans (evidence-based), and use of Motivational Enhancement Therapy with a focus on the person, not the diagnosis.

L'Abate, L. L., Farrar, J. E., & Serritella, D. A. (1992). *Handbook of differential treatments for addictions*. Boston, MA: Allyn & Bacon.

This book provides information on a variety of addictions that they describe as socially destructive (alcohol, substance abuse, tobacco, domestic violence, sexual abuses and offenses), socially unacceptable (interpersonal/love, eating disorders), or socially acceptable (gambling, workaholism, exercise, spending, religion, codependency).

McGovern, M. (2009). *Co-occurring addiction and mental health disorders: A handbook for recovery*. Hazelden: Center City, MN.

This book is written specifically for the client who believes they may have a co-occurring disorder. There are 17 short, easy-to-read chapters that describe the assessment, treatment, and recovery process.

Mueser, K. T., Noordsy, D. L., Drake, R. E., & Fox, L. (2003). *Integrated treatment for dual disorders: A guide to effective practice* New York, NY: Guilford Press.

This is an excellent workbook that generally describes co-occurring diagnosis and then provides information on working with this population in the assessment and treatment process including individual, group, and family therapy. Its appendix contains 16 educational handouts and 20 assessment and treatment forms.

National Institute on Drug Abuse (NIDA). (2010, September). *Comorbidity: Addiction and other mental illnesses*. (NIH Publication No. 10–5771). Rockville, MD: NIDA.

This publication provides an excellent summary of comorbity.

National Institute on Drug Abuse (NIDA). (2011, September). *Comorbidity: Addiction and other mental disorders*. (NIDA InfoFacts). Rockville, MD: NIDA.

This brief document describes co-occurring disorders in a general, concise approach.

Smith, T. (2008). *A balanced life: 9 strategies for coping with the mental health problems of a loved one*. Center City, MN: Hazelden.

This book is written for the family and friends of a loved one who struggles with mental illness. It provides nine strategies to help the individual

cope with the daily realities of this situation within a balanced lifestyle. It incorporates a Higher Power concept.

Solomon, J., Zimberg, S., & Shollar, E. (Eds.). (1993). *Dual diagnosis: Evaluation, treatment, training, and program development* (pp. 39–53). New York, NY: Plenum Press.

This book covers theory, research, and practice with co-occurring diagnosis. Specific suggestions are made regarding assessment and treatment of the dually diagnosed.

Substance Abuse and Mental Health Services Administration. (1994). *Assessment and treatment of patients with coexisting mental illness and alcohol and other drug abuse* (DHHS Publication No. 94–2078). Rockville, MD: Author.

This publication has nine chapters that provide basic information on co-occurring diagnosis and treatment (issues, collaboration, medication) and a separate chapter on specific diagnoses (mood disorders, anxiety disorders, personality disorders, psychotic disorders).

Substance Abuse and Mental Health Services Administration. (1998). *Substance abuse disorder treatment for people with physical and cognitive disabilities*. Rockville, MD: Author.

This 156-page publication examines treatment issues, screening issues, treatment planning, service delivery, community links and case management, and organizational commitment. It has appendixes of bibliography, information, referral, and alcohol and drug problems as related to the American Disabilities Act.

Substance Abuse and Mental Health Services Administration. (2002). *Report to congress on the prevention and treatment of co-occurring substance abuse disorders and mental disorders* (www.samhsa.gov). Rockville, MD: Author.

This report is divided into five chapters: characteristics/needs, impact of federal block grants, prevention, evidence-based practices, and a 5-year action blueprint.

Watkins, T. R., Lewellen, A., & Barrett, M. C. (2001). *Dual diagnosis: An integrated approach to treatment*. Thousand Oaks, CA: Sage.

This book covers general issues related to co-occurring diagnosis and then provides separate chapters on assessment and treatment on specific disorders in relation to substance abuse (schizophrenia, depression, bipolar, personality disorders, anxiety disorders).

Depression

Center for Substance Abuse Treatment (CSAT). (2008). *Managing depressive symptoms in substance abuse clients during early recovery*. Treatment Improvement Protocol (TIP) Series, No. 48. DHHS Publication No. (SMA) 05–3922. Rockville, MD: Substance Abuse and Mental Health Services Administration.

This manual is the first TIP manual using a new format that describes working with this population in three parts for substance abuse counselors (Part 1: counseling methods and frameworks), program administrators (Part 2: provision of administrative support for part 1 to be integrated), and clinical supervisors (Part 3: online literature review that is updated every 6 months for 5 years and can be accessed at www.kap.samhsa.gov).

Eating

Schwartz, M. F., & Cohn, L. (Eds.). (1996). *Sexual abuse and eating disorders*. New York, NY: Brunner/Mazel.

This book provides an excellent overview of the overlap of the issues between sexual abuse and eating disorders.

Stromberg, G., & Merrill, J. (2006). *Feeding the fame*. Center City, MN: Hazelden.

This book tells the stories of 17 celebrities who struggled with eating disorders and are in the process of recovery. It does an excellent job of personalizing and demystifying the struggle with eating disorders. The celebrities come from all types of careers (political, journalistic, acting, writing, modeling, religious, entertaining, sports, paranormalistic).

Substance Abuse and Mental Health Services Administration. (2011a). *Clients with substance use and eating disorders*, HHS Publication No. (SMA) 10–4617.

Rockville, MD: Substance Abuse and Mental Health Services Administrations.

This publication provides an overview of eating disorders based on the *DSM-IV-TR*.

Thompson, J. K., Heinberg, L. J., Altable, M., & Tantleff-Dunn, S. (1999). *Exacting beauty: Theory, assessment, and treatment of body image disturbance*. Washington, DC: American Psychological Association.

This book provides an excellent overview of theoretical approaches (societal/social, interpersonal, feminist, behavioral, cognitive, and integrative) that explain eating disorder prevalence. It has 36 scales, surveys, and questionnaires that can be used with this population.

Gambling

Grant, J. E., Odlaug, B. L., & Potenza, M. N. (2009). Pathologic gambling: Clinical characteristics and treatment. In R. K. Ries, D. A. Fiellin, S. C. Miller, & R. Saitz (Eds.), *Principles of addiction medicine* (pp. 509–517). Philadelphia, PA: Wolters Kluwer.

This book chapter specifically focuses on the behavioral addiction of gambling that includes definitions, diagnostic criteria, and treatment.

Heineman, M. (1993). *When someone you love gambles*. Center City, MN: Hazelden.

This 20-page pamphlet is easy to read and concisely describes an overview of gambling.

Behavioral Addictions

Harvard Medical School Special Report. (2008). *Overcoming addiction*. Boston, MA: Harvard Health Publications.

This 48-page booklet succinctly describes behavioral addictions in three pages.

L'Abate, L. L., Farrar, J. E., & Serritella, D. A. (1992). *Handbook of differential treatments for addictions*. Boston, MA: Allyn & Bacon.

This book provides information on a variety of addictions that they describe as socially destructive (alcohol, substance abuse, tobacco, domestic violence, sexual abuses and offenses), socially unacceptable (interpersonal/love, eating disorders), or socially acceptable (gambling, workaholism, exercise, spending, religion, codependency).

Sandberg, K. M., Richard, T. E., & Erford, B. T. (2013). *Assessing common mental health and addiction issues with free-access instruments.* New York, NY: Routledge.

This book is designed to provide counselors with efficient free-access instruments that assess common diagnostic categories. Seven of the eight chapters focus on specific disorders: anxiety; mood; addiction and related; AD/HD, disruptive, impulse control, obsessive compulsive, and related; autistic and schizophrenic spectrums; eating; and trauma and stressor-related.

Shoptaw, S. J. (2009). Sexual addiction. In R. K. Ries, D. A. Fiellin, S. C. Miller, & R. Saitz (Eds.), *Principles of addiction medicine* (pp. 519–530). Philadelphia, PA: Wolters Kluwer.

This book chapter discusses the behavioral addiction of sexual activity that includes definitions, diagnostic criteria, and treatment.

Yip, S. W., & Potenza, M. N. (2009). Understanding "behavioral addictions" insights from research. In R. K. Ries, D. A. Fiellin, S. C. Miller, & R. Saitz (Eds.), *Principles of addiction medicine* (pp. 45–61). Philadelphia, PA: Wolters Kluwer.

This book chapter provides a concise overview of nine behavioral addictions that includes definitions, diagnostic criteria, and treatment.

SUGGESTED RESOURCES

Substance Abuse
Toolkits

Center for Substance Abuse Treatment (CSAT). (2003). *Co-occurring disorders: Integrated dual disorders treatment: Implementation resource kit.* Rockville, MD: Author.

Support Groups

Double Trouble in Recovery (DTR)
c/o Mental Health Empowerment Project

271 Central Avenue
Albany, NY 12209
Phone: (518) 434-1393
www.bhevolution.org/public/doubletroubleinre covery.page

Dual Diagnosis Anonymous
320 North E. Street
Suite 207
San Bernardino, CA 92401
(909) 888-9282

Dual Recovery Anonymous
World Network Central Office
P.O. Box 8107
Prairie Village, KS 66208
Phone: (913) 991-2703
E-mail: draws@draonline.org
www.draonline.org

Eating
Support Groups

Overeaters Anonymous
P.O. Box 44020
Rio Rancho, NM 87174
Phone: (505) 891-2664
www.oa.org

This organization focuses on compulsive overeating from a 12-step program perspective.

Gambling
Toolkits

www.samhsa.gov.
SAMHSA has a Problem Gambling Toolkit that also contains advice for family members.

Support Groups

Debtors Anonymous
General Service Office
P.O. Box 920888
Needham, MA 02492-0009
Toll-free: (800) 421-2383 U.S. only
Phone: (781) 453-2743

Fax: (781) 453-2745
E-mail: office@debtorsanonymous.org
www.debtorsanonymous.org

Gamblers Anonymous
P.O. Box 17173
Los Angeles, CA 90017
Phone: (626) 960-3500
www.gamblersanonymous.org

Gam-Anon
P.O. Box 157
Whitestone, NY 11357
Phone: (718) 352-1671
www.gam-anon.org

These organizations are based on the 12-step recovery program.

Behavioral Addictions
Sexual Activity
Support Groups

Sex Addicts Anonymous
International Service Organization of SAA
P.O. Box 70949
Houston, TX 77270
Phone: (800) 477-8191
E-mail: info@saa-recovery.org
www.saa-recovery.org

Sexaholics Anonymous (SA) International
Central Office
P.O. Box 3565
Brentwood, TN 37024
Toll-free: (866) 424-8777
Phone: (615) 370-6062
Fax: (615) 370-0882
E-mail: saico@sa.org
www.sa.org

These organizations center on compulsive sexual activity from a 12-step program focus.

Shopping
Support Groups

Debtors Anonymous
General Service Office

P.O. Box 920888
Needham, MA 02492-0009
Toll-free: (800) 421-2383 U.S. Only
Phone: (781) 453-2743
Fax: (781) 453-2745
E-mail: office@debtorsanonymous.org
www.debtorsanonymous.org

WEBSITES

Substance Abuse

National Institute on Drug Abuse
www.drugabuse.gov

This website provides general information on drug abuse and addiction.

National Institutes of Mental Health
www.nimh.nih.gov

This website provides information on understanding and treating mental illness.

Substance Abuse and Mental Health Services Administration (SAMHSA)
www.samhsa.gov

This website provides a variety of information and resources on substance abuse and mental health.

Treatment Improvement Exchange (TIE)-(SAMHSA funded)
www.treatment.org

This website provides information on the treatment of addiction with a special topics section that addresses concerns such as co-occurring disorders, gambling, and homelessness.

Gambling

National Center for Responsible Gaming
1299 Pennsylvania Avenue NW, Suite 1175
Washington, DC 20004
Phone: (202) 552-2689
Fax: (202) 552-2676
E-mail: contact@ncrg.org
www.ncrg.org

This website provides research on gambling disorders.

National Council on Problem Gambling
730–11th Street NW, Suite 601
Washington, DC 20001
Phone: (202) 547-9204
Fax: (202) 547-9206
www.ncpgambling.org

This website provides general information and information on treatment and research with respect to gambling.

Behavioral Addictions
Sexual Activity

The Society for the Advancement of Sexual Health (SASH)
P.O. Box 433
Royston, GA 30662
Phone: (706) 356-7031
Fax: (866) 389-3974
E-mail: sash@sash.net
www.sash.net

This website provides general information regarding sexuality with specific information on sexual addiction.

CHAPTER 5

THE CORE TREATMENT PROCESS FOR ADDICTIONS

PERSONAL REFLECTIONS

Treatment for addiction is both a science and an art. While the counselor needs to use interventions that have been shown to be effective, the counselor also needs to apply them with a sensitivity and compassion for the difficulty in breaking out of the addictive cycle. One aspect of it being an art is in having a positive "contagion" effect with addicts and their loved ones who come to counseling. They often are discouraged, frightened, angry, and hopeless because of their struggle with the addiction. Therefore, the counselor needs to find a way to stay calm in the form of counseling (crisis, individual, group, family) being used to respond to the addiction. This group of clients and their significant others can easily and quickly accelerate a situation into a crisis because of the suffering they have experienced and are experiencing as a result of the addiction. This is why as counselors it is so important that we learn how to "stay steady in a storm." Each of us varies on how we do this, but what is important is that we think about how we stay calm in stressful situations and then practice that stance. It is important because our clients and their significant others can catch that calmness from us; we can be "contagious" in a positive way. As I have told my students: "Early in my career of working with addicted clients and their family members, I realized somebody was going to have to stay calm in the room, and it looked like it had to be me."

OBJECTIVES

1. To learn basic crisis counseling approaches.
2. To understand stages of group development as they apply to addicted clients.
3. To examine family dynamics as they relate to addiction.

The 2011 National Survey on Drug Use and Health (Substance Abuse and Mental Health Services Administration [SAMHSA]) reports 21.6 million (8.4%) of people age 12 or older needed treatment for an illicit drug or alcohol use problem. These findings highlight the important need for treatment of alcohol/drug addiction.

This chapter examines four aspects of addiction treatment counseling: crisis intervention, individual, group, and family. Because of the frequency of group counseling in the addiction

counseling field both historically and currently, specific exercises for use by the addiction counselor are provided in the group counseling section. The chapter begins with an overview of two philosophies toward addiction, harm reduction and the recovery movement that, if adopted by the counselor, impacts all four of these core treatment processes. The harm reduction philosophy is controversial within the addictions field—there is a continuum of reactions ranging from the view that it enables the addiction to the perspective that it is the only realistic approach to addressing addiction. The reader may need to examine one's own reactions to this philosophy and let the welfare of the client guide the amount of influence of the harm reduction philosophy on the treatment of the addiction. In this chapter, each section is followed by a case study and an exercise reflecting that particular philosophy or framework.

PHILOSOPHICAL APPROACHES

Harm Reduction

From the harm reduction perspective, the emphasis is on reducing problems with usage rather than the amount of alcohol/drugs the individual is using (Kinney, 2003; Shaw, Ritvo, & Irvine, 2005; Tiderington, Stanhope, & Henwood, 2013). It tries to approach use of drugs/alcohol as a reality that occurs; drug use is here to stay, so we need to focus on reducing its effects, and some forms of use are safer than others (Shaw et al., 2005). It is a benefit to the individual and society to reduce the harm connected to the using behavior; both individual and community quality of life is the most important, not necessarily abstinence (Shaw et al., 2005).

The harm reduction approach is based on public health principles avoiding judgment about using and focusing instead on reducing harm in practical ways (Cheung, 2000). It is a public health philosophy that involves many different strategies (Denning, 2005). Examples of a harm reduction approach include programs for designated drivers and needle exchange programs (Kinney, 2003). In addition to the needle exchange programs (that reduce the transmission of HIV/AIDS and hepatitis C), the other most familiar form of harm reduction approaches is methadone maintenance that does not require abstinence but focuses on reducing the dangers an addict faces in the street lifestyle (Shaw et al., 2005).

Historically, the harm reduction approach was used to guide policy in Europe and Australia, but in the United States it was present only in an underground fashion in the 1960s and 1970s until it became formalized in the 1980s (Faupel, Horowitz, & Weaver, 2004). According to Denning (2005), in the late 1970s and early 1980s when hepatitis B was killing intravenous drug users in Europe, the Netherlands implemented strategies to try to save people's lives. Amsterdam, Holland, and England in the 1970s and 1980s had increases in illicit drug use with limited effectiveness of abstinence-based treatment programs (Tatarsky & Marlatt, 2010). At the same time, the United Kingdom and Australia were beginning similar programs of needle exchange and methadone maintenance, and in the late 1980s these programs emerged in major U.S. cities. There were three phases of the harm reduction approach in the United States: (1) in the 1960s, the first phase focused on health problems related to nicotine and alcohol; (2) in the 1990s, the second phase focused on HIV/AIDS prevention in injection drug users; and (3) the third phase, in which we are currently engaged, looks at legal and illegal drugs from a public health view (i.e., drug education to adolescents, programs that are harm reduction–based or abstinence-based) (Erickson, 1999). Keep in mind that the United States has a long, entrenched history of using the disease model of addiction to treat alcoholism that has an emphasis on abstinence (Larimer et al., 2012) and abstinence is not necessarily a goal of addiction treatment from the harm reduction perspective (Tatarsky & Marlatt, 2010).

There are various controversies with regard to harm reduction. First, the struggle with harm reduction approaches intensifies with illegal drug use and specific populations such as adolescents and pregnant addicts. The type of drug and drug use population can elicit moralistic responses to usage that advocate prohibitionist or abstinence-based approaches to education/prevention and/or treatment. Second, there are concerns that a harm reduction approach will result in legalization of a drug ("Do Mainstream Treatment, Harm

Reduction Mix?," 2001). As a result of these concerns, harm reduction programs may face discrimination in the United States. A good example of this discrimination is with syringe exchange programs that often involve providing clean syringes, information on how to inject into and care for veins, warnings about bad drugs available, information on wound care, and social services available (Denning, 2005). Although syringe exchange programs are successful in reducing HIV as well as other infectious diseases (Phillips, Stein, Anderson, & Corsi, 2012; Vickerman, Martin, Turner, & Hickman, 2012), these programs may be illegal in states and face threats from the police and raids by them (Denning, 2005). However, there are also groups that are pro harm reduction. One such group is the Harm Reduction Coalition (HRC), a peer-based, consumer-led organization that looks at policy and advocacy issues, street outreach, and treatment revision; it has newsletters, brochures, and conferences available (Denning, 2005). Contact information for this organization is included at the end of this chapter.

Denning (2005) outlines nine main principles of harm reduction:

1. Reduce the harm of drug use and prohibition of it.

2. Avoid punitive sanctions for what a person puts in their body.

3. View drugs as being used for many reasons and remember that all use is not abuse.

4. Remember that people can make rational life decisions while they are using.

5. Know that denial is unconscious and a result of shame and punitive sanctions.

6. Work with people's ambivalence rather than confront it because resistance is normal in response to change.

7. View addiction as a relationship providing support to the addict and that treatment, while it can provide support, cannot be as "consistently useful" (p. 493) as that relationship.

8. Remember that change is slow, relapse is common, and people need to stay connected in relationships throughout this process.

9. View success as any positive change.

Harm reduction therapy is unique to America and has been formally in existence for 12 years (Tatarsky & Marlatt, 2010). The harm reduction philosophy has a potential to be viewed as a barrier or bridge by addiction counselors. Although the harm reduction approach runs counter to the moral model of addiction, it can be a bridge with the psychological, sociocultural, medical, and biopsychosocial models of addiction discussed in Chapter 1. Given the prevalence of the biopsychosocial model of addiction, the harm reduction model has the potential to enhance this model in terms of prevention, treatment, and aftercare of addiction. The nine principles earlier can be used as guides for the counselor who wants to use them in treatment of the addicted client.

One of the benefits to this model is the pragmatic approach to addiction treatment. Lifelong abstinence may not be attainable for some clients, or the clients may not be motivated by abstinence (Rotgers, 2003). A harm reduction approach may assist the client in eventually achieving abstinence but do so in manageable steps (Rotgers, 2003); the counselor establishes goals collaboratively with the client to address the substance abuse problems (Rubin, 2003). This approach is a good match for the motivational interviewing and brief intervention approaches discussed in Chapter 9, as well as the stages-of-change model discussed throughout this book.

When adopting this type of approach, a counselor needs to be careful of two main dangers. First, there is the danger of going to an extreme and believing that all clients in all circumstances can be treated from a harm reduction perspective. Using the welfare of the client as a guide, a counselor may need to take a direct stand or intervention of abstinence in order to act in the best interests of the client. Second, the counselor needs to continually monitor enabling behavior toward the client. This may be offset by dialogue with colleagues, supervisors, and/or mentors to ensure that assessment, treatment, and aftercare interventions are not reducing consequences to the using behavior and are keeping drug use as a primary focus. The question that faces the counselor is: "When is this approach reducing harm and when is it enabling?" (Shaw et al., 2005). The emphasis is on reduction of harm that can be done in a manner that fits a mainstream treatment model (e.g., letting people stay in treatment after a relapse or stay when on methadone). One example of the integration of the 12-step philosophy and methadone maintenance treatment, that includes discussion of the barriers and bridges in this integration, is provided by Ronel, Gueta, Abramsohn, Caspi, and Adelson (2011).

Eight recommendations for collaboration between blending mainstream addiction treatment and harm reduction approaches are ("Do Mainstream Treatment, Harm Reduction Mix?," 2001):

1. Respect the client (nonjudgmental).

2. Reduce consequences of drug abuse in the community.

3. Be creative in ways to reach potential clients.

4. Decrease consequences for those who use.

5. Provide treatment to clients and loved ones caught in the addiction cycle.

6. Do not view relapse as treatment failure.

7. Provide substance abuse treatment to clients receiving prescribed medication for medical/psychiatric conditions.

8. Provide comprehensive services by working with other systems.

Teamwork, communication, and consideration of the complexities of the individual client's situation are necessary in this type of work.

One possible augmentation to treatment is the involvement of self-help groups with a harm reduction focus such as Methadone Anonymous. (The reader can refer to Chapter 8 for guidelines on the selection of self-help groups and the resource section for support groups at the end of this chapter.) Although Methadone Anonymous uses the 12 steps of Alcoholics Anonymous (AA), a core difference is in the Step 1 wording of the groups. Methadone Anonymous states "We admitted we were powerless over *illicit drugs, including alcohol,*" while AA states, "We admitted we were powerless over *alcohol—that our lives had become unmanageable.*" The wording of Step 1 is important because historically individuals on methadone maintenance have experienced prejudice against their use of methadone when attending traditional 12-step support groups such as AA and Narcotics Anonymous (Gilman, Gillanter, & Dermatis, 2001). The word *illicit* is used intentionally by Methadone Anonymous as an invitation to individuals who are on methadone maintenance—it is meant to welcome them to a support group specifically designed for their recovery that involves the use of methadone (Gilman et al., 2001). Although abstinence from alcohol and other drugs is advocated by Methadone Anonymous, this group views methadone as a tool of recovery that may or may not be discontinued during a person's recovery process (www.methadonesupport.org). Finally, the only Methadone Anonymous steps that have the same wording as AA are steps 2, 4, and 10. Clarification of the differences in the wording of the steps can be made by comparing the AA steps listed in Chapter 8 with those listed at the Methadone Anonymous website (www.methadonesupport.org). In general, the wording changes are with substituting terms such as "God" with "Higher Power" or deleting phrases such as "praying only for knowledge of His will for us and the power to carry that out" (Step 11).

In 1995, Advocates For the Integration of Recovery and Methadone, Inc. (A.F.I.R.M.) was formed to promote Methadone Anonymous in order to integrate 12-step philosophy into methadone treatment (www.methadone-anonymous.org).

This group consists of a variety of methadone maintenance treatment providers and interested consumers, individuals, and other groups. (See Case Study 5.1.)

them to make choices and have control over their treatment in contrast to traditional treatment where clients are told what to do or superficially consulted about their treatment. The underlying

CASE STUDY 5.1

You have a client who is not interested in being abstinent, but who wants to have fewer problems in life around chemical usage. Which of Denning's nine main principles of harm reduction apply in this situation and why?

EXERCISE 5.1

With a peer, discuss your view of the harm-reduction theoretical orientation. Specifically, which aspects of it do you agree with and which ones do you disagree with?

Recovery Movement/Recovery Model

The recovery movement/recovery model is not limited to the addiction area, but addresses mental health problems in general. The term *recovery* started in the field of addictions and has been adopted by the mental health field to look at mental illness as being a struggle from which one can recover; the recovery movement is a grassroots initiative that encourages concepts of strengths and empowerment for individuals who have mental health problems to help them recover from mental illness (National Association of Social Workers [NASW], 2006). This movement has also been called *addiction recovery management* and *sustainable recovery management* that has a strengths-based approach that merges the old and the new treatment approaches into a recovery focus (van Wormer & Davis, 2013).

The NASW (2006) summarizes the Recovery Model that shares the views of the recovery movement, as follows. It is a concept of treatment where consumers (clients) make decisions and have most of the choice and control about their mental health care. This model blends well with the social work orientation of approaching clients from a strengths-based perspective and empowers

premise is that clients experiencing treatment choice and control will transfer this approach to their lives and take more initiative in living their daily lives. This model has become increasingly influential in the mental health field with regard to national and state policies regarding mental health delivery systems (White & Evans, 2013).

White and Evans (2013) provide a summary of this recovery approach to the addictions counseling field as follows. They present "recovery" as a new organizing construct in the addiction counseling field. Treatment is being viewed within a larger context (personal, family, community, wellness, quality of life). Recovery is tied into a network of support systems (religious/spiritual, mutual aid societies, cultural/political mobilization). Institutions such as recovery homes, schools, industries, ministries, and cafés are emerging. New recovery service roles (support specialists, coaches, peer specialists) have also emerged. Research that is recovery-based is being asked for, and is challenging traditional research institutions such as NIDA and NIAAA that are more pathologically oriented. The authors also state that the construct has been described by critics as: amorphous, redundant, faddish, unscientific, impractical, and dangerous. They state that the "recovery revolution" needs to address these criticisms by clearly defining recovery, examining how the orientation changes treatment, defining how the recovery roles are different from previous service roles, and providing performance evaluation frameworks for roles/organizations/systems.

NASW (2006) makes five specific suggestions to mental health professionals who want to incorporate the Recovery Model into their clinical practice [note that the word *consumer* is used where some counselors use the word *client*]:

1. Do not talk about the consumer in the third person when they are present.

2. When a consumer makes a treatment request to the mental health professional, the mental health professional should not ignore it or refuse it, but first ask the consumer to elaborate on the request and help them think through the benefits and consequences of their decisions. The professional's role is more supportive than decision-making.

3. Be aware of body language and communication skills that communicate the consumer is a part of the dialogue.

4. Respect the consumer's different cultural views.

5. Focus on empowerment and self-actualization goals of the consumer.

Because of the current strong influence of the recovery philosophy and model in mental health treatment, the addiction counselor needs to become familiar with the approach and work within its framework. In this author's experience with traditional addiction treatment that has kept in mind the welfare of the client, traditional treatment did and does focus on recovery involved in many of the areas White and Evans presented (2013) (larger context, network of support, different roles) as well as being committed to the five guidelines above in working with addicted clients (NASW, 2006). The strengths-based perspective is a core component to the recovery process in such systems. The author also believes that a caution needs to be heeded in applying this practice to addicted clients. Typically addicts have a high need for control; it is not uncommon for them to enter treatment with an attitude that they will tell the counselor what they need and how to do it. As a result, the counselor needs to be careful in working with this population to keep in mind their tendency to want total control over treatment and to balance a recovery philosophy with holding the addicted client responsible for their behavior and not allowing them to have total control over their treatment. (See Case Study 5.2.)

CASE STUDY 5.2

Your client has come to your session describing exactly what type of treatment she needs and how you and your agency need to provide it. How would you use the five NASW guidelines to incorporate the Recovery Model into your practice and yet avoid the client dominating and controlling all aspects of the treatment?

EXERCISE 5.2

Discuss in small groups the pros and cons of the Recovery Model with regard to the population with whom you intend to work.

CRISIS INTERVENTION

A crisis is a situation where known problem-solving techniques are not available to the client (Slaikeu, 1990). It has also been defined as "a perception or experiencing of an event or situation as an intolerable difficulty that exceeds the person's current resources and coping mechanisms" (James, 2008, p. 3). It has three components: the event, the client's perception of the event, and failure of the client's normal methods of coping (Kanel, 2007). At least temporarily the person is unable to find relief in the situation (Hoff, Hallisey, & Hoff, 2009).

When someone has increased stress and decreased coping skills, there is an increased chance of a crisis (Greenstone & Leviton, 1993). For example, the client may be unable to recall a previous technique used at the time of the crisis, the client may not know a technique that would help in the crisis, or the client may be helpless in the circumstance and unable to use any coping techniques in order to survive the situation. A crisis is dangerous because the person may end up in a situation of homicide or suicide, but it is an opportunity because the person is reaching out for assistance (James, 2008). The crisis, then, gives the client an opportunity to have a negative or positive outcome from the experience. With a negative outcome, the client does not come through the crisis with new knowledge and coping skills, whereas with a positive outcome the client uses the opportunity to obtain new knowledge and coping skills.

The earlier the addicted person is in recovery, the more prone he or she may be to crisis situations. G. Buelow and Buelow (1998) state that chemically dependent individuals typically have a history of poor impulse control/judgment and extremes in mood, and that early in recovery a possible coexisting mental illness can emerge (an illness that drugs either covered up or made worse) and be impacted by the drugs taken or withdrawal from those drugs. These characteristics can make a client early in recovery even more

susceptible to experiencing a crisis. In terms of a client's life history, there are several factors that indicate a crisis-prone person: drug use, legal problems, housing changes, physical injuries, unstable work, financial problems, relationship problems (marital, little support, high alienation), impulsive behavior, low self-esteem, mental/emotional problems, and repetition of mistakes (Greenstone & Leviton, 1993). All of these factors are common in the lives of addicted individuals, thereby meeting the authors' definition of a crisis-prone person.

Addicted individuals often need assistance in learning what a crisis is. In some ways, particularly early in recovery (defined here as less than 2 years of sobriety), everything for the addicted individual may feel like both a danger and an opportunity (a trigger). The individual is learning to live without alcohol/drugs and, as a result, may simply be more sensitive to the environment and the feelings being experienced. Thus, there may be many triggers to a crisis that can emerge from one specific factor or a multiple of factors that appear in the client's life in either a clustered or a serial fashion (Greenstone & Leviton, 1993).

There is also the reality for an addicted person early in recovery of the impact of the pressuring forces (i.e., legal, family, medical) that led to the desire to become sober. These individuals and systems may have placed increasing pressure on the addict to get sober, resulting in the addicted client feeling in crisis, feeling raw as he or she faces the consequences of the alcohol/drug use. The counselor plays an important role as an anchor in the addicted client's life by assisting the individual in determining whether the situation is or is not a crisis situation. Crisis is complex—different components interact—both within and outside of the individual; therefore, the counselor needs to carefully sort out the components of the crisis with the client.

The addicted individual needs to learn how to cope with a crisis—that is, how to deactivate the triggers of the crisis situation. The counselor is charged with helping the client find ways to calm him or herself, reach out for support from others, and stay sober throughout the situation. These coping strategies can be and need to be taught to clients, regardless of whether the counselor believes the situation is actually a crisis.

The addicted individual also needs to learn what types of situations trigger crisis reactions. Once the crisis has passed, the counselor can help the client examine his or her thoughts and feelings that indicated that the situation was urgent. An awareness of these triggering events can cue the counselor as to coping skills that need to be learned by the client and that respect the client's own "soft spots" in the recovery process. McMullin (2000) describes four cognitive methods to use in a crisis situation: a quick perceptual shift, a marathon session (3 to 4 hours focused on cognitive methods), brief cognitive restructuring, and using various cognitive restructuring techniques (e.g., coping statements, here-and-now perceptions) that are active and direct.

Crisis therapy involves assessment, planning, implementation, and follow-up that is woven into therapy (Hoff et al., 2009). James (2008) names five counselor characteristics that are helpful in crisis situations: life experiences, poise, creativity/flexibility, energy/resilience, and quick mental reflexes. Especially in working with addicted clients, the counselor needs to remain calm and supportive throughout the sessions. The calmness is crucial in that the client can catch it from the counselor. "When in doubt, breathe"; that is, when a counselor does not know what to do in a client situation or experiences an emotionally intense client situation, the first thing to do is calm down. It is important to avoid judgment (e.g., "That is not a crisis") and simply to listen to the client's story. The client will need assistance in sorting out and prioritizing issues to determine whether the situation is a crisis and what needs to be done to address the circumstances. Finally, the counselor needs to help the client develop self-compassion both during and after the crisis. The client must learn that it is fine to reach out for assistance from others and that even if the client overreacted to the situation, the important thing is that he or she made an effort to stay sober and learn from the experience.

Possible accompanying struggles for the addicted client include problems dealing with authority figures, difficulty trusting others, being emotionally reactive, and having poor impulse control. The counselor needs to be aware that the addicted client may view the counselor as an authority figure who cannot be trusted, based on previous experience the client has had with authority figures. Based on previous interpersonal experiences, the client may generally struggle with trusting others as well as be emotionally reactive and experience poor impulse control in interpersonal relationships. By remaining calm and supportive, the counselor can create an oasis for the client during the crisis. The counselor should keep in mind these tendencies in order to understand that it may take longer for an addicted individual to make a connection with a counselor in a crisis situation and calm down when facing a crisis situation.

Short–Term Counseling

Slaikeu (1990) breaks crisis counseling into two components: first-order intervention (psychological first aid) and second-order intervention (crisis therapy). The main focus of psychological first aid is to help the client begin coping. Slaikeu lists five components to this process:

1. *Psychological contact.* The counselor connects with the individual through the use of communication skills.

2. *Problem exploration.* The counselor looks at the crisis experience in terms of what led up to it, the strengths and weaknesses of the client, and what followed the crisis.

3. *Solution exploration.* The counselor helps the client prepare to address the crisis situation by looking at possible alternatives.

4. *Concrete action taken.* The client decides to take some action to address the crisis through the support and direction of the counselor.

5. *Follow-up.* The counselor and client have contact to see whether the action taken helped the client's needs.

The themes of support and empowerment run throughout psychological first aid. This stage has also been called emotional first aid, where the intervention's focus is to disrupt the dysfunctional behavior cycle and help the person return to previous levels of functioning. Such intervention requires the counselor to take action right away by establishing a calm, stable presence, assessing the situation, and helping the client make decisions (Greenstone & Leviton, 1993). Weaver (1995) echoes this approach by encouraging counselors to be calm, obtain and give necessary information, listen, be honest, and decrease negative feelings and decompensation. The addiction counselor plays an important role of being present for the client throughout the crisis and helping the client see that he or she can survive this difficult situation sober.

During second-order intervention (crisis therapy), the counselor focuses on resolution of the crisis. Here, Slaikeu (1990) presents a BASIC personality profile to facilitate counselor assessment:

- *Behavioral.* This area focuses on the client's behavior in terms of strengths and weaknesses as well as behavioral antecedents and consequences.

- *Affective.* The counselor assesses the client's feelings about these behaviors.

- *Somatic.* The counselor assesses the client's physical health through sensations experienced.

- *Interpersonal.* This area focuses on examining the quality of various relationships in the client's life.

- *Cognitive.* The counselor assesses the thoughts and self-talk of the client.

The counselor using this framework with addicted clients is often using components of relapse-prevention work. For addicted clients, a crisis situation is often paired with an urge to use. It is important that the counselor be aware that the addicted client in crisis may see only one way to cope with the situation: Use alcohol/drugs. This myopic view of coping may be present for the client despite the length of his or her sobriety. As a result, the client should use the BASIC profile to examine the urge to use as well as to evaluate the crisis situation.

Slaikeu (1990) continues by encouraging the counselor to apply the BASIC profile to four specific crisis-resolution tasks: surviving the crisis physically, being able to express one's feelings about the crisis, mastering the crisis cognitively, and learning to make adjustments behaviorally and interpersonally that will have an impact on the client's future. The BASIC profile information gathered by the counselor will guide the development of the crisis-resolution tasks. As stated under the BASIC profile, the counselor should verify that the client is also focused on tasks to stay sober as well as survive the crisis.

Finally, James (2008) describes a six-step model for crisis intervention that encourages assessment throughout the process. The listening aspect is inherent in the first three steps (problem definition, client safety assurance, provision of support), and the last three steps are action focused (an examination of alternatives, development of plans, and obtaining a positive action commitment).

The counselor needs to use these frameworks as a way to organize the crisis. Additionally, they are helpful structures to use to relax oneself in a crisis situation in order to focus on strategic interventions for the welfare of the client.

Common Addiction Recovery Crises

Kanel (2007) organizes common drug abuse crises as medical, legal, psychological, and spiritual. Often, addicted individuals have interpersonal problems such as marital problems, separation or divorce problems, domestic violence, parenting issues, and sexual orientation concerns. They may also have extensive trauma related to experiences such as rape and physical or sexual abuse, as discussed in Chapter 6. They may also be dual-diagnosed or diagnosed with a life-threatening illness such as HIV/AIDS. Consequences such as financial or legal concerns that result from their using may also be an issue. Finally, these individuals may be suicidal or homicidal. Although the other areas may be effectively addressed through the crisis therapy previously discussed, a special emphasis is placed on suicidal and homicidal tendencies of the client.

Suicidal Tendencies

The strong relationship between alcohol and drug use and suicide underscores the importance of the counselor to assess suicidal tendencies and possible means of intervention when working with this population. G. Buelow and Buelow (1998) report that chemically dependent individuals commit suicide at 4 times the national average, and Kinney (2003) states that 65% of suicide attempts are alcohol related. With chemically dependent clients, the counselor needs to remember that the tendency of impulsive behavior combined with a sense of hopelessness can be a lethal combination. Before a discussion of suicide assessment, it is necessary to review the types of suicide-related groups as described by Kinney.

Kinney (2003) describes four groups of individuals in relation to suicide: completers, attempters, threateners, and parasuicidals. The name of each group describes its members accurately. Completers are people who kill themselves with that intention. Attempters are those who kill themselves but did not intend to do so. Threateners are those who threaten suicide, use it as a weapon, and may or may not follow through on the threat. Parasuicidal individuals are those trying to get rid of emotional pain but not trying to kill themselves when they harm themselves.

These groupings may assist the counselor in the assessment of the suicidal client by helping to clarify the intention of an attempt and thus the issues that need to be addressed in the intervention and counseling. Yet, the counselor needs to remember that all suicidal tendencies need to be examined in a serious, thoughtful, careful manner.

Many times, clients who are suicidal have ambivalent feelings about hurting themselves; the counselor must work to find that part of the client that wants to remain alive. Shea (2002) describes it as a complex, stressful process of weighing pros and cons by a person who would not choose suicide if he or she had better solutions. To connect with the part of the client that wants to live, the counselor must first watch for signals of possible suicidal tendencies.

One such means for assessment is the SAD PERSONS scale (Patterson, Dohn, Bird, & Patterson, 1983). This scale focuses on 10 factors that are correlated with suicide:

1. *Sex.* Males are more likely to complete suicide and choose more lethal means.

2. *Age.* Individuals under age 18 and over age 35 are higher risk groups.

3. *Depression.* Clients who are depressed are more likely to commit suicide, especially if they begin to feel better and have more energy after being severely depressed.

4. *Previous attempts.* Clients who have attempted suicide before may find it easier to attempt again.

5. *Ethanol.* The presence of alcohol/drugs is connected with suicide.

6. *Rational thinking loss.* A person with thought disorders may not be able to find ways to cope with the crisis.

7. *Social supports lacking.* If a client feels isolated and does not have enough relationships of meaning, there is an increased chance of suicide.

8. *Organized plan.* If a client has an organized plan, the lethality level is high.

9. *No spouse.* Single individuals are more likely to commit suicide.

10. *Sickness.* If a client has a serious physical illness, he or she is more prone to commit suicide.

Another way to assess suicide potential is to memorize three questions to ask clients who seem to feel hopeless:

1. Are you thinking of hurting yourself?

2. How would you hurt yourself?

3. What stops you from hurting yourself?

The first question communicates an openness by the counselor to discuss this topic. The second question addresses the means of the attempt. The third question focuses on what the client values about living, what gives life hope and meaning. Asking these questions in a calm, direct manner may assist the counselor in clarifying the lethality of the situation. For example, a client thinking of suicide who has a plan, access to means, and nothing of value to self that would inhibit an attempt is at high risk for suicide. Yet, although these questions may clarify the level of lethality, any suicidal intention should be taken seriously, and a counselor may need to consult with a supervisor or colleague to assist in lethality assessment (Zaro, Barach, Nedelman, & Dreiblatt, 1996). J. L. Johnson (2004) states that the counselor needs to make every reasonable effort legally and ethically to keep the client from committing suicide; those efforts include appropriate screening, lethality assessment of immediate risk, remaining with the person during a high-risk time, involving family and friends in around-the-clock supervision, and making an involuntary hospitalization. "When assessing lethality, the counselor can ask him/herself: 'Can I go home tonight and get a good night's sleep trusting this person won't harm themselves?' This self-reflective question may assist the counselor in determining if everything that needs to be done by the counselor is being done" (G. A. Miller, 2012a, p. 127).

Interventions on suicidal clients can be carried out several ways (Sunich & Juhnke, 1994). G. W. Lawson, Lawson, and Rivers (2001) advocate choosing the least restrictive alternative. Generally, focusing on developing support and exploring alternatives is helpful. Options include increasing the frequency of the counseling sessions (Zaro et al., 1996) and involving family and friends (G. Buelow & Buelow, 1998). If clients' risks appear low or moderate, it may be appropriate to ask them to sign a contract agreeing not to attempt suicide for a specific period of time and agreeing to take some action (e.g., contact the counselor if they decide to hurt themselves). This contract may be written or verbal. For moderate-to-high-risk clients, hospitalization and medication may be required.

The counselor needs to remember that confidentiality is waived in a situation such as this, and it may be helpful to notify close friends and family of the client's intent. Also, counselors need to understand their own reactions to suicide (attitudes, biases, responses) in order to be psychologically, logically, and emotionally available to clients (Shea, 2002). Counselors can find assessing suicide to be challenging and anxiety producing (Schechter & Barnett, 2010) and mental health counselors are undertrained in suicide prevention (Jackson-Cherry & Erford, 2014). Finally, Corey, Corey, and Callanan (1998) recommend that counselors know their own limits in working with suicidal clients as well as carefully document their clinical work with these clients. Weaver (1995) expands the self-care emphasis for counselors engaged in this intense work within the context of disaster mental health counseling. The author suggests that counselors know their own stress warning signs, be aware of a need to take breaks and take small breaks during the work, use positive self-talk, care for their bodies, and reach out to others for support. (See Case Study 5.3.)

CASE STUDY 5.3

John is a 26-year-old single man. He was divorced 4 years ago and since that time has dated a number of women. He has been in private practice therapy (with the same counselor) since his divorce. He sobered up at the time of his divorce and has remained alcohol/drug-free. He attends a weekly 12-step group (Narcotics Anonymous) and has a sponsor whom he contacts frequently. Two years ago, John tried to kill himself: He had a gun to his head and called his therapist for help. He was committed to a psychiatric hospital. This attempt followed the breakup of a relationship. He has little contact with his family and few friends. Today, John is calling his counselor because he does not want to live anymore. His most recent relationship ended earlier today because of his overcontrolling, demanding nature.

1. How well does John fit the SAD PERSONS scale?
2. What questions would you want to ask John to determine his level of lethality?
3. What are your intervention options with John?

EXERCISE 5.3

Complete the following four statements about suicide:

1. My experiences with suicide in my personal life have been. . . .
2. My experiences with suicidal clients have been. . . .
3. When a client gives me indication of suicidal tendencies, my first emotional reaction is. . . .

Finally, discuss with another person any of the responses that surprised you.
4. My main concerns with working with a suicidal client are. . . .

Now complete these same statements by replacing the word suicide with homicide.

Homicidal Tendencies

Some of the factors positively correlated to homicidal behavior are similar to those of suicidal behavior: sex (males are more likely to commit homicide), history of violent behavior, excessive use of alcohol/drugs, and psychotic or paranoid disorders (Wicks, Fine, & Platt, 1978). In addition, these clients may exhibit reckless behavior or be accident-prone, have a sense of failure and low self-esteem, and have neurological problems, especially if there has been a head injury (Wicks et al., 1978). Hoff (2009) summarizes the literature by encouraging counselors to look at assessment based on factors such as statistics (e. g., more men), personality (e.g., aggression), situations (availability of weapons), and how these three areas interact with one another. Kanel (2007) adds asking if the client is involved in active or passive violent/dangerous behavior.

The process of assessment is similar for homicide. The counselor can use these three questions to assess the lethality level:

1. Are you thinking of hurting someone?
2. How would you hurt this person?
3. What stops you from hurting this person?

Again, these questions will get at openness to discuss the topic, the means, and the values/issues. The counselor can use the answers to the last two questions to clarify the lethality of the situation. As with suicide threats, all homicide threats need to be examined in the same serious, thoughtful, careful approach. The same strategies for effectively intervening and coping with the stress of this situation discussed in the section on suicide apply here as does the self-reflective question ("Can I go home tonight and get a good night's sleep trusting this person won't harm another?" [G. A. Miller, 2012a, p. 129]). In addition, intervention in a homicidal threat requires that the counselor not only examine the need for hospitalization and medication but also notify the individual whom the client has threatened to harm. This crisis situation overrides the commitment to confidentiality, as evidenced in the case of *Tarasoff v. Regents of the University of Individual Therapy* can be very important for California (Bersoff, 1976) as discussed more fully in Chapter 13.

INDIVIDUAL THERAPY

Individual therapy can be very important for the recovering addict. It is here where the addict can learn to apply both general and specific recovery techniques to his or her own life situation. As J. L. Johnson (2004) states, individual therapy potentially provides a safe, confidential context where the client can sort out very sensitive and personal problems. The counselor who is both willing and able to assist the client in this critical personalization process can provide the client with an anchor in recovery. An aspect of this personalization is to examine common issues faced by addicts in recovery. Margolis and Zweben (1998) summarize these issues and ways counselors can assist with them as:

- Taking in the reality of being a recovering addict (counselor helps by working with the stigma of it in the person's life).

- Having euphoric recall about alcohol/drug use (counselor assists by looking at triggers).

- Using other drugs (counselor views this as a warning sign for relapse).

- Developing new social networks to encourage abstinence (counselor supports and guides this process).

- Learning to cope with feelings and having ambivalence (counselor helps develop coping strategies).

These issues are a part of the recovery process and are discussed in Chapter 7, "Relapse Prevention." While general issues of recovery are helpful in guiding therapy, DiClemente (2003) cautions counselors to be aware of the variation among addicted individuals both in terms of addicted behavior and the number of living problems they have, both addiction-specific and general. The variation among clients and their problems requires careful assessment and intervention by the counselor.

In helping personalize the recovery process for the client, the counselor needs to determine how willing the client is to change his or her alcohol/drug use and personal issues. W. R. Miller and Rollnick (1991) recommend that a counselor listen carefully in the session, ask open-ended questions that encourage thinking, check out assumptions, and periodically determine the client's stage of change (precontemplation, contemplation, preparation, action, or maintenance). Connors, Donovan, and DiClemente (2001) provide specific therapeutic interventions for each stage of the model.

When addressing personality issues at a deep level, G. Buelow and Buelow (1998) recommend waiting until the therapeutic relationship is strong, the client is committed to recovery, and the client has a support network beyond the counselor to turn to for support. Van Wormer and Davis (2008) encourage the use of strength-based approaches, such as motivational interviewing and solution-focused therapy discussed in Chapter 9, where the counselor assists the client in finding their strengths and competencies.

In addition, individual therapy can assist clients in being drawn back into the human community, which can support and care about them after experiencing the isolation that comes with addiction. For example, counselors can positively influence clients' AA attendance (Brown University Digest of Addiction Theory and Application, 2009). AA can be viewed as a place where clients experience a supportive human community. If counselors are interested in encouraging AA attendance, Finley's book, *Integrating the 12 Steps into Addiction Therapy* (2004), describes how the 12 steps can be fused into addiction therapy. This integration can create a bridge between treatment and recovery self-help groups where peer role modeling, ongoing support, a social environment, lifelong aftercare, and available educational resources are accessible and free to the client. Schenker (2009) has also written a book that can facilitate such integration, *A Clinician's Guide to 12-Step Recovery*, which explains the 12-step program to counselors and how they can work with it.

Individual therapy with individuals who are addicted will probably flow out of the theoretical framework of the counselor, as discussed in Chapter 2. However, whatever the counselor's theoretical framework, awareness of some similarities among addicted individuals may enhance individual therapy by the use of specific approaches. These approaches include genuine counseling, collaborative relationships, and challenging interactions. Individual therapy also involves making sure that the client is in an appropriate treatment setting. Two streams of information on client treatment matching, the American Society of Addiction Medicine (ASAM) placement criteria and Project MATCH, are discussed at the end of this section in terms of their impact on individual counseling.

Genuine Counseling

Being genuine with clients is an important element in counseling all clients and is even more

critical when working with addicted individuals. Because addicts often have difficulties in interpersonal relationships and especially in trusting others, the genuineness of the counselor can be useful in facilitating the therapeutic relationship.

A counselor working with addicted individuals needs to be very direct, honest, and genuine. For numerous reasons, addicts are able to spot phoniness and insincerity relatively quickly, or as I have stated to my students, "Whether due to causes of nature or nurture, they have good 'baloney sniffers.'" They will not trust someone who exhibits these behaviors of phoniness or insincerity. For a counselor to establish a therapeutic relationship where healing around addiction issues can occur, there needs to be a core of honesty to the relationship. One part of this core honesty is to "name" the problem that the client faces and then help the client learn how to live with this problem in his or her recovery. The counselor does not deny or minimize the problem, but addresses it in a straightforward, supportive fashion. For example, if the client has a historically difficult relationship with a stepmother, in counseling the counselor can help the client state and clarify the problems in the relationship and through the counseling process, help the client find ways to live with this reality. Some self-help philosophies describe this as "learning to live with life on life's terms." This process can also help the client examine what he or she is doing that contributes to the problem. Back to the example, the client can look at behaviors that seem to exacerbate the problems with the stepmother.

Another part of this core of honesty involves the counselor's being direct about what he or she feels and thinks concerning the client. The counselor needs to determine how much self-disclosure fits his or her personal style of therapy, as discussed in Chapter 13. Kinney (2003) cautions the counselor to be professional and disclose in a thoughtful way that is appropriate, therapeutic, and facilitates a human connection. Regardless of the amount of the disclosure, the counselor needs to be congruent with the addicted client. If the client finds discrepancies among the counselor's thoughts, feelings, and behaviors, the client may simply write off the counselor as another individual who will not be helpful to him or her. A counselor who is genuine with the addicted client will find that this genuineness paves a solid baseline for clinical work. An addicted client who trusts the counselor will give that counselor a lot of room—a lot of trust to address and work on personal issues.

A second important core component is the establishment of a collaborative relationship. Many addicted individuals are suspicious and distrustful of authority figures. This lack of trust may be based on family of origin or later life experiences that led to or evolved from their experiences with addiction. The counselor who tries to hide behind or use a rigid, authoritarian stance with addicted clients will have a difficult time helping the addicted individual trust. However, if the counselor begins to work with clients in a more collaborative manner, the addicted clients are more likely to be honest in sessions and work closely and deeply with the counselor on the issues that fuel the addiction.

Collaborative counseling means that the counselor may present ideas and options to the client but always stresses the client's right to make a choice. Although it may be difficult for the counselor to allow a client to make mistakes in the treatment or recovery process of addiction, the empowerment experienced by the client communicates a deep respect for individual choice. Motivational interviewing can be useful in this process (W. R. Miller & Rollnick, 2013). Basically, the counselor can use five principles to enhance motivation to change alcohol/drug usage or address personal issues: express empathy, develop discrepancy, avoid arguments, roll with resistance, and support self-efficacy (W. R. Miller & Rollnick, 2002). Additional aspects of motivational interviewing that can facilitate this process (W. R. Miller & Rollnick, 2013) are discussed in Chapter 9. Margolis and Zweben (1998) provide excellent

therapeutic approaches and interventions for developing a commitment toward and establishing abstinence.

Addicted individuals have tendencies to push the limits on relationships with others as well as have excuses for their behavior in an attempt to avoid consequences. Counseling with addicted clients requires the counselor to be clear and firm about limitations and consequences. If a counselor does not provide this type of structure to the addicted client, the counseling will not help the addict with the addiction. The counselor needs particularly to examine personal views on relapse and any consequences in counseling given for this behavior, as discussed in Chapter 7.

One of the main difficulties in working with addicted individuals can be the challenging interactions that arise with them. As discussed earlier, addicts may not be able to determine what a crisis is, so they may inadvertently burn out counselors and others in their lives with their most current crisis. An adage sometimes used by counselors of addicted individuals is that they "want what they want when they want it." Therefore, if the addicted individual decides in that moment that he or she wants help, then that is typically the expectation of the addict. Often, there is a lack of willingness to delay gratification or trust the process that individuals are trying to help them even though a delay is involved. The combination of urgent demands for help with a general distrust of authority can make the addicted client very difficult to counsel.

A counselor working with this population in an individual setting needs to set firm, yet supportive, limits with the client. The counselor needs to stay calm, yet be honest and communicate clearly with the client about the difficulties of client behavior in their interaction. By maintaining a calm, steady influence with clients, the counselor can teach them to slow down the reaction process and learn some helpful communication and social interaction skills as well as provide them with honest feedback about their interpersonal style so they can learn their strengths and weaknesses in relation to others. This is where the concept of compassionate accountability is so necessary. The counselor needs to hold the client accountable for behaviors with compassion. Consequences may need to be given for behavior, but they can be given in a spirit of compassion. The communication of the "what" of the message can be facilitated by the "how" of its delivery.

For example, the counselor may need to give the client consequences for a relapse, but this can be done in a nonjudgmental manner where the client has an opportunity to learn from his or her mistakes. Some clients may draw an urge from a counselor to be treated special—in that the counselor may not want to hold the client accountable for behavior. Both extremes of special treatment can be hurtful to the client. Rather, the counselor needs to practice compassionate accountability, which is a middle ground between the extremes. A red flag should go up for a counselor to practice compassionate accountability anytime there is an urge to treat a client differently than the counselor typically treats addicted clients—whichever extreme direction to which the counselor is drawn. At this warning sign, a counselor may want to consult with a colleague, supervisor, or mentor about the client's case to enhance treatment effectiveness.

Finally, the aspect of matching the client with the appropriate treatment is important. The ASAM Patient Placement Criteria is the most widely used criteria and it provides comprehensive guidelines for working with addiction-disordered clients with regard to their placement, continued stay, and discharge. The ASAM handbook, which was most recently published in 2013, is an excellent reference for counselors, because it outlines the specific criteria that need to be met for different aspects of treatment (admission, ongoing stay, discharge, etc.) at all levels of treatment for both adolescents and adults (Perkinson, 1997, 2008). Because these criteria are being increasingly used in treatment programs throughout the United States (Shulman, 1997),

counselors would be well advised to obtain a manual for reference in the assessment and treatment process.

In 1989, the National Institute on Alcohol Abuse and Alcoholism (NIAAA) began Project MATCH (Matching Alcoholism Treatment to Client Heterogeneity), involving 1,726 treatment centers throughout the United States, including women (25%) and minorities (15%; NIAAA, 1997). The two main arms of the study were outpatient clients who came from the community and aftercare clients who had just completed treatment (inpatient or intensive day hospital; NIAAA, 1997). Clients were randomly assigned to three types of treatment: 12-step facilitation (TSF), cognitive-behavioral therapy (CBT), and motivational enhancement therapy (MET; NIAAA, 1997). No control group was used, because the project was focused on comparing treatments and because of the ethical dilemma of refusing to treat clients who need treatment (Mattson & Fuller, 1997).

Results of the study were summarized by NIAAA (1997): (1) patient treatment matching is not needed for treatment effectiveness, except that clients with few or no psychiatric problems were able to stay sober longer with TSF than CBT; (2) drinking and negative consequences were reduced in all three treatments; and (3) clients with previously supervised abstinence (aftercare clients) were better able to maintain abstinence than outpatient clients. Counselors, then, may not need to be as concerned with the type of treatment the client receives for the addiction as much as that it be delivered by competent addiction professionals and to be aware that psychiatric problems and supervised abstinence may play a role in the abstinence of clients. The National Institute on Drug Abuse (1999) outlines principles of effective treatment that encourage individualized, accessible, comprehensive, ongoing, and adequate time length of treatment. They also recommend counseling and medication as needed. Finally, they encourage awareness of dual disorders, problems, clients not needing to be voluntary, and that recovery can be a long process.

Treatment Plans

As Kinney (2003) states, although counselors typically dislike the process of documenting client care, it is necessary to view the process as providing care for the client, because records (previous chart notes, progress notes, discharge summaries, etc.) are an important way to communicate with other professionals. Good client records communicate a professionalism by the counselor, enhance funding for therapy, and ensure that the unique personal factors of the client are included in the therapy plan.

The documentation of a client's care may be the only way another professional views a counselor's work. General suggestions on documentation are noted in Chapter 13 in the discussion of legal and ethical issues of counseling. Careful, accessible documentation can facilitate professional respect for the counselor and assist the counselor if he or she is contacted to defend or explain his or her clinical work ethically or legally.

Careful documentation can also make a significant difference in funding for treatment. Counselors need to balance the truth within the context of therapy funding. There may be variation on how the truth is documented that makes a difference in treatment funding. The counselor may need to learn the language of the funding source to translate the need for care into words that increase the chance for funding. The counselor may want to consult with the funding source about acceptable terminology and consult with other addiction professionals as to how they ethically address this issue.

Before discussing the development of treatment plans, some general guidelines about paperwork need to be mentioned. First, if a counselor works at an agency, it may be prudent to ask the medical records personnel or the director for a model client chart. This request will communicate a seriousness about documentation and a willingness to work within the constraints of the system and provide an opportunity for the counselor to learn how to efficiently and effectively provide client care for agency records. A thorough examination of a model record's components (progress notes, treatment plan, discharge summary) can be an excellent training tool for a counselor.

Second, the progress notes need to match the treatment plan. The progress notes should reflect the ongoing work of the therapy. Progress notes not only provide legal and ethical defense of client care but also help a counselor quickly focus on clinical issues that need to be addressed in a session. A coordination between progress notes and the treatment plan enhances the welfare of the client, because it ensures that a specific area is not missed.

Third, there are a variety of chart note formats. One such method is the SOAP format. Cameron and turtle-song (2002) describe this method in detail. **S** stands for subjective; the information is recorded as relayed to the counselor by the client and others involved in the case. While client quotes can be useful, the authors suggest using as few as possible and making them brief. The **O** stands for objective, and this section needs to be written in a way that can be measured. This section contains observations by the counselor and written materials from outside sources. The **A** represents assessment, which is the counselor's clinical perspective: the psychiatric diagnosis from the *Diagnostic and Statistical Manual of Mental Disorders* (*DSM-5*; American Psychiatric Association, 2013) and clinical impressions for ruling in and ruling out diagnoses. The **P** stands for plan: an action plan and diagnosis, including date the client will return, session content, client progression, and focus of the next session. Cameron and turtle-song suggest that the counselor remember these are legal documents, record information while it is fresh, keep track of all contacts, and sign the document.

The counselor may want to chart with this overall perspective: Imagine that the client sits on one shoulder and an attorney sits on the other, with both reading what is written. The client can always read his or her chart, so the information needs to be written with a respect for that right; and the information can always be requested legally, so the counselor needs to prepare for what is written to be a part of the public record.

Agencies, funding sources, and addiction professionals record some or all of their information by computer. This can be an additional stress for a counselor, depending on the reliability of the computerized system, the adequacy of and access to computer technological support, and the counselor's own comfort and familiarity in working with computerized record keeping as well as learning the system used by the agency/funding source. In such situations, the counselor may need to allow for additional time in working with a computerized system (especially when a new one is installed), work with the frustration as it presents itself, and advocate for self and others, if necessary, to be provided with additional training and supports in order to work adequately with the system. Addiction professionals may also find it helpful to consult with their professional licensing/certification group for ethical guidelines regarding working with computerized records.

The treatment plan serves as a rudder for the client work, assisting both the client and the counselor in keeping a balanced focus on issues. It also helps the client and counselor prioritize issues that need to be addressed. Because addicted clients can present with both complicated and extensive problems, the treatment plan can prevent both client and counselor from becoming overwhelmed in the therapy process. The counselor can use the treatment plan as a way to educate the client about how to address problems in a systematic, paced manner so a balance is found between ignoring problems and becoming overinvolved with them. This education can be new lifestyle information for the addicted client, who may be more familiar with the tendency to go to extremes when addressing problems. Table 5.1 provides a sample treatment plan.

Table 5.1   Treatment Plan

A. Behavioral strengths (generic):
   1.
   2.
B. Behavioral problem areas (generic):
   1.
   2.
C. Education/employment
   1. Problem (behavioral)
   2. Goal (behavioral)
   3. Method (type of treatment)
   4. Measurement (behavioral)
D. Legal
   1. Problem (behavioral)
   2. Goal (behavioral)
   3. Method (type of treatment)
   4. Measurement (behavioral)
E. Financial
   1. Problem (behavioral)
   2. Goal (behavioral)
   3. Method (type of treatment)
   4. Measurement (behavioral)
F. Spiritual
   1. Problem (behavioral)
   2. Goal (behavioral)
   3. Method (type of treatment)
   4. Measurement (behavioral)
G. Medical
   1. Problem (behavioral)
   2. Goal (behavioral)
   3. Method (type of treatment)
   4. Measurement (behavioral)
H. Relationships: family/marriage/social
   1. Problem (behavioral)
   2. Goal (behavioral)
   3. Method (type of treatment)
   4. Measurement (behavioral)
I. Addiction recovery
   1. Problem (behavioral)
   2. Goal (behavioral)
   3. Method (type of treatment)
   4. Measurement (behavioral)
J. Sexuality
   1. Problem (behavioral)
   2. Goal (behavioral)
   3. Method (type of treatment)
   4. Measurement (behavioral)

Nine overall suggestions for writing a treatment plan in this format are:

1. Put the history on one page (to increase the chances others will read it).

2. Make the goals within the treatment time frame.

3. Make the goals realistic and achievable.

4. Focus on the presenting problem and contributing causes.

5. Think of the problem and the goal as the opposite of one another and state them in behavioral terms. [For example, if the problem is "using alcohol and drugs," the goal is to "stay sober."]

6. Think of the method as the "noun" or the form of treatment (e.g., Alcoholics Anonymous meetings).

7. The measurement needs to match the progress notes, have a date, and be clear as to how often it will occur and its completion date. The measurement needs to be an observable client change of their behavioral or emotional state.

8. If there is an area that is not a problem for the client, clearly designate that by stating N/A (not applicable).

9. When the assessment is complete, if the counselor does not know if an area is a problem, information on that area needs to be obtained to determine if it is a problem area that needs to be included in the treatment plan.

The sample treatment plan begins with two generic strengths and two problem areas to help both counselor and client focus on main strengths and struggles of the client. While the treatment goals need to be based on the problem, the treatment plan needs to affirm the client by being anchored in client strengths (two generic strengths) and avoid overwhelming the client with the number of problems the client may be facing (two main problem areas).

The problem needs to be clear and behavioral—the opposite of the goal. For example, to help create an observable goal, it may help to ask the client a question such as, "How would you identify or know that things had changed positively for you in counseling?" after they have described their problem to you. The method is the type of treatment intervention (individual/group/family therapy, self-help meetings). The measurement is sometimes called the *objectives*: The behavioral measures of whether the goal is being reached ("Client will attend Alcoholics Anonymous meetings once a week"). Perkinson (2004) suggests having at least one objective tied to each goal. The chart notes will reflect the progress of the treatment plan. Thus, the development of a good treatment plan is necessary for client welfare. Shaping the treatment plan needs to be done with a consideration for the new language of change for the client (R. Hood, personal communication, August 16, 2009). Perkinson (2004) reminds us that the focus is on what the client needs to do to stay sober and suggests that counselors ask themselves three questions in the process of developing goals:

1. What is the patient doing that is maladaptive?

2. What does the patient have to do differently?

3. How can I help the patient behave in a new way? (p. 55)

The suggested readings at the end of this chapter provide a review of some excellent books on documentation. The counselor should remember the importance of individualizing and personalizing the treatment plan for each client. The danger of using documentation texts is that the counselor can develop a formula for treatment plan writing that forgets the individual client and the client's needs. Such documentation texts can be extremely beneficial for the therapeutic process if the counselor uses them flexibly with a respect for individual differences.

One final notation about treatment plans. This author has often found issues of spirituality and sexuality as common in working with addicts. The concept of spirituality is discussed more in Chapter 12, but briefly, it is looked at in the treatment plan as a section where general trust/mistrust in the world and others can be addressed. In the treatment plan, this can be examined as how one relates to something big-

done with the guide being how to assist the client in staying sober. With staying sober as the number-one priority, the counselor can approach these issues and back off of them if necessary in order to prevent a relapse. The counselor and client need to work closely so that these issues are neither avoided nor addressed in an untimely manner. (See Case Study 5.4.)

CASE STUDY 5.4

Jerry has been in individual counseling for his addiction because he has been unable to attend any group sessions due to his work schedule. Whenever he meets with his counselor, he appears angry and belligerent. He has told his counselor he feels miserable being sober and angry that he cannot drink. He said he cannot believe that his counselor is in this "racket" for anything other than the money. When Jerry gets upset in an individual session, he simply gets up and leaves the session.

1. If you were the counselor, how would you approach Jerry about his behavior?
2. What would make it difficult for you to work with someone like Jerry?
3. What limits would you set on Jerry's behavior, and how would you set them?

EXERCISE 5.4

Using the little information you have on Jerry, write up a treatment plan for him using Table 5.1 as a guide. Which general areas need to be addressed? For areas that you do not have enough information, make a list of questions you would want to ask him to obtain the necessary information to complete a treatment plan.

ger than oneself, which could be a community of other individuals or a Higher Power of some type. If the client is willing and it seems appropriate, the area of religion can be examined here also in terms of experiences and beliefs that can have an impact on the client's recovery.

The concept of sexuality, discussed more in depth in other chapters throughout the text, is also important to examine in the treatment plan because of how commonly addicts experience wounds in this area. Both spirituality and sexuality need to be raised in a thoughtful, respectful manner where the timing of approaching and examining such issues needs to be

GROUP THERAPY

Group therapy is a common form of therapy used in chemical dependency treatment centers in the United States (Capuzzi & Gross, 1992), due to the roots of the addiction field in AA and the therapeutic community, both of which use substantial group work to help people change (Margolis & Zweben, 1998). Kinney (2003) reports that group therapy is sometimes viewed as a treatment of choice for addicted clients because of the power of groups and the ability for a client to learn about him- or herself by interacting with others, getting social support and feedback, and receiving hope for change. Vannicelli (1995) states that group therapy brings clients together who share the common problem of addiction, thereby helping clients stay vigilant about recovery. The author also points out that the popularity of group therapy may be in relation to its cost effectiveness.

Furthermore, a common difficulty for addicted individuals is interpersonal problems (Capuzzi & Gross, 1992). For this reason, group therapy can be very healing for an addict's recovery process. As Yalom (1985) states, group therapy is a microcosm of the real world. Therefore, how an addict operates in the real world will show up in the group, allowing the addicted individual to work through those issues differently. Addiction is a disease of isolation. Group treatment can decrease the addicted client's sense of isolation (Kinney, 2006). Therefore, group therapy is a potentially powerful healing oasis where addicted individuals can learn how to form and maintain relationships with others.

Because of the prevalence of group work, it is critical that addiction counselors have a basic understanding of group counseling approaches and techniques. This section discusses types of groups, group stages, leader techniques, specific issues, and therapist self-care. In addition, specific group exercises that can be used with addicted clients are provided; these and additional group exercises are included in the author's text, *Group Exercises for Addiction Counseling* (2012), which is based on "tried and true" group exercises used by experienced addiction counselors.

Setup and Maintenance of a Group

Corey (1995) discusses different types of counseling groups: educational, vocational, social, and personal. Addiction groups may be a combination of educational, social, and personal types. Also, there are more structured groups that focus on a theme of recovery from addiction. For example, Greanias and Siegel (2000) talk about ways to

work with dual-diagnosis clients within a group context. Also, group work has been discussed from a motivational interviewing perspective (Ingersoll, Wagner, & Gharib, 2002; Velasquez, Stephens, & Ingersoll, 2006). Ten specific areas to examine in the creation of a group are (Corey, 2004b):

1. Type

2. Population

3. Goals

4. Need

5. Rationale

6. Leader/co-leader

7. Screening and selection procedures

8. Pragmatics: number of members, location, length, open/closed

9. Topic and focus

10. Group norms (ground rules)

The leader of an addictions group needs to determine the goal for the group and then look at how to set up norms to encourage the achievement of that goal.

These norms should be clearly stated in the pregroup interview. If possible, it is a good idea to interview individuals who are going to join the group before they attend their first session. A 15- to 20-minute interview can allow the leader time to educate the client about the purpose and norms of the group, as well as allow the client to obtain a sense of the leader and the group. A balance between safety and risk needs to be discussed with each member. Yet, members need to be encouraged to "do life differently." This means that in the group they can experiment with other people on being different. For example, if the client is normally quiet, the client could work at talking more in the group. This encouragement may assist clients in breaking out of lifelong interactional patterns.

Some authors have specific suggestions for a pregroup interview. In this interview, the addiction professional can determine whether the client is appropriate for the group, hear the client's concerns and hopes, and provide group orientation (Margolis & Zweben, 1998). Vannicelli (1995) suggests that information may need to be given in this pregroup interview for clients who have been exposed to self-help groups without previous exposure to group therapy. These clients need to be educated about differences in the therapy group: stricter group norms on time and attendance, clearer boundaries, more accountability, cost, discussion of outside group contacts, discussion of group process, focus on and communication of feelings, and exploration of the past and present.

Many times, however, addiction counselors do not have the luxury of a pregroup interview. In these cases, it is helpful for the leader to make some type of contact with the individual either prior to or in the group, even if it is as simple as shaking the person's hand and introducing himself or herself. Even the smallest personal contact can facilitate the trust with a new group member and help make the group feel comfortable for the client. If a new member joins a group without a pregroup interview, the other group members can educate that individual to the norms of the group as a part of the group process.

If the counselor does not have the luxury of determining group membership, this issue must be discussed within the work environment. A counselor may face having someone in the group who is very disruptive to the group process. This issue needs to be discussed with a supervisor to determine a policy for handling this difficulty. The counselor also needs to look at having reasonable expectations for himself or herself as group leader, the members, and group goals. If the counselor is expected to work with whomever is in the group without previous contact, the counselor may need to simply do the best possible in the present moment of the group session.

A leader must be careful in setting the tone for the group. One of the important bases of a group is the norms that are established. For instance, the leader needs to make sure that people attend the group, and if they cannot, they must know that it is their responsibility to contact the leader. It is helpful to ask members to attend the group five or six times to get a feel for the average group before deciding whether they like or dislike the group. Group members must know that they cannot be sexual with one another in the group because of how such a relationship would affect the dynamics of the group. They need to understand that if they do want to be involved with another group member, it is best to bring up the issue with the leader, who must then consider separating the individuals into different groups. Group members also need to be told the importance of confidentiality as well as the leader's limitations on enforcing such confidentiality. Margolis and Zweben (1998) provide an example of group rules and expectations (see Table 5.2).

If a member leaves the group, the leader should allow the group and member a chance to say goodbye. If a member needs to leave the group and there is not a chance for the group to say goodbye, the leader may ask the member whether he or she wants a statement to be read to the group or, at the very least, allow the group a chance to acknowledge the absence of the member in the next session.

It is also important to make sure that there are enough chairs in the group for everyone, including members who are not present. Even though it may sound odd to have empty chairs in the group for individuals who are not there, it communicates an important message to the group that members are still part of the group, even if they cannot make it to one session. For example, a leader may leave an empty chair in the group for a member who drops out of the group while the group discusses this member leaving the group and then remove the chair once the discussion is complete. This provides a ritual for acknowledging the presence and absence of group members. Also, the leader

Table 5.2   Group Rules and Expectations

Our groups are one of the most lively and powerful parts of our program, but to keep them working well, we ask for certain commitments:

1. Come on time.

2. Do not come intoxicated.

3. Notify your group leader if you will be absent or you know you will be late. Other group members are usually concerned about those missing.

4. Keep the identities of the members in strictest confidence. You can share anything you like about what you experience in the group, but not about others.

5. Be open to looking at yourself and your behavior and to giving and receiving feedback. It is especially important to discuss any alcohol or drug use in the group.

6. Although contact with other group members outside group can be beneficial, please do not become involved in any relationship outside group that would interfere with your ability to be honest and explore issues in the group. Romantic or sexual relationships with other group members is an obvious example but not the only type of relationship that can be an impediment.

7. A minimum of 3 months' participation is needed to learn to use the group, more to receive full benefits. Please give 1 month's notice if you plan to terminate the group.

8. There is a list of group members' names and telephone numbers because we think you are an important support system for one another. This list must be kept strictly confidential.

I give/do not give (circle one) permission to have my name on the group list given to members. (First names only on the list.) I have read and agree to the above rules and guidelines: Name: _____ Date: _____

Source: Treating Patients with Alcohol and Other Drug Problems: An Integrated Approach, by R. D. Margolis and J. E. Zweben, 1998, Washington, DC: American Psychological Association. This form can be used or reproduced without permission from the publisher or the authors.

needs to be aware of how different chairs in the group can contribute to group dynamics. If there is an extremely comfortable chair, group members may show sibling rivalry over that chair by coming early to group to obtain access to it, claiming it as "my chair," or quietly develop resentments toward another client who tends to occupy the chair. There is no need for all chairs to be the same, but if there are differences among the chairs, the group leader can use these differences to be aware of and comment about the group process metaphorically.

A leader needs to decide how to open and close sessions to see whether these actions will reinforce targeted behaviors. The counselor needs to find a way to open and close sessions that is comfortable for himself or herself and respectful to the types of group members. The counselor can choose the same types of opening and closing statements or

different ones. The counselor may begin each week by saying, "Let's go around the room and have each person say one word about how easy or difficult it has been for you to stay sober this week," and end the session by saying, "Let's hear from each person, in one sentence, what you learned in group today about staying sober." It is important that the counselor make these choices consciously, because they set a tone for how clients enter and exit the group each session.

Corey (2004b) provides some excellent suggestions for beginning and ending general group sessions that can easily be translated to addiction-specific groups. The use of exercises in the group also needs to be examined. Although exercises can be helpful in providing clients with a framework for the group (thereby reducing their anxiety), they may also reinforce dependency on the leader. G. A. Miller's (2012) text, *Group*

Exercises for Addiction Counseling, also provides exercises for opening and closing a group. A counselor needs to find a balance between over-using and underusing exercises in a group.

Group leaders also need to examine how they own their power. This form(s) of power will hinge on factors such as the leader's theoretical frame-work, personal preference of a power form, job title, and client population. Seven possible forms of power the leader can choose from are:

1. *Coercive*, which is based on *fear*. Failure to comply with the leader results in punishment for the members.

2. *Legitimate*, which is based on *leader position*. The leader has the right to expect that sug-gestions are followed by group members.

3. *Expert*, which is based on the leader possessing *expertise*, *skill*, and *knowledge*. The leader is respected for having these traits.

4. *Reward*, which is based on the leader's *ability to reward others*. The leader will provide positive incentives for client compliance.

5. *Referent*, which is based on the leader's *per-sonality traits*. The leader is liked and admired for his or her personality.

6. *Information*, which is based on the leader's access to *valuable information*. The information the leader has is wanted or needed.

7. *Connection*, which is based on the leader's *connections with others who are influential or important in terms of the organization* (inside or outside of the organization). Group members want to have the positive aspect of the con-nections and avoid the negative aspects.

The first five are from French and Raven (1959), the sixth one is from Raven and Kruglanski (1975), and the seventh one is from Hersey and Blanchard (1982). Leaders may have: (1) more than one form of power they use with a group, (2) a favorite form of power, and/or (3) need to change the form of power they typically use because of the type of group they are counseling or the membership of the group. What is critical for a leader is to know and consciously use power for the welfare of the client(s) and for one's own self-care as a counselor.

If a counselor has a co-leader in the group, the dynamics of this relationship can have a powerful effect on the group. The communica-tion between co-leaders must be very honest and open with issues being addressed between them. If there are communication problems, they will be acted out in a group, just as marital problems in a family are acted out in the children's behav-ior. The co-leaders become parents in the group, because the group is a re-creation of the family of origin (Yalom, 1985). These pro-jections will be strengthened if one co-leader is male and one is female. However, these projec-tions can be present even if the co-leaders' genders are the same. One co-leader will typi-cally be viewed as the stereotypic mother (car-ing, supportive, nurturing), and the other co-leader will typically be viewed as the stereotypic father (worldly, disciplinary). Leaders can use these projections to assist clients in healing from their family of origin issues, but they need to not let any difficulties between them as leaders be acted out with group members. The co-leaders need to discuss how they will deal with differ-ences both inside and outside the group (e.g., How much do we tell the children about our marital problems and how do we tell them?).

Finally, group leaders need to be sensitive to issues related to disabilities that may impact the degree to which clients feel welcomed to groups. Roth (2013) provides an overview of ways group leaders can ensure the welcoming of clients with disabilities into a group. The leader is like an orchestra conductor who is responsible for the material, the environment, and guidance related to the group. Generally, the leader needs to be sensitive to using inclusive language, acknowl-edging the disability (but avoiding detailed questions), asking if assistance is needed or wanted, and speaking directly to the client.

Some of Roth's (2013) guidelines for group leaders follow. *Specific group strategies for individuals who are blind or have vision loss* include: introducing self and letting your location be known by a light arm touch; asking if they want to be guided to their group location (that includes physical guidance and specific verbal directions); if there is a guide dog, creating room for a guide dog near their feet and reminding group members to not distract the dog from his/her work, and having introductions made by name so the client can learn to identify group members by their voice. *Specific group strategies for individuals who use a wheelchair* include: moving other chairs to make room for the wheelchair maneuvering necessary; avoiding leaning on the client's wheelchair, and asking if assistance is needed to move. *Specific group strategies for individuals who are deaf* include: having an ASL interpreter in the group sitting directly across from the client and speaking directly to the client in regular voice speed and tone.

Specific Addiction Group Issues

Relapse. When working with addicted individuals in a group, the leader needs to address relapse issues. For example, each leader needs to think about the conditions under which individuals who relapse will be allowed to remain in the group (Capuzzi & Gross, 1992). There is a thin line between compassion for how difficult it is to change a habit and encouraging the addicted individual to continue using. Relapse is understandable if an individual has a commitment to sobriety and is willing to learn from the relapse by exploring it in the group therapy context, as well as possibly individually with the therapist (G. Miller, Kirkley, & Willis, 1995). It is important that group members accept consequences for their relapses. It is best that these consequences be clearly outlined in the group before the relapse occurs.

Countertransference. For example, the counselor in the pregroup interview tells each recovering client that he or she is expected to remain sober, but if a relapse occurs, the client must let the counselor know of the relapse. This relapse would then be discussed openly in the group to determine what needs to be done differently to help the client stay sober. The client must understand that relapse does not automatically mean dismissal from the group (assuming the counselor is able to make such a promise) but that repeated relapses mean that the client's recovery is not working and treatment alternatives may need to be explored with the counselor as well as the group.

Vannicelli (1995) also cautions group leaders about the issues of countertransference regarding substances. In particular, the author cautions counselors who are in recovery to (1) remember their role is different from a 12-step meeting, especially in terms of client welfare; (2) address the smell of alcohol in a group openly even if he or she is uncertain as to who has been drinking; and (3) negotiate recovery contracts so they are supportive rather than automatic or formula-based.

Typically, addicts have problems with authority figures, trusting others, emotional reactivity, and impulse control. Problems with authority figures are discussed in the following section, Therapist Self-Care. The other three themes, which need to be monitored throughout the group development stages, are discussed briefly here.

Mistrust of others. Because trust of others may be a serious issue, the group leader needs to work hard at *encouraging individuals to be both honest and respectful* toward one another throughout the group sessions. An atmosphere of such honesty will assist members in trusting one another. At the same time, addicted members need to learn to work with their emotional reactivity and their poor impulse control. They must be *encouraged to listen to their emotions and their impulses but to delay acting on them* until they have seriously anticipated the consequences of their behavior. Thus, clients learn to recognize and express their emotions in ways that are honest and respectful toward others. Two areas that may pose problems in a group with addicted individuals are denial and resistance (Capuzzi & Gross, 1992). Group members who have denial need to be confronted on the discrepancies of their behaviors, thoughts, and feelings. This does not have to be a highly emotional confrontation; in fact, a *calm, neutral, confrontational, behaviorally oriented approach* may help the client hear the confrontation less defensively. If possible, it is highly effective to have members confront one another on the presence of denial or resistance. Again, however, such confrontation, while honest, also needs to be respectful and caring. The counselor should note, however, that resistance in an addicted individual may be healthy in that the client may be aware that there is not enough support in his or her life to address such issues. The client may not be willing to look at specific issues at that time because he or she does not have the necessary resources internally or externally to address them. In such a case, the counselor may encourage the client to state this limitation to the group and work with the client on building internal and external supports that would allow for such issues to be addressed.

Stages of Group Development

Different group theorists frame group development in various stages (Corey, 2012; Corey, 2004a, 1995; Yalom, 1985). The framework used in this chapter is Corey's (1995, 2012), which discusses four group stages: Initial Stage—Orientation and Exploration (Stage 1), Transition Stage—Dealing with Resistance (Stage 2), Working Stage—Cohesion and Productivity (Stage 3), and Final Stage— Consolidation and Termination (Stage 4). The counselor needs to remember that these group stages are not fixed or clear-cut. Groups may show evidence of going back and forth between the stages, depending on membership changes in the group or issues that arise in the group. Also, when group membership changes each

group, the group leader may need to look at each session as one where each of these stages is touched on in that session. Thus, although there may not be a carryover from group session to group session in terms of group development, group development primarily occurs in each session because the group is so significantly changed in terms of membership each time. This perspective can reflect the approach advocated earlier where the group leader has expectations that are reasonable given the context of the group.

Stage 1

The first stage of group development is what may be called the cocktail party stage, where members are nervous about attending the group. During this stage, members generally are involved in superficial chitchat that does not reveal much about themselves. As Corey's (1995, 2012) title (Orientation and Exploration) implies, members are trying to orient themselves to the group and explore how they are expected to function within the group. A central issue for members is the theme of trust (Corey, 1995, 2012). As members are determining group rules and norms, they are also trying to determine a sense of whether they belong in this group and whether they will be accepted by the other group members as well as by the group leader.

Addiction clients may show these initial group development behaviors in specific ways. For example, superficial chitchat may be "junkie of the year" competition bragging. Here, a client may talk with other clients about how many different types of drugs he or she used, how much of certain drugs has been taken, or how many consequences have been experienced (e.g., the number of DUIs). This information sharing may appear both deep and meaningful, but the client is truly sharing information that, to some degree, is already known by the counselor and other individuals in the client's life. This chitchat may serve as a distraction from the painful issues in the client's life that led to or resulted from the addiction. At the same time, this information is important for the client to share to determine how similar or dissimilar he or she is to other group members and to determine whether these members will be judgmental. The group leader, then, who is aware of the need for such information to be shared by members, also needs to monitor whether this information sharing is an avoidance technique being used by the clients. If it appears to be an avoidance technique, the counselor will need to set limits on this type of sharing and encourage group members to share at a more personal level.

Stage 2

Stage 2 of group development is often a difficult stage for both clients and the leader. In this stage of group development, the leadership of the group is challenged. Prior to this stage, the leader may have looked like an omnipotent parent to members (Yalom, 1985). During Stage 2, members are questioning the leader's ability to direct the group. The members are really trying to find out how safe the group is for them. Knowledge of this level of safety emerges from struggles with power and control. Typically, this challenge is initially directed to the leader, in part, to determine how the leader acts when stressed in situations. It is a parallel process to what a person may do in an intimate relationship to find out how safe he or she is with an individual by fighting with the individual or, staying with the family metaphor, how safe the kids are when the parent(s) is upset. Once the leader has been challenged, group members will repeat this process with other group members. Group members will not confront one another until the leader is challenged because of the need to see how conflict is addressed in the group. These conflicts will show how the leader responds to conflict and how other members in the group act when they are challenged.

At this stage of development, addicted clients may challenge group leaders in a variety of ways.

The leaders, if not recovering addicts, may be asked what they know about addiction and how they dare to work with addicts when they have never faced these issues. If leaders are recovering addicts, they may be challenged by being asked what types of drugs were done or how long they used. Leaders may also be challenged on gender or ethnicity differences, again questioning how well they can understand the struggles of the members. Vannicelli (1995) elaborates on specific challenges to leadership from a 12-step perspective. These challenges include the client's having an overzealousness of AA 12-step programs, being too literal about 12-step philosophy (e.g., slogan resistance in which the client uses slogans to avoid addressing personal issues such as live in the present rather than address past issues), using 12-step program terminology in a defensive manner (e.g., "I just have to let go of it"), and using program labels to avoid experiencing conflict or differences (e.g., "alcoholic behavior"). Whatever the form of the challenge, leaders are questioned on their competence. This questioning process reflects the underlying anxiety of the group members and the level of resistance or willingness they have to discuss concerns at a deeper level. Group leaders, while responding to questions directed to them, also need to redirect the focus from themselves by refocusing the group's attention to the underlying anxiety and resistance and processing this anxiety and resistance with the group.

Many times, addicted clients have a poor history with conflict resolution. Often they come from families or drug use experiences where conflict was unchecked and resulted in violence physically, emotionally, or psychologically. The addiction counselor needs to keep this tendency in mind when working with addicted clients so that the group is a safe place where clients learn that conflict does not mean violence and that they can learn conflict resolution techniques. At this stage, the counselor can use conflict that occurs as a natural part of group process to teach clients to handle conflict in a different manner. Counselors need to encourage clients to be aware and express their issues with conflict, requiring the counselor to watch the verbal and nonverbal behavior of clients during group sessions. Thus, the counselor may need to encourage confrontation from clients to the leader so the counselor can be a role model for how to handle conflict and set norms for how conflict will be handled in this group.

There may be times that in spite of "doing it all right" that the group leader may find the group simply becomes stuck at this stage until something, such as membership of the group, changes. This is where discussion with supervisors or colleagues can be beneficial to determine if anything more can be done in the group and how to address the "stuckness" of the group. Sometimes there are subgroups that have formed in the group (known or unknown to the leader) that inhibit the group development or perhaps the group has a severed personality disordered member or members that are causing the group to be stuck at this stage. If these unfortunate circumstances are a reality for the counselor, it may be best to look at facilitating the group from a four part perspective until there is a shift in the group: do limited processing in the group, contain the negative impact of the forces present on the group development, lower one's expectations of the group, and practice self-care.

Stage 3

In the working stage of group development, Stage 3, group cohesion has developed, and members trust and feel close to one another. Members share information about themselves on a deep and meaningful level. In the context of the group, they are now willing to look at issues with which they have struggled. Members are comfortable being direct and confrontational with one another. The leader is seen by group members in a more realistic light of having both strengths and weaknesses.

In working with addicts at this stage of group development, the leader may find members willing to discuss their personal issues in depth. Rather than simply discussing drugs they have used, they may be willing to discuss the shameful and embarrassing actions they took to obtain drugs. They may discuss how they felt as children growing up in alcoholic homes. Issues that emerge are discussed with expression of vulnerability and openness. At this stage, members are willing to be supportive and share their own places of pain with others in the group.

Stage 4

In the final stage of group development, members are facing issues of termination and attempting to integrate their experiences in the group into their daily lives. Strong feelings about termination may emerge for members, as well as concerns about how well they may apply these group experiences to their lives. Themes of loss and grief may appear. The loss of loved ones through death or through the consequences of their drug use may be present. Feelings of abandonment and betrayal may also emerge. The leader, for example, might be accused of not really caring for the addicted individuals, because the group will end and they will not be able to see the leader again.

Leader Skills at Developmental Group Stages

One of the main areas that will assist a group in developing is this ability of the therapist to work with the group's transference on his or her leadership role (characteristics projected onto the leader). As Yalom (1985) states, the leader must remember that the transference is connected to the role. At the same time, the leader also needs to be aware that struggles with the leadership will be shaped by the traits and style of the leader. These projections are examined in terms of group development stages and self-care practices of the leader.

During the first stage of group development, the leader is closely watched by group members. When the leader enters the room, the members might become very quiet, and during discussions, members may turn often to the leader for feedback and suggestions. Group leaders will likely react differently to this focus of attention. For some, it may be uncomfortable to be under the magnifying glass of the group. These leaders may need to learn how to relax and be themselves when in the spotlight. Others who like to have the spotlight and be seen as having all the answers may need to proceed cautiously with feedback to members. In short, these leaders need to keep their egos in check for the sake of the group development and encourage members to be responsible for themselves.

The primary goal for the leader in the first stage of group development is to help the members feel comfortable in the group by making the group an inviting place for them to attend. The leader should allow members to have superficial conversations while also inviting them to look at deeper issues. The leader must closely monitor his or her own behavior so the norms being set for the group are the ones the counselor wants to have set.

During the second stage of group development, the leader encourages criticism from the group members. Here, the leader is monitoring for verbal and nonverbal signs of disagreement with the leadership. It is important for the leader to facilitate such challenges so that the group members learn how to confront one another in the group and learn that they are safe even if they challenge the authority structure of the group. The counselor knows that it is impossible to please all members of the group at this stage. Like the parent of an adolescent, whatever action he or she takes, the group members will find some fault with it. If the therapist is caring, the group may say it wants more authority. If the counselor is authoritative, the group may say that it wants more flexibility. The group attack on the leadership will never be unanimous (Yalom, 1985), but to some degree, it will be personal.

The leader must acknowledge his or her flaws and possibly apologize to the group. The group will be closely watching the leader to see how he or she deals with being confronted. By remembering that the members are transferring their projections from previous experiences with authority figures, the leader will be less likely to be overwhelmed by the experience. It may also help to remember that allowing the group the process of challenging the leadership is exactly what will help the group move into the working stage.

Thus, it is necessary for the counselor to learn how to take on the criticism of the group. He or she must model an openness to feedback and find a way to ground himself or herself during the challenge. This process of anchoring may vary among group leaders. Some may find it helpful to take a deep breath before responding to criticism. Others might place both feet on the floor and uncross their arms while doing a visualization that they are connected to the earth and that they will survive this confrontation. Whatever means of self-care is practiced by the leader, it is imperative that he or she not strike back at the group member(s) who is doing the challenging. He or she must realize that the individual is simply the mouthpiece of the challenge for the group—the one individual speaking is also speaking for others. The counselor, then, needs to encourage other members to speak their dissatisfaction with the leadership so that one individual does not monopolize the group and run the danger of becoming a scapegoat in the group.

Because many addicted clients have had negative experiences with authority figures, Stage 2 is critical in an addictions group. The leader needs to firmly guide the group through this stage of development by being honest, open, and willing to work through the challenge. Becoming resistive or defensive can stop the group at this stage of development.

During Stage 3 of group development, the leader turns over different leadership functions, such as beginning and ending the group, establishing the focus of the group session, or maintaining the physical aspects of the group space (chair arrangement, room temperature). This may be difficult for leaders who have a high need for control, but it is important for the group members who have grown in their sense of autonomy. During Stage 4 of group development, the leader must be comfortable with issues of death and loss. The leader needs to help members process their own grief reactions to the group ending as well as allow himself or herself a chance to grieve the ending of the group.

An important part of self-care skills as a leader is allowing yourself some supports in being a therapist. The feedback of trusted colleagues, a supervisor, or a mentor will assist in this area. Finally, it is helpful for the group leader to recognize the stages of group development that are more comfortable for him/her than others. If we think of the leader as the parent, parents are typically more comfortable with some developmental stages of raising a child than others. Recognition of where one's strengths and weaknesses lie with regard to the group's developmental stages and what is required of him/her as a leader can assist the counselor in "playing to one's strengths" and augmenting one's weaknesses.

Group Leader Techniques

Group leaders can facilitate the transitions in the stages of group development by acknowledging the need for certain factors to be present and encouraging the presence of those factors in the group. Because two of Yalom's (1985) 11 therapeutic factors for group development—installation of hope and universality—seem especially related to the issues of addicted clients, they are discussed here.

Installation of hope is a very powerful tool in working with addicted clients. These individuals may have previously tried to address their addiction and found themselves back in it despite their best efforts. If a leader can communicate hope to clients, this hope may assist them in making important changes in their lives. The leader's belief in the client's ability to change may assist with the client's motivation level as well as provide the client with support to make changes around addictive behavior. For example, the leader can

simply encourage clients to do it differently in the context of group—that is, to try different behaviors in an attempt to achieve and maintain sobriety. This experience can lead to what Yalom (1985) calls the corrective emotional experience: The client heals from a previous trauma by re-experiencing the emotions in the group and having a chance to reflect on them. For example, a client may have let down many people in attempts to be sober and, as a result, has been ostracized from significant others because of the addictive behavior. If a client relapses in a group and has the experience to process feelings and thoughts about the relapse within an honest, caring, supportive group that holds the client responsible for the relapse behavior, the client may experience hope about staying sober. In addition, the client has the corrective emotional experience of still being cared for and supported by the group to make another attempt at recovery.

Universality is the sense that the individual is not unique in his or her problems or situations (Yalom, 1985). This sense can reduce a feeling of social isolation for the addicted individual. One way for this sense to be encouraged is for the therapist to work in the here and now. In other words, the therapist is aware of what is happening in the group at the present moment and watches for items of similarity among members. Commenting on such similarities can assist with the sense of universality, which can provide a strong basis for the group to explore specific issues related to addictions because of the experiences they have in common.

In addition, the experience of universality can be healing in and of itself because of the tendency for addicted individuals to be isolated from others as a result of their addiction and related behaviors. The universality can provide the addict with the sense of belonging to a community. For example, a client who has had extramarital affairs related to alcohol/drug use may have been isolated from his or her partner, children, church members, neighbors, and friends, who thought the affairs were a statement on what a bad person the addict is. Coming to a group and hearing how others made the mistake of having extramarital affairs may be healing for the addicted client and encouraging for him or her to discuss other issues related to dependency.

Leaders may find some other group techniques helpful when working with clients who are addicted. Connors et al. (2001) state that while the history of substance abuse treatment has been confrontational in style in order to break the client's denial about substance abuse problems, such a style can result in client resistance or treatment dropouts. Rather, the authors advocate a supportive, empathic, client-centered style that invites clients to change. In general, group leaders need to listen actively; reflect meaningfully; facilitate goal achievement; and clarify, summarize, empathize, interpret, question, confront, support, diagnose, evaluate, and terminate appropriately within the group context. One technique that is helpful to group development is called linking. In this technique, the leader watches for ways to encourage interaction among the members by connecting the words and actions of one member to the concerns of another. This focus on common concerns among group members can facilitate the cohesion of the group (G. Corey & Corey, 1992).

Another technique is blocking, which is helpful in group development because the leader blocks member behaviors that work against group cohesion. At the same time, the leader does not attack the individual client demonstrating those behaviors in the group. G. Corey and Corey (1992) report some behaviors that need to be blocked: asking too many questions, gossiping, telling stories, invading privacy, and breaking confidences. For example, the leader can block too many questions by interrupting with a refraining comment such as, "It seems that the group members are wanting to know you better. What would you like us to know about you?"

Finally, group leaders need to use techniques that are a good match with the characteristics of the addicted clients with whom they work (Capuzzi & Gross, 1992). Leaders need to be directive by being focused and disciplined, which is important for addicted clients who may have low frustration tolerance and impulsiveness. They also need to confront both indirectly and directly to help clients break self-defeating patterns. Leaders must also be tolerant toward emotionalism expressed by members and nondefensive, especially concerning anger and hostility. By being directive, respectfully confrontive, tolerant, and nondefensive, leaders can assist groups in becoming more cohesive as well as provide addicted clients with role-modeling behaviors that are helpful to their recovery process. (See Case Study 5.5.)

CASE STUDY 5.5

You have taken over an aftercare group from a female counselor. You have no control over the size of the group (the agency simply places people in the group by the night they can attend), and there are 16 members. You sat in on the group once before, taking over facilitation of the group alone. You noticed that the former leader did not allow the group members to go into their feelings very deeply. You sensed a lot of frustration in the group toward the leader and other group members.

1. What group norms will you need to change in the group, and how will you go about changing them?
2. What level of development is this group in?
3. What would you expect to happen in the group if you encourage members to express their emotions at a deeper level?

EXERCISE 5.5

The following group exercises can be used in an addiction counseling group to facilitate treatment. Also, Hagedorn and Hirshhorn (2009) describe experiential group activities that can be used with addictive clients.

Disease. Have a client sit in the middle of the group, and have another client (representing the disease of addiction) approach the first client and try to entice him or her to use. As the two get closer, have a few other clients (who represent people who are important and supportive of the client's staying straight), who are standing behind the seated client, respond to the disease's message, forcing the disease to be drowned out because the others are so loud that the disease's message cannot be heard.

Family sculpting. Have a group member volunteer to have his or her family of origin sculpted. This member can choose different group members to represent family members. These individuals should all stand at the center of the group. The counselor should help the volunteer client to arrange people physically in the group to represent how they are in relation to the client. Then the client should add himself or herself to the sculpture. The counselor asks the client first and then other family members for reactions to how they feel as they stand in that posture. After processing the volunteers' reactions, the counselor should have the remaining group members respond to what they have seen. Finally, the group members need to process their own individual thoughts and reactions to the exercise.

Image. Have clients take a brown paper bag and cut and paste pictures and words on the outside of the bag that demonstrate the image they try to show the world. Then have them cut out pictures and words that represent what they try to hide from the world and have them place these on the inside of the bag. Then have group members discuss how hard they work to hide their secrets from others and their fears if they were to tell others what is inside their bag.

Music. Have group members bring in lyrics of a song that they believe represents them or some aspect of their life as it relates to their active addiction or addiction recovery. Have the group look for common themes of use and recovery between the songs.

Peer pressure. Have one member role-play being at home and watching TV while three other clients try to get the client to use with them. Have these four group members sit in the middle of the group. After the role play, ask the four members first for their reactions to the experience, and have the remaining group members give each of the role-play members feedback with a particular emphasis on what the client watching TV did that was positive in resisting the peer pressure.

Self-esteem. Have group members write their names and one or two things they have proudly accomplished in their life on a 3-by-5-inch card. Have group members exchange cards and introduce the other person and his or her accomplishments to the group. During the introduction, have the person being introduced stand; following the introduction, have the group applaud the individual.

Serenity Prayer. On a board, draw one circle that contains the phrase from the Serenity Prayer, "the courage to change the things I can," and on another section, "to accept the things I cannot change," written outside the circle. Ask each member to contribute something for the outside of the circle in terms of life problems with which they struggle. Then ask each member to contribute something for the inside of the circle that they can do to address the problem. Clients may need to help one another come up with ideas about what they can do about the problem.

Triggers. Have one person identify a substance abuse trigger and describe five strategies that help him or her deal with that trigger. Then have other members in the group discuss similar strategies for triggers that they have used in recovery.

Using versus abstinence. Have two empty chairs in the middle of the group. Have a client sit in one chair and try to entice the person in the other chair into using. Then have the client sit in the other chair and try to entice the person into staying straight.

FAMILY THERAPY

Addiction does not occur in a vacuum, and many times family can play an important part in both the active addiction and recovery process for the addicted client. A family may affect abuse and overdose incidents, drug usage role modeling (parental), the need of drug abuse for homeostasis, and the enabling of the active addiction (Stanton & Heath, 1997). There are basically two functions for substance abuse in a family system: (1) the abuse is primary and in itself causes problems within the family; and (2) the abuse is a symptom of lacking skills or needs that have not been satisfied (McIntyre, 1993). The counselor needs to determine how the family uses alcohol/drugs in the system to determine how to most effectively intervene. When the counselor does intervene, the family, and family members, need to be given choices about how to address the addiction—the counselor can view it as providing them with a buffet of options. The counselor also needs to warn the family that once consequences for the addictive behavior are given, it is like Russian roulette; no one knows what chain reaction it may send off. Therefore, once a family or family members decide to interrupt the homeostasis, they need to be clear that they are letting go of the outcome of their intervention.

Family therapy is a way of looking at problems from the view of the overall system and intervening on interactions within the system

(Stanton & Heath, 1997). The National Institute on Drug Abuse (NIDA; 2003a) recommends that family therapy be used with discretion. In situations where substance abuse has a strong positive correlation with family interactions, the counselor may want to use family therapy. Here it can help a family expect change, try out new ways of acting, learn about the system dynamics, involve the strengths of members, and look at the relationship of substance abuse within the family. NIDA also advocates that even if long-term family therapy is not done, there can be benefits from one or two sessions of family therapy, especially when the therapy is present-focused, educational in nature, and the problem to be addressed is specific and solution-focused. However, NIDA advocates hesitation in its use when: (1) other members are active in their own substance abuse or have denial about the client's substance abuse or (2) there is a history of violence or excessive anger.

Counselors who do use family therapy need to be educated about family systems, dysfunctional patterns, and power and communication problems (NIDA, 2003a). Therefore, just because a counselor has been trained to work with addicted clients does not mean he or she is qualified to handle the complex dynamics of working with the issues of an addicted family. Also, counselors trained to work with families may not be qualified to handle the complex dynamics of addiction within a family context. Counselors need to ethically examine their training and experience in working with addicted families to determine whether they are qualified to work within this therapy modality and the depth to which they can work as a family therapist. In the suggested readings at the end of this chapter, two books on family therapy may be helpful to the client who wants to learn more about family therapy approaches in general: Patterson, Williams, Grauf-Grounds, and Chamow (2009); and Winek (2009).

Following education and training in these counseling areas (individual, family systems, substance abuse), application involves a powerful, dramatic paradigm shift for the counselor in terms of theory, technique, and outcomes. Therefore, counselors need to be prepared to experience such shifts and when they occur, make use of consultation and supervision to assist in the blending of these paradigm shifts.

This section addresses types of addictive families, basic concepts of family counseling, general techniques of family counseling, the term codependency, and the recovery process of the family.

Types of Addictive Families/Developmental Stages

Understanding the type of addicted family with whom the counselor is working can assist in understanding the type of overall approach to take with the family. McCrady, Epstein, and Sell (2003) report that most treatment of addiction currently follows one of three models: family disease, family systems, or behavioral. The family disease model views addiction as a disease, encourages family members to examine their own issues, and addresses concepts, discussed later in this section, such as codependency and enabling. The family systems model looks at how the addiction functions in the family, with treatment examining aspects such as roles, rules, boundaries, communication, problem solving, and behavioral treatment to encourage abstinence. The behavioral model looks at behaviors of the family that precede and reinforce use, with

treatment trying to change what occurs before and after use as well as address relationships in terms of themes, communication styles, and how the drug keeps the relationship stable. The discussion of family therapy here is a blend of these three models with Kaufman's model as a baseline for discussion.

Kaufman (1985) describes four types of alcoholic families: functional, neurotic enmeshed, disintegrated, and absent. The *functional alcoholic family* has a stable system. In this type of family, drinking is usually in its early phase and is connected to conflicts that are social or personal in nature. The recommendation for counseling with this type of family is educational in nature (Kaufman, 1985).

The *neurotic enmeshed family* may be regarded as the stereotypic alcoholic family, where drinking is either a symptom of family problems and/or a means to cope with family problems. This type of marriage has sometimes been labeled the "alcoholic marriage" (Doweiko, 1990). Communication is indirect, fighting is frequent, marital partners compete with each other, and the nonalcoholic is in charge in the family (Kaufman, 1985). It is recommended that the family of this type be educated as well as have therapy that is behavioral, structural, and psychodynamic.

The *disintegrated family* is one where there is some temporary separation between the alcoholic and the other family members. This is generally the neurotic enmeshed family that has progressed to a later stage of development. Here, it is recommended that the focus be on the individual, with some exploration of potential family support.

The fourth type of family is the *absent family*, where there is permanent separation between the alcoholic and his or her family. In this family system, there is basically no longer a family to whom the addict can turn. Here, the counselor can be most effective by helping the addicted individual develop new support systems.

Family issues may also emerge during the addicted person's recovery process and come to counseling to address those issues. McIntyre

(2004) describes three phases of recovery (and their related problems) for the addicted family: early recovery, which occurs over the first 1 to 2 years (the family is attempting to restabilize), middle recovery, which is from years 3 to 5 (therapy problems range from affairs to behavioral disorders), and ongoing recovery, which emerges during years 4 or 5 (spiritual, philosophical, value issues emerge).

Understanding the developmental stage of a family can also inform the counselor as to how to approach therapy with a family in terms of prognosis. G. Buelow and Buelow (1998) frame treatment of families within their developmental stages: early abusive, middle dependent, and late deteriorative. In the early abusive stage, the family holds the value of sobriety even when members abuse drugs. Treatment prognosis for the family at this stage is good. In the middle dependent stage, the drugs have been integrated into the daily functioning of the family, and the counselor needs to realize that progress with the family at this stage may be slow. In the late deteriorative stage, the family dysfunction is severe, with family members split off from one another. Here, it is advocated that the counselor take on an educator or consultant role. Family development can also be viewed within the context of the stages-of-change theory as discussed in Chapter 9. DiClemente (2003) and Connors et al. (2001) provide specific suggestions for applying stages-of-change approaches to family therapy.

The counselor who can accurately assess the addicted family in terms of type and developmental stage can more readily determine the appropriate techniques to be used in the family intervention. Some basic concepts and techniques follow.

Basic Concepts of Addiction Family Counseling

Overall, the counselor needs to look for homeostasis: how the family stays in balance. This means the family needs to examine and possibly change its boundaries, rules, roles, and values to help find a new balancing point for itself (Fisher & Harrison, 1997). In terms of boundaries, the family needs to look at how it is divided both inside and outside the system (i.e., the types of rules that guide the family; Kaufman, 1985). Rules around communication patterns and cross-generational coalitions need to be understood (McIntyre, 1993). As to roles, the family needs to examine what conditions led to the alcohol/drug use, who the scapegoat (identified patient) is, who acts out the family pain, and what triads exist in the family to keep symptom behavior alive (Kaufman, 1985).

Individuals in the family will likely need help in understanding the role they play in the system (McIntyre, 1993). This awareness can help them understand themselves and the system better, and thereby be freer to make choices about their behaviors rather than automatically responding according to the role they have been assigned or taken on. One way to facilitate awareness is to help them look at family of origin issues on alcohol and drugs (McIntyre, 1993). Without realizing it, parents may be bringing their unresolved alcohol/drug use issues from their family of origin to their family of creation. This information can be beneficial in examining the alcohol/drug use impact on the family.

J. L. Johnson (2004) summarizes Wegscheider's (1981) work describing chemically dependent family roles of "the chemically dependent person, chief enabler, hero, family scapegoat, lost child, and family mascot" (p. 141). These roles are what their labels describe: The addict is focused on the addiction, the chief enabler is focused on being responsible for the family staying stable, the hero is the star of the family who saves the family image, the family scapegoat is the person who gets into trouble to keep the focus off the family's problem with addiction, the lost child is the one who is quiet and blends into the background of the family, and the family mascot is the one who distracts the family and provides relief through humor. In some treatment work with addicted clients and their families, these roles are used to educate the family about how the dynamics of addiction have played out in the family. The counselor using such terms needs to remember they are not based on scientific evidence, nor are they clinical terms. As Kinney (2003) cautions with the term of codependency, these roles may best be used as metaphors in family therapy that provide families with terms that may help them begin to look at how their interactions impact one another.

Finally, the counselor needs to look at family strengths and determine who will be involved in therapy. The counselor looks for the strengths the family has developed through the process of addiction (McIntyre, 1993). Knowledge of the strengths can assist the counselor in finding cornerstones on which the family therapy can be built. One of the items of concern may be how much to involve the children. Perhaps the children need to be involved in order to understand the impact on them, but not necessarily involved in any work that does not directly concern them (e.g., marital problems). Another area of concern may be determining who forms the family to be involved in family therapy. Both current and family of origin can be complicated in working with addicted individuals because of factors such as divorce and remarriage or long-term involvement with a significant other. In such a complicated situation, the counselor and client may need to determine who the client considers to be family and which of those family members may be the most helpful in family therapy.

Related to the inclusion of family members in therapy is network therapy. This therapy is a combination of individual and group therapy that uses psychodynamic and cognitive-behavioral approaches in individual therapy while the client is engaged in a group support network that consists of family members and peers (Galanter & Brook, 2001). In this therapy, family and peers join the therapy sessions at intervals in order to provide a network of support to the addict that is cohesive, discourages denial, and encourages treatment compliance (Galanter & Brook, 2001). Involvement of the family in therapy can assist in the treatment of the addiction (Rowe, 2012).

Techniques

Although treatments for specific populations are discussed in Chapter 10, some general transtheoretical techniques for family therapy are discussed here. Margolis and Zweben (1998) report that it is common for abstinence to be a baseline for effective family therapy work to occur. With abstinence as a baseline, the authors then suggest six techniques be used with family members:

1. *Joining.* The counselor connects with each member in an attempt to understand his or her perspective. With this technique, the counselor is not trying to directly change the family structure but work within it and build on the strengths of the family.

2. *Stabilization.* The counselor is helping the addicted person obtain abstinence or at least reduce use so functioning is enhanced. Abstinence contracts (minimum of 20 days) may be used to determine how sobriety impacts all members of the family, behavioral goals for the addicted person are mutually set by everyone involved in therapy (these goals may be based on a harm reduction rather than abstinence-based approach), and a therapy regime (e.g., attendance at self-help meetings) is established.

3. *Education.* The family is educated both about the addictive process and the recovery process. Areas such as craving, time spent on recovery, self-help group referrals, trust rebuilding, relapse plans, and warning signs for relapse need to be openly discussed with the family.

4. *Family systems and structural analysis.* The counselor helps the family examine what does not work in the family, what contributes to the problem, and helps the family find other ways to function.

5. *Alternative coping strategies.* The main strategy here is the counselor teaching the family members how to talk about emotions in an honest and respectful manner.

6. *Relapse prevention.* The counselor helps each family member form and implement a plan on how to handle a relapse by the addict and how they might help prevent it.

These techniques may be used within specific contexts. For example, addiction treatment centers may have family weeks to help families both support and confront each other. G. Buelow and Buelow (1998) recommend that before these intensive weeks, the counselor should meet with the family to discuss confidentiality issues, set limits on focusing on those behaviors that will bring the family closer together, and provide ground rules for the group. Such guidelines can help treatment of the family be both effective and respectful. Note that some specific approaches to family therapy with substance-abusing adolescents are discussed in Chapter 10; a review shows promising in-home and in-community work with this population (Rowe, 2012). Also, Zimmerman and Winek (2013) provide a variety of group activities that can be used with families in their text, *Group Activities for Families in Recovery.* This author has also found G. A. Marlatt and Gordon's (1985) relapse-prevention model and related techniques, which are discussed in Chapter 7, to assist family members in examining their enabling behaviors. [Note that the initial use in this model is equivalent to the family member's break in their "abstinence" of their enabling behavior.]

Codependency

Codependency, a term that often comes up when discussing marital and family therapy, is a controversial topic in the addictions field. Zelvin (1993) reports that the term started in Minnesota in the 1970s, when individuals close to alcoholics/addicts were seen as affected by the addiction and requiring assistance. Some theorists estimate that 96% of Americans are codependent (Zelvin, 1993).

Doweiko (1990) defines a codependent person as someone trying to connect with the addicted individual to obtain personal strength. The behaviors are related to relying too much on others to have emotional needs met, thereby resulting in dysfunctional relationships (Daire, Jacobson, & Carlson, 2012). In essence, the codependent individual focuses on the addict's need(s) to the point of not noticing his or her own needs. It has been described as "hyperempathy" where one is overly concerned about what others think and feel; a "pathological altruism" (Oakley, 2012). Zelvin (1993) describes codependency as the result of not developing completely as an individual and thereby focusing externally to obtain a sense of fulfillment. Both Doweiko and Zelvin recommend viewing codependency on a continuum. Doweiko's model views those on the ends of the continuum as being totally dependent on others for a sense of self-worth (e.g., being a people pleaser) to totally disregarding the feedback of others. Zelvin lists three aspects of a codependent person: focusing too much on the opinions of others, not knowing what he or she likes or wants, and being drawn to relationships where others are needy.

The other view of codependency is that it does not exist, or at least not in the framework just described. Collins (1993) reports that no research empirically supports the construct, and Kinney (2006) encourages its use as a metaphor rather than a "proven scientific concept" (p. 206). Kasl (1992) describes codependency as a lack of personal development, where codependent individuals do not have an internal sense of power and security, do not believe in their ability to exist on their own, have strong feelings of being alone and responsible, and are uncomfortable with being assertive. There is an argument that the definitions of codependency blame the victim (Kasl, 1992; van Wormer, 1989). Kasl states that stereotypic codependent behavior of submissiveness and passivity are reinforced in women (e.g., codependency is the oppression of women internalized).

Although some counselors and writers of self-help books use the term codependency, the diagnosis is not listed in the *DSM-5*. Myer, Peterson, and Stoffel-Rosales (1991) state that there is a lack of consensus about codependency because of the lack of specific criteria describing codependent behavior. To use the term clinically requires more precision and more clinical research to support the term (Mannion, 1991). Counselors may avoid the argument of whether codependency is a diagnosis by working within the client's frame of reference. Kinney (2003) encourages the use of the term as a metaphor rather than a scientific concept in order to practice good care for our clients. If a client uses this term to describe himself or herself, it would be wise for the counselor to ask what the client means by the term. It would also be wise for the counselor to be careful in using this term so that clients do not think they are being diagnosed clinically.

Until further research is obtained, it may be best to use descriptions of the symptoms (poor boundary setting, lack of assertiveness skills, overfocus on others, relationship problems around power and control, or extremes in complementary role behaviors) rather than the term codependency. Even without the label of codependency, the counselor can help the individual become more aware, accepting, reflective, and responsible concerning self (Whitfield, 1997). Codependency is an attempt by a person to cope with the addict's behavior in maladaptive ways (Margolis & Zweben, 1998). If a woman in a heterosexual relationship functions well, she is expected to stay and "save" her "sick" partner (Peled & Sacks, 2008).

Although counselors should be cautious in labeling clients as codependent, the use of the concept of enabling in therapy may assist family members and significant others in examining their own behavior concerning the addicted individual. Enabling is the process of encouraging the alcohol/drug use by unintentional

behavior (Zelvin, 1993). Enabling describes behavior that keeps the addicted person from experiencing the consequences of his or her use, thereby encouraging the addictive behavior (Margolis & Zweben, 1998). It involves preventing the addicted individual from experiencing the consequences of chemical usage by making excuses for behavior, lying to others for the benefit of the addict, attempting to control the addict's behavior, taking over the addict's roles, protecting the addict from consequences, and rescuing the addict from trouble (Perkinson, 1997, 2008; Zelvin, 1993). The process of enabling fuels the addicted person's denial about the presence of an addiction problem, the belief that the chemical usage is controllable, and the belief that responsibility for the problem lies within the control of non-addicted individuals (Perkinson, 1997, 2008; Zelvin, 1993).

Margolis and Zweben state that the counselor must look at what helps and hurts family functioning; jargon such as codependency and enabling can keep family members from anger expression, problem clarification, and effective conflict resolution. The counselor can assist the family and significant others as well as the addicted client in the recovery process by encouraging all members to take responsibility for themselves and allow others to experience the consequences of their behaviors. If family members and significant others can recognize and cease their enabling behavior of the addiction, the vicious cycles of addiction can be broken or hampered, because the outside supports for the addiction are gone.

One such approach in breaking out of the tendency to enable the addicted person is the Community Reinforcement and Family Training (CRAFT) approach (Smith & Meyers, 2004). O'Farrell, Murphy, Alter, and Fals-Stewart (2008) provide a summary of this learning theory approach where family members learn to positively reinforce and provide negative consequences to decrease alcohol/drug use. It encourages family members to have less stress and more enjoyment in their lives. It also helps family members recognize (a) dangerous situations (so safety is increased for the family) and (b) teachable moments (when the addict may be more open to obtaining assistance for their substance abuse problem).

Children of Alcoholics

There are similar struggles when looking at the characteristics of the children of alcoholics, sometimes called adult children of alcoholics (ACOAs). The self-help groups of ACOA began in the 1970s and are not affiliated with AA or Al-Anon (Doweiko, 1996). Theorists who believe that ACOA issues exist describe these individuals as not trusting themselves and struggling with boundaries, awareness of feelings, impulse control, trust of others, and guilt over parental alcohol use (Doweiko, 1990). The belief is that these individuals struggle in the present because of a dysfunctional alcoholic system in which they were raised.

The critics of the existence of ACOA issues state that this viewpoint is another victim-blaming perspective that keeps the focus of the issues away from the individual (Doweiko, 1990). Once again, there is a struggle with using this label with clients, because there is not enough specific, behavioral criteria to substantiate the use of such a label (Doweiko, 1990). Kinney (2003) states there is no research to support the assertion that specific personality traits organize this group of individuals or that problems and adult experiences can be entirely explained by growing up in an alcoholic home. Mackrill, Elklit, and Lindgarrd (2012) found a lot of variation in their sample's childhood experiences and levels of distress. Counselors should use the term ACOA with great caution, because it is not listed in the *DSM-V*, and there is no consistent pattern of behavior on which to base the diagnosis. Also, if a client is using this term, it is important to ask the client what it means to him or her and then use that definition to help guide treatment planning.

Recovery Process

Regardless of terms counselors use to describe the impact of being involved closely with an individual who is addicted, it is important to have a healing process for the person who cares about someone who is addicted. A core concept is that of enabling, where the nonaddict encourages the addict's chemical use by buffering the addict from the consequences of the addiction (Zelvin, 1993). The counselor needs to help the significant other examine how the problem of addiction is being fed by enabling behavior.

Zelvin indicates that it is common for people not to see themselves as having any kind of problem connected with the addiction. If family members and significant others do not receive treatment, they may undermine the addict's treatment (Stanton & Heath, 1997). Zelvin (1993) states that two goals in treating the individual are (1) to stop the enabling behavior so that the addict can feel the full consequences of usage and (2) to enhance the sense of self-responsibility. One way to help meet these goals is to support the individual in attending self-help groups (Al-Anon, Nar-Anon, Co-Anon, Families Anonymous, Codependents Anonymous [CoDa], and ACOA; McIntyre, 1993; Zelvin, 1993). (See Chapter 8 for suggestions on how to help clients find the best group for themselves, along with a list of support groups that may be contacted for information.)

Al-Anon developed from conversations among wives of alcoholics when their husbands were at AA meetings. These women met and talked about their own problems of living with alcoholic men. At some point in these conversations, they decided to apply the 12 steps to their own lives. In 1948, the Al-Anon Family Group modified the 12 steps and 12 traditions to meet the needs of families of alcoholics. The only change to the 12 steps was that the word alcoholics in the 12th step became others. In 1957, Al-Anon was modified for the concerns of teens. It used the same 12 steps as Al-Anon and encouraged the view that the teenager had not caused the alcoholic to drink.

Codependents Anonymous and Adult Children of Alcoholics meetings may also be helpful to clients. Whether the diagnoses of codependency or ACOA exist or not, clients may find comfort in attending these meetings that offer them support and encouragement in their daily lives.

Markowitz (1993) comments on working with children of addicted families, suggesting that young children look at their denial about the impact of the alcohol/drug usage as well as allow themselves a chance to become angry and have their reactions to the usage supported. With adult children, the author recommends addressing the following issues in therapy: compulsivity, low self-esteem, shame, lack of self-awareness, and boundary problems. (See Case Study 5.6.)

CASE STUDY 5.6

The Jones family has an alcoholic/prescription-addicted mother who has been brought to addiction treatment by her husband. She has been a successful treatment client in that she has examined her addiction and has been attending self-help groups during her short time of recovery. Shortly before discharge from the treatment program, her family has been brought in for a counseling session. Her husband and her two teenage daughters do not see why they needed to come in, because now that Mrs. Jones is sober, they do not anticipate any more family problems.

1. How would you address the denial and resistance that the family is experiencing?
2. What options of treatment would you offer this family in terms of counseling? Self-help groups?
3. If the family refuses all treatment options, what areas would you address with your addicted client before she leaves treatment?

EXERCISE 5.6

Write your own definitions of codependency and enabling. Try to make your definitions as specific as possible in terms of measurable behavior. Then write where you learned those definitions (e.g., personal experience, self-help books or groups, friends/family members, TV talk shows). Now write out how you may ethically use these concepts within the context of counseling.

SUMMARY

In this chapter, specific areas common in the treatment of addiction are discussed: crisis intervention as well as individual, group, and family therapies. Two philosophical perspectives, harm reduction and the recovery movement/recovery model, are also presented because of their potential impact on counseling. An overview of basic concepts is provided, with suggestions on how to apply these concepts to counseling.

QUESTIONS

1. What are some of the controversies associated with use of the harm reduction model?

2. What are the basic tenets of the recovery movement/recovery model?

3. What are some important aspects of crisis counseling with addicted clients?

4. What are the five components of psychological first aid?

5. What are the four main goals of crisis resolution?

6. How are assessments of suicides and homicides similar and different?

7. How are interventions on suicides and homicides similar and different?

8. What are the stages of group development?

9. What are some issues common to addiction groups?

10. How can a leader care for himself or herself during the different stages of group development?

11. What are common issues among addicted families?

12. What is the controversy about codependency? Adult children of alcoholics?

READINGS/RESOURCES/WEBSITES

SUGGESTED READINGS

General

National Institute on Drug Abuse (3rd ed.) (2012). *Principles of drug addiction treatment* (NIH Publication No. 12–4180). Rockville, MD: Author.

This publication provides a basic overview of addiction and addiction treatment approaches with various populations.

Harm Reduction

Denning, P. (2005). Harm reduction tools and programs. In R. H. Coombs (Ed.), *Addiction counseling review* (pp. 487–509). Mahwah, NJ: Erlbaum.

This chapter is an excellent summary of harm reduction theory and approaches.

Tatarsky, A., & Marlatt, G. A. (2010). State of the art in harm reduction psychotherapy: An emerging treatment for substance misuse. *Journal of Clinical Psychology, 66*, 117–122.

This introduction is in an issue of the journal that focuses on harm reduction psychotherapy.

Recovery Movement/Model

Substance Abuse and Mental Health Services Administration (SAMHSA). (2010). *Recovery-oriented systems of care (ROSC) resources guide*. Rockville, MD: Author.

This resource guide provides an overview of ROSC and how the systems are at the core of the new health care environment in terms of prevention, intervention, treatment, and posttreatment.

van Wormer, K., & Davis, D. R. (2013). *Addiction treatment: A strengths perspective* (3rd ed.). Belmont, CA: Brooks/Cole.

This book has 13 chapters divided into four sections: an introduction and the biology, psychology, and social aspects of addiction from a strengths perspective.

White, W. L., & Evans, A. C. (2013). Toward a core recovery-focused knowledge base for addiction professionals and recovery support specialists. Available from www.facesandvoicesofrecovery.org

This article provides a table comparing core knowledge and skills for professionals that contrast traditional approaches with recovery-oriented approaches: present focus with missing dimensions.

Crisis

Hoff, L. A. (2009). *People in crisis: Clinical and diversity perspectives* (6th ed.). New York, NY: Routledge.

This book is an overview of crisis work. It is divided into three sections: understanding crisis intervention, specific crises, and suicide/homicide/catastrophic events.

Jackson-Cherry, L. W., & Erford, B. T. (2014). *Crisis assessment, intervention, and prevention*. Boston, MA: Pearson.

This book has 14 chapters divided into two sections: elements of crisis intervention and special issues. The special issues section has a chapter on substance abuse.

James, R. K. (2008). *Crisis intervention strategies*. Belmont, CA: Thomson Brooks/Cole.

This book provides an overview of crisis intervention. It has four sections: theory and application, handling specific crises, workplace, and disaster. There is a specific chapter related to addiction.

Miller, G. A. (2012). *Fundamentals of crisis counseling*. Hoboken, NJ: Wiley.

This book has nine chapters: overview, models, disaster mental health counseling, settings/diagnoses, assessment, additional therapies, multicultural counseling, and self-care.

Shea, S. C. (2002). *The practical art of suicide assessment: A guide for mental health professionals and substance abuse counselors*. Hoboken, NJ: Wiley.

This book has three sections: an overview, suicidal ideation, and assessment. It has helpful appendices on assessment documentation, safety contracts, and suicide-prevention websites.

Individual

Finley, J. R. (2004). *Integrating the 12 steps into addiction recovery: A resource collection and guide for promoting recovery*. Hoboken, NJ: Wiley.

This book has a section that explains the need for integration and a section of homework assignments available off the accompanying CD that can assist clients in the transition to 12-step groups.

Margolis, R. D., & Zweben, J. E. (1998). *Treating patients with alcohol and other drug problems: An integrated approach*. Washington, DC: American Psychological Association.

This 358-page book has an excellent section on techniques a counselor can use to encourage abstinence.

Schenker, M. D. (2009). *A clinician's guide to 12 step recovery: Integrating 12 step programs into psychotherapy*. New York, NY: Norton.

This book has 12 chapters that are designed to educate the clinician about the core components of 12-step recovery programs and how to integrate them with one's clinical practice. Chapters address topics such as the history of AA, what happens in meetings, common treatment issues as they relate to AA, and critiques and challenges.

Shaw, B. F., Ritvo, P., & Irvine, J. (2005). *Addiction & recovery for dummies*. Hoboken, NJ: Wiley.

This book has 20 chapters divided into five sections: the detection of addiction, taking initial steps, treatment approaches, a recovery life, and 10 ways to help a loved one and self-help resources. It is written to a layperson.

Group

Corey, G. (2012). *Theory and practice of group counseling* (8th ed.). Belmont, CA: Brooks/Cole.

This book has 18 chapters divided into three sections: basic group process overview, theoretical approaches, and integration and application.

Engleberg, I. N., & Wynn, D. R. (2013). *Working in groups* (6th ed.). Boston, MA: Pearson.

Although this book is not focused on therapy groups, it offers an interesting and different perspective on group interaction and development that may be helpful to the counselor. The 12 chapters address different aspects of groups that may be familiar to the counselor (communication, development, membership, diversity, leadership, conflict/cohesion) as well as unique ones (creative problem solving, critical thinking, meetings, technology/virtual).

Jacobs, E. E., Masson, R. L., & Harvill, R. L. (2009). *Group counseling: Strategies and skills* (6th ed.). Belmont, CA: Thomson Brooks/Cole.

This book has 18 chapters that cover group development as well as chapters on specific techniques, problem situations, and working with specific populations.

Kelin, R. H., & Schermer, V. L. (Eds.). (2000). *Group psychotherapy for psychological trauma*. New York, NY: Guilford Press.

This book focuses specifically on trauma in terms of group work.

Malekoff, A. (2004). *Group work with adolescents: Principles and practice* (2nd ed.). New York, NY: Guilford Press.

This book has 17 chapters on group work with the adolescent population. Chapter 9 has an appendix that provides information on group manuals specifically designed for this age group.

Substance Abuse and Mental Health Services Administration. (2005). *Substance abuse treatment: Group therapy*. Treatment Improvement Protocol (TIP 41) Series (DHHS Publication No. SMA 05–3991). Rockville, MD: Author.

This book has seven chapters that discuss substance abuse treatment groups in general, types of common groups, placement criteria for clients, group development and tasks, stages of treatment, group leadership, and training supervision.

Wagner, C. C., & Ingersoll, K. S. (2013). *Motivational interviewing in groups*. New York, NY: Guilford Press.

The 21 chapters of this book are divided into three sections: foundations (five chapters), group development (seven chapters), and applications to specific groups (nine chapters).

Wenzel, A., Liese, B. S., Beck, A. T., & Friedman-Wheeler, D. G. (2012). *Group cognitive therapy for addictions*. New York, NY: Guilford Press.

This book divides 10 chapters into three sections: background (related to cognitive therapy), session components, and summary and integration.

Yalom, I. D., & Leszcz, M. (2005). *The theory and practice of group psychotherapy* (4th ed.). New York, NY: Basic Books.

This book provides an in-depth look at group counseling.

Family

Patterson, J., Williams, L., Grauf-Grounds, C., & Chamow, L. (2009). *Essential skills in family therapy*. New York, NY: Guilford Press.

This book has 11 chapters that describe the interview, assessment, treatment, and termination process with families. It has separate chapters on working with families with children, couples, and a family with a mentally ill member.

Substance Abuse and Mental Health Services Administration. (2005). *Substance abuse treatment and family therapy*. Treatment Improvement Protocol (TIP 39) Series (DHHS Publication No. SMA 05–4006). Rockville, MD: Author.

This manual is divided into six chapters: substance abuse treatment and family therapy, impact of substance abuse on families, approaches to therapy, integrated models for treating family members, specific populations, and policy and program issues. It has a helpful appendix on assessing violence (domestic, child abuse).

Substance Abuse and Mental Health Services Administration. (2006). *What is substance abuse treatment? A booklet for families*. DHHS Publication No. SMA 06–4126. Rockville, MD: Author.

This short booklet (31 pages) explains substance abuse and its treatment, as well as speaks to family members about typical reactions they may have. It has a helpful glossary and resource section at the end.

Winek, J. L. (2009). *Systemic family therapy: From theory to practice*. Thousand Oaks, CA: Sage.

This book is divided into five sections: history and development, first-generation models, systemic models, postmodern models, and processes and outcomes. It provides an overview of family therapy with brief summaries on effectiveness research on adolescent substance abuse, and alcohol abuse.

Support Groups

For self-help groups and their publications, see Chapter 8.

Conyers, B. (2003) *Addict in the family: Stories of loss, hope, and recovery*. Center City, MN: Hazelden.

This is written to the family member from a disease-model perspective. Stories are interwoven into the text of information about addiction.

Kellermann, J. L. (1969). *A guide for the family of the alcoholic*. Center City, MN: Hazelden.

Although written some time ago, this book provides a helpful guide on coping with alcoholism in a family.

W. C. (1994). *Detaching with love*. Center City, MN: Hazelden.

This short booklet is written by an Al-Anon member who, at the time of publication, had been in Al-Anon for 27 years and had two sons and a husband in recovery.

Williams, T. (1993). *Do's & don'ts for family members: How to pull your life together when you're suffering*. Center City, MN: Hazelden.

This short booklet has helpful, simple suggestions on coping with addiction dynamics in one's family.

Williams, T., & Swift, H. A. (1992). *Free to care: Recovery for the whole family*. Center City, MN: Hazelden.

This short booklet describes family dynamics as they apply to a family struggling with addiction in simple language.

RESOURCES

Alcohol and Substance Abuse

Support Groups (Abstinence-Based)

See Chapter 8's support group section.

Support Groups (Harm Reduction)

Methadone Anonymous

Advocates For the Integration of Recovery and Methadone, Inc. (A.F.I.R.M.)

Phone: (888) METH7-86

E-mail: fchristie@afirmfwc.org

http://www.methadone-anonymous.org

Videos

A & E (Producer). *Investigative reports: Inside Alcoholics Anonymous* [DVD]. Available from aetn.com/shop

This 50-minute DVD provides an overview of Alcoholics Anonymous.

Alcoholics Anonymous (Producer). (1990). *Hope: Alcoholics Anonymous* [Video]. Available from alcoholicsanonymous.org

This 15-minute video provides an overview of Alcoholics Anonymous through the eyes of a male celebrating his first year of sobriety.

Hazelden (Producer). (2004). *Steps 1, 2 and 3 for Adults* [DVD]. Available from www.hazelden.org

These three DVDs are each 12 minutes in length, and each covers one of the first three steps of Alcoholics Anonymous.

HBO Documentary Films (Producer). (2007). *Addiction* [4 DVDs]. Available from www.hbo.com/docs

This four-DVD set is divided into (a) discs 1 and 2 (90 minutes) that focus on "What Is Addiction?," "Understanding Relapse," "The Search for Treatment: A Challenging Journey," and "The Adolescent Addict"; and (b) discs 3 and 4 (270 minutes) that have four interviews with addiction professionals, three sections on treatment, one section on drug court, and one about a mother.

Workbooks

Berghuis, D. J., & Jongsma, A. E. (2014). *The addiction progress notes planner* (5th ed.). Hoboken, NJ: Wiley.

This book is a guide to documenting the therapeutic process and can assist in eligibility determination of reimbursable treatment. It complements *The Addiction Treatment Planner*, fifth edition (2014), also published by Wiley.

Finley, J. R., & Lenz, B. S. (2014). *Addiction treatment homework planner* (5th ed.). Hoboken, NJ: Wiley.

This book has 100 homework assignments for chemical and nonchemical addiction treatment issues. It has all of the forms on a CD.

Jongsma, A. E., Peterson, L. M., & Bruce, T. J. (2014). *The complete adult psychotherapy treatment planner* (5th ed.). Hoboken, NJ: Wiley.

This book covers numerous diagnoses and has two sections specifically on chemical dependency: chemical dependence and chemical dependence-relapse. For each one it provides behavioral definitions, long-term goals, short-term objectives/therapeutic interventions, and diagnostic suggestions. It provides a section on how to write a treatment plan as well as two samples of treatment plans.

Group Therapy

Workbooks/Exercises

Carrell, S. (2010). *Group exercises for adolescents* (3rd ed.). Thousand Oaks, CA: Sage.

This book provides numerous exercises for working with adolescents.

Connors, G. J., Donovan, D. M., & DiClemente, C. C. (2013). *Substance abuse treatment and the stages of change* (2nd ed.). New York, NY: Guilford Press.

This book has a section on group treatment that discusses "resolution-enhancing" exercises that can assist clients in addressing their ambivalence about

their alcohol and drug use (good or less good things about use, decisional balance, looking back/looking forward, exploring goals, the "miracle question").

DeLucia-Waack, J. L., Bridbord, K. H., Kleiner, J. S., & Nitza, A. G. (2006). *Group work experts share their favorite activities: A guide to choosing, planning, conduction, and processing* (Rev. ed.). Alexandria, VA: Association for Specialists in Group Work.

This 189-page workbook has group activities for each stage of group development (orientation, transition, working, termination).

Dossic, J., & Shea, E. (1988). *Creative therapy: 52 exercises for groups I*. Sarasota, FL: Professional Resource Exchange.

Dossic, J., & Shea, E. (1990). *Creative therapy: 52 exercises for groups II*. Sarasota, FL: Professional Resource Exchange.

Dossic, J., & Shea, E. (1995). *Creative therapy: 52 exercises for groups III*. Sarasota, FL: Professional Resource Exchange.

Each of these books has 52 exercises that are clearly described in terms of how to use them in a group context.

Fleming, M. (1995). *Group activities for adults at risk for chemical dependence*. Minneapolis, MN: Johnson Institute.

This 113-page workbook has numerous exercises that can be used in a group setting for substance-abusing clients.

Ingersoll, K. S., Wagner, C. C., & Gharib, S. (2002). *Motivational groups for community substance abuse programs*. Richmond, VA: Mid-Atlantic ATTC (804–828–9910) mid-attc@mindspring.com

This book addresses the application of motivational interviewing to group therapy with substance abusers.

Metcalf, L. (1998). *Solution-focused group therapy*. New York, NY: Free Press.

This book addresses the application of solution-focused therapy to a group setting. It has an excellent admission interview form and forms for notes for the client and therapist to complete after each session to monitor clinical work from a solution-focused perspective.

Miller, G. A. (2012). *Group exercises for addiction counseling*. Hoboken, NJ: Wiley.

This book has four sections: introduction, philosophy and practice of group work, group exercises, and resources. Group exercises are a compilation of "tried and true" group exercises used by experienced addiction treatment group counselors.

Mueser, K. T., Noordsy, D. L., Drake, R. E., & Fox, L. (2003). *Integrated treatment for dual disorders*. New York, NY: Guilford Press.

This book has a helpful section (four chapters) on group interventions with persuasion, active treatment, social skills training, and self-help groups when working with dual-disordered clients.

Ragsdale, S., & Saylor, A. (2007). *Great group games*. Minneapolis, MN: Search Institute.

There are 175 exercises formed around the stages of group development that can be used for all ages.

Reddy, L. A. (2012). *Group play interventions for children*. Washington, DC: American Psychological Association.

This workbook provides strategies for teaching prosocial skills in the context of child group play. Although it focuses on children in general, it could be beneficial in working with the children in families where there are issues with alcohol/drugs. It is divided into four sections: Part I has five chapters that describe the "nuts and bolts"; Part II has 43 group play skill sequences; Part III has 67 group play interventions within eight teaching modules; and Part IV addresses closing comments and future directions.

Rosengren, D. B. (2009). *Building motivational interviewing skills: A practitioner workbook*. New York, NY: Guilford Press.

This workbook is designed for counselors to develop the skills of motivational interviewing.

Tomlin, K. M., & Richardson, H. (2004). *Motivational interviewing and stages of change*. Center City, MN: Hazelden.

This 231-page book has seven chapters: the first two focus on basic information and the integration of both of these models, the next four chapters involve change activities that can be used by counselors with different populations and counseling contexts (adolescents, family)—one chapter specifically focuses on application to special populations—and the last chapter on integrating these approaches into one's clinical setting.

Rohnke, K., & Butler, S. (1995). *Quicksilver*. Dubuque, IA: Kendall/Hunt.

This book consists of activities and adventure games that can be used with groups.

Velasquez, M. M., Maurer, G. G., Crouch, V., & DiClemente, C. C. (2001). *Group treatment for substance abuse: A stages-of-change therapy manual*. New York, NY: Guilford Press.

This 222-page book has three sections: The first section provides an overview of the stages-of-change model, and the next two sections cover the five stages, providing thorough outlines for each session.

Zimmerman, J., & Winek, J. L. (2013). *Group activities for families in recovery*. Los Angeles, CA: Sage.

This workbook is divided into three parts: introduction, structure of family group, and curriculum. The curriculum section includes family structure, family identity, sober fun, health, anger, communication, and parenting.

Icebreaker Exercises

Chat Pack. Available at www.questmarc.com

These cards each have a question on them.

Conversations to Go. Available at www.moonjar.com

These cards come in a box (encouraging people to think outside the box), and each has a question written on it.

The Feelings Playing Cards. Available at www.time-promotions.com

Each card has a cartoon face and an emotion written on it.

Soul Cards1 & 2. Available at www.touchdrawing.com

> These picture cards can be used to facilitate discussion.

WEBSITES

Harm Reduction

Harm Reduction Coalition (New York; Oakland, CA)
22 West 27th Street, 5th Floor
New York, NY 10001
(212) 213-6376
E-mail: hrc@harmreduction.org

Or

1440 Broadway, Suite 510
Oakland, CA 94612
E-mail: hrcwest@harmreduction.org
www.harmreduction.org

This national advocacy organization provides free online resources (DVD and printed material for a minimal fee) to improve the quality of life of individuals and their communities affected by drug use (publications, reports, podcasts, videos, webinars, resource list by state, and a blog).

Suicide

American Association of Suicidology (AAS)
www.suicidology.org

One can join this organization. The website has facts, warning signs, support groups, crisis centers, a bulletin board (members only), and a bookstore.

American Foundation for Suicide Prevention (AFSP)
www.afsp.org

This website has statistics and suicide survivor information.

SA/VE-Suicide Awareness/Voices of Education
www.save.org

This website has suicide-prevention education, advocates for suicide survivors, and has information on developing a group for suicide survivors.

Suicide . . . Read This First
www.metanoia.org/suicide

This website attempts to reduce the stigma around having suicidal thoughts so the reader is open to receiving help.

Support Groups

See Chapter 8's support group websites.

Group Therapy

Association for Specialists in Group Work
www.asgw.org

This website provides general information about this division of the American Counseling Association. It also has available a variety of resources for counselors, such as videos and their journal. A counselor can join this national division by joining the American Counseling Association.

Family Therapy

American Association for Marriage and Family Therapy
www.aamft.org

This is the website for the American Association for Marriage and Family Therapy that has general information on marriage and family therapy. It also has links to therapists, practitioner resources, and publications.

CHAPTER 6

TREATMENT-RELATED ISSUES AND COUNSELING APPROACHES

This chapter reviews topics that can be difficult to read about: sexual issues, HIV/AIDS, intimate partner violence (IPV), and homelessness. These topics can be very difficult to work with in counseling settings. As counselors we can easily soak up the toxins connected to the stories of our clients. Sexual issues, HIV/AIDS, IPV, and homelessness not only have their inherent toxins in the client's story, but they can also stir our own personal experiences in relation to these topics. What is necessary for each of us is to respect our wounds and how we can be wounded in hearing our clients' stories. Even if we have not experienced a similar trauma or struggle ourselves, we are exposed to hearing the incredible cruelty inflicted on human beings by human beings (that may involve our client as either the survivor or perpetrator or both) or the harsh realities human beings face in living. We need to know our limits in working in these areas, follow those limits, and nurture ourselves as we witness and attempt to be a part of the healing journey for our clients.

I have also found that some specific counseling approaches are helpful in my process of staying grounded personally and professionally in working in these areas. While I choose counseling approaches that enhance the welfare of the client addressing these issues, I also need to consider those that help me remain calm and focused in the emotional storms my client experiences and guide both of us to a safe place where healing can occur. In my work with trauma survivors, I have often found an emotional rigidity where the survivor is stuck in negative, catastrophic feelings and believing that he/she will feel this way forever. I have simply made a commitment to ride out these emotional storms with my clients because cognitive interventions were unable to touch the depth of the client's entrenchment in this negative emotional state.

I have found issues related to the treatment of addiction to be some of the most honorable work I have done as a counselor. I have a deep respect for the bravery of these human beings who explore the nightmares they have experienced or are experiencing while attempting to remain sober. I continue to be in awe of their willingness to trust me on the frightening, overwhelming journey when their whole being may be telling them to not trust anyone given their experiences or their situation.

OBJECTIVES

1. To understand the impact of sexual, HIV/AIDS, IPV, and homelessness issues on addicted clients.
2. To learn some counseling approaches (DBT, Seeking Safety, Grief Counseling) that may be used in response to these issues.
3. To learn about drug court and how this may be a helpful resource to addicted clients.

This chapter reviews four areas that are often related to addictions treatment: sexual issues (rape, sexual abuse), HIV/AIDS, intimate partner violence (IPV), and homelessness. These areas are summarized in terms of general findings, with specific recommendations made for addiction counseling. As in Chapter 5, each section is followed by a case study and exercise to facilitate understanding of the material.

Reading this information may be overwhelming for a counselor because of the numerous issues that may interact with addiction. The following overview is meant to serve as a reference in working with addicted clients. No counselor can remember to work with all of these issues all of the time, but an awareness of the possible presence of these issues, combined with careful listening to the client's story, can provide a holistic approach to addiction counseling. Also, addicted clients often present with some of these issues overlapping. For example, an addicted client may have a childhood history of sexual abuse, a history of being raped, and be currently involved in an intimate partner violence situation that has resulted in their becoming homeless. "Drug-using populations have a high exposure to traumatic events" (Afful, Strickland, Cottler, & Bierut, 2010, p. 47). Substance abusing female clients may have childhood and/or adult histories of violent trauma. The counselor may need to carefully prioritize these issues with the client so that neither are overwhelmed by the number, depth, nor overlapping nature of the problems. Focusing on recovery from substances as the core issue and addressing the other issues with flexible prioritizing as they contribute to the client's abstinence, combined with the knowledge of referral resources and the willingness to refer to them, can help the counselor and the client stay afloat in the complicated situation of recovery presented.

There is also a section on specific counseling approaches that can be helpful in working on these areas. These are dialectical behavior therapy (DBT), Seeking Safety, and grief counseling. Because many times addicted clients may be involved in legal issues related to their drug use

(and possibly related to the issues discussed in this chapter), there is a section within counseling approaches on drug court. Although this section is not a specific counseling approach, this information may be useful to the counselor who needs to address legal issues as a part of the treatment plan. Again, each section is followed by a case study and exercise.

SEXUAL ISSUES

Sexually related struggles may take different forms in the addiction treatment and recovery process. Three areas of possible concern are discussed in this section: rape, sexual abuse, and HIV/AIDS. Although these areas are not inclusive of all of the potential sexual concerns of addicted individuals, these three areas are common ones that may emerge in the treatment of addiction. For example, childhood trauma is linked to posttraumatic stress disorder (PTSD), substance abuse, and violence (Lisak & Miller, 2003) and cocaine dependence has been linked to increased risk exposure to trauma and PTSD (Afful, Strickland, Cottler, & Bierut, 2010). A general overview of each area, as well as counseling approaches specific to addictions, is provided.

Some overall comments on sexual trauma work, as experienced by the author in working with substance abusing clients, are as follows. The counselor needs to focus on listening to the survivor's story and not be pulled into a solution or judging approach. The survivor may have extreme emotional reactions to the trauma where the counselor needs to create a space where these emotions can be discharged in counseling as well as assist the survivor in finding people and places in the addiction recovery network that allow for the expression of intense emotion. The counselor can assist the client by being a touchstone of safety of reassurance and the survivor, like a CD that has a scratch on it, may need to perseverate on the experience. The survivor may also turn to rituals and practices that appear to be of an obsessional-compulsive nature in order to make oneself feel safe (i.e., having daily contact with a 12-step sponsor and attending a 12-step meeting at least once a day). While long range, the counselor may need to assist the survivor in finding more of a lifestyle balance, initially, this emotional expression and behaviors may be needed by the client to achieve and maintain sobriety. In the short term, the counselor can use various intervention strategies such as those of a spiritual nature, as discussed in Chapter 12, or cognitive-behavioral strategies, discussed in Chapter 9 that may assist with client tendencies such as catastrophizing and hopelessness. The client can also learn some of the triggers for potential substance abuse relapse, discussed in Chapter 7, that are related to the trauma. For example, a client may report feeling small, vulnerable, and unsafe and not know why. The counselor, who helps the client identify these trauma-related feelings, can help the client respond to these feelings in a self-soothing manner without initially understanding the trauma-related triggers.

Rape

The threat of rape shapes women's lives in the daily choices they make (Cahill, 2001). Forcible rape is underreported in official statistics, especially when it involves someone known to the victim (e.g., acquaintance, date, marital, group, and gang), because of personal reactions to threats of the rapist and feelings of shame and fear (of rejection from others, publicity, embarrassment, courtroom experiences, etc.; J. M. MacDonald, 1995). Women are the most frequent victims (90%), and in most assaults the victim knows the rapist (Bureau of Justice Statistics, 2004). While in college, 1 in 5 young women are the victim of sexual assault, and the statistics for teenage girls show that 1 in 9 are forced to be sexual (Gilletter, 2012). Rarely is rape fabricated because of the stigma attached to it (Russell & Bolen, 2000). However, about half of women who report rape experiences (that meet the

legal definition of rape) do not label it as such (McMullin & White, 2006).

Underreporting of rape may also be related to other factors. For males (5% to 10% of sexual assault victims are male), underreporting may be due to fear of not being believed, a lack of treatment, confusion about their sexual identity, and gender role expectations (Kassing & Prieto, 2003). Like females, they experience similar reactions such as PTSD and treatment from others who blame them for the rape; however, male rape has been researched only more recently (Fisher & Pina, 2013).

The relationship between alcohol consumption and rape has been demonstrated, particularly among college students (Parrot, 1991a, 1991b; Testa & Hoffman, 2012). At least half of them involve alcohol use with the majority of them being "incapacitated rape" where the woman is too intoxicated to resist (Testa & Livingston, 2009). Those women with PTSD symptoms, who use substances to reduce their distress, may also be at greater rape risk (Messman-Moore, Ward, & Brown, 2009). In general, alcohol and drug use may increase the risk of rape/sexual assault due to impaired judgment and problem-solving abilities (Hien, Litt, Cohen, Miele, & Campbell, 2009). Specifically, in a study of PTSD with methadone patients, the most common stressor for women was rape (Villagomez, Meyer, & Lin, 1995).

Frazier, Harlow, Schauben, and Byrne (1993) report that women who blamed themselves and external forces for the rape experienced more distress in the recovery process. Avoidant strategies (e.g., suppression) are connected with less successful recovery (Littleton & Breitkopf, 2006). In contrast, women who had a sense of control over their futures and belief that they could avoid future assaults were more successful in the recovery process. Cognitive restructuring resulted in less distress, whereas higher distress was connected with the expression of emotion. Gilmartin (1994) suggests that although crisis counseling can be helpful in terms of assisting the victim to attach blame on the perpetrator(s) and access resources, the counselor needs to be careful not to minimize the woman's experience and her sense of the impact of that experience on her. Alcohol use may also increase in response to the rape (McMullin & White, 2006), and women may use prescription drugs to cope by self-medicating (Sturza & Campbell, 2005).

Counseling Approaches

Gilmartin (1994) encourages society to look at the long-range effects of rape and to look at how symptoms such as drug and alcohol abuse/addiction may be metaphors for the struggles of victims recovering. The author suggests that these symptoms may indicate that the victim's view of herself and the world has been altered or even shattered. How she viewed and organized the world may be forever changed. Rapes can be traumatizing and devastate the person, leaving them vulnerable to PTSD (Sturza & Campbell, 2005). The authors also mention the medicalization of rape for some rape survivors whose doctors prescribed them medication when they discussed rape, resulting in the survivor feeling blamed and silenced.

Counselors working with individuals who have been raped must be sensitive in processing the experience with the individual. They must connect sensitively with these victims by caring for them both during and after they relate their story and by avoiding simplistic responses (Gilmartin, 1994). Rather, therapists need to hear and empathize with the broad range of thoughts and emotions the victim may be experiencing. Because of the frequency of substance use and rape, counselors need to assess addicted clients for being raped and having raped.

Triggers from trauma may cause intense emotional reactions (Rothschild, 2000). Such reactions may result in substance abuse. Counselors, then, need to make sure they assist survivors in examining rape experiences so they can assist them in coping with the triggers for substance abuse. Such assessments may assist in the client's recovery, because underlying issues such as PTSD and violent tendencies can then be addressed. The counselor needs to suspend stereotypes and myths about rape during the assessment so information is not missed (e.g., males are not overlooked in rape assessments or women who do not label these experiences as rape).

The format of therapy is also a consideration. While sexual violations and trauma survivor treatment has historically focused on survivor treatment in an individual format, family treatment and interventions can provide a multisystemic relational approach that may also be beneficial for the survivor (Tuttle, 2011). A resource for creative therapies that are nonverbal (particularly body actions) that may assist trauma survivors in their healing process by providing them with avenues to express their trauma is Brooke's (2007) *The Use of Creative Therapies with Sexual Abuse Survivors.* (See Case Study 6.1.)

CASE STUDY 6.1

Trudy is a 22-year-old female who has come in for outpatient chemical dependency treatment. She has been involved with the program for about two weeks and has just completed her first step on powerlessness over her addiction. She turns in her written first step to you. You notice that Trudy has an item written about the powerlessness she experienced at a fraternity party in college. Her comments seem vague and unclear. In your next individual session, you ask Trudy to clarify that section of her first step and she begins to cry. She tells you that she went to a fraternity party when she was a sophomore in college, had too much to drink, and passed out. She woke up in a bedroom in the fraternity house while someone was having sex with her. She said the experience terrified her, but she did not fight back, even though three more males raped her after she woke up. She said she did not press charges against them for three reasons: (1) she was drunk and felt like she was responsible for what happened, (2) she knew most of the males who raped her and described them as "basically good guys," and (3) one of the males she knew the best came in after the rape ended, cried, apologized, and begged her not to file charges against them. Trudy flunked out of college that semester because of her heavy drinking and her inability to concentrate on her studies after the rape. She never returned to college. She did not tell anyone about the rape until this conversation with you.

1. What would be your overall response to Trudy's story?
2. How would you address her rape as a part of her treatment plan?
3. What concerns would you have for Trudy in her recovery because of her being raped?

If you were providing addiction counseling to the young man who apologized to her for having raped her, shift the three questions as follows:

1. What would be your overall response to his story?
2. How would you address his raping her as a part of his treatment plan?
3. What concerns would you have for him in his recovery because of his being a rapist?

Note any cognitive or emotional shifts you felt in terms of your reactions to treating a survivor or perpetrator of rape.

EXERCISE 6.1

Imagine you are working with a survivor of rape in an addiction counseling setting. What issues of countertransference might emerge for you out of your own personal or professional experiences in working with this population? Now do the same for working with a perpetrator of rape. How might you handle this countertransference so you are serving the best interest of your client?

Sexual Abuse

There are at least three difficulties with accuracy in the prevalence rates of sexual abuse. First, in terms of gender, females are studied more than males, boys may underreport (abuse does not fit stereotype, fears related to homosexuality, girls more easily seen as victims, etc.), and females may be abused in a less direct manner (Gonsiorek, Bera, & LeTourneau, 1994). Second, because of a lack of a clear definition of childhood sexual abuse, the statistics can be interpreted only within each study's definition of sexual abuse (Russell & Wilsnack, 1991). Third, research methodology problems (sensitivity of interviewers, number of subjects, randomness of subjects, etc.) affect the results (Russell & Wilsnack, 1991).

Despite the variation of sexual abuse statistics, counselors working in the area of addiction need to remember that childhood sexual and physical abuse increases the chance of a substance use disorder (Brown & Anderson, 1991; Danielson et al., 2009; Downs, Capshew, & Rindels, 2004; Zweben, 2009). Childhood abuse appears to be a risk factor for alcohol and drug problems in adolescent and adult years (Downs & Harrison, 1998; Sartor et al., 2013); it is the best predictor of female alcohol dependence, and drug use medicates the depression and low self-esteem that result from childhood sexual abuse (van Wormer & Davis, 2008). SAMHSA (2000b) recommends that counselors screen for trauma when PTSD, major depression, or mood disorders are present, and that this screening be done throughout the treatment process. Before doing an assessment, SAMHSA recommends the treatment team look at length of abstinence, commitment to recovery, and relapse potential.

Sexual abuse can have a variety of *effects* on the client. Finkelhor (1986) describes short- and long-term effects of sexual abuse for *female* survivors. Short-term effects include fear, anxiety, depression, anger, hostility, and inappropriate sexual behavior. Long-term effects are depression, self-destructive behavior, anxiety, sense of isolation and stigmatization, low self-esteem, a tendency toward revictimization, substance abuse, difficulty trusting others, and sexual maladjustment. Common to both are anxiety, depression, and sexual concerns. *Males* may commit more aggressive acts, experience sexual identity confusion, have insecurity about masculinity, recapitulate the victimization, have more aggressive fantasies about others, and express more sexual interest in children (Gonsiorek et al., 1994). They may also have intimacy problems, discomfort with emotions, and feelings of alienation and anger (Kia-Keating, Sorsoli, & Grossman, 2010). Rosen, Ouimette, Sheikh, Gregg, and Moos (2002) summarize the research by stating that most women and a large minority of men in substance abuse treatment have survived physical or sexual abuse that is connected to interpersonal problems and co-morbidity, with PTSD predicting poorer addiction treatment outcome.

SAMHSA (2000b) states that two symptoms to look for in substance-abusing clients include:

1. *Childhood symptoms.* Depression, dissociative responses, aggressive behavior, poor parental

relationship(s), difficulty trusting others, extreme passivity, passive-aggressive behavior, inappropriate age/sexual formation, blackout time frames, excessive nightmares or fears (fear of the dark, need for door locks).

2. *Family characteristics.* Substance abuse (parents), battering, child protective service involvement, foster care/relative placement, severe discipline, trauma from separation and loss.

Counseling Approaches with Survivors

This section of counseling approaches addresses those related to the experience of the *survivor*.

Many addicted women are survivors of childhood sexual abuse (Hurley, 1991; Orrok, 1992) and may develop an addiction in response to sexual abuse (E. S. Blume, 1990). Similar relationships between addictions and compulsive behaviors and sexual abuse seem to be present for men (Bruckner & Johnson, 1987; Dimock, 1988; Krug, 1989; Olson, 1990; Urquiza, 1993).

When a counselor works with a client who is chemically dependent, it is important to ask whether the individual has ever been sexually abused. A good approach to asking this question is: "Has anyone ever touched you in a way that felt sexual and was uncomfortable for you?" This open question does not frame the answer in terms of sexual abuse, which is critical, because some clients may not realize that what was done to them was abusive. When a counselor asks this type of question and informs the client that this type of question is routine in an interview, the client may understand that the counselor is simply asking for information rather than suggesting that the client has been sexually abused (Knapp & VandeCreek, 1997).

In the late 1980s and early 1990s, claims of false memory syndrome became more frequent. The basis of this syndrome is that many cases of abuse are lies or distortions made by counselors (Gonsiorek et al., 1994), resulting in increased lawsuits (Knapp & VandeCreek, 1997). Therefore, counselors who ask about sexual abuse in their clients need to be careful about how they ask about the abuse. No specific cluster of symptoms automatically means a person was sexually abused. The counselor needs to find a balance between neglecting to address a significant childhood experience and assuming abuse happened without vivid memories or other evidence (Knapp & VandeCreek, 1997). A counselor using ethical standards, consultation, and supervision in conjunction with good clinical practices (firm boundaries, informed consent, careful diagnosing, clear diagnosis and treatment documentation, proven therapy techniques, and concern for future client-family connections) can find a balance between these extremes (Knapp & VandeCreek, 1997).

In the area of assessment and diagnosis, a counselor needs to let the client's story lead the counseling and let the client label whether he or she has been sexually abused. The counselor can always work with the client on the symptomatic problems and let go of the label of abuse. As Briere (1989) states, the counselor does not have to be the litmus test of truth. When abuse is suspected or self-reported, the counselor needs to establish an egalitarian relationship that is paced by the client (Briere, 1989). Rather than focusing on the label of sexual abuse, the counselor can focus on the presenting problems of the client. A safe environment needs to be established (Ratican, 1992), where trust is a core part of the therapeutic relationship (Hall, Kassees, & Hoffman, 1980). The counselor must be willing to completely accept the survivor and any feelings he or she has (Potter-Efron, 1989), as well as encourage the survivor to practice self-care (Armsworth, 1989). "The counselor needs to believe the client and create an oasis that will facilitate a discussion of shame and possibly misplaced responsibility in response to the abuse" (G. Miller, 1997, p. 2). The counselor needs to gather information on thoughts, feelings, understandings, and memories of the abuse; how it is being reacted to and addressed now; and the coping strategies of the client (SAMHSA, 2000b). Recommendations also include that the counselor carefully evaluate the appropriateness of group therapy and family therapy and that the counselor not be the one to

confront the perpetrator in family therapy. The counselor needs to be empowering, open, non-judgmental, consistent, and set good boundaries with the client. Two basic ingredients in effective counseling with a sexual abuse survivor are trust and self-care.

The survivor can learn to trust another by developing a relationship with a counselor (G. A. Miller, Sack, & Simmons, 1994). Also, the survivor needs to learn the symptoms of the abuse and to practice self-care. For example, if a survivor tends to have outbursts of anger when something reminds her of the abuse, she needs to learn to recognize this as a symptom of the abuse having a current impact on her. In doing so, she will learn that such behavior does not control her, but rather guides her into self-care. Survivors also need to learn how to calm themselves. This process of self-care is important for addicted survivors so that they do not turn to alcohol and drugs to self-medicate.

It seems most prudent to treat sobriety as a first priority, because a sense of self-efficacy can be strengthened (Briere, 1989; Evans & Schaefer, 1987). Yet, when survivors stop using alcohol and drugs, they often have memories and flashbacks of the abuse (Bass & Davis, 1988; Briere, 1989) and may relapse in their addiction to cope with the memories of sexual abuse (Evans & Schaefer, 1987; Root, 1989). J. Littrell (2000) encourages counselors to help clients think about the trauma in a way that helps them feel that they have control over their lives and be optimistic in the sense they still believe in a just world. The survivor may need to be sober a while in order to address the trauma (Washton & Zweben, 2008). Therapy with the sexual abuse survivor, then, is a dance between the issues of addiction and sexual abuse: addressing the sexual abuse issues until signs of addiction relapse are present, and then focusing on the addiction until the recovery process is stabilized and the sexual abuse issues can be examined once again (G. A. Miller et al., 1994). An example of trauma work using action therapy, with addicted women who have shown mental health stability in an assessment, is the use of psychodrama (reenacting real-life themes), drama therapy (imagined themes to look at other choices), and role training (new skills and behaviors are practiced; Uhler & Parker, 2002). Recent research with male survivors examined what improved their ability to seek out and maintain supportive relationships (what they labeled "relational recovery" because it helped them heal through relationships with pets, children, adults, or others who had suffered similarly) (Kia-Keating et al., 2010). The authors found that these men developed relationships where they felt safe, belonged, worked out relational dynamics (e.g., boundaries), and learned to accept themselves. Counselors working with male survivors may want to explore the presence of such relationships in their clients' lives.

Because many substance-abusing clients also have PTSD, joint treatment is recommended, because PTSD symptoms (flashbacks, etc.) can interfere with treatment and substance abuse can aggravate the PTSD (Mathias, 2003). Brady (2001) states that 30% to 60% of substance abuse clients have PTSD and reports three categories of PTSD symptoms: (1) intrusions (flashbacks, nightmares about the trauma), (2) hyperarousal (anxiety that is shown by a hypervigilance and edginess), and (3) avoidance (staying away from anything that might trigger memories). The goal in therapy is to reduce symptoms in each of these areas.

The client needs to be informed that painful memories can result in strong reactions, and the counselor needs to make sure there are supports available for crisis response when the client returns home (SAMHSA, 2000b). Hodges and Myers (2010) also recommend that with female survivors, counselors help clients develop quality of life coping skills as a foundation from which to process their abuse experiences—this same strength-based approach may be equally effective with male survivors. Also, the counselor needs to consider cultural factors, language differences, and gender issues in working with these clients.

The survivor and the counselor need to learn what the particular high-risk relapse situations are for the client in order to prevent relapse (G. A. Marlatt, 1985a). These situations are different for each survivor. For some, it may be a visit home; for others, it may be running into the perpetrator or someone who looks like the perpetrator. The counselor can help the survivor learn what the high-risk situations are by showing the survivor how to self-monitor (i.e., become aware of times of intense emotional reaction or an unexplainable reaction to circumstances). The survivor can then report the situation and reaction to the counselor, and together they can determine what seemed to trigger the response. One framework for relapse vulnerabilities is unknown, surfacing memories; emerging feelings (abuse related and general); experiences and problems in life with addictive behaviors absent; and the emergence of addictive behaviors in other forms (Young, 1995).

The counselor and survivor can then work on approaches to cope with high-risk situations. Some examples of coping behaviors are encouraging self-talk, contacting a recovery sponsor or mentor, learning to detach from intense feelings (experiencing them without acting on them or repressing them), and developing missing coping skills such as assertiveness (G. A. Miller et al., 1994). The three recovery S's (G. A. Miller et al., 1994) are (1) *sobriety* becomes top priority, (2) *strengthening* the addict's functioning, and (3) *signs* of relapse are monitored. Throughout the counseling, the therapist needs to keep in mind the different effects that gender may have on the sexual abuse experience.

In the recovery process, a counselor will often refer a client to a self-help program or the client will already be involved in one. (Chapter 8 examines different self-help groups. In attempting to help an addicted survivor find a good match, the counselor needs to keep in mind the survivor's issues and, as outlined in Chapter 8, process the experience of the self-help groups with the survivor.)

An example of adapting a self-help program to benefit survivors is provided by G. A. Miller et al. (1994), who suggest how counselors may translate the 12 steps for addicted female survivors. In the first two steps, which address powerlessness—a feeling familiar to survivors—the counselor can assist the individual in understanding that acknowledging addiction powerlessness frees the survivor and helps develop a sense of personal power (without drugs). In the third step, which uses the phrase "God as we understood Him," the survivor may need to find a group that uses the word *Her* rather than *Him*, or a group that translates this phrase in a broad, spiritual sense, or perhaps work on this issue alone. In the fourth and fifth steps, which encourage the person to admit flaws, and in the sixth and seventh steps, which look at removing flaws in oneself, the survivor may need to be reminded that she did not cause the abuse and that the effects of the abuse need to be viewed with compassionate accountability: The survivor is responsible for personal actions, but she was doing the best she could to survive under the circumstances. In the eighth and ninth steps, where amends need to be made, a survivor needs to be reminded that she should be at the top of the amends list, because she experienced the most pain of the addiction. Finally, with the last two steps, which are the recovery maintenance steps, the client needs to understand that mistakes will be made, to learn to communicate spiritually in a comfortable way, and to care for herself and others. These self-help group adaptations can also be applied to male survivors.

This example of finding a way to translate a self-help recovery program can be done with any self-help group. The counselor simply needs to work with the client on reactions to the recovery program and have the client translate concepts in a way that is helpful to the client's staying sober. Finally, counselors need to consider how difficult it can be to work with such violent stories and care for themselves along with caring for their clients throughout the counseling process—this may be especially true for counselors in addiction recovery themselves who have childhood trauma issues.

Counseling Approaches with Perpetrators

When a counselor is treating a perpetrator of sexual abuse, it is very likely that the perpetrating client has previously worked with a sexual abuse offender expert; if not, the client needs to be referred to one to address the perpetration issues. This recommendation for a sexual offender specific assessment of treatment cannot be emphasized enough. Unless a counselor is specifically trained in this area, it is important to work closely with other counselors who have been. The counselor needs to remember that the client has a problem with both alcohol/drugs and sex offending, and treatment must focus on both areas, or the problems may continue to feed into each other.

In a baseline theoretical framework, Finkelhor (1986) presents four preconditions that have to exist for the offender to sexually abuse; the first two must be present for the second two to occur. The first two are that the offender has to be motivated to abuse (be interested in sexually abusing another) and overcome any internal inhibitions about abusing (e.g., the incest taboo). The second two are that the offender must overcome external obstacles against abusing (e.g., abusing in the presence of others) and has to overcome the child's resistance. Although alcohol or drugs can assist the offender in overcoming internal inhibitions against abuse, the motivation to abuse still must be present. Offenders in treatment, then, cannot simply brush off the abuse as something that happened when they were drinking/using. Obviously, a second problem is present besides the problem with alcohol/drugs.

The *Juvenile and Family Court Journal* (National Task Force on Juvenile Sexual Offending, 1988) provides a philosophy of managing and treating sex offenders. The first aspect of this philosophy is to make the community safe; therefore, there may be limits on confidentiality of sessions (e.g., the offender's plan to abuse someone). Second, treatment needs to complement the legal sentence given by the court, not reduce or void it. Third, treatment should fit the risk potential of abuse by the offender. Fourth, denial needs to be confronted and guilt must be admitted. Fifth, sex offenders need long-term treatment and follow-up. Last, a coordinated, multidisciplinary team is needed to address these issues.

The counselor working with a perpetrator needs to work as part of a multidisciplinary team and in conjunction with the legal system so the perpetrator's behavior can be held accountable. Also, in family treatment, in addition to the counselor needing to report sexual abuse to the authorities, the counselor needs to address these issues directly and make sure the children are safe (McIntyre, 2004). Therapists will likely need to confront the "teflon defenses" (projection and denial) used by most perpetrators by pointing out inconsistencies and holding the perpetrators

accountable for their behavior. The counselor working with the addiction aspects of the client's problems needs to stay focused on that aspect and not allow the client to use the addiction as an excuse for offending behavior.

In terms of self-help recovery, the counselor must assist clients in finding groups that hold them accountable for personal behavior. The counselor may also need to translate program philosophy so clients do not use it to minimize perpetration acts (e.g., "I was powerless over my behavior because I was drinking").

Sexual abuse counseling, whether with the perpetrator or the survivor, needs to be incorporated into addiction counseling to promote a complete recovery process. It is important that the addictions counselor be aware of these issues and their relationship with addictions through training, supervision, and/or consultation with colleagues. (See Case Studies 6.2 and 6.3.)

CASE STUDY 6.2

Sharon is a 40-year-old female who has had two previous addiction treatments. She has come to counseling because of work complaints: She has difficulty communicating with her supervisor. Sharon states that the stress is so high at her work that she often thinks about using alcohol/drugs. As she talks in counseling about her supervisor, she mentions that he looks a lot like her uncle, who sexually abused her from ages 8 to 12. When encouraged to talk more about her concerns, she describes her problems with her supervisor with intense affect, but describes her childhood sexual abuse with a sharply contrasting flat affect. She states that she does not want to discuss her childhood experiences any more during the session. The day after her first counseling session, she calls you in the early morning, crying heavily. She reports sleeping only for brief periods during the night, wakened by nightmares of her uncle sexually abusing her. She states she is afraid that she will return to using alcohol and drugs.

1. What would be your first priority in working with Sharon?
2. In the short term, how would you balance her memories of the abuse and her addiction recovery?
3. What would be your long-range plan for working with the client?

   Shift the client in this scenario to a male. How might gender influence your answers to the three questions listed?

EXERCISE 6.2

To enhance survivor awareness, have the survivor take a few moments to jot down responses to the following six questions:

1. What do I know about myself that I did not know 5 years ago?
2. How did I learn this new knowledge about myself?
3. How do I know when I am in a dangerous situation?
4. How does my body tell me when I am in a dangerous situation?
5. What situations from my past have taught me cues about dangerous situations?
6. How do I care for myself during and following a dangerous situation?

CASE STUDY 6.3

Now imagine that you have Sharon's uncle as a client. He has experienced a lot of shame, guilt, and remorse during the time he has been sober in his clinical work with you, and he has just admitted in your session that he sexually abused her. He is afraid he will return to using alcohol and drugs if he does not address this issue.

1. What would be your first priority in working with him?
2. In the short term, how would you balance his memories of the abuse and his addiction recovery?
3. What would be your long-range plan for working with the client?

Again, answer these three questions with your client being a male. Are there any changes in your answers?

Next, how might your answers shift if the perpetrator for your female client and your male client change if the perpetrator was female?

EXERCISE 6.3

To enhance perpetrator awareness, use the same exercise for survivors (6.1). Have the perpetrator take a few moments to jot down responses to the following six questions:

1. What do I know about myself that I did not know 5 years ago?
2. How did I learn this new knowledge about myself?
3. How do I know when I am in a dangerous situation (of perpetrating again)?
4. How does my body tell me when I am in a dangerous situation?
5. What situations from my past have taught me cues about dangerous situations?
6. How do I care for myself during and following a dangerous situation?

Again, note any cognitive or emotional shifts in your reaction to treating a survivor or perpetrator in treatment for chemical dependency.

HIV/AIDS

NIDA (2006) provides the following summary of the current knowledge of HIV/AIDS that is anchored in a review of research findings. About 1 million people in the United States live with HIV/AIDS, but because HIV reporting is not mandatory, it is difficult to know the exact number. In terms of the United States and District of Columbia, the Centers for Disease Control and Prevention's HIV/AIDS Surveillance Report (2007) estimated that 1,106,400 people were living with HIV infection, with 21% undiagnosed, 1.1 million people were living with diagnosed or undiagnosed HIV/AIDS, and 35,962 people were diagnosed with AIDS [in the United States, 1.2 million individuals live with HIV and 1 in 5 do not know they are infected (DeAngelis, 2013)]. In 2011, 8 of the 10 states with the highest HIV diagnosis rates were located in the South and the South had 49% of the HIV diagnoses (while the South only has 37% of the population of the United States), and the highest HIV-related mortality and morbidity rates (Reif et al., 2012). Reif et al. (2012) suggest that high poverty rates, HIV-related stigma, and sexually transmitted diseases (STDs) contribute to both HIV incidence and mortality.

Initially, it was men who had sex with men (MSM) (typically white, urban) and intravenous drug users (IDUs) who were primarily infected with the virus. "The virus has now spread to young minority populations who may never have held a job, may have dropped out of school and may have problems with substance abuse" (DeAngelis, 2013, p. 30). New infections are occurring more frequently with individuals who are: MSM, women, or in racial/ethnic minorities (NIDA, 2012).

The link between HIV/AIDS and drug abuse/addiction has been apparent from the start of the epidemic. At present the new infections of MSM are due to high-risk sexual behavior that is linked to methamphetamine and other club drugs. IDU infection has dropped off in the past few years, while heterosexual transmission has increased.

While intravenous drug use is recognized as an avenue for infection, it is less apparent that: (1) drug use can lead to high-risk sex with partners who are infected by the virus because of the intoxicated person's decrease in judgment and inhibition, and (2) drugs can speed up the progression of HIV and its consequences. Depression and substance abuse are the most common HIV-associated comorbidities that are related to poor adherence to treatment of the disease (Safren et al., 2012).

Monti and Operario (2009) state that there is a decrease in the number of deaths since the mid-1990s due to highly active antiretroviral therapy (HAART) [also called HIV ART (HIV antiretroviral therapy) (Phillips et al., 2013)]; the decrease in AIDS mortality also means that there are more people living longer who might transmit the disease. There are still about 50,000 HIV infections yearly (Centers for Disease Control and Prevention [CDC], 2013). Factors that increase the number of cases that are related to unsafe sexual practices are: little/no condom use, multiple partners, and women who are dependent financially on marriage or prostitution (Sulis, 2009).

There are specific populations especially at risk (NIDA, 2006). AIDS is the leading cause of death to African Americans between 25 and 44, possibly due to a lack of awareness of the infection until later in the development of the disease. The Centers for Disease Control and Prevention's HIV/AIDS Surveillance Report (2007) states that Blacks are disproportionately impacted by HIV more than any other U.S. ethnic group, attributing this to related ethnicity issues such as poverty, stigma, high STD rates, and drug use; this tendency has continued (CDC, 2013a). While in the past new infections were lower for Hispanics than Whites and Blacks, Hispanics account for 17% of the new infections. People from ages 13 to 24 are at risk, especially in minority populations due to sexual experimentation and drug abuse as well as "generational forgetting" (NIDA, 2006, p. 4), where they do not recognize the dangers of HIV/AIDS.

Another population at high risk is women. Women are diagnosed later in AIDS progression and have poorer treatment access (van Wormer & Davis, 2008). Also, women can transmit the virus to babies before or during birth or through breast-feeding (van Wormer & Davis, 2008). In terms of ethnicity, African-American women and Latinas are disproportionately affected when compared to women of other ethnic groups (CDC, 2013b). More women are being diagnosed with AIDS because they are having sex with HIV-infected men and they are sharing drug paraphernalia with HIV-infected individuals (Zweben, 2009). Zweben (2009) states that while condoms are a major method in reducing HIV infection, women must have men agree to condom use or women need to say no to having sex. The author points out that due to low self-esteem and poor communication skills, women may not negotiate condom use well; this may be particularly true for younger women. Also, women may fear emotional or physical assault if they do assert themselves.

Because a person can be infected for years and not know it, the best prevention is drug treatment; community outreach, testing, and counseling; and early detection (routine screening) (NIDA, 2006). The American Psychological Association has a website that may encourage clients to have HIV testing: http://psychologybenefits.org/2013/06/27/6-reasons-why-you-should-consider-getting-tested-for-hiv/. Also, prevention with people with HIV, called *prevention with positives*, has shown that health-care providers who talk with clients about their specific situations in an objective, empathic, and nonjudgmental manner enhance prevention conversations with clients (Koester et al., 2012).

A main barrier to HIV/AIDS prevention is legislation (van Wormer & Davis, 2008). For example, many states prohibit carrying more than a few condoms and make carrying more than a few grounds for prostitution arrests—these are used for harassment because courts typically do not uphold these arrests (K. Norins, personal communication). Also, while needle-exchange programs can help reduce HIV/AIDS infection, 47 states have laws against distributing and possessing syringes. Some authors have advocated the addressing of human rights and structural changes legally, particularly regarding HIV nondisclosure prosecution and HIV exposure and transmission (Phillips et al., 2013).

With regard to treatment, HAART is excellent because it is a customized combination of medications from different drug classifications that both delays symptoms and helps people live longer (NIDA, 2006). Some research indicates that other factors, at least in North America, may positively influence adherence—factors such as being older, White or Hispanic, and higher social capital (perceived) (Phillips et al., 2013).

Finally, there needs to be a discussion on the Hepatitis C virus (HCV) because co-occurrence of HIV and HCV is more prevalent in those individuals who have a substance abuse disorder (Batki & Nathan, 2008). The hepatitis viruses (A, B, C) all impact the liver. A is contracted through feces, primarily contracted through food sources; B through sex, sharing needles, and childbirth; and C through IDU use and equipment and blood transfusions before 1992 (as well as many types of blood contact) (K. Norins, personal communication). Batki and Nathan (2008) provide a summary of the hepatitis C virus that is currently more prevalent than HIV.

Hepatitis C is a viral infection that attacks the liver and is transferred by blood contact. It is serious for some, but has no long-term effects for others. It may result in cirrhosis, cancer, or failure of the liver and is the leading cause of liver transplants. Prevention recommendations include not sharing needles or drug works, having hepatitis A and B vaccinations, and practicing safe sex. Injection drug use is a major conduit for HIV and new HCV infections. When HIV and HCV co-occur, HIV accelerates HCV; end-stage liver disease is the leading cause of morbidity and mortality with people with HIV/AIDS.

Triple-diagnosis clients (HIV or HCV, substance abuse disorder, psychiatric disorder) create diagnostic problems and require special treatment. Counselors need to be sensitive, then, to the presence of HCV as well as HIV in their substance-abusing clients.

History and Development of the Disease

There are different theories as to the origin of HIV (human immunodeficiency virus) (Kalichman, 1998). Zhu et al. (1998) reported that HIV-1, the dominant form prevalent in the epidemic globally, "may have evolved from a single introduction into the African population not long before 1959" (p. 594), but the factors that stimulated the initial spread were still unknown. However, it appears a common ancestor of HIV-1 was acquired by humans in a "cross-species transmission under natural circumstances, probably predation" (Worobey et al., 2008, p. 663) and that the "rise of cities [roads] may have facilitated the initial establishment and the early spread of HIV-1" (Worobey et al., 2008, p. 663).

HIV can lead to acquired immunodeficiency syndrome (AIDS). The HIV reproduces itself by taking over the protein-producing functions of the host cell. The protein receptors of the immune system cells are the CD4 receptors, through which HIV enters in order to reach the protein receptor. Naturally, the immune system uses white blood cells to address invading organisms: The helper cells tell the immune system to be alerted. After HIV enters the helper cells, utilizing them as a factory for self-protection and ultimately destroying them, the suppressor cells provide stronger signals, which make the immune system less able to respond to the organism invading the body. After infection occurs, HIV reproduces itself by integrating HIV RNA (protein) into the DNA of its host cell, the very cells that normally fight infection (disease). Thereby, HIV is able to both hide within a healthy-appearing cell body (CD4) and utilize that cell body via its proteins as a virus-producing factory. HIV eventually destroys that immune cell and releases multiple (50 to 100) HIV copies into the bloodstream to infect cells. Simply stated, soon after initial infection, HIV makes cells that retreat to protected areas of the biological system, which act as reservoirs; if HIV infection is reduced, these cells release to repopulate the system with the virus (K. Norins, personal communication). The person infected with HIV or who has AIDS, then, is more susceptible to infections that might otherwise not be life threatening (APA, 1996a). Basically, then, HIV attacks one's immune system until eventually the immune system does not respond to infection or illness. That means that many people do not die of HIV but of opportunistic infections.

Classification

HIV is now considered a chronic illness (Stoff, Mitnick, & Kalichman, 2004). The development of HIV infection to AIDS can take from at least 1 to 15 years (Bartlett, 1993), but antibody testing for the virus can reveal it within 3 months of infection and viral RNA testing (PCR) more rapidly (K. Norins, personal communication).

The Centers for Disease Control and Prevention (CDC) (2009) describe the general stages a person may experience in their HIV infection before they develop AIDS. The earliest stage is called *infection*. This occurs immediately after infection, where HIV may enter cells and make copies of itself before the immune system has a chance to react. Flu-like symptoms may be experienced at this stage. The next stage is *response*. At this stage the body is responding to the virus by making antibodies. This is labeled seroconversion, where the person moves to an HIV-positive status from a negative one. The following stage has *no symptoms* as asymptomatic infection is occurring. This means that the person has HIV, the HIV may be causing the individual damage, but the individual does not feel it. The next stage is *symptoms* (symptomatic infection), where symptoms develop such as an infection of *pneumocystis carinii* pneumonia (PCP). Finally, AIDS is the diagnosis given when CD4 levels drop such that life-threatening illness occurs or is likely to occur (K. Norins, personal communication).

In 1993, the CDC revised its definition of AIDS. The new definition does not focus on manifestations of the virus, but on the CD4 cell count being below 200 (Kain, 1996) and/or the presence of an opportunistic infection. AIDS is diagnosed when the CD4 cell count is below 200 (normally a healthy person has a CD4 cell count that ranges from 500 to 1800) or if HIV is present with diseases such as tuberculosis or PCP (CDC, 2009).

The most commonly used HIV test measures antibody production, as do most tests for virus infection. This is much less expensive than detecting virus (Saag, 1992). The test called ELISA (enzyme-linked immunosorbent assay) looks for HIV antibodies. If results are positive, results are confirmed by a Western blot, another test looking for antibodies. As Saag (1992) points out, these two tests reduce the chances of misdiagnosis to a low probability. After a negative HIV antibody test, testing should be repeated in 3 months, because antibody production can take that long to occur. Other viral tests are being used, one of which is polymerase chain reaction (PCR), which can detect infections directly following the exposure to HIV. The PCR will not pick up the infection for at least 4 days. Unfortunately, these tests are very expensive, thereby limiting widespread use.

Transmission

There are six routes of HIV transmission and therefore six risk behaviors: anal intercourse, vaginal intercourse, oral-genital contact, prenatal transmission, injection drug use, and blood transfusion (Kalichman, 1996). In regard to sexually related risk, condom use, particularly the use of latex condoms, helps protect the individual against HIV (Conant, Hardy, Sernatinger, Spicer, & Levy, 1986). Although latex condoms (and nonlatex condoms, not natural skin condoms, made from polyisoprene) greatly reduce the risk of contracting the virus, they do not eliminate it (K. Norins, personal communication). Due to improper storage or use, condoms can break, slip off, or have undetectable tears. Also, only lubricants that are oil free and water based should be used with condoms, because oil products will break down the latex (Voeller, Coulson, Bernstein, & Nakamura, 1989).

HIV can be transmitted to babies by crossing the placenta, having contact with blood and vaginal fluids during delivery, and during breastfeeding (CDC, 1989). Babies can be tested for HIV using the PCR method. However, perinatal transmission can be substantially reduced (almost eliminated) via testing during pregnancy and treatment of the mother and baby to present infection (K. Norins, personal communication).

The virus can also be transmitted when injection equipment such as needles and syringes are used by an infected person and shared with others. Because drug use is considered deviant (Mondragon, Kirkman-Liff, & Schneller, 1991), HIV-infected drug users often experience a double discrimination. In the United States, individuals who received blood transfusions between 1978 (onset of the epidemic) and 1984 (first HIV antibody test became available) are at the highest risk for infection (Kalichman, 1998).

Ramifications

HIV/AIDS is not considered terminal now, because early detection of HIV and adherence or compliance to a medication regimen ends the automatic death sentence. Note, however, that people still die of HIV/AIDS due to medication resistance, not taking medication at all, or taking medication inconsistently (K. Norins, personal communication).

Early diagnosis allows for treatment to begin before the immune system is disabled, therefore protecting the body from opportunistic infections. This is why testing and an appropriate medication regimen are critical. Even though it may not be viewed as a terminal illness, HIV/AIDS may be similar in its ramifications to other terminal illnesses. Moynihan, Christ, and Silver (1988) point out that HIV/AIDS has an impact on younger people and has both a unique disease process and unique social context. Other authors indicate that social support for someone who has HIV/AIDS is inhibited (Turnell, 1989), and the presence of HIV/AIDS may involve more litigation for the individual (J. T. Huber, 1993). Kegeles, Coates, Christopher, and Lazarus (1989) report that HIV/AIDS-infected individuals commonly experience discrimination from others. This prejudice is in conjunction with fear of contracting the virus, risk group characteristics, and culturally negative attitudes toward death (Kalichman, 1998).

Often, individuals who have HIV/AIDS experience social rejection when they have a strong need for social support (Herek & Glunt, 1988; King, 1989). HIV/AIDS-infected individuals are often excluded from society (Bickelhaupt, 1986; Durham & Hatcher, 1984; Newmark, 1984; Nichols, 1985), as well as have a tendency to isolate themselves (McDonell, 1993). They may also experience discrimination in their employment and in their treatment from medical and mental health professionals.

Viney, Henry, Walker, and Crooks (1989) find that HIV/AIDS-infected individuals often feel helpless. Biller and Rice (1990) report that grief is compounded by multiple losses and lack of time between the losses. Kain (1996) indicates that some of the losses include physical attractiveness, employment, mobility and physical functioning, friends and significant others who react to their being HIV-positive, future, and self (not knowing who they are due to all of the changes experienced).

Counseling Approaches

The approach to treatment of HIV/AIDS-infected individuals hinges on several factors: where the client is in the process of having the disease, discrimination experienced around the disease, and losses with the disease.

In terms of the process of having the disease, the counselor should be familiar with the medical terms and conditions associated with the HIV/AIDS disease. There are numerous texts available that can assist counselors with this understanding

as well as classic texts such as *Understanding AIDS: A Guide for Mental Health Professionals* (Kalichman, 1998) and *Positive: HIV Affirmative Counseling* (Kain, 1996). A counselor would also be well advised to work as closely as possible with the client's physician or another physician/medical professional who is familiar with the medical diagnosis and treatment associated with the disease. Such information may facilitate the counseling approaches used in therapy by providing the therapist with current information about the client's physical condition. Issues related to that condition can be processed in counseling. However, clients need to be their own advocates and make their own treatment decisions, because currently, treatment tends to be very individual and personalized, with collaboration being critical from the beginning. While in the past there may have been intermediaries between doctors and clients, this situation is rarer now if it exists at all. The medical personnel and the client need to collaborate so any intervention taken is one where the client is on board from the beginning, willing to make a commitment to change. The client's understanding being improved through dialogue with pharmacists and doctors could result in improved outcomes of adherence and treatment (Racey et al., 2010).

This is where interventions that consider the stages-of-change model and motivational interviewing, discussed in Chapter 9, are helpful. Regarding overall treatment, the client drives the treatment decisions, and the counselor can facilitate the process of collaboration between the client and the medical personnel by keeping in mind the client's level in the stages-of-change model and use motivational interviewing strategies as appropriate. Also, in terms of reduction of risky sexual behavior, there is evidence that motivational interviewing strategies (in terms of time and number of sessions) are helpful (Chariyeva et al., 2013).

As Burke and Miller (1996) indicate, counselors need to work at separating their own countertransference issues from the client's counseling concerns. For example, when a client who has

HIV/AIDS comes in for counseling, the counselor may assume that the client has death and dying issues. This may not be the client's reality, but rather what the counselor anticipates he or she would struggle with if diagnosed with HIV/AIDS. Other authors indicate that counseling may be negatively affected by the issues of the counselor: fear and denial (Rinella & Dubin, 1988), coping ability (Amchin & Polan, 1986), and loss and grief (Cho & Cassidy, 1994). Some mental health professionals may have negative attitudes toward these clients, similar to those of laypeople, because of homophobia, anxiety about death, and negative stereotypes about drug users (Kalichman, 1998). On the flipside, because of advances in HIV treatment, counselors may minimize the trauma of being infected and the discrimination their clients face (K. Norins, personal communication). Counselors need to examine, on their own, and possibly with the assistance of colleagues and supervisors, their reactions to homosexuality, death, and/or drug users to reduce the impact of these biases on counseling.

Although familiarity with common issues facing individuals who have HIV/AIDS is important, the counselor also needs to remember to take the individual story into account. A counselor can easily stereotype an HIV/AIDS client based on reading literature and research written on the topic rather than clarifying the issues as perceived by the client. For example, the therapist may read that individuals who have HIV/AIDS experience discrimination at the workplace; however, the client may work in an environment that is very supportive. Therefore, even though there may be common experiences among individuals who have HIV/AIDS, the counselor needs to remember these tendencies do not apply to all such clients.

Client issues that might need to be addressed in counseling include, but are not limited to, positive test results, disclosure of positive test results to others (and possibly related disclosure of sexual preference [gay, lesbian, bisexual] and drug use history), diagnosis of AIDS, and issues related to dating and sexuality, loss, physical problems, medical treatment, helplessness and dependency on others, rational suicide, plans for death, spirituality, substance abuse, and quality of life (Kain, 1996; Kalichman, 1998). Additionally, clients may have issues that need to be addressed with regard to ongoing sexual activity (K. Norins, personal communication). Finally, because of the view shift from terminal illness to manageable disease, clients can stay in longer or re-enter the workforce (Dahlbeck & Lease, 2010)—this shift in context invites challenges to some clients that can be explored through the use of MI, DBT, and job skills training (DeAngelis, 2013).

With the increase in medication therapy options, counseling issues have expanded to include the individual's (a) returning to work, (b) not dying when anticipated and thus living with consequences evolving from decisions based on that anticipation (e.g., selling off his or her insurance policy), (c) believing the government has a cure, but it is not being given to patients, and (d) struggling with disclosure of being infected because of possible severe consequences (e.g., losing his or her career). Given this list of concerns, it would be easy for a counselor to become overwhelmed when working with a person who is diagnosed as HIV-positive. Thus, it may be best for the counselor to work within the context of the individual's story and find out early in the counseling process, as well as ongoing, what the client feels will be the best approach to take in counseling and how to prioritize the issues being faced. As Szasz (1994) indicates, counselors need to ask clients what they want, and if it seems reasonable, help them attain that wish or some sort of compromise.

When the HIV/AIDS client is also addicted, there are additional twists to the counseling process. People who have psychiatric problems, substance abuse, and HIV may have an increase in their disability, distress, risky behavior, and have fewer coping skills (Stoff et al., 2004). Also, dual-diagnosis clients may have the virus undetected and may be involved in high-risk behaviors (Parry, Blank, & Pithey, 2007).

If the client is still using alcohol/drugs, the counselor should facilitate the client's receiving additional treatment for these concerns. Although the client may believe that the alcohol/drugs are helping with coping with the diagnosis (Greene & Faltz, 1991), the alcohol/drugs are actually preventing the client from addressing the issues being faced and may increase HIV-transmitting behaviors (Kalichman, 1998). Monti and Operario (2009) report that some evidence suggests that alcohol may impact one's immune function and thereby increase the susceptibility to HIV, as well as be a risk for not following safe-sex behaviors. However, addiction treatment that best fits the client's needs must be chosen (discussed in Chapters 5 and 9). For example, Springer (1991) recommends the harm reduction model, which is based on preventing HIV/AIDS as a higher priority than preventing drug use and avoiding a narrow focus on drug abstinence. The basis of this approach is that a focus on reduction of harm rather than abstinence may enhance communication about drug use and decrease the spread of HIV/AIDS. It is not a model that encourages drug use, but one that focuses on reduction of harm in a manner most appealing to the client. For example, rather than making abstinence a requirement for help, the counselor may initially focus on helping the person use less dangerously (i.e., avoid drinking and driving, use clean needles, etc.). Or the counselor may want to address other behavioral issues as part of counseling, such as barebacking and circuit party. *Barebacking* is the street term for anal sex without condoms. *Circuit party* is a party that is held over a weekend that involves recreational sex and intense substance use (Barrett & Logan, 2002). Both of these behaviors may need to be assessed and addressed in counseling with a gay client.

For the client who has recently stopped using alcohol/drugs or who has been sober for some time, the HIV/AIDS diagnosis may bring up issues of remorse, guilt, resentment, self-pity, loss, and hopelessness. The client may feel punished for past mistakes. Also, those who have been clean may now face having to take mood-altering addictive drugs to cope with their physical decline, which may seem strangely ironic. Finally, these clients may feel discrimination by helping professionals, whose personal issues arise when dealing with someone who has the HIV/AIDS diagnosis. For example, a helping professional may assume that the individual at some level deserves the illness because of involvement in risky sexual behaviors in the past. While such an attitude may not be expressed verbally, the client may detect judgmentalism, thereby making it difficult to share the struggles experienced by having an HIV/AIDS diagnosis.

This discrimination may also be present with those who have the triple diagnosis of addiction, mental health problems, and HIV/AIDS. The counselor working with the addicted individual who also has HIV/AIDS (and possibly a third mental health diagnosis) needs to look at the client in a multifaceted manner. Even though it is hopeful that clients can live with AIDS with treatment, the counselor may need to address countertransference issues that surface around an HIV/AIDS case diagnosis, such as medical choices, sexual orientation, and death. As stated previously, the counselor can address these issues in his or her own therapy, in conversation with colleagues who have resolved such issues, and/or with a supervisor who has previously addressed such concerns.

The client's concerns can work as an anchoring point in developing a treatment plan. What struggles is the client currently facing? What issues does the client anticipate or fear facing in the future? The counselor also needs to look at the setting in which the client is receiving addiction treatment. Who is supportive to the client in that setting? Are there other individuals who are HIV-positive and addicted with whom the client can connect? Are there individuals within the setting who need to be educated about an HIV-positive diagnosis? What are agency policies on working with someone who has HIV/AIDS? On leaving treatment, what community resources are present for the client? The importance of maintaining hope—by religion, work or vocation, or support of family and friends—is necessary for the HIV/AIDS client (B. A. Hall, 1994). Such community of support has been shown to assist HIV/AIDS clients to "take control" of its impact in their lives, resulting in their finding meaning and a will to live (Balthip, Boddy, Kong-In, & Nilmanat, 2011).

Most important of all, the client who has tested HIV-positive needs to be treated the same as any client who enters therapy: with respect and compassion. Respect does not mean that the counselor avoids confronting the client on possible treatment issues (e.g., viewing the diagnosis as a death sentence), thereby reducing the importance of addiction treatment and recovery from the client's perspective. Rather, respect means that the counselor works with the client on issues pertinent to the recovery process and keeps the welfare of the client at the forefront of treatment. The counselor who is not able to work through personal prejudices needs to make coworkers and supervisors aware of this limitation. The counselor who has been able to address such concerns and is able to work with the HIV-positive client with compassion can invite health into the addicted individual's life, especially if the counselor works through his or her own countertransference issues that arise.

When working with substance-abusing clients in general, counselors need to have a system in place for testing for tuberculosis and Hepatitis C. SAMHSA (2000c) makes the following recommendations:

- Medical treatment:

    a. Work on a team due to the complexities of these issues.

    b. Have staff examine the needs, relapse potential, and culture with regard to each client.

    c. Adhere to drug regimens and educate the client as needed.

    d. Conduct risk assessments and provide education and counseling to clients.

    e. Test for HIV if the client is engaged in risky behaviors, had a sexually transmitted disease, has shared injection equipment, or has symptoms that might show infection.

    f. Assess behaviors connected to HIV transmission.

    g. Have a thorough medical history done.

    h. Discuss medication issues related to antiretroviral therapy, chronic pain, and alternative therapy vaccines.

    i. Address gynecological problems.

    j. Address nutritional needs.

- Mental health:

    a. Address psychiatric symptoms caused by substance abuse, HIV/AIDS, medications taken to treat HIV/AIDS, or preexisting disorders (treat or refer them for treatment).

    b. Work cooperatively with medical personnel.

    c. Have goals that the client can achieve.

    d. Be sensitive to culture and ethnicity.

    e. Assess mental health in the context of the client's problem.

    f. Be sensitive to medications used: diagnose carefully; see that medications are started slowly and at low dosage; know the symptoms of drug interactions; be sensitive to prescription medications that could be used in a suicide attempt; make sure a Hepatitis A and B vaccine is given if necessary, because most intravenous drug users are positive for Hepatitis C, and the CDC recommends this vaccine for people who test positive; and use support groups.

- Case management: Work on a multidisciplinary team (choose who is on the team, examine the nature of the team, develop team norms, have one person lead the team, evaluate the group, address how to work with barriers, and look for resources for the client).

- Counseling:

    a. Examine your own attitudes and experiences.

b. Obtain needed training.

c. Look for other areas to address in terms of priority: "substance abuse treatment, medical care, housing, mental health care, nutritional care, dental care, ancillary services and support systems" (p. xxiv).

d. Ensure confidentiality with test results.

e. Keep in mind socioeconomic status and acculturation level with different cultural groups.

f. Use support services.

g. Examine views of death and dying, end-of-life health care options, and preparing children for the loss of parents.

- Ethically: Have someone with whom to resolve ethical dilemmas.

- Legally:

a. Be familiar with federal and state laws on disability in order to advocate against discrimination clients may experience in obtaining services.

b. Consider federal and state laws regarding confidentiality.

c. Examine the "duty to warn" issues carefully.

Finally, clients in substance abuse treatment need to be informed of the following (K. Norins, personal communication):

- A monogamous relationship is best in terms of prevention.

- If the client or his or her partner has not been tested 12 weeks following a sexual encounter with someone else, there is no way of knowing if the client or the partner is infected with the virus. Testing needs to be done 12 weeks after any other partner.

- The client needs to be aware that individuals are most infectious within the first 12 weeks they have been infected.

- Anyone who has HIV/AIDS can be reinfected because of different subclades of HIV, and the disease can then progress more quickly.

- There have been medical advances that have resulted in medication that requires doses only once a day and a reduction in pill load.

- If medication can be used to attain a nondetectable viral load in the mother, babies can be delivered without being infected when medication is also administered to the mother during delivery and to the baby for 4 to 6 weeks following birth. (See Case Study 6.4.)

CASE STUDY 6.4

William is a 25-year-old male who has used drugs intravenously. He shared needles with his older brother, who died of AIDS about 1 year ago. William entered chemical dependency treatment because he was diagnosed 1 week earlier as being HIV-positive (he had seen a doctor at a public clinic because he felt ill). He decided to come to treatment because he wanted to die with more peace than his brother did. After 3 weeks in treatment, he told his counselor in an individual session that he saw no point in trying to stay drug free. He said he was going to die no matter what, and he wanted to die without any anxiety (e.g., being high on heroin). William shared that he had always felt down about life since his teenage years, and he did not know "what possessed me a few weeks ago" to think that life could be any different.

1. What tentative co-occurring diagnosis might you give William?
2. What would be your first intervention strategy with him?
3. What overall plan would you develop for dealing with his issues?
4. Are there any portions of his story that would make it difficult for you to work with him?

EXERCISE 6.4

Imagine the setting in which you work or anticipate working as a counselor. If you saw a client who was triple diagnosis (substance abuse, mental health, HIV/AIDS), how would you answer the following four questions:

1. Where would you begin your treatment approach?
2. What limitations might you experience working with this person?
3. What limitations might there be in the system where you work as you work with this person?
4. How might you overcome these limitations in yourself? In the system?

INTIMATE PARTNER VIOLENCE

Intimate partner violence (IPV) has also been called *domestic violence* and *household terrorism* (van Wormer & Davis, 2008). Intimate partner violence is verbal, psychological, or physical force that is intentionally used by a family member toward another family member (SAMHSA, 1997). Violence is more commonly caused by family members or partners than strangers (Acierno, Coffey, & Resnick, 2003). Greene and Bogo (2002) describe two types of IPV: (1) patriarchal terrorism (violence is used for control over the partner, typically males are perpetrators), and (2) common couple violence (violence can be started by either person and emerges as an argument escalates without the dynamic of control being present). Patriarchal terrorism, in comparison with common couple violence, typically involves more severe violence and fear of the perpetrator. Patriarchal terrorism is focused on in this chapter.

IPV and chemical abuse/dependency appear to be two issues that overlap. They commonly coexist, which means that women and children are in danger (Bednar, 2003; Macy & Goodbourn, 2012). U.S. Department of Justice statistics (2005) found offenders were more likely to be drinking or using drugs. Alcohol/drug use may be high in battering situations, but there does not appear to be evidence that it *causes* battering (National Woman Abuse Prevention Project, 1989; Walker, 1984). Some perpetrators may lose impulse control when using, whereas others use it to excuse their behavior or justify behavior they have planned (Jacobson & Gottman, 1998). In addition, some women who are battered have alcohol/drug use problems (Eberle, 1982); that is, women who abuse substances may find partners who do the same or they self-medicate their situation through using alcohol/drugs (Gomberg & Nirenberg, 1991). The National Woman Abuse Prevention Project found that 7% to 14% of battered women have alcohol abuse problems. Therefore, alcohol and drugs are frequently involved in IPV situations, whether it is the batterer or the victim or both using them. An example of this overlap of the two areas is with female batterers who use alcohol/drugs, where counselors are encouraged to assess and treat for both problems when one (the battering) is presented (Stuart et al., 2013).

Because the use of substances is considered a risk factor for intimate partner violence and failure to deal with IPV issues can result in relapse of substance use (SAMHSA, 1997), the counselor who works with individuals who are addicted needs to understand how the dynamics of IPV interact with addiction. The counselor also needs to work in a coordinated, teamwork approach with IPV specialists in the community to control the behavior of batterers and assist survivors in being safe. Some examples of such collaboration include: (a) substance abuse treatment centers and women's shelters (Macy & Goodbourn, 2012; van Wormer & Davis, 2008) and (b) legal and mental health assistance resources (Wright & Johnson, 2012).

The two fields, chemical dependency and IPV, have typically not worked closely with each other. The Minnesota Coalition for Battered Women (MCBW; 1992) states that there is a lack of services for women in IPV situations that adequately address both areas. There are also barriers between these programs (Levy & Brekke, 1990; Rogan, 1985; J. Wright & Popham, 1982) that are based on different points of view and a lack of experience (Bennett & Lawson, 1994). Bennett and Lawson found in their study that substance abuse programs are less likely to refer to domestic violence programs, and they further state that conflict around how self-control is interpreted is one of the largest problems: IPV programs view the violence as intentional and hold the batterer totally responsible for the violence, whereas the addictions programs studied believed in the disease model of addiction, which indicates that the addict is not in control of his or her behavior. Additionally, barriers include a lack of training in both areas, limited monies, and fragmented systems (government, legal, policy) (Macy & Goodbourn, 2012) and difficulties accessing basic safety services (housing, legal, crisis, medical) (Edmond, Bowland, & Yu, 2013).

G. Miller (1997) provides a summary of the barriers and bridges between the fields:

- Barriers:
  a. Philosophical differences (sobriety first versus safety first).
  b. Stereotypes (of the helping professionals of both fields) toward one another.
  c. Disagreement about systemic violence (each partner has an equal part), mediation (each person has equal power), codependency (each person has equal responsibility for the violence), and causal views of substance abuse and violence (which comes first).

- Bridges:
  a. Hold clients responsible for their behavior and choices.
  b. Avoid making moral judgments about behavior and choices.
  c. Emphasize the impact of behavior and choices on the client and others.

G. Miller (1997) recommends that counselors in both areas be aware of their myths and stereotypes of one another, attend training in the other area to be aware of broad warning signs, and know counselors in the other area with whom they feel comfortable seeking consultation and making referrals. This view is also supported by a review of the literature done by Macy and Goodbourn (2012)—they also make additional recommendations for future practice and policy that the reader may find helpful.

Diagnosis/Assessment

Findings such as those just discussed underscore the importance of counselors becoming aware of the dynamics of IPV. The overlap requires a counselor to assess for both (van Wormer & Davis, 2008). If the violence is not assessed and addressed in addiction treatment and/or recovery, the addicted individual may be more prone to relapse. Also, if the violence is not adequately addressed, the family may believe that once the addict sobers up, the violence will stop. The indications are that an addicted individual with a propensity for violence has two problems: the addiction and the violence (MCBW, 1992). Because of the high frequency of males with substance abuse problems and IPV in treatment settings, both need to be addressed for treatment to be effective. There is some evidence that a history of childhood physical abuse is related to IPV perpetration (Edwards, Dixon, Gidycz, & Desai, 2013), therefore, counselors working with clients who have a history of childhood physical abuse may want to assess for the presence of IPV. Safety must be assessed quickly in treatment so anyone at risk is protected (Washton & Zweben, 2008). Once again, although a general addiction professional can do a broad screening for domestic violence, the professional needs to be ready to consult and refer to a domestic violence expert if it is determined to be present.

Before working with individuals in IPV situations, the counselor would be well served to examine any personal beliefs about IPV. The MCBW (1992) states three common myths about IPV: (1) battering occurs because of low self-esteem in the batterer; (2) battering occurs because the batterer loses control of emotions; and (3) battering is a disease. The MCBW responds to those myths by pointing out that many individuals with low self-esteem do not batter, the batterer batters in order to maintain control, and violence is a learned behavior.

Although both men and women have the potential to be batterers, 95% of all domestic violence assaults are crimes committed by men toward women (National Coalition Against Domestic Violence, n.d.). As a result, the following discussion for assessment primarily focuses on men as batterers and women as victims. Note that women most vulnerable are single, separated, or divorced and that the poor and people with limited education may appear more on records because they do not have the resources to prevent the record keeping ("Countering Domestic Violence," 2004).

The counselor working with an IPV situation needs to be able to make an assessment both of the batterer and of the victim, because either individual could be the client. Assessment instruments are provided by SAMHSA (1997). A counselor using such instruments to assess for IPV needs to remember that all violence is not physical, as demonstrated in the power and control wheel (see Figure 6.1). An example of a scale that can be used for psychological and emotional abuse in women is the Women's Experiences Battering Scale (WEB; P. H. Smith, Earp, & DeVillis, 1995). Brekke (1987) advocates an approach called *funneling*, which means bringing up the topic of abuse gradually to obtain complete information. This technique can be applied both to batterers and victims. The counselor may also find it more beneficial to interview the couple separately to obtain information about the violence. Otherwise, the victim may say little in the session out of fear of being abused later. In the case of the batterer, the counselor can look for some specific indicators (Brekke, 1987): hostility, rigid view of sex roles, patriarchal attitude, history of family of origin abuse, sense of women victimizing him, lack of significant nonfamily relationships, jealousy (extreme), difficulty recognizing emotions other than anger, and dependency on partner for emotional needs (extreme).

SAMHSA (1997) makes 11 specific suggestions in the assessment of batterers:

1. Ask questions about violence (in the third person) to determine whether the person ever views it as justified.

2. Make questions specific and concrete.

3. Be direct and candid.

4. Learn typical excuses batterers give for behavior.

5. Do not allow substances to be blamed for violence.

6. Consider a collateral interview done by an IPV expert with the partner to determine dangerousness.

7. Have the batterer sign a no-violence contract during treatment.

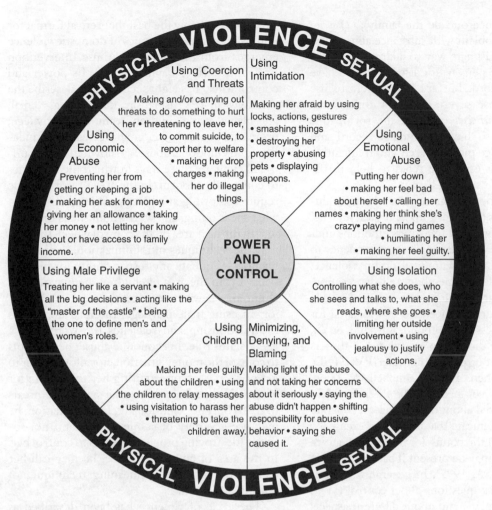

Figure 6.1 Power and Control Wheel

Source: Domestic Abuse Intervention Project, 202 East Superior Street, Duluth, Minnesota 55802 (218) 722-2781. www.theduluthmodel.org Reprinted by permission.

8. Examine the relationship between substance use and violence (when it occurs, how much occurs when using, what substances/feelings occur before violence occurs, and the possible use of substances to recover from violence).

9. Develop strategies with the client to manage behaviors and emotions based on information that develops from examination of the relationship between substance use and violence.

10. Watch for batterers using a 12-step philosophy to excuse violence.

11. Refer to Batterers Anonymous groups only after there is focused treatment on battering and a period of nonviolence.

Gondolf (1992) describes three types of batterers: (1) *typical* (have an absence of mental illness/ personality/substance abuse disorders, criminal record, or violence outside the family); (2) *socio-pathic* (have a problem with substance abuse, view violence as a legitimate way to address concerns, and possibly are personality disordered and have no criminal record, but are more likely to use weapons or cause severe injury or threaten to kill); and (3) *antisocial* (are like the sociopathic category but also have a criminal record and engage in violence more severely and frequently). A counselor can use these types to help in the assessment process of the batterer.

In the woman, the counselor can look for different symptoms (Brekke, 1987): physical injuries, depression, being afraid to express emotions and/or sexual intimacy, depersonalization, tendency to be passive, history of family of origin violence, hostility toward family members, self-deprecation, concern for children's safety (extreme), and suicide attempts. The survivor needs to be evaluated for PTSD and depression (Edmond, Bowland, & Yu, 2013), especially those who are substance abusers because of the strong overlap between IPV, PTSD, and SUDs (Cohen, Field, Campbell, & Hien, 2013). The survivor needs to be interviewed in private, to be asked about the violence in concrete ways, and communicate that there is no excuse for the violence; and the counselor needs to be aware that child abuse may be present if partner abuse is present (SAMHSA, 1997). In general, the counselor needs to ask questions about control (Who controls the money?) and about different aspects of abuse (e.g., psychological) besides physical, remembering that battered women may not look abused. Overall, the counselor needs to understand the type of IPV experienced, the relationship dynamics, the social support network available, child maltreatment history, early dating violence, and current mental health functioning (Bogat, Garcia, & Levendosky, 2013).

Psychologically battered is a term that has been used to describe women who have not been physically or sexually assaulted, but do experience "fear, loss of control, and entrapment" (Coker, Smith, McKeown, & King, 2000, p. 553). The counselor needs to let the woman know her story is believed and that she is not responsible for the situation. Probably the best theoretical format for understanding the dynamics of domestic violence emerges from the Domestic Abuse Intervention Project (Pence & Paymar, 1993). Its power and control wheel has eight sections that describe the dynamics of IPV: isolation; minimizing, denial, and blame; using children; using male privilege; economic abuse; coercion and threats; intimidation; and emotional abuse, as shown in Figure 6.1.

All eight areas are ways in which the man tries to control the woman. In the area of isolation, he requires knowing at all times where she is going, what she is doing, and with whom she is interacting. In the next area on the control wheel, the man may use techniques of minimization, denial, and blame to eliminate any responsibility for his own behavior. In the area of children, he may use the children as pawns to control the woman's behavior. In using male privilege, the man dominates the relationship and relegates the woman to a lesser status role. In economic abuse, he attempts to control the money situation, not allowing her to get or keep a job or requiring her to ask him for money. In the area of threats, he may make threats to try to hurt her emotionally. In intimidation, he may use a variety of subtle (looks) and not-so-subtle (destroying property) means to control her. In the area of emotional abuse, he may call her names or find other demeaning techniques of putting her down.

The cycle of violence has been described as having three phases (Walker, 1979). In Phase 1, there is an increase in tension between the partners, as evidenced in increased fighting. In Phase 2, the battering occurs in any of the eight forms listed in the power and control wheel. In Phase 3, the relationship enters a calm phase, where the male is remorseful for his behavior. It is in the third phase that the batterer who uses alcohol/drugs may report that the abuse occurred because he had been high or drunk.

Counseling Approaches

Walker (1980) says that counselors often have inadequate training in addressing domestic violence. Some view the problem as a family problem (MCBW, 1992) or one caused by addiction concepts such as codependency (Frank & Golden, 1992): Neither concept holds the batterer wholly accountable for the violence. Viewing the problem as a family one and involving techniques such as mediation is based on an equal relationship, which is the opposite of the IPV situation (Golden & Frank, 1994). Therapists who work in that modality may actually endanger the battered woman (A. Jones & Schechter, 1992). In the labeling of codependence, the battered woman is a blamed victim again, in that she may be viewed as sharing the responsibility for the violence or as staying in the relationship because of something internally wrong with her. The label does not take into account the reality of the situation she faces with the batterer (Frank & Golden, 1992). The danger of these labels for the batterer is that he may view his violence as due to the woman's participation in the violent behavior (family problems, codependence issues, etc.).

As discussed in other chapters on addiction, the counselor needs to be aware of how his or her countertransference issues may emerge. Male counselors, for instance, might dismiss the violence experienced by the woman as not as intense as she describes it because of a lack of empathy for the oppression of women or a lack of awareness of their own struggles with anger. Female counselors, for example, might become angry at the woman for not leaving or might lack an understanding of how IPV can erode a woman's self-esteem and confidence. In male or female counselors, past experiences with family members or friends who left or did not leave abusive situations may influence their view of the struggle (e.g., wanting their clients to do the work that their loved ones were not able to do in their own lives).

If the counselor experiences intolerance when counseling a battered woman, the counselor needs to examine the need to resolve the situation quickly, as well as learn to live with the fear of being concerned about the client's safety. The battered woman's choices and control need to be respected. Information on available resources such as shelter, legal, and housing need to be provided, as well as an awareness of how the client perceives these resources and who tends to use them. Providing information on what she can expect with the referral process to resources can also assist the client in accessing additional supports.

The counselor needs to stress safety throughout the counseling process and, if the battered woman decides to stay in the situation, help her figure out how she can make it most safe for herself. The counselor needs to see the primary counseling role as one of providing information and support. Yet, counselors need to know their own limits in working in this area and find a balance between providing concrete options and information and forcing their own opinions.

The counselor can also ask the following three questions in ongoing work with a client in this situation:

1. Have you been hurt (slapped, pushed, shoved) or threatened since I last saw you?

2. Tell me the obstacles around your leaving.

3. What am I doing that is helpful/not helpful? Or, is this helpful? Does this make sense?

Washton and Zweben (2008, p. 228) add two additional questions:

1. Do you feel safe in your current relationship?

2. Is there a partner from a previous relationship making you feel unsafe now?

The counselor can focus on five statements as a guide when a woman says she cannot leave a violent situation:

1. I am afraid for your safety (gets at denial of danger and excuses).

2. I am afraid for the safety of your children (may help motivate the client).

3. It will only get worse (provides a reality check).

4. I am here for you when you are ready to leave (provides information and support).

5. You do not deserve to be abused (provides education and support).

Before discussing specific treatment approaches with survivors, the counselor needs to be aware of barriers in the survivor's escape or survival with regard to the violence. These barriers include abuser retaliation, inconsistent legal responses, lack of shelters, low income, loss of child custody, lack of housing, societal expectations, the myth of gender equality, and limited or negative assistance from family clergy and counselors (MCBW, 1992).

The MCBW (1992) states six requisites for counselors working with survivors:

1. Safety of the woman should always be top priority.

2. The goal of counseling should be to empower the woman.

3. The therapy should be client based, with a focus on mutuality.

4. The therapy needs to take into account sociopolitical forces that are larger than the woman and her history and relationship.

5. Ethnicity and culture need to be considered in the counseling process.

6. The counselor should never take a stance of blaming the victim.

The woman whose partner is in addiction treatment needs the therapist to think of her safety and advocate for her in clinical decisions. She also needs to be given the option of participation in the man's treatment and told that addiction and battering are separate issues (MCBW, 1992). The woman in addiction treatment needs to be educated about the different issues of battering and addiction, be provided with an advocate, and be given information about support for surviving the battering situation (MCBW, 1992). Although a woman might drink or use drugs to cope with the battering, she needs to be reminded repeatedly that she cannot make the best decisions of survival for herself and her children if she is drunk or high.

It may be best for the counselor to assess all women, whether they or their partners are in addiction treatment or recovery, for IPV. Women may not report abuse due to feelings of shame, humiliation, and fear (Hien et al., 2009). Some of these indicators are outlined by SAMHSA (1997): history of treatment relapse or noncompliance, untreated injuries (face, neck, throat, breasts) or inconsistent or evasive answers about injuries, pregnancy complications, physical problems that are stress or anxiety related, and sadness, depression, or talk of suicide. If the woman does admit to IPV, she needs to be believed by the counselor, and a safety or protection plan needs to be developed for her. Even if the woman insists that the violence will not occur again, the counselor needs to encourage her to prepare for the worst and give her a chance to rehearse what she will do if the violence does occur.

A safety plan needs to include (Hodges, 1993) hiding extra money, car keys, and important papers in a safe place she can access quickly; keeping a packed suitcase hidden somewhere (inside or outside the house, at a friend's or relative's, etc.); having phone numbers of the local shelter and support network individuals available; giving a signal to children or neighbors that the police should be called; and knowing where to go in case of an emergency. It may underscore the seriousness of her situation and help her to clarify these thoughts if the counselor draws up a simple checklist form that addresses each of these areas. Also, online guidelines are available at www .ncadv.org/protectyourself/SafetyPlan.php.

Women may address the issue of battering either individually and/or in groups. Emphasis should be on encouraging safety, giving gifts to themselves, moving out of the situation at the individual's own pace, working with the fear of failure, stressing positive aspects of the woman and her life, enjoying laughter, and sharing and being supportive to others (M. S. Goodman &

Fallon, 1995). It is also critical to emphasize that the woman assert her rights, process her difficulties leaving, set boundaries with others, make decisions, and work through her feelings (Goodman & Fallon, 1995). In addition to a focus on safety, counselors also need to help survivors reduce how much they minimize the abuse (Bogat et al., 2013). Van Wormer and Davis (2008) encourage the use of the stages-of-change and motivational interviewing models to assist survivors in feeling empowered and having options. Survivors who have more psychopathology, distress, and social support may be more ready to change and thus seek services (N. Johnson & Johnson, 2013). Therefore, counselors who want to enhance the chances for treatment effectiveness may want to assist the survivor in building a strong support network.

Most critically, the counselor needs to work at providing the battered woman with information about the IPV situation and then work at letting her make her own decisions. It is very important for the counselor to avoid conveying information in a critical, judgmental attitude that may cause her to blame herself further and to isolate from others. Rather, the counselor needs to give the client a safe place to talk about the violence and her options because of the complexity of the decision to stay in or leave the relationship (Hien et al., 2009). In a group, same-sex groups that are nonconfrontational are helpful (SAMHSA, 1997). Also, in residential treatment, communication needs to be monitored, because the batterer may continue to harass her in treatment. Two resources are the National Domestic Violence Hotline (800-799-SAFE; www.ndvh.org) and the National Coalition Against Domestic Violence (303-839-1852; www.ncadv.org).

As to the batterer, the counselor needs to take a different focus. Many times, batterers underestimate the violence and/or shift the blame to the survivor and/or other life circumstances (Adams & McCormick, 1982). The counselor needs to avoid being seduced by the defense mechanisms of projection and denial and hold the batterer accountable for his behavior. Also, as mentioned earlier, batterers who are also addicted need to be educated that the violence is a separate problem that needs to be addressed and that battering is a crime (MCBW, 1992). If possible, the counselor can refer the client to a program that works specifically with batterers or to an integrated treatment program that addresses both issues (Bednar, 2003). Because of how significantly these areas can overlap, it is recommended to have simultaneous treatment for both issues rather than what typically occurs at present, which is sequential or separate treatment (Langender, 2013). Holding substance abusing batterers accountable for both areas may enhance their awareness of the areas and their overlap as well as enhance treatment effectiveness (Langender, 2013).

The violence by the batterer is an intentional act to gain power, and the goal in therapy is to stop the violent behavior (Edelson & Tolman, 1992). It is important to assess how the man has been abusive—how severely and how often. The batterer may experience intimate relationships with women as being dangerous and uncontrollable; this view, in combination with a high power need and a low verbal ability to assert himself, results in violence (Edelson & Tolman, 1992). Batterers also seem to have high levels of depression and suicide (Ganley & Harris, 1978), are angrier than nonviolent men (Barnett & Planeaux, 1989), and have negative, sexist attitudes toward women (Edelson & Tolman, 1992).

Group intervention with batterers may be helpful, because they are receiving support from other men to be nonviolent: This holds them accountable for the violence and helps them learn ways to be nonviolent (Edelson & Tolman, 1992). The batterer's attitudes have to change to being responsible for all abusive behavior, having empathy for their partners, accepting confrontation from others, being aware of their socialization process (Edelson & Tolman, 1992), and being more aware of violence cycle cues (e.g., situational, cognitive, emotional, and physical). They need to sign an agreement to be nonviolent, become aware of their emotions (particularly those underlying the anger), learn to manage their arousal, take time-outs when upset, restructure their thoughts, and learn assertiveness and conflict resolution skills (Edelson & Tolman, 1992). Van Wormer and Davis (2008) recommend the use of the stages-of-change and motivational interviewing models in batterers' groups to establish rapport and invite behavior change. Female batterers treated in groups have reported that the connections and bonds they formed in the group (with both other participants and facilitators) and the anger management and negative emotion management skills were helpful to them (T. Walker, 2013).

Couples treatment should occur only when (1) the man has made a commitment to be nonviolent, demonstrated this commitment by participating in treatment for the battering, and shown a commitment to nonviolence over time; (2) the woman feels safe; and (3) the couple wants to stay together (Edelson & Tolman, 1992). This treatment requires time, energy, and commitment on the part of the couple. A counselor would probably be most effective by requiring an evaluation of the couple before beginning work with them by an expert in the area of IPV to determine whether couple's counseling is appropriate. Van Wormer and Davis (2008) recommend couples and family counseling only after successful treatment of the batterer, with safety being the top consideration.

Related Issues

Robinson (2003) states that violence toward women by men is due to sexism, relationship power differentials, and cultural/religious beliefs that encourage the imbalance of power in the relationship. Other issues such as family, religious, legal, and multicultural aspects enter into the reality of addressing IPV issues. Each of these is briefly examined here to heighten the counselor's sensitivity to these concerns.

A battered woman can experience a wide range of family reactions to the domestic violence. Family members may offer support (emotional, physical, and financial), advice, transportation, and care

of children. However, some family members of the battered woman may take a cold, detached stance with regard to assisting. Because of the batterer's control over the survivor, contact with the family may be limited, which may make bringing up the topic of abuse awkward and result in the family blaming the survivor for the abuse (MCBW, 1992). The counselor needs to assess the client's relationship with family, regardless of whether the client is the batterer or the survivor. The closeness of the client to family and how strongly the family views the situation will affect the client's views and decision-making process.

Battered women who are involved with religion may bring religious issues into the counseling setting (Whipple, 1987). Walker (1979) and Straus, Gelles, and Steinmetz (1980) report that IPV occurs across different religions. Although religions have cultural values, there may be a lot of variety within a religious group as to the beliefs it adheres to (Hines & Malley-Morrison, 2005). Concepts such as faith, forgiveness, submission, and a lack of acceptance of divorce may encourage a battered woman to remain in the relationship regardless of the level of damage to her and/or her family (Whipple, 1987). Depending on the woman's religion, other idiosyncratic aspects of her religion may be a place of struggle for her. The counselor is advised to:

- Have the woman educate the counselor about her religion in general. (If appropriate, the counselor might do some research on the religion.)

- Have the woman educate the counselor about the specific religious creeds that seem to inhibit her taking an active response to IPV.

- Work with the woman to find disagreement in religious creeds or in the lives of other parishioners that question any directives to remain in the IPV situation.

- Work with the woman to find positive directives about relationships and views of women in religious creeds as well as in lives of other parishioners.

- If possible, offer to connect the woman with a religious figure of her faith who has an understanding of IPV issues to facilitate a processing of spiritual concerns.

Women survivors have also reported that their spirituality helped them move from a survival mode to resiliency and healing (Drumm et al., 2013). Counselors, then, may want to use some of the techniques discussed in Chapter 12 to facilitate spiritual resources for the client.

For the counselor working with a batterer, a similar process can be followed. Even though the steps are similar, the counselor can work to help the batterer see that he does not have a right to perpetuate the violence.

All counselors must be aware of legal issues surrounding IPV concerns. Some state bar associations (e.g., North Carolina Bar Association, 1995) publish legal guides for survivors of IPV. The counselor needs to determine how the law defines IPV, provides protection against IPV, and allows for criminal and/or civil charges to be filed. If the counselor does not have the time to obtain all of this information, it may be helpful to contact the state bar association, a local attorney, or a local IPV shelter for a summary of use of the legal system to hold batterers accountable for their behavior and/or to support survivors of the abuse. Another option is to contact the National Coalition Against Domestic Violence or the state coalitions in which the counselor works. If the counselor works at an agency, it may be beneficial to have someone at the agency become specialized in domestic violence situations, given the frequency of the crossover between substance abuse and IPV.

Knowledge of the legal issues is critical in assisting individuals in IPV situations. Many states have temporary orders of protection or temporary restraining orders that protect women from future abuse (Ferraro, 1993). Civil protective orders (CPOs) are the most widely used response

(Wright & Johnson, 2012). Some batterers respond to social controls and public humiliation; legal charges may reach them in ways that other information does not. However, it is important to keep in mind that a restraining order is just a piece of paper and that some batterers have no respect for or fear of the law. Survivors need to know what their rights are and the limits of legal protection so that they can make decisions that are best for them. There is evidence that supports improved mental health in survivors that have a CPO (Wright & Johnson, 2012). In addition, it is helpful to know of local attorneys, magistrates, and judges who have an understanding of IPV.

Five possible legal considerations for clients are:

1. Have legal representation or consultation with an attorney who is familiar with family law and the local legal system.

2. Be aware that filing a protection order will start a civil lawsuit and could set off a legal chain reaction, so legal consultation about the ramifications of filing could be helpful.

3. If filing for a protection order does not work or is not a good option, a legal representative may be able to recommend other laws to the client.

4. The client needs to be serious about filing claims: using the law to protect herself against the threat of violence, and if she decides to later drop the case, dropping it through legal channels rather than being a no-show.

5. If photo documentation is used, provide good pictures with a close-up of the injury and an overall shot of the area so it is obvious that the close-up is of the woman. Labels for the pictures need to include information such as: on the front, her name, date of photo, explanation of the picture; and on the back, name and title of person who took the photo, date of the assault, and how the assault occurred (e.g., punched repeatedly in the face). If a woman has just experienced a beating, she may want to have the photos taken as the bruises rise. She

may want to keep the pictures in her record or take them with her.

Minorities are not immune to battering. Individuals from sexual orientation or ethnic minorities typically experience discrimination and may be concerned about the increase in discrimination they may face if they discuss the IPV situation. Regarding gay/lesbian populations, IPV is under-reported, and there is evidence of a relationship between IPV and alcohol/drug abuse (Cabaj, 2008).

Peterman and Dixon (2003) summarize some of the realities facing the gay/lesbian population on IPV: (a) IPV is involved in 25% to 30% of all same-sex relationships; (b) it is the third highest-ranking health problem among gay men; and (c) it occurs in one of four lesbian relationships. If gays and lesbians discuss the battering in their relationship, they will also be coming out to the counselor about their sexual preference at the same time. This reality may inhibit their disclosure of the battering in the counseling relationship. Also, Leeder (1988) reports that many of the dynamics of violence are similar to heterosexual couples, but the counselor needs to be especially aware of counter-transference issues related to sexual orientation, whatever the counselor's sexual orientation.

Finally, Benowitz (1986) states that lesbians in abusive relationships may have difficulty admitting to the battering because of fears of community reactions and the belief that lesbians cannot be abusers, so it is ignored or silenced in the lesbian community (Peterman & Dixon, 2003). Police may ignore the reality of gay/lesbian battering because of their homophobia and may be less likely to intervene on the violence because of a tendency to see this group as deviant and thereby experiencing violence as a way of life (Ferraro, 1993). They may also believe that this group deserves to be battered due to internalizing the culture's negative view of them (Peterman & Dixon, 2003).

Once they do reach out for help, there may be complications. For example, lesbian abusers may go to shelters under the guise of being victims to find their partners, and gay men may find few shelters that will take them or can only give them hotel vouchers (Peterman & Dixon, 2003). Also, legal and social services are typically designed to meet the needs of heterosexual couples; therefore, gays and lesbians are not supported or protected in the same way as heterosexuals (Peterman & Dixon, 2003). Lastly, Hines and Malley-Morrison (2005) state there is little data on transgender IPV, possibly because of the small number of individuals who make up this population.

As to racial minorities, the findings are conflicting as to if there is higher, same, or lower percentages of incidents of IPV (Hien et al., 2009). E. White (1994) reports that even though African-American women can be sensitive to the oppression and racism that African-American men experience, this does not mean that the woman needs to tolerate abuse. In traditional Latino immigrant families, when typical gender roles are threatened, there may be an increase of violence (Hien et al., 2009). IPV is also an issue in Asian and South Asian immigrant groups. When an ethnic minority woman does consider reporting the abuse, she may also be aware that, historically, police have oppressed people of color and have higher arrest rates for racial minority groups (Ferraro, 1993). Furthermore, these oppressed groups may be viewed by police as deviants who experience violence as a way of life, thereby inhibiting police intervention on the violence (Ferraro, 1993).

Depending on the individual's ethnic minority, there may be other barriers to reporting violence. Immigrant women may be more isolated, increasing the odds of ongoing family violence (Hien et al., 2009). The individual may experience cultural and/or language barriers, be afraid of deportation, and experience poverty limitations (North Carolina Coalition Against Domestic Violence, 1995). The counselor needs to be aware of how each of these areas may inhibit the individual from addressing the battering situation. The counselor needs to approach the ethnic minority client with these different factors in mind.

Another consideration is the geographic area in which the client lives. G. Miller, Clark, and

Herman (2007) report some of the issues related to IPV in a rural setting and make recommendations to professionals working with survivors in those settings.

Finally, Hines and Malley-Morrison (2005) discuss the vulnerability of the disabled to IPV. The authors state that a physical or mental disability can make an individual vulnerable to abuse. In particular, they are vulnerable to abuse from their caregivers. They state it is unclear if this population is more mistreated than women who are not disabled; however, there is evidence that women who are disabled physically may have longer periods of physical and sexual abuse.

Counselors working with addicted individuals need to keep in mind the frequent crossover between the areas of IPV and substance abuse.

Focus on IPV issues needs to occur at all levels of addiction counseling: assessment and diagnosis, treatment, and recovery. (See Case Study 6.5.)

HOMELESSNESS

Since the early 1980s, research with the homeless has shown high rates of mental illness and substance abuse, both severe in nature and more common with this population than in the general population (Koegel, Burnam, & Baumohl, 1996). Homeless people have been called resistant to treatment, but it may be more related to not seeing treatment as pertinent until their basic needs of food and shelter are provided for (SAMHSA, 1997).

CASE STUDY 6.5

June is a 41-year-old female who has entered addiction treatment for the third time. She has been sent to treatment each time by her husband of 23 years. He threatens to leave her if she does not stop the pills and the alcohol, so she goes to treatment. After 2 weeks of treatment, she has confidentially admitted to you that she has trouble staying sober because her husband beats her frequently. She reveals that she never told any of her previous counselors about this situation, because she did not want to admit that she had an affair during the early years of her marriage. June says that her husband began beating her when she told him about the affair shortly after it happened. She stated that he agreed not to bring it up in her treatment if she did not bring up his abuse. He tells her he would never have beaten her if she had not had an affair.

June is afraid to call an IPV shelter or take out a restraining order on her husband because of his threats of violence ("I'll kill you if you leave me"). She says he is a churchgoing man who is very kind to her in public but very critical of her in private. According to June, the pills and the alcohol help her forget the pain and cope with her life. She drinks with her husband and says that he does not mind her alcohol use, but he does not like her taking Valium and Xanax because she becomes "listless." They have one son, age 22, who, according to June, was never hit by his father and never witnessed his father's violence toward his mother.

1. What aspects of June's story are typical for a survivor of IPV?

2. What would be your first priority in counseling her?

3. How would you help June address the IPV situation?

4. What internal and external barriers inhibit June from addressing the IPV situation in a different way?

EXERCISE 6.5

Take turns responding with another person to each of seven items regarding IPV:

1. I believe I have (would have) an easier time working with (choose batterers or survivors) because. . . .
2. Working with survivors, my main strength is and my main weakness is. . . .
3. The best counseling I did with a survivor was. . . .
4. The most difficult counseling I did with a survivor was. . . .
5. Working with perpetrators, my main strength is and my main weakness is. . . .
6. The best counseling I did with a perpetrator was. . . .
7. The most difficult counseling I did with a perpetrator was. . . .

Now respond to the same statements with regard to rape and sexual abuse.

Alcoholism is common among homeless people, because they drink to cope and to socialize (Daly, 1996). Homelessness causes stress, and people use alcohol and drugs to cope with the stress (van Wormer & Davis, 2008). The subculture of homelessness allows for heavy drinking (Schutt & Garrett, 1992).

There is a relationship between homelessness and mental illness. Often, the chronically mentally ill have been deinstitutionalized, which may result in alcoholism (Daly, 1996). However, while homelessness may cause mental health and substance abuse problems, these problems may also cause homelessness (Koegel et al., 1996). For most homeless alcoholics, heavy drinking is present before the homelessness (Schutt & Garrett, 1992). Their problems of homelessness, substance abuse, and mental health may all interact to make treatment for these problems difficult: Mental health and substance abuse issues may keep them from homeless programs, and their homelessness may keep them from receiving help from mental health and substance abuse programs (Oakley & Dennis, 1996).

Additionally, street drugs such as crack may cause the homeless to be dangerous and violent (Director, 1995). Counselors working with the homeless population or clients who have a history of homelessness need to be sensitive to the possibility that the client has one or both (substance abuse and mental health) problems. Having a broad assessment instrument for substance abuse as a regular part of the intake process with someone who is homeless or has a history of it can help the counselor determine if a referral is needed to determine if a substance abuse problem is present. The corollary is true for mental health issues. For example, the inclusion of a mental status exam discussed in Chapter 3 can assist in the determination of a referral need for further assessment. Because co-occurring diagnosis is especially common in the homeless, in prisons, and in mental hospitals, both broad substance abuse and mental health instruments need to be included when counselors are working with these populations.

Scheffler (2004) states that the first priority is to help the person obtain housing, which enhances substance abuse treatment. This approach is called the "Housing First" one that has a harm reduction focus in contrast with the "Treatment First" (treatment that requires abstinence) (Henwood, Padgett, & Tiderington, 2013; Padgett, Stanhope, Henwood, & Stefancic, 2011), with the Housing First approach having a more positive impact (Padgett et al., 2011). Also note that in a review of the literature, Hwang, Tolomiczenko, Kouyoumdjian, and Garner (2005) found that case management resulted in less substance use, supporting coordinated treatment programs for the homeless. Case management services include engaging the clients, developing a plan, doing crisis intervention, networking, monitoring needs and progress, and advocating for them (Scheffler, 2004).

Homeless clients may be difficult to treat because of the high rates of mental illness and substance abuse (Koegel et al., 1996) in combination with their state of homelessness. Programs that focus on their homelessness may be reluctant to treat these individuals because of their mental health and/or substance abuse problems, and the state of homelessness may complicate working with them in mental health and substance abuse programs (Oakley & Dennis, 1996). Also, the homeless often have practical problems (i.e., housing, food, money), are mobile, and have a general mistrust of helping agencies (Schutt & Garrett, 1992). In addition, they often have health problems, are unemployed, have criminal histories (both as victims and perpetrators), are cross-addicted, and are socially isolated. These numerous problems may cause counselors not to view them as "good" patients (Stahler, 1995). Often, they are placed at the end of waiting lists for treatment because of a lack of money and identification (Joseph & Paone, 1997).

Counseling Approaches

Homeless clients often provide misinformation about their alcohol/drug use (Schutt & Garrett, 1992). Counselors attempting to obtain information from homeless clients about their alcohol/drug usage need to (Schutt & Garrett, 1992):

- Ask the client questions that make him or her think about use history.

- Ask a cluster of questions about the usage rather than relying on only one.

- Remember that long-term effects of usage and withdrawal from the substance(s) may affect the client's recall.

- Establish good rapport and practice patience because of the high possibility that the client may have both substance abuse and mental health problems.

- Be aware of the tendency to be duped into believing the client has more awareness of his or her substance abuse problem than he or she actually does.

Intervention with the homeless can be difficult for reasons stated previously (their numerous problems) as well as their tendency to miss appointments and referrals, their high recidivism rates, and difficulty in connecting them with helping agencies (Schutt & Garrett, 1992). One place the homeless may readily appear is in detoxification centers. Detoxification centers were started as alternatives to incarceration for publicly intoxicated individuals because of the 1971 Hughes Act (Uniform Alcoholism and Intoxication Treatment Act) to decriminalize public intoxication. Although sometimes jail is the only place available for publicly intoxicated individuals, when they are placed in detoxification centers, they have a safe, respectful place where they can withdraw and the chance for others to intervene regarding their usage. A detoxification center, then, may be a place that counselors can begin the process of intervention on the homeless client.

Beginning in the 1980s, NIAAA and NIDA researched the treatment of homeless clients with substance abuse problems. Stahler and Stimmel (1995) review 14 of these funded projects in terms of their treatment effectiveness, service dosage effects, and client characteristics with regard to treatment effectiveness. Overall, the research results indicate that traditional abstinence-based programs are not as effective with this population as ones that have a harm reduction emphasis, a careful assessment of the client and his or her needs, flexibility to meet a variety of needs and motivational levels, and a counseling style that allows for relapse (Oakley & Dennis, 1996). The findings also indicate that addiction treatment needs to include the meeting of the client's basic needs; high dropout rates should be expected; clients tend to improve over time even with small amounts of treatment (e.g., the control groups); clients need longer-term treatment; and clients who have more education and less severity in terms of substance abuse, criminal trouble, and social isolation have more positive treatment results (Stahler, 1995). There is some indication that substance abuse treatment may especially be helpful to the homeless who have PTSD or a major depressive disorder (Austin, McKellar, & Moos, 2011).

Five ways counselors may enhance the intervention process on the homeless client in the treatment process include (Schutt & Garrett, 1992):

1. Carefully match the client and the agency.

2. Give the client pertinent information about the referral, especially by giving the name of a contact person.

3. Make sure they have all necessary documents for the referral.

4. Arrange transportation to the referral agency.

5. Follow up with the referral agency once the intake has been done.

Oakley and Dennis (1996) also make several recommendations for both counselors and agencies that work with the homeless population. First, counselors need to address both substance abuse and mental health issues at the same time. Second, systems such as mental health, social services, and legal agencies need to work together, because many of the clients have interaction with all of them. Next, agencies need to reach out to these clients in a nonthreatening manner that cultivates their motivation for help. Fourth, agencies need to bring services to these clients over time and be flexible in types of services and styles of service delivery. Finally, nine general treatment strategies include:

1. Involving clients in their assessment and treatment process.

2. Educating clients on their conditions.

3. Using peer groups for support and role modeling.

4. Cautiously discussing medication with them.

5. Emphasizing harm reduction techniques (i.e., decrease substance use, change to less dangerous ingestion mode, switch drugs, have a more healthful life, etc.).

6. Using case managers to arrange care.

7. Helping them find jobs or meaningful activities.

8. Providing treatment sensitive to their cultures.

9. Being suspicious of easy solutions to the problems of homelessness.

Counselors working with this population need to be cognizant of all the struggles their clients may be experiencing. Viewing recovery from substance abuse problems as a process may facilitate a compassion that results in increased motivation with the homeless client. (See Case Study 6.6.)

CASE STUDY 6.6

Ray is a 40-year-old male who has come to a local homeless shelter. He has a bulbous nose, tremulous hands, and appears quite disheveled. During the intake process, he rarely looks at the interviewer and instead focuses his eyes on the floor. His answers are short and lack detail. Ray says he cannot remember the last time that he had something to drink or how much he normally drinks. He seems suspicious and defensive about the questions about his drinking.

1. What would you focus on as a top priority with Ray?
2. How would you attempt to establish rapport with Ray?
3. What concerns might you have with the accuracy of Ray's substance use history and why?

EXERCISE 6.6

Imagine that you have just lost your home as a result of unexpected unemployment. You and those who were living in the home with you do not have anywhere to go and you have no funds on which to draw. As you reach out to assistance to others (personal, professional), you experience judgmental attitudes that blame you for your homelessness. Process in a dyad how you believe this would impact your attitude, particularly in terms of collaboration and trust, and your behavior toward others.

SPECIFIC COUNSELING APPROACHES

As stated in the beginning of this chapter, three counseling approaches (dialectical behavior therapy, Seeking Safety, grief counseling) are presented in this section because of their potential usefulness in addressing the areas previously discussed in this chapter. Additionally, the section on drug court is included because of the frequent overlap of addiction and legal issues.

Dialectical Behavior Therapy (DBT)

Goldstein (2004) reports, in a review of the research, that there is a range in the overlap between chemical dependency and borderline diagnoses, with the most common frequency being more than 55%. Goldstein (2004) provides a summary of this overlap as follows. There are potentially three reasons for this overlap: (1) a borderline personality disordered individual may have deficits that make him or her vulnerable to alcohol/drugs; (2) chemically dependent and borderline diagnoses may have similar symptoms; and (3) both may be caused by similar circumstances/factors. Both disorders are difficult to treat, and

borderline personality disordered clients have more problems (i.e., self-injurious, suicidal).

Goldstein (2004) summarizes the difficulties in working with borderlines with regard to defenses and problem areas. Typically they are confusing and unpredictable clients who view people and situations in extremes. Six defenses they typically use are:

1. Splitting (all good/all bad).

2. Denial.

3. Idealization.

4. Devaluation (see self and/or others as bad).

5. Omnipotent control.

6. Projective identification (projecting one's own anger onto someone else who then has to be controlled).

They also have problems in the following areas: impulse control, anxiety tolerance, affect regulation, negative feelings, inability to self-soothe, fears of abandonment, self-esteem regulation, superego (may feel bad about behaviors, but cannot stop the action), interpersonal relationships (intense, unstable), perceptions of reality (distorted), and self-cohesion (may decompensate under stress). DBT was originally designed for borderline personality disordered clients (Rizvi, Steffel, & Carson-Wong, 2013).

Dialectical behavior therapy (DBT) was developed by Dr. Linehan in the 1970s (Dimeff & Linehan, 2008). A summary of the history and makeup of DBT follows (Dimeff, Comtois, & Linehan, 2009; Wheelis, 2009). During the 1970s, behavior therapy was being used to help chronically suicidal clients develop skills to create a meaningful life. The problem that emerged in the application of behavior therapy with borderline personality disordered clients is that the clients were both sensitive to criticism and had emotional dysregulation. As a result, they did not feel validated in terms of their needs and experiences by their counselors. The challenge became to find a way to both accept the client's needs and experiences and introduce change.

It is based on three theories: biosocial, behavioral, and dialectical philosophy (Rizvi et al., 2013). The phrase *dialectical polarity* means to synthesize two opposites; the two opposites here are change and acceptance. The challenge to the counselor became to persuade clients to change and to strategically use the oppositions to change that arise in counseling and in the counseling relationship. The philosophy became to not accept any proposition as a final truth or something that cannot be questioned.

DBT has five components to its treatment:

1. Increase client's motivation to change.

2. Increase client's capabilities.

3. Generalize new client behaviors.

4. Structure the environment.

5. Increase counselor capacity and motivation.

It uses four modes of treatment: individual, group, phone, and counselor consultations. It also involves a hierarchy of targets; the highest with this population, substance-abusing borderline clients, is to have a decrease in drug use and the behavioral patterns related to it. These behavioral targets include a decrease in physical discomfort (abstinence/withdrawal) and urges/cravings, an avoidance of opportunities and cues for abuse, and an increase in community reinforcement (Dimeff & Linehan, 2008). It has been shown to be effective with substance-dependent clients who have a borderline personality disorder (Dimeff, Comtois, & Linehan, 2003) and to improve their emotional regulation (Alelrod, Perepletchikova, Holtzman, & Sinha, 2011).

The counselor working with this population needs to help the client feel safe, set limits and structure, be aware there may be a trauma history, and manage countertransference (stay calm) (Goldstein, 2004). Dimeff and Linehan (2008) add that the counselor needs to talk about the client's tendency to have a "butterfly attachment problem" (meaning that they attach like a butterfly) and the importance of addressing it immediately in counseling. They specifically suggest developing a list with the client of where the counselor can look if the client becomes lost, increasing contact in the first few months of counseling, bringing therapy to the client, and shortening or lengthening counseling sessions.

Abstinence is viewed differently from the DBT perspective. Dimeff, Comtois, and Linehan (2009) define "dialectical abstinence" as the counselor accepting abstinence when the client is off of the alcohol/drugs and accepting a relapse by being nonjudgmental and keeping a problem-solving approach (the client uses cognitive self-control strategies and learns from mistakes). The counselor focuses on ways to encourage abstinence in the client and a willingness to maintain the abstinence. Dimeff and Linehan (2008) describe two approaches to abstinence: (1) having the client make a 100% *commitment* to abstinence for a specific period of time and then renewing the commitment, and (2) asking the client to "cope ahead" by preparing for high-risk situations.

Specific techniques that can be used for the newly abstinent client experiencing a crisis are the *Wise Mind ACCEPTS Skills* and *Self-Soothing the Five Senses* (Dimeff et al., 2009; Linehan,

1993). The *ACCEPTS Skills* are using the following seven distractions to get through the crisis:

1. **A**ctivities.

2. **C**ontributing (e.g., being altruistic).

3. **C**omparisons (comparing oneself to others who are struggling more in life).

4. With opposite **E**motions (doing something that stirs opposite emotions).

5. **P**ushing away (denying the problem temporarily).

6. With other **T**houghts (focusing on something else such as thought repetition).

7. Other **S**ensations (distracting self with body sensations).

Self-Soothing the Five Senses can be used when the client cannot or does not want to do the ACCEPTS skills. This means using vision, smell, taste, hearing, and touch as avenues to self-soothe. There is an exercise on this approach in Chapter 13.

DBT can be especially helpful in the counseling of substance abusing clients who also are diagnosed with borderline personality disorders. (See Case Study 6.7.)

CASE STUDY 6.7

Your client is a young female in her early 20s who is addicted to methamphetamines. She has a history at your agency of alienating the staff and burning out counselors because of her emotional intensity. You are aware she has a diagnosis of borderline personality disorder and a severe trauma history. You are seeing her for the first time, and you have been warned about her from other counselors. You want to give her a fair start with you.

1. What are some overall approaches you would use to establish a relationship with her?

2. How would you approach the "butterfly attachment" problem right away?

3. In terms of abstinence, how would you use commitment and the "cope ahead" approach?

4. How might you use the ACCEPTS skills in treating her (especially in crisis situations)?

5. How might you use the exercise of "Self-Soothing the Five Senses" as another crisis management approach?

EXERCISE 6.7

Think of the difficulties you might have in working with someone who abuses alcohol/drugs and is also diagnosed as having a borderline personality disorder. In particular, how might you get caught in countertransference when your client either idealizes or demonizes you? How would you manage your emotions? Discuss your thoughts and feelings with another person and develop a strategy for coping with the emotional intensity of working with this type of client.

Seeking Safety

Ross (2008) states that posttraumatic stress disorder (PTSD) is the most studied anxiety disorder in relation to substance use and psychotherapy. PTSD and SUD are strongly related and these clients have serious, urgent clinical needs that both require attention (Najavits, 2007). In a review of the research, Saladin, Back, and Payne (2009) report that many clients who have PTSD and a substance abuse disorder only receive treatment for the substance abuse. Yet, they also report that integrated treatment has become more common in the past 10 years, and research supports the finding that early treatment of trauma may increase chances of long-term recovery. These findings may support the view that substance abuse is a form of self-medicating in response to the presence of PTSD symptoms.

"Seeking Safety is the most widely known and empirically studied integrated CBT" (cognitive-behavioral therapy) (Saladin et al., 2009, p. 1255). It decreases PTSD and substance abuse when they co-occur (Hien, Cohen, Miele, Litt, & Capstick, 2004; Najavits, Weiss, & Shaw, 1997). It is trauma-specific for clients who have both a substance abuse and trauma history (Zweben, 2009). "It is an early-stage intervention designed to stabilize the patient (create safety) with respect to both substance abuse and PTSD, integrated within a manualized but flexible treatment approach" (Zweben, 2009, p. 473).

Seeking Safety was started in 1993 to treat the dual diagnosis clients (PTSD and SUD) (Najavits, 2007). It was grant-funded through NIDA and the therapy was developed through a trial-and-error process through several research studies (Najavits, 2002). Although its main focus is on safety (from substances, dangerous relationships, extreme symptoms), it is also described as *present, problem-oriented, brief, time-limited, structured, directive,* and *collaborative,* with an emphasis on decreasing current symptoms (Najavits, 2002, 2007). It has 25 sessions and has educational and coping skills components that are focused on helping clients have more control in their lives (Saladin et al., 2009).

Counselors can use various methods to assist clients in learning the skills (i.e., experiential exercises, role plays, identification of role models, replaying scenes, involvement of safe others, making tapes).

Each topic in the book (Navatis, 2002) has: a summary, clinician orientation, quotation, handouts, and tough cases (Navatis, 2007). It was originally developed for adult women in a group context, but it has been expanded to men and adolescents, as well as an individual therapy context (Saladin et al., 2009).

It is a program that is meant to give clients hope. Krinsley (2007) encourages counselors to ask themselves:

- Why do I want to work with these clients?

- How do I hold people accountable?

- How am I with intense emotions?

Krinsley (2007) also encourages counselors working with this population to:

- Be aware of the presence of roles of victim, perpetrator, bystander, and rescuer.

- Watch for transference and countertransference issues.

- Balance support and accountability.

- Give clients control whenever possible.

- Provide an all-out effort as a counselor.

- Practice self-care.

- Maintain boundaries.

- Use motivational enhancements.

This counseling approach, then, can be readily used by counselors who are working with clients who have both substance abuse and PTSD issues. (See Case Study 6.8.)

Grief Counseling

Grief is the client's reaction to a significant change or loss (G. A. Miller, 2012a). It involves strong

CASE STUDY 6.8

Your client is a middle-age woman who feels no hope for herself in terms of her addiction recovery. She has tried substance abuse treatment several times and feels she has failed each time because of her inability to achieve any long-term abstinence (more than 6 months). She has a significant trauma history and has been diagnosed as having PTSD.

1. How could you see the Seeking Safety program as being helpful to her?
2. How would you explain the program to her?
3. Would you place her in individual therapy, group therapy, or both? And why?
4. What would be your main focus in applying the Seeking Safety program to her situation?

EXERCISE 6.8

Imagine the most horrific trauma history a client could have. Keeping that scenario in mind, how would it be difficult for you to hold your client accountable for his or her behavior? What would you do to ensure that you could hold your client accountable while providing support? Share your reactions with a colleague and look for similar themes regarding accountability that you share.

emotion that cannot be controlled and an emotion that involves the feelings of helplessness and passivity (Leming & Dickinson, 1998). Grief is normal and natural in response to loss; it is also "messy" and unique to each client. Grief has its own life force of an ebb and flow (G. A. Miller, 2012a).

Grief issues may arise for clients as they address the issues discussed in this chapter (sexual, HIV/AIDS, IPV). This author's experience in working with addicted individuals has been that grief presents itself frequently in at least three ways: (1) unresolved grief (i.e., death of a family member, trauma-related), (2) grief as a result of losses that occur in sobriety (i.e., changes in significant relationships), and (3) consequences due to their alcohol/drug use (i.e., DSS removal of children, loss of driving license, imprisonment).

Counselors need to recognize and work with these issues as they emerge in the recovery process. Counselors do not need to be trained as grief therapists to effectively work in this area; they are practicing within their area of competence if they focus on the welfare of the client and the

relationship between the alcohol/drug use and the loss the client has experienced. Grief and trauma processing often overlap in counseling (Neimeyer & Wogrin, 2008) as indicated in the following example. A counselor working with a sexual abuse trauma survivor may find the client grieving the loss of the father she will never have because of his rape of her when she was a child; this loss may have led to the alcohol/drug use that helped her live with the reality of the father she had. Now that she is sober, she may need to allow herself to grieve her losses related to both the alcohol/drug use and the trauma.

As discussed previously in this book, the counselor needs to thoughtfully and carefully explore grief issues of the addicted client because they can readily overwhelm the recovering client. The counselor needs to assess the client's internal and external resources and the stability of their recovery when determining *when* and *how* to process the grief. It may be in the best interests of the client for the counselor to simply note—for oneself, with the client, or for future counselors—the need to address grief issues in more depth in the future. To make the determination as to the appropriateness of dealing with these issues, the counselor needs to be aware of the many ways grief can manifest itself so it does not remain hidden in the addiction treatment process.

Miller (2012, p. 167) summarizes Worden's (2009) four descriptions of the manifestations of grief:

1. *Feelings* (sadness, anger, guilt/self-reproach, anxiety, loneliness, fatigue, helplessness, shock, yearning, emancipation, relief, numbness).

2. *Physical sensations* (hollowness, tightness, over-sensitivity to noise, depersonalization, breathlessness, weakness, decreased energy, dry mouth).

3. *Cognitions* (disbelief, confusion, preoccupation, sense of deceased's presence, hallucinations).

4. *Behaviors* (sleep and appetite disturbances, absentminded behavior, social withdrawal, dreams of the deceased, avoidance of reminders of the deceased, searching and calling out, sighing, restless overactivity, crying, visiting places/carrying objects that are reminders of the deceased, treasuring objects belonging to the deceased).

Stroebe, Hansson, Stroebe, and Schut (2001) add the following five indicators of loss:

1. Susceptibility to illness.

2. Problems with memory and concentration.

3. Despair.

4. Depression.

5. Loss of pleasure.

Although these two lists are not exhaustive checklists of manifestations of grief, addiction counselors can use them as potential indicators of grief issues present and assist clients in identifying and addressing both the manifestations and the grief issue(s).

Worden's (2009) four tasks of mourning may also be helpful to the counselor when working with grief issues in the addicted client. Although these four tasks are connected to the death of someone significant to the client, they are translated here to grief issues connected to addiction counseling. In the *first task*, the addicted client needs to accept the reality of the loss and what it means to him/her. In the previous example, the survivor needs to take in that she will never have the nurturing father she wanted as a child. In the *second task*, the client needs to work through the pain of the grief with awareness of barriers to this work: messages (internal, external) that block its expression (i.e., "It happened a long time ago"), an urge to avoid feeling the emotions (i.e., "I don't have any feelings about the incident"), or taking a geographical cure of some type ("I am going to alcohol/drugs or I will just keep really busy"). In the *third task* of adjusting to absorbing the loss into the reality of his/her life, the addicted client may need to examine the impact of the loss particularly on sense of self and sense of the world. The client in the example may look at how being raped at a young age by her father shaped how she looked at herself and the world-especially in looking at it leading to her alcohol/drug use and now in her recovery process. In the *fourth task*, the client "emotionally relocates" meaning the client proceeds on with life and is no longer locked in the grief. In the example, the client sees herself, in recovery, as more than the trauma and its impact and instead focuses on how she now chooses to view the world and herself thereby impacting her behavior and interactions with others. These stages are not necessarily linear or completed—as stated earlier, grief is messy. What is critical is that the counselor assist the client in exploring these grief issues and provide the client with techniques that can be used when they emerge in the recovery process.

Counseling can be a safe place where the addicted client has an opportunity to grieve the loss with a witness (or in the case of marital/family/group counseling, witnesses). Depending on the counselor's theoretical orientation, various techniques can generally be used in addressing grief issues. Any exercises that can assist in the "emotional thawing out" may be useful (role play, expressive arts, experiential activities, etc.). Exercises that encourage the client to look at the meaning of the loss in terms of self-identification and interaction with others may also be helpful. General reflection and questioning techniques, such as discussed in Chapter 9 in the section on Motivational Interviewing, may facilitate the grief work. Shallcross (2009) reminds counselors that: Each client has a unique way of processing their grief, clients' cultures impact their grief process, and clients' shattered perceptions and meanings need to be explored with a commitment to assist them in finding new meanings. Additionally, all interventions need to be developmentally appropriate for the client (Sandovai, Scott, & Padilla, 2009).

Miller (2012, p. 169) summarizes some of the specific techniques counselors may want to use in grief counseling as stated by Shallcross (2009) and Worden (1991).

Shallcross (2009) summarizes the techniques used by grief counselors and experts as:

- Identifying client strengths

- Honoring the relationship, but moving on in life

- Recognizing that the grief may resurface

- Using three generation genograms to trace loss/grief experiences

- Writing a dialogue letter

- Using a keepsake in session to stimulate discussion

- Making booklines that document the grief journey

- Creating resilient images in the client's mind

- Journaling

- Using the empty chair technique

- Providing opportunities for emotional expression through art

- Practicing rituals

Worden (1991) adds the following techniques to this list:

- Using language that evokes emotional responses from clients and a reality check for them

- Role-playing

- Cognitive restructuring

- Developing a memory book. (See Case Study 6.9.)

CASE STUDY 6.9

Your client has returned from a military tour of duty in a war zone. While he has not experienced any outward disabilities as a result of his service, he shows evidence of PTSD symptoms. Both you and your client are aware that he has both addiction and PTSD issues, but as you address them in treatment, you notice he has a deep sense of melancholy. This melancholy is most intense when he talks about how he tried unsuccessfully to talk with his father, who was also a war veteran, prior to his recent death, about his war experiences.

1. What questions might you ask him, based on indicators of loss, to determine if he is feeling grief over his father's death?

2. Assuming he has unresolved grief with his father's death, how would you incorporate the four tasks of mourning into his treatment plan?

3. What techniques might you use in counseling to help him explore and address his grief issues?

4. How would you carefully balance addressing his grief with his addiction recovery?

EXERCISE 6.9

Think of a loss that pierced your heart with grief; one that you thought you might not survive. Note all the ways the grief manifested itself in your life and how you tried to run away from the grief. Where do you see yourself in the four tasks of mourning? Are there any of the techniques listed that you believe would help you heal even more in the grief?

Addiction counselors can use these techniques in various forms of counseling (individual, group, marital/family). For the addicted client who is experiencing grief, these techniques can facilitate and stabilize the recovery process.

Drug Court

There is a strong relationship between crime and drug abuse that typically involves at least three types of offenses: those involving drug possession/sales, those with a direct relationship to the abuse of drugs (such as stealing), and a lifestyle related to offenses that encourages offenders to be involved in illegal activity (NIDA, 2006). Approximately 56% to 66% of people in prison in the United States in 2005 met diagnosable criteria for a substance abuse disorder (James & Glaze, 2006), and of those on probation in 2006, 37% had served a drug offense sentence (Glaze & Bonczar, 2007). Incarceration is ineffective in treating addiction or reducing criminal recidivism (Hora & Schma, 2009).

Drug courts were developed because of overcrowded jails and a hope to decrease the revolving-door recidivism in crime (Cosden, 2008). The first U.S. drug court was developed in Miami/Dade County in 1989 (Leffingwell, Hendrix, Mignogna, & Mignogna, 2008). There are now more than 2,000 (National Association of Drug Court Professionals [NADCP], 2008). Drug court is a "judicially supervised, treatment-driven program for nonviolent substance abusing criminal offenders" (Hora & Schma, 2009, p. 1514). It involves community-based drug abuse treatment and court supervision (Cosden, 2008). It is an intense program that involves an exchange of court-supervised treatment and case management for prosecution and/or incarceration (NIDA, 2008). The criminal justice system is used as leverage in treatment (Ritvo & Causey, 2008).

Drug court involves a team of professionals from court, probation, treatment, and police who meet weekly to discuss participants in the program (van Wormer & Davis, 2008). The National Association of Drug Court Professionals (NADCP) has guidelines for drug courts that involve rapid treatment entry, treatment and court services being integrated, frequent drug testing, and use of sanctions and awards. It serves a range of clients who have a range of drug/alcohol and other problems (Cosden, 2008). It is abstinence based and focuses on the family of the participant as well as the participant (van Wormer & Davis, 2008).

Most drug courts have three phases: abstinence phase (weekly attendance in court), treatment phase (meets with judge twice a month), and relapse-prevention phase (monthly court dates) (Hora & Schma, 2009). The participant appears regularly before the judge, who gives praise and encouragement for treatment, progress, and success as well as immediate sanctions for treatment failure or program violation (Leffingwell et al., 2008): "carrots and sticks" (Hora & Schma, 2009, p. 1514). Often a written contract is involved (Hora & Schma, 2009). The judge develops a close relationship with the participant and, while receiving feedback from the team, makes the final court decisions (Hora & Schma, 2009). Drug court is more informal than regular court (there is more of a conversational interaction with the judge) and is sometimes called "Happy Court" by judges because their work is more enjoyable since they are able to be a part of a participant's success (K. Laws, personal communication, 2009).

It tends to cost more, but recidivism is decreased, thereby resulting in lowering costs judicially and to victims of crime (Mitchell, Wilson, Eggers, & MacKenzie, 2012; NIDA, 2008; Rempel, Green, & Kralstein, 2012). Recent research has found enhanced recidivism rates for clients who: are older, are female, have ethnic minority status, and have serious criminal histories (Brown, 2011). Drug court also increases the time participants stay in treatment; they abuse drugs less frequently than others on probation; and they have lower re-arrest rates (NIDA, 2008). Leffingwell et al. (2008) report 10 positive aspects to drug court:

1. Collaboration among different disciplines.

2. A change in the culture of both traditional judicial and treatment approaches.

3. Use of evidence-based practices (learning principles such as timely and consistent reinforcement and punishment).

4. Effectiveness with substance-abusing criminal offenders.

5. Cost effectiveness, especially regarding incarceration.

6. Provision of opportunities to be sober and avoid prison to overly represented groups in prison, such as minority ethnic groups.

7. Balanced protection of the public with compassion for the addict.

8. Involvement of new technology (alcohol and drug monitoring).

9. Problem-solving courts to problems other than alcohol/drug use.

10. Professional satisfaction among those involved with drug court.

Veterans' courts have been appearing in the United States since 2008. The court takes into account risk factors for criminal acts by veterans: substance abuse, homelessness, unemployment, and mental health and relationship issues. Holbrook (2011) provides a summary of veterans' courts. In 2008, Judge Robert T. Russell presided over the first court designed to meet the needs of veterans; it had emerged from his experience as a Buffalo, New York judge where he had noticed that there was an increasing number of defendants who were military veterans that responded well to other military veterans. The veteran court pairs defendants with mentors (both veterans) and with service providers who understand the needs/challenges of veterans. In 2010 the American Bar Association adopted a policy supporting these courts and developed establishment principles. As of 2011, there were approximately 40 courts in 21 states.

The third type of court discussed in this section is *juvenile drug court*. Two-thirds of adolescents in the juvenile justice system have co-occurring disorders, with more than 60% of them having substance use disorders (SAMHSA, 2013). SAMHSA (2013) provides the following overview of these courts. Juvenile drug courts emerged from the adult drug court model. Originally, the same model was used for juveniles as adults, however, the goals, approaches, and resources for these two populations were quite different. Some of these differences include developmental differences and typically less entrenchment in criminal activity for adolescents. There is increased involvement of family, school, and community organization partnerships.

A counselor may want to familiarize him- or herself with local and state drug courts by finding out general information about them (location, structure, types of acceptable participants). This information may assist in working with substance-abusing clients who may want to become involved with drug court or who are currently involved. Also, a counselor might consider applying to become a part of the drug court team as a part of his or her professional work in the substance abuse field. (See Case Study 6.10.)

CASE STUDY 6.10

Your client, who has been working with you generally on counseling-related issues, has chosen the option of being involved with drug court rather than being returned to prison for a recent relapse that involved a drug-related charge. You have never been involved with drug court, and you are not sure of its benefits. You would like to learn about it to be helpful to your client, but you do not know how to begin to educate yourself about drug court.

1. Where would you start to get information?

2. What biases do you believe you would have about drug court? (positive, negative)

3. How might you collaborate with drug court in terms of your client's treatment?

EXERCISE 6.10

Find out where the closest drug court is in your area. Contact a local professional related to drug court and ask if you could sit in on a session. Attend the local drug court and be aware of what you liked and did not like. Process the experience with someone who is familiar with drug court on a professional level.

SUMMARY

This chapter gives an overview of four areas often related to substance abuse and dependence: sexual issues (rape, sexual abuse), HIV/AIDS, intimate partner violence (IPV), and homelessness. No counselor can be an expert in all of these areas, but it is necessary for counselors to have some broad awareness of each area in order to better serve clients. A broad awareness that these issues may coexist with a substance abuse problem can assist in client welfare. Once a counselor is sensitive to such issues being present, the counselor can then turn to colleagues, supervisors, or mentors for consultation on working with this population and determine whether additional treatment components are needed to address this area of concern (i.e., referral for assessment and treatment). Effective treatment and aftercare, including relapse prevention, rely heavily on the thoroughness of the counselor's assessment.

Struggles with related issues such as these can result in a relapse in substances, which can cause the client to feel like a failure. Although accurate assessment does not guarantee a client's sobriety, the counselor can be assured that addressing the issues as part of the treatment plan has fulfilled his or her responsibility as a counselor.

Also included in this chapter is an overview of specific counseling approaches that may be used in response to these issues: DBT, Seeking Safety, and Grief Counseling. Counselors may find they enhance the effectiveness of their general approach to therapy through the use of these approaches. Finally, within this section, information is presented on drug court because these four issues sometimes involve legal issues with clients that are directly related to their alcohol and drug use—drug use that may be a result of struggles with these issues or in conjunction with them.

QUESTIONS

1. What do counselors need to generally do in addressing issues of rape with both survivors and perpetrators in treatment?

2. What are the effects of sexual abuse in men? In women?

3. What are the differences in counseling work with a perpetrator of sexual abuse and a survivor?

4. What are the transmission processes of HIV/AIDS?

5. What are common issues for clients with HIV/AIDS?

6. What is the difference in counseling focus between a batterer and a survivor of IPV?

7. When is a couple's treatment of IPV appropriate?

8. What multicultural concerns arise about IPV?

9. How may homelessness overlap with addiction issues?

10. What issues are unique in the substance abuse assessment process with the homeless? The substance abuse treatment process?

11. What are the core components of DBT? Seeking Safety? Grief Counseling?

12. How might DBT enhance addiction counseling work? Seeking Safety? Grief Counseling?

13. How are "change" and "acceptance" core components of DBT?

14. What is the main focus of the Seeking Safety counseling approach?

15. How may grief counseling overlap with addiction treatment issues?

16. What is the main purpose of drug court? Veterans' court?

READINGS/RESOURCES/WEBSITES

SUGGESTED READINGS

General Trauma

Briere, J., & Scott, C. (2006). *Principles of trauma therapy*. Thousand Oaks, CA: Sage.

This book is divided into two sections: trauma effects and assessment and clinical interventions.

Foa, E. B., Keane, T. M., Friedman, M. J., & Cohen, J. A. (2009). *Effective treatments for PTSD: Practice guidelines from the International Society for Traumatic Stress Studies* (2nd ed.). New York, NY: Guilford Press.

This book is divided into five sections: assessment and diagnosis (two chapters); early interventions (three chapters); treatment for chronic PTSD (15 chapters; children/adolescents/adults, various treatment approaches); treatment guidelines (18 sections); and conclusions.

Hien, D., Litt, L. C., Cohen, L. R., Miele, G. M., & Campbell, A. (2009). *Trauma services for women in substance abuse treatment*. Washington, DC: American Psychological Association.

This book has three sections: the relationship between trauma and substance abuse; the impact of trauma on functioning; and strategies for implementation.

Ogden, P., Minton, K., & Pain, C. (2006). *Trauma and the body: A sensorimotor approach to psychotherapy*. New York, NY: Norton.

This book is divided into two sections: theory and treatment. The theoretical section has seven chapters that look at thoughts, feelings, and sensorimotor reactions to trauma. The treatment section has five chapters that provide the counselor with information on how to apply the theory to clinical practice with trauma survivors.

Rothschild, B. (2000). *The body remembers: The psychophysiology of trauma and trauma treatment.* New York. NY: Norton.

This book is divided into two sections: theory and practice. The theoretical portion describes the main impacts of trauma on the mind and body. The practice section provides the counselor with practical suggestions on working with trauma survivors.

Rothschild, B. (2010). *8 keys to safe trauma recovery: Take-charge strategies to empower your healing.* New York, NY: Norton.

This book contains strategies of empowerment for trauma survivors.

Sexual Abuse

Professional

Cunningham, C., & MacFarlane, K. (1991). *When children molest children: Group treatment strategies for young sexual abusers.* Orwell, VT: Safer Society Press.

This book contains simple activities for children ages 4 to 12 that counselors can use in addressing sexual offender behaviors in young children. It has three sections (interventions, skills/competencies, progress measures), with accompanying exercises the counselor can use in group counseling.

Treatment–Related Issues

Gonsiorek, J. C., Bera, W. H., & LeTourneau, D. (1994). *Male sexual abuse: A trilogy of intervention strategies.* Thousand Oaks, CA: Sage.

This book covers basic information on male sexual abuse with specific counseling suggestions.

Substance Abuse and Mental Health Services Administration. (2000). *Substance abuse treatment for persons with child abuse and neglect issues.* Rockville, MD: Author.

The seven chapters in this manual cover areas that include working with these issues: screening, assessment, treatment, therapeutic issues, breaking the cycle, and legal concerns.

Personal

Bass, E. (Ed.). (1983). *I never told anyone: Writings by women survivors of child sexual abuse.* New York, NY: Harper.

This book has 33 stories of survivors of sexual abuse that are organized by the type of perpetrator (fathers, relatives, friends/acquaintances, strangers).

Bass, E., & Davis, L. (1988). *The courage to heal: A guide for women survivors of child sexual abuse.* New York, NY: Harper & Row.

This book was written for female survivors. It has five sections (taking stock, the healing process, changing patterns, survivor supporters, and courageous women) that provide information as well as questions and exercises to assist the survivor in the healing process.

Lew, M. (1988). *Victims no longer: Men recovering from incest and other sexual child abuse.* New York, NY: Harper & Row.

This book has five sections (general information, information about men, survival, recovery, and other people/resources). Each section provides information and the story of a survivor.

Lew, M. (2004). *Victims no longer: The classic guide for men recovering from sexual child abuse.* New York, NY: Harper Paperbacks.

This book describes how culture inhibits men's ability to see abuse and obtain treatment for it.

Mendel, M. P. (1995). *The male survivor: The impact of sexual abuse.* Thousand Oaks, CA: Sage.

This book has eight chapters that each provide information on male sexual abuse and are accompanied by a survivor's story. The final chapter discusses the male survivor in general.

HIV/AIDS and Infectious Disease

Barret, B., & Logan, C. (2002). *Counseling gay men and lesbians: A practice planner.* Pacific Grove, CA: Brooks/Cole.

This book is a general counseling book for working with the LGBT population. It includes chapters on identity development, couples counseling, youth, spiritual, parenting, and health issues.

Cabaj, R. J. (1997). Gays, lesbians, and bisexuals. In J. H. Lowinson, P. Ruiz, R. B. Millman, & J. G. Langrod (Eds.), *Substance abuse: A comprehensive textbook* (3rd ed., pp. 725–733). Baltimore, MD: Williams & Wilkins.

This chapter provides a succinct summary of issues facing the LGBT population in relation to substance abuse.

Kalichman, S. C. (1996). *Answering your questions about AIDS*. Washington, DC: American Psychological Association.

This book provides answers to common questions about AIDS in terms of general information on the virus, transmission, testing; sex and drugs; people at risk; caretakers; ethics; and prevention.

Kalichman, S. C. (1998). *Understanding AIDS: Advances in research and treatment* (2nd ed.). Washington, DC: American Psychological Association.

The first section of this book covers virology, epidemiology, and clinical manifestations. The second section covers psychological, neurological, and social concerns. The third section looks at adjustment in the sexual, psychological, and social areas.

National Institute on Drug Abuse (NIDA). (2012, July). *Drug abuse and HIV*. (NIH Pub. 12–5760) Rockville, MD: NIDA.

This publication provides a condensed, current overview of HIV as it relates to drug abuse.

Perez, R. M., DeBord, K. A., & Bieschke, K. J. (2000). *Handbook of counseling and psychotherapy with lesbian, gay, and bisexual clients*. Washington, DC: American Psychological Association.

This book has 18 chapters divided into three main sections: social and theoretical perspectives, counseling and therapy, and therapy/theory/research issues. The therapy section addresses therapist issues; individual, couples, and group therapy; and issues related to aging, adolescents, and family.

Savin-Williams, R. C. (2001). *Mom, Dad. I'm gay: How families negotiate coming out*. Washington, DC: American Psychological Association.

This book has nine chapters that discuss LGBT concerns within the context of the family. Especially helpful are the chapters that examine the relationship between different family members (e.g., daughters and fathers).

Substance Abuse and Mental Health Services Administration. (2000). *Substance abuse treatment for persons with HIV/AIDS*. Rockville, MD: Author.

This manual has 10 chapters that cover a wide range of treatment concerns, including prevention, medical and mental health treatment, integration and coordination of services, counseling recommendations, legal and ethical issues, and funding and policy concerns.

Substance Abuse and Mental Health Services Administration. (2003). *A provider's introduction to substance abuse treatment for lesbian, gay, bisexual, and transgender individuals*. Rockville, MD: Author.

This publication is an excellent resource for working with the LGBT population in terms of substance abuse treatment. It is divided into three main sections: an overview, a clinician's guide (the coming-out process; health issues; and clinical issues with lesbians, gay males, bisexuals, transgender individuals, youth, and families), and a program administrator's guide.

Substance Abuse and Mental Health Services Administration. (2011). *Drugs, alcohol, and HIV/AIDS: A consumer guide*. Rockville, MD: Author.

This short brochure provides core information that includes agency contact information (phone numbers, websites).

Intimate Partner Violence

Professional

Edelson, J. L., & Tolman, R. M. (1992). *Intervention for men who batter: An ecological approach*. Newbury Park, CA: Sage.

This manual is designed to provide practical suggestions to the counselor who wants to counsel batterers.

Goodman, M. S., & Fallon, B. C. (1995). *Pattern changing for abused women: An educational program*. Thousand Oaks, CA: Sage.

This text provides an overview of domestic violence counseling theory and approaches. The accompanying workbook has helpful exercises that a counselor can use in working with this population; one especially helpful handout is "Your Bill of Rights."

Hines, D. A., & Malley-Morrison, K. M. (2005). *Family violence in the United States: Defining, understanding, and combating abuse*. Thousand Oaks, CA: Sage.

This book has 12 chapters that address definition issues, cultural contexts, religious contexts, child physical abuse, child sexual abuse, child neglect, wife abuse, husband abuse, GLBT abuse, elder abuse, hidden types of abuse, and effective responses.

Knapp, S. J., & VandeCreek, L. (1997). *Treating patients with memories of abuse: Legal risk management*. Washington, DC: American Psychological Association.

This book presents suggestions on how to treat clients who have been abused from a risk management perspective. It provides helpful guidelines for practice in working with this population.

Leventhal, B., & Lundy, S. E. (1999). *Same-sex domestic violence: Strategies for change*. Thousand Oaks, CA: Sage.

This book is divided into four sections: personal stories, legal perspectives, organizing coalitions and building communities, and providing services.

Miller, G., Clark, C., & Herman, J. (2007). Domestic violence in a rural setting. *Journal of Rural Mental Health, 31*, 28–42.

This journal article provides a summary of barriers that face intimate partner violence survivors in a rural setting along with specific counseling examples. Recommendations are made to rural healthcare professionals.

Minnesota Coalition for Battered Women. (1992). *Safety first: A guide for battered women*. St. Paul, MN: Author.

This is a useful book for survivors of intimate partner violence because it provides both theoretical and practical information and suggestions.

Substance Abuse and Mental Health Services Administration. (2012). *Substance abuse treatment and domestic violence*. (TIPS Manual 25) Rockville, MD: Author.

This manual summarizes the knowledge base of intimate partner violence (male batterers to female survivors), the relationship between substance abuse and intimate partner violence, and how to screen for it in treatment. It also provides instruments that can be used for assessment.

Personal

NiCarthy, G. (1987). *The ones who got away: Women who left abusive partners*. Seattle, WA: Seal Press.

This book has 33 stories of women from all different walks of life who left their abusers. There is also a chapter on the lessons the women who leave provide and a chapter on why they left and how they were able to stay away.

NiCarthy, G. (1997). *Getting free: You can end abuse and take back your life*. Seattle, WA: Seal Press.

This book provides general information on intimate partner violence with exercises to facilitate the survivor's awareness. There are chapters on teen abuse, lesbian abuse, and emotional abuse.

White, E. C. (1994). *Chain, chain, change: For black women in abusive relationships*. Seattle, WA: Seal Press.

This book has nine chapters that attempt to provide information to the reader to assess if she is in a violent relationship and actions she may choose to take. There is also a chapter on lesbians and abuse.

DBT

Dimeff, L. A., Comtois, K. A., & Linehan, M. M. (2009). Co-occurring addiction and borderline personality disorder. In R. K. Ries, D. A. Fiellin, S. C. Miller, & R. Saitz (Eds.), *Principles of addiction medicine* (4th ed., pp. 1227–1237). Philadelphia, PA: Wolters Kluwer.

This book provides a concise overview of DBT as applied to a substance-abusing borderline population.

Dimeff, L. A., & Linehan, M. M. (2008). Dialectical behavior therapy for substance abusers. *Addiction Science & Clinical Practice, 4*, 39–47.

This article provides a concise overview of DBT as applied to a substance-abusing borderline population.

Substance Abuse and Mental Health Services Administration. (2012). *Dialectical behavior therapy: An informational resource*. Rockville, MD: Author.

This document is a part of a series of evidence-based practices; it provides a general overview of DBT.

Seeking Safety

Najavits, L. M. (2002) *Seeking safety: A treatment manual for PTSD and substance abuse*. New York, NY: Guilford Press.

The manual has a chapter that provides an overview of PTSD and substance abuse and a chapter that discusses how to conduct the treatment. The remainder of the manual focuses on treatment topics.

Grief Counseling

Harvard Health Publications (2010). *Coping with grief and loss*. Boston, MA: Harvard University.

This booklet provides an overview of grief and ways to cope with it as well as a section on the terminally ill and a section on making arrangements related to the loss of someone.

Lewis, C. S. (1961). *A grief observed*. San Francisco, CA: Harper.

This book focuses on issues related to life, death, and faith one faces in loss.

Neimeyer, R. A. (2002). The language of loss: Grief therapy as a process of meaning reconstruction. In R. A. Neimeyer (Ed.), *Meaning reconstruction & the experience of loss*. Washington, DC: American Psychological Association.

This book chapter provides a helpful outline and techniques of using narrative therapy within the context of grief work.

Worden, W. (1991). *Grief counseling & grief therapy*. New York, NY: Springer.

This book provides an excellent overview of grief counseling.

Drug Court

Berg, I. K., & Shafer, K. C. (2004). Working with mandated substance abusers: The language of solutions. In S. L. A. Straussner (Ed.), *Clinical work with substance-abusing clients* (pp. 82–102). New York, NY: Guilford Press.

This chapter provides an overview of applying solution-focused approaches to a mandated substance abusing population.

Hora, P. F., & Schma, W. G. (2009). Drug courts and the treatment of incarcerated populations. In R. K. Ries, D. A. Fiellin, S. C. Miller, & R. Saitz (Eds.), *Principles of addiction medicine* (4th ed., pp. 1513–1520). Philadelphia, PA: Wolters Kluwer.

This book chapter provides an overview of drug courts.

Leffingwell, T. R., Hendrix, B., Mignogna, M., & Mignogna, J. (2008, Spring). Ten things to love about drug courts. *Addictions Newsletter*, *15*, 11–12.

This short article succinctly describes 10 overall aspects of drug courts.

National Institute on Drug Abuse. (2007). *Principles of drug abuse treatment for criminal justice populations: A research-based guide*. (NIH Publication No. 07–5316). Rockville, MD: Author.

This 33-page pamphlet elaborates on 13 principles of treatment for criminal justice populations.

RESOURCES

General Trauma

Videos

Cavalcade Productions (Producer). (1998). *Trauma and substance abuse I: Therapeutic approaches* [Video]. Available from www.cavalcadeproductions.com

This 46-minute video discusses ways to work with substance abuse trauma survivors.

Cavalcade Productions (Producer). (1998). *Trauma and substance abuse II: Special treatment issues* [Video]. Available from www.cavalcadeproductions .com

This 40-minute video discusses the issues of counter-transference, codependency, crisis, and relapse.

Cavalcade Productions (Producer). (2005). *Numbing the pain: Substance abuse and psychological trauma* [Video]. Available from www.cavalcadeproductions.com

This 30-minute video examines how substance abuse has assisted survivors in their lives and the ways therapy can provide challenges and benefits to the survivor.

CNS Productions (Producer). (2008). *In & out of control* [Video]. Available from www.cnsproductions.com

This 38-minute video provides general information about emotional, physical, and sexual violence.

Workbook

Williams, M. B., & Poijula, S. (2002). *The PTSD workbook*. Oakland, CA: New Harbinger.

This book has 15 chapters. Each chapter has exercises that facilitate awareness about the impact of the trauma on the survivor and ways to heal from the trauma.

Rape

Video

Fanlight Productions (Producer). (1992). *Surviving rape: A journey through grief* [VHS]. Available from www.discover-films.com

This 32-minute film discusses the healing process from rape within the five stages of grief through the stories of five women.

Workbook

Rosenbloom, D., & Williams, M. B. (2010). *Life after trauma: A workbook for healing* (2nd ed). New York, NY: Guilford Press.

This workbook is meant for trauma survivors in general. It has eight sections that have accompanying exercises to facilitate awareness in trauma survivors. It also has a prologue with suggestions on how to use the book and an epilogue on long-term healing. Finally, it has appendices on self-care in

health care settings, recommended readings, the psychotherapy process, and suggestions to counselors on how to use the book.

Sexual Abuse

Support Groups

Adult Survivors of Child Abuse (ASCA)
The Morris Center
P.O. Box 14477
San Francisco, CA 94114
(415) 928-4576
E-mail: info@ascasupport.org
www.ascasupport.org

Adult Survivors of Child Abuse (ASCA) is a self-help program for adult survivors of child abuse that has a *Survivor to Thrive Manual* and a list of individual and group meetings by city.

Incest Survivors Anonymous (ISA)
P.O. Box 17245
Long Beach, CA 90807-7245
(562) 428–5599
www.lafn.org/medical/isa/

This is a 12-step support group organization that has literature packets available in English and Spanish.

Survivors of Incest Anonymous
World Service Office
P.O. Box 190
Benson, MD 21018-9998
(410) 893-3322
www.siawso.org

This is a 12-step self-help recovery program for adult survivors of sexual abuse as children.

Videos

Fanlight Productions (Producer). (2006). Talk to me: Teens speak out about sexual violence [[DVD]. Available from www.fanlight.com

This 33-minute DVD is a summary of powerful stories of teenagers who have been sexually abused.

KB Films (Producer). The healing years [DVD]. Available from www.bigvoicepictures.com

This 52-minute DVD has a summary of different women's stories of sexual abuse and incest. A former Miss America tells her story.

Workbooks

Carter, W. L. (2002). *It happened to me: A teen's guide to overcoming sexual abuse*. Oakland, CA: New Harbinger.

This book has five sections, with exercises in each section meant to help teenagers become aware of their reactions to sexual abuse they have experienced.

Davis, L. (1990). *The courage to heal workbook*. New York, NY: Harper & Row.

This workbook is designed for women and men who have survived sexual abuse. It has three sections (healing survival skills, taking stock, and healing aspects). Each section has subsections, with specific exercises meant to help the survivor learn about self and heal from the sexual abuse.

Rosenbloom, D., & Williams, M. B. (1999). *Life after trauma: A workbook for healing*. New York, NY: Guilford Press.

This workbook is meant for trauma survivors in general. It has eight sections that have accompanying exercises to facilitate awareness in trauma survivors. It also has a prologue with suggestions on how to use the book and an epilogue on long-term healing. Finally, it has appendices on recommended readings, the psychotherapy process, and suggestions to counselors on how to use the book.

Intimate Partner Violence

Videos

Domestic Abuse Intervention Project (Producer). *Power & control: A woman's perspective*. [Video]. Available from www.theduluthmodel.org

This 1-hour video discusses power and control issues from a woman's perspective through interviews with survivors.

Domestic Abuse Intervention Project (Producer). *Power & control: The tactics of men who batter* [Video]. Available from www.theduluthmodel.org

This 40-minute video discusses power and control issues from a man's perspective through interviews with perpetrators.

Workbooks

Fall, K. A., & Howard, S. (2004). *Alternatives to domestic violence* (2nd ed.). New York, NY: Brunner/Routledge.

This is a homework manual for participants in a battering intervention group. It has 12 chapters meant to facilitate self-awareness through exercises for each chapter.

Goodman, M. S., & Fallon, B. C. (1995). *Pattern changing for abused women*. Thousand Oaks, CA: Sage.

This text provides an overview of intimate partner violence counseling theory and approaches. The accompanying workbook has helpful exercises that a counselor can use in working with this population; one especially helpful handout is "Your Bill of Rights."

Rosenbloom, D., & Williams, M. B. (1999). *Life after trauma: A workbook for healing*. New York, NY: Guilford Press.

This workbook is meant for trauma survivors in general. It has eight sections that have accompanying exercises to facilitate awareness in trauma survivors. It also has a prologue with suggestions on how to use the book and an epilogue on long-term healing. Finally, it has appendices on recommended readings, the psychotherapy process, and suggestions to counselors on how to use the book.

DBT

Workbooks

Bein, A. (2014). *Dialectical behavior therapy for wellness and recovery: Interventions and activities for diverse client needs*. Hoboken, NJ: Wiley.

This book has six chapters written for the clinician that are readily applicable for DBT counseling interventions. Interventions are provided throughout the text with the final chapter having 15 lessons and activities. It has one chapter that focuses on substance abuse recovery.

Linehan, M. M. (1993a). *Cognitive-behavioral treatment of borderline personality disorder*. New York, NY: Guilford Press.

This book comprehensively describes this treatment approach.

Linehan, M. M. (1993b). *Skills training manual for treating borderline personality disorder*. New York, NY: Guilford Press.

This book comprehensively describes this treatment approach in terms of skills, teaching strategies, and discussion topics in groups.

Marra, T. (2004). *Depressed & anxious: The dialectical behavior therapy workbook for overcoming depression & anxiety*. Oakland, CA: New Harbinger.

This book has nine chapters. The first is an overview of DBT. The remaining eight are meant for the client to use as exercises (dialectics of anxiety and depression, feelings, "there must be something wrong with me," meaning making, mindfulness skills, emotional regulation, distress tolerance skills, and strategic behavioral skills).

McKay, M., Wood, J. C., & Brantley, J. (2007). *The dialectical behavior therapy skills workbook*. Oakland, CA: New Harbinger.

This is written for the client. It provides an overview of DBT in the introduction and 8 of the 10 chapters are focused on specific skill development (basic and advanced) in four areas (distress tolerance, mindfulness, emotion regulation, interpersonal). Additional chapters are on mindfulness and organizing the different skill areas learned.

Seeking Safety

Videos

There is a set of five training videos available through the Seeking Safety website.

www.seekingsafety.org

Workbook

Najavits, L. M. (2002). *Seeking safety: A treatment manual for PTSD and substance abuse*. New York, NY: Guilford Press.

The manual has a chapter that provides an overview of PTSD and substance abuse and a chapter that discusses how to conduct the treatment. The remainder of the manual focuses on treatment topics.

Exercises

Card Deck of Safe Coping Skills

Available at www.seekingsafety.org

These cards are based on the concepts used in the Seeking Safety approach.

Grief Counseling

Videos

Fanlight Productions (Producer). (1992). *Encounters with grief*. Available from www.fanlight.com

This 13-minute film tells the stories of a mother, widow, and widower regarding death.

Fanlight Productions (Producer). (1997). *Grief in America*. Available from www.fanlight.com

This 55-minute film tells seven stories from the lives of individuals who vary in terms of age, ethnicity, and religion. It has an educational focus and explores the impact of unresolved grief and the role of religion.

Fanlight Productions (Producer). (1998). *Surviving death: Stories of grief*. Available from www.fanlight.com

This 47-minute film has seven individuals from different ethnic groups (Caucasian, Chinese, Native American) discuss their experiences with loss and recovery that ended on a hopeful note.

Client-Oriented Books and Workbooks

Bozarth, A. R. (1990). *A journey through grief: Gentle, specific help to get you through the most difficult stages of grieving*. Center City, MN: Hazelden.

This 51-page book speaks to the person grieving. It provides practical, "how to" suggestions.

Gilbert, K. (2001). *From grief to memories: A workbook on life's significant losses*. Silver Spring, MD: Soras.

This 208-page book has numerous exercises that clients can use in the grief process. It provides helpful resources at the end of the book.

Kemp, C. O. (2000). *A book of hope for the storms of life*. Franklin, TN: Wisdom.

This short book is written from a Christian perspective and is meant to be uplifting to someone in grief.

Lewis, C. S. (1961). *A grief observed*. San Francisco, CA: Harper.

This 76-page book focuses on the issues related to life, death, and faith that one faces in loss.

Neeld, E. H. (1990). *Seven choices: Finding daylight after loss shatters your world*. Austin, TX: Centerpoint Press.

In this 345-page book, the author describes seven phases that mark the grieving process. Based on her experience of having lost her husband to death, the author discusses these seven phases through her story and that of others and ends each section by discussing the choice of value in this phase.

Rich, P. (2001). *Grief counseling homework planner*. New York, NY: Wilcy.

This 240-page workbook is divided into 14 sections that cover basic areas of grief work. Each section has a number of exercises that can be used by counselors doing grief work (disk included).

Wise, L. (2001). *Inside grief*. Incline Village, NV: Wise Press.

This 109-page book has 44 stories and poems in an anthology covering many different forms of loss. It is a very powerfully written book that could be used in bibliotherapy with clients.

York, S. (2000). *Remembering well: Rituals for celebrating life and mourning death*. San Francisco, CA: Jossey-Bass.

This 216-page book has nine chapters that offer family members and helping professionals ideas on planning services and rituals that both honor the person who is deceased and fit those attending the service. There are three resources at the end of the book: blessing and preparing a body, five services people created, and readings/prayers/blessings.

Zonnebelt-Smeege, S. J., & DeVries, R. C. (2001a). *The empty chair: Handling grief on holidays and special occasions*. Grand Rapids, MI: Baker Books.

In this 222-page book, the authors write from a Christian perspective on the loss of a spouse based on both of their personal experiences of having lost a spouse. It is written to the grieving person. It has sections on "Helpful Suggestions" throughout the book.

Zonnebelt-Smeege, S. J., & DeVries, R. C. (2001). *Getting to the other side of grief: Overcoming the loss of a spouse*. Grand Rapids, MI: Baker Books.

This 91-page book is written from a Christian perspective for people in the pain of grief as it relates to death. It has five sections divided into three parts (reflections on personal experiences, suggestions on managing grief, a Christian meditation and prayer). There is a nice candle-lighting ceremony at the end (one that is secular and one that is Christian).

Drug Court

Workbooks

Hazelden. (2005). *Client recovery workbook*. Center City, MN: Author.

This 143-page workbook has five sections: getting started, you and your team, 12-step and other group meetings, AA/NA/CA recovery basics, and getting ready to go off probation/parole or leaving the safety of the drug court. It has 52 exercises, each of which has an introduction and a set of questions.

Hazelden. (2005). *Client cognitive skills workbook*. Center City, MN: Author.

This 148-page workbook has eight parts: mapmaking, criminal and addiction history, becoming aware of your inner maps, learning to think about your thinking, learning to think about your behaviors, socialization, what works/what doesn't, and how to change. It has 45 exercises designed to facilitate self-exploration.

Hazelden. (2005). *Client life skills workbook*. Center City, MN: Author.

This 100-page workbook has four parts: have a plan, plan the work, the many parts of the plan, and work the plan. There is a good, simple explanation of the stages-of-change model on page 11. It looks at recovery in a holistic way. There are 52 exercises designed to facilitate the client's self-exploration.

Substance Abuse and Mental Health Services Administration. (1996). *Relapse prevention with chemically dependent criminal offenders, counselor's manual* (Technical Assistance Publication Series 19; DHHS Publication No. SMA 06–4217). Rockville, MD: Author.

This 181-page booklet provides general information on addiction, relapse prevention treatment, a guide to professionals on how to use the workbook, and an appendix workbook on relapse prevention that has 27 exercises.

WEBSITES/PHONE CONTACTS

Rape

Rape, Abuse, & Incest National Network (RAINN)
E-mail: info@rainn.org
www.rainn.org

This website provides information on rape, abuse, and incest regarding services, education, and advocacy.

Sacred Circle—National Resource Center to End Violence against Native Women
www.sacredcircle.com

Men Can Stop Rape—Creating cultures free from violence

www.mencanstoprape.org

This website provides support for men who are interested in promoting cultures that are free of violence, specifically men's violence against women.

Sexual Abuse

After Silence
www.aftersilence.org

This website has a support group, message board, and chat room.

Posttraumatic Stress Disorder Alliance
www.ptsdalliance.org

This website has general information on PTSD as well as articles and support group information.

Rape, Abuse, & Incest National Network (RAINN)
E-mail: info@rainn.org
www.rainn.org

This website provides information on rape, abuse, and incest regarding services, education, and advocacy.

Sacred Circle—National Resource Center to End Violence against Native Women
www.sacredcircle.com

This website provides information on sexual assault in American Indian and Alaskan Native tribal communities.

SAMHSA
www.ncadi.samhsa.gov

This website provides the TIP series and their related products. Two helpful, free brochures are *Helping Yourself Heal*. One is written for recovering men (DHHS Publication No. SMA12–4134) who have been abused as children and one for recovering women (DHHS Publication No. SMA13–4132).

Survivorship
E-mail: info@survivorship.org
www.survivorship.org

This website provides resources for survivors of ritualistic abuse, mind control, and torture.

HIV/AIDS and Infectious Disease

AIDSinfo
www.aidsinfo.nih.gov

American Foundation for AIDS Research

www.amfar.org

This website is for the American Foundation for AIDS Research and has news/features, research, and events.

American Psychological Association
www.apa.org/pi/aids

This website links the reader to their Office on AIDS that provides information, training, and technical assistance with regard to HIV/AIDS and related topics.

The Centers for Disease Control and Prevention
www.cdc.gov/hiv/dhap.htm

This is the website for The Centers for Disease Control and Prevention that provides information on addressing the HIV/AIDS epidemic.

Department of Health and Human Services
www.aidsinfo.nih.gov

This website for the Department of Health and Human Services AIDS *info* provides general information on AIDS.

Harm Reduction Coalition
www.harmreduction.org

This is the website for the Harm Reduction Coalition. This website provides links to needle-exchange programs in the United States. Its overall mission is to advocate for individuals and organizations impacted by drug use.

National AIDS Hotline
(800) 342–2437
National Institute of Allergy and Infectious Diseases
www.niaid.nih.gov

This is the website for the National Institute of Allergy and Infectious Diseases, whose focus is to understand, treat, and prevent infectious disease. It has a section on HIV/AIDS.

Office of HIV/AIDS and Infectious Disease Policy (OHAIDP)
www.aids.gov

This is a government website that provides overall information about HIV/AIDS.

Intimate Partner Violence

The Domestic Abuse Intervention Project
www.theduluthmodel.org

This website provides overall information on intimate partner violence from the Duluth Model-Domestic Abuse Intervention Project.

The Domestic Violence Initiative for Women with Disabilities
www.dviforwomen.org

This website provides information regarding domestic violence within the disabled population of women.

The Institute on Domestic Violence in the African-American Community
E-mail: nidvaac@umn.edu
www.dvinstitute.org

This website provides information on family violence in the African-American community and provides an avenue where individuals can state their perspectives.

Jewish Women International
www.jewishwomen.org

This website provides information on programs, education, and advocacy within the Jewish population.

Minnesota Coalition for Battered Women
www.mcbw.org

This organization provides general information, books, stickers, pins, posters, referrals, trainings, research, networking, and legislative lobbying.

Mending the Sacred Hoop: Technical Assistance Project
www.mshoop.org/ta-project/

This website provides training and technical assistance to American Indians and Alaskan Natives in the effort of eliminating intimate partner violence in this population.

National Coalition Against Domestic Violence
www.ncadv.org

This website provides information helpful at the regional, state, and national levels. Information includes safe homes/shelters, policy development and legislation, public education, and technical assistance.

National Latino Alliance for the Elimination of Domestic Violence
www.dvalianza.org

This website provides information on intimate partner violence in the Latino population.

Sacred Circle—National Resource Center to End Violence against Native Women
www.sacredcircle.com

This website provides information on intimate partner violence in American Indian and Alaskan Native tribal communities.

Homelessness

Homeless Assistance Hotline
(800) 483-1010
Homeless Resource Center
www.homeless.samhsa.gov

This SAMHSA website provides an overview of information and resources regarding homelessness.

National Coalition for Homelessness
www.nationalhomeless.org

This website is a national personal and professional network that is focused on preventing and ending homelessness while meeting immediate needs and protecting civil rights of the homeless.

DBT

Behavioral Tech
www.behavioraltech.org

This website provides information on workshops, training (intensive, online), and educational products related to DBT.

Seeking Safety

Seeking Safety
www.seekingsafety.org

This website provides general information about the Seeking Safety approach. It includes article and training information on the topic.

Grief Counseling

American Hospice Foundation
www.americanhospice.org

This website provides onsite training workshops, articles, resources, and publications.

Ashley Foundation
www.theashleyfoundation.org

This website helps teenagers face cancer with education and support.

Association for Death Education and Counseling
www.adec.org

This website provides education, care, research, and counseling information regarding death.

The Compassionate Friends
www.compassionatefriends.org

This is the website for the national, nonprofit, self-help support group for families grieving the death of a child.

Counseling for Loss and Life Changes
www.counselingforloss.com

This website provides counseling resources as well as articles and books.

Griefshare
www.griefshare.org

An online support center that can direct individuals to Griefshare groups in their home communities.

The Grief Recovery Institute
www.grief-recovery.com

This website provides programs and workshops for individuals dealing with loss as well as articles, books, and other resources. It also provides training for professionals.

National Hospice and Palliative Care Organization
www.nhpco.org

This website focuses on end of life care and facilitating access to hospice care.

Drug Court

National Association of Drug Court Professionals (NADCP)
www.nadcp.org

The National Association of Drug Court Professionals (NADCP) provides general information about their organization at this website.

National Drug Court Institute
www.ndci.org

The National Drug Court Institute provides education, research, and scholarship for drug court intervention programs. This website provides information on how to access these resources.

Restorative Justice
www.restorativejustice.org

The Restorative Justice website provides resources such as crime victim support. The focus of this group is to repair the harm done by crime.

The National Institute on Alcohol Abuse and Alcoholism (NIAAA)
www.niaaa.nih.gov

The National Institute on Alcohol Abuse and Alcoholism (NIAAA) website provides general information on alcohol use as well as resources helpful to the counselor.

National Institute on Drug Abuse (NIDA)
www.nida.nih.gov

The National Institute on Drug Abuse (NIDA) website provides general information about drug abuse as well as numerous resources.

Substance Abuse and Mental Health Services Administration (SAMHSA)
www.samhsa.gov

The Substance Abuse and Mental Health Services Administration (SAMHSA) website assists in treatment location and services as well as providing resources (publications, etc.) on substance abuse.

CHAPTER 7

RELAPSE PREVENTION

PERSONAL REFLECTIONS

Relapse-prevention work can be very encouraging work for addiction counselors. In this work, we can help people prevent relapse by simply becoming aware of unique internal and external personal triggers for relapse. This awareness can free our clients to make choices that assist them in becoming and staying sober. When awareness is paired with the learning of coping skills to help them in high-risk situations, clients can make empowering choices that assist them in obtaining and maintaining their sobriety. For all the areas of addiction work where a counselor may experience powerlessness and frustration, this is truly an area of hope and encouragement, because a counselor can watch miracles happen and observe the resilience of the human spirit.

Sometimes a counselor can negatively impact this important work by expressing views to the client that convey a message that relapse is a "normal" part of recovery. This view can actually end up enabling alcohol and drug use by encouraging relapse in the client through the underlying message that "everybody relapses in recovery." It is more appropriate and respectful to send a message that "relapse may happen but does not have to happen."

Often in addiction counseling, there can be clarification of the counseling approach to be taken with a client by translating the situation to a scenario of another disease. For example, in terms of relapse prevention with the disease of cancer, a doctor talking with a newly diagnosed cancer patient regarding treatment options would probably not say, "We can go ahead and treat the cancer, but chances are, no matter what we do, it will probably come back." In fact, we might say that such a doctor is inhumane to deliver such a message.

Instead, we would respect a doctor who says to the patient, "You have cancer. Now, let's look at everything we can do medically in terms of treatment to find the best, most effective treatment package to stop this disease in you. This treatment package includes everything you can do and everything I and the medical profession can do to stop this disease from coming back. If it comes back, then let's deal with it, but for now, let's work together as a team and give it everything we can to eradicate it."

OBJECTIVES

1. To examine your approach to relapse-prevention work.
2. To understand a relapse-prevention framework for use.
3. To determine counseling techniques that can be used in relapse-prevention work.

Two thirds of addicted clients relapse within weeks or months of beginning treatment and more than 85% relapse within a year of treatment (Sinha, 2011). Addiction has been called one of the most prevalent psychiatric disorders; it has a chronic, relapsing tendency (Sinha, 2011). Addiction relapse happens more quickly (within days or months) than with other psychological disorders (Brandon, Vidrine, & Litvin, 2007).

The addicted person can easily relapse because the alcohol/drugs *work*: The alcohol/drug use is reinforcing because the addicted person gets the effect they want. Therefore, it makes it hard to change their behavior of using the alcohol/drugs (Mackay, Donovan, & Marlatt, 1991).

Relapse-prevention work has increasingly become a part of U.S. treatment programs (Margolis & Zweben, 1998). Although it is often a specific focus of a treatment program in a group format, it can be used easily in individual sessions and in various clinical contexts (Washton & Zweben, 2006). Relapse does not mean that treatment is not working, the person is not trying, or the person will never be able to live without the active presence of the disease (Hanson, 2002). For example, drug craving can be stirred by three types of stimuli: priming (having "just one"), experiencing environmental cues for use, and acute or chronic stress (Hanson, 2002).

In the 1970s, relapse was typically not discussed by addiction professionals, and in the 1980s it was seen as people reverting to denial or not working their program (Post, 1996). The past two decades have focused more on relapse and the view of it as a process rather than an event (Brandon et al., 2007). For example, factors such as co-occurring disorders, pain, grief, money, sexual abuse, and eating disorders are considered possible contributing factors to the relapse. G. A. Marlatt and Witkiewitz (2005) state that the main goal of this work is to focus on the relapse with prevention or management techniques. The techniques used include education, therapeutic confrontation, and the development of coping skills (Schenker, 2009; Washton & Zweben, 2006). Relapse-prevention work has been shown to be generally effective and most effective with the use of alcohol or polysubstances, medication, and when the client is evaluated right after treatment (Irvin, Bowers, Dunn, & Wang, 1999). To make long-term, positive changes in addictive behaviors, relapse needs to be prevented or curtailed (Hendershot, Witkiewitz, George, & Marlatt, 2011).

COUNSELOR APPROACHES

Although relapse is common when clients try to break out of a habitual pattern of behavior (Prochaska, DiClemente, & Norcross, 1992), the counselor working on relapse issues with a client walks a fine line. The counselor wants open communication with the client, building trust so that the client will bring up relapse situations in counseling sessions. However, the counselor does not want to encourage relapse or enable the client to use by reinforcing excuses for using behavior. The counselor, then, needs to create an atmosphere of trust so that the client feels comfortable discussing actual or potential relapses, as well as create an environment of accountability where the client looks at how choices resulted in relapsing behavior. Washton and Zweben (2006) underscore the importance of the counselor's attitude toward the relapsing client. They encourage counselors to be empathic, concerned, and focus on a problem-solving approach where the client can learn from his or her mistakes.

Depending on experience in the area of addictions (personal, professional), as well as training and professional orientation, various terms and definitions may be used for a break in abstinence for the addicted individual. There is no consensus on the term (Hendershot et al., 2011). However, three terms commonly used are *slip*, *lapse*, and *relapse*; each of these terms is briefly examined here.

Sometimes self-help groups and addiction professionals use the term *slip* to discuss resumed drug usage. A slip is viewed as a one-time use that might be accidental and about which the person feels bad (Margolis & Zweben, 1998). Slips are "incidental, impulsive, and unplanned" (Washton & Zweben, 2008, p. 211). There are two difficulties with the use of this term. First, the term may encourage the client to view drug-taking behavior as accidental and outside of personal control. Related to this view, clients may view a slip as the same as a relapse, which may result in a self-fulfilling prophecy (G. A. Marlatt & Gordon, 1985). Second, a slip may not distinguish clearly between a lapse and a relapse. A lapse is different from a relapse. A *lapse* means the addict breaks the commitment to abstinence but does not return to previous levels of use; this is the initial setback (Witkiewitz & Marlatt, 2004). *Relapse* involves an activation of the addictive process where the addict resumes drug use at previous levels (Witkiewitz & Marlatt, 2004). It is a "slip that has gotten out of control" (Washton & Zweben, 2008, p. 211). This usage occurs after a series of maladaptive responses on the part of the addict (National Institute on Drug Abuse, 1994b).

Because of the lack of clear definition between a lapse and a relapse, viewing relapse as a continuum may be most helpful in the treatment process (National Institute on Drug Abuse, 1994b). The *Technical Assistance Publication (TAP 19)* (SAMHSA, 1996) describes relapse as a process, not an event, where the addicted person cannot cope with life sober. The counselor needs to help the client in treatment determine the warning signs that occur long before a relapse so the client can interrupt the process (TAP 19). Washton and Zweben (2008) describe distinctions as being important in that actions can be taken before a full-blown relapse occurs.

Note that other terms that have been used are *jump* (Washton & Stone-Washton, 1990), which describes more of a deliberate usage that may have been preplanned, and *binge*, which is a time-limited episode (Margolis & Zweben, 1998). Whatever terminology is used by the counselor, it is important to help the client look at the experience and learn from it to decrease the chances of reoccurrence. This chapter examines how the counselor can create an encouraging environment for the client to discuss (a) relapse, both in terms of prevention of and recovery from a relapse, (b) specific relapse-prevention models, and (c) specific counseling techniques.

Facilitation of Discussion

It may be best to start a discussion of the relapse or relapse potential by using a model of behavior change, such as Prochaska et al.'s (1992) five stages

of addictive behaviors: precontemplation, contemplation, preparation, action, and maintenance. This five-stage model, the stages of change, is the most widely known component of the transtheoretical model (TTM) (Miller & Rollnick, 2009). Discussion of this model may provide a framework through which the relapse can be viewed, as well as a common language for the counselor and client to discuss the relapse. Sometimes a sixth stage, *relapse*, has been included in this model that means the client has recycled through the stages and counselors need to help clients get to the action and maintenance stages as soon as possible (Miller, Forcehimes, & Zweben, 2011).

The *precontemplation* stage is apparent by the lack of intention to change the behavior. At this point, the person is unaware of or underestimates the level of the problem and is resistant to changing it. During the *contemplation* stage, the individual is aware of the problem, is thinking about changing, but has not made a commitment to take any action to address the problem. In this stage, the individual is weighing how much it will cost to address the problem and whether the price is worth the change. In the *preparation* stage, the individual is planning to take some action to make the behavior change and has tried to change the behavior (without success) in the past year. During the *action* stage, the individual is making overt changes to address the addictive behavior by committing time and energy to the changes. In the authors' definition of this stage, the individual's addictive behavior has been changed anywhere from a day to 6 months. Finally, in the *maintenance* stage, the individual is preventing relapse of the addictive behavior by continuing the change process through stabilized behavior.

DiClemente et al. (1991) point out that in this spiral cycle of change, the addicted individual can learn from mistakes made in the recovery process and make changes in the recovery plan based on what was learned about changing the behavior. In addition, because the client's readiness to change is related to the outcome of treatment (Prochaska et al., 1992), the counselor needs to evaluate how ready the client is to make a change

(Shaffer, 1997). Prochaska and colleagues recommend that therapists determine the current change level of their clients and then use that to determine the type of treatment intervention that can have an impact on relapse prevention. For example, a client at the contemplation stage may benefit more from therapy sessions that focus on the benefits and losses of making a behavior change than on action that needs to be taken to change the addiction. Further examples of application of this theory can be found in Prochaska et al. (1992) and in Chapter 9 of this text.

Understanding where the client is in terms of stage of change can assist the counselor in assessing whether relapse is a concern for the client and how to approach a discussion of relapse prevention or recovery even though, in the strictest definition of the model, relapse does not emerge as a concern until the maintenance stage. Yet, it is possible that a concern about relapse may appear in each of the stages, although it may appear differently. For example, in the first three stages, clients may have some denial or concern about changing the behavior, because they may not see themselves as able to make such a change successfully. While in the action or maintenance stages, the client might worry about relapse, because a commitment has been made to change. In the earlier stages, the counselor may need to carefully introduce the concept of relapse (not encouraging it or denying it), whereas in the later stages the counselor may need to invite the client to discuss concerns.

Connors, Donovan, and DiClemente (2001) state that relapse is a clinical issue, because clients may move back in stages in response to a relapse, with most clients returning to contemplation or preparation stages. Also, they state it is important to address, because it helps a client stay at the maintenance stage of change. Motivational interviewing strategies that address ambivalence, making decisions, and a commitment to change help clients through initial change stages (Miller & Rollnick, 2002). These strategies can also assist clients in the action stage and relapse prevention (DiClemente, Garay, & Gemmell, 2008). The client, through motivation, has enhanced facilitation through the stages of change, because the tasks of that stage have been accomplished (DiClemente, 2003).

Enabling Behavior

During relapse-prevention work with a client, whether in prevention of or recovery from a relapse, counselors need to check for enabling behavior that encourages relapse by asking themselves six questions:

1. Am I telling the client that relapse is expected for all addicts?

2. Am I avoiding giving the client consequences for the choice to use?

3. Do I think that I would drink/use if I were in the same situation?

4. Am I keeping information about the relapse from others (e.g., intimate partners, bosses, parole officers) whom I have agreed to update on the client's recovery process?

5. Do I find myself avoiding examination of the relapse situation with my client?

6. Do I avoid telling colleagues about the relapse because of how I, the client, the quality of our therapy work, or the impact on treatment may be viewed?

If the answer to any of these questions is yes, then the counselor needs to examine (alone or with a colleague or supervisor) the possibilities of enabling the client usage. The first question is critical because, as stated previously, the counselor does not want to encourage relapse, but also does not want to deny the possibility of it. As stated earlier, the counselor may want to introduce the relapse concept in the early stages of change, but be careful about sending a message to the client that all addicts relapse. Such a message is like telling a medical patient, "Treatment for your heart attack is not going to work the first time. You will have more heart attacks in the future." Rather, the counselor needs to send a message of realistic hope of change to the client that may be captured in the adage: "Hope for the best; prepare for the worst."

Three guidelines may assist a counselor in avoiding enabling behavior:

1. Question yourself and your motive in counseling in relapse situations.

2. Examine your history of caretaking of addicts.

3. Use supervision and critical-thinking colleagues to question your reactions to relapse.

These guidelines are not a guarantee against enabling, but they can assist the counselor in keeping a balance between being judgmental and enabling during relapse-prevention work.

but the client needs to be held accountable for the behavior. Thus, the client must learn to take responsibility for recovery choices and be aware of individual recovery soft spots or relapse triggers. Triggers that seem to be associated with relapse are stress, negative emotions, positive emotions, interpersonal conflict, social pressure, other substance use, and drug-related cues that stimulate cravings (National Institute on Drug Abuse, 1994b). Gordon (2003) labels them as anger and frustration, stress, positive emotional states, overconfidence, psychiatric co-morbidity, severity of addiction, and social pressure/environmental cues. Substance abusers commonly report these reasons for relapse: "stress, negative mood and anxiety, drug-related cues, temptations and boredom, and lack of positive environmental contingencies (e.g., job, family relationships, responsibilities)" (Sinha, 2011, p. 399).

Three Practical Suggestions to Help Clients Avoid Relapse

1. Ask clients to think of the worst time they had using.

2. Guide the client in "following the drink through" to its typical end experience.

3. Assist the client in addressing high-risk situations by deciding to always avoid them, avoid them for a while, or act differently when in them.

Note: The first two techniques may assist the client in coping with the euphoric recall of the usage.

View of Relapse

In terms of accountability, the actual or potential relapse for the addicted client can be viewed as a signal that something has gone wrong with the client's recovery. Some clients may avoid looking at the relapse by stating that they just slipped or that they do, after all, have a disease and then want to move off the topic. Certainly, the therapist wants to avoid being judgmental of the relapse,

The relapse does not need to be viewed as a treatment failure (G. A. Marlatt & George, 1984) but, rather, as an experience from which the client can learn and a chance to intervene in the relapse process (Mackay & Marlatt, 1990–1991). The relapse is more than an event; it is a "dynamic, ongoing process" (Hendershot et al., 2011; van Wormer & Davis, 2008). DiClemente (2003) describes relapse as a part of changing behavior, where we often learn new behaviors in successive approximations; a spiral movement where the client recycles through the stages of change. Although it is understandably difficult to discuss relapse, the counselor is not facilitating the recovery process by letting a phrase such as *I just slipped* or *I have a disease* suffice as an explanation of the relapse. To intervene in the addictive process, the counselor needs to help the client find the words to describe the relapse experience so it can be thoroughly examined in counseling, thereby allowing for an appropriate intervention.

Creation of a Trustworthy Atmosphere

The creation of a trustworthy atmosphere requires a nonjudgmental approach by the counselor in order to discuss a relapse and further relapse potential. For a client who is genuinely attempting to change behavior, a relapse can elicit a tremendous amount of negative thoughts and feelings. Trust in the counselor is absolutely necessary for the client to discuss thoughts of breaking the abstinence or actual behavior of breaking it. For example, cocaine addicts may be hesitant to report their urges because of social and clinical consequences, i.e. it is an illegal drug and they may have legal concerns as well as concerns that urges may be viewed as not being committed to or motivated for treatment (Paliwal, Hyman, & Sinha, 2008).

The component of relapse can make the work with recovering addicts very frustrating. It is difficult to work with clients on their recovery, mutually enjoy the success of their changes, and then face their relapses with them in a nonjudgmental fashion. There are opportunities for countertransference issues to emerge in this aspect of recovery. Rather than examine the components of the relapse situation, the counselor may simply begin to assume that the client is not motivated or is not ready to recover from his or her addiction. There are also opportunities for transference where the client may blame the counselor for not doing enough to help him or her stay sober. Although the disappointment may be shared by both counselor and client, the counselor needs to maintain a nonjudgmental stance in order to work through countertransference and transference issues and thereby guide the individual into a discussion about the relapse situation. Probably the best source of nonjudgmentalism for the counselor is awareness of any personal habit (overeating, smoking, gambling, drinking coffee, watching television, etc.) he or she has tried to change. Struggling with his or her own habitual tendencies may help the counselor have compassion for the ongoing struggle it takes to change behavior. The client, struggling to change an addictive behavior, may sense this compassion in the counselor or at least feel comfortable talking with a counselor who has engaged in a self-examination process.

In addition, addicted clients often legitimately ask counselors how they can understand the recovery process. If a counselor has examined his or her own habitual tendencies, the counselor may choose to let the client know that he or she understands how difficult it is to change a habit, even though it may be a different habit from the one with which the client is struggling.

Clients, then, need assistance in becoming aware of, making decisions about, and preparing to change their addictive problem. Therapists need to understand that clients may need to cycle through the stages of change several times before the behavior change is maintained. An awareness of this reality of changing addictive behaviors may assist both therapists and clients in being realistic about the difficulties that accompany changing an addictive behavior.

RELAPSE-PREVENTION MODELS

Although there are numerous relapse-prevention models (Rawson, Obert, McCann, & Marinelli-Casey, 1993), two are reviewed specifically because of their popularity among counselors and/or their vigor. The first reviewed is Gorski's CENAPS model (it is frequently used in chemical dependency treatment centers). The second model is the Marlatt and Gordon model (it is a foundational model for the field of addictions upon which many of the other relapse-prevention models are based).

Gorski's Center for Applied Sciences Model

Gorski's developmental model of recovery (DMR) (Gorski, 1989a, Gorski, 1989b, Gorski, 1990; Gorski & Miller, 1986; M. Miller, Gorski, & Miller, 1982) has been used extensively in private chemical dependency treatment centers (Rawson et al., 1993). Although Gorski's work provides many clinical recommendations within a cognitive-behavioral view (Gorski, 1992), it lacks a specific methodology that can be examined in research (Rawson et al., 1993). Gorski's work has focused on alcohol and cocaine addiction. The model addresses client responsibility in terms of awareness of relapse triggers, the process of relapse, and coping behaviors other than the use of alcohol/drugs. The Gorski model came from the "clinical world" while the Marlatt model came from the "research world" (Gordon, 2003).

Gorski was one of the first addiction professionals to produce relapse-prevention materials that encouraged the view of relapse as a mind state occurring before usage, with warning signs that were internal and behavioral in nature (Margolis & Zweben, 1998). Gorski's model is linked closely with the 12-step recovery program, which may explain in part why it has been used extensively in private chemical dependency treatment centers. Although it is popular among clinical treatment providers for the past 25 years, little empirical research has been done on the model (Miller & Harris, 2000).

In this model, recovery is viewed as developmental, and relapse prevention is viewed from a biopsychosocial perspective (G. W. Lawson, Lawson, & Rivers, 2001). It views addiction as a disease rather than a bad habit (Gordon, 2003). "Key components of Gorski's Center for Applied Sciences (CENAPS) model include assessment, identification, and management of warning signs for relapse, planning for recovery, and early intervention training for relapse." (Brandon et al., 2007, p. 273). At the core of this model is a 37-step warning sign progression that indicates the client's closeness to a relapse.

Gorski's (1989a) model has six stages:

1. *Transition*. There is a denial of an alcohol problem in that individuals believe they can control it, but they leave this stage when they realize they cannot.

2. *Stabilization*. The individuals know they have a problem but cannot quit using.

3. *Early recovery*. The individuals realize they need to make internal change and learn to cope without the drug.

4. *Middle recovery*. They become aware of the need to find a balance in life and begin to look at mending relationships and career issues.

5. *Late recovery*. They learn the maladaptive living patterns they learned as a child (learn to recognize, recover from, and solve current problems).

6. *Maintenance*. The individuals view addiction as a problem they will have all of their lives, resulting in the need for a daily recovery and growth.

Relapse prevention, then, is based on where the person is in the developmental model. Gorski (1990) describes nine principles of relapse-prevention work:

1. *Self-regulation*. Activities of daily living are stabilized.

2. *Integration*. The relapse risks are examined in terms of self-defeating behaviors, relationship-building, decreased pain, and creation of a relapse history.

3. *Understanding*. The person has accurate information about what contributes to a relapse in general.

4. *Self-knowledge*. The person can see the warning signs of relapse.

5. *Coping skills*. The person learns to avoid high-risk situations, address self-talk, and examine core beliefs that are unreliable.

6. *Change*. This involves taking a daily inventory of warning signs by having goals for a day and looking at any related problems at the end of the day.

7. *Awareness*. The person maintains the inventory of change.

8. *Significant other support*. This support helps with the relapse prevention.

9. *Maintenance*. Updates of the relapse-prevention plan are done.

Gorski and Miller (1988) list 14 mistaken beliefs about relapse and how a counselor may counter them in counseling. For example, mistaken belief number 2 is: "Relapse comes on suddenly and without warning" (Gorski & Miller, 1988, p. 6). The authors suggest that the counselor assist the client in examining what happened long before the alcohol/drug usage.

More information on specific ways the counselor can use the DMR and the principles can be found in the CENAPS workbooks listed on Gorski's website (www.cenaps.com). Although DMR uses cognitive-behavioral strategies as the Marlatt model described following does, it views stress as the major cause of relapse (Gordon, 2003). Gorski has also applied his relapse-prevention approach to topics such as brief therapy (Gorski, 1998), managed care (Gorski, 2003), and specific populations, such as African Americans (Williams & Gorski, 1997).

Marlatt and Gordon's Relapse-Prevention Model

The relapse prevention (RP) model (G. A. Marlatt & Gordon, 1985) is described as a self-management program that tries to increase the chances of a habit change being maintained. Research studies have supported the model both theoretically and practically (Hendershot et al., 2011; Larimer, Palmer, & Marlatt, 1999; Miller, Westerberg, Harris, & Tonigan, 1996), and it has been described as the most influential model in relapse prevention (DeJong, 1994). It has remained an influential cognitive-behavioral model in the addiction treatment field (Hendershot et al., 2011). The goal is to teach clients how to anticipate and cope with actual and potential relapse by increasing client awareness and choice about behavior, capacity for coping and self-control, and confidence/mastery/self-efficacy (A. Marlatt, 2000). It examines the surrounding events for initial drug use that follows a time of abstinence (DeJong, 1994). The model provides a conceptual understanding as well as treatment strategies (Hendershot et al., 2011). The model can be applied as maintaining a specific change or as a global lifestyle change. The specific interventions help the client with regard to the high-risk situations (anticipate and cope with them) while the global aspect encourages a positive, balanced lifestyle change in the client (Hendershot et al., 2011).

With regard to a specific habit, the goal is broken into two parts: (1) anticipation and prevention of a relapse after changing an addictive behavior and (2) recovery from a lapse before a full relapse; this event is called a *prolapse*—the behavior is corrected before it reaches a full blown relapse (Hendershot et al., 2011). The goal here is to help clients maintain the change in behavior long range and reduce harm if the client does have a break in abstinence (Dimeff & Marlatt, 1998). The proponents of the model (G. A. Marlatt & Gordon, 1985) believe it can be used on any addictive behaviors that consist of a compulsive habit pattern where the individual attempts to obtain immediate gratification. The model is based on social learning theory and uses treatment approaches that are cognitive and behavioral (Quigley & Marlatt, 1999). It is based on self-control that uses behavioral skill-training and cognitive interventions in an attempt to obtain the behavior change (Sandberg & Marlatt, 1991).

This social learning theory model is based on four assumptions:

1. Addiction is an overlearned, maladaptive habit pattern.

2. Behavioral determinants and consequences have an impact on behavior.

3. People are not responsible for developing a habit or for not simply being able to stop it.

4. Escape from the addiction cycle hinges on changing habits through participation and responsibility.

The process of changing a habit involves three stages: (1) commitment and motivation, (2) implementation of the specific behavioral change, and (3) long-term maintenance of the behavioral change. The individual's view of the maintenance stage contributes significantly to the recovery process.

Relapse is viewed as a two-step process. Step 1 is a lapse, where the person violates the behavioral goal that has been set. In Step 2, the relapse, returning to the target behavior existing at the pretreatment level depends on the individual's perception of the cause of the initial lapse. The lapse is a chance for the client to learn from the temporary setback (Hendershot et al., 2011). For example, the client may view himself or herself as a hopeless failure at staying sober after having one joint of marijuana (leading to a relapse of previous higher levels of marijuana use), or the client may view himself or herself as having made a mistake and needing to learn what preceded the marijuana use in order to prevent a relapse. The focus of RP is to assist people in viewing relapses as mistakes they can learn from rather than a behavior for which they are to be judged or punished.

Relapse is a decision-making process: What occurs before and after the initial lapse is critical, and there are many opportunities that may increase or decrease the risk of relapse. A successful recovery from an addictive behavior is based on a high motivation to change and a high degree of self-efficacy. Self-efficacy consists of the self-

judgments made about a person's competency to adequately perform in a particular task situation (Bandura, 1977). Self-efficacy affects behavior, thought patterns, and emotional arousal. Motivation is important because it underlines the commitment made to achieve a goal. Self-efficacy complements motivation by outlining how individuals can reach that goal and the degree to which they believe they can obtain the goal. For example, a client may be highly motivated to quit using alcohol and drugs because of family and legal problems. If the client can picture himself or herself as able to cope in different high-risk situations (high self-efficacy), there is a good chance of the client staying sober.

Most addictive behaviors involve a motivational conflict: Immediate gratification is desired but conflicts with the desire to avoid delayed negative effects. An addiction assists people in coping with natural emotional reactions that are unpleasant or aversive by decreasing the awareness of them. It is not the quitting of addictive behavior that is difficult, but the staying quit that is difficult to maintain (Connors, Donovan, & DiClemente, 2001). Relapse frequently occurs when the person enters a high-risk situation (with regard to the addictive behavior). Often, seemingly irrelevant decisions (SIDS) are a part of the addicted person's decision chain, where choices result in exposure to the drugs and a risk of relapse (National Institute on Drug Abuse, 1994b). When the person enters a high-risk situation, does not know how to cope in the situation, and experiences diminished self-efficacy and positive outcome expectancies of the addictive behavior, a relapse is highly likely, as shown in Figure 7.1. The high-risk situation means that the client is vulnerable to the addictive behavior and that contexts can include emotional or cognitive states, environment, or physiological states; these can vary across behaviors, clients, and within a client over a time period (Hendershot et al., 2011). Three high-risk behaviors connected to relapse are negative emotional states, interpersonal conflict, and social pressure (G. W. Lawson et al., 2001). Outcome expectancies are the client's

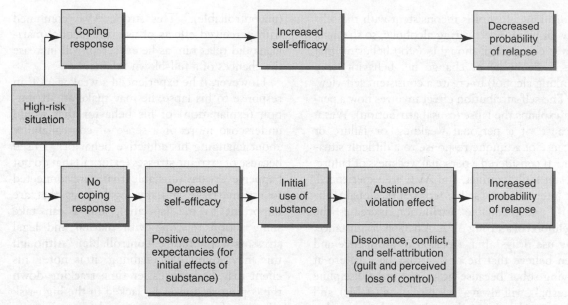

Figure 7.1 A Cognitive-Behavioral Model of the Relapse Process.

Source: Relapse Prevention, p. 38, by G. Alan Marlatt and Judith R. Gordon (Eds.), 1985, New York, NY: Guilford Press. Copyright 1985 by Guilford Press. Reprinted with permission.

anticipation of the future experience of using as well as craving (Witkiewitz & Marlatt, 2004).

To continue with the example of the client who wants to stay sober because of legal and family problems, the individual has a fight with his wife in the morning and then goes to court for the DUI and receives a severe sentence. This may be a high-risk situation, because he feels that he is trying to change, yet his changes do not seem to make a difference in his life situations. He may not know how to cope with these stressors other than using alcohol and smoking marijuana. His lack of coping responses affects high self-efficacy level: He does not view himself as able to stay sober with all of these stressors. He also begins to have positive outcome expectancies of drinking alcohol and smoking marijuana (e.g., "If I just drank and smoked a joint, I could relax and figure out how to handle this situation"). He uses alcohol (two beers) and marijuana (one joint) as a natural outcome of being in a high-risk situation, not knowing how to cope without the use of alcohol/marijuana, experiencing low self-efficacy

(cannot see himself as being able to persist at staying sober), and expecting positive outcomes from using alcohol/marijuana (being able to relax and think clearly).

After the initial use, the individual experiences an abstinence violation effect (AVE), the psychological effect of violating the abstinence rule. AVE hinges on cognitive dissonance and the self-attribution effect. It is increased in its likelihood if one views relapse from a dichotomous perspective or does not take situational factors into account (Hendershot et al., 2011). Cognitive dissonance is the discrepancy between what people believe about themselves and how they behave. This discrepancy requires individuals to change either their thoughts or behaviors in order to reduce the dissonance and have a consistent view of themselves.

For example, a person who wants to stop drinking alcohol enters an addiction treatment program and makes a commitment to herself that she will never drink again. On leaving treatment, there is a lapse: She has a beer. The behavior of drinking alcohol is inconsistent with the self-view of being a recovering alcoholic, so she must either change her thoughts (stop believing that she is alcoholic) or change her behavior (stop drinking alcohol) to create a consistent self-view.

The self-attribution effect involves how a person explains the lapse (causal attribution). Was it because of a personal weakness or failure or because of a unique response to a difficult situation? If considered a personal weakness or failure, greater guilt, conflict, and AVE are experienced: An internal (self), stable (constant), global (general), uncontrollable attribution increases the likelihood of a strong AVE. A person, for instance, may use drugs after a period of abstinence and then believe that he or she may be a failure at staying sober because he or she lacks discipline (internal), will always lack discipline (stable), and will never be able to learn how to be more disciplined (global, uncontrollable).

On the other hand, if a person can explain the lapse as a unique response to a difficult situation, he or she will experience weaker guilt, conflict, and AVE: An external (environment), unstable (changeable), and specific and controllable causal attribution decreases the likelihood of an intense AVE. Because a stronger AVE will increase the chances of relapse, the AVE in response to the lapse is a critical intervention point. Returning to our same client who lapsed by drinking two beers and smoking a joint, his behavior is considered a lapse, because before treatment, he drank half a case of beer and smoked half an ounce of marijuana daily. If he returns to his pretreatment level of use, it is considered a relapse. At this point, however, he has only had a lapse into his addictive behavior. What determines whether he returns to his pretreatment level of use is the AVE he experiences. If he experiences a strong AVE, he may make an attribution (an explanation) of his behavior that would underscore a sense of uncontrollability about changing the addictive behavior: "I used because I am a failure as a human being (internal), and I will always be a failure at staying sober (stable) no matter what situation I am in (global) or what others and I try to do

(uncontrollable)." This strong AVE combined with perceived effects of use (the alcohol/marijuana did relax him as he expected) will increase the chances of a full-blown relapse.

However, if he experienced a weaker AVE in response to his lapse, he may make an attribution (explanation) of his behavior that would underscore more of a sense of controllability about changing his addictive behavior: "I used because of extreme stresses (external) that do not happen every day (unstable) that were connected to my marriage and my legal status that are important to me (specific), and I can take some action to cope with marital and legal stressors in the future (controllable)." Although this may sound like enabling, it is not. This client may have an easier time tracking down the coping responses he lacked in the high-risk situation if he does not get caught in an intense, seemingly endless AVE, which will only encourage further relapse and a sense of hopelessness and uncontrollability in making a change about the addictive behavior.

The RP model attempts to take a realistic, practical approach to recovery from an addiction. Viewing relapse as a normal part of recovery allows counselors to step out of a parental, authoritarian role with clients. As stated previously, however, the counselor needs to emphasize that relapse is *not* a requirement of recovery. Focusing on the likelihood of relapse provides counselors and clients with the opportunity to develop prevention plans so relapse does not occur. Counselors can use this relapse-prevention model within their own theoretical framework. For example, this social learning model has been used with psychoanalytic theories (D. S. Keller, 2003).

Finally, this model has been reconceptualized in a way that specifically addresses the complex, dynamic, and unpredictable process of addiction (Witkiewitz & Marlatt, 2004, 2007). The revision of the model emerged from six areas core to the model (triggers/specific situational events; similarities/differences of lapse and relapse determinants; individual reactions/conceptualizations of a lapse leading to a relapse; possible set-up for a high-risk situation; points of intervention to prevent a relapse; treatment preparation to reduce relapse) as well as studies that questioned the original model design (Marlatt, Bowen, & Witkiewitz, 2009). In this reconceptualization, relapse is viewed as a fluid process with multi-dimensional and dynamic determinants that interact with one another; the factors of timing and event interrelatedness are emphasized (Witkiewitz & Marlatt, 2007). In the relapse process, there are feedback loops that "allow for the interaction between coping skills, cognitions, affect, and substance use behavior" (Witkiewitz & Marlatt, 2007, p. 22). This new, dynamic model (Hendershot et al., 2011) focuses on the high-risk situation where *tonic* (stable) and *phasic* (transient) influences intertwine in a complex manner thereby determining if a relapse is going to occur. *Tonic* processes include *digital risks* (family history, social support, dependence), cognitive processes, and physical withdrawal, while *phasic* processes include cognitive and affective processes, how one copes in the situation, and the substance use behavior and consequences. Motivation is implicitly included in the model as motivation for a positive behavior change or to engage in the problem behavior (Witkiewitz & Marlatt, 2004).

Assessment of the relapse requires that it be viewed as a process that involves different determining factors that need to be assessed frequently in counseling as well as assessment of the different determining causes (Brandon et al., 2007). The multidetermination is important because there is variation within and across individuals with regard to relapse. Therefore, long-term monitoring is needed once a relapse has occurred. Because relapse is frequent and rapid, the assessment for it needs to happen a short time following treatment (weeks, months) to determine if the client is susceptible to relapse (Sinha, 2011). Also,

additional clinical symptoms such as "history of trauma and high stress, and drug craving" (Sinha, 2011, p. 402) need to be used as markers in identifying clients in treatment who may be even more susceptible to relapse. For example, childhood trauma was found as predictive of cocaine relapse in women, but not men (Hyman et al., 2008). Assessment can lead to treatment interventions regarding the teaching of specific coping skills such as job finding, social skills, emotional regulation, behavioral self-control, and coping with cravings and urges (Miller et al., 2011).

It is easy with a complex, interactive theory for both the counselor to become lost in its application. To avoid this, think of tonic processes as those aspects that determine *who* is vulnerable and phasic ones as determining *when* the relapse occurs. The counselor can assess if the client is vulnerable to a relapse and in what types of circumstances that vulnerability may come to fruition. In the Marlatt model, the emphasis is placed on clients learning coping skills that can be used in high-risk situations as well as learning from previous lapse(s) and relapse(s) (Brandon et al., 2007).

The author has found specific approaches in applying the model to assess the client with regard to relapse prevention. *First*, it is helpful to focus on the most emotional relapse experienced by the client in order to facilitate the details of the experience. For example, many people in the United States will be able to remember the details of where they were/what was happening if they hear the date, September 11, 2001, in contrast to other dates they may hear. *Second*, try to gather the information in as stark a description as possible in order to focus on the critical elements of the relapse. *Third*, focus on the actual drug use because clients may readily go into tangential information that is related to the drug using experience, but not necessarily core for the assessment. The counselor needs to "rein the client in" with regard to the storytelling in a gentle, but firm manner. Using close-ended questions may help the counselor contain and focus the story. At the same time, counselors need to be aware that "tangential information" may be clinically relevant for noting an underlying "wound" that needs to be addressed in future treatment. *Fourth*, balance the retrieving of information with the scales of being aware of the client's potential sensitivity in discussing the use and being time efficient. *Finally*, and possibly most importantly, the counselor needs to be acutely aware that talking about the lapse/relapse may trigger another lapse/relapse. This can be monitored by: (a) watching the client's nonverbal behaviors, (b) periodically checking in with the client about thoughts and feelings related to the assessment process, and (c) making sure the client is knowledgeable about user-friendly coping skills that include a community of support.

Although there are many cues and anticipated consequences that the client has to take in and process in a high-risk situation, the counselor can help the client, especially early in the recovery process, by focusing on a few broad internal and external factors that the client can watch for in and outside of oneself. If the client has a coping response that is effective in combination with social support, positive affect, and negative outcome expectancies, the client may have an increase in self-efficacy and an ability to remain abstinent (Witkiewitz & Marlatt, 2005). Again, the counselor can help the client by memorizing a few general coping responses to apply in a high-risk situation.

For example, a client may attend a social function anticipating that no alcohol or drugs may be present. At the actual function no use is occurring, but when the client steps outside to have a cigarette, she discovers that people are using drugs outside the back of the building (*high-risk situation*). In this situation, the client remembers she can call her sponsor (*coping response*), which calms her momentarily, and she begins to see herself as

able to stay sober in this situation (*increased self-efficacy*). However, when she reaches for her cell phone to call her sponsor, she finds the phone is dead. In this feedback loop, the memorized coping response is not going to work (*no coping response*). She experiences a meltdown where she feels emotionally overwhelmed with the belief she cannot stay sober in this situation because her coping response does not work (*decreased self-efficacy*). She begins to ask the other people to share their drugs with her to help calm her initial anxiety about being in this social situation sober and now the increased anxiety she is experiencing since her coping strategy did not work (*positive outcome expectancies*).

At that point, she notices someone she met in a self-help group come to the back of the building for a cigarette and notices he also looks anxious around the drug use. She approaches him and tells him she is having a hard time at the social function, especially since she stepped outside and found herself around others using drugs. He smiles at her, thanks her for her honesty, and tells her he is having the same problem. Her reaching out to him (*coping response*) and his supportive response (*social support of her recovery*) results in her feeling more hopeful (*positive affect*) about staying sober in the situation (*increased self-efficacy*). They begin to talk about the negative outcomes that would result from their use of the drugs (*negative outcome expectancies*). This results in a *decreased probability of relapse* for both of them. This example shows the complexity and dynamics involved in a relapse situation and the importance, then, of obtaining as much information as possible from the client about high-risk situations. At the same time, it is important that the counselor not overwhelm or frustrate the client during the gathering of information by becoming bogged down in the details of the relapse situation. That is why it can be highly beneficial to the client if the counselor can help the client determine a few general internal and external factors that can increase vulnerability to relapse and a few general coping skills that can be applied across various high-risk situations.

COUNSELING TECHNIQUES

The main emphasis in relapse prevention is for the counselor to assist the client in becoming more self-aware. The relapse-prevention activities need to be personal. Clients need to take the abstract theory of relapse prevention and, with the help of the counselor, apply it to their own life. This personalization will result in an increased self-awareness. The self-awareness can generally be encouraged by the counselor by asking clients to watch themselves through techniques such as timing the length of the urge to use or logging of recovery experiences. Marlatt and Kristeller (1999) call this *urge surfing*. In this imagery technique, the client labels the urge in terms of sensations and cognitions and detaches from the urge. Therefore, the client becomes aware of the urge, accepts it, but does not act on it or fight it (Marlatt & Witkiewitz, 2005).

Treatment that is based in mindfulness may assist in the prevention of relapse (Brandon et al., 2007). Mindfulness is defined as "observing, seeing one thing in the moment" (Marra, 2004, p. 100) and as an emptiness: "to have an empty mind, a mind free of determinative, categorical conceptualizations" (Craig, 2007, p. 11). Or as Zgierska et al. (2009) describe it, "as the intentional, accepting and non-judgmental focus of one's attention on the emotions, thoughts and sensations occurring in the present moment" (p. 2). Mindfulness assists in the mind-body connection in a manner Siegel (2009) describes as brain hygiene. The "urge surfing" technique is a mindfulness practice that can be used in high-risk situations. The client's awareness and acceptance of thoughts, senses, and emotions leads to greater tolerance, compassion, and self-efficacy with regard to oneself. Bowen et al. (2006) found mindfulness meditation helped a prison population cope with relapse, because they were mindful of urges to use in the present moment.

A specific form of mindfulness is mindfulness meditation that is considered a form of complimentary or alternative medicine (CAM) (Barnett &

Shale, 2013). The client focuses on breathing while being aware of the present. The four common components of meditation address location (quiet), posture (specific and comfortable), attention (focus), and attitude (open). The authors caution counselors and their clients to be trained appropriately through legitimate organizations that offer certificates in the practice of meditation. Witkiewitz, Marlatt, and Walker (2005) propose that integrating mindfulness meditation techniques with relapse prevention will strengthen addiction treatment as well as be cost-effective because it is inexpensive and accessible. In a systematic review of the literature on mindfulness meditation (Zgierska et al., 2009), the authors concluded that there were positive outcomes across studies supporting it as an effective treatment for clients with substance use, misuse, or disorders. A later study (Witkiewitz & Bowen, 2010) found mindfulness-based relapse prevention (MBRP) to assist in reduction of substance use as connected to responses (cognitive, behavioral) to depressive symptoms.

Also, experiential activities such as role-plays (acting out relapse-triggering scenarios), guided imagery (focusing on positive thoughts and images while simultaneously imagining the difficult situation; Cormier & Cormier, 1998), and empty chair (carrying on a dialogue with opposing parts of the self by being the opposite self in each chair) can help a client personalize the relapse-prevention process through increased self-awareness. In addition, the counselor can suggest that the client "follow the drink (drug) through" to facilitate awareness of possible use consequences. Finally, Figure 7.1 can be used with a client who has relapsed by asking the client to recall the worst relapse experienced in order to cognitively and emotionally understand the application of the model to the client's recovery process.

An increased self-awareness can assist the client in recognizing danger signs of relapse and developing a personal continuum of difficult recovery situations. Early in recovery, this self-awareness may appear as a hypervigilance where the client is overly aware of high-risk situations.

This sensitivity needs to be discussed and to some degree encouraged by the counselor so the client knows that such behavior may be helpful in anticipating potential high-risk situations. For example, when a client is invited to a party, because of the client's use history, the client may assume alcohol or drugs will be at the party. Such an assumption can help the client realize that whether alcohol or drugs are present, vigilance may help the client prepare for the worst and not be taken unaware in such a situation.

Marlatt and Gordon's Relapse-Prevention Model

Marlatt and Gordon (1985) outline an intervention procedure for preventing relapse. An overview of the RP model is provided by Larimer et al. (1999). Counselors are encouraged to help clients learn seven specific target behaviors:

1. Situations that are high risk for them.

2. Skills to cope in high-risk situations.

3. Relaxation and stress management skills.

4. Examination of positive outcome expectancies: realistic outcomes of addictive behavior (sometimes described in self-help groups as "follow the drink through [to its inevitable outcome]").

5. Immediate and delayed effects of the addictive activity.

6. Action to take if a relapse occurs.

7. Control over behavior through programmed relapse.

Marlatt and Gordon (1985) also recommend global recovery strategies, including examination of the client's lifestyle, development of positive addictions or substitutions for the addictive behavior, creation of an "observatory role" where clients learn from their urges to use rather than act on them, and development of the client's "relapse warning system" so early-warning signals of

relapse can be heard. For example, during the process of treating a middle-age woman who is addicted to prescription medication and alcohol, the therapist will want to examine situations where she may have difficulty avoiding the use of prescription medication and/or alcohol to cope. The therapist should determine coping skills the client might lack, her view of the effects and consequences of her pill and alcohol use, and the action and control she needs to take to prevent a relapse. Also, the therapist will want to help this woman examine her overall lifestyle in terms of balance, positive addictions, capacity to self-monitor, and presence of a relapse warning system. Marlatt (2000) recommends that the RP approach be individualized so interventions are carefully chosen that fit the client's problem and lifestyle.

This approach can also be matched with stages of change in treatment. Three additional suggestions are to (1) help the client choose a combination of techniques, (2) focus on techniques one at a time, and (3) balance verbal approaches with nonverbal ones. In 2002, Marlatt, Parks, and Witkiewitz developed *Clinical Guidelines for Implementing Relapse Prevention Therapy* that the reader may find useful. Marlatt's cognitive-behavioral *Relapse Prevention* video (American Psychological Association [APA], 1997) provides an excellent example of the application of relapse-prevention techniques in an individualized manner. Also, the *Inventory of Drinking Situations* (Annis, Graham, & Davis, 1988) helps identify places of client vulnerability based on the Marlatt model. Two specific techniques that may assist in this process of relapse-prevention planning with a client are the decision matrix and mapping.

The *decision matrix* (G. A. Marlatt, 1985a) is a chart that compares the consequences of quitting with continuing the addictive behavior. Table 7.1, for example, shows a decision matrix for a person who wants to quit smoking. The matrix has eight cells that are divided into two sections. The first section, which has four parts, looks at the positive and negative consequences for stopping (or remaining stopped) the addictive behavior. Both immediate and delayed consequences of stopping

Table 7.1 Decision Matrix for Smoking Cessation

	Immediate Consequences		Delayed Consequences	
	Positive	Negative	Positive	Negative
To stop smoking or remain abstinent	Increased self-efficacy. Social approval. Improved physical state. Financial gain.	Denial of gratification. Withdrawal discomfort. Frustration and anger. Weight gain.	Enhanced self-control. Improved health (absence of disease). Financial gain. Absence of social disapproval.	Denial of gratification (becomes less intense).
To continue or resume smoking	Immediate gratification. Removal of withdrawal discomfort. Consistent with past self-image. Weight loss.	Guilt and attribution of no control. Social censure. Negative physical effects. Financial loss.	Continued gratification.	Decreased self-control. Health risks. Financial loss. Continued social disapproval.

Source: Relapse Prevention, p. 38, by G. Alan Marlatt and Judith R. Gordon (Eds.), 1985, New York, NY: Guilford Press. Copyright 1985 by Guilford Press. Reprinted with permission.

are addressed. Staying with the example of the middle-age woman, the therapist could use the matrix to understand the client's view of the consequences and effects of her addiction (see comments in parentheses):

- Immediate positive consequences to stopping or remaining stopped in terms of the addictive behavior. (She likes feeling "clear-headed and energetic.")

- Immediate negative consequences to stopping or remaining stopped in terms of the addictive behavior. (She does not like the feelings of anxiety she experiences when she is without pills or alcohol and in a stressful situation.)

- Delayed positive consequences to stopping or remaining stopped in terms of the addictive behavior. (She hopes to earn back her children's respect by being sober.)

- Delayed negative consequences to stopping or remaining stopped in terms of the addictive behavior. (She is afraid she will not be able to cope with the anxiety every day of her life she is sober.)

The second section, which has four parts, looks at the positive and negative consequences for continuing (or resuming) the addictive behavior. Again, both immediate and delayed consequences are addressed:

- Immediate positive consequences to continuing or resuming the addictive behavior. (She enjoys the feeling of relaxation she experiences when she takes pills and alcohol.)

- Immediate negative consequences to continuing or resuming the addictive behavior. (Her children will not let her visit her grandchildren if she resumes her chemical usage.)

- Delayed positive consequences to continuing or resuming the addictive behavior. (She will feel capable to cope with her anxiety in stressful situations.)

- Delayed negative consequences to continuing or resuming the addictive behavior. (Her children will lose respect for her again and possibly forever.)

In this example, high-risk situations include those that the woman finds stressful and those when she uses pills and alcohol to cope with the stress. She lacks the stress management skills that could help her cope with the anxiety. If she can learn some stress management skills, which will help her stay sober, she may be able to choose actions in stressful situations that will allow her to control her behavior (stay sober) and work at regaining the respect of her children and the contact with her grandchildren, which are so important to her. By developing such a relapse warning system for high-stress situations and by learning to observe herself for signs of tension, the client can work at developing a more balanced lifestyle that incorporates some positive addictions to stress management activities.

The counselor and client need to work together on completing this matrix early in the treatment process to determine the client's motivation level and goals. Also, the matrix will help the counselor learn the values and level of commitment of the client that may not have been articulated. Knowledge of these values and commitment level may enhance the client's motivation to change the addictive behavior by clarifying appropriate interventions. In the author's use of this intervention, the matrix exercise is especially useful with clients who like to process experiences in a cognitive, logical format.

Another relapse-prevention technique is called *mapping* (G. A. Marlatt, 1985a) or "relapse road maps" (Marlatt & Witkiewitz, 2005, p. 5), where the possible outcomes resulting from a high-risk situation are discussed by the counselor and the client. The client and therapist draw a relapse-prevention map for the client. This map shows where the individual is and where he or she wants to go. The process leading to the final goal of abstinence from the addiction can be mapped out, so the client gets an overall view of his or her recovery process.

Figure 7.2 provides an example of a general mapping strategy. The left side of the diagram is called the "*Road of No Use*" and the right side is called the "*Road of Use*." Both sides of the diagram can be used to facilitate awareness. The goal of this exercise is to increase client awareness of relapse

components so the client can learn from previous relapses and avoid future ones; it can help increase the client's awareness of the antecedents and consequences to both non-using (*Road of No Use*) and using (*Road of Use*) behavior. Both roads can be used to exemplify the internal and external strengths and vulnerabilities of the client and his/her recovery resources.

The counselor needs to fill in empty map boxes on both roads with words or pictures based on the information elicited from the sample script questions for each of the boxes. The map can assist the therapist in learning the aspects of relapse prevention that the client may be neglecting in his or her recovery. Also, mapping may help clarify whether a client needs to always avoid certain situations, avoid them for awhile, or decide to enter a situation and be different (e.g., not use alcohol or drugs). Finally, the continuity loop in the diagram is symbolic for how the client will potentially face high-risk relapse situations throughout their addiction recovery.

The author has found this to be especially beneficial for clients who feel limited in their language expression as well as clients who enjoy experiential, expressive activities since this exercise can easily involve drawing, collage work, etc. For example, a collage exercise using only pictures in the mapping process can enhance client awareness in an individual or group counseling setting.

In the previous example, the counselor and the client determined that a final destination for the client is to regain the respect of her children and contact with her grandchildren. Keeping these goals in mind, the client and counselor can anticipate high-stress situations for her based on her past use history and current life situation. Discussions can focus on what could lead the client to wanting to use pills and alcohol and what would happen to her if she does so. Although the outcome may be similar to using the decision matrix, some clients may feel more comfortable with this exercise than one that lists short- and long-term effects, or the same information obtained in two different exercises may facilitate the client's awareness of relapse prevention. Both the *decision*

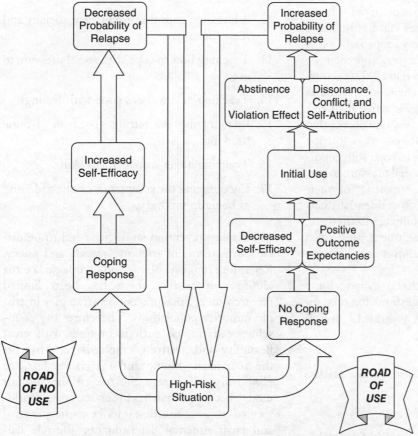

Counseling Goal: Increased Client Awareness of High-Risk Situations

{*Seemingly Irrelevant Decisions*: Fertile Ground for High-Risk Situation}

Figure 7.2 Relapse Prevention Mapping Exercise.

Sample Relapse Prevention "Road of Use" Exercise Script

Seemingly Irrelevant Decisions: "What decision(s) did you make that led up to the high-risk situation?"

High-Risk Situation: "Tell me about just one high-risk situation—preferably the most emotionally upsetting relapse you had when you were trying to stay sober. Describe the situation in as much detail as possible (i.e., who was there, where were you, what alcohol/drugs were present)."

No Coping Response: "What is it you did not know how to do in this situation? What skills were you lacking?"

Decreased Self-Efficacy: "Tell me how you could not picture yourself as staying sober."*

Positive Outcome Expectancies: "How did you expect the alcohol/drugs to help you?*

[*=Use these two areas in combination to understand the set-up for the initial use]

Initial Use: "What was the first break in your abstinence?" (i.e., first drink of alcohol)

Abstinence Violation Effect: "What happened right after your initial use in terms of your thoughts and feelings about staying sober?" (i.e., anger at self for using, shame about using)

Dissonance, Conflict, Self-Attribution: "How did you explain to yourself that you were using again even though you had been trying hard to stay sober? "

Increased Probability of Relapse: "Tell me about that point in your relapse when you gave up on abstinence—you found you had broken your commitment to it, gave up, and returned to your normal alcohol/drug use level."

matrix and *mapping* can assist clients in preventing a relapse from occurring in their recovery or in learning from a relapse that has occurred. Therefore, both of these techniques can be used in a general anticipatory recovery approach or a relapse-specific, reflective recovery approach.

In summary, Daley and Marlatt (1997) encourage counselors to help their clients see relapse as both an event and a process, identify high-risk factors and coping strategies, be aware of cues that can set off cravings, find different ways to cope with negative emotions, learn to cope with cognitive distortions, be aware of social pressure to use, develop a social network supportive of their behavior change, help those in residential treatment make the transition to outpatient/aftercare, consider pharmacological treatment, develop a balanced lifestyle, and develop a lapse/relapse plan.

Washton and Zweben (2006) include some of these factors in their suggestions for relapse-prevention strategies. They suggest 17 overall strategies counselors can use:

1. Educating about relapse and relapse prevention.

2. Enhancing awareness of warning signs.

3. Being aware of substance-specific factors that may trigger relapse.

4. Avoiding the presence of the abstinence violation effect (AVE).

5. Increasing awareness of seemingly irrelevant decisions (SIDS).

6. Addressing the fantasy of controlled use.

7. Addressing the resistance to abstinence from all mood-altering drugs.

8. Dealing with "pink cloud" or "honeymoon" recovery feelings.

9. Creating a balanced lifestyle.

10. Encouraging the presence of visible reminders of the negative consequences of use.

11. Monitoring alcohol and drug use (urine testing).

12. Addressing gaps that are present socially and recreationally.

13. Teaching how to cope with social pressure to use.

14. Teaching new ways to cope with feelings.

15. Encouraging the letting go of all-or-none thinking.

16. Teaching anger management skills.

17. Encouraging the acceptance of one's identity as being in recovery.

Relapse-prevention strategies need to be discussed in terms of *ethnicity*, *gender*, and *family*. Regarding *ethnicity*, Blume and Garcia de la Cruz (2005) caution that there has been limited research on relapse-prevention strategies in ethnic minority populations. Therefore, the counselor needs to use such techniques with great flexibility and a strong emphasis on what fits the individual. Blume and Garcia de la Cruz (2005) also encourage the use of the Marlatt model, because it matches the collectivistic worldview of ethnic minorities: It looks at interpersonal and environmental determinants, lifestyle balance, positive addictions ("alternative activities," p. 56), and identification with the majority/minority cultures. They also suggest that the counselor assess the acculturation level of the client and consider the use of alternative activities, community leaders, and oral traditions such as storytelling (e.g., possibly using traditional stories about relapse prevention).

Regarding *gender*, Gordon (2003) summarizes the differences as follows: (a) women relapse less than men because of a tendency for greater involvement in group counseling and a willingness to seek treatment; (b) cocaine-addicted clients and those in alcoholism treatment reported different triggers for relapse (women = negative emotions, interpersonal problems; men = positive feelings); (c) female cocaine-addicted clients had more impulsive relapses while men justified and rationalized more after their relapse; and (d) male alcohol treatment clients reported a return to drinking alone while female clients reported drinking with female friends/romantic partner. Gordon (2003) recommends, then, that treatment for relapse prevention may need to emphasize different skills based on gender.

Finally, Washton and Zweben (2006) discuss *family* issues as they relate to relapse prevention, defining family in as broad a fashion as possible. They suggest considering issues of enabling behaviors that encourage the addiction, preoccupation with the addict's behavior (codependency), domestic violence, need for a family therapist, perceived loss of the addict to the self-help movement, avoidance of major decisions in the first year of recovery, sexual problems, and power balance.

Ten Most Common Dangers

An excellent overall counseling technique (National Institute on Drug Abuse, 1994a) to use with addicted individuals is an awareness of common dangers that addicts face in general when they are:

- Around familiar drugs, drug users, or drug-related settings.
- Experiencing negative feelings.
- Celebrating positive feelings.
- Experiencing boredom.
- Getting high on any mood-altering substance.
- Experiencing physical pain.
- Focusing on getting high.
- Having a lot of money all of a sudden.
- Taking prescription medication that causes a high.
- Believing that occasional drug use (without problems) is possible.

Because these are general relapse areas for the addicted individuals, it is important to find out which of them are specifically dangerous for your client. For example, a particular client may not struggle with experiencing positive feelings or negative feelings in general, but he or she may have an especially difficult time handling the feeling of loneliness.

TIPS for Coping with Stressful Situations

The National Institute of Drug Abuse (1994a) developed the acronym *TIPS* to remind addicts of how to cope with difficult situations: **T**ruth, **I**nformation, **P**riorities, and **S**upport. *Truth* means that the addict needs to let others know honestly about the current struggle being experienced. *Information* encourages the addict to obtain facts about the situation at hand rather than react on assumptions or emotions. *Priorities* means that the addict sees the number-one priority as staying sober and focusing on what is really important to him or her. *Support* reminds the addict to turn to others for support when in a difficult situation. This acronym may be helpful for the addicted person and the counselor to memorize. In terms of relapse prevention, the client and counselor can examine the high-risk situation from this perspective: What truth does the client need to speak, what information needs to be obtained, what priorities need to be set, and what support needs to be drawn?

HALT

HALT is another helpful acronym for clients and counselors used in some self-help groups (National Institute of Alcohol Abuse and Alcoholism, 1995a). This acronym warns about potential relapse by reminding the addict to not get too **H**ungry, **A**ngry, **L**onely, or **T**ired. When using this acronym with clients, discuss how they can recognize how they behaviorally act out these feelings: What are they like when hungry, angry, lonely, or tired? If they can pinpoint behavioral indicators of HALT, these behaviors can be alerts for them to stop and practice self-care in response to that need. For example, if a client learns through self-observation or feedback from others that when he or she is hungry there is a tendency to be more edgy with others, then the client can watch for edgy behavior and then respond to the hunger. If the client cannot be so precise, he or she may simply want to use the acronym as a general self-care checklist when feeling out of sorts or off-balance. For example, if the client is upset, he or she may try to address each of the areas (eat something, take a deep breath, talk with a friend, rest) until something helps him or her feel more in balance. This simple acronym may assist addicted clients when they find themselves in an upsetting situation that they do not know how to handle; it may remind them of simple self-care steps they can take to prevent relapse.

Relapse prevention is critical to the recovery process. To assist clients in maintaining their sobriety, therapists need to help them anticipate and prepare for difficult recovery situations. The various techniques discussed (decision matrix, mapping, 10 most common dangers, TIPS, HALT) can assist clients in resolving their ambivalence about staying sober. (See Case Study 7.1.)

CASE STUDY 7.1

Frank is a 45-year-old male who is married for the third time. He completed 1 year of college and has worked the night shift at a local factory for 20 years. All of Frank's friends are from his workplace, and their main recreational activity is focused on drinking. His first two wives left him because of his drinking, and his third wife is currently threatening to leave him for the same reason. Frank has four children (two from each of his previous marriages), but none of his children have contact with him because of his aggressive personality when he is drinking. Frank's third wife has been in Al-Anon for 3 of the 5 years they have been married. She arranged an intervention for him for his drinking, and he entered inpatient treatment primarily because "I love my wife and I will do anything to keep her."

During Frank's past few days in treatment, his wife admits during the family session that she has been having an affair with one of his best friends from the plant and that she arranged for Frank to go to treatment so she could leave the marriage without a guilty conscience. Frank is devastated by the news, and that afternoon one of his drinking buddies calls him at the treatment center and invites him to a retirement party for one of their friends at the plant. The party is scheduled for the day after Frank leaves treatment.

Frank decides to not tell anyone about the retirement party. He and his counselor make arrangements for him to live with another male who is new to recovery. When Frank leaves treatment, he goes to his house to collect the items he needs for his new apartment. His wife is there, but she refuses to talk with him. Frank has difficulty sleeping that night and has a lot of angry fantasies about seeking revenge on his wife and friend. When he gets to the retirement party, he sees his old friend who is involved with his wife. He decides to drink a beer ("to get some courage"). He then walks over to his friend and hits him as he calls him names. His friends separate the two men, and some of them go with Frank to a local bar. Frank feels very ashamed that he drank, cannot imagine that he can live through the humiliation he feels about his wife's infidelity, and believes the alcohol has made him feel stronger and more confident about handling the situation.

After a couple of months of drinking at his old rate, Frank contacts you for help.

1. How would you help Frank talk about his relapse?

2. How do you recognize the different aspects of the relapse-prevention model (high-risk situations, lack of coping responses, decreased self-efficacy, positive outcome expectancies, lapse, (initial use of substance) AVE, perceived effects of use, (dissonance, conflict, and self-attribution) increased relapse probability)?

3. What coping behaviors would you work on with this client?

4. What changes does Frank need to make in his lifestyle?

5. What would you want to help Frank do with regard to positive addictions and/or substitutes?

6. How might learning the observer role help Frank?

7. How will learning early-warning relapse signals help Frank?

8. How would you help Frank use techniques such as decision matrix, mapping, 10 common dangers, TIPS for coping?

CASE STUDIES OF SPECIAL POPULATIONS

Often addiction does not stand alone. It is frequently accompanied by additional issues such as domestic violence, sexual abuse, and behavioral addictions such as eating disorders and gambling. Marlatt and Donovan (2005) provide chapters in their edited book that address relapse prevention with some of these special populations: eating disorders, gambling disorders, sex offenders, and sexually risky behaviors. Although these concerns are discussed at length in Chapters 4 and 6, some case studies of these special populations are presented here to facilitate the understanding of relapse prevention with regard to accompanying issues. (See Case Studies 7.2–7.5.)

CASE STUDY 7.2

Jeanette is a 22-year-old amphetamine addict who came to treatment at her doctor's recommendation. She had been obtaining amphetamines over the past five years by seeing different doctors for prescriptions ("doctor shopping") and by going to different pharmacies. One of the pharmacists notified one of her physicians of her amphetamine use, and she was confronted by that doctor about her addiction during her next visit. Her doctor also asked her at that time about the bruises on her body, and she admitted that her husband of two years beats her. She begged her doctor and her treatment counselor not to confront her husband, because she is afraid a confrontation of the issue will accelerate the violence.

She has done well in inpatient treatment, has attended both AA and Women for Sobriety (WFS) self-help groups, has a sponsor/mentor in each of the self-help groups, and will be returning home in a couple of days. Although she is aware that she used drugs in part to cope with the violence (she used amphetamines to get more things done at home and at work so he would not be angry with her), she refuses to discuss the domestic violence in her home, and her husband refuses to attend family sessions at the treatment center.

As her aftercare counselor, answer the following six questions:

1. What would be a main concern to address with Jeanette immediately in her aftercare plans?
2. What high-risk situations might Jeanette face when she returns home?
3. What coping responses might she lack?
4. What evidence is there of decreased self-efficacy and positive outcome expectancies?
5. Do you see Jeanette as needing to make a lifestyle change in order to remain sober? If so, what changes do you see her needing to make, and how would you recommend that she make them?
6. Which counseling techniques (decision matrix, mapping, 10 common dangers, TIPS for coping) would you see as appropriate to use with her at this time?

CASE STUDY 7.3

Suzi is a 30-year-old female who had one previous addiction treatment 5 years ago. She was able to stay sober for 1 year. Her treatment was court-ordered because of a DUI. She has come to you for counseling because she recently started drinking heavily again after a visit home over the holidays (during the previous 4 years, she says her drinking was limited to the weekends, but now she is back to daily drinking). She wants to quit drinking and using drugs again, but she wants to do it through private counseling with you rather than a formal treatment center, which she believes is a financial rip-off. She warns you that she is a "loser" when it comes to sobering up, because treatment did not work for her, nor did Alcoholics Anonymous or Narcotics Anonymous, and her family has always told her she is a loser who will never be able to make anything of herself.

Suzi is single and lives alone. She is the middle child of three girls and denies any family history of alcoholism. She says that when she sobered up the first time, she started to have trouble having sex with men she dated, and she had bad dreams of her father forcing her to have sex with him. She does not remember specific incidents of sexual abuse beyond her dreams. She does not have these dreams when she is drinking (her drug of choice is alcohol, although she says she has tried "everything") and reports being afraid that she will have the bad dreams again when she sobers up for a while. Suzi states that she has problems when she visits her family, which she does only on holidays, when she is sober. She says her father has a habit of French kissing her "hello" and "good-bye," which she does not mind when she is drinking, but did mind that year that she was sober. She is unable to talk at length about what happened during her last visit home over the holidays: She begins to cry uncontrollably when she is asked about it. All she can state is, "This time it was more than French kissing."

As her private therapist, answer the following six questions:

1. What are the high-risk situations for Suzi in her addiction recovery?
2. What is her abstinence violation effect?
3. What positive outcome expectancies do you think may precede Suzi's initial use?
4. What may need to change in terms of her coping responses and her environment for her to stay sober?
5. How might the observer role help Suzi learn to stay sober?
6. Which counseling techniques (decision matrix, mapping, 10 common dangers, TIPS for coping) would you use in your work with this client?

CASE STUDY 7.4

Jeff is a 55-year-old man who admits to being addicted to alcohol and barbiturates. He also admits to being bulimic since his early 20s. He has never been married and has always lived with his mother. He describes his relationship with his mother as a love/hate one: His mother dominates him (which Jeff resents), but Jeff says he does not believe he could live without his mother. Jeff says his mother ignores every assertion or boundary he has made in the relationship. He believes his addiction and his eating disorder are fused: He drinks to avoid the shame of his eating disorder.

Jeff has just entered the halfway house and is open to working on his issues. He says he does not see himself as being able to stay sober, because he knows he needs alcohol and barbiturates to be able to live with his mother. Due to financial constraints, Jeff will return to live with his mother when he leaves the halfway house in 6 weeks.

As his primary halfway house counselor, answer the following seven questions:

1. What are high-risk situations for Jeff?
2. What coping responses might he lack in those high-risk situations?
3. How do you perceive his self-efficacy level in terms of his recovery, and how might that be a dangerous match with his positive outcome expectancies of the alcohol and drugs?
4. Based on his story, what are some possible abstinence violation effects Jeff may experience after using?
5. What positive addictions or substitutes might Jeff look at incorporating into his life?
6. What might be some early-warning signals for him in terms of a relapse?
7. Which of the counseling techniques (decision matrix, mapping, 10 common dangers, TIPS for coping) might you use with this client?

CASE STUDY 7.5

Franklin is a 50-year-old addict who is in treatment with you on an outpatient basis. He has been able to maintain abstinence from alcohol and drugs for the past 5 years. However, in his last session with you, he reports that he believes he has a gambling addiction. He said he took a test on the Internet that indicated he had a problem, and he has been confronted by his self-help group and his sponsor on how often he gambles and how much money he has lost in his recovery to gambling. He says he is very ashamed of how much money he has lost and his compulsion to gamble. He believes if he were working a better program of recovery, that this (gambling) would not be an issue for him.

1. Which stage-of-change level do you believe he might be at in terms of his alcohol/ drug problem? His gambling problem?

2. Assuming that he has a gambling problem to some degree, how might you use the Marlatt model of relapse prevention to help him gain awareness of his problem?

3. What concerns would you have that his gambling problem may result in a drug/ alcohol relapse according to the Marlatt model? How could you see them potentially interacting in high-risk situations?

4. How might you use mindfulness strategies, such as urge surfing, to assist him with his gambling problem and related shame issues?

CO-OCCURRING DISORDERS

Orlin and Davis (1993) report that a longer time frame may be needed with the co-occurring disorders population (discussed extensively in Chapter 4) to achieve abstinence because of the presence of two chronic problems. For example, in a study with injection drug users, relapse happened more quickly for those individuals who struggled with factors such as homelessness and HIV seropositivity (Shah, Galai, Celentano, Vlahov, & Strathdee, 2006). Evans and Sullivan (2001) report high relapse rates with this population. Sinha and Schottenfeld (2001) report that 65% to 75% of treatment clients have addiction and psychiatric problems (i.e., antisocial personality, anxiety, affective disorders) and that they have a higher relapse rate. Zimberg (1993) states that relapse may be more common with this population because of how difficult it is to stabilize both problems at the same time. Although these

authors make excellent points about relapse and co-occurring disorders, the therapist must be careful about not enabling relapse in a co-occurring disordered client while attempting to create a compassionate atmosphere in which to address recovery issues.

As with other clients, Daley (1995) notes that the causes of relapse (i.e., lifestyle problems, interpersonal factors) are often multiple. Daley also recommends similar therapeutic strategies: understanding that relapse is a process; identifying the high-risk factors for the individual; helping the individual cope with cravings, cues, and social pressures; and assisting the individual in developing a recovery network. Ries (1993) suggests that three psychopharmacological considerations be given when working with the co-occurring disorders client who is on medication: the medication's abuse potential, aspects of the medication that may help recovery, and aspects of the medication that may hinder recovery. Daley (1995) stresses that a nonjudgmental attitude and a strong therapeutic alliance can make a significant difference in the recovery of a co-occurring disordered client.

The following case study concerns a client with co-occurring disorders. Following the case study is a list of questions to assist in applying the relapse-prevention model. The specific co-occurring disorder is not given, because sometimes in treatment the behavior indicating a co-occurring disorder is present, yet the counselor needs to continue working with the client until a psychological evaluation can be done that clarifies the specific disorder. (See Case Study 7.6.)

CASE STUDY 7.6

Jane, as discussed in Chapter 4, is a 50-year-old woman who has had a 12-year history of severe alcoholism with four hospital detoxifications and four chemical dependency treatments, none of which had any significant impact on her drinking. She was court-ordered to treatment for her third DUI. After 2 weeks in the treatment center, the staff noted that Jane rarely was seen sleeping. At night, she would walk up and down the halls of the treatment center. She was also becoming more agitated in group therapy, where she alternated between being very quiet, yet agitated (unable to sit still) and becoming very hostile when confronted or probed for information about herself by the counselor or other clients. She was the topic of most staff meetings, as counselors complained about how frustrating it was to work with her. There was discussion in the meetings of discharging her. The other clients increasingly refused to associate with her because of her highly critical manner and her tendency to be emotionally explosive.

As her primary therapist, answer the following four questions:

1. Without knowledge of her specific mental health diagnosis, how are you limited in helping Jane with relapse prevention?
2. What steps would you need to take to obtain clarification of her mental health problems?
3. What additional information might you want to obtain or explore to ensure that all co-occurring disorders issues are addressed?
4. Based simply on the behavior she is showing, even though you do not know her mental health diagnosis, what appears to be a high-risk situation(s) for Jane, and what appear to be some coping responses she lacks?

SUMMARY

Relapse prevention is a necessary component of the recovery process from addiction. With the reality of fewer therapy sessions being covered by insurance companies and the ongoing process required to break out of an addiction, relapse prevention is a crucial aspect of treatment, because it helps the client anticipate problems in advance, thereby reducing the chance of relapse. The use of relapse-prevention approaches can increase the efficiency of addiction treatment.

QUESTIONS

1. What is the balance a counselor needs to find in working with relapse-prevention issues?

2. What are the five stages of addictive behaviors?

3. What is the main goal of the Marlatt RP model?

4. What are the two main parts of a specific habit-change goal according to RP?

5. The RP model is based on which four social learning theory assumptions?

6. According to the RP model, what are the three stages of changing a habit?

7. What is the distinction between a lapse and a relapse?

8. What do the terms *self-efficacy* and *AVE* mean, and what roles do they play in the RP model?

9. What are seven things counselors need to do to help their clients change specific target behaviors?

10. What four counseling techniques can be used in relapse prevention?

EXERCISES

Exercise 7.1

Interview someone who has experienced a relapse with alcohol/drug usage. This person should not be a close friend, relative, or client in order to enhance the chance the person will discuss the relapse factors in detail. Tell the person this interview is a learning experience, not a professional consultation. Also talk with the person about the types of supports they have in their lives in the event the interview stirs old wounds.

Ask the individual to choose the most memorable relapse (if he or she has had more than one) to work with in this exercise. You are asking the person to take you to the one situation and slow it down. [Note that the client who has had more than one relapse may jump from talking about one to another. If possible, keep asking the client to focus in on just one that was emotional so the themes of the relapse emerge more strongly and clearly.]

Walk him or her through the Marlatt model (Figure 7.1) in terms of the bottom part of the model. Begin with the initial use (What was the

person's first break in abstinence?). Then ask about the preceding components focusing on obtaining as much information as you can obtain about the high risk situation. Clarify the components (internal, external) that led to the relapse with the awareness that the model is not perfect, so it may not fit the client's story exactly (some aspects of the model may simply be absent from the assessment). Rather, gather the greatest amount of information as possible without frustrating the client or becoming bogged down in unnecessary details. Also, be aware that the client may not remember all aspects to the relapse story; just focus on what is remembered. The important thing is to look for the client's internal and external strengths and weaknesses to better understand his or her vulnerabilities.

Once the interview is done, review and critique the fit of the model to the client's story with a teacher, colleague, or supervisor. Discuss the interventions you may use to address the internal and external factors you believe need to be addressed. Use of the decision matrix and mapping may be helpful in the discussion.

Exercise 7.2

Stay with the same client story as in Exercise 1 and answer three questions:

1. Which of the 10 most common dangers apply in this situation?

2. How might TIPS have been helpful to this person?

3. How did HALT apply in this situation?

Exercise 7.3

Shift Exercise 7.1 to a self-exploration exercise. Apply the Marlatt model to yourself in terms of a habitual pattern of behavior you have struggled with changing. If possible, choose one where you have relapsed and been successful at eventually maintaining a changed behavior.

READINGS/RESOURCES/WEBSITES

SUGGESTED READINGS

Gorski, T. T., & Miller, M. (1986). *Staying sober: A guide for relapse prevention.* Independence, MO: Herald House/Independence Press.

This book explains the theory of the relapse-prevention model of Gorski.

Marlatt, G. A., & Gordon, J. R. (1985). *Relapse prevention: A self-control strategy for the maintenance of behavior change.* New York, NY: Guilford Press.

This book describes the theoretical and research basis for the relapse-prevention model presented.

Marlatt, G.A., Parks, G.A., & Witkiewitz, K. (2002). *Clinical guidelines for implementing relapse prevention therapy.* Retrieved from http://www.bhrm.org/guidelines/RPT%20guideline.pdf

This document provides specific intervention strategies the counselor can use to integrate relapse prevention therapy into treatment.

National Institute on Drug Abuse. (1994). *Clinical report series: Relapse prevention* (NIH Publication No. 94-3845). Rockville, MD: Author.

This booklet describes theories, strategies, and approaches of relapse prevention with sections on working with special populations and implementation issues.

RESOURCES

Workbooks

Daley, D. C., & Marlatt, G. A. (1997). *Managing your drug or alcohol problem: Client workbook.* San Antonio, TX: Psychological Corporation.

This book has three sections: self-assessment, change issues and strategies, and progress measurement. Exercises are incorporated throughout the workbook. An appendix provides information on self-help groups.

Daley, D. C., & Marlatt, G. A. (2006a). *Overcoming your alcohol or drug problem: Effective recovery strategies: Therapist guide* (2nd ed.) New York, NY: Oxford University Press.

In this book of 21 chapters, the authors look at assessment and treatment (including two chapters on dual disorders), as well as issues and strategies regarding change and measuring progress.

Daley, D. C., & Marlatt, G. A. (2006b). *Overcoming your alcohol or drug problem: Effective recovery strategies: Workbook* (2nd ed.) New York, NY: Oxford University Press.

This workbook is a complement to the above-mentioned therapist guide that includes exercises the client can use as therapy to address the areas discussed in the therapist guide.

Fanning, P., & O-Neill, J. T. (1996). *The addiction workbook: A step-by-step guide for quitting alcohol and drugs*. Oakland, CA: New Harbinger.

The 12 chapters in this book cover topics such as self-assessment, preparation, finding help, and addressing areas such as nutrition, exercise, relaxation, feelings, spirituality, communication, and making amends. Exercises are incorporated throughout the topics.

Gorski, T. T. (1992). *The staying sober workbook: A serious solution for the problem of relapse* (Rev. ed.). Independence, MO: Herald House/Independence Press.

This workbook contains 37 exercises for relapse prevention in the areas of assessment, warning sign identification, management of warning signs, and recovery planning. The workbook follows the Gorski relapse-prevention model.

Gorski, T. T. (1995). *Relapse prevention counseling workbook: Managing high-risk situations*. Independence, MO: Herald House/Independence Press.

This workbook has eight sections: warning sign identification, warning sign analysis, situation mapping, thought management, feeling management, behavior and situation management, recovery planning, and final evaluation. Activities and exercises for each area reflect the Gorski model. Also included is a list of resources and a treatment plan for relapse prevention.

Hazelden Community Corrections Project. (2005).

This project includes three workbooks that may be helpful to the counselor working with the correctional population. Each one involves a number of self-reflection exercises that can be completed by the client through writing in the text. The workbooks are as follows:

Beazley, H. (2005). *The Hazelden community corrections project: Client recovery workbook*. Center City, MN: Hazelden.

This workbook has five sections: starting a recovery program, working with the drug court, participating in group meetings (such as 12-step), learning about the basics of 12-step recovery, and leaving the legal system.

Harberts, H. (2005). *The Hazelden community corrections project: Client life skills workbook*. Center City, MN: Hazelden.

There are four sections in this workbook that focus on the development of a transition plan for the client: developing the plan, fine-tuning the plan, focusing the plan even further, and applying the plan.

Horvath, A. T. (2003). *Sex, drugs, gambling, & chocolate: A workbook for overcoming addictions* (2nd ed.) San Luis Obispo, CA: Impact.

This workbook provides general information about the addictive process and working with cravings in recovery. It has been described in reviews as straightforward, practical, and applicable to various habitual patterns of behavior. It views addiction as a changeable habit and is written from a 12-step alternative, harm reduction focus. The 13 chapters contain exercises that can be used to facilitate personal awareness by covering topics such as the costs and benefits of addiction, cravings, and building a new life. Each chapter includes an overview, discussion, questions, and projects for the reader to consider. The appendices list numerous resources for the reader.

Mattson, K. (1992). *A relapse prevention workbook for women*. Center City, MN: Hazelden.

This booklet has simple exercises designed to assist women in preventing relapse through awareness of themselves.

Minnesota Department of Corrections (2005). *Client cognitive skills workbook*. Center City, MN: Hazelden.

The eight parts of this workbook are anchored in a cognitive-behavioral framework with the last three sections focusing on interpersonal relationship dynamics.

National Institutes of Health. (1993). *Recovery training and self-help: Relapse prevention and aftercare for drug addicts*. (NIH Publication No. 93-3521). Rockville, MD: National Institute on Drug Abuse.

This manual is designed to help establish a relapse prevention program. It has numerous handouts to facilitate client awareness.

Perkinson, R. R. (2011). *Chemical dependency counseling: A practical guide* (4th ed.). Los Angeles: Sage.

This 880-page book has 16 sections and 68 appendices. It has a specific appendix on relapse prevention exercises.

Shaw, B. F., Ritvo, P., & Irvine, J. (2005). *Addiction & recovery for dummies*. Hoboken, NJ: Wiley.

This book has two chapters that may be beneficial for clients to read about relapse prevention. It is written in an easy-to-understand language and covers basic recovery barriers (Chapter 15) and handling slips and relapses (Chapter 16).

Swanson, J., & Cooper, A. (1994). *Identifying your high-risk factors: The complete relapse-prevention skills program*. Center City, MN: Hazelden.

This program section has a pamphlet, workbook, and video that look at patterns of thinking and behavior as well as social situations.

Swanson, J., & Cooper, A. (1994). *Coping with emotional and physical high-risk factors: The complete relapse-prevention skills program*. Center City, MN: Hazelden.

This program section has a pamphlet, workbook, and video that examines high-risk factors (feelings, cravings, physical problems), with the workbook assisting in the development of a relapse-prevention plan.

Swanson, J., & Cooper, A. (1994). *The complete relapse prevention skills program: Coping with personal and social high-risk factors*. Center City, MN: Hazelden.

This section of the program addresses ways to have fun sober, be confident, and handle conflicts.

Williams, R. E., & Kraft, J. S. (2012). *The mindfulness workbook for addiction: A guide to coping with the grief, stress, and anger that trigger addictive behaviors*. Oakland, CA: New Harbinger.

This workbook has three parts that cover main concepts and skills, losses, and moving forward. It has 10 sections of exercises that cover: emotions, thoughts, behaviors, mindfulness, loss, addiction, connecting addiction and loss, mindful grieving, relationships, and recovery/relapse prevention/beyond.

Videotapes/DVDs

American Psychological Association (Producer). (2006). *Cognitive-behavioral relapse prevention for addictions* [DVD]. Available from www.apa.org/videos

This 45-minute video shows G. Alan Marlatt, PhD, applying his model of relapse prevention in an individual setting.

Balcony Releasing and Freedom Behind Bars Production (Producer). (2008). *The Dhamma Brothers* [DVD]. Available from www.dhammabrothers.com

This 70-minute video contains numerous personal stories of individuals in prison. It describes an intervention on alcohol/drug abuse with the meditation technique of Vipassana that teaches how to observe sensations in the body, but not react to them.

David Donnenfield Productions (Producer). (1998). *Changing from the inside* [Videotape]. Available from www.pariyatti.com

This 30-minute video describes a meditation program (based on the technique of Vipassana) for inmates at a minimum-security jail. Some of the participants are addicts.

WEBSITES

www.cenaps.com
This is the home page that provides overall information on Gorski's CENAPS program. Some areas of information are calendar of courses, home study programs, and publications.

www.tgorski.com
This website has numerous books and articles available on Gorski's CENAPS program as well as information on training and consulting.

www.draonline.org/index.html
This website describes Dual Recovery Anonymous, a 12-step fellowship for individuals who have both an emotional or psychiatric illness and chemical dependency. It focuses on relapse prevention to help reduce the risk for alcohol/drug use and the symptoms of the emotional/psychiatric illness. The website for specific information on relapse prevention for this group is www.draonline.org/relapse.html

SELF-HELP GROUPS

OBJECTIVES

1. To have a basic understanding of the 12–step model of addiction recovery.
2. To have a working knowledge of alternative, abstinence–based, national self–help groups.
3. To be able to assist clients in finding a group that is beneficial to them.

This chapter examines the historical development, basic concepts, use in counseling, strengths, and limitations of national self-help groups in the United States. Suggestions are made to counselors on how to familiarize themselves with self-help groups and their importance in therapy. These groups are also called self-help support groups (SHSG) (Dadich, 2010) and mutual help groups (MHG) (Kelly & Yeterian, 2008). Next, 12-step groups, in order of their emergence (Alcoholics Anonymous, Narcotics Anonymous, Cocaine Anonymous, Marijuana Anonymous, Crystal Meth Anonymous, Heroin Anonymous) and 12-step alternative groups (Women for Sobriety,

16 Steps, Rational Recovery, Secular Organizations for Sobriety, and Self-Management and Recovery Training [SMART Recovery®]) are reviewed. The chapter concludes with a section designed to help counselors match their clients with the self-help group that best meets clients' needs. A listing of major 12-step groups (for both addicts and their families/significant others) and alternatives to 12-step groups appears in the end-of-chapter listing of Resources. The Methadone Anonymous group is discussed in Chapter 5 in the harm reduction section and the Pills Anonymous group is discussed in Chapter 11 with regard to pain management. The use of self-help groups for

family members and significant others are briefly mentioned in Chapter 5. The section at the end of this chapter, matching self-help groups to meet client needs, can be used with minor modifications to assist family members and significant others in finding the best self-help group for themselves.

Note that during times of treatment funding restrictions, self-help groups may be the only or main support available to addicts at no cost. The importance of these groups, during such times, grows substantially. In terms of effectiveness, Dadich (2010) summarizes research findings that highlight the benefits of SHSGs for substance use issues. Finley (2004) states that 12-step groups can add to the treatment of the addicted individual as well as fill in treatment gaps for the client that include aftercare as long as the client needs it. Powell and Perron (2010) state that these groups can affirm and compliment the professional work of agencies through collaboration and interaction.

Also note that there are some groups that are national and abstinence-based that are not included in this chapter; their exclusion is not meant to be discriminatory or imply that they cannot be helpful to clients, but they are not included because they have a specific focus on an aspect related to recovery such as spiritual orientation or cultural identification. The counselor is encouraged to assist the client in the choice of self-help groups in a manner that promotes the welfare of the client. It is simply important for the counselor to consider the availability of such groups in the area where the client lives as well as assisting clients in the inclusion of the philosophy of these groups in a style that is beneficial to the client and not overwhelming or confusing.

SUGGESTIONS FOR COUNSELORS

Counselors' perspectives on self-help groups may widely vary. Some examples of such perspectives follow. Recovering counselors (addicted and/or

involved in an addictive system/relationship), who experience(d) the healing power of these groups, may view these self-help groups as *the answer* to addiction as it plays out in the life of the addict or their loved ones. At the other extreme, counselors unfamiliar with these groups may have projections based on Hollywood movies, television, the Internet, etc. which often show addicts at extremes: strictly focused on *not* using alcohol and drugs rather than developing a balanced lifestyle that inherently inhibits the use of alcohol/drugs, and/or baring the most intimate details of their lives rather than speaking in general themes of life struggles in a group setting. Counselor projections, then, can result in countertransference reactions to the use of self-help groups as augmenting therapy can negatively impact the welfare of the client.

In avoiding such extreme projections, the counselor needs to be aware of his/her own biases as well as the potential benefits of these groups. Self-help groups can benefit clients by providing them with: (a) support to *change their behavior* (whether others outside the self-help group believe they can and sometimes in spite of horrendous life circumstances) (*Don't drink*); (b) avoidance of isolation by being in a *community of others* trying to change their self-defeating behavior and hearing their stories (*Go to meetings*); and (c) *philosophical readings* that support a balanced lifestyle (*Read the Big Book*). The statements in parens are often used as a three-part answer in traditional 12-step self-help groups in response to the question: "How does one stay sober?"

If a counselor is new to the addiction field of self-help groups or is familiar with primarily one model, it may be overwhelming to try to become familiar with all of the self-help recovery programs. Some practical suggestions for becoming involved in this area follow:

1. *Become familiar with one 12-step model of recovery.* This recommendation is not based on a bias toward 12-step models, but on the reality that these groups have been around the longest of any of the self-help groups and,

therefore, tend to be widespread and well rooted. Typically, then, most recovering clients will have access to them.

a. Readings

   i. *Read a core chapter from the main text of the 12-step group.* For example, read the *Alcoholics Anonymous* chapter titled "How It Works," which informs the reader of the basic concepts of the philosophy.

   ii. *Read a story of someone in recovery in the main text of the 12-step program.* Reading a story can assist the counselor in understanding some of the struggles and hope in recovery. It can personalize the addict to the counselor and thereby break through some of the counselor's stereotypes about the addicted person. A listing of some books recommended by the author is provided in Appendix 8A.

   iii. *Read a recovery meditation book.* There are numerous meditation books in the self-help section of bookstores or published by organizations such as Hazelden. Reading such a book daily can assist the counselor in knowing how meditation reading can benefit an addicted client.

b. Attend an open 12-step meeting

Attending an open meeting can help the counselor understand some of the dynamics of the meetings that can help the addicted person stay sober: hearing others' stories of hope and change, learning coping skills for addressing discrimination experienced, receiving encouragement and support to stay sober, and so on. The counselor needs to remember, however, that each meeting is different and is organized on a self-help basis. Thus, the time or location may be changed without notice, and the group may vary in its openness to newcomers. Yet, both positive and negative experiences from attending an open meeting can assist a counselor in discussing the barriers and bridges his or her client may experience. In addition, by attending an open meeting, a counselor is sending a message of openness to the recovering community.

2. *Become familiar with at least one 12-step alternative self-help group.* Ideally, a counselor would become familiar with each of the alternative-based programs; however, because of time and energy constraints, it may be most feasible for the counselor to become familiar with at least one alternative group. When choosing one, the counselor should look at two aspects that may influence the practicality of the choice: (1) the main addicted population with whom the counselor works, and (2) alternative programs that are the most readily available to clients (physically or by computer access).

The counselor needs to examine his or her caseload for the typical client. For example, if a counselor typically works with addicted women, it may be helpful to learn about the Women for Sobriety program. The counselor can have knowledge of and access to information that can augment the recovery of the addicted individual. Such information may be especially helpful for the client who struggles with the 12-step model.

Another method of choosing an alternative program could be availability to clients. There may be no reason to learn about an alternative program if no such group exists in the area in which the counselor works or if clients have no access to the group in terms of transportation or computer.

Once the counselor chooses an alternative group to study, the same guidelines for learning about 12-step groups apply: (1) read core literature available (philosophy, stories of recovery, daily readings), and (2) attend an open meeting of the group if available. When talking with clients about alternative groups, the counselor may need to be careful about stepping on toes with regard to allegiance to the 12-step model. For example, a client may feel disloyal to the 12-step philosophy by reading literature about other models or attending other groups, or the 12-step recovering community may feel threatened if a counselor encourages a client to explore alternative programs of recovery. This does not mean that a counselor should not encourage exploration of this area but that the counselor needs to be aware of potential backlashes (that can occur both within and outside of a client) in exploring alternative groups with a client. Also, the counselor needs to determine if the client is a good match for the alternative program. The philosophy and values of the program are reflected in the words used in the literature (i.e., steps), and simply by reading the program's literature, the counselor can broadly screen if the client might be open to the program. For example, the 16 Steps uses the word "goddess" in its steps. A counselor in reading the steps may be aware that the client may close off from further information about the program simply by reading that one word. Finally, as stated in the introduction, the counselor needs to avoid overwhelming or confusing the client by providing too many alternatives or conflicting philosophies of recovery to the client.

When discussing the use of self-help in psychotherapy, Norcross (2003) encourages counselors to avoid "professional-centrism," expand how we define *self-help* (books, autobiographies, movies, Internet, groups), and incorporate the concept of self-help from the beginning of therapy. He argues that self-help can include client education, motivation, empowerment, reinforcement, and social support. Dadich (2010), in a research study involving young people (20 to 29 years) in 12-step groups, found that group involvement, in addition to providing support and connectedness, also provided an opportunity to learn.

Margolis and Zweben (1998) state five self-help group benefits for clients:

1. Existence of a social network not focused on use.

2. Encouragement of a free personal development process.

3. Widespread existence of groups.

4. Provision of a sense of belonging and encouragement of hope.

5. Availability of support around the clock.

Lawson, Lawson, and Rivers (2001) report that self-help groups can essentially provide the client with a sense of family. For some clients who have no sense of family or who have current difficulties with their families, self-help groups may provide a surrogate family where the addicted person can share his or her struggles with recovery without criticism or blame and within the context of support. This is not to encourage the addicted person to avoid family issues, but rather to allow him or her to address those issues when they can be comfortably and safely addressed in the addict's recovery. Self-help groups can provide role models to show the addict how to effectively address family issues.

12-STEP GROUPS

The history, basic concepts, and the 12 steps for six groups—(Alcoholics Anonymous, Narcotics Anonymous, Cocaine Anonymous, Marijuana Anonymous, Crystal Meth Anonymous, Heroin Anonymous)—are reviewed, followed by discussion of types of meetings, use of 12-step groups in counseling, and strengths and limitations of this type of self-help group. An additional overview of the 12-step programs (history, philosophy, structure, etc.) is provided in a chapter by Schulz, Williams, and Galligan (2009) in the book *Principles of Addiction Medicine*, fourth edition.

Alcoholics Anonymous

In 1931, American Rowland H. saw Dr. C. J. Jung in Switzerland for his alcoholism and was advised that he needed a religious/spiritual experience in order to overcome his drinking problem. Rowland then returned to America and joined the New York Oxford Group, a group of non-denominational Christians. In 1934, Rowland introduced Ebby T., another alcoholic, to the Oxford Group; Ebby introduced his friend, Bill Wilson, who later became a cofounder of Alcoholics Anonymous (AA), to the Oxford Group (Judge, 1994). Following his visit with Ebby about the Oxford Group and Ebby's ability to stay sober, Bill was admitted to a hospital under the care of psychiatrist Dr. William Silkworth (Nace, 1997).

In May 1935, AA began when cofounders Bill Wilson (Bill W.), a failed Wall Street stockbroker, and Dr. Bob Smith (Dr. Bob), a surgeon, met in Akron, Ohio, where Bill Wilson was attempting a stock takeover bid that failed. Afraid he would resume drinking, Bill Wilson contacted a local Oxford Group minister who was listed in a church directory. By contacting the minister and eventually a woman named Mrs. Henrietta Sieberling, Bill obtained the name of another alcoholic in the area, Dr. Bob, whom he met at Mrs. Sieberling's house (Nace, 1997). Mrs. Sieberling arranged the meeting (McClellan, 2011). One month after Bill W. and Dr. Bob met, Dr. Bob had his last drink (Judge, 1994), and AA was born on June 10, 1935. The first successful groups of AA were in Akron, New York, and Cleveland (Alcoholics Anonymous World Services, 1953). From 1935 to 1939, AA attracted 100 members. Those who attend AA typically maintain abstinence more than those who don't attend meetings (Schenker, 2009).

Kelley (2005) describes a core component of self-help groups as "helping you helps me" (p. 15). Bill W. and Dr. Bob used this philosophy to guide the principles for the organization that emerged in 1939, when it received its name "Alcoholics Anonymous" from its book that discussed a theory of alcoholism, the 12 steps, and stories of alcoholics (Alcoholics Anonymous World Services, 1976). This publication ended AA's connection with the Oxford Movement and other religious groups (Schulz et al.,

2009). The book is better known in recovering communities as the *Big Book*.

The program of AA is based on the concept of one alcoholic helping another, especially during periods of stress (Kurtz, 1988). W. R. Miller, Forcehimes, and Zweben (2011) encourage further clarification of the AA program by describing the difference between the actual AA *program* and the AA *fellowship*. The AA program consists of the beliefs and practices written (i.e., the 12 Steps and 12 Traditions discussed later) while the fellowship consists of the members' interactions supportive of the recovery process (sharing life experiences, socializing, and helping each other).

Regarding the fellowship, in the early years of its development, the alcoholics helping one another consisted predominantly of Caucasian, middle-class males who had been professionals (Robertson, 1988), with the typical member being an alcoholic male with a nonalcoholic wife (McClellan, 2011). Although the fellowship did not exclude women, "some early male members were ambivalent, even hostile, toward the participation of alcoholic women" (pp. 342–343), and there were assumptions that women who drank heavily were promiscuous (McClellan, 2011). As a result, alcoholic women were mentored at times by the nonalcoholic wives of male members, resulting in potentially less sexual complications, but keeping women from an individual mentoring relationship with another alcoholic. As the number of women grew in AA, male member attitudes toward them changed and the fellowship in general became more open to women (McClellan, 2011). *A Biography of Mrs. Marty Mann: The First Lady of Alcoholics Anonymous*, provides a powerful story of one woman's experiences with AA in its early days (S. Brown & Brown, 2001).

The General Service Office of AA has literature, videos, and meeting directories available. For readers who are interested in the organizational structure of AA, Robertson (1988) provides an excellent summary. Basically, each group of AA is self-supporting and guided by the 12 Traditions of Alcoholics Anonymous (Alcoholics Anonymous World Services, 1953). The 12 Steps, which were drawn from the Oxford Group concepts (Kurtz, 1988), serve as the backbone of AA for the individual member.[1]

12 Steps

1. We admitted we were powerless over alcohol—that our lives had become unmanageable.

2. Came to believe that a Power greater than ourselves could restore us to sanity.

3. Made a decision to turn our will and our lives over to the care of God, *as we understood Him*.

4. Made a searching and fearless moral inventory of ourselves.

5. Admitted to God, to ourselves, and to another human being the exact nature of our wrongs.

6. Were entirely ready to have God remove all these defects of character.

7. Humbly asked Him to remove our shortcomings.

8. Made a list of all persons we had harmed, and became willing to make amends to them all.

9. Made direct amends to such people wherever possible, except when to do so would injure them or others.

10. Continued to take personal inventory, and when we were wrong promptly admitted it.

11. Sought through prayer and meditation to improve our conscious contact with God, *as we understood Him*, praying only for

knowledge of His will for us and the power to carry that out.

12. Having had a spiritual awakening as a result of these steps, we tried to carry this message to alcoholics, and to practice these principles in all our affairs.

The 12 Steps are principles that serve as guidelines for the recovering client. The 12 Traditions, published in 1946 and confirmed in 1950 at the First International Conference of AA (Alcoholics Anonymous World Services, 1953), are guidelines for the development of the fellowship of AA.[2]

12 Traditions

1. Our common welfare should come first; personal recovery depends upon AA unity.

2. For our group purpose, there is but one ultimate authority—a loving God as He may express Himself in our group conscience. Our leaders are but trusted servants; they do not govern.

3. The only requirement for AA membership is a desire to stop drinking.

4. Each group should be autonomous except in matters affecting other groups or AA as a whole.

5. Each group has but one primary purpose—to carry its message to the alcoholic who still suffers.

6. An AA group ought never endorse, finance, or lend the AA name to any related facility or

---

[1] The Twelve Steps and Twelve Traditions are reprinted with permission of Alcoholics Anonymous World Services, Inc. (A.A.W.S.). Permission to reprint the Twelve Steps and Twelve Traditions does not mean that A.A.W.S. has reviewed or approved the contents of this publication, or that A.A. necessarily agrees with the views expressed herein. AA is a program of recovery from alcoholism only—use of the Twelve Steps and Twelve Traditions in connection with programs and activities that are patterned after AA, but which address other problems, or in any other non-AA context, does not imply otherwise.

[2] The Twelve Steps and Twelve Traditions are reprinted with permission of Alcoholics Anonymous World Services, Inc. (A.A.W.S.). Permission to reprint the Twelve Steps and Twelve Traditions does not mean that A.A.W.S. has reviewed or approved the contents of this publication, or that AA necessarily agrees with the views expressed herein. AA is a program of recovery from alcoholism only—use of the Twelve Steps and Twelve Traditions in connection with programs and activities that are patterned after AA. but which address other problems, or in any other non-AA context, does not imply otherwise.

outside enterprise, lest problems of money, property, and prestige divert us from our primary purpose.

7. Every AA group ought to be fully self-supporting, declining outside contributions.

8. Alcoholics Anonymous should remain forever nonprofessional, but our service centers may employ special workers.

9. AA, as such, ought never be organized; but we may create service boards or committees directly responsible to those they serve.

10. Alcoholics Anonymous has no opinion on outside issues; hence the AA name ought never be drawn into public controversy.

11. Our public relations policy is based on attraction rather than promotion; we need always maintain personal anonymity at the level of press, radio, and films.

12. Anonymity is the spiritual foundation of all our traditions, ever reminding us to place principles before personalities.

Alcoholics Anonymous is the largest self-help group (Hester & Miller, 2003) and inspired the development of numerous self-help groups in the United States (i.e., Narcotics Anonymous, Cocaine Anonymous, Al-Anon, Overeaters Anonymous, Sexaholics Anonymous, Emotions Anonymous, and Codependents Anonymous). AA is the help resource most commonly used in the United States for alcohol problems (SAMSHA, 2006). Narcotics Anonymous, Cocaine Anonymous, and Marijuana Anonymous are discussed because of their specific focus on drug use recovery. Self-help groups for addicted individuals and their family members/significant others are listed at the end of this chapter.

Narcotics Anonymous

Narcotics Anonymous (NA) was founded in July 1953 in southern California and opened a World Service Office in Los Angeles in 1972 (Narcotics Anonymous, 1982). It views itself as similar to AA, but its definition of the problem is "addiction" rather than a specific substance "alcohol" (Narcotics Anonymous, 1982).

Narcotics Anonymous essentially uses the same 12 Steps of AA with a few revisions: (1) In Step 1, the word *alcohol* is replaced by *our addiction*; (2) the word *we* is added to the beginning of Steps 2 through 11; and (3) the word *alcoholics* in Step 12 is replaced by *addicts* (Narcotics Anonymous, 1982). The organization has its own main book, *Narcotics Anonymous* 1982, which is similar to the *Big Book* of AA in that it has information on addiction and stories of addicts. NA is also guided by 12 Traditions similar to AA's 12 Traditions, with minor alterations: (1) *NA* is substituted at times for *AA*, or *AA* is simply deleted, and (2) the word *alcoholic* is replaced with the word *addict*.

When referring clients to NA, Gifford (1991) suggests that the time of the organization's formation be taken into account: AA was formed in a more conservative time than NA. The author also suggests that NA has a broader definition of addiction and a more diverse membership. Because of these differences, Gifford (1991) states that NA may work better for adolescents than AA. While these descriptions of differences between the two types of 12-step groups may be accurate, each counselor needs to determine differences between the groups based on the local area information rather than basing perceptions only on tendencies reported in the literature.

Cocaine Anonymous

Cocaine Anonymous (CA) was founded in 1982 in Hollywood, California. CA uses AA's text, and members are encouraged to translate the words related to alcohol to include cocaine. A storybook, *Hope, Faith, and Courage*, based on the stories of cocaine addicts, and various literature are available to its members. It uses the 12 Steps of AA, revising Step 1 (*alcohol* is replaced with *cocaine and all other mind-altering substances*) and Step 12 (*alcoholics* is replaced with *addicts*). CA also uses the 12 Traditions of AA, replacing the following phrases: *AA* with *CA*, *alcohol* with *addict*, *Alcoholics Anonymous* with *Cocaine Anonymous*, and *drinking* with *using cocaine and all other mind-altering substances*. They hold a yearly conference.

Marijuana Anonymous

Marijuana Anonymous (MA) was founded in June 1989, when delegates from Marijuana Smokers Anonymous, Marijuana Addicts Anonymous, and Marijuana Anonymous met in Morro Bay (between San Francisco and Los Angeles) to unify their programs into a 12-step recovery program. In addition to in-person meetings, they hold meetings by phone (once daily for 5 days a week) and online (www.ma-online.org). MA uses the 12 Steps of AA, revising Step 1 (*alcohol* is replaced with *marijuana*) and Step 12 (*alcoholics* is replaced with *marijuana addicts*). MA also uses the 12 Traditions of AA, replacing the following phrases: *AA* with *MA*, *alcoholic* with *marijuana addict*, *Alcoholics Anonymous* with *Marijuana Anonymous*, and *drinking* with *using marijuana*. They have: (1) a newsletter, *A New Leaf*, that includes stories of addicts (issues up to 2010 are published on their website) and (2) a main text, *Life with Hope: A Return to Living through the Twelve Steps and Twelve Traditions of Marijuana Anonymous*, that describes the 12-step program.

Crystal Meth Anonymous

Crystal Meth Anonymous (CMA) was founded in 1994 in West Hollywood, CA, at the West Hollywood Alcohol and Drug Center. They have locations in 100 metropolitan areas in the United States as well as locations in Canada, Australia, and the United Kingdom. Its first world conference was held in 2008 in Park City, Utah. CMA uses the 12 Steps and 12 Traditions of AA replacing the word *alcohol* with *crystal meth*. Many groups use the *Big Book* of *Alcoholics Anonymous* as a guiding text while other groups use the *Narcotics Anonymous Basic Text* or texts from other 12-step fellowships. They have stories of recovery in their text, *Crystal Clear: Stories of Hope*.

Heroin Anonymous

Heroin Anonymous (HA) was founded in 2004, in Phoenix, Arizona, at Hope House, a halfway house for alcoholics and addicts. It exists in 19 states in the United States and will have its first convention in 2014. It offers a mail start-up kit if one wants to begin a group. HA uses the 12 Steps and 12 Traditions of AA with the emphasis on one heroin addict helping another. It uses the *Big Book* of *Alcoholics Anonymous* as a guide and offers the *Bulletin*, a monthly publication. It offers a Facebook page as well as a website (www.heroinanonymous.com) where one can share opinions, stories, and comments.

Types of Meetings

There are different types of 12-step meetings (P. N. Johnson & Chappel, 1994) available to clients (the naming of these types may vary by locale):

1. In *open* meetings, generally one recovering person speaks to the group about his or her addiction and recovery story, and nonaddicts can attend and listen. These meetings are for people who generally want to learn more about addiction.

2. *Closed* meetings are for addicted individuals only.

3. *Discussion* meetings tend to focus on a topic discussed by those addicts in attendance; these meetings are called *participation* meetings in California.

4. In *speaker* meetings, one addicted person speaks to the audience about his or her addiction and recovery story; the speaker meeting may be open or closed.

5. In *step* meetings, the topic for discussion is one of the 12 steps; typically, these meetings are for addicted individuals only.

6. In *Big Book* meetings, a chapter from *Alcoholics Anonymous* is read and discussed.

Alcoholics Anonymous provides a pamphlet, *The A.A. Group: Where It All Begins*, that describes how a group functions and how one can start a group. In this pamphlet, different types of meetings are defined. These meetings include: open, closed, discussion, speaker, beginners, step/tradition/*Big Book*.

Medallions

Medallions, or "chips," are generally used to acknowledge a length of recovery. These lengths of time vary from group to group. Sometimes a beginner medallion or a "white chip" is given to someone new or returning to recovery. Typically, they are given at intervals of 1, 3, 6, 9, 12, and 18 months and then yearly. In some groups, a celebration of cake and coffee at the end of the meeting is given for members. A short video, *Hope: Alcoholics Anonymous* (Alcoholics Anonymous, 1990), demonstrates this process of celebration. Table 8.1 describes the general format of an AA meeting.

Use in Counseling

In a discussion about AA and NA, Humphreys (1993) warns counselors of two main potential difficulties in integrating 12-step groups and counseling: (1) a tendency to view the healthy individual differently (abasement versus self-responsibility), and (2) a difference in helping responses (community/free/mutual problem versus individual/paid/not mutual problem). Despite these differences, Humphreys urges counselors to find ways to use 12-step programs based on principles of separate yet respectful and cooperative views. For example, the counselor may help clients see that being responsible for themselves includes

Table 8.1   AA Meeting

Typical characteristics of an AA meeting, although this may vary from group to group:
Social interaction (greeters)
   Chairperson calls meeting to order
      (Introduces self by first name and label of alcoholic)
      (Possible opening with the Serenity Prayer)
   Welcome new members (visitors)
   Reading from *Alcoholics Anonymous* (section of "How It Works")
   Announcements relevant to AA
   Introductions of new or returning people
   Meeting (discussion/speakers)
   Giving of medallions
   Closing (Lord's Prayer, spoken while holding hands)

Adapted from *Handbook of Alcoholism Treatment Approaches*, third edition, by R. K. Hester and W. R. Miller, 2003, Boston, MA: Allyn & Bacon.

the capacity to be humble and to see themselves realistically. The counselor may also need to explain the difference between the accessibility and the lay feedback in self-help groups and the process and goals of therapy to help the client determine ways he or she can appropriately have needs met in the different settings. Schenker (2009) wrote an excellent book that bridges counseling and 12-step programs by explaining the philosophy of AA and how it can be integrated into the practice of counseling through the provision of specific strategies/techniques the counselor can use. The following discussion focuses on ways counselors may use these programs in conjunction with counseling. Take note that counselors may also facilitate the integration of the 12-step program with counseling by applying the 12 steps to one's own life. An example of a text that can be helpful in that process is Hirschfield's (1990) *The Twelve Steps for Everyone . . . Who Really Wants Them* and Osten and Switzer's (2014) *Integrating 12-Steps and Psychotherapy*.

Generally, 12-step groups may work well with addicted clients in that they can provide support for recovery (Dadich, 2010; Flores, 1988), reduce a sense of isolation (Dadich, 2010; Talbott, 1990), and help the client develop a sense of self-regulation (Khantzian & Mack, 1994). In addition, they may provide an overall support to therapy (Bristow-Braitman, 1995; P. N. Johnson & Phelps, 1991; Riordan & Walsh, 1994) and provide a framework for cognitive restructuring (Steigerwald & Stone, 1999). As stated previously in this chapter, Powell and Perron (2010) propose that these groups augment counseling effectiveness; however, they caution agencies to remember that these groups are heterogeneous and vary on a continuum of benefits to clients. Their caution is the reason for counselors to carefully assess the health of the specific group attended by the client; assessment suggestions to the counselor are made later in this chapter.

Counselors need to be aware of the importance of self-help group referrals. If clients are not encouraged to experience self-help groups while in counseling, they are not likely to do so after counseling ends (W. R. Miller et al., 2011). An effective referral to these groups does not require the counselor to be recovering from an addiction and attending local self-help groups. Rather, it requires the counselor to provide information on these groups and their literature; encourage 12-step meeting attendance and 12-step literature reading; and talk with clients about their unique reactions to the meetings/readings. Such discussions will assist the counselor in making the best 12-step recovery match for the client.

There are different avenues for exploring individual client reactions to 12-step groups. Four such options are as follows. First, Finley (2004) provides an excellent text of exercises that counselors can use with clients to facilitate the awareness and integration of the 12-step program into treatment. Second, W. C. Moyers' (2012) *Now What?* is a text written in layperson's language that explains addiction and recovery from a 12-step perspective. Third, Chapters 11 and 12, Twelve-Step Programs and Joining Self-help and Support Groups, of *Addiction Recovery for Dummies*, provides a helpful overview, highlights main points, and provides self-reflective questions to facilitate involvement. A fourth option is the use of Twelve-Step Facilitation (TSF) to bridge counseling and,

specifically, the 12-step group of AA. This focused approach is evidence-based and supported by research. Counselors can use a therapy manual (Nowinski, Baker, & Carroll, 1995) and/or an online training site (Sholomskas & Carroll, 2006) to learn the TSF approach. The approach uses techniques to encourage involvement in and benefits from 12-step participation (Ries, Galanter, Tonigan, & Ziegler, 2011). The counselor helps the client accept that they are alcoholic and committed to AA.

Le, Ingvarson, and Page (1995) encourage counselors to remember that AA is not a recovery program that fits all clients and to examine their counseling theory and determine how well AA fits into that theory. Additionally, the counselor may find it helpful to take the following initiatives. First, counselors may read materials such as *Alcoholics Anonymous, Narcotics Anonymous*, and *Life with Hope;* attend open AA, NA, and MA meetings; and, if possible, talk with members of these groups who have been involved in the program for several years so they can assess the fit between their counseling theory and the 12-step approach. Second, counselors need to be knowledgeable about the different types of 12-step groups available in the local community in order to appropriately make a client referral to a 12-step group. Finally, counselors can use concepts that emerge out of the 12-step program that may facilitate therapy and the recovery process. For example, because emotional self-regulation appears critical to addiction recovery, as discussed in Chapter 5, the reader may want to use the concept of emotional sobriety that is based in the 12-step program at the end of this chapter in Appendix 8B. The components of the resource (definitions, symptoms, theories, exercises, applications to clinical populations) were used by the author in a 2013 training for addiction counselors.

Strengths

The 12 steps are referred to as "suggested" steps in the "How It Works" chapters of both *Alcoholics*

Anonymous (Alcoholics Anonymous World Services, 1976) and *Narcotics Anonymous* 1982, as well as the MA book, *Life with Hope* (2001). This notation allows recovering clients the ability to use the steps as they apply to themselves and their lives, avoiding absolute prescriptions against which addicted clients may rebel.

Membership

The only requirement for membership in AA is a desire to stop drinking (Tradition 3; and in NA, CA, and MA, the desire to stop using). The recovering client can begin and end membership based on his or her desire to change behavior. There are no dues or fees, so help for recovering clients is free and easily accessible. Typically, 12-step groups "pass the basket" (Tradition 7) at the end of the meeting for costs such as coffee and rental space; individuals are invited to contribute what they can.

Accessibility and Familiarity

Another main strength of a 12-step program, particularly AA, is that it is widely used for treatment of addiction (Le et al., 1995), making it very accessible for clients. It was first used in inpatient treatment in 1950, and a few years later the 28-day treatment model (5 days detox plus therapy) evolved into what has been called the *disease* concept of treatment, the Willmar model, the Hazelden model, and the Minnesota model (Lile, 2003). Particularly for clients in rural areas and those clients who travel frequently, knowledge of accessibility to a recovery program may provide the client with a sense of security. In addition to the ease of accessibility is the familiarity of the program for those clients who have received addiction treatment in the United States: Most of the substance abuse treatment programs in the United States use the 12 steps in some capacity in their program (Bradley, 1988). Previous exposure to the program can facilitate the transition from addiction treatment to community support self-help groups. Finally, because AA is so widespread, there are numerous special-interest groups within AA for sexual orientation

(gays/lesbians), professionals (attorneys, physicians, nurses, etc.), gender, and groups such as Two Hatters (recovering counselors). Also, there is an AA meeting in print for Spanish-speaking individuals.

Valverde and White-Mair (1999) describe AA as a highly ethical organization because it encourages the concept of powerlessness, anonymity, nonjudgmentalism, first-person storytelling, relationship with a Higher Power, and emphasizing a daily focus of recovery.

Spiritual/Religious Emphasis

A strength of the 12-step program, for clients who view themselves as spiritual or religious, is its focus on spirituality. Spirituality, from the 12-step perspective, is viewed as "both the fundamental deficit leading to the development and maintenance of addiction and the cornerstone of recovery" (Kranitz, Holt, & Cooney, 2009, p. 149). Therefore, while the absence of spirituality can lead to addiction, its presence can assist the addicted client in maintaining sobriety. In support of the inclusion of spirituality as it relates to both prevention and treatment, the authors summarize research showing the protective dynamics of spirituality and religion on alcohol/drug use as well as helping people in the recovery process from addiction.

Limitations

Walters (2002) lists 12 reasons that alternatives to AA need to be used, including high attrition rates, motivation being connected to "hitting bottom," religious connotations, external locus of control (spiritual), use of the disease model, and a focus on defects of character, powerlessness, loss of control, abstinence, self-labeling as an alcoholic, dependence on the group, as well as inconclusive research on its effectiveness. Lile (2003) states three general concerns that may impact clients. First, the discussion of usage in meetings may stimulate cravings for the client. Second, the catch phrases might be irritating to the client (e.g., Easy Does It, One Day at a Time). Third, the client may develop a substitute dependency. The author suggests that counselors help clients focus on the core of an individual's story, not just the usage; understand that the phrases are meant to be cognitive interventions; and view the dependency as a temporary state.

Rigidity

One of the limitations of a 12-step program is connected to one of the strengths: interpretation and application of the 12 steps. Although the literature discusses the steps as being "suggested," individual AA, NA, CA, and MA groups may interpret the steps as more absolute: They may offer a rigid interpretation of the steps to clients and demand that the client follow the steps as defined by the group or group members. If such experiences arise, the counselor and client may need to discuss ways the client can handle uncomfortable encounters with more rigid interpretations of the steps. For example, a group may interpret *Higher Power* to mean a Christian God and strongly discourage group members from discussing any other form of Higher Power in meetings. The counselor and client may determine together how comfortable the client, who is not Christian, feels in the group. Is it worth it to find a way to stay in the group, and how can he or she remain true to his or her own spiritual beliefs? If the client wants to remain in the group, discussion between the counselor and client may focus on how the client shares spiritual beliefs in the meeting in a manner that is respectful to him or her. If it is too uncomfortable for the client, the counselor and client may want to work together to find a group that will be more receptive to the client's spiritual beliefs.

Open Membership

Because there are no selection criteria for membership, clients need to remember that anyone can be at a self-help meeting. It is important for counselors to stress the *anyone* so that clients approach step meetings with a somewhat protective stance, similar to one they would take in any social setting, rather than openly and freely trusting individuals simply because they are at the meeting. Clients need to be aware that there are no inherent safeguards against individuals at meetings taking advantage of their vulnerability, such as sexually or financially.

Previous Negative Experiences

Another limitation may be the client's previous treatment and/or self-help group history. Previous exposure to a 12-step program may have been an unpleasant experience or left the client unimpressed, resulting in the client not being open to attending meetings. It is helpful for the counselor to process the client's emotions and experiences in the counseling session to determine if the reaction is one that can be resolved or if it is simply more helpful to refer the client to another self-help group. Because of the availability of 12-step meetings, it is important for clients at least to develop a tolerance for these meetings so that, in the event of a recovery crisis, the client has different supports on which to rely. Also, counselors must respect the limits of their clients: If the client simply is not able to draw support from a 12-step group, exploration of other available self-help groups may be necessary.

Limited Applicability

One criticism of the AA program is its basis in Caucasian, middle-class, male culture, which has resulted in questioning its applicability to other groups. In interviewing some of the critics of AA, Judge (1994) reports two concerns: struggle with the wording of the 12 steps and "isms" experienced in self-help groups. In terms of the wording, both AA and NA use the word *Him* when discussing God in the 12 steps. For some clients, this language may be viewed as sexist and limiting of their concept of God (Higher Power). Another common wording struggle is in the word *powerless* in Step 1: Critics argue that oppressed groups do not need to learn about powerlessness but how to own their power (Judge, 1994). For clients who struggle with such wording, the counselor may assist the client in translating the word so it is less offensive or may explore alternative self-help groups that are less offensive to the client.

An example of translating the 12 steps for sexual abuse survivors is provided by G. A. Miller, Sack, and Simmons (1993). For example, a female sexual abuse survivor may struggle with the concept of powerlessness in Step 1 of AA. Her therapist can help her learn to differentiate between the powerlessness of the sexual abuse and the powerlessness of her chemical dependency. Experiencing the powerlessness of her chemical dependency can free her from its abusiveness. Alternative self-help groups, which may be a better match for clients, are explored later in this chapter.

"Isms"

The second area of concern presented by Judge (1994) is with the "isms" experienced in some 12-step groups. An *ism* is defined as a negative bias and stereotype that discriminates against a certain population (e.g., sexism, racism, and homophobia). A group may espouse openness, yet in its own meetings it may have only a select group of individuals who attend (i.e., Caucasian heterosexual males). Because there are no specific selection criteria for membership, clients need to be aware that some "isms" may operate in a group, and if those "isms" make the client uncomfortable, he or she may need to find another support group that does not practice discrimination. Schenker (2009) reports that the program has been limited in reaching women and ethnic minorities. The author also states that one way the program has adapted to the needs of women has been through the creation of women-only meetings.

Some groups even struggle with having clients with "other" problems in their group. For example, an AA group may not want its members talking about the use of other drugs. To enhance acceptance by the group, some therapists have recommended that clients identify themselves as other group members identify themselves (Robertson, 1988) and share stories that involve drugs that group members are comfortable discussing. Groups may also have a bias against members

taking any medication, including prescribed medication that is not addictive. For clients who have dual disorders, this type of feedback may be hazardous to their recovery. Counselors may need to caution their clients about this possible reaction to their medication use.

Spiritual/Religious Emphasis

A final limitation of a 12-step program, for some clients, is its spiritual/religious dimension. The program of AA has been criticized as being based in Christianity, given its Oxford Group roots (Judge, 1994). The wording in the 12 steps of AA, NA, CA, and MA involves the word *God*, which is followed by the phrase *as we understood Him*. This attached phrase sometimes helps clients relax in the reaction (G. A. Miller et al., 1993). For other clients, though, this phrase, in combination with some self-help groups that begin and/or end meetings holding hands and praying the Lord's Prayer or the Serenity Prayer, may simply be too religious for them. Once again, it is important for the therapist to discuss whether the client wants to develop some sort of tolerance for these group tendencies or whether another self-help group might be more helpful to the client.

12-STEP ALTERNATIVE GROUPS

The following five groups (Women for Sobriety, 16 Steps, Rational Recovery, Secular Organizations for Sobriety, Self-Management and Recovery Training [SMART Recovery®]) are 12-step alternatives that are national, abstinence-based programs that currently encourage the existence of self-help groups that embody their philosophy–except for Rational Recovery that began with the encouragement of self-help groups and later began to discourage their existence. As discussed previously in this chapter, such alternative groups may be helpful to the client as a replacement for 12-step groups or as an augmentation of 12-step groups' literature, etc.

Women for Sobriety

Women for Sobriety (WFS), the first national self-help program specifically for alcoholic women, was started in 1976 by Jean Kirkpatrick. Kirkpatrick's (1978) book, *Turnabout: Help for a New Life*, describes her recovery process from alcoholism and the evolution of WFS. Kirkpatrick used Emerson, Thoreau, and Unity Church philosophies in conjunction with cognitive-behavioral techniques and emphases on the support of peers and health promotion to develop WFS principles (Horvath, 1997). The WFS program was based on the belief that women alcoholics have problems and needs different from those of male alcoholics—particularly in self-value, self-worth, and reduction of guilt. The shame and stigma of women alcoholics (guilt, humiliation) are addressed through positive affirmations to improve self-image. Three dynamics present that facilitate behavioral change are positive reinforcement through approval and encouragement, cognitive strategies such as positive thinking, and using the body as a recovery resource through relaxation techniques, meditation, diet, and physical exercise.

Kaskutas (1994) states that women who attend the WFS program describe it as a supportive, nurturing, and safe environment that focuses on emphasizing the positive, building self-esteem, and addressing women's issues. It focuses on self-enhancement rather than fear-based strategies of change. The program also advocates individual application of the steps to the members' lives. The program encourages groups to be limited to fewer than 10 members (6 to 8) so that participation and confidentiality are possible. Each group typically has co-moderators who facilitate the group and a secretary/treasurer. Donations are used to assist the group in functioning. Videos, cassette tapes, literature, and monthly newsletters (*Sobering Thoughts* is their official publication) are available to its members. It also has a pen pal program that matches individuals with someone who is also working a WFS program.

Basic Concepts

The WFS program is based on a 13-statement program designed to assist a woman in addressing her alcoholism and lifestyle by encouraging her emotional and spiritual growth. Members are encouraged to use the 13 statements in any order they wish to use them. These Thirteen Statements of Acceptance are currently written as follows (Kirkpatrick, 1990).[3]

1. I have a life-threatening problem that once had me.

2. Negative thoughts destroy only myself.

3. Happiness is a habit I will develop.

4. Problems bother me only to the degree I permit them to.

5. I am what I think.

6. Life can be ordinary or it can be great.

7. Love can change the course of my world.

8. The fundamental object of life is emotional and spiritual growth.

9. The past is gone forever.

10. All love given returns.

11. Enthusiasm is my daily exercise.

12. I am a competent woman and have much to give life.

13. I am responsible for myself and my actions.

The 13 statements are formed into the six levels of the New Life program (see Figure 8.1). Level I focuses on acceptance of the disorder (Statement 1). Level II emphasizes changing negative thought patterns and tendencies toward guilt by focusing

---

[3]Since 1976, the wording of the Thirteen Statements has been changed to assist members in applying the program to their lives as follows: Statement 1 (from drinking problem to life-threatening problem), Statement 2 (from negative emotions to negative thoughts), Statement 10 (from returns twofold to returns), Statement 12 (from others to life), and Statement 13 (from sisters to actions).

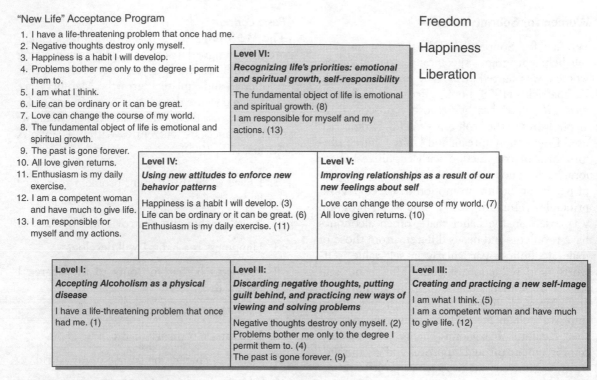

"New Life" Acceptance Program

1. I have a life-threatening problem that once had me.
2. Negative thoughts destroy only myself.
3. Happiness is a habit I will develop.
4. Problems bother me only to the degree I permit them to.
5. I am what I think.
6. Life can be ordinary or it can be great.
7. Love can change the course of my world.
8. The fundamental object of life is emotional and spiritual growth.
9. The past is gone forever.
10. All love given returns.
11. Enthusiasm is my daily exercise.
12. I am a competent woman and have much to give life.
13. I am responsible for myself and my actions.

Freedom

Happiness

Liberation

Level VI:
Recognizing life's priorities: emotional and spiritual growth, self-responsibility

The fundamental object of life is emotional and spiritual growth. (8)
I am responsible for myself and my actions. (13)

Level IV:
Using new attitudes to enforce new behavior patterns

Happiness is a habit I will develop. (3)
Life can be ordinary or it can be great. (6)
Enthusiasm is my daily exercise. (11)

Level V:
Improving relationships as a result of our new feelings about self

Love can change the course of my world. (7)
All love given returns. (10)

Level I:
Accepting Alcoholism as a physical disease

I have a life-threatening problem that once had me. (1)

Level II:
Discarding negative thoughts, putting guilt behind, and practicing new ways of viewing and solving problems

Negative thoughts destroy only myself. (2)
Problems bother me only to the degree I permit them to. (4)
The past is gone forever. (9)

Level III:
Creating and practicing a new self-image

I am what I think. (5)
I am a competent woman and have much to give life. (12)

Figure 8.1 New Life Program

Source: Women for Sobriety, Inc., P.O. Box 618, Quakertown, PA 18951–0618. Reprinted with permission.

on new problem-solving approaches (Statements 2, 4, and 9). Level III encourages the creation of a new self-image (Statements 5 and 12). Level IV involves the emergence of new attitudes resulting in new behaviors (Statements 3, 6, and 11). Level V stresses the improvement of relationships (Statements 7 and 10). Level VI emphasizes the priorities in the individual's life, which are spiritual and emotional growth and taking responsibility for self (Statements 8 and 13).

A WFS Certified Moderator, who is a volunteer, facilitates the groups. The group format is typically as follows:

- The moderator opens the meeting and the Thirteen Statements of the New Life Program and the Statement of Purpose are read.

- Each woman introduces herself and says something positive about herself.

- The meeting discussion topic comes from a Weekly Topic Guide that accompanies the Group Starter Kit or from other WFS literature.

- The meeting ends with a joining of hands and recitation of the group motto: "We are capable and competent, caring and compassionate, always willing to help another, bonded together in overcoming our addictions."

Note that literature is given to the woman at her first meeting.

In 1994, Men for Sobriety (MFS), a self-help program based on the same 13 statements, was started by Dr. Kirkpatrick at the request of some men (Horvath, 1997). The focus is on issues experienced by men in recovery (Horvath, 1997). Meetings are currently held in major U.S. cities such as Washington and Boston.

Use in Counseling

The WFS and MFS organizations can be used effectively to support the recovery process and to complement therapy. In terms of recovery, again, clients can increase their sense of support, reduce their sense of isolation, and increase their self-regulation through involvement. As to therapy, the counselor needs knowledge of the philosophy of the organization, available local groups, and the fit of the philosophy with the counseling approach taken in recovery.

Strengths

As with 12-step groups, anyone can call himself or herself a member of WFS or MFS. There are no dues or fees for membership, so support is easily accessible. There are online chat groups where one can receive daily encouragement to stay sober. It may be especially beneficial for minority individuals who have experienced oppression (e.g., women, ethnic minorities, and gays/lesbians) to have a focus of empowerment. It may also be helpful to those who have unsuccessfully tried other self-help groups.

Spiritual/Religious The spiritual dimension, although mentioned in Statement 8, is not emphasized as much as in 12-step programs. This de-emphasis may make WFS a better match as a recovery program for the client who has religious/spiritual issues or does not see them as a critical component for his or her recovery.

Limitations

As with any self-help group, clients need to be reminded that because membership is not screened, anyone can be present at the meetings. Again, then, clients need to be aware of their potential vulnerability with such open membership.

Limited Accessibility Probably the main limitation of the program is its accessibility to clients. Because it is not as widespread as 12-step groups, there may not be as many meetings available to clients.

16 Steps

In 1985, Charlotte Kasl informed her 12-step women's recovery group that she could no longer say the 12 steps because they did not feel right to her, particularly because of the religious and ego-deflation wording of the steps (Judge, 1994; Kasl, 1992). Kasl summarized the struggles she and others experienced with the 12 steps in her 1990 *Ms.* magazine article, "The Twelve Step Controversy." Her book, *Many Roads, One Journey: Moving Beyond the Twelve Steps* (1992), is based on 7 years of workshops, projects, and interviews related to addiction recovery. Note that she has written an excellent text, *Yes, You Can: A Guide to Empowerment Groups* (Kasl, 1995), that guides the reader in the process of setting up such groups.

In the introduction to her book, Kasl (1992) states she is writing (1) for women and minorities, whom she views as having been historically neglected in addiction recovery approaches; and (2) to support individuals who want to use new healing models in addiction recovery. She describes her model as one based on empowerment and discovery. Her book has four main sections that examine the recovery controversy, the diversity of addiction, the recovery models, and the other healing opportunities such as the 16 steps.

Basic Concepts

Kasl (1992) reports that she intentionally wrote the 16 steps in the present tense, because she believes healing is a process people go through together. On her website she writes: "The 16-step empowerment model is a holistic approach to overcoming addiction that views people in their wholeness-mind, body and spirit. A fundamental basis of this model is flexibility and an openness which leads to continually ask: What works? Who does it work for? and How can we help it work better?" (Kasl, 2011, para. 1; http://charlottekasl.com/16-step-program/).

Kasl (1992) lists 12 common 16-step group guidelines, including structure (purpose, format, and length), time sharing, moderator, group focus, collection and dispersion of dues, confidentiality, meeting place and time, member commitments, coping with severe member problems, giving notice of leaving the group, and letting go of individuals who leave the group.

Use in Counseling

As stated previously for other groups, the 16-step group can also provide the recovering client with additional support, a decreased sense of isolation, and an increase of self-regulation. Again, the counselor needs to have an understanding of how the 16 steps work, available groups in the area, and how well the philosophy matches the counseling approach.

Strengths

The 16 steps have the common self-help group advantages: Anyone can join without dues or fees, there are no membership requirements, and help can be obtained at times when the counselor may not be available. The empowerment emphasis, which may appeal to those who have experienced oppression, may help clients develop their sense of power and esteem, as well as understand the role of the culture in encouraging their addiction. It may also be a helpful program for clients who have had negative experiences with other self-help programs.

Spiritual/Religious   The 16 steps may be desirable for clients with spiritual beliefs that are not necessarily Judeo-Christian. Because of the emphasis on different spiritual beliefs, the group may provide a variety of recovery role models. Participants will hear not only Judeo-Christian views at meetings but also other religious and spiritual perspectives that may be healing. The flexible interpretation encouraged for the steps may assist rebellious clients in working the steps in their daily lives.

Limitations

As with all self-help groups, the counselor needs to remind the client that anyone can be a member of these groups. This strategy may help the client

retain healthy boundaries concerning group members.

Limited Accessibility   One of the principal limitations of this model is its accessibility. Because of its relative newness in comparison to the other self-help groups, it may not be available for individuals in terms of location and/or frequency of meetings.

Complicated Language   The wording of the steps may be too complicated for some clients. Also, clients who come from traditional Judeo-Christian backgrounds may struggle with some of the openness of the spiritual language.

Rational Recovery

Rational Recovery (RR) groups were started in 1985 by Jack Trimpey; in 1989, he published *Rational Recovery from Alcoholism: The Small Book*. In the preface of his book he discusses how, as a clinical social worker, he heard clients discuss their difficulties with the AA 12-step program, how he could not make sense of AA for himself, and how he decided to use his training as a rational emotive therapist to become his own therapist and encourage others to become their own therapists. Trimpey was able to overcome his drinking problem by using a rational approach (Horvath, 1997). The RR program is based, then, on Albert Ellis's (1962) rational emotive therapy.

Basic Concepts

A client does not have to be abstinent to be a member of RR, but the program does encourage the use of a strategy called *addictive voice recognition training* (AVRT®; Rational Recovery, 1992) and has an Internet crash course available on AVRT®. In this strategy, the client is aware of his or her rational voice and his or her addictive voice (also called the *beast*) and learns to control them to make rational choices. Addiction is viewed, not as a disease, but "as a maladaptive voluntary response to stressors, and will view veterans of the program as cured, not recovering." (Schenker, 2009,

p. 230). Sobriety spreadsheets are used to track irrational thoughts that kick off using urges. Relapses are viewed more as learning experiences than failures. There are no steps, per se, to the program. In the appendix section of *The Small Book*, Trimpey provides an example of 13 steps, but he does not recommend them as steps that should summarize the program for everyone. These statements are not listed here at the request of RR, because the organization views them as obsolete (L. E. Trimpey, personal communication, November 25, 1997). Because RR is not a step program, Trimpey suggests that the reader make up his or her own RR ideas. The RR program has literature, videos, and a meeting directory available as well as its own journal, the *Journal of Rational Recovery*. The AVRT® Internet crash course is free. Since 1993, RR focuses more on educating people about AVRT® (Horvath, 1997). Current views on RR are summarized in *Rational Recovery: The New Cure for Substance Addiction* (Trimpey, 1996).

On December 31, 1998, RR declared a recovery group–free America by 2000, encouraging RR groups and other self-help groups to disband, because they are not necessary for recovery. Although some RR groups are still reportedly in existence, the RR founders advocate the nonexistence of groups due to a concern that the addicted person will become dependent on them. The organization still has its resource materials available for customers. In addition, RR has developed a network to work for social change in the addictions field (Rational Recovery Political and Legal Action Network; RR-PLAN).

Use in Counseling

As stated with the previous self-help groups, RR can provide the client with recovery support, thereby decreasing isolation and increasing self-regulation. However, Trimpey, on his website states: "By its nature, *AVRT® is not and cannot be a professional tool. AVRT® is not a form of counseling, therapy, or addiction treatment.* If AVRT® is offered as a professional service, diluted as an adjunct to any other recovery methodology or treatment, or included in the program of a recovery group, its fundamental meaning is radically changed" (Trimpey, 2013, para. 5; https://rational.org/index.php?id=94).

Strengths

Similar to the other self-help groups, RR may be a helpful referral for clients who have had negative experiences with other self-help groups. Galanter, Egelko, and Edwards (1993) write that the majority of members they studied were men who had previously attended AA.

Focus The RR program makes help available to individuals struggling with addiction issues and may especially appeal to individuals who value looking at issues logically and rationally.

Spiritual/Religious The program may appeal to clients who do not want to focus on a spiritual or religious dimension of recovery. No mention is made of this area as a necessary aspect of recovery.

Limitations

For individuals who need group support, this organization may be limited in its helpfulness unless there is a group that focuses on RR concepts in their area.

Limited Guidance The program encourages clients to read RR literature, make their own interpretations of recovery, and trust their own logic. Therefore, RR may not be helpful to those who require more guidance in their recovery and those who are well defended about their addiction and/or other personal problems.

Secular Organizations for Sobriety

James Christopher is the founder of Secular Organizations for Sobriety/Save Our Selves (SOS). In his own addiction recovery process, he wrote "Sobriety with Superstition," a 1985 *Free Inquiry* magazine article (Kasl, 1992), and in 1986 he began SOS, which was originally called Secular Sobriety Groups (SSG; Christopher, 1997).

Basic Concepts

The groups are open to people struggling with any type of addiction problem and their family members and friends (Kasl, 1992). Through attending meetings, family members and friends, as well as the addict, can learn about the addiction cycle (Christopher, 1997). Addiction is viewed as a cycle involving a physiological need, a learned habit, and the denial of both; the sobriety cycle involves recognizing and accepting the addiction and making sobriety the top priority of the addict's life (Christopher, 1992). The philosophy is one of empowerment and esteem building based on abstinence and secularism. The SOS program (Christopher, 1988) offers six guidelines:[4]

1. To break the cycle of denial and achieve sobriety, we first acknowledge that *we are alcoholics.*

2. We *reaffirm* this truth daily and accept without reservation—one day at a time—the fact that, as sober alcoholics, we cannot and do not drink, *no matter what.*

3. Since drinking is not an option for us, we take whatever steps are necessary to continue our sobriety priority lifelong.

4. A high quality of life—the good life—can be achieved. However, life is also filled with uncertainties; therefore, we do not drink regardless of feelings, circumstances, or conflicts.

5. We share in confidence with each other our thoughts and feelings as sober alcoholics.

6. Sobriety is our priority, and we are each individually responsible for our lives and our sobriety.

Meetings are organized according to the group members. There are no rigid guidelines or procedures. The organization offers a newsletter, which is printed four times a year, as well as literature, audiotapes, videotapes, a meeting directory, and a yearly national conference. Sponsorship is not encouraged, because SOS does not believe in one person telling another how to live life. Current information on SOS is available in the *Sobriety Handbook: The SOS Way* (Christopher, 1997).

Use in Counseling

As with other self-help groups, SOS can provide support for recovery while decreasing social isolation and increasing self-regulation. Again, counselors need to be familiar with the philosophy of the group, how it matches their counseling philosophy, and knowledge of available groups in the area.

Strengths

The SOS program allows anyone to be a member and does not charge any dues or fees, so help is available to anyone who chooses to attend. It encourages empowerment and self-esteem building, which may be helpful to clients who have little or no experience owning their power and who have poor self-concepts. It may also be appealing to individuals who have had negative experiences with other self-help organizations. It has a 24-hour online meeting. Note that five concepts have been updated to incorporate addictions to substances other than alcohol:

1. The first guideline adds "or addicts" at the end.

2. The second guideline now reads: "We reaffirm this truth daily and accept without reservation the fact that, as clean and sober individuals, we cannot and do not drink, or use, no matter what."

3. In guideline 3, the wording "or using" is added after drinking.

4. The word "high" is deleted and the phrase "or use" is added after the word "drink" in the fourth guideline.

[4]Source: *How to Stay Sober: Recovery without Religion* by James Christopher (Amherst, NY: Prometheus Books). Published in 1988. Reprinted by permission of the publisher.

5. In guideline 5, the words "clean individuals" are substituted for the original words of "alcoholics."

Spiritual/Religious The program may be helpful to clients who feel they do not have spiritual or religious needs that require addressing in their addiction self-help program. A spiritual/religious focus to recovery is not encouraged.

Limitations

As with other self-help groups, anyone can attend SOS meetings. In addition, the openness of who may attend (addicts as well as their family members and friends) may be uncomfortable for some clients.

Limited Accessibility These group meetings are likely to be held in major metropolitan areas, so SOS may also have the problem of limited accessibility for clients in certain areas. It is not as widespread as some of the 12-step programs.

Limited Guidance The program does not offer sponsorship and encourages flexibility in recovery interpretation and at meetings. As a result, SOS may not offer enough structure for some clients.

Self-Management and Recovery Training (SMART Recovery®)

In 1994, in order to maintain its not-for-profit status and to continue to provide free self-help meetings, SMART Recovery® came into being and ended its prior connection with RR, which continues to exist as a for-profit program. SMART Recovery® focuses on providing free self-help meetings (both face-to-face and online) for those seeking to overcome addictive behaviors. The program includes a cognitive-behavioral approach, combined with Albert Ellis's (1962) rational emotive behavior therapy. The program offers specific tools and techniques in its four-point program.

SMART Recovery® 4-Point Program® (http://www.smartrecovery.org/intro/)

The 4-Point Program® offers specific tools and techniques for each of the program points:

1. Building and Maintaining Motivation

2. Coping with Urges

3. Managing Thoughts, Feelings, and Behaviors

4. Living a Balanced Life

Basic Concepts

The SMART® organization focuses on cognitive-behavioral approaches to changing self-destructive behavior: Controlling thoughts and emotions can result in empowerment to abstain. The emphasis of SMART® is on motivation, coping skills, rational thinking, and lifestyle balance. The basis of the program is the belief that to recover from chemical dependency, a person needs to be motivated, learn to resist urges as well as learn new ways to cope, and develop a positive lifestyle. The SMART® organization stresses the present and the change of self-destructive behaviors in the present. It does not believe that addiction is a disease, but it is an abstinence-based program. Sobriety is viewed as a choice, and relapse is seen as a learning opportunity. Religion and spirituality may be helpful to an individual but are not viewed as a part of the SMART® program. SMART® does not have any steps to follow, but it advocates nine ideas:[5]

1. I'm not "powerless" over alcohol or drugs, or other addictive behavior. I can certainly use some help, but I believe I can beat this problem, like millions of other people have.

2. Booze and other drugs don't jump into my body. I choose to use them, so I can choose not to and make it stick.

---

[5]Source: Reprinted by permission, SMART Recovery® Self-Help Network, 7537 Mentor Avenue, Suite #306, Mentor, OH 44060.

3. My substance use hurts me and others. I may feel good for a short time, but I suffer more in the long run. It is the "buy now—pay later" plan of life.

4. SMART® can help me achieve my goal of sobriety, but I gain power by accepting personal responsibility for my life and what I put into my body.

5. Getting drunk or high is a way of indulging myself and trying to cope with stress, frustration, and anger. It's just not worth it!

6. There are better ways of coping with life than intoxicating myself. Once I learn these, I will be willing to give up my addictive behavior permanently.

7. It makes sense to seek help to learn new approaches because whatever I've been doing hasn't been working.

8. I can learn from others and enjoy their support without depending on the group for the rest of my life.

9. Once I have mastered the proven methods of self-management offered by SMART®, I can recover, graduate from the program, and get on with my life.

Groups meet 1 or 2 times per week for about 90 minutes. Coordinators of the groups are volunteers who have been trained by SMART®. Some of them have a history of chemical dependency problems and some do not; SMART® says it is not necessary for the coordinators to be in recovery, because the focus of the program is educational mental health. Groups have a volunteer advisor who is a mental health professional to help with crisis or special situations. Donations are welcomed but not required for attendance. Individuals are not expected to attend the groups for the rest of their lives; they can attend for as long as they want, however.

Through dialogue, group members look at their drinking problem as well as their personal problems. One person presents one problem at a time, and the group attempts to help the person solve the problem. One of the tools that a client is likely to encounter at a SMART Recovery® meeting is also used in Rational Emotive Behavior Therapy, referred to as an ABC:

• What is the **A**ctivating event? What did I do? What did others do? What happened to me? What idea occurred to me?

• **B**elief: What is it that I believe about A, the activating event?

• **C**onsequences: What am I feeling or doing that is not working for me? Am I feeling anger, depression, anxiety, low-frustration tolerance, self-pity, and so on? Am I behaving in a way that doesn't work for me? (drinking, attacking others, moping).

• **D**ispute: Is there any evidence that my B, belief, is true? Is my B, belief, rational or irrational? If the belief is irrational, what rational belief can I use to replace it?

• Are there more **E**ffective new, more accurate, rational self-statements for our dysfunctional beliefs?

Use in Counseling

Like the other self-help groups discussed, SMART® can provide a client with a sense of belonging and encouragement to change addictive behavior. This self-help group's philosophy would be an excellent match for a counselor who is comfortable working within a cognitive-behavioral framework. Again, a counseling referral needs to account for its philosophy and availability of the group for the client.

Strengths

As with the other self-help groups, SMART® allows people simply to say they are members; fees are not charged. It may be a good referral for clients who have had negative experiences with other self-help groups. Also, having trained volunteers and a mental health professional advisor would possibly screen out individuals who do not belong in the group or may contribute to poor health in the group. It has online meetings and a message board on its website.

Focus
This program may appeal to clients who like to look at life rationally and focus on a problem. The structure of the meetings may be beneficial to some clients.

Spiritual/Religious
Individuals who do not want to have religious or spiritual beliefs as a part of their recovery program may do well in this program. However, SMART® does not prohibit people from having these components as a part of their recovery program.

Limitations
The main limitation with SMART® is that it may be available only to clients who live in large metropolitan areas.

MATCHING SELF-HELP GROUPS TO MEET CLIENT NEEDS

Humphreys and Rappaport (1994) describe a *self-help group* as a voluntary group where each member is both the helper and helpee. All of the self-help groups reviewed seem to have some additional common factors: Each encourages (1) individuals to examine the need for a behavior change, (2) education of self about the addictive process as interpreted by the specific program, (3) some contact with others in similar situations, and (4) a personalization of the recovery process.

Before asking questions to understand a client better, a sensitive therapist may experience empathy for a client attending a new self-help group by imagining the following scenario: You walk into a room of strangers, and, simply by entering the room, you are admitting that you have a problem that everyone in the room knows you have because you are there and this problem is one you have tried to address and failed. This sense of vulnerability and openness to strangers is commonly felt by individuals who are breaking an addictive pattern.

Helping a client find a group requires counselors to have knowledge of their own theoretical orientation, knowledge of the self-help group's philosophy and availability, and knowledge of the client. Counselors are encouraged to spend some time determining the match of their theoretical orientation with the various self-help group philosophies. The availability of the various self-help groups, both nationally and locally, may temper the use of them in counseling. The counselor and client may develop a mix-and-match approach in terms of combining various literature with available meetings. The caution here is that the counseling not overwhelm the client with recovery options and information.

To facilitate a match to such a group, all counselors need to be sensitive to clients' self-help group experiences, lifestyles, and values in order to make the best match possible. In addition, the group needs to fit the client in terms of the client's stage of change as discussed in Chapter 9 and the client's culture (Norcross, 2003). (See Case Study 8.1.)

CASE STUDY 8.1

Your client is a 30-year-old, single, educated, Caucasian male who lives alone. He does not believe in God and has an aversion to any hint of organized religion. He is so sensitive to it that when he saw a Serenity Prayer plaque in the agency office, he almost left the agency rather than come in for treatment. He wants to become sober, and you believe that he needs a self-help group for support. Assuming that each of the national abstinence-based groups is available, answer the following three questions in response to this case:

1. Which self-help group would you most likely recommend?
2. What would be your rationale in the referral?
3. Would you consider blending self-help groups (e.g., using literature from one group and encouraging attendance at another)? If so, which ones would you blend and why? Also, how would you help your client not become confused with this blending?

Questions to Ask

Four questions can be used directly in an interview with a client or can be used as a mental checklist by the counselor in terms of making a referral:

1. *What types of self-help groups are available where you live and/or work?* The counselor needs a list of all of the different types of self-help groups available in the client's community. This list needs to be shared and reviewed with the client. In some cities, lists of self-help groups are specific (nonsmoking, gay/lesbian, etc.) in their descriptions. In this situation, the client can review the descriptors of the group and determine the type of group he or she wants to try. Even if the therapist believes that the client is being too particular about the type of group, it is important that the client choose a group where the client anticipates feeling the most comfortable. After attending the chosen group, the individual may be more open-minded about attending another group. If a list of local groups is not very descriptive, the client will simply need to try the group and determine if it is one where he or she feels comfortable.

If clients are being treated in one location and live in another, it is important that they attend groups in the area where they plan to attend both during and after addiction treatment. If this is difficult to arrange (e.g., the client is in a different state for treatment), it is critical to provide the client with a link in the hometown community for a similar self-help group. Sometimes, individuals do not want to attend groups near their homes for anonymity

reasons. Some therapists may take issue with this approach; however, it is most important that clients attend groups in a setting where *they are comfortable* rather than one where their therapist believes they would or should be comfortable.

If a client has an extremely hectic schedule, it may be easier to attend a meeting during a work lunch hour or before or after work. Some work environments may allow meetings to be held in the workplace and, if a client is comfortable, meet someone who can be supportive in the work environment. Some clients have employers participate actively in their treatment program, and these employers may work with the clients on lunch-hour extensions or connections with other recovering individuals in the company. For clients with child-care responsibilities, fitting their recovery meetings with their work schedule may assist them in attending meetings. Finally, an individual who travels frequently may need to obtain a national and/or international directory of self-help groups to locate a meeting in the area where he or she is traveling. Many groups have a contact person who can be reached prior to travel.

2. *When you look at your life, where and how is it easiest to fit into meetings?* The feasibility of meetings is critical for clients. Given their values, lifestyles, and commitments, it is important that the counselor find a position between enabling clients to miss meetings (e.g., believing all of the reasons they cannot attend) and insisting that they attend meetings despite their life situation (e.g., expecting a single

parent with children to attend 90 meetings in 90 days). If the client cannot attend any meetings in a week for numerous reasons, the therapist can tentatively assume that the client is being resistant. In this case, the therapist needs to explore the resistance with the client. Possibly the client is afraid to go to a meeting alone, angry at being required to attend meetings, or overwhelmed with life responsibilities. Encouraging clients to express their feelings about attendance at self-help group meetings can result in enhanced counseling. A discussion of apparent resistance may also encourage clients to discuss pragmatic recovery roadblocks (e.g., no babysitter available).

Some counselors may believe that a person needs to spend most recovery time in self-help meetings. This viewpoint is fitting in particular circumstances. First, early in a person's recovery, attendance at as many self-help meetings as possible may be necessary to build supports for making a change. Also, attending meetings may provide the client with a time filler, because he or she is no longer involved in securing and using alcohol or drugs. Finally, attending various meetings helps clients become exposed to different groups, different individuals, and different ways of being sober. However, the counselor needs to remember that clients did not necessarily sober up to spend all of their free time in meetings; they also need to build or rebuild relationships with significant others in their lives and learn to have fun without alcohol and drugs. Overall, clients need to attend as many recovery meetings as needed to stay sober. A minimum self-help group meeting of once a week is a good guideline to use.

3. *How comfortable are you with giving out your phone number/e-mail address to members of the self-help group?* Often, members of self-help groups share their phone numbers/e-mail addresses with one another. Those who are attending a group for the first time should think about their comfort level with sharing their phone numbers/e-mail addresses and then rehearse responses to such a request with their counselors if they do not want to share their numbers/addresses. Usually, individuals share only their first names and their phone numbers/e-mail addresses.

4. *How comfortable are you with being touched in a self-help group?* In some self-help groups, it is common for members to hug each other and/or hold hands at the closing of the meeting. The new member in a group may need to consider how to respond to being touched in a group. This area may be of significant concern to the recovering person who has been physically and/or sexually abused.

Assessing a Group's Personality

Self-help groups, like individuals, have unique personalities. Often, clients need to attend the same group for five or six meetings to learn how the group tends to operate and the types of individuals in the group. Attending a meeting more than once can assist a client in developing a commitment to the recovery process, enhancing tolerance toward others, and developing impulse control.

After attending a meeting for the first time, there are a series of eight questions that can help the counselor and client assess the health of the group. The counselor can approach this area by asking the client to "walk me through the meeting step by step":

1. What was the meeting like overall? (friendly? hospitable?)

2. What was the meeting like physically? (safe part of town? easy parking? comfortable room? too much smoke in the room?)

3. How were you greeted? (respectfully? friendly?)

4. Was there anyone in the group with whom you felt particularly comfortable? (potential sponsor/mentor?)

5. What was the topic of the meeting? (relevant to recovery?)

6. Did everyone participate in the meeting? (everyone spoke?)

7. Did you feel comfortable with the person (people) who seemed to direct the meeting? (reasonable leader?)

8. Did you go early and/or stay late at the meeting? (visit informally with others?)

These questions provide examples of how a group's health can be assessed. Some meetings are simply more open to newcomers, individuals who are in treatment, or those court-ordered to self-help groups. Some meetings, because of their location or openness to new members, may in time become overwhelmed with new individuals in recovery and have few members who can serve as recovery role models for clients. The overall atmosphere of the meeting might help the client decide to seek a meeting in a different location or one that is more compatible with the client's needs. For example, some meetings may be held in an undesirable part of town, and if the client needs to park some distance away from the building, this may increase the chances that the client will not attend or will not feel safe. An example of a difficult meeting room condition is that some meetings allow smoking, and it may be very difficult for the client to tolerate cigarette smoke.

Even though many self-help groups are committed to anonymity, it is legitimate for the client to describe individuals at the meeting without using names. For example, a client may describe a meaningful discussion at a meeting by saying, "A divorced woman with two children said she has a hard time trusting a Higher Power because of her life experiences." Finding out who greets the newcomers and how they are greeted may help the counselor determine the appropriateness of the meeting for the client. Many types of people attend self-help groups; clients must understand that they cannot automatically trust all individuals who attend them. Some group members may approach new members with the intention of using them somehow (i.e., financially or sexually); self-help groups are not free from the social influences that exist at any social gathering. Finding out who felt trustworthy to the client may indicate client issues as well as strengths. A female client, for example, may trust only males and may need to be encouraged to trust some women in the group.

The questions that focus on topic, participation, and leaders in the group will assist the client in determining the norms of the group. This may be difficult to assess after one meeting, but these questions will heighten the client's awareness of the meetings attended and provide clues as to which groups are more comfortable for the client than others. A self-help group that gently but firmly encourages all members to participate can assist recovering clients in developing skills such as reading (if they read materials at the meeting), public speaking (if they need to introduce themselves), and social skills (conversing with others, setting boundaries, etc.). The final question about going early and/or staying late may also assist a client in fitting in with the group. Going early and/or staying late may allow the individual to participate in preparing the room for the meeting and provide him or her with both a sense of ownership in the meeting (assembling and disassembling the meeting room) and a chance to visit informally with others.

Guidelines for Healthy and Unhealthy Groups

These guidelines, in part, are determined by the comfort level of the client in the group. However, some general rules may be applied based on the previously stated questions. The following six indicators of an unhealthy group are based on observations of more than one meeting:

1. An unwelcoming sense to the group.

2. No greetings for newcomers or greetings that seem manipulative in nature.

3. An unhappy, negative tone to the majority of the group members.

4. An unwillingness by group members to discuss practical, optimistic approaches to recovery issues.

5. Dominance by one or a few individuals who do not encourage participation by others.

6. A general lack of participation and/or interest in the meeting.

Kasl (1992) describes unhealthy groups as those that limit outside involvement, reading material, disagreement with the group, members from having different group roles, member discussion ("robot talk" or "jargon"), and member choices (on involvement in the group). She also describes these groups as grandiose, paranoid, lacking self-reflection, and having sexual needs met within the group.

By contrast, a healthy self-help group leaves the newcomer feeling as though his or her presence was both wanted and needed by the group. This begins with genuine greetings by the group and continues with an optimistic, how-to recovery approach in the meeting, which involves the participation of everyone in the group who wants to participate. Individuals who belong to a healthy recovery self-help group are enthusiastic about the meeting and very willing to be supportive to one another.

Kasl (1992) describes healthy groups as flexible, open to self-scrutiny, having a clear focus, using conflict management approaches, and retaining a sense of humor. She also states that members in these groups want to participate at a personal level through regular attendance and to feel respected as a whole person, not exploited. Table 8.2 provides six suggestions for the use of self-help groups.

Some self-help groups (e.g., AA) strongly encourage sponsorship, whereas others (e.g., RR, SOS) do not believe it is necessary. A sponsor is someone who has been in AA longer than the client and can guide him/her on applying the 12-steps to his or her life (Schenker, 2009). Because self-help groups do not keep track of who sponsors whom, sponsorship is an option for group participation, whether the group endorses it formally or not. Sponsorship is helpful in terms of providing a recovery role model for the client and

Table 8.2   Overall Suggestions in the Use of Self–Help Groups

1. Have a knowledge of the various 12-Step model and 12-Step Alternative abstinence-based self-help groups in one's area.

2. Learn about at least one 12-Step model and one 12-Step Alternative model that fits with one's theory of counseling and one's client population.

3. Have a professional contact within the 12-Step and 12-Step Alternative groups that can inform the counselor of information on local groups, that is, meeting times and locations, "personalities" of the groups.

4. Have copies of meeting schedules for both 12-Step and 12-Step Alternative groups available in the waiting room and counseling office.

5. Have free literature available on 12-Step and 12-Step Alternative groups for clients.

6. Help clients determine a group in terms of matching it with therapy.

someone the client has permission to contact if recovery issues surface. Because it is not necessary to have a sponsor to be in a self-help group, it is truly an option for the client. Regardless of whether a client formally asks a person to be a sponsor, the client can watch for an individual (or individuals) in self-help groups who seems to be living the recovery life the client aspires to live. The counselor can encourage conversations and activities with this individual, who may provide the client with a strong role model, a recovery mentor. Fagan (1986) indicates that sponsors may be a significant component in the recovery process, especially early in recovery.

Some groups recommend same-sex sponsors to help the individual learn about recovery. However, this recommendation may also exist to discourage sexual relations in such an intimate relationship, and such a recommendation assumes a heterosexual bias. It may be best for the counselor to help the client choose a sponsor based on the qualities of the potential sponsor and to assist the client in considering the possible impact of gender on his or her choice of a sponsor.

The process of sponsor selection can be approached in several ways. For instance, a sponsor can be either temporary or permanent. A temporary sponsor is one that helps the client through early recovery until a permanent sponsor can be obtained (Schenker, 2009). If the counselor is familiar with different individuals in recovery in the local community, a temporary sponsor can be arranged for the client. In this sponsorship, it is understood by both individuals that the relationship is only a tentative one that will stop as soon as the individual obtains a permanent sponsor. The danger of a counselor arranging for a sponsor is twofold: The sponsor may be linked with the client's treatment, and the client may learn a passive approach to recovery. Clients make seek out sponsors (temporary or permanent) on their own through a variety of avenues: asking for a sponsor during a meeting, approaching someone before or after a meeting, or checking a posted list of available sponsors (Schenker, 2009).

Counseling can help in selecting and maintaining a sponsor for the client. Initially, the counselor can assist in sponsor selection by using knowledge of the client as a rudder in the discussion of available sponsors in order to help the client choose the most appropriate sponsor. Once a sponsor is chosen, the counselor can check in periodically with the client with regard to the sponsorship relationship. In these periodic check-ins, the counselor can help the client examine problems, expectations, and feelings regarding the relationship in order to enhance the positive impact of sponsorship on the client's recovery process (Schenker, 2009). Discussion of sponsorship can also help the counselor evaluate the client's commitment to the recovery process: regular, frequent contact with a sponsor may indicate a strong commitment to the recovery process.

Asking an individual to be a temporary sponsor can be helpful to both the client and the sponsor. It allows both individuals to try on the relationship and determine if the match is a good one; the relationship can simply dissolve and does not have to be addressed unless the client so desires.

Questions to Ask

If a client decides to obtain a sponsor, he or she may find it helpful to ask the potential sponsor these six questions:

1. Would you be willing to sponsor me in the self-help program?

2. What do you think it means to be a good sponsor?

3. What expectations would you have of me if I were your sponsee?

4. How often could I contact you about recovery questions?

5. Are there certain times of the day or week that you would not want me to contact you?

6. Have you ever sponsored anyone before?

Questions such as these may prevent misunderstandings and conflicts about the sponsor/sponsee relationship. The client can discuss the potential sponsor's answers with the counselor to determine the quality of the match. Even though the client may obtain appealing answers from the potential sponsor, it is important that the client watch the sponsor's behavior over time to see if the verbal responses match the sponsor's behavior, at least most of the time. For example, a sponsor who promises accessibility to a client and then is usually unavailable for recovery support can be both frustrating and discouraging to the client. The counselor can use the following guidelines in helping the client find a match.

Guidelines for a Healthy/Unhealthy Sponsor/Mentor

There are no absolute guidelines for the healthy sponsor/sponsee relationship, because recovering clients have very different needs. An appropriate sponsor for one client may be inappropriate for another. There are some tendencies, however, that may discourage a client's recovery process. An unhealthy sponsor may be:

- An individual who promises *always* to be available for the person.

- An individual who views sponsorship as a legitimate means to control another person.

- An individual who uses sponsorship as a means to use a person in recovery (i.e., for sexual or financial gratification).

- An individual who discourages the person to think for himself or herself; rather, the individual tells the person what to think and how to act.

- An individual who has unrealistic expectations of the person's recovery.

- An individual who is unavailable to the person.

- An individual who is highly critical and judgmental of the person.

- An individual who has a relatively short recovery time (less than a year sober).

By contrast, the healthy sponsor is realistic in the expectations of self as well as the sponsee and views sponsorship as a role modeling of recovery. Firm, clear boundaries are set between the sponsor and the sponsee, preventing the sponsee from being used by or using the sponsor. A healthy sponsor is also one who is willing to explore the options facing the sponsee rather than approaching problem solving simplistically. Finally, a healthy sponsor is one who is available and supportive to the sponsee and one who has some significant time in recovery so that the sponsee can draw on the sponsor's experiences.

SPECIAL ISSUES

Three special issues are discussed in this section: small-town concerns, anonymity, and online meetings/discussion groups. These issues are raised because they may add a unique aspect to

a client's recovery that needs to be considered in the counseling process.

Small-Town Concerns

Several issues arise in relation to small-town recovery concerns. First, there may be a limited number of types of self-help groups and a limited number of self-help meetings in general. Small towns may have only AA meetings available. For the client to whom this self-help type of group does not seem an option, the counselor can work with him or her at developing a tolerance toward the philosophy and translate it into a language that makes sense to the client. For the counselor who is unable to do this translation, it may be helpful to suggest that the client approach the most open individual at a meeting for assistance with the program—a person who has been sober a few years and views the recovery process as unique to each individual. Attendance at meetings can also be supplemented with readings from another type of self-help group.

When a counselor in a small town makes a referral to a self-help group, it is important to warn the client that meetings may be listed as active, but meetings may have stopped because of a small number of participants. This warning may be helpful to the client who goes to a meeting at a listed site and then discovers no one is there. Also, if a client attends one meeting in a small town and presents a list of potential meetings, typically a member of the self-help group can let the client know which groups are still active.

Another small-town concern is the amount of anonymity provided by the meeting. Generally, people in a small town know one another's business. This may include where and when the self-help groups are held. All clients referred to self-help groups in small towns need to keep this fact in mind. Some clients may prefer to drive to a different location or a larger city for self-help meetings to preserve their anonymity.

Finally, the topics discussed in a small-town meeting may need to be discussed between the counselor and the client before the client brings them up in a meeting. Even general discussions of individuals and organizations in a small town may cause others to know exactly who and what is being discussed at the meeting. It may be more helpful to clients who do not want others to know their specific concerns to talk in the meeting about general themes and save the details of the recovery struggle for their sponsor and/or counselor.

Anonymity

Generally, members of self-help groups make a commitment not to talk specifically about who is present at a meeting. This encourages people to share freely in a group. Clients need to understand that there is no guarantee of anonymity in a group and that what they say may be talked about outside

of a meeting. Although this may inhibit clients in their speech, it is critical that they be informed of the nonregulatory function of self-help groups.

Online Meetings/Discussion Groups

Clients using electronic forms of communication for support need to be aware that these forms of communication may have different ramifications than sharing information at an in-person, self-help group meeting. They may assume anonymity (and to some degree confidentiality) when in reality there is no guarantee of anonymity/confidentiality once information is sent out electronically through the Internet. This may be a special concern for those involved with illegal drug use. (See Case Study 8.2.)

CASE STUDY 8.2

Your client is a female, ethnic minority individual who is raising four children on her own in a rural area. She has severe financial restrictions in terms of treatment, so she needs to be discharged from treatment earlier than you would like to see her discharged. She needs to find self-help group support as quickly as possible so she has support to stay sober, because she does not know any recovering addicts.

1. Which self-help group philosophy do you think matches her best?

2. What type of group would you look for to enhance the match for her recovery needs?

3. How would the realities of her life shape the type of group you believe she would need to find?

4. What important pieces of information, about the self-help group referral you are making, would you give her before she attends her first meeting?

5. What questions would you ask her before and after attending the meeting that you believe would facilitate the referral?

SUMMARY

This chapter reviews 12-step groups (AA, NA, CA, MA, CMA, HA) and five alternatives to 12-step groups (WFS, 16 Steps, RR, SOS, SMART®) in terms of their history, basic

concepts, strengths, and limitations. Each group has in common a desire to help people break out of their habitual patterns with alcohol and drugs. Each group also varies in terms of its development and philosophy. Counselors referring clients to these groups need to be aware of the strengths and limitations of each group in order to assist clients in locating a group that meets the clients' idiosyncratic recovery needs.

The counselor can facilitate the addicted person's recovery through knowledge of self-help groups. The counselor needs to be wary of overloading the client with too many recovery options. However, especially during times of economic struggle for the client personally or the society at large (thereby impacting mental health service accessibility), self-help groups can augment a client's resources in staying sober. The recovering community can help clients tap into a support that is bigger than self that can assist clients in knowing when they are out of balance.

By providing the client with an oasis where information and reactions to self-help groups can be sorted out, the counselor can provide an invaluable service to the client. For example, the counselor can help the client survive a typical "pink cloud" reaction in recovery where he or she thinks "all recovering people are wonderful and there are no problems anywhere" and learn how to live within a community of support where there is a blend of strengths and weaknesses. Also, a sensitivity toward specific issues such as barriers to attendance (distance, openness to gays/lesbians, etc.) and caution about what is shared on the Internet in chat rooms or in meetings with others can be beneficial in the long run to the individual's recovery.

QUESTIONS

1. What are the names of 12-step programs that help people recover from alcohol/drug addiction?

2. What are five self-help groups other than 12-step groups?

3. Which characteristics of different self-help groups are helpful to some clients?

4. Which characteristics of different self-help groups are not helpful to some clients?

5. How do individual factors such as race and gender affect the effectiveness of some groups?

6. What information would a counselor need to know about a client in order to make an adequate referral to a self-help group?

7. How can a counselor determine if a self-help group is a good match for a client?

8. What characteristics describe a healthy group? An unhealthy group?

9. What characteristics define a healthy sponsor/mentor? An unhealthy sponsor/mentor?

10. What are some self-help group concerns specific to small towns?

EXERCISES

Exercises 1, 2, 5, and 6 focus on the addicted individual. Exercises 3 and 4 can be used both with addicts and their loved ones. With exercises 1 and 2, there is no right or wrong choice—only a clinical rationale is required to explain the choice.

Exercise 8.1

Match the following individual descriptors with the most appropriate self-help groups by making an "X" under the group heading. Then discuss with a peer why that choice was made.

Descriptor	12 Steps	WFS	16 Steps	RR	SOS	SMART®
Has desire to stop using						
Travels frequently						
Lives in a small town						
Is an ethnic minority						
Is female						
Is nonreligious/aspiritual						
Is nonreligious/spiritual						
Is religious/spiritual						
Likes structure/order						
Is highly self-critical						
Has high shame/guilt						
Has low self-esteem						
Has little sense of power						
Is cognitive focused						
Does not like the 12 steps						

Exercise 8.2

Your client may have difficulty with the following problems. For each listed problem, check the program(s) you believe would most effectively address this problem. Then in the checked box, briefly note why you made that choice.

Programs

Problem	12 Steps	WFS	16 Steps	RR	SOS	SMART®
Denial of drug impact						
"Know-it-all"						
Angry						
Anxiety about present and/or future						
Ashamed/guilty						
Defensive						
Mistrustful						
Overly sensitive						
Proud						
Secretive						
Relapse						

Exercise 8.3

Attend an open 12-step meeting. Note all of your reactions from beginning to end as to:

1. Finding out information on the meeting time and location

2. Getting to the meeting

3. Being received by others at the meeting

4. Being in the meeting

5. Leaving the meeting

6. Whether you believe you would ever return to such a meeting and why or why not

Exercise 8.4

Attend another meeting with a sensitivity to the barriers you would experience in the same five reaction areas listed in Exercise 8.3 if you were deaf, blind, or otherwise physically challenged. Discuss your awarenesses with a colleague, focusing on how you would try to work with these barriers in your recovery process if you were addicted and living with such physical challenges.

Exercise 8.5

Obtain information on a 12-step alternative model in terms of philosophy, local meeting site (s), and where you can easily/readily receive such information *as though you were an addicted client.* Discuss in a dyad your responses to the following statements:

> I chose this group because its philosophy . . .

> I anticipate difficulty in being involved in this group in my area because . . .

> I would work around these access barriers by . . .

Then imagine you are currently involved with a 12-step program and want to augment your 12-step philosophy with the alternative model:

> I could use this information to improve my recovery process in the following ways . . .

Exercise 8.6

Examine the language of the steps outlined for 12-step groups and the alternative groups (that have steps or guidelines) in answer to these four questions:

1. What philosophy of addiction recovery is evident in the language used?

2. What values are reflected in the language used?

3. Who, in terms of clients, might be alienated by this language?

4. What type of client might be drawn into this approach by the language used?

READINGS/RESOURCES/WEBSITES

SUGGESTED READINGS

Al-Anon Family Groups. (1973). *Al-Anon faces alcoholism.* New York, NY: Author.

Al-Anon Family Groups. (1990). *Alateen: Hope for children of alcoholics.* New York, NY: Author.

Al-Anon, (1995). *How Al-Anon works for families and friends of alcoholics.* Virginia Beach, VA: Author.

Alcoholics Anonymous World Services. (1953). *Twelve steps and twelve traditions.* New York, NY: Author.

Alcoholics Anonymous World Services. (1976). *Alcoholics anonymous* (3rd ed.). New York, NY: Author.

Christopher, J. (1988). *How to stay sober: Recovery without religion*. Buffalo, NY: Prometheus Books.

Christopher, J. (1992). *SOS sobriety*. Buffalo, NY: Prometheus Books.

Cocaine Anonymous. (1993). *Hope, faith and courage*. Los Angeles, CA: Author.

Crystal Meth Anonymous (2012). *Crystal clear: Stories of hope* (4th ed.). Los Angeles, CA: Author.

Finley, J. R. (2004). *Integrating the 12 steps into addiction therapy*. Hoboken, NJ: Wiley.

Hirschfield, J. (1990). *The twelve steps for everyone . . . who really wants them*. Center City, MN: Hazelden.

Kasl, C. D. (1992). *Many roads, one journey: Moving beyond the 12 steps*. New York, NY: HarperCollins.

Kasl, C. D. (1995). *Yes, you can: A guide to empowerment groups*. Lolo, MT: Author.

Kirkpatrick, J. (1978). *Turnabout: Help for a new life*. New York, NY: Doubleday.

Kirkpatrick, J. (1981). *A. fresh start*. Dubuque, IA: Kendall-Hunt.

Kirkpatrick, J. (1990). *Stages of the "new life" program*. Quakertown, PA: Women for Sobriety.

Knaus, W. (1995). *SMART Recovery®: A sensible primer*. Mentor, OH: SMART®.

Marijuana Anonymous. (2001). *Life with hope: A return to living through the twelve steps and twelve traditions of Marijuana Anonymous*. Van Nuys, CA: Author.

Moyers, W. C., (2012). *Now what?* Center City, MN: Hazelden.

Narcotics Anonymous. (1982). *Narcotics Anonymous*. Sun Valley, CA: CARENA.

Schenker, M. D., (2009). *A clinician's guide to 12-step recovery*. New York, NY: Norton.

Secular Organizations for Sobriety/Save Our Selves. (1997). *Sobriety handbook: The SOS way*. Oakland, CA: LifeRing Press.

Trimpey, J., (1989). *Rational recovery for alcoholism: The small book*. New York, NY: Delacorte.

Trimpey, J., (1996). *Rational recovery: The new cure for substance addiction*. New York, NY: Pocket.

RESOURCES

12–Step Support Groups

Adult Children of Alcoholics World Service Organization, Inc. (ACA)
P.O. Box 3216
Torrance, CA 90510
(310) 534-1815
(562) 595-7831 (alternate phone)
E-mail: info@adultchildren.org
www.adultchildren.org

Al-Anon Family Group Headquarters (Al-Anon)
1600 Corporate Landing Parkway
Virginia Beach, VA 23455
(757) 563-1600
(757) 563-1655 (fax)
E-mail: wso@al.anon.org
www.al-anon.org

Alcoholics Anonymous World Services, Inc. (AA)
P.O. Box 459
New York, NY 10163
(212) 870-3400
www.aa.org

Cocaine Anonymous World Services (CA)
CAWSO, Inc.
21720 S. Wilmington Ave., Suite 304
Long Beach, CA 90810-1641
or
P.O. Box 492000
Los Angeles, CA 90049-8000
(310) 559-5833
(310) 559-2554 (fax)
E-mail: cawso@ca.org
www.ca.org

Co-Dependents Anonymous (CODA)
CODA, Fellowship Services Office
P.O. Box 33577
Phoenix, AZ 85067-3577
(602) 277-7991 (meeting information only)
(888) 444-2359 (toll-free)
(888) 444-2379 (Spanish toll-free)
E-mail: outreach@coda.org

www.coda.org
www.coda.org/spanish

Crystal Meth Anonymous
Northern California
(415) 692-4762 (NorCal CMA Infoline)
www.norcalcma.org

Families Anonymous, Inc.
701 Lee St., Suite 670
Des Plaines, IL 60016
(847) 294-5877
(847) 294-5837 (fax)
E-mail: famanon@FamiliesAnonymous.org
www.FamiliesAnonymous.org

Heroin Anonymous World Services
5025 N. Central Avenue, #587
Phoenix, AZ 85012
www.heroinanonymous.org

Marijuana Anonymous World Services
P.O. Box 7807
Torrance, CA 90504-9207
(800) 766-6779
E-mail: office@marijuana-anonymous.org
www.marijuana-anonymous.org

Nar-Anon Family Group Headquarters, Inc.
(Nar-Anon)
22527 Crenshaw Boulevard, #200B
Torrance, CA 90505
(310) 534-8188 or (800) 477-6291
(310) 534-8688 (fax)
E-mail: naranonWSO@gmail.com
or wso@nar-anon.org
www.nar-anon.org

Narcotics Anonymous World
Services (NA)
P.O. Box 9999
Van Nuys, CA 91409
(818) 773-9999
(818) 700-0700 (fax)
www.na.org

Alternatives to 12–Step Programs

Rational Recovery Systems
Lotus Press
P.O. Box 800
Lotus, CA 95651
(530) 621-4374 (8 A.M. to 4 P.M.)
(530) 621-2667
www.rational.org

Secular Organizations for Sobriety (SOS)
4773 Hollywood Boulevard
Hollywood, CA 90027
(323) 666-4295
(323) 666-4271 (fax)
E-mail: sos@cfiwest.org
www.cfiwest.org/sos/index.htm

16 Steps
Dr. Charlotte Kasl
Many Roads, One Journey
P.O. Box 1302
Lolo, MT 59847
(406) 273-6080
E-mail: contact@charlottekasl.com or
charlottekasl@yahoo.com
www.charlottekasl.com or www.mixedbag.us/
16steps.htm

SMART Recovery®
7304 Mentor Avenue, Suite #F
Mentor, OH 44060
(440) 951-5357
(866) 951-5357
(440) 951-5358 (fax)
www.smartrecovery.org

Women for Sobriety (WFS)/Men for
Sobriety (MFS)
P.O. Box 618
Quakertown, PA 18951-0618
(215) 536-8026
(215) 536-9026 (fax)
E-mail: newlife@nni.com
www.womenforsobriety.org

APPENDIX 8A: STORIES OF RECOVERY

12-Step Groups

1. *Alateen.* The book *Hope for Children of Alcoholics* contains a section of stories for the teenage children of alcoholics.

2. *Al-Anon.* The book *Al-Anon Faces Alcoholism* has a section titled "Those Who Live with the Problem," which contains stories of the loved ones of addicted individuals. The book *How Al-Anon Works for Families & Friends of Alcoholics* has a section on Al-Anon experiences that has numerous stories of family members and friends who have lived with alcoholics/addicts.

3. *Alcoholics Anonymous.* In the book *Alcoholics Anonymous*, Part II contains stories of alcoholics in recovery.

4. *Cocaine Anonymous.* In the book *Hope, Faith, and Courage*, the entire book, except the prelude, consists of cocaine addicts' recovery stories.

5. *Crystal Meth Anonymous.* In their text, *Crystal Clear: Stories of Hope*, addicts share their stories of recovery.

6. *Marijuana Anonymous.* In their newsletter, *New Leaf*, and their book, *Life with Hope*, they publish the stories of addicts in recovery.

7. *Narcotics Anonymous.* In the book *Narcotics Anonymous*, the Book Two section contains stories of addicts in recovery.

Alternatives to 12-Step Programs

1. *Secular Organizations for Sobriety (SOS).* The book *SOS Sobriety* has a section titled "Welcome to SOS," which contains stories of individuals in recovery.

2. *Women for Sobriety.* The book *Turnabout* is essentially the story of the founder, Jean Kirkpatrick.

Alcoholics/Addicts

1. In his autobiography of his addiction and recovery, *Broken*, William Cope Moyers, son of journalist Bill Moyers, tells his story with a short section of the book that contrasts the different societal reactions to his diagnoses of addiction and cancer.

2. In the book, *The Harder They Fall*, Stromberg and Merrill (2005) record the stories of 21 celebrities in terms of their addiction and recovery.

Alcoholics/Addicts and Family

1. In Sheff's (2007) *Tweak*, he describes his story of addiction to and recovery from methamphetamines as a young man.

2. In Sheff's (2011) *We All Fall Down*, he follows up on his 2007 book with an update on his addiction and recovery from methamphetamines.

3. In Sheff's (2008) *Beautiful Boy*, the father of the *Tweak* author describes his responses to his son's addiction and recovery.

Family

1. In *Terry*, George McGovern tells his story of living with his daughter's struggle with alcoholism that resulted in her death.

APPENDIX 8B: EMOTIONAL SOBRIETY

Emotional Sobriety: Sustaining Long-Term Recovery

Definitions of Emotional Sobriety

1. The presence of a quality emotional recovery where one lives in balance and maturity through the practice of self-awareness and self-regulation.

2. "Slow, steady rethinking about all the people, places and things that once did—and could again—throw us off kilter" (Herbert, 2012).

3. "We have learned how to tolerate our intense emotions without acting out in dysfunctional ways, clamping down and foreclosing on our feeling world, or self-medicating. Self-medicating and compulsive behaviors reflect a lack of good self-regulation" (Dayton, 2007, p. xviii).

4. "Everything in moderation" (Dayton, 2007, p. xxix).

Symptoms of a Lack of Emotional Sobriety (Dayton, 2007, p. 13)

1. Underdeveloped skills of self-regulation.

2. Inability to regulate strong feelings such as anger, rage, anxiety, sadness.

3. Lack of ability to regulate mood, appetite.

4. Lack of ability to regulate behavior.

5. Not being able to put strong emotions into perspective.

6. Lack of ability to regulate substances or self-medicating behaviors.

7. Inability to live in the present.

8. Lack of ability to regulate activity level (chronically over- or underactive).

9. Inability to live comfortably in intimate relationships.

10. Lack of resilience or the ability to roll with the punches.

11. Tendency to try to get rid of painful emotions through defensive strategies such as transference (transferring painful feelings from a relationship from the past onto a relationship in the present), projection (projecting unwanted feelings outside the self onto another person or situation, disowning them), and splitting (throwing unwanted feelings out of consciousness).

Theory (Dayton)

Signs of Emotional Sobriety (Dayton, 2007, pp. 12–13)

1. Well-developed skills of self-regulation.

2. Ability to regulate strong emotions.

3. Ability to regulate mood, appetite.

4. Ability to maintain a perspective on life circumstances.

5. Ability to regulate potentially harmful substances or self-medicating behaviors.

6. Ability to live in the present.

7. Ability to regulate activity levels.

8. Ability to live with both social and intimate connection.

9. Resilience, the ability to roll with the punches.

10. Ability to regulate personal behavior.

11. Ability to own and process unwanted or painful emotions rather than disown them, split them off, or project them outside the self.

Exercise for Signs of Emotional Sobriety (Dayton) (developed by Geri Miller, PhD)

I would like to develop stronger emotional sobriety by focusing on the items above with which I currently struggle in my daily life (circle all items that apply):

1. Well-developed skills of self-regulation.

2. Ability to regulate strong emotions.

3. Ability to regulate mood, appetite.

4. Ability to maintain a perspective on life circumstances.

5. Ability to regulate potentially harmful substances or self-medicating behaviors.

6. Ability to live in the present.

7. Ability to regulate activity levels.

8. Ability to live with both social and intimate connection.

9. Resilience, the ability to roll with the punches.

10. Ability to regulate personal behavior.

11. Ability to own and process unwanted or painful emotions rather than disown them, split them off, or project them outside the self.

I currently show emotional sobriety by exhibiting these signs *regularly* in my daily life (list all the numbered items above that apply):

_____

_____

Application to Client Population
I see my clients frequently struggling with the following aspects of emotional Sobriety (list all the numbered items above that apply):

_____

_____

Discuss in small dyads/small groups, ways to encourage the expression of emotional sobriety in one's client population.

Theory (Dayton)

Solutions for Coming into Balance (Dayton, 2007, p. 14)

1. Learn the skills of mind, body, and emotional self-regulation.

2. Resolve childhood wounds so they don't undermine self-regulation.

3. Learn effective and healthy ways of self-soothing and incorporate them into daily life.

4. Learn effective ways to manage stress.

5. Maintain a healthy body; get daily exercise, rest, and proper nutrition.

6. Process emotional ups and downs as they happen and learn to consciously shift feeling and thinking states.

7. Learn to use the thinking mind to regulate the feeling, limbic mind.

8. Develop inner resources: quiet, meditation, spiritual pursuits.

9. Develop outer resources: work, hobbies, social life, community.

Exercise for Solutions for Coming Into Balance (Dayton) (developed by Geri Miller, PhD)

List three of the above balancing solutions that you "shine" at:

_____

_____

_____

Write a short paragraph on how you learned these solutions:

_____

_____

_____

_____

_____

Application to Client Population
List ways you may help your clients learn balancing solutions based on your own personal experience in this area:

_____

_____

_____

_____

_____

_____

_____

_____

Theory (Dayton)

A. Critical Components: Flexibility, Adaptability, Resilience

Exercise for Critical Components (Dayton) (developed by Geri Miller, PhD)
Complete the following statements.

1. I show my *inflexibility* in life by (list behaviors):

_____

_____

_____

_____

2. I show my *flexibility/adaptability* in life by (list behaviors):

_____

_____

_____

_____

3. The following are roles where I find it hard to be flexible/adaptable and the reasons why:

Role	Reasons for being inflexible/adaptable
_____	_____
_____	_____
_____	_____
_____	_____

4. My goal is to become more *flexible/adaptable* in my life by (action taken/behavior changed):

_____.

Application to Client Population
I see my clients frequently struggling with inflexibility in the following ways:

_____

_____

_____

Discuss, in small dyads/small groups, ways to encourage the expression of flexibility in one's client population.

Theory (Berger)

12 Smart Things to Unhook Emotional Dependency

1. Know yourself—and how to stay centered.

2. Stop allowing others to edit your reality.

3. Stop taking things personally.

4. Own your projections as an act of integrity.

5. Confront yourself for the sake of your integrity. Practice:

   a. *Self-support* (encourage self as we are),

   b. *Self-soothing* (maintain perspective), and

   c. *Self-compassion* (acceptance of imperfection).

6. Stop pressuring others to change, and instead pressure yourself to change.

7. Develop a healthy perspective toward yourself, your feelings, and your emotional themes.

8. Appreciate what is.

9. Comfort yourself when you are hurt or disappointed.

10. Use your personal compass to guide your life.

11. Embrace relationship tensions as the fuel for personal growth.

12. The "problem" is not the real problem.

Exercise (developed by Geri Miller, PhD)

Based on 12 Smart Things to Unhook Emotional Dependency (Berger)
Rate yourself on a scale of 1 (lowest you have ever practiced this item) to 5 (highest you have ever practiced this item).

1. I know myself and how to stay centered.

   1   2   3   4   5

2. I edit my own reality rather than have others edit it.

   1   2   3   4   5

3. I keep a balanced perspective rather than take things personally.

   1   2   3   4   5

4. I own my projections as an act of integrity.

   1   2   3   4   5

5. I confront myself for the sake of my integrity. I practice:

   a. *Self-support* (encourage self as I am)

       1   2   3   4   5

   b. *Self-soothing* (maintain my perspective)

       1   2   3   4   5

   c. *Self-compassion* (accept my imperfection)

       1   2   3   4   5

6. I pressure myself to change rather than others.

   1   2   3   4   5

7. I have a healthy perspective toward myself, my feelings, and my emotional themes.

   1   2   3   4   5

8. I appreciate what is.

   1   2   3   4   5

9. I comfort myself when I am hurt or disappointed.

   1   2   3   4   5

10. I use my personal compass to guide my life.

    1   2   3   4   5

11. I embrace relationship tensions as the fuel for personal growth.

    1   2   3   4   5

12. I view the "problem" as not the real problem.

    1   2   3   4   5

In a dyad, discuss those items above that are your *current strengths* and *current "soft spots."* Discuss the *internal and external barriers* to enhancing your emotional sobriety.

Application to Client Population

I view the *current strengths* (generally) in my clinical population as the items above:

_____

I view the *current "soft spots"* (generally) in my clinical population as the items above:

_____

Ways that I may encourage the decrease of emotional dependency in my clients are:

_____

Theory (Mathieu, 2011)

Addicts: ". . . sensitive individuals with mindsets that gravitate toward symptom relief" (p. 6).

American Culture: focuses on quick fix

Spiritual Bypass:

1. ". . . a defense mechanism by which we use spiritual practices or beliefs to avoid our emotional wounds, unwanted thoughts or impulses, or threats to our self-esteem" (p. 2).

2. Apply spiritual tools or principles "alcoholically."

3. ". . . wears a mask or presents a false spiritual self that represses aspects of that person's true self" (p. 40).

4. "Bypass involves grasping rather than gratitude, arriving rather than being, avoiding rather than accepting" (p. 40).

Warning Signs:

1. Unconscious Manipulation

2. Magical Thinking

3. Isolation

Goals:

1. Humility

2. Acceptance

3. Balance

Exercise for Spiritual Bypass (Mathieu) (developed by Geri Miller, PhD)

Develop a spiritual development timeline from birth to your present age.

1. Begin with early perceptions of spirituality (i.e., family religious affiliations and beliefs).

2. Note significant shifts in your spiritual journey as it relates to different areas of your life that may seem pertinent: age, peers, environment, physical/mental problems, drug/alcohol abuse, drug/alcohol recovery, relationship changes, loss.

3. Note times/periods in your spiritual development where you experienced a bypass.

4. Note on your timeline ways you emerged from that bypass.

Application to Clinical Population
What are ways you see your clients demonstrate a spiritual bypass?

_____

_____

Annotated References

Berger, A. (2010). *12 smart things to do when the booze and drugs are gone. Center* City, MN: Hazelden.

In 179 pages, the author elaborates on 12 smart things one can do to unhook from emotional dependency.

Dayton, T. (2007). *Emotional sobriety: From relationship trauma to resilience and balance*. Deerfield Beach, FL: Health Communications.

In this 281-page book, there are 23 chapters that cover various aspects of emotional sobriety.

Dayton, T. (2012). *Emotional sobriety: From relationship trauma to resilience and balance (Workbook)*. www.tiandayton.com

This 71-page workbook includes 16 exercises that are designed to enhance the reader's application of the concepts explained in *Emotional sobriety: From relationship trauma to resilience and balance*.

Herbert, W. (2012). The nuts and bolts of emotional sobriety. *Scientific American Mind, 23*, 66–67.

This article provides a brief overview of the components of emotional sobriety.

Mathieu, I. (2011). *Recovering spirituality: Achieving emotional sobriety in your spiritual practice*. Center City, MN: Hazelden.

In this 183-page book, the author has 13 chapters, a conclusion, and an epilogue that clarifies the concepts of spiritual bypass and emotional sobriety and how they may interact in someone's recovery process. Three recovery stories (including Bill Wilson's) are woven throughout the text as examples of the interactions of these concepts. There are suggestions throughout the text on methods to achieve emotional sobriety.

Ray, A. (2012). *Practice these principles: Living the spiritual disciplines and virtues in 12-step recovery to achieve spiritual growth, character development, and emotional sobriety*. Denver, CO: Outskirts Press.

This 237-page book integrates the spiritual principles of recovery with the steps to facilitate the practice of the spiritual principles in one's daily affairs.

ELABORATION ON SPECIFIC THERAPIES AND TECHNIQUES RELEVANT TO ADDICTION COUNSELING

PERSONAL REFLECTIONS

I focused this chapter based on my experiences as a counselor, an educator, and a counselor trainer in answer to my guiding question of "What works with addicted clients?" in my counseling office, classrooms, and counselor training sites. I encourage the reader to continue the exploration of other therapies in depth with the guiding question of "What works with *my* addicted clients?" Even when it is "proven" that techniques are effective, we need to apply them thoughtfully and judiciously in our work with clients.

This chapter is an exciting one to me because these four therapy approaches and evidence-based practices can be readily used in the addictions field. When I began as an addictions counselor, we had very few theories and techniques to draw from for counseling addicts. These approaches speak to how open the addictions field has become to using what works for each individual—what is healing for that person caught in the throes of addiction. As a result, addicts can see the same counselor and yet experience a different emphasis in counseling as well as participate in different techniques. This allows a tremendous amount of freedom and flexibility for both the counselor and the client in treating the addiction.

OBJECTIVES

1. To learn more in depth about four therapies and evidence-based practices in the addictions field.
2. To learn techniques from these therapies and practices that can be readily used with clients.
3. To determine which theories and techniques best fit your counseling approach.

This chapter explores one core concept of counseling, client resilience, four therapy approaches and techniques (positive psychology, the stages-of-change model, motivational interviewing, and brief therapy) as well as evidence-based practices. Each area is complementary to the others and is a current counseling concept with great potential for use in the addictions counseling field: resilience naturally leads to a discussion of positive psychology—both of which can assist clients in moving in their stage of change—and motivational interviewing and brief therapy are interwoven in the dynamics of resilience, positive psychology, and stages-of-change. Client resilience is examined from the perspective of how counselors can encourage resilience to facilitate change. Positive psychology is explored to emphasize the shift from pathology to wellness that can encourage change. The stages-of-change model can assist counselors in matching the appropriate level of intervention to the client's readiness for change. The spirit and techniques of motivational interviewing are explored in terms of involving clients in counseling. Brief therapy and related techniques, as divided into psychodynamic, cognitive and behavioral, and strategic and systemic, is described. The section on evidence-based practices is meant to be an overall review of current approaches.

CLIENT RESILIENCE

It is important to understand the concept of resilience because it is core to the recovery process from addiction. We do not know the exact mechanisms that explain the chronic, compulsive nature of addictions, but we do know that neurologically stress has a toxic effect on the brain that can have a negative impact on recovery (Alim et al., 2012). Therefore, we need to understand more about resilience and how it operates neurologically (Alim et al., 2012). Our goal, as counselors, is to help the addicted client learn how to cope effectively with stress without returning to the use of alcohol/drugs; that is, how resiliency evidences itself in relation to addiction. Because reliance is defined as the absence of the pathology (Alim et al., 2012), that means that in addiction, resilience means the absence of the substance use (Larm, Hodgins, Tengstroem, & Larsson, 2010). Resilience, then, can play an important role in preventing addiction as well as preventing relapse.

Note that while there has been more interest in resilience in the past 20 years, the absence of a consistent definition and ways to measure it has resulted in confusion (Kolar, 2011). For example, in psychology, positive psychology looks at it as a virtue while humanistic psychology views it holistically in relation to other virtues and the environment (it can be seen as either a virtue or a vice) (Friedman & Robbins, 2012). In light of the confusion and disagreement regarding the definition and composition of resilience and because of its importance in the recovery process, it is necessary to clarify the general concept of resilience

here in order to encourage it in our clients' recovery process.

Resilience is ordinary, not magical (Masten, 2001). Resilience means we get up once more than we are knocked down; it helps us cope with life. The philosophy of resilience is summarized through the five main concepts of resilience (Discovery Health Channel & APA, 2002):

1. People can learn to be resilient, to "bounce back."

2. The development of resilience is personal and unique.

3. Being resilient does not preclude difficult times.

4. Resilience is not something that is extraordinary.

5. Resilience is ongoing, requiring time and effort.

Ryff and Singer (2003) examine resilience as an outcome and a dynamic process. The outcome definition of resilience is: "the *maintenance, recovery, or improvement in mental or physical health following challenge*" (Ryff & Singer, 2003, p. 20). This definition is different than an absence-of-illness approach because of the presence of positive aspects, such as positive connections with others (mental) and healthy diet (physical). The authors also define resilience as a dynamic process: "successful *engagement* with difficult events and experiences" (Ryff & Singer, 2003, p. 20). In their research, people who flourished under expected and unexpected change had factors (psychological, social) that protected them. They had "coping strategies, flexible self-concepts, quality relationships with others, positive comparison processes" (Ryff & Singer, 2003, p. 23).

Resilience may involve a "reserve capacity," which means the person's potential to change and grow (Staudinger, Marsiske, & Baltes, 1995). Growth that occurs after trauma may result in a different self-perception, respect for one's own vulnerability, closer relationships with others as well as an increased appreciation of the significant individuals in their life, more self-disclosure, and a different view/philosophy of life (Tedeschi & Calhoun, 1995). Thriving is the concept that describes a person being better off following a traumatic experience (Ryff & Singer, 2003).

Resilient people show they can adapt positively to life's adversities. Resilience is "the process of adapting well in the face of adversity, trauma, tragedy, threats, or even significant sources of stress—such as family and relationship problems, serious health problems, or workplace and financial stressors" (Discovery Health Channel & American Psychological Association [APA], 2002, p. 2).

Three models of resilience, as summarized by Zolkoski and Bullock (2012), are: *compensatory* (factors that neutralize exposure to the risk, i.e., adults moderating the substance use of young people in a poverty situation), *challenge* (moderate stress that encourages mobilization of resources, i.e., the children in poverty, instead of doing drugs, reach out to their teachers for assistance in avoiding drug use and developing other interests), and *protective* (immunity v. vulnerability-stress and personal attributes are related to adaptation—i.e., parents impact the substance use of their children in the context of poverty). The counselor can use these models in assisting the addicted client in achieving and maintaining sobriety by looking for compensatory factors, making challenging factors "livable," and reducing the stress and enhancing adaptive personal attributes. We are looking at resilience as consisting of two broad categories: risk factors and protective factors (Lee et al., 2013). A counselor examining the risk factors and the protective factors present for the client can facilitate their recovery process.

The counselor especially needs to look for internal aspects of the client that encourage resilience, as well as external aspects of the client's life; these need to be explored because both have been shown to contribute to resilience (Kolar, 2011). In summarizing a review of the literature, Kolar (2011) states there are three interactive level factors involved in resilience: "*individual-level factors* (personality characteristics, talents, skills), *social-level factors* (family and peer network relationships, the degree of support that can be gathered from these relationships), and *societal-level factors* (community, school environment, cultural norms, institutional and other outside supports)" (p. 426).

Dialogue with a counselor can assist clients in assessing and naming these internal and external factors, *and* how they interact, so clients can play to their strengths and incorporate these factors with intentionality into their life. This process can encourage hopefulness in clients for change. Based on the summary by Ryff & Singer (2003), each of us can develop or increase our resilience in facing life situations through an integration of the following four areas: learning and using new coping strategies, having a flexible self-concept, developing and maintaining quality relationships with others, and having ways to make positive comparisons within ourselves and in relation to others.

Regarding positive comparisons, if we face a difficult life situation, we can not only survive it, but we can thrive by having intra- and inter-feedback loops that assist us in our resilience. In the intra-feedback loop, our self-talk, our self-concept may need to change, as well as how we compare ourselves to others. For example, we may need to say to ourselves, "*This* is the *new* me and I cannot compare my insides (how I am feeling/thinking in this situation) with other people's outsides (how others appear to be handling life well)." This intra-feedback loop is connected to the interfeedback loop, where we are open to receiving feedback on the success of our coping strategies and the types of relationships that we need in these circumstances. Addicted clients may need to say to themselves and others: "This is the new, sober me, and I need to have people in my life who will be supportive to my staying sober no matter what happens to me in life. I also need to have people who will give me honest feedback on how I am coping and the quality of the relationships in my life."

When working with addicted individuals, counselors can also help clients develop resilience by informing them that they can learn to be resilient no matter what life circumstances or experiences they have had. Counselors need to go beyond examining and addressing the client's deficits and help them find ways to be self-protective and adaptively change in response to difficult situations (Leadbeater, Dodgen, & Solarz, 2005). For example, treatment interventions that focus on coping and problem-solving skills and social support can help an addict avoid relapse (NIDA, 2006). Some of the research that has provided evidence of the protective factors of resilience in terms of substance use and abuse with various populations include: adolescents (Isganaityte & Cepukiene, 2012); college students (Johnson, Dinsmore, & Hof, 2011); women (Hernandez & Mendoza, 2011); and adults in treatment (Shumway, Bradshaw, Harris, & Baker, 2013).

There are several frameworks of specific factors for the facilitation of resilience. The benefit of such frameworks is that they remind you to check for the presence or absence of such factors in your clients' lives, thereby facilitating their addiction recovery in terms of sobriety and a balanced lifestyle. Two of these frameworks are examined here.

One such framework is as follows: Factors that contribute to resilience are caring and supportive relationships, a capacity for the development of realistic plans and taking the steps necessary to create those plans, a positive self-view and confidence, communication and problem-solving skills, and the ability to manage intense feelings and impulses (Discovery Health Channel & APA, 2002; see Table 9.1).

A second framework is focused on stress. Stress can contribute to drug abuse or relapse, whereas behaviors that are healthy can help the addict handle the stress of life (NIDA, 2006). An example of commonsense suggestions for addiction recovery in handling stress include maintenance of personal hygiene, exploration of one's senses, and incorporating exercise (Shaw, Ritvo, & Irvine, 2005). A third framework the counselor can use to build resilience in the client is the use of the 10-item list (Table 9.1).

Table 9.1 Ten Ways to Build Resilience

1. Make connections.
2. Avoid seeing crises as insurmountable problems.
3. Accept that change is a part of living.
4. Move toward your goals.
5. Take decisive actions.
6. Look for opportunities for self-discovery.
7. Nurture a positive view of yourself.
8. Keep things in perspective.
9. Maintain a hopeful outlook.
10. Take care of yourself.

Adapted from the Discovery Health Channel and American Psychological Association, 2002.

Overall, then, the counselor can assist in the development of three resilience factors by helping clients:

1. *Develop a more positive view of themselves.* Individual tendencies (e.g., being positive) are important in having resilience (Eisenberg & Wang, 2003).

2. *Develop supportive relationships.* Interpersonal relationships that nurture the person's qualities that are resilient are a critical component of resilience (Caprara & Cervone, 2003).

3. *Learn to make plans, learn problem-solving skills, and manage intense feelings.* Human strength, resilience, is framed as persevering, hanging on and letting go, and experiencing growth changes in oneself (Carver & Scheier, 2003).

The Discovery Channel and APA have developed a packet called *Aftermath: The Road to Resilience* in conjunction with their *The Road to Resilience* project that provides community-based tools and information to facilitate resilience in individuals and communities. Substance abuse professionals can easily access this information for integration into their theory or practice by calling (800) 964-2000 or going online to www.apa.org/helpcenter/road-resilience.aspx

POSITIVE PSYCHOLOGY

People need to have a positive reason to live and "positive psychology aims to help people live and flourish rather than merely exist" (Keyes & Haidt, 2003, p. 3). While the term positive psychology has been in existence for over a century (Taylor, 2001), positive psychology has emerged strongly since the 1990s. It is called *positive* because it focuses on strengths rather than weaknesses and health rather than sickness (Woolfolk & Wasserman, 2005).

It has similarities to humanistic psychology that has examined what it means to flourish as a human being through the works of individuals such as Maslow (who studied the character strengths and virtues of self-actualized individuals) and Rogers (who explored the concept of a person who was fully functioning and had well-being and optimal functioning) (Joseph & Murphy, 2013; Robbins, 2008). Yet, there is an ongoing, current tension between humanistic psychology and positive psychology that has been discussed in the literature (K. Schneider, 2011; Waterman, 2013). This tension exists because while there is crossover between the two areas (i.e., Maslow, Rogers), there are deep philosophical differences between them (Waterman, 2013).

Also, as positive psychology has increased in its popularity, it has been criticized for: (1) consisting of a "Pollyanna-style 'happiology'" (Hart & Sasso, 2011, p. 91), (2) having limited effectiveness research primarily focused on groups such as healthy college students (Krentzman, 2013) and application of the approach before there has been enough research to support it (Azar, 2011), and (3) being divided in its views, ambiguous, and ambivalent (Kristjansson, 2010). The field of positive psychology has, in part, responded to these criticisms by: increasingly examining the concept of resilience as it applies to individuals in difficult situations (this is in response to being described as being "happiology" and elitist) and drawing on the concept of *eudaimonia* (Hart & Sasso, 2011), a

core concept of Aristotelian ethics (Woolfolk & Wasserman, 2005). Briefly, eudaimonia means living more completely or realizing human potential (Ryan, Huta, & Deci, 2008). In this type of living, one pursues goals and values for their own sake and behaves autonomously in a mindful, aware manner that meets psychological needs (Ryan et al., 2008). One has meaning and self-realization, and experiences well being in that they are fully functioning (Ryan, et al., 2008). One lives life in a deep, satisfying, full way rather than only having positive feelings (Deci & Ryan, 2008).

As it continues to evolve, positive psychology needs to continue to address its criticisms and clarify its focus. One example of this is Ciarrocchi's (2012) statement: "Positive psychology will need to decide whether it wants to play a role in extending its study of character strengths and virtues to the moral dimension of what it means to live a quality life amid the gifts and burdens of affluence" (p. 434).

Currently, positive psychology has professional meetings, undergraduate and graduate courses on the topic at universities, a master's degree in Positive Psychology through the University of Pennsylvania in Philadelphia, master's and doctoral degrees at Claremont University in California, and research centers at both the University of Pennsylvania and Claremont University. In 2008, the U.S. Army, in its Comprehensive Soldier Fitness Program, began using some of its core tenets (Azar, 2011).

Two different frameworks, selected by the author, may assist the reader in understanding the shift in counseling focus. In the first framework, positive psychology focuses on three areas: *positive subjective experiences* (i.e., hope, flow—a concept explained later in this section), *personality traits* (character strengths and virtues such as life perseverance and wisdom), and *social institutional qualities* that strengthen these subjective experiences and personality traits (Robbins, 2008; Seligman, Steen, Park, & Peterson, 2005). In another framework, the concepts have been named slightly differently and encompass four areas: "(1) positive emotions (happiness, gratitude, fulfillment), (2) positive individual traits (optimism, resiliency, character strengths), (3) *positive relationships among groups*, and (4) enabling institutions (schools, worksites) that foster positive outcomes" (Kobau et al., 2011, p. e1).

Overall, positive psychology was developed to enhance well-being and optimal functioning in people who were already healthy: Seligman, as quoted in the Harvard Mental Health Letter (2008), described it as a "Build what's strong approach." The goal of positive psychology is to promote the good in life (stay happy, find meaningful work, volunteer for good causes), not just fix the wrong (Kogan, 2001). Basically, then, positive psychology shifts the counseling question from "What is wrong about people?" to "What is right about people?" This question incorporates an examination of the attributes, assets, and strengths of the person (Kobau et al., 2011). Positive psychology provides a framework and an encouragement to understand and use this counseling approach (Snyder, Berg, & Thompson, 2003) because it focuses on assets and affirmations (Kobau et al., 2011). Positive psychology examines *positive experiences* (defined as why one time is better for a person than another), *personality*, and *environments* (Seligman & Csikszentmihalyi, 2000) and encourages clients to develop positive emotions, experiences, and traits (Harvard Mental Health Letter, 2008).

Positive psychology is about *valued experiences*, *positive individual traits*, and *civic virtues*. Valued experiences have to do with the past (experiencing well-being, contentment, satisfaction), the future (having hope and optimism), and the present (having a sense of *flow* and happiness). Related to these valued experiences is the concept of flow. Flow is the focus in a task that involves concentration, skill, perseverance, and is enjoyed for its own sake with a sense of harmony and self-integration (Csikszentmihalyi, 1990). Positive individual traits include capacity for love and vocation, courage, interpersonal skill, aesthetic sensibility, perseverance, forgiveness, originality, future mindedness, spirituality, talent, and wisdom. Group *civic virtues* are those of responsibility,

nurturance, altruism, civility, moderation, tolerance, and work ethic. An example of the interplay between positive individual traits and group civic virtues is Alcoholics Anonymous (AA). AA, a spiritual recovery movement, is a social system with behavioral norms that provides people with new, transcendent life meaning (Galanter, 2007).

Positive psychology encourages the counselor to look more completely at the individual rather than focusing only on the suffering (Seligman et al., 2005). For example, the book *Character Strengths and Virtues: A Handbook and Classification* (*CSV*; Peterson & Seligman, 2005) was developed to be a contrast to the *DSM-IV-TR*. The classification system is based on six virtues (wisdom, courage, humanity, justice, temperance, and transcendence) with strengths under each virtue. The following brief summary of Seligman and Csikszentmihalyi's philosophy (2000) clarifies this shift in focus.

From this perspective, buffers against mental illness include courage, future-mindedness, optimism, interpersonal skill, faith, work ethic, hope, honesty, perseverance, and capacity for flow and insight. To help people does not simply mean to cease or reduce suffering, but also to help them live a fuller life. Psychology may have had a negative focus in the past because (1) negative emotions and experiences may have been naturally responded to first by the profession for survival reasons; (2) we may take for granted the conditions needed to live; and (3) American culture may have evolved to a stable, prosperous, and peaceful place that allows for an examination of the positive. Seligman and Csikszentmihalyi (2000) encourage counselors to find ways to help people flourish and grow.

One aspect of positive psychology that fits well with the models discussed in this chapter is that of hope. Snyder et al. (2003) state that we learn hope and counselors encourage hope by helping clients define goals (make markers of progress), find ways to achieve those goals despite barriers (assignments both in and out of session), and be motivated to use those ways to achieve goals (self-talk, physical exercise, self-narratives).

We can help clients set goals, become immersed in what they are doing, pay attention to what is happening in and around them, and enjoy what is happening in the here and now. This approach helps clients become self-assured with how they fit in the world, focus on the world in an alert and open stance, and discover new solutions to problems by allowing the problem to emerge (Csikszentmihalyi, 1990). Seligman (2002) described the "pleasant life" (maximizing pleasure and having positive feelings), the "good life" (one is abundantly and authentically gratified by using their signature strengths—it incorporates the concept of "flow"), and the "meaningful life" (being intertwined with something outside of self). Happiness is defined as including positive emotion, being engaged in life, and having a meaningful life (Seligman, 2002). Seligman's more recent work (2011) focuses less on happiness and instead emphasizes a four-factor life of well being that consists of positive emotions, engagement, accomplishment, and relationships.

Some of the concepts of positive psychology, such as self-efficacy, have been well researched and supported (Harris, Thoresen, & Lopez, 2007). However, even though the overall clinical impact of positive psychology requires more research, the current encouragement is to include the techniques in traditional therapy (Harvard Mental Health Letter, 2008). For example, in the treatment of depression, positive psychology techniques are being used at the University of Pennsylvania to increase positive emotions, the strengths of the client, and the client's sense of meaning (Harvard Mental Health Letter, 2008). In addition to reducing depressive symptoms, it has been shown to help with one's sense of well-being and psychological well-being (Bolier et al., 2013).

To facilitate its integration into therapy, Kauffman (2006) suggests four guiding principles:

1. Change the negative focus to a positive one.

2. Encourage the use of a language of strength.

3. Balance the positive and negative.

4. Develop hope-building strategies.

Counselors can help clients learn more helpful, constructive ways of thinking and how they use language, and simply, by looking at the client's strengths and resources, there may be motivation to change (Harris et al., 2007). One way to do this is through an examination of language and problem conceptualization (Harris et al., 2007). Gelso and Woodhouse (2003) recommend this be done by commenting on client's strengths, reframing client weaknesses as strengths, and viewing symptoms as responses that are logical when framed in the client's historical life context. Also, the framework of counseling can be changed to have the assessment process include a more expansive case conceptualization that includes the strengths of the person and important factors in the environment (Harris et al., 2007).

Finally, five specific examples of positive psychology techniques (Seligman et al., 2005, p. 416):

1. Gratitude visit

2. Three good things in life

3. You at your best

4. Using signature strengths in a new way

5. Identifying signature strengths

In the *gratitude visit* exercise, the client has 1 week to write and send a letter of gratitude to someone they have never thanked for their kindness. *Three good things in life* requires the client to write down three things that went well in a day and why—for 1 week. *You are at your best* has the client write a story about a time they were at their best and look for the strengths in the story and review the story once each day. *Using signature strengths in a new way* means taking the inventory of character strengths online (www.authentichappiness.sas.upenn.edu), receiving feedback on one's top five strengths, and then for 1 week using one of these strengths in a new and different way each day. *Identifying signature strengths* is a shorter version of the previous technique where the client simply uses their strengths more often in a week.

Addictions counselors can easily incorporate a positive psychology approach into their work. The approach enables counselors to help clients find valued experiences (past, present, future), develop positive individual traits, develop civic virtues, find out what is right about them, flourish and grow, and develop a sense of hope and flow. Csikszent-mihalyi (1990, 2008) states that counselors can assist clients in developing an *autotelic* self (self-contained), where flow experiences can occur almost anywhere. Krentzman (2013) describes positive activity interventions (PAIs)—exercises that encourage positive feelings, thoughts, and behaviors—that can be especially helpful with addicted clients. These are the gratitude intervention of *Three Good Things* (described earlier) and the optimism intervention, *The Best Future Self* (the client writes down their experiences—after they think about their life in the future—where they have worked hard, succeeded at their life goals, everything has gone well, and their life dreams are realized). (See Case Study 9.1.)

STAGES-OF-CHANGE MODEL

Although the stages-of-change model is discussed in Chapter 7, "Relapse Prevention," it is important to consider how it relates to matching intervention with client motivation level. The stages-of-change model is the most widely known component of the transtheoretical model (TTM), which emerged in the early 1980s alongside motivational interviewing (MI); although they are different models, there is a natural fit between them (W. R. Miller & Rollnick, 2009). Prochaska, DiClemente, and Norcross (1992) report that change happens for people when the right process happens at the right time. Therefore, addiction counselors need to determine their clients' stage level of change and find the interventions that fit the particular stage: *precontemplation, contemplation, preparation, action, maintenance,* and *termination* (De Biaze Vilela, Jungerman, Laranjeira, &

CASE STUDY 9.1

Roger, in his mid-30s, was referred for an assessment of his addiction because of an argument with his girlfriend: She says if he does not cut out all of his chemical use, she is breaking up with him. He has come to the session quite defensive, claiming that he does not have a drinking or drug problem. Roger says he normally does not drink alcohol, but when he feels a lot of stress in his life with work and his girlfriend, he drinks more than he should. He is divorced and has three children by his previous two marriages. His father was a heroin addict and his mother a "pothead." His parents are still married and use marijuana a few times a week. Roger reports he uses marijuana with them, and the three of them strongly believe that marijuana is not addicting and should be legalized. He says he does not plan to change any of his using behavior, because he rarely uses alcohol (maybe once every 6 months), and he does not see his daily use of marijuana as a problem. He admits to having used too much alcohol, speed, and cocaine in the past, but views himself as having cut back successfully to the point where he does not currently experience negative consequences of his use.

1. Would you see Roger as a good candidate for positive psychology? Why or why not?
2. Using the positive psychology perspective (what are his strengths?), how would you approach Roger in the interview?
3. What is "right" about Roger?
4. Which theoretical technique(s) of positive psychology would you use to help Roger develop or enhance his sense of hope?

Callaghan, 2009). The interventions are focused on the tasks that need to be addressed at that stage in order for the client to move to the next stage. In a qualitative study based on the recovery experiences of nine addicted individuals, Hansen, Ganley, and Carlucci (2008) describe how the TTM can be used as a model for addiction recovery. Research has supported the application of the model to the addiction process involving alcohol and drugs (Heather, Hoenekopp, & Smailes, 2009; Heather & McCambridge, 2013). However, there has also been research criticizing the model for being too simplistic with regard to behavioral change and calling these categories "artificial" (D'Sylva, Graffam, Hardcastel, & Shinkfield, 2012). As with any theoretical model, then, the counselor can use TTM as a guide in counseling that may work with some clients and not with others.

At the *precontemplation* stage, the client has no intention of changing behavior. Here the client has little, if any, awareness of the problem, even though others might be aware of it. Resistance is core to this stage (Prochaska & Norcross, 2002). The task is for the client to be motivated emotionally and intellectually; to become more aware of the behavior and alternative behaviors (Harvard Mental Health Letter, 2008).

In the *contemplation* stage, the client is aware there is a problem and is thinking seriously about changing it but has not made a commitment to do so (Prochaska & Norcross, 2002). Here the client is examining the cost of changing the problem in terms of the effort and energy he or she will need to expend, as well as the loss involved. The task, then, is cognitive in nature with the focus on making some preliminary change decisions (Harvard Mental Health Letter, 2008).

During the *preparation* stage, the client is planning to take action within a month and has tried to take action without success in the past year. Small changes have been made, but not significant enough action has occurred (Prochaska &

Norcross, 2002). Again the task has a cognitive focus, but here more realistic goals and timelines are brought up (Harvard Mental Health Letter, 2008).

In the *action* stage, behavior, experiences, and/or environment are changed by the person to address the problem. This stage involves time and energy commitment by the client, resulting in behavior changes recognized by others (Prochaska & Norcross, 2002). The task here is to focus on the behavior (Harvard Mental Health Letter, 2008).

In the *maintenance* stage, relapse is prevented and change is consistent for at least six months (Prochaska & Norcross, 2002). The task at this stage is to make sure there is the presence of support and reinforcement for the change with an emphasis on problem-solving (Harvard Mental Health Letter, 2008).

In the *termination* stage, the change is complete, and relapse does not need to be prevented: There is no temptation, and the client is confident of the change (Prochaska & Norcross, 2002). The bias of this author is that this stage is not necessarily a very helpful one with alcoholics and drug addicts, who, as a tendency, rarely completely resolve their ambivalence about using. Due to this perspective, this author did not discuss this stage in Chapter 7. It is important to note, however, that the counselor can assist the client in "leaning strongly in the direction of change, of abstinence"—creating internal and external worlds that are so locked in place that it would be difficult to resume the addictive behavior easily.

Clients may spiral through these change stages, learning from their relapses (Prochaska et al., 1992). Counselors need to look at where the client is in terms of willingness to change to determine appropriate treatment intervention (Prochaska et al., 1992). Littrell provides a simple assessment questionnaire that can be readily used with clients (1998).

The counselor needs to use change process interventions that will help the client move from one stage to another. The change processes are both internal and external; these experiences and activities help clients move through the stages (DiClemente, 2003). One type involves thinking and feeling (which are more critical for moving through precontemplation and contemplation), and the other involves behaviors focused in commitment and action (which are more important in preparation, action, and maintenance stages). The first type (thinking and feeling) involves five areas: raising consciousness, arousing emotion, reevaluating self, reevaluating environment, and being socially liberated. The second type (behavior oriented) includes five areas: "self-liberation, stimulus generalization or control, conditioning or counterconditioning, reinforcement management, and helping relationships" (DiClemente, 2003, p. 35).

Some of these processes in conjunction with the stages (Prochaska, 2012; Prochaska & Norcross, 2002) need elaboration. From precontemplation to contemplation, *consciousness raising* is useful when the client recognizes how change may be beneficial and therapy might be helpful (i.e., bibliotherapy, confrontation). Also, *self-reevaluation* is useful when clients begin to examine what they value and how they view themselves. In *dramatic relief*, the client experiences the feelings about both the problems and solutions through grief exercises or role-play scenarios. Moving from contemplation to preparation requires a change process of *self-liberation*, where the client begins to believe that change can happen through commitment (willpower) therapy that encourages decisions and commitment. Moving to the action stage requires the presence of *reinforcement* and *counterconditioning* (replace behaviors with healthier ones). Maintenance requires *stimulus control* so that the client is aware of relapse.

Table 9.2 provides a descriptive summary of these stages, as they apply with the addicted client, with regard to the client, counselor, and interventions.

Some of the recommendations that Prochaska and Norcross (2001) make in general to counselors are to assess the client's stage level, avoid treating everyone as though he or she is in the action stage, set realistic goals, and have the change process match the stage. Two related concepts presented by DiClemente (2003) that clients need to consider are the *decisional balance* and *self-efficacy*. Decisional balance impacts the early stages of change, because the client is weighing the benefits and costs of change. As to self-efficacy, clients view themselves as able to persist at change, thereby impacting the action and long-term change stages. The author also brings up the concept of *temptation* as related to self-efficacy in that there needs to be an awareness of the degree of the client's urge to engage in a habit in a certain situation.

Counselors can use these stages of change and change processes readily in counseling. By knowing the stage of change of the client, the counselor can choose a change process that is fitting and then provide the most appropriate, effective counseling possible for the client. This approach also fits into a brief therapy model in that the counselor is employing only the necessary and appropriate interventions needed by the client. However, important cautions in the use of this model are provided by Littell and Girvin (2002). The authors note that change is not always linear and that successful change also depends on the nature and complexity of the behavior as well as the presence of additional problems, stressors, and/or supports. They also note that the behavior needs to be viewed within a cultural context. Finally, the stages-of-change model can be used in the assessment process to choose motivational interviewing strategies (Scheffler, 2004). The match of interventions with the client's stage of change can reduce resistance and treatment dropout, and increase effectiveness of treatment through the development of a treatment plan that fits the client (Washton & Zweben, 2006). Recent research has underscored the importance of counselors monitoring the client's stage of change and using strategies to intervene on low motivation whenever it occurs in the treatment process (Heather & McCambridge, 2013). (See Case Study 9.2.)

Table 9.2 Specific Application of the Stages-of-Change Model to Addiction Treatment

Stage	Description of Client	Description of Counselor	Counseling Process Interventions (Internal/External)
Precontemplation	—Has no intention of changing his or her addictive behavior —Has little, if any, awareness of the alcohol/drug problem, even though others are probably aware of it —Is resistant to change	—Helps the client to become aware of his or her addictive behavior —Helps the client become motivated to be abstinent	—Any activities (individual, group, family, couples therapy) that invite thinking and feeling regarding alcohol/drug use: 1. Raise consciousness (i.e., bibliotherapy, confrontation) 2. Arouse emotion (i.e., grief exercises, role-play scenarios) 3. Encourage self-evaluation (i.e., values, self-view) 4. Encourage environment evaluation 5. Liberate socially (change social environment in terms of people, activities, places)
Contemplation	—Has awareness of alcohol/drug problem —Is seriously considering changing behavior —Lacks commitment to change behavior —Is thinking of the effort, energy, and loss involved in behavior change	—Helps the client make preliminary change decisions about alcohol/drug use —Helps the client become motivated to be abstinent	—Any activities (individual, group, family, couples therapy) that invite thinking and feeling regarding alcohol/drug use that invites client decisions and commitment to abstinence: 1. Raise consciousness 2. Arouse emotion 3. Encourage self-evaluation 4. Encourage environment evaluation 5. Liberate socially (change social environment in terms of people, activities, places)
Preparation	—Plans to become abstinent within a month —Has unsuccessfully tried to be abstinent in the last year —Has made small changes with regard to alcohol/drug use	—Brings up realistic goals regarding abstinence —Brings up timelines regarding abstinence	—Any behavioral activities (individual, group, family, couples therapy) that invite commitment and action regarding alcohol/drug use: 1. Encourage a self-liberation perspective of the freedom from alcohol and drugs 2. Encourage stimulus generalization or control-behavioral choices to stay sober 3. Provide conditioning or counterconditioning that encourages abstinence—replace alcohol and drug using behaviors with sober behaviors (i.e., instead of spending time with using friends, spend time with sober friends)

Stage		
Action	—Has changed behavior, experiences, and/or environment resulting in being abstinent —Has committed time and energy to being abstinent —Has abstinent behavior recognized by others	—Focuses on supporting abstinent behavior	4. Provide reinforcements for being abstinent 5. Assist in developing helping/nurturing relationships; create a community that supports sobriety —Any behavioral activities (individual, group, family, couples therapy) that invite commitment and action regarding alcohol/drug use especially in becoming aware of preventing relapse: 1. Encourage a self-liberation perspective of the freedom from alcohol and drugs 2. Encourage stimulus generalization or control–behavioral choices to stay sober 3. Provide conditioning or counterconditioning that encourages abstinence 4. Provide reinforcements for being abstinent 5. Assist in developing helping/nurturing relationships; create a community that supports sobriety
Maintenance	—Has been abstinent for at least 6 months —Needs support and reinforcement to remain abstinent —Requires assistance with problem-solving with regards to maintaining abstinence (relapse prevention)	—Focuses on supporting abstinent behavior especially with regard to relapse prevention	—Any behavioral activities (individual, group, family, couples therapy) that invite commitment and action regarding alcohol/drug use: 1. Encourage a self-liberation perspective of the freedom from alcohol and drugs 2. Encourage stimulus generalization or control–behavioral choices to stay sober 3. Provide conditioning or counterconditioning that encourages abstinence 4. Provide reinforcements for being abstinent 5. Assist in developing helping/nurturing relationships; create a community that supports sobriety

CASE STUDY 9.2

George is a 21-year-old college student who has been referred to you because he has been suspended from the university he attends because of an alcohol/drug-related charge. He has been told that he cannot be considered for reenrollment as a student until he has therapy to address his alcohol/drug use. In your first session with him, you talk with him about the need to do a formal alcohol and drug assessment because of his desire to return to his studies at the university. In response to your description of the assessment process, George tells you that he does not see himself as having a problem with alcohol/drugs. He tells you that he was at a party on campus that was busted by the campus police, and he believes they simply overreacted to the presence of drugs at the party and arrested him and a few others.

1. Which stage of change do you see George at?
2. Which process(es) of change would you use with George based on his stage of change?
3. How would you build this process(es) into the counseling sessions?
4. What realistic goals would you set with him?

MOTIVATIONAL INTERVIEWING

W. R. Miller and Rollnick (2002) developed motivational interviewing (MI) within the context of addiction treatment during the 1970s and 1980s, when a highly confrontational approach was used with addicted individuals. This approach also viewed the client as bearing full responsibility to be motivated for treatment and the recovery process; the client was seen as needing to hit bottom in order to be motivated to change (DiClemente, Garay, & Gemmell, 2008). Yet, in reality, clients often come to treatment ambivalent about receiving help (DiClemente et al., 2008). MI does not tell people what to do and thereby reduces resistance and engages the individual and empowers them (Saarnio, 2011). "MI is based on a way of being or spirit, which is foundationally client-centered; emphasizing client as expert and the creation of a safe space in which clients can freely unpack, explore, and sort through often conflicting and contradictory views of change" (Westra & Aviram, 2013, p. 277).

In 1991, W. R. Miller and Rollnick published the first edition of their book on MI that focused on the addictions field. Since then, MI has been used in other helping professional areas, an international organization of MI trainers has developed (www.motivationalinterviewing.org), and MI has its own website (www.motivationalinterview.org). Motivational Interviewing is a way of being (that includes skills) that develops over time with ongoing training and guidance—workshops alone may not suffice for the development of the way of being and skills related to MI.

It has been used in a variety of settings for different health concerns (Bagoien et al., 2013) and is frequently paired with other approaches such as inpatient alcohol/drug treatment (Moyers & Houck, 2011). Because of this flexibility in intervention applications, it is difficult to know the exact mechanisms of change; therefore, additional theory-based research is needed to clearly understand the variables operating in its effectiveness (Barnett, Sussman, Smith, Rohrbach, & Spruijt-Metz, 2012) as well as causal tests of theories that pull out the unique impact of MI (Morgenstern et al., 2012).

A few examples of its effectiveness, as demonstrated in research studies, follow. In reducing substance use, it has been demonstrated as effective in single sessions (Berman, Forsberg, Durbeej, Kaellmen, & Hermansson, 2010) and in primary care settings (Van Buskirk & Wetherell, 2013) as well as with cormorbid substance use clients (Bagoien et al., 2013), adolescents (Jensen et al., 2011), juvenile offenders (Doran, Hohman, & Koutsenok, 2011), and correctional clients (Craig, 2012). However, it is important to note that there is some indication that some clients may not benefit from MI: those with severe substance dependence (Raistrick, 2007), those already motivated to change (Adams & Madson, 2006; Raistrick, 2007), and those with numerous problems that have different stages-of-change (Patterson & Buckingham, 2010).

W. R. Miller and Rollnick (2009) state 10 things MI is not. It is:

1. Not anchored in the transtheoretical model (TTM).

2. Not "A way of tricking people into doing what they don't want to do" (p. 131).

3. Not a technique.

4. Not a decisional balance (an examination of the pros and cons of change, but more of trying to find the client's motivation to change).

5. Not requiring assessment feedback (MI was paired with structured personal feedback based on intake assessment treatment in Project Match that was called *motivational enhancement therapy*).

6. Not a form of cognitive-behavior therapy.

7. Not simply client-centered counseling.

8. Not easy, but it is simple.

9. Not what counselors are already doing.

10. Not a panacea designed to address all the client problems a counselor faces.

Rather, the MI approach is both a spirit and style of counseling; it is more than a series of techniques. There is a relational component that stems from empathy and the interpersonal spirit of MI, and there is a technical component that emerges from evoking and reinforcing change talk (W. R. Miller & Rose, 2009).

It is an *interaction* more than a therapy (Sorbell, 2009). It incorporates a combination of directive and client-centered approaches with an emphasis on helping behavior change occur through exploration and resolution of ambivalence. In a review of the history of MI, Tober and Raistrick (2007) state that Miller combined an "agenda-driven, directive style while maintaining a non-confrontational approach" (p. 6). The counselor has a strong impact on treatment by encouraging the spirit of counseling—the atmosphere created that invites change. The approach is optimistic, hopeful, and strengths-based (van Wormer & Davis, 2008). It has been described as practical, accessible, and grounded in theory and research, as well as providing treatment strategies that help clients become motivated to change (Arkowitz, Westra, Miller, & Rollnick, 2008). Walters, Rotgers, Saunders, Wilkinson, and Towers (2003) report four research-based conclusions related to motivation:

1. Desire, confidence, and free choice to change seem to be the best ingredients for behavior change.

2. Counselors need to find out what reinforces a person to change and with the client develop an acceptable plan for change.

3. It is important to remember that some moments are more teachable (the client is willing to accept feedback and try new behavior) than others.

4. The interaction between the counselor and client can have a significant impact on motivation.

Counselors can use MI throughout the counseling process. It can be used to engage the person in treatment initially, as a style of relating throughout treatment, and as an approach whenever ambivalence about change arises during treatment. While the techniques are helpful, the *spirit* of the approach is emphasized. In the spirit of the approach, MI involves *collaboration* between counselor and client, *evocation* for change within the client, and *autonomy* about the change (Adams & Madson, 2006; W. R. Miller & Rollnick, 2002).

The four general principles of MI are (W. R. Miller & Rollnick, 2002):

1. Empathy

2. Discrepancy

3. Self-efficacy

4. Rolling with resistance

Empathy is incorporated into the general spirit of MI. W. R. Miller and Rollnick (2002) focus on Rogers's factors of accurate empathy, nonpossessive warmth, and genuineness (Rogers, 1951). By creating an atmosphere of acceptance, the counselor sets an important basis for inviting change. The expression of empathy involves reflective listening and a capacity to suspend assumptions and advice and really listen to the other person (W. R. Miller & Rollnick, 2002). It avoids argumentation and rather focuses on learning as much about the client's perspective as possible. This is a very respectful process where the counselor works hard to hear the client's story and not rewrite it in terms of biases, stereotypes, or countertransference. The client genuinely feels heard and respected. A comfortable environment is established through empathy and nonjudgmentalism, so the client does most of the talking about the process of change (Sorbell, 2009). *How* the counselor says statements (empathy) and *what* the counselor says (content) is critical in developing a comfortable environment where the client is willing to discuss the problem openly (Sorbell, 2009).

Motivation is not a stable trait that cannot change, but is sensitive to interactions with others, especially others with whom they are emotionally involved (Daley & Zuckoff, 1999). We tend to change for what we love, so in order to invite change, it is necessary to determine what the client loves—partner, children, career, and so on—that can help the client develop motivation to be different or break out of the habitual pattern of behavior. Some clients may need to be taught values and motivators for change because addiction has distorted their "healthy loves," if they were ever present. This type of learning for these kinds of clients may occur in communities of recovery where the clients live and learn on a daily basis. Motivation is a readiness to change (Sorbell, 2009), and it is complex (DiClemente et al., 2008). It is also important to recognize, however, that some of our clients need to be taught healthy values that enhance the quality of life for themselves and others. It is also important to remember that values are culture-bound, and counselors, in order to meet the needs of clients, need to examine what is important and what is valued by their clients (Añez, Silva, Paris, & Bedregal, 2008).

Counselors can help the client become motivated to change by enhancing any *discrepancies* between what the client is doing and what the client desires to do (values), a discrepancy between who the client is and who the client wants to be. Typically, in a conflict between behavior and value, the behavior will change (W. R. Miller & Rollnick, 2002). In this counseling approach, ambivalence is viewed as a natural, normal process of change, in which the counselor's role is to help the client explore the ambivalence. This is the same decisional balance discussed in the stages-of-change model and the decision matrix for relapse prevention discussed in Chapter 7.

This discrepancy needs to be paired with self-efficacy, a person having the confidence that he or she can change (W. R. Miller & Rollnick, 2002). *Self-efficacy* means that clients believe themselves able to persist at change and draw on internal and external supports that will help them do that. You help the client recognize the need for change and maintain the belief that change is possible (Miller & Rollnick, 2002). The counselor also needs to assess the level of importance and confidence the client has regarding making the change.

If the discrepancy is large, the change is seen as important, and the client maintains self-efficacy, the client is less likely to engage in defense mechanisms such as denial, rationalization, or projection (W. R. Miller & Rollnick, 2002). From this perspective, denial is viewed as a normal reaction in a client to a counselor being aggressive in attempting to help the client change (Walters et al., 2003). *Resistance* is viewed as a natural part of change and a marker in the session where the counselor recognizes the need to do something different to engage the client in the process of change. Resistance is not met head on, but rather the counselor focuses on joining the client in order to understand the resistance better (W. R. Miller & Rollnick, 2002). *Discord* is the current term being used with resistance being considered the manifestation of a discord between the counselor and the client (W. R. Miller & Rollnick, 2013).

It may be helpful to examine this process in an example. An addicted client is in session with an addiction counseling professional. The counselor uses a client-centered approach that invites the client to relax and explore the problem with the counselor. The counselor then enhances the discrepancy between the client's values and behaviors, helping the client argue the pros and cons for change rather than the counselor taking one approach and the client taking the opposite. Resistance and power struggles are thus avoided between counselor and client. Instead, the counselor can invite a discussion of how the addictive behavior conflicts with a value(s) of the client. The counselor begins with "what is," which helps the client compare it to "what could be," and encourages the client to engage in "change talk" (talking about a commitment to change), thereby reducing client resistance and increasing self-efficacy.

W. R. Miller and Rollnick (2002) warn of six specific traps to avoid in sessions:

1. Engaging in a question-and-answer format.

2. Taking sides on the change issue.

3. Playing the expert.

4. Labeling the problem.

5. Developing a premature focus.

6. Blaming the client for the behavior.

The four processes of MI are engaging, focusing, evoking, and planning (W. R. Miller & Rollnick, 2013). *Engaging* is the process of establishing a helpful connection and working relationship. *Focusing* is the process where the counselor develops and maintains a specific direction in the conversation about change. *Evoking* means eliciting the client's own motivation(s) for change and is the heart of MI. *Planning* involves developing a commitment to change and formulating a concrete plan of action. W. R. Miller and Rollnick (2013) encourage the use of five communication skills, core MI skills (the first four are housed within the acronym OARS) that are considered prerequisite skills to being proficient in MI. These five skills that are used throughout MI are:

1. Asking **O**pen questions.

2. **A**ffirming the client (in terms of change attempts, strengths, etc.).

3. **R**eflective listening.

4. **S**ummarizing.

5. Informing and advising (with permission).

Counselors are probably familiar with the first four strategies. In their video series, W. R. Miller and Rollnick (Moyers, 1998) clarify these four opening strategies. Open questions are those that, either as questions or statements, elicit the client's story: There is an avoidance of questions that will result in dichotomous answers. Affirmations need to be genuine. While reflections are restating what the client has said, they are very important and key to empathic listening. Summary statements are basically a longer reflection. It is critical that the counselor remember the importance of affirmations to the client. It can be easier for clients to look at change when they feel acknowledged for what is good and right about themselves. However, the counselor needs to be cautious about what is being affirmed so reinforcements are being given with an intentional awareness and focus. For example, a counselor may not be able to say to a parent who has had children removed by the Department of Social Services, "You are a good parent," but the counselor may be able to affirm, "You sound as though you love your children deeply." Also, the OARS acronym can be used to help the counselor keep in balance in a session by doing a quick internal check on how much each of the techniques has been used in the session. The fifth strategy, informing and advising, addresses the reality that sometimes the client will ask for information or advice or that the counselor believes it is necessary. In these situations, it is given only with permission of the client and the client has the room to decide how relevant the information is to his/her situation (W. R. Miller & Rollnick, 2013).

The ambivalence about change, as discussed previously, involves two types of talk: *sustain talk* (the person's arguments for not changing) and *change talk* (the person's statements in favor of change) (W. R. Miller & Rollnick, 2013). Eliciting *change talk* requires some explanation. In *change talk*, the client engages in discussion in the session that reflects a language emphasizing change. The client basically makes an argument or states reasons for change. Here the client recognizes the problem, has concern about it, is intending to change, and is optimistic about changing (W. R. Miller & Rollnick, 2002). The client's Desire ("I want to do this . . ."), Ability/Self-efficacy ("I can see myself doing this . . . "), Reason ("I need to change because . . ."), Need ("I need to do something"), and Commitment ("I will make this change") (DARN-C) stirs change talk (W. R. Miller, 2004). The client speech impacts behavior change, and the counselor impacts this speech (Moyers et al., 2007). There are seven methods for eliciting change talk in a client:

1. *Asking evocative questions.* These questions encourage expressions of the client's views and concerns.

2. *Using the importance ruler.* Ask the client to rate on a scale—from 0 (not at all) to 10 (extremely)—the importance of change in the behavior and to follow it with questions: "Why are you at __ (insert number here) and not zero?" and "What would it take for you to go from __ (insert number here) to __ (a higher number)?" This scale can also be used to ask the client how confident he or she is about making the change.

3. *Exploring the decisional balance.* The client weighs the pros and cons of change, and the counselor helps the client explore this balance.

4. *Elaborating.* When the client gives a reason to change, ask for clarification, an example, a description when the change last occurred, or ask, "What else?"

5. *Querying extremes.* Ask the client for extremes in terms of concerns about his or her behavior (and others) or the best consequences that could result from making a change.

6. *Looking back.* The client looks back to a time when the problem behavior didn't exist and compares it to the present.

7. *Looking forward.* The client looks to the future to describe how a change would impact the future or what it will be like in the future if no change is made.

This approach fits well in the addiction counseling field, and many of the techniques can be easily and readily applied to counseling sessions. Remember, however, that it is critical to have the *spirit* of MI present throughout the counseling process in order for the approaches to be effective. The MI approach is an excellent blend with brief therapy, because an atmosphere of collaboration in a client-centered, yet directive, approach can result in the most effective therapy within a short time period. MI is a therapy style that helps clients examine their ambivalence. A general overview of motivational assumptions is provided in *Enhancing Motivation for Change in Substance Abuse Treatment* (Treatment Improvement Protocol #35; Substance Abuse and Mental Health Services Administration, 1999b).

Through the Blending Initiative, the National Institute on Drug Abuse (NIDA) and the Substance Abuse and Mental Health Services Administration's (SAMHSA) Center for Substance Abuse Treatment (CSAT) merge service and science to improve treatment. They developed the Motivational Interviewing Assessment: Supervisory Tools for Enhancing Proficiency (MIA:STEP) Products: Briefing Materials, MI Assessment Protocol, Teaching Tools for Assessing and Enhancing MI Skills, Supervisor Tape Rating Guide, Demonstration Materials, and Supervisor Training Curriculum. They also created Promoting Awareness of Motivational Incentives (PAMI), which has a video, Power-Point presentations, and a tool kit to assist in developing awareness of motivational incentives. Both sets of materials can be obtained by contacting one's local Addiction Technology Transfer Center (ATTC) (www.attcnetwork.org/index. asp). Group therapy MI approaches are discussed in Chapter 5. (See Case Study 9.3.)

CASE STUDY 9.3

Annette is a 30-year-old, married woman. She has been married 2 years. She is a mental health counselor (master's degree in counseling). She has been sober for 4 years. Her drug of choice was a mixture of cocaine, pot, and alcohol. She met her husband at a Narcotics Anonymous (NA) convention when she had been sober for $1^1/_2$ years. They do not have any children. They are very involved in the NA community where they live.

About a month ago, Annette was watching a film on television about sexual abuse. She began to have trouble sleeping at night and could not remember much about her dreams. She could only remember a dark-haired male coming into her room and kissing her sexually. She wakes up terrified and has trouble breathing. She has not slept through the night since she watched the show on abuse. She has trouble falling asleep, wakes up every few hours terrified, and does not want to get up in the morning.

Recently, she was at a family gathering and her dark-haired brother playfully came up behind her and said "Boo!" She immediately screamed and automatically shoved him away from her. She was very embarrassed because everyone at the family gathering stopped and stared at her. She does not know what came over her, but she said she has not been able to talk to her brother without crying since they were at the gathering a week ago. They had previously been close, with him being very supportive of her recovery. She is the second child of three children, the only girl, and her older brother is the one who terrifies her now.

Although she has no legal problems at present, she has a history of arrests for selling drugs. She said she was never a major drug dealer, but she was busted for selling drugs to some people she knew at the university. She said she has never had any trouble being sexual and had enjoyed sex a great deal until watching the film on TV. She reports having no interest in sex now and is very afraid when her husband even holds her. She said he is frustrated with her current change in behavior but is trying hard to be understanding. She currently has a urinary tract infection and is on medication from her physician. She has come in for counseling because in the past few days she has come very close to relapsing.

1. What characteristics of resilience do you see Annette having?
2. From a positive psychology view, write a paragraph describing Annette that focuses on her strengths.
3. Where do you see Annette in terms of stages of change?
4. How would her stage-of-change level influence your treatment approach?
5. How could you see motivational interviewing as being beneficial to Annette?

BRIEF THERAPY

Although brief therapy may be currently popular because of mental health or managed health-care systems constraints, it did not emerge because of these influences. In a historical review of its development, Bloom (1997) reports that *planned* short-term psychotherapy began in the early and mid-1960s along with the community mental health movement: there was a need to provide efficient, effective, and prompt counseling to as many individuals as possible, and it was found that short time spans of counseling could result in significant changes for clients. This type of therapy is also labeled *solution-focused therapy*; the differences in terminology have occurred because of managed health care and different theoretical orientations (Bloom, 1997). It became popular in the late 1980s and the 1990s when counselors and insurance companies became interested in it because it was viewed as efficient, effective, and less costly (Nugent, 1994). At present, counselors may be open to using this therapy approach because agencies and health care systems may encourage or require them to use it, it may assist in managing large caseloads in a professional, realistic manner, and they believe that the counseling goals can be achieved in a shorter period of time.

Brief therapy focuses on specific goals within a limited number of counseling sessions to enhance a client's coping abilities so he or she can manage future situations in an improved manner (Nugent, 1994). A summary of the overall approach of brief therapy follows (Bloom, 1997; Koss & Shiang,

1994; Littrell, 1998; Preston, 1998). Brief therapy has a focus on the here-and-now with assessment focusing on the problem, what the client has tried and what resources are available. Goals are time limited, concrete, and they focus on symptom reduction and increased coping as well as a change plan and the involvement of homework. Interventions are flexible, prompt, and early, with the therapist being active and directive. Counselors focus on more limited interventions with the individual, which can occur in daily life; see the complaints as legitimate in and of themselves; believe that therapy can be too long; and view therapy as just one important aspect of someone's life (Bloom, 1997).

Brief therapy invites a shift in perspective. First, counselors see themselves as *consultants to clients* about problems in sessions while the main therapy work happens outside of the sessions in the clients' day-to-day lives. Second, *clients become their own therapists* by counselors emphasizing what is positive and including the client's view on the need for change. Third, counselors are human with their clients in the here-and-now through approaches such as *therapist immediacy* (in the session the counselor discloses to the client feelings about the client, the counselor's self in relation to the client, or the therapy relationship for the purpose of understanding/experiencing/resolving interpersonal conflicts) (Kasper, Hill, & Kivlighan, 2008).

Brief interventions have shown to be effective in alcohol and drug use disorders (Fals-Stewart, & Lam, 2008; Oegel, & Coskun, 2011; Zahradnik et al., 2009) and may be a helpful alternative to traditional treatment, which can be costly in terms of money, time, and intensity (Osborn, 2001). Mild or moderate problems with alcohol may be especially responsive to brief interventions that focus on moderation or abstinence, with moderation potentially evolving into abstinence (Glaser & Edmondson, 2000). Brief therapies have been used with addicted individuals to (a) encourage them to go to treatment and (b) intervene on their use (McLellan, 2008; Smock et al., 2008; Szapocznik, Zarate, Duff, & Muir, 2013). The short length and lack of need for client treatment compliance has made brief interventions appealing, especially to helping professionals in medical settings such as family medicine and emergency medicine (Alcoholism & Drug Abuse Weekly, 2011; Bray, Kowalchuk, Waters, Laufman, & Shilling, 2012; Gonzales et al., 2012; Hankin, Daugherty, Bethea, & Haley, 2013; McLellan, 2008). In a recent study supported by NIAAA (D'Onofrio et al., 2012), brief interventions were found to decrease alcohol use over a 12-month period. NIAAA (1999) highlights the importance of setting up goals around using behavior, follow-up, and timing in order for brief interventions to be effective; timing is related to the person's readiness to change, as discussed in the section on stages of change. Note that in 2005 NIAAA published a short brochure on brief interventions that explains its use of MI approaches to reduce the harm of alcohol/drug usage in a client's life.

When working with addicted clients, you may legitimately ask: How can I use brief therapy with such a long-standing, deeply entrenched problem as addiction? The first part of the answer is that the approach requires a shift in perspective as outlined above. In reality, counselors do not know whether they will see their clients from session to session, so each session needs to be viewed as a one-time opportunity to have some impact on the clients' lives: Counselors need to make the most out of the sessions with their clients.

Second, changing habits requires small, successive changes over time with support for such changes to occur. You, as consultant, can help the client make changes with the addiction (avoid using alcohol/drugs) while assisting the client in creating a support network to change through education (bibliotherapy), treatment (relapse prevention), and community support (self-help groups). As stated previously, you would be active and direct in sessions, intervene promptly and early in treatment, focus on the here and now with specific time-limited goals to reduce addiction symptoms, and enhance coping abilities for staying sober. The counselor assesses the client's problems and resources regarding the addiction (level of addiction, reality problems, motivation, number of previous treatments, and responses to treatment), obtains necessary information to treat the addiction, and is flexible in treatment, particularly concerning relapse. The therapy that focuses on one primary issue, the addiction, may result in both the client and counselor experiencing less pressure to produce extensive change and encourage the client's willingness to change and celebrate small victories with the counselor (Talmon, 1990). The addiction therapy may be brief in that several sessions may occur within a short time period with follow-up visits, or sessions may be spread out over a longer time period.

Third, brief therapy can also assist in the establishment of realistic goals with the client. This can reduce later frustration for both you and the client, avoid potential power struggles, and benefit you both in terms of achieving the agreed-on goals. For example, the counselor who is assigned court-ordered clients who are not interested in being sober as a long-term goal can use this information to develop a realistic treatment plan. While the client may be ordered to be abstinent during the treatment, the counselor can focus on educating the client about addiction and motivating him or her in terms of remaining abstinent as outlined in the stages-of-change model. This realistic focus may prevent power struggles regarding different views about addiction and recovery and may result in the client's being more motivated to seek treatment.

The remainder of this section focuses on techniques of brief therapy that can be applied to addiction counseling. Prior to discussing three planned short-term psychotherapy theoretical approaches and related techniques (*psychodynamic*, *cognitive and behavioral*, and *strategic and systemic*), two overall approaches that can be useful with brief therapy are presented. The first is the FRAMES approach (W. R. Miller & Sanchez, 1994): **F**eedback, **R**esponsibility, **A**dvice, **M**enu, **E**mpathy, and **S**elf-efficacy. Hester and Bien (1995) clarify these aspects of counseling in terms of the substance-abusing client. Therapeutic *feedback* may be needed because the client may not have noticed the negative feedback of alcohol/ drug usage for a number of reasons: (1) addicted clients may not be aware of negative consequences because the consequences are delayed while the positive effects of using alcohol/drugs are more immediate, and (2) clients did not absorb the information, because it was given in a negative and judgmental manner. By contrast, a counselor using the words "addiction" and "disease" invites client responsibility for current usage, but not for the development of the substance abuse problem (Friedman & Fanger, 1991). As to *responsibility*, the counselor encourages client awareness that he or she is responsible for the choice to use or not use, thereby avoiding power struggles. If the client gives permission to hear *advice*, the counselor needs to give the advice in a nonjudgmental manner. *Menu* in the acronym means that the client is presented with options for changing substance-using behavior. The *empathy* that you convey by listening to the client's story is helpful in the establishment of a collaborative relationship in counseling. Encouraging a sense of *self-efficacy*, where the client can view him- or herself as able to change the substance-using pattern conveys a critical "hopeline" for the client.

The second is Bloom's (1997) guidelines for focused single-session therapy that may assist the addicted individual in obtaining clarity about the addiction as well as assist the counselor in making the assessment and possible referral for the client. These 10 guidelines are:

1. Focus on a problem.

2. Present simple ideas.

3. Be active in the latter part of the session (avoid self-disclosure, ask open-ended questions, learn the language the client speaks, provide simple information, and have the responsibility of the communication lie with the client).

4. Explore and present tentative interpretations.

5. Use empathy.

6. Be aware of the time.

7. Minimize factual questions.

8. Do not focus too much on the event that brought the client to counseling.

9. Avoid side issues.

10. Do not overestimate what the client knows about himself or herself.

A few of Bloom's (1997) objectives need to be emphasized in working with addicted clients. First, you have a ready-made focus on the client's problem: It is an addiction. However, depending on the reasons why the client is referred for counseling (e.g., referred by another rather than self-referred), the counselor may need to help the client develop a problem focus that is appealing to both the referral source and the client. Learning the language spoken by the client can also facilitate a problem focus. Metaphors used by the client or interests or values expressed can be used by the counselor to communicate information about addiction recovery. For example, the client who is in treatment only because a court order states that he must get counseling may, in conversation, express an interest in car racing. You may use this interest as a way to provide information about recovery: Like a car needs oil to run, an addict needs to attend treatment and self-help groups to stay sober. Simple information and ideas are also important in counseling. A person new to the recovery process may be overwhelmed by the consequences of use and intense emotions, so the simpler the information is presented, the more likely it will be remembered. Finally, avoidance of side issues may be necessary, especially with individuals who have been referred to counseling by others.

In addition, Bloom posits that the counselor (1) acknowledge the work the client has already done outside of the session, (2) be aware of the client's strengths, (3) help build social supports, (4) educate the client when necessary, (5) add additional therapy sessions if necessary, and (6) have a follow-up plan. These six guidelines need to be directly translated to addiction counseling work. The counselor needs to help the client examine the ways in which he or she has tried to stop using and how these strengths can be used at this point in recovery (1 and 2). The importance of social networks needs to be stressed, especially with a recovering community that makes sense to the client and can help the client stay sober (3). The development of a solid relapse-prevention plan is also necessary to determine when future counseling will occur and what other ingredients are necessary in the client's life to help recovery occur (4, 5, and 6). This chain reaction of therapy may be especially helpful with addicted clients in terms of breaking their denial of addiction and helping them explore what recovery may mean for them.

Some useful techniques with addicted clients that emerge from three planned short-term psychotherapy theoretical approaches (*psychodynamic, cognitive and behavioral*, and *strategic and systemic*) are presented here.

The theoretical concepts from Davanloo's *psychodynamic* theory (Bloom, 1997; Davanloo, 1980) may be of most assistance with addicted clients who are in the triangle of conflict or the triangle of person. The "triangle of conflict" has one of the following items at each point on the triangle: impulse, anxiety, or defense. The client experiences an unacceptable impulse, which increases anxiety, which results in a defensive reaction (using alcohol/drugs). The counselor needs to assist the client in determining the impulses leading to the anxiety that results in the chemical usage behavior. For example, a recovering addicted client may have a lot of difficulties with his father.

When he has contact with his father, his impulse is to get upset, which may increase his anxiety, which may result in his using alcohol/drugs to defend against the anxiety.

The second triangle is the "triangle of person." At each point on the triangle is one of the following: past, present, or future. In this triangle, significant people are considered a part of each of these, and the client's reactions toward the therapist are similar to those reactions experienced in the past or in the present. This triangle may assist you in understanding the client's transference and enable you to work with it more effectively. For the addicted client, issues with a significant female in his or her life (e.g., mother, intimate partner) may be projected onto a female counselor. A counselor with this understanding can assist the client in breaking out of these interactional patterns by pointing them out to the client and encouraging the client to try out different behaviors.

Although Davanloo's theory (Bloom, 1997; Davanloo, 1980) does not suggest the triangle be used in this manner, the concept of the triangle can also be used to help the client determine supportive individuals in his or her life. Counseling can assist the client in determining which people were significantly helpful in the past and/or the present, so any useful connections can be enhanced in counseling. For the addicted client who may have severed or scarred relationships with others, examining these relationships may assist the client's recovery process. Determine whether some of these relationships can be built into the client's current support network, as well as the types of individuals the client finds supportive so he or she can more actively seek them out.

One version of *cognitive-behavioral therapy* is Ellis's rational emotive psychotherapy where actions are viewed as the results of beliefs (Bloom, 1997; Ellis, 1962). Here, direct, active therapy may involve homework assignments and bibliotherapy, and confrontation of cognitive, emotional, behavioral problems by examining the beliefs that occur between the experience and the emotion. This brief therapy approach can be very useful with addicted clients, because they may hold highly irrational beliefs about what their chemical usage does for them and how it affects others. Ellis (1992) recommends focusing on the problem drinking and the dysfunctional beliefs causing the drinking and then using rational emotive therapy (RET) techniques to intervene.

Another version of *cognitive-behavioral therapy* is Beck's view of depression as a result of distortions of self, the world, and the future (Beck, 1976; Bloom, 1997). These schemas, or ways of viewing the world, emphasize failure while minimizing success. This form of therapy examines the client's automatic thoughts, explanations of life events, assumptions of the world, and development of new responses from new assumptions. Beck (Beck, 1976; Bloom, 1997) states that the counselor should be trustworthy, communicate well, and have confidence that the client's situation can change. In terms of specific techniques, the counselor needs to help the client identify automatic thoughts (identify what occurs between the event and the client's reaction to it by use of something such as a record of reactions to events), identify the client's underlying assumptions, use questions to increase awareness, and involve homework assignments that may assist in increasing awareness.

This form of therapy may be especially beneficial for the addicted client because it focuses on addressing hopelessness, which many addicts experience. It also provides the addicted client with a sense of control and self-observation, underscoring the reality that the addict has choices about life. For example, when an addicted client wants to use, help the client determine what the automatic thoughts were in the situation where the urge was experienced ("Oh, no. I didn't think they would be serving alcohol at a work function"), what underlying assumptions may be present ("I will never be able to live through this situation sober"), and help the client through questions ("How have you been able to stay sober before in previous situations?") and homework ("Watch yourself the next time you have an urge

and become aware of the thoughts and feelings you have during the experience. Keep a log of these experiences and we will review them in your next session").

An example of cognitive-behavioral strategies with addiction counseling is seen in the area of relapse prevention. (Chapter 7 discussed a relapse-prevention model in detail.) Relapse-prevention treatment involves techniques of homework, bibliotherapy, guided imagery, role play, and self-monitoring (Giannetti, 1993). Clients need to identify situations that may trigger a relapse, avoid triggers to relapse, substitute rewards, test new skills, picture themselves in a relapse-provoking situation to develop a coping plan, and develop realistic long-term goals.

The third category is *strategic and systemic*. The theory focused on here is de Shazer's solution-based brief therapy (Bloom, 1997; de Shazer, 1985), which began in the mid-1970s. This form of therapy emphasizes solutions rather than problems in marriage and family therapy. There are three main objectives: change clients' perceptions, change clients' behavior, and help clients access their strengths. The focus is on finding an exception to the problem (i.e., discovering when the problem does not exist). The counselor must look at the symptoms, the exceptions, and then apply interventions. Specification of goals is viewed as critical to the process. Often, in the first session, the miracle question is asked: "If a miracle occurs tonight while you are asleep and the problem is eliminated, how will you know the next morning? How will others know? What will you be doing differently or saying differently?" These questions stress healthy functioning and the client determining his or her own solutions to the problem (Kingsbury, 1997); they also help determine the values of the client that may assist in motivation for change. It is also important that the sessions involve homework to help the client determine a successful solution to the problem (C. H. Huber & Backlund, 1992) and to develop supports for the change (Preston, 1998).

Berg and Miller (1992) outline steps for using this form of therapy with substance abusers.

These steps emphasize the importance of a good therapeutic relationship; development and implementation of treatment goals; and focusing on interviews, treatment interventions, and maintenance of change. The overall goal is to help the client use available resources and strengths to increase the frequency of times when drugs are not used by studying exceptions to the client's use (Stevens-Smith & Smith, 1998). Berg (1995) points out that clients often have periods when they do not use, so this information about what they do that helps them stay sober is already available, whether these exceptions are deliberate (the client intentionally tries to stay away from using and can explain the steps taken to attain abstinence) or random (the client cannot explain the steps taken to achieve abstinence). In the case of deliberate exceptions, you can help the client plan to retake the same steps, and with random exceptions, you can help the client learn to predict times of recovery to enhance a sense of control (Berg, 1995). In this type of philosophy, the client does not need to fix what works, does need to do more of what does work, and has to do something different if he or she tries something that does not work (Berg & Miller, 1992). As to doing things differently, your intention should be to encourage the client to simply make a small change in the behavior (Littrell, 1998).

The treatment can be one session or a series of brief sessions that occur over time in the individual's recovery (Berg, 1995). Whether in individual or group counseling, the miracle question is used to establish goals. Scaling questions (scales of 1 to 10 or 1 to 100 are used to describe the intensity of the clinical issues experienced) are used to determine progress, and behavioral tracking is done to determine what steps have helped the client stay sober (Berg, 1995). For example, after asking the addicted client the miracle question, scaling questions could be used as follows: "On a scale of 1 to 10, 10 being the highest point, in what settings do you have the greatest urge to use, and what point on the scale would you assign to each of those settings?" and "In the past week, using a scale of 1 to 10 again, scale the most stressful interaction you

had with someone and describe that experience." Also, "What would it take to reach a 10 goal?" Additionally, asking clients questions about significant others can be helpful: how they rate their progress and where they see themselves in terms of change (Berg, 2000). These techniques can aid the counselor in determining the extent of difficulty of the client's clinical issues.

Clients may view their situation as stable, they may not believe there is anything they have not tried, and they may look at their particular situations as uncontrollable (C. H. Huber & Backlund, 1992). For clients who view their situations as stable, focus on helping them recognize exceptions to the stability and then reinforce a successful solution to the problem (Huber & Backlund, 1992). As stated previously, addicted clients who believe they can never be sober need to look at times they have been able to stay sober and build on the successful components of those attempts at sobriety. For example, with an addicted client with a tendency to relapse, it may be helpful to explore times they did *not* relapse in response to high-risk situations: what resources inside or outside of them made a difference and how can they incorporate these changes in their lives with more intentionality? For clients who believe they have tried everything to cope with the situation, they may be encouraged to try something different (e.g., attending Women for Sobriety rather than AA); follow-up with them can determine how successful that change was (Huber & Backlund, 1992). For clients who feel as though their situations are uncontrollable, it may be helpful to focus on what they did to try to make a difference in their situations, again focusing on the successful aspects of their solutions (Huber & Backlund, 1992). Addicted clients who believe they cannot have an impact on their recovery may need to examine carefully attempts at sobriety in terms of one day rather than a lifetime.

In terms of multicultural counseling, brief therapy may not work with all individuals from all cultural settings: brevity and diversity in counseling may not be a good match for some clients (Steenbarger, 1993). Cross-culturally, brief therapy has been used successfully in crisis intervention work to relate hope, develop support, and increase self-esteem (Pedulla & Pedulla, 2001). A good example of its effectiveness in alcohol and drug abuse treatment is brief strategic family therapy (BSFT) that is showing promising results in reducing Hispanic youth drug abuse (Szapocznik, Schwartz, Muir, & Brown, 2012; Szapocznik & Williams, 2000). Depending on the effectiveness of the match of brief therapy for the individual, it can be either empowering or disempowering. The addiction counselor, then, needs to keep these application considerations in mind from a multicultural perspective (See Case Study 9.4).

research, clinical expertise, and patient characteristics/culture/preferences are all involved and integrated, research is the priority (Norcross, Hogan, & Koocher, 2008a). The goal of EBP is to reduce the research and practice gaps and increase the ability to help clients and avoid harming them (Gambrill, 2010). Because research is the top priority, counselors start with the research available about treatment approaches; then they integrate the research information about the treatment approaches into their expertise (their practice) and take into account pertinent client variables. The counselor, based on his or her expertise, makes

---

CASE STUDY 9.4

Jane is a 26-year-old woman who has been court-ordered to treatment because of her second DUI. She is single, has no children, works as a court reporter, and has a bachelor's degree in English. Jane has come to see you in individual counseling for two sessions (intake and one general session) and has been in outpatient addiction treatment group counseling for 1 week. She does not speak at all in the group session and answers questions only briefly in individual sessions. She avoids eye contact, speaks in a soft tone, and does not express or show affect. She is very articulate, using words at times with which you are unfamiliar.

1. What aspects of her story would make her a good candidate for brief therapy?

2. What aspects of her story would make her a poor candidate for brief therapy?

3. Would your brief therapy approach be different in individual counseling as compared to group counseling? If so, what aspects would be different and why?

4. Apply the FRAMES model to your work with her.

5. Which specific techniques from the three brief therapies would you use with her in the individual sessions? Provide your rationale for your choice.

6. Which specific techniques from the three brief therapies would you use with her in the group sessions (and again provide your rationale)?

EVIDENCE-BASED PRACTICES (EBPs)

Evidence-based practice is "the integration of the best available research with clinical expertise in the context of patient characteristics, culture, and preferences." (APA Task Force on Evidence-Based Practice, 2006, p. 273). While

the final decision about the best practice with the client by weighing the different components: research-supported treatment, his or her expertise, and client variables. Counselors may find SAMHSA's National Registry of Evidence-Based Programs and Practices referenced at the end of this chapter to be helpful in the selection of EBPs.

In part, the demand for evidence-based practices has emerged because of a desire to contain costs, whether in a public or private system (D. Dobson & Dobson, 2009). Health maintenance organizations (HMOs) and insurance companies promote EBP guidelines in order for clients to receive the best treatment (practice) available, and reimbursement may hinge on application of best practice to the client (Blume, 2005). Some of the additional reasons for its emergence include: gaps in clinical application of research findings, variations in clinical practice, not using services that were helpful as well as not stopping services that were ineffective or harmful, access to databases on the web and systematic, rather than peer, review (Gambrill, 2010).

In the 1990s, researchers showed a tendency to want to identify empirically supported treatments for therapy (Chambless & Ollendick, 2001). It emerged out of the field of medicine (van Wormer & Thyer, 2010). It began in Great Britain and then moved to Canada, the United States, and now internationally (Norcross et al., 2008). The need for treatment to be effective, time-limited, and emphasize empirical outcomes, then, has opened the counseling field to the application of evidence-based practices to mental health treatment in the form of manuals and observation checklists (due to the need to standardize treatment in order to measure treatment outcome) as well as professional guidelines for therapists (Norcross et al., 2008). Regarding the future of the mental health and substance abuse treatment, Norcross et al. (2008) state: "What earns the privileged designation of 'evidence-based' will increasingly determine, in large part, what we practice, what we teach, and what research wins funding" (p. 4).

Behavioral therapies and cognitive-behavioral therapies are not the only EBPs, however, because they are more readily measurable (they are anchored in behavior), they may dominate the EBP therapy approaches. Cognitive-behavioral therapy is one of the strongest EBPs. It has been shown to be effective with these disorders: depression, bipolar (once the person has been medically stabilized), schizophrenia (once the person has been medically stabilized), anxiety disorders, personality disorders (e.g., dialectical behavior therapy), and chronic pain (Blume, 2005). Although cognitive-behavioral therapy is discussed in Chapter 2, a brief review of this approach and techniques based on D. Dobson and Dobson's work (2009) follows.

Dobson and Dozois (2001) describe four principles of cognitive-behavioral therapy:

1. *Access hypothesis.* We can access our own thoughts and be aware of them.

2. *Mediation hypothesis.* Emotions are mediated by our thoughts in response to situations.

3. *Change hypothesis.* We can change our response to situations by knowing our thoughts and our emotional responses to them.

4. *Realistic assumption.* There is an objective reality that is outside of our awareness, and one can learn to more accurately determine what that reality is and respond accordingly, rather than through one's own misperception of it.

D. Dobson and Dobson (2009) state that cultural factors present in North America have also been a welcoming format for cognitive-behavioral therapies. These eight factors include:

1. A focus on individualism.

2. A tendency to have a lack of community connection.

3. Easier access to information.

4. A possible decrease in stigma for having mental health problems.

5. An increased acceptance for obtaining mental health treatment.

6. A tendency for people to view the self as a consumer wanting a good product in therapy.

7. Cost containment concerns.

8. A focus on efficiency and effectiveness in a faster-paced society.

A focus on getting the most for one's money from systems and the presence of specific cultural factors has increased the use of cognitive-behavioral approaches being used by counselors. First, there are basic principles of cognitive-behavioral therapy. These are that (a) we can access our own thoughts and be aware of them; (b) our emotions are mediated by our thoughts—if we change our thoughts we can change our emotions; and (c) we can more accurately assess reality rather than react to our perceptions of reality.

The authors caution that counselors can be closed to this approach because they do not have enough information or experiences with it, have biases about it, misinterpret literature or training received in this area, or use approaches with which one is more experienced and/or knowledgeable. Eight typical negative (untrue) beliefs held by counselors about cognitive-behavioral therapy are that it:

1. Is too rigid, structured, and not individualized enough because of manualization.

2. Has tools that can be inserted into any theoretical framework.

3. Lasts 6 to 20 sessions.

4. Lacks an emphasis on emotions in therapy.

5. Is psychoeducational in nature, thereby is only a place to start therapy.

6. Addresses the symptom of the problem, not the problem.

7. Is antifeminist because of the emphasis on the logical.

8. Ignores social context in the examination of problems. (See Case Study 9.5.)

While the four therapies that have been included in this chapter are EBPs, the only one listed for positive psychology on the SAMSHA website is "Say It Straight" (SIS)—a communication training program for substance abuse prevention. An overview of evidence-based addiction treatment is provided in P. M. Miller's (2008) *Evidence-Based Addiction Treatment*. Because of the current prevalence of the use of evidence-based practices, the reader is encouraged to approach this area with an open-mindedness and challenge any myths or negative beliefs held about these practices of therapy.

CASE STUDY 9.5

Your client has very limited English skills and little education. You would like to use a cognitive-behavioral approach toward his struggle with depression that worsens when he stops using alcohol/drugs.

1. What considerations would you need to take into account in applying such an approach to his situation?
2. What adaptations might you consider in applying this approach to his depression?
3. What agencies would you contact for an EBP that would best apply to your client?

SUMMARY

The concept of client resilience, four therapies (positive psychology, stages-of-change model, motivational interviewing, and brief therapy), and evidence-based practices have been discussed in this chapter. Each of these concepts/therapies/practices can be helpful within different addiction treatment contexts (individual, couple, family, or group) and different stages of addiction treatment (assessment, treatment, or relapse prevention). The counselor using specific techniques of these therapies needs to have some focused training in this area of therapy or at least be supervised by someone who has been trained in these techniques, as well as know the clients with whom these therapies may be most beneficial. Although these therapies, as well as all therapies, may not be able to serve the needs of all addicted clients in all situations, they are helpful, additional tools that an addiction counselor can use in treating a client.

QUESTIONS

1. Define:

   Resilience

   Positive psychology

   The stages-of-change model

   Motivational interviewing

   Brief therapy

2. What are the main principles in each of these areas: positive psychology, stages of change, motivational interviewing, brief therapy?

3. What are the main techniques in each of these areas: positive psychology, stages of change, motivational interviewing, brief therapy?

4. What are the three main areas involved in EBPs?

EXERCISES

Exercise 9.1

Use Table 9.1 as a checklist for ways you were resilient when experiencing a difficult period in your life. Which of the "10 Ways to Build Resilience" did you expand in order to enhance your survival of your difficulties and thrive? How did you expand them?

Exercise 9.2

As you think of this difficult period of time in the previous exercise, write out what were the strengths inside of you (traits, thoughts, feelings, etc.) and outside of you (environmental supports such as social supports, philosophies, reading materials, etc.) that assisted you (or would assist you) in surviving the experience. What provided you with a sense of hope? Then, shift to the present and answer the question: "What is right about me?"

Exercise 9.3

Think of a habitual pattern of behavior you have attempted to change. Diagnose yourself in terms of stages of change at this present time. If you are dissatisfied at your stage of change, how might you use the processes for change to assist you in moving to a different stage? Discuss your thoughts with another person.

Exercise 9.4

Get into a triad. Have one person be the client, one be the therapist, and one be an observer. Spend at least 15 minutes in this role play (5 minutes of role play, 5 minutes of processing with the triad, and 5 minutes discussing within the larger group facilitated by a leader/trainer). Have the *client* discuss a personal concern (the client can always stop the role play if it becomes uncomfortable) or one the client has heard frequently in the population with which they work. Have the *therapist* practice at least one aspect of the OARS and, if possible, a change talk strategy. Have the *observer* watch the therapist and: (1) focus on his/her strengths, (2) write down the number and examples of open-ended questions asked, affirming statements made, reflections made, and summary comments made, and (3) any indicators of change talk. During the processing, have the time divided into the client giving the counselor feedback first, then the counselor discussing the experience, and finally, the observer. Each person needs to focus on the strengths of the counselor and what they believe was helpful to the client—and since the flip side of one's strengths is one's weakness, the counselor is also learning about their weaknesses. Finally, the last 5 minutes can be processed in a larger group about what are common themes of effectiveness throughout the different role plays. If there is time, each person can switch roles and have the experience of playing each of the three roles.

READINGS/RESOURCES/WEBSITES

SUGGESTED READINGS

Brief Therapy

Bloom, B. L. (1997). *Planned short-term psychotherapy: A clinical handbook* (2nd ed.). Boston, MA: Allyn & Bacon.

This book provides a comprehensive summary of the three main branches of short-term therapy: psychodynamic, cognitive and behavioral, and strategic and systemic. For each of the three main branches, the author provides helpful examples that can be used by the counselor in sessions.

Pichot, T. (2009). *Solution-focused substance abuse treatment*. New York, NY: Routledge.

This book has nine chapters that apply solution-focused therapy to substance abuse treatment. The

Exercise 9.5

Get into a triad. Have one person be the client, one be the therapist, and one be an observer. In using the format in the previous exercise, practice at least one of the brief therapy strategies (psychodynamic, cognitive and behavioral, strategic and systemic) in a role play situation where the client is an addicted person.

Exercise 9.6

Go to the SAMSHA website (www.nrepp. samhsa.gov) and choose an evidence-based practice that you believe would be most helpful to the client population with whom you currently work or anticipate working. Write out the pros and cons of the application of this practice given your theoretical orientation and your counseling practice.

topics include an overview of treatment and solution-focused therapy, assessment, case management, group therapy, practice issues, and forms and handouts.

Evidence-Based Practices

Dobson, D., & Dobson, K. S. (2009). *Evidence-based practice of cognitive-behavioral therapy*. New York, NY: Guilford Press.

This book has nine chapters that review cognitive-behavioral approaches to therapy with a practical application focus on assessment and treatment. It has excellent appendices on the Cognitive Therapy Scale and articles examining the efficacy of this therapy from general to specific disorders.

Miller, P. M. (Ed.). (2009). *Evidence-based addiction treatment*. Burlington, MA: Academic Press.

The 23 chapters in this book are divided into six sections: introduction, assessment and treatment monitoring, treatment methods, special populations, treatment in action, and the future.

Norcross, J. C., Hogan, T. P., & Koocher, G. P. (2008). *Clinician's guide to evidence-based practices: Mental health and the addictions*. New York, NY: Oxford University Press.

This book has 10 chapters that describe evidence-based practice and explores approaches, interpretation of research, ethics, and dissemination. There is a CD included with the book.

van Wormer, K., & Thyer, B. A. (Eds.). (2010). *Evidence-based practice in the field of substance abuse: A book of readings*. Los Angeles, CA: Sage.

This book has 17 chapters divided into five sections: introduction, substance abuse assessment, interventions (gender, culture), treatment, and policy.

Motivational Interviewing

Arkowitz, H., Westra, H. A., Miller, W. R., & Rollnick, S. (Eds.). (2008). *Motivational interviewing in the treatment of psychological problems*. New York, NY: Guilford Press.

This book has 13 chapters: The first is an overview of MI and the next 12 each address the application of MI to a specific psychological problem.

Hohman, M. (2012). *Motivational interviewing in social work practice*. New York, NY: Guilford Press.

This book has 10 chapters that describe MI and its integration with the practice of social work, with five of the chapters focusing on specific MI concepts and techniques.

Miller, W. R., & Rollnick, S. (2013). *Motivational interviewing* (3rd ed.). New York, NY: Guilford Press.

This third edition has 28 chapters divided into seven sections of defining/describing it, engaging, focusing, evoking, planning, applying it, and evaluating it. The book is helpful in understanding the spirit of motivational interviewing and provides techniques of motivational interviewing that can easily be applied by the clinician. It has a helpful glossary and bibliography at the end of the text. At www.guilford.com/p/miller2 one can obtain a comprehensive MI bibliography, two annotated case examples, reflection questions for each chapter, a personal values card sort, and a glossary of terms.

Naar-King, S., & Suarez, M. (2011). *Motivational interviewing with adolescents and young adults*. New York, NY: Guilford Press.

This book has 22 chapters divided into three sections: the guide (eight chapters that are reviews of basic MI concepts and techniques), side trips (12 chapters on application to specific issues and populations), and choosing your own path (two chapters on ethics and proficiency development).

Wagner, C. C., & Ingersoll, K. S. (2013). *Motivational interviewing in groups*. New York, NY: Guilford Press.

The 21 chapters of this book are divided into three sections: foundations (five chapters), group development (seven chapters), and applications to specific groups (nine chapters).

Positive Psychology

Csikszentmihalyi, M. (2008). *Flow*. New York, NY: Harper.

This book provides an in-depth description of this concept.

Harvard Mental Health Letter. (May, 2008). Positive psychology in practice. *Harvard Mental Health Letter, 24*, 1–3.

This short newsletter succinctly provides a current overview of positive psychology.

Lopez, S. J., & Snyder, C. R. (Eds.). (2003). *Positive psychological assessment: A handbook of models and measures*. Washington, DC: American Psychological Association.

This book provides an overview of research in positive psychology within five areas: cognitive, emotional, interpersonal, religious/philosophical, and positive processes/outcomes/environments.

Seligman, M. E. P. (2011). *Flourish*. New York, NY: Free Press.

This 368-page book, which is conceptual and research-based, focuses on a four-factor life of well being consisting of positive emotions, engagement, accomplishment, and relationships.

Seligman, M. E. P., & Csikszentmihalyi, M. (2000). Positive psychology: An introduction. *American Psychologist, 55,* 5–14.

This article provides a helpful overview of the general concepts of positive psychology.

Resilience

Csikszentmihalyi, M. (2008). *Flow.* New York, NY: Harper.

This book provides an in-depth description of this concept.

Miller, B. (2011). *The woman's book of resilience: 12 qualities to cultivate.* York Beach, ME: Conari Press.

This book has 12 chapters that is meant through text and exercises to assist the reader in developing resilient qualities.

Stages of Change
Overview

Prochaska, J. O., DiClemente, C. C., & Norcross, J. C. (1992). In search of how people change. *American Psychologist, 47,* 1102–1114.

This article provides a description of the stages-of-change model.

Group

Velasquez, M. M., Maurer, G. G., Crouch, C., & DiClemente, C. C. (2001). *Group treatment for substance abuse: A stages-of-change therapy manual.* New York, NY: Guilford Press.

This 222-page book is divided into three sections. In the first section there are three chapters that discuss the model, strategies for change, and making the interventions. The second section outlines the 14 precontemplation, contemplation, and preparation sessions. The third section outlines the 15 action and maintenance sessions.

Special Populations
Adjustment Disorders

Araoz, D. L., & Carrese, M. A. (1996). *Solution-oriented brief therapy for adjustment disorders: A guide for providers under managed care.* Philadelphia, PA: Brunner/Mazel.

This 162-page book outlines working with adjustment disorders (according to the *DSM-IV*) in terms of diagnosis and therapy. It has an especially helpful chapter titled "Teaching Patients Self-Therapy" that includes nine cognitive-behavioral practices clients can use.

Couples

Halford, W. K. (2001). *Brief therapy for couples.* New York, NY: Guilford Press.

This 288-page book describes self-regulatory couple therapy (SRCT) that enhances a couple's self-directed change. A framework for less than 25 sessions is provided with intervention guidelines.

Group

Metcalf, L. (1998). *Solution-focused group therapy.* New York, NY: Free Press.

This 242-page book applies the solution-focused approach to group therapy with ideas and worksheets for group work. It has a chapter on out-of-control behaviors that include eating disorders and alcohol and drug use. There is a helpful exercise on one's perception of how change happens, as well as an admission interview and group process notes for both client and counselor.

RESOURCES

Brief Therapy
Workbooks—Alcohol

Cohen-Posey, K. (2000). *Brief therapy client handouts.* New York, NY: Wiley.

This workbook includes a disk with 100 handouts that facilitate the application of core brief therapy concepts covered in two sections (relationships, disorders) that include 10 chapters.

Cohen-Posey, K. (2011). *More brief therapy client handouts*. Hoboken, NJ: Wiley.

This 265-page book has a CD that has 200 handouts (exercises, handouts, self-assessments) covering three main sections (quiet mind, thinking mind, between minds) in eight chapters.

Miller, S. D., & Berg, I. K. (1995). *The miracle method*. New York, NY: Norton.

This 172-page book has a solution-focused approach that is applied to problem drinkers, providing an alternative perspective from the disease and 12-step models that are written to the client. It has exercises that can be used to facilitate self-examination.

Schultheis, G. M. (1998). *Brief therapy homework planner*. New York, NY: Wiley.

This 239-page book includes a disk that has 62 homework assignments. It has 18 sections that extensively cover numerous brief therapy concepts; there is one section that focuses on relapse prevention.

Workbooks—General

Cade, B., & O'Hanlon, W. H. (1993). *A brief guide to brief therapy*. New York, NY: Norton.

This 202-page book provides an overview of the theory of brief therapy and a description of common techniques, such as framing, pattern, paradox, and metaphor interventions.

DeJong, P., & Berg, I. K. (2013). *Interviewing for solutions* (4th ed.). Pacific Grove, CA: Brooks/Cole.

This 324-page book applies the solution-focused approach to interviewing and later sessions. It has an appendix of tools for protocols (feedback, first session, later session, involuntary clients, crisis interviews) as well as helpful questions with goal development, exceptions, involuntary clients, and coping.

Littrell, J. M. (1998). *Brief counseling in action*. New York, NY: Norton.

This 246-page book provides counselors with theoretical explanations of solution-focused therapy with exercises that can be used to facilitate its application with clients. There is also a modification of the stages-of-change model with client quotations that is helpful in understanding the stages, as well as a four-item assessment of a client's stage level.

National Institute on Alcohol Abuse and Alcoholism (NIAAA). (July, 2005). *Alcohol alert: Brief interventions*. Rockville, MD: Author.

This short publication provides an overview of brief interventions (short individual sessions) that can be used regarding alcohol and drug use.

Substance Abuse and Mental Health Services Administration (1999). *Brief interventions and brief therapies for substance abuse*. Treatment Improvement Protocol (TIP 34) Series (DHHS Publication No. SMA 03–03810). Rockville, MD: Author.

This 234-page book provides an overview on brief therapies and interventions used in addiction counseling.

Evidence-Based Practices
Workbooks

Nejad, L., & Volny, K. (2008). *Treating stress and anxiety: A practitioner's guide to evidence-based approaches*. Norwalk, CT: Crown.

This workbook (and CD) covers cognitive-behavioral techniques to reduce stress and anxiety and enhance life quality. It has exercises, handouts, and worksheets; the handouts and worksheets can be printed from the CD.

Motivational Interviewing and Stages of Change
Workbooks

Rosengren, D. B. (2009). *Building motivational interviewing skills: A practitioner workbook*. New York, NY: Guilford Press.

This workbook is designed for counselors to develop the skills of motivational interviewing.

Tomlin, K. M., & Richardson, H. (2004). *Motivational interviewing and stages of change*. Center City, MN: Hazelden.

This 231-page book has seven chapters: The first two focus on basic information and the integration of both of these models, the next four chapters involve change activities that can be used by counselors with different populations and counseling contexts (adolescents, family)—one chapter specifically focuses on application to special populations—and the last chapter on integrating these approaches into one's clinical setting.

Positive Psychology
Workbooks

Froh, J. J., & Parks, A. C. (2012). *Activities for teaching positive psychology: A guide for instructors*. Washington, DC: American Psychological Association.

This 173-page text has enjoyable, interactive classroom activities for high school, undergraduate, and graduate students in addition to extensive reading lists.

Special Populations

Berg, I. K., & Reuss, N. H. (1998). *Solutions: Step by step*. New York, NY: Norton.

This 185-page manual describes solution-focused therapy and discusses special treatment situations (codependents, relapsers, mandated clients, women, etc.) as they relate to substance abuse. It provides examples of interactions through transcripts. Its appendix contains 16 worksheets that can be used with clients (including a recovery checklist and worksheet that examines recovery from a holistic perspective).

Cohen-Posey, K. (2000). *Brief therapy client handouts*. New York, NY: Wiley.

This 185-page manual has exercise worksheets for working on relationship issues (emotions, family, marriage, parenting) and disorder-related issues (e.g., panic, OCD, moods, anger, ADD/ADHD, self-discovery). A CD is included.

Schultheis, G. M. (1998). *Brief therapy homework planner*. New York, NY: Wiley.

This 221-page manual has 62 homework assignments that match 30 behaviorally based problems from *The Complete Adult Psychotherapy Treatment Planner* (2nd ed.) that can be used to facilitate the solution-focused approach in counseling. It has a separate section on relapse prevention. A CD is included.

Videotapes/DVDs
Motivational Interviewing

American Psychological Association (Producer). (2003). *Drugs and alcohol abuse: William Richard Miller, PhD* (APA Psychotherapy Videotape Series III) [Videotape]. Available from www.apa.org/videos

The entire video is more than 100 minutes and is broken into three segments: a discussion between the host and Dr. Miller, a therapy session with a real client, and a question-and-answer period with Dr. Miller regarding the session.

Theresa B. Moyers, PhD (Producer). (1998). *Motivational interviewing: Professional training videotape series* (A-F) [Videotapes]. Available from www.motivationalinterviewing.org

This six-tape series (A–F) provides basic information on motivational interviewing through lecture/discussion by Miller and Rollnick and role-play situations with clients struggling with habitual patterns of behavior. The six tapes cover (A) Introduction to Motivational Interviewing (41 minutes); (B) Phase 1: Opening Strategies (two cassettes)—Part 1 (OARS) (39 minutes) and Part 2 (Change Talk) (51 minutes); (C) Handling Resistance (62 minutes); (D) Feedback and Information Exchange (55 minutes); (E) Motivational Interviewing in Medical Settings (48 minutes); and (F) Phase 2: Moving Toward Action (37 minutes). The tapes that cover the core MI techniques are the B tapes.

Miller, W. R., Rollnick, S., & Moyers, T.B. (2013). *Motivational interviewing-3*. [DVD] Available from www.motivationalinterviewing.org

This DVD training set is an update on the 1998 series described above.

Stages of Change

Hazelden (Producer). (2004). *Stages of change* [DVD]. Available from www.hazelden.org, this 2-hour video is a thorough overview of the stages-of-change model in a lecture format.

WEBSITES

Brief Therapy (Solution-Focused)

Solution-Focused Brief Therapy Association
www.sfbta.org

This website for the therapy association provides general information as well as information on conferences, products, training, research, etc.

Evidence-Based Practices

Evidence-Based Behavioral Practice
www.ebbp.org/

This website has training resources to bridge the gap between research and practice.

National Institute on Alcohol Abuse and Alcoholism
www.niaaa.nih.gov

This website has general information on evidence-based practices.

National Institute on Drug Abuse
www.drugabuse.gov

This website provides general information on evidence-based practices.

Substance Abuse and Mental Health Services Administration (SAMHSA)
www.nrepp.samhsa.gov

This site has the National Registry of Evidence-Based Programs and Practices that provides information on mental health and substance abuse interventions (prevention and treatment) that are scientifically based and practical.

Professional Organizations

American Association for Marriage and Family Therapy
www.aamft.org

American Counseling Association (ACA)
www.counseling.org

American Psychological Association (APA)
www.apa.org

National Association of Social Workers
www.socialworkers.org

These general websites have links for information on evidence-based practices.

Motivational Interviewing

Addiction Technology Transfer Center
www.attcnetwork.org/index.asp

This website provides information on one's local Addiction Technology Transfer Center (ATTC) that has access to the *Motivational Interviewing Assessment: Supervisory Tools for Enhancing Proficiency* (MIA:STEP) *Products* [Briefing Materials, MI Assessment Protocol, Teaching Tools for Assessing and Enhancing MI Skills, Supervisor Tape Rating Guide, Demonstration Materials, and Supervisor Training Curriculum] and *Promoting Awareness of Motivational Incentives* (PAMI) *Products* [video, PowerPoint presentations, and a tool kit].

Motivational Interviewing
www.motivationalinterview.org

This website provides information on clinical issues, has a library, and contains training-related information.

SAMHSA
www.nrepp.samhsa.gov/pdfs/MI_Booklet_Final.pdf

This website links to the SAMHSA National Registry of Evidence-Based Programs and Practices (2012) document: *Motivational Interviewing: An Informational Resource*.

Positive Psychology

American Psychological Association
www.apa.org

This general website has links to different divisions' focus on positive psychology.

Positive Psychology Center at University of Pennsylvania
www.positivepsychology.org
www.ppc.sas.upenn.edu

These websites are for the Positive Psychology Center at the University of Pennsylvania in Philadelphia. They provide general information on positive psychology, opportunities in this area of study, conferences, educational programs, teaching and research resources, and research information. For example, the Authentic Happiness home page (www.authentichappiness.sas.upenn.edu) provides information on theories, initiatives, presentations, and media as well as opportunities to take different questionnaires.

Positive Psychology at School of Behavioral & Organizational Sciences at Claremont Graduate University in California
www.cgu.edu/pages/4571.asp

This website provides information on the two concentrations in positive psychology, developmental and organizational, at the master's and doctoral levels, as well as information on the Quality of Life Research Center (QLRC), an institute for research in positive psychology.

Resilience

American Psychological Association
www.apa.org/helpcenter/road-resilience.aspx

This website provides an overview of information on resilience with links to specific aspects related to resilience.

CHAPTER 10

CULTURALLY SENSITIVE ADDICTION COUNSELING

PERSONAL REFLECTIONS

The multicultural aspect of counseling has involved some of my best and worst experiences in my different roles as a counselor, educator, or trainer. My interest in multicultural counseling has only heightened over the years as I often heard and read the words of professionals describing this area in an almost euphoric, idealistic recall manner that makes it sound easy. Those descriptions are not my experiences as a counselor, an educator, or a trainer. Rather, I have found this area demands me to be brave because all of us, it seems, come to this area with our own baggage made up of our own mixed bag of personal and professional experiences that fall on a continuum of positive to negative. We also live in a time where, in the words of an experienced counselor in response to hearing my struggles to rewrite this chapter on multicultural counseling: "Everyone gets upset with these discussions and it is so hard to discuss these concerns because no one wins."

We need to have compassion for ourselves and our clients as we stumble bravely and honestly to build bridges across our differences while respecting those differences. This is an important, delicate balance that can be hard to find in an increasingly politically correct world that can inhibit honest, genuine interactions. Additionally, while we need to have high standards for ourselves in this area, when we come short of those standards, we need to address our mistakes and learn from them.

We know we cannot reach perfect multicultural counseling, but I believe we can make amazing progress in ourselves, our clients, and the world by "reaching for the stars." I have witnessed such progress in myself, clients, students, and trainees, which is why I believe that each of us can learn and grow and make a meaningful difference in our worlds. As I have said to my students: "It is a mess, but we are in it together."

OBJECTIVES

1. To learn an overall perspective on multicultural counseling and some techniques to facilitate multicultural counseling.
2. To become familiar with alcohol and drug use assessment, treatment, and aftercare issues as they relate to gender, ethnicity, sexual orientation, disability, and age (adolescents, the elderly).
3. To integrate an approach and techniques into assessment, treatment, and aftercare issues with regard to gender, ethnicity, sexual orientation, disability, and age.

"Culture is the sum total of a group's life ways" (el-Guebaly, 2008, p. 45). Cultural differences need to be valued, not feared (McFadden, 1999). Because our view of the world shapes how we assess and the action we take, counselors need to be aware, knowledgeable, and have skills of multicultural counseling to help clients (Lee, 2003). In an interview, Courtland Lee, a multicultural

302 CHAPTER 10 CULTURALLY SENSITIVE ADDICTION COUNSELING

counseling expert, described five cultures that influence each of our clients (Shallcross, 2013). The first is the *universal* culture of being a human being. The second is the *ecological* culture (way of life) that our geographical environments guide. The third is that humans live in different *countries* that have various "rules, regulations, customs, and laws" (p. 37) that must be followed. Fourth are *regional* differences within a country. The fifth is the *racioethnic* culture into which the client has been born. All five of these cultural influences need to be taken into account as the counselor approaches the client in establishing a therapeutic alliance and working in the client's best interest.

Therefore, counselors need to look at how people are alike (universal culture) and different at the same time (Edwards, Johnson, & Feliu, 2003). This cultural sensitivity is described by Lopez et al. (1989) in four stages of counselor development:

1. The counselor is unaware of cultural differences.

2. The counselor has increased awareness of the client's culture from his or her own perspective but may not see it from the client's view.

3. The counselor is hypervigilant in cultural considerations, yet may not see how the client's behavior is connected to culture.

4. The counselor is more culturally sensitive by developing hypotheses about behavior based on the client's culture but is also open to testing these hypotheses.

Multicultural counseling involves counseling strategies to build bridges between the cultural differences of counselor and client. This type of counseling can be very difficult because of the struggle to understand the world from a completely different viewpoint. A person's culture is often fused with who that person is as an individual.

Even for those people who have had cultural experiences different from those with whom they were originally exposed, it is difficult at times to understand how individuals think and act the way they do.

Multicultural counseling, then, involves specific challenges to the counselor. It requires the counselor to have an awareness of self, others, and different cultures, as well as to be flexible, open, perceptive, and willing to learn in order to build a bridge between the differences. It does not require counselors to personally give up their value systems to work with clients, but it does require counselors to know their limitations and then either "stretch" themselves or be willing to refer clients with whom they cannot work.

Because each person is a product of the culture in which he or she was raised, all counselors need to learn to work with individuals who are different from themselves. No one can be all things to all people. Three items are important to keep in mind with multicultural counseling. First, it may be more comfortable to work with people of some cultures than with others. No counselor can work with all individuals from all cultures equally well. Second, there is a danger that when a counselor learns things about different cultures, the counselor will end up stereotyping individuals based on what was learned about that culture. It is most important that the counselor hear the individual's story of what it was like for him or her to grow up in the United States (or another country) and then work within that viewpoint. Clients need to have their own cultural experiences heard by counselors. Third, some individuals are more comfortable going beyond the limits of their culture than others—more willing to learn and try ways of living that are outside of their cultural experience because of their personality or life experiences. This tendency applies to both counselors and their clients.

When working with culturally different individuals in counseling, then, the therapist must determine the clients' comfort levels for trying something different from what they have known. Initially, it may be more comfortable for clients to be exposed to counseling theories and techniques that fit well with their traditional cultures, but as they proceed in counseling, they may be willing to try something different. For example, a female client from an Asian culture may initially be most comfortable with client-centered counseling techniques in an individual setting, but as she progresses in counseling, she may become comfortable with joining a counseling group that is more confrontational in its style.

Multicultural counseling needs to be discussed in relation to addiction because addiction transcends many differences among people resulting in a subculture related to drugs. Addicted individuals belong to cultures that help define who they are and what they do (Reid & Kampfe, 2000). An example of the effectiveness of such sensitivity to culture in the addictions field is the prevention program "Keepin' it R.E.A.L." developed for urban middle-schoolers (National Institute on Drug Abuse [NIDA], 2003b).

Figure 10.1 describes an overall multicultural substance use/abuse counseling assessment and treatment guide that is an interactive, ongoing process. The reader may find it helpful in organizing the information presented in this chapter. This guide is an example of how a counselor may approach multicultural counseling while keeping in mind a substance abuse counseling perspective. The counselor can address what is not known about the client and his/her culture by: gathering information, obtaining formal training, consulting with colleagues, mentors, supervisors, etc. Again, it can be overwhelming to learn and integrate the multicultural and substance abuse counseling information available (information that is possibly conflicting and changing) as it relates to gender, race/ethnicity, sexual orientation, disability, and age (adolescents, the elderly) and the culture that accompanies these substance abusing populations. The counselor again needs to be aware of the need to pace oneself (remember: "Progress, not perfection") and address the areas in the diagram in terms of practical limitations on time, energy, and money.

A word of caution: Be wary about finding a pat formula for multicultural counseling. It is more feasible to develop a counseling approach that encourages an adaptive counseling style. In a recent multicultural training, a participant in my training talked with me confidentially about a difficult multicultural work situation he had experienced. He said, "I wanted to talk with you about this sticky situation because I wanted to know if there was something else, some 'magic formula' that could have happened to help the situation." I said, "There is no magic formula. This is the magic: We get into the mess and help/guide/support each other as best we can. *We*, you and I, create the 'magic formula' with our clients in the *context* of the situation through genuine, honest *dialogue* where we are humane and civilized with one another."

This chapter examines different aspects of multicultural counseling. First is an overview of multicultural counseling, followed by an examination of the impact of drug abuse and addiction on different groups. As in Chapters 5 and 6, each section is followed by a case study and exercise to facilitate understanding of the material. At the end of the chapter, three overall multicultural exploration exercises related to substance use/abuse are provided. The danger in writing a chapter of this nature is that it may further stereotypes for different populations. Therefore, the reader is encouraged to tentatively absorb the tendencies of these findings and use them *only* if they enhance the therapeutic relationship and promote the welfare of the client.

DEFINING MULTICULTURAL

One of the difficulties with multicultural counseling is that even the definitions vary. Here, *multicultural* is defined as working with differences. Differences, for example, may be in ethnicity or sexual orientation; whatever the context of the differences between client and counselor, the emphasis is on the fact that there are differences between the two.

Reid and Kampfe (2000) provide an excellent summary of the history of multicultural counseling. The authors state that it began seriously in the early 20th century as counselors examined the

Overall Clinical Focus: Welfare of the Client [determines priority of and approach for addressing issues]

Guiding Questions for each quadrant: "What approach gathers the most useful information?"
"What helps the person stay sober?"

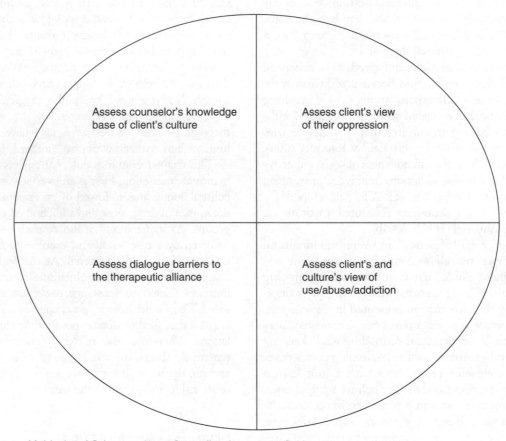

Figure 10.1   Multicultural Substance Abuse Counseling Assessment Guide.

needs of minority clients as it related to their vocation. In the 1950s, following legislation making segregation illegal, counselors focused on assimilating into mainstream America using techniques that came from a mainstream perspective with little or no success, because the client's cultural contexts were not considered. The 1964 Civil Rights Act opened discussions on how factors such as race influenced the therapeutic relationship, more counselor diversity resulted

in an openness to being more sensitive to diversity issues, increased cultural tolerance of differences was reflected in counseling, and desegregation of schools showed the deficiency of what was known about cross-cultural clients. The expansion of the definition of minority groups to women, gays/lesbians/bisexual/transgender, and disabled individuals occurred in the 1970s. In the 1980s and 1990s, multicultural counseling theory showed a refinement of the theory, because counselors who came from different cultures helped develop it, resulting in an increased sensitivity to culture. For example, Amodeo and Jones (1997) include regional, religious, social class, age, and resettlement differences in their multicultural perspective.

SOCIAL–ENVIRONMENTAL ASPECTS

One approach to developing multicultural counseling methods is to develop a culturally sensitive environmental framework. An excellent, classic environmental aspect framework was developed by Koss-Chioino and Vargas in 1992. This framework encourages counselors to take four areas into account when working with individuals from different cultures: poverty, racism (or "isms") and prejudice, acculturation, and normative behavior.

A counselor needs to be aware of these social-environmental aspects and the impact they may place on counseling. When a client is from a different culture, the counselor needs to be careful not to assume that he or she has the same cultural advantages as the counselor. It is equally important for the counselor to avoid assuming that the client has had fewer cultural advantages than the counselor. Even when the counselor and client have similar cultural experiences, it is necessary for the counselor to maintain an open-minded approach, allowing the client's story to emerge rather than making assumptions about the client. For example, even if two women working together in therapy are the same ethnicity and age, if they were raised in different parts of the United States, their perspectives on how a person should live and act in the world are probably quite different. A counselor assuming almost complete sameness between them as counselor and client could miss ways in which they are different, which in turn could affect the therapeutic alliance. Extreme assumptions about clients must be avoided.

The four socioenvironmental aspects (poverty, racism/prejudice, acculturation, normative behavior) are reviewed in the following section,

with some adaptations for working with addicted individuals. It is followed by a section on cultural diversity in America.

Poverty

Sometimes, different groups experience oppression along with their different cultural experiences. For example, women, people of color, and gays and lesbians may be oppressed as well as come from a different culture than that of the counselor. Women, for instance, who in their oppression have different cultural experience than that of men, often experience poverty as a part of their oppression. Ethnic minorities, the disabled, GLBT individuals, and the elderly often live below the poverty line (American Psychological Association, 2006). Oppressed groups of individuals often experience different struggles in conjunction with their societal status, such as poverty. "Concentrated poverty, after declining [in America] in the 1990s, swung back upward in the 2000s. Almost nine million people live in 'extreme poverty' neighborhoods" (Parry, 2012). Joblessness and the housing crisis have had significant impacts (Parry, 2012).

Jensen (2009) makes important points about poverty. First, even the word *poverty* has a tendency to elicit strong emotions and questions. Second, poverty is complex and is "a chronic and debilitating condition that results from multiple adverse synergistic risk factors and affects the mind, body, and soul" (Jensen, 2009, p. 6). Third, a problem created by poverty leads to another problem resulting in horrific consequences. For example, a lack of money may drive a parent to steal food for their children and result in their being arrested for stealing. Fourth, four risk factors need to be considered as possibly present for individuals and families living in poverty: emotional and social challenges, acute and chronic stressors, cognitive lags, and health and safety issues. Finally, the author identifies six types of poverty that may be helpful in assessing and addressing the poverty and its impact on counseling the individual, couple, and family living in poverty:

1. *Situational* (usually temporary and caused by sudden crisis or loss, i.e., divorce, health issues, disasters).

2. *Generational* (at least two generations where there is an absence of tools to help them move out of the poverty).

3. *Absolute* (focus is on daily survival due to a lack of necessities such as water, food, shelter).

4. *Relative* (insufficient income in terms of average living standards).

5. *Urban* (present in populations over 50,000 where stressors include issues such as crowding, violence, noise, and overtaxed services).

6. *Rural* (present in populations under 50,000 where stressors include service access, disability support, and educational opportunities).

Both the type and experience of poverty may have a significant impact on their treatment. For example, for a recovering individual to be referred to self-help groups in the community, the issue of not having transportation to such groups because of a lack of money may arise. This may be especially true for the client who lives in a rural setting. The reality of poverty, then, may have a significant effect on the individual's treatment plan and recovery process.

Isms and Prejudice

Individuals from different cultural groups may also experience an "ism" or prejudice about their status in the society. *Isms* is a term used here to summarize the prejudicial biases of individuals toward others. Oppressed individuals may be directly attacked physically or verbally for who they are, or they may experience systematic attacks by a system being organized around values that are unfamiliar to them. Discrimination is a chronic stressor for poor, racial/ethnic minority,

and female clients and has a negative effect on mental health (Lo & Cheng, 2012). For example, racism changes social status, creates barriers to receiving services, and causes both psychological and health problems that result in higher mortality (Lo & Cheng, 2012).

Experiencing these "isms" and prejudices may cause an individual to approach those who are considered mainstream with anger, bitterness, and distrust. If the counselor is considered mainstream by the client (e.g., by look, dress, or speech), then the counselor may find a need to stretch to assist the individual in trusting him or her. (The same may be true if the client is the one who is considered mainstream and the counselor is of the oppressed group.)

Additionally, clients may experience *internalized oppression*, which is the "mostly unconscious belief in the superiority of those more representative of the dominant culture" (Tisdell, 2003, p. 147). A Jewish mentor commented on a woman's internalized oppression: "You lost your wail; your song is a minor key, and you've been trying to fit into a major key" (Tisdell, 2003, p. 153). In response to this comment, the woman realized her internalized oppression: "I had learned to hate who I was, and I did not even know it" (Tisdell, 2003, p. 153).

Finally, in his classic work, Friere (1989) describes the concept of *horizontal violence*, where individuals of an oppressed group have internalized the oppression of the dominant culture and attack individuals of their same oppressed group, i.e., women attacking women as an expression of their internal hatred for being a woman.

These aspects of oppression (discrimination, internalized oppression, horizontal violence) need to be sensitively addressed in addiction counseling. They can influence the entire continuum of counseling (assessment, treatment, aftercare) with oppressed populations. Therefore, the counselor needs to be aware of these dynamics at all points on the continuum and determine, in terms of welfare of the client, how and when to address such concerns. For example, in the assessment process, the discrimination experienced by the client may make it difficult to trust the counselor with the truth about one's use—such mistrust may again emerge in the treatment and aftercare process when a relapse occurs. The counselor may also need to carefully invite the client to examine how aspects such as horizontal violence may impact the client's recovery process, i.e., women having difficulty trusting other women.

Acculturation

With regard to acculturation, a model of integration breaks cultural contact status into four areas. These areas are: *assimilation* (no desire to maintain cultural identity), *separation* (maintain cultural identity), *marginalization* (little interest in being involved in the dominant culture), and *integration or biculturalism* (maintain cultural identity and be involved in dominant culture also) (Berry, 2002). Addicted clients, who belong to oppressed populations, can fall into any one of these four areas. A counselor needs to be aware of where the client falls on the continuum of acculturation. A counselor also needs to be sensitive about the amount of encouragement given in developing the client's cultural identity, i.e. such a level of processing too early in recovery may need to occur after the client has some stable time in recovery (Mohatt, Allen, & Thomas, 2007). Such encouragement may be facilitated by counselor understanding of the different acculturation models.

Earlier acculturation models looked at how the person assimilates into the dominant culture. These were theoretical models that described a person's involvement in their culture and how the marginalized group was influenced by the dominant culture (Valentine-Barrow, Adcock, & Jenkins, 2011). In contrast, *unilinear* models viewed the person as leaving their cultural practices to incorporate new ones (Valencia & Johnson, 2008). Additional models of acculturation summarized by Valentine-Barrow, Adcock, and Jenkins (2011) are: *bidimensional* (person is highly involved in both cultures), *bilinear* (rituals and practices are exchanged between both cultures), and *orthogonal* (acculturation is independent with its own factors and changes that may/may not impact the culture).

A perspective on where the client/culture is regarding acculturation (theoretical, unilinear, bidimensional, bilinear, orthogonal) may assist the counselor in helping the client develop a healthy cultural identity. For example, in terms of their substance use, addicted individuals may be, as outlined in the unilinear model, leaving their cultural practices regarding alcohol/drug use through either the entry into or the exit from the active addiction. The client may start using alcohol/drugs that breaks him or her away from a culture that prohibits all use of alcohol/drugs. Or, clients, by becoming sober, may be breaking away from their culture that encourages substance abuse. The counselor who understands this may need to assist clients, then, into reconnecting with their healthy culture-of-origin practices that support the recovery process or helping them disengage from unhealthy culture-of-origin practices that inhibit their recovery process.

Individuals who are considered outside of the mainstream may also have difficulty adjusting to the predominant cultural values to which they are exposed. It may be helpful to ask these individuals who they identify with in order to understand how they may be feeling alienated. Even individuals who have "made it" may struggle with these issues, because they may believe that somehow they have sold out and/or that they have missed specific things because of their standing outside of the mainstream culture.

In terms of substance use and abuse, this is where the messages that clients have received from the culture with which they identify can impact their approach to assessment, treatment, and aftercare. They may believe, for example, from their cultural identification, that if they only had a strong enough belief in God, they would not have any difficulties with alcohol and drugs. This strong belief may make it difficult for them to receive professional assistance throughout the continuum of treatment. If a counselor has an awareness of the clients' view and their culture's view of substance use and abuse, this can assist in the process of providing help to them in a manner that feels respectful to their views.

Normative Behavior

Acculturation also brings up the issue of normative behavior. What is normal? What is typical for the environment in which an individual lives? How much of an adjustment should a person be required to make to fit in? These difficult questions need to be examined at the onset of counseling, yet easy answers may not emerge. However, counselors who examine these concepts increase their chances that they will be free of cultural biases about normative behavior. What are the differences between what the client and the counselor consider as normative behavior? The counselor needs to assist the client in being aware of these issues and then determine at what level the client wants or needs to adjust to these pressures. Some clients may be more flexible in terms of adjusting to different environments, whereas others will refuse to do so. It is important for client welfare that the client be exposed to a continuum of options and feel empowered to choose the best option(s).

As stated previously, it is important to understand the normative views of the client and their culture with regard to substance use and abuse. These views may make assessment, treatment, and aftercare an even more complicated process for both the counselor and the client if they are not named and addressed in the counseling process.

American History of Cultural Diversity

Murphy (1995) wrote a humorous article about the ease of forming opinions of others based on a lack of knowledge. He reports that the American Jewish Committee once included a group called Wisians (a nonexistent group) in an attitude survey. About 40% of survey respondents gave opinions on this nonexistent group. The author concludes that possibly what humans need is a nonexistent "scapegroup" for our negative projections on others—a scapegroup that could help meet our judgmental needs but not be harmful to any specific group.

Schwarz (1995) reports that the United States has a diversity myth that it promotes internationally.

This is the myth that there is a long history of tolerance and harmony in the United States regarding different cultures. Schwarz attacks the myth with examples about race, ethnicity, and North–South differences. This history of oppression toward specific cultural groups, such as racial minorities and gay and lesbian populations (Vacc, DeVaney, & Wittmer, 1995), has resulted in negative experiences among specific U.S. cultural groups. Minority groups are discriminated against and then blamed for their social conditions that stem from the discrimination (e.g., victim blaming; Atkinson & Hackett, 2004). Therefore, counselors working with different cultural groups need to understand the history of that group's experience in the United States to provide some perspective for the struggles of different individuals in counseling.

This myth of diversity and the need to understand the history of a group's experience is discussed in a recent interview with Dr. Ronald Takaki, a multicultural expert (Adams & Welsch, 2007). In this interview, Dr. Takaki states that diversity is America's manifest destiny. What this means is that there needs to be a dignity given to our differences. In this approach, our differences are recognized, appreciated, and accepted, thereby enriching all of us. With regard to substance use and abuse, the uniqueness of the clients and their culture needs to be respected in order to instill or reinstall a sense of dignity to the individual no matter what they have done in the course of their substance use and abuse.

BREAKDOWN OF COMMUNICATION

If an individual is from an oppressed group, it may be more difficult to establish sincere communication lines between the client and the counselor. The history of negative experiences may make it much easier to distrust than to work on a relationship with each other. This may be true regardless of whether the counselor or the client is from an oppressed group.

The breakdown of communication often seems to be based on schemata. *Schemata* means the systems of knowledge a person has about certain areas, such as types of people and situations (Mook, 1987). One type of schemata is person schemata, where the impressions of a group of people are overly simple, rigid, and generalized (e.g., stereotypes). Personal and social experiences are used as the sources of information about a group of individuals, and then that fixed knowledge of information is used to judge current experiences with individuals from that group (Fiske & Taylor, 1983). Simply stated, a person is caught in stereotypes of individuals from that group. Barriers to multicultural counseling include such stereotypes that reflect a difference in values between counselor and client; counselor stereotypes of clients (including misdiagnoses); counselor ethnocentrism, lack of awareness of own culture, and both counselor and client resistance (Hays & Erford, 2014).

Multicultural counseling requires the therapist to examine his or her perceptions of others and listen carefully to their stories to determine whether he or she is typecasting others. To prevent the limitation of stereotypes, therapists must accommodate their beliefs about an individual to new information received about the person. This typecasting requires heightened attention by the substance abuse counselor because in addition to the stereotypes of the oppressed population, the counselor may also have stereotypes of how and why that population uses and abuses certain drugs as well as their chances for recovering from their use, abuse, or addiction.

MULTICULTURAL COMPETENCE/ MULTICULTURAL ORIENTATION

Multicultural competence means that the counselor has awareness, knowledge, and skills that allow for "work with others who are culturally different from self in meaningful, relevant, and productive ways" (Pope, Reynolds, & Mueller, 2004, p. 14).

Historically, Atkinson, Morten, and Sue (1993) report that to develop cross-cultural competence, counselors must examine their own attitudes, beliefs, knowledge, and skills in terms of awareness of their own cultural values and biases, awareness of the client's worldview, and intervention strategies that fit the client's culture. Also, Cross, Bazron, Dennis, and Isaacs (1989) developed a similar framework where the counselor can be culturally incompetent, culturally sensitive, or culturally competent in terms of cognitive, affective, and skills dimensions, with overall effects ranging from destructive, neutral, and constructive, respectively. In this latter framework, the culturally competent counselor is knowledgeable (cognitive), committed to change (affective), highly skilled (skill), and has a constructive effect on the counseling.

More currently, D. W. Sue and Sue (2013) state that a critical component of cultural competency means that the counselor explore and discuss intense emotions related to sociodemographics because those emotions may block us from hearing our clients who are oppressed. In Shallcross' (2013) interviews with multicultural counseling experts, various aspects of multicultural competence were raised. Coker states: "The bottom line is that you can't grow up in a racist, sexist, homophobic, etc., society and not have vestiges of it yourself. All human beings do. But it's what we do with that knowledge and those feelings that are the keys to being a very effective counselor" (p. 34). Another expert, Mariska, encourages counselors to have a basic curiosity about their clients that is echoed in Lee's following statement: "Cultural competency is best achieved by standing in the other person's shoes." Pope cautions: "'competent' implies that they are complete, finished" and instead advocates the view of counseling as a jigsaw puzzle where the more puzzle pieces the counselor has about the client, the more effective the counselor can be in session.

SAMHSA (2000a) provides standards on providers of mental health counseling in terms of knowledge, understanding, skills, and attitudes specifically with four underserved/underrepresented groups (African Americans, Hispanics, Native Americans/Alaska Natives, Asian/Pacific Islander Americans). These competencies include knowledge and/or skills in these 10 areas:

1. Client population background

2. Clinical issues

3. Appropriate treatment

4. Role of the agency/provider

5. Communication skills

6. Quality assessment

7. Quality care and treatment plan formulation and implementation

8. Quality treatment provision

9. Counselor use of self and knowledge in treatment

10. Counselor attitude that is respectful and open to working with others different from self

Whichever theoretical framework is adopted to encourage a multicultural counseling approach, the goal is for the counselor to develop a capacity to work with individuals who are different from him or her. As discussed previously, Shallcross (2013) interviewed various multicultural counseling experts and summarized their views that focused on the overall goal of achieving multicultural counseling competence. The main theme emerging from these interviews was that counselors need to constantly work, throughout their careers, on studying and developing themselves in this area. In this article, one expert, Brooks, suggested that multicultural competence be viewed like professional certification where one obtains it and then has to *maintain* it. Another expert, Bemak, stated that the American Counseling Association division of the Association of Multicultural Counseling and Development has established baseline multicultural counseling competencies for counselor training that have advanced the counseling field; yet, a possible

limitation to multicultural counseling is that these competencies may be applied in a superficial manner that does not incorporate the complex, deep multicultural issues that emerge. Bemak advocated "authentic, honest discussions—not politically correct discussions. We have to take risks and be honest with each other in talking about these issues of diversity and race. We need to get it on the table rather than brushing over it" (p. 33). We need to look at the development of ourselves as being multiculturally competent from the perspective of having an ongoing commitment to learning and being willing to have deep and genuine humane discussions and interactions in this area. The following section discusses some pragmatic approaches to facilitate multicultural counseling.

Typically mental health professional organizations, such as the American Psychological Association, encourage multicultural competencies (MCCs) in four areas: education, training, research, and practice (*Clinician's Research Digest*, 2013). A recent shift in this area is to *multicultural orientation* (MCO) as summarized in the September issue of the *Clinician's Research Digest* (2013). This term means that the counselor's "*way of doing*" (knowledge/skills necessary for working with diversity) is augmented by a "*way of being*" (counselor humility is combined with an other-oriented focus). This means that no matter what level of expertise the counselor has in the multicultural area, the counselor needs to demonstrate *cultural humility* in the interpersonal relationship with each client by "asking questions when uncertain and expressing curiosity about clients' backgrounds, experiences, and worldviews" (*Clinician's Research Digest*, 2013, p. 5). Although it may be especially helpful with clients who come from a different culture, it can also be useful with clients in general because it breaks up cultural assumptions the counselor may make about the client and instead encourage counselors to collaborate with their clients with regard to their cultural experience. For example, it may be a powerful therapeutic alliance bridge when counselor and client come from different genders; however, it may be just as useful of an approach when counselor and client come from the same gender. The tenets of a respectful curiosity shown the client communicates a desire to understand the world from the client's perspective. As curiosity is described by Waehler (2013): "Usually each client has so many different life variables that I am endlessly intrigued by the unique combination that have become intertwined within each client's life" (p. 352). The author goes on to state: "When I have a better understanding of my client's worldview and cultural assumptions, I begin to shape an experience of a 'different' culture, one construed intentionally (by me) in a way that will invite this client to be more reflective of who she/he is and the choices that she/he makes (and can choose to *not* make)" (p. 353).

An instrument counselors may use to measure the concept of *cultural humility* is the Cultural Humility Scale, a 12-item scale used by the client to rate the counselor (Hook, Davis, Owen, Worthington, & Utsey, 2013). While early in its development, this scale has shown good reliability and construct validity across three sample populations.

In terms of substance abuse counseling, counselors need to be committed to multicultural competence by having an ongoing commitment to staying current on the types of drugs used and the pattern of use by specific oppressed populations. They also need to stay current on effective prevention, assessment, treatment, and aftercare interventions with these populations. Regarding multicultural orientation, the counselor needs to remember that no matter how much they know about the client's cultural group(s) and addiction, each client needs to be approached humbly with a respect for them as a unique human within their culture that includes their experience in the drug culture.

DIALOGUE

Again, in his classic work, Friere (1989) describes dialogue as different from a communiqué where one person is above another without empathy; rather, dialogue is a horizontal relationship between two people who are empathically joined in a search. Burbules (1993) describes the necessary components of dialogues as respect, concern, interest, commitment, open participation (nonauthoritarian), continuous, developmentally sequenced, and exploratory and interrogative in nature. Oakeshott (1991) describes dialogue as conversation that lacks debate, does not attempt to discover the truth, is taken at face value, is unrehearsed, and is intellectual as well as rich in both seriousness and playfulness.

All of these definitions of dialogue combined indicate that it is a process where two individuals are involved. A counselor attempting to work within a multicultural context needs to be able and willing to create a dialogue-friendly atmosphere so schemata and stereotypes do not dominate the direction of the sessions and yet issues are openly discussed. Counselor *broaching* means that the counselor invites a counseling environment of emotional safety where counselor and client can move from superficiality to intimacy in order to have a relationship where race, ethnicity, and cultural implications for the client can be openly discussed in dialogue (Day-Vines et al., 2007). Broaching looks at how sociopolitical factors impact the concerns the client brings to counseling; how cultural meaning becomes attached to phenomena. The responsibility for inviting such dialogue falls to the counselor; the counselor who shows an openness to explore diversity in sessions can help clients be empowered, feel even more connected to the counselor, and have improved outcomes.

How can a counselor create a dialogue-friendly atmosphere? Initially, it is helpful for the counselor to be aware of differences between himself or herself and the client. As stated previously, it is beneficial if the therapist has knowledge of the culture in which the client lives and the impact of that culture on the client's life. This awareness of potential or explicit differences will assist the counselor in maintaining an openness to learning about the client rather than relying on stereotypes.

In addition, interpersonal factors such as genuineness, empathy, and unconditional positive regard (Rogers, 1987) can establish a solid baseline from which the therapist can work in counseling. If a client believes the counselor is genuine, empathic to the client's struggles, and holds a positive view of the client, many differences can be bridged. Chung and Bemak (2002) provide 10 dimensions to developing cultural empathy with a client:

1. Being genuinely interested in the culture.

2. Having some awareness of the client's culture.

3. Appreciating cultural differences in the client.

4. Including culture as a part of treatment.

5. Understanding the dynamics of family and community.

6. Including indigenous healing components in treatment.

7. Knowing the history of the client's cultural group (including sociopolitical).

8. Knowing adjustments that had to be made psychologically in a move to another culture.

9. Being sensitive to ongoing discrimination experienced by the client.

10. Focusing on empowering the client.

Some specific suggestions on enhancing dialogue when communicating with clients who are not familiar with the "mainstream culture and language" being used by the counselor and/or the treatment agency are offered by Prince and Hoppe (2000, pp. 20–22) who developed guidelines for business:

• Speak clearly and a little more slowly than you usually do.

• Use an even tone of voice.

• Pronounce your words clearly and enunciate carefully.

• Use the simplest and most common words in most cases.

• Avoid slang and colloquial expressions.

• Use stories and analogies that are universally understood.

• Use inclusive language and avoid terms and labels that may be offensive.

• Be aware of language uses in other cultures.

• Use simple language and complete thoughts when writing to a person from another culture.

• Pay special attention to language during phone calls and when leaving voice mail messages.

Also note that there may be differences in the dialectic of the English-language and the nonverbal social language behavior (Mohatt et al., 2007).

Another important factor is the role the counselor takes at a critical moment in therapy: Is the counselor a compassionate authority individual or a critical one? This role is also discussed in Chapter 13 in relation to organizational dynamics. In multicultural counseling, there are invariably places of conflict and differences. What is important is the approach taken by the counselor at those times. Rather than focusing the blame on someone for the event, which is the stance of the critical authority individual, it is more important that the counselor focus on what has occurred and its impact on the client and the counseling relationship. A sincere apology for the misunderstanding between the counselor and client can deeply facilitate the therapeutic relationship. In addition, a careful, thoughtful, respectful processing of the event can assist clients in trusting the counselor in therapy and learning about patterns of their own behavior.

So-called commonsense approaches are also helpful in therapy. Asking a client "What would you like to be called?" for example, in terms of identification of ethnicity, or sexual orientation and then remembering to use that term is respectful. Also, gently and respectfully asking a client who is the only member of a specific group or culture, "What is it like to be the only ____ in this place?" is helpful. If it seems inappropriate to ask, the counselor may simply want to use these questions to guide the counseling process. Finally, when there is a disagreement or conflict of some type, the counselor may not know what occurred that caused the client to withdraw; however, the counselor may feel a qualitative shift in the therapeutic relationship. This experience can be described as a glass wall that drops down between the counselor and the client. The client may or may not appear engaged with the counselor, but it feels to the counselor that he or she has been shut out. At that point, it is necessary for the counselor to ask, "What happened here?" to learn what may have been offensive or alienating to the client. Note that Achara-Abrahams et al. (2013, p. 269) offer a trauma-sensitive phrase "such as 'what happened to you?' rather than 'what's wrong with you?'" These general approaches can simply be invitations by the counselor. The counselor can be responsible only for the effort, not the outcome. The client may have the understandable response of not wanting to educate the counselor about his or her opinions on how to be treated as part of his or her cultural group. However, many clients may respond to a sincere human outreach that is asking for assistance in how to treat a client with respect.

The danger for all counselors in multicultural counseling is experiencing a lack of compassion based on ignorance and fear. To operate out of ignorance and fear not only limits the counseling but also is hurtful to the client. When counseling struggles appear to be based in cultural differences, the counselor needs to process the struggle carefully with the client. It is helpful to take a deep breath and then proceed into the dialogue about the conflict with honesty, setting limits, and taking time to discuss the issues. The conflict and discussion need to be personal. At this point in the encounter, the counselor needs to show his or her humanness. The amount of disclosure required may vary from counselor to counselor, but what is most necessary is that the client feel the counselor's willingness to hear about the conflict and the counselor's commitment to attempt to work through it.

I have found it helpful in high-stress multicultural situations where emotions are intense to: (1) stay calm (examine what I am afraid of and work at calming myself down), (2) set a few, simple limits (for example, let go of a time frame and be committed to staying with the process until the situation is calmer by cancelling/rescheduling/reassigning other appointments or responsibilities), and (3) encourage/model/practice self-care (examine my thoughts, feelings, and behaviors and respond to them in a self-compassionate manner). Additionally, I "name" the problem (stating it is present and my perception of it), make "I" statements, and focus on behaviors (mine and the client's/clients'). My overall approach is to slow down reactions (mine and the client's/clients') in order to invite behavior that is thoughtful rather than emotionally reactive. Sometimes it is more helpful to contain the emotions until a time or setting where everyone is calmer rather than process the emotional reactions at such a highly charged time.

While not specifically addressed as relating to substance abuse counseling, each of the areas discussed previously (dialogue, therapeutic alliance, language [communication] enhancement, compassion, commonsense approaches, and a calm approach) are critical in substance abuse counseling. As discussed in Chapter 5, addicts typically have difficulty with authority figures, trust, emotional reactivity, and impulse control. Such aspects can have a strong impact on multicultural counseling where differences are already present—these differences can easily be exacerbated until they spiral out of control. This is why the substance abuse counselor needs to keep these approaches at the forefront of the overall counseling as well as the following section on general counseling suggestions.

GENERAL COUNSELING SUGGESTIONS

Counselors who desire to be sensitive and effective with individuals from other cultures need to be aware of several areas. First, they must be aware of their own cultures and how that affects their life. Second, they need to be aware of the social-environmental aspects that may be experienced by some groups, including the history of treatment of these groups in the United States. Third, counselors need to work at continually creating a dialogue-friendly atmosphere to facilitate counseling across different cultures.

It may be helpful for a counselor to use a framework such as *broaching* to assess his or her comfort level in discussing multicultural issues with clients. In this framework, there are five counselor broaching styles: *avoidant* (minimize differences), *isolating* (simple, superficial), *continuing/incongruent* (limited empowering skills), *integrated/congruent* (part of professional identity), and *infusing* (a way of being in the world) (Day-Vines et al., 2007). Such self-examination can lead the counselor to examine through supervision, mentoring, or with colleagues ways to develop more professionally in order to enhance dialogue in session with clients.

As Edwards et al. (2003) state, counselors need to be respectful in differences and similarities, empathic to struggles, and patient with issues such as reimbursement, session limits, and speed of problem resolution. Fourteen specific multicultural counseling suggestions follow:

1. Provide a respectful, open environment, particularly concerning cultural differences.

2. Be flexible.

3. Be an expert in the field of counseling, but not in the clients' lives.

4. Establish a relationship of trust with a client. Do not pretend you know what you do not know.

5. Remember that a person can be a part of several cultures at one time.

6. Say, "I do not know what it is like to be . . . ."

7. Ask clients to teach you what you do not know.

8. Do not create issues, but address them if they arise.

9. Do not fight with people, but respond to their statements; do not let things go by.

10. Share your own experience of a communication breakdown if it occurs.

11. Apologize when you are wrong.

12. Learn how to deal with people who do not like you.

13. Turn to other counselors for support.

14. Remember the commonalities among all people.

ASSESSMENT, TREATMENT, AND AFTERCARE ISSUES

Amodeo and Jones (1997) discuss the importance of looking at addiction within the culture of the client and present a framework for assessment of use that covers five areas pertaining to the client's culture:

1. The general attitudes/values/behavior connected to use.

2. Determination of criteria that defines use as a problem, the consequences for it, the responsibility for it, and how it may be enabled or hidden.

3. When and where help is sought as well as reinforcers for change.

4. Culture-specific relapse and consequences for it.

5. Who is thought of as successful and when an intervention is successful.

These five areas should be kept in mind as gender, race/ethnicity, sexual orientation, disability, and age (adolescents, the elderly) are discussed within the area of addiction. El-Guebaly (2008) recommends doing a cultural assessment of clients to learn their subjective view of the world, the illness's meaning to them, and recovery expectations they have. This assessment includes cultural identity, explanation of the illness, social stressors and supports, as well as similarities and differences culturally between the professional and the client, in order to understand factors such as transference and countertransference. Awareness of cultural factors can enhance treatment (Westermeyer, 2009). Finding out who the client's role models were around alcohol/drug use, how the client was socialized into using, early use experiences, and if use was linked to developmental tasks (i.e., recreation, dating, etc.) can facilitate the treatment process.

It may be helpful here to review Lee's five-culture framework as adapted to addiction counseling (Shallcross, 2013). Our addicted clients are a part of the *universal* culture in that they are human beings. Therefore, they need to be treated with care and respect no matter what they have done in the process of their addiction. Second, we need to understand their *ecological* culture (way of life) that their geographical environments guide. For example, how has "living on the streets" impacted their behavior in terms of trust and survival that can spill over into their treatment process? Third, the "rules, regulations, customs, and laws" (p. 37) of the country (countries) in which they have used drugs may have an impact on their treatment. An example is a client who is determined as noncompliant in a treatment facility (i.e., has relapsed) may be required to go to prison if discharged from the facility. Finally, *racioethnic* culture into which the client has been born can impact the entire treatment process as outlined in Figure 10.1. Again, these cultural influences need to be taken into account as the counselor approaches the client in establishing a therapeutic alliance and working in the client's

best interest specifically within the context of the continuum of addiction counseling.

Some final, overall comments need to be made here before advancing to the specific populations. First, the "isms" experienced by the client may make recovery harder, but they are not an excuse to use. Second, compassionate accountability needs to be practiced here: the counselor needs to name the wrong of the "ism" with the client and address it as a part of the recovery process, i.e. how it is handled by the client. Third, the client, unfortunately, needs to examine how to work with the "ism" in recovery as a part of a relapse prevention plan, but with a focus that it is inherently wrong, unjust, and yet, cannot be allowed to take the client "under." Finally, while addiction complicates multicultural counseling, it does not make recovery impossible or improbable, but simply requires the counselor to be even more committed to assisting the client in developing internal and external resources to address the reality of the discrimination the client may or does experience. One of these resources oppressed groups sometimes find helpful is a spiritual dimension that is discussed in Chapter 12. Such a dimension to recovery sometimes provides our clients with an oasis of support in living with the discrimination and oppression they experience. All of these suggestions need to be tentatively and sensitively applied to counseling especially if the "ism" experienced was at the hands of the same population to which the counselor belongs in terms of gender, race/ethnicity, sexual orientation, disability, and age. This sensitivity is powerfully captured in the statement made by an African-American woman to a Caucasian woman in a "talking stick" circle: "[I am sorry] . . . that someone who looks like me has caused you so much pain" (Tisdell, 2003, p. 224).

Reading the following sections can be depressing because of the harsh statistics and the barriers to assessment, treatment, and aftercare that each of these groups uniquely face. It may be necessary for the reader to practice self-care (as discussed in Chapter 13) by reading small sections at a time and taking breaks. It may also be overwhelming because of the amount of information presented on the different groups. The reader is encouraged to look at this section in the book as a reference section that can be used when working with an individual from that population rather than absorbing all of the content areas presented at once.

Gender

Before discussing the different ways that assessment, treatment, and aftercare need to shift to enhance treatment of addicted women, it is necessary to review historically important research on women's ways of relating to others. It is also important to keep in mind that there is little research that has been done on alcoholic women (Thurang, Fagerberg, Palmstierna, & Bengtsson, 2010).

A woman develops and has life experiences within her relationships (J. B. Miller, 1986). J. B. Miller (1976) describes a woman's sense of self as being organized around her relationships: making and maintaining them. This sense of connectedness leads to a woman's sense of herself as well as her moral views (Surry, 1985). A woman's self, then, is organized and developed within important relationships in her life (Surry, 1985). Furthermore, it is as important for a woman to be understood by the significant others in her life as it is for her to understand them. The mutuality of relationships is the basis for the individual woman's growth and awareness (Surry, 1985). McClelland (1975) defines power for a woman as having the strength and capacity to care for and give to others in her life. Van der Walde, Urgenson, Weltz, and Hanna (2002) state that this perspective on women's relationships includes both how society and the individual woman views herself. The typical stereotypes of female addicts have been described as the "pathology and powerlessness" story: Women are viewed as pathological (promiscuous/lazy/selfish) or powerless (weak/scared/trapped) (Anderson, 2008). Asking a woman simply at any stage of the recovery process (intake, assessment, treatment, aftercare), "What are people in your life

saying about you with regard to your use?" can unfold core stories and emotional reactions to the stigma and barriers she may be experiencing.

Considering this viewpoint of women's development, a woman in the different phases of treatment needs to be viewed with an awareness of her relationships with others in terms of her self-development and her sense of power. For example, a woman may have difficulty during an assessment (e.g., telling the truth about her chemical usage for fear that it may have an impact on the raising of her children). During the treatment phase, she may have difficulty concentrating on treatment concerns because she is worried about loved ones in her life. Finally, during aftercare, a woman may have difficulty thinking about what is best for her because she is concerned about the well-being of those she loves. Counseling with women, then, may need to focus on her multiple identities, consciousness-raising, an equal therapeutic relationship, and assistance in learning to value and validate themselves (Forrest, 2004).

Also important in terms of treatment is helping the woman organize her recovery around some treatment guidelines based in this developmental perspective. The recovery process needs to be made personal for her, in the context of her relationships, in a manner that makes sense to her. She may not see a reason for sobering up for herself, but she may see a reason in sobering up for the sake of those individuals she loves. She may be able to stay with the recovery process more if she is both confronted *and* supported, at the same time, by her counselor; this encourages her to look at her issues within the context of a professionally therapeutic, supportive relationship. She may also be able to stay involved in the recovery process better if she develops a social network of important relationships with individuals who are meaningful to her and to her recovery.

Some therapists believe that a woman needs to connect with other women as early as possible in order to stay sober. These connections are important for women in recovery in order to address the issues of sexism as they arise. As discussed previously, chemically dependent women are stigmatized because they (a) are alcoholic, therefore, are immoral or their addiction is their fault; (b) are measured against higher moral standards than men; and (c) experience sexual stigma related to their chemical usage (e.g., they are promiscuous) (S. B. Blume, 1997). These stereotypes can evidence themselves in the daily lives of women alcoholics in various ways. For example, the stereotype of being promiscuous may place a woman at a higher risk for being sexually assaulted or raped (van der Walde et al., 2002).

Such stigma may be best understood by another recovering chemically dependent woman. However, sometimes women sober up with such a high mistrust of other women that the only individuals they will listen to are males. This mistrust may emerge from negative experiences with other women due to competing with them for drugs, money, or intimate partners, or negative experiences in general with other women. A counselor needs to reflect on the importance of whether the woman hears the message of recovery no matter who delivers it or whether the individual delivering it is more important than the message. This is not a dichotomous clinical choice that needs to remain constant through a woman's recovery process. It may be more pragmatic initially to engage the woman in a therapeutic relationship where she trusts the individual, male or female, and then during her recovery process, encourage her to rely on the support of other females who understand the sexism she may face in the general culture and/or in the recovering community in which she lives.

A qualitative study provided support for the following theoretical and research statements regarding women that can guide the assessment and treatment process (Thurang et al., 2010):

- Caring treatment (meaning kind, dignified, professional, and welcoming) results in a decreased sense of disgrace and an increase in self-confidence.

- Caring is an exchange between the client and the counselor where the client both lets go of responsibility (allows treatment to occur) and takes on responsibility (accepts responsibility for one's recovery process).

- Immediate access to help and regular meetings are important.

- Adjustment of care to the woman's needs; listening seriously to her; being emotionally sensitive, open and honest with her all result in decreased shame/disgrace and increased self-esteem.

- Provision of a medical diagnosis and treatment for the disease results in lessened feelings of disgrace, loneliness, and guilt.

- Counselor view of the woman as an "important human being" (p. 703).

- Assistance in developing a new "family" and taking control over and establishing a regular routine in her life are important.

- Conversations between counselor and client and a sense of mutual responsibility are beneficial.

Assessment

Results from the 2011 National Survey on Drug Use and Health state the rate for substance dependence or abuse in females aged 12 or older was 5.7% (alcohol and illicit drug use) (SAMSHA, 2012). Zweben (2009) points out that we know more about the biomedical effects of alcohol than illicit drugs on women. In terms of alcohol, men have a greater tendency to drink and drink more than women, but women are more vulnerable to the harmful effects of alcohol (Harvard Medical School Special Report, 2008).

Pape (1993) states that addiction is a serious problem among women, who are often treated disparagingly for becoming addicted. Women who are addicted are more likely to have used substances to cope with negative emotions, needed help earlier for emotional problems, attempted suicide, and during childhood internalized their struggles (Haseltine, 2000). The author also states that women use to decrease stress and self-medicate, and in comparison with males, they have less money and family support and are more likely to have employment and family problems and have a partner who drinks. In addition, they have inadequate insurance and treatment resources, as well as many unknowns in the research about women and addiction (Straussner & Brown, 2002). Fifteen known facts about women and addiction are:

1. Because women have more fat, they absorb alcohol faster and become intoxicated more quickly on the same amount of alcohol as a male (Harvard Medical School Special Report, 2008a; S. Johnson, 1991; van der Walde et al., 2002).

2. Women taking birth control pills have higher blood alcohol levels when drinking because the liver metabolizes both the pills and the alcohol (M. K. Jones & Jones, 1984).

3. Women have more pure alcohol enter their bloodstream because of differences in the stomach's capacity to oxidize alcohol, production of less alcohol dehydrogenase, the enzyme that breaks alcohol down (Frezza et al., 1990; Harvard Medical School Special Report, 2008a; van der Walde et al., 2002).

4. Women develop alcohol dependency more quickly than men (telescopic effect; Brady & Back, 2008; Harvard Medical School Special Report, 2008a).

5. Women do not need to use as much alcohol for as long a time as men to develop alcohol-related physical consequences (Harvard Medical School Special Report, 2008a; Pape, 1993; Thurang et al., 2010) and are more at risk for developing cirrhosis of the liver (Harvard Medical School Special Report, 2008a; van der Walde et al., 2002).

6. Alcoholic women have more gynecological problems than nonalcoholic women (Wilsnack,

1973), specifically when in childbearing age, that is, "infertility, miscarriage, spontaneous abortion, and fetal alcohol syndrome and effects" (van der Walde et al., 2002).

7. Women may begin drinking alcohol heavily because of a specific circumstance or stressor; they may use to self-medicate (Jamison, Butler, Budman, Edwards, & Wasan, 2010; Straussner, 1985; van der Walde et al., 2002).

8. Women are more likely to come from families with a history of alcoholism (Harvard Medical School Special Report, 2008a; Pape, 1993).

9. Many women who abuse alcohol have a history of sexual abuse (Harvard Medical School Special Report, 2008a; Hurley, 1991; Orrok, 1992; van der Walde et al., 2002), physical abuse in adulthood (Harvard Medical School Special Report, 2008a), and abuse/trauma/relationship problems (Magnusson et al., 2012).

10. Women are more likely to attempt suicide (Pape, 1993; Thurang et al., 2010).

11. The majority of tranquilizers, antidepressants, and amphetamines are prescribed for women (D. J. Davis, 1990; Simoni-Wastila & Strickler, 2004).

12. Women may be more susceptible to cognitive problems related to drinking (Harvard Medical School Special Report, 2008a; van der Walde et al., 2002).

13. There may be higher sexual dysfunction (due to trauma) before using as well as sexual ambivalence, leading women to use alcohol as a way of helping them be sexual (van der Walde et al., 2002), but it is difficult to know whether this is the antecedent or consequence of using.

14. Women tend to be overly responsible, view themselves as causing problems others have, deny their needs, and internalize pain (van der Walde et al., 2002), with alcoholic, married

women and mothers having more guilt and shame than men in similar situations (Angove & Fothergill, 2003).

15. Risk factors for substance abuse in women include emotional problems and psychiatric comorbidity (Thurang et al., 2010; Zilberman, 2009).

Finally, when compared to abstinent or moderate-drinking women, heavy-drinking women have increased chances of osteoporosis, premature menopause, infertility/miscarriage, hypertension, and cardiovascular disease (Harvard Medical School Special Report, 2008a). Also, alcohol use in general may increase a woman's chance to develop breast cancer (Harvard Medical School Special Report, 2008a).

The National Institute on Drug Abuse (NIDA, 2002) found that women may be more sensitive to drug rewards and that struggles with psychosocial factors (abuse, depression, PTSD, significant other relationships, partner violence) may have a strong role in why women begin and continue to use. Also, women who abuse substances tend to be unmarried, be unemployed, have a history of abuse, struggle with self-esteem and a sense of powerlessness, and begin drinking in response to a relationship crisis (Kohn, 2002). Women may start abusing substances because of male partners' influence (Bright, Ward, & Negi, 2011).

Spelman (1988) states that gender is mixed with race, class, and sexual orientation: "All women are women, but there is no being who is only a woman" (p. 102). Treatment needs to address how each woman identifies culturally, racially, and ethnically (Bright, Osborne, & Greif, 2011; Gray & Littlefield, 2002). It is also important to note that minority women may face additional cultural or language barriers (Kohn, 2002). Some comments need to be made about specific racial/ethnic minority groups discussed earlier in this chapter.

African American and Latina women are less likely than Euro American women to seek substance abuse treatment (Alvidrez, 1999). African American women experience greater impact from trauma that is connected to poverty, social isolation, and stressful environments (Grant, 2011). Also, African American women have lower treatment retention (Davis & Ancis, 2012).

Latinas are a heterogeneous population who come from Latin and Caribbean cultures, yet they share the same language, a belief in family connections, and typically have been raised Catholic (Mora, 2002). Gilbert (1991) found that Latinas who are more acculturated into U.S. mainstream society and younger Latinas drink more and use more drugs. SAMHSA (1998c) found that "Other Latina" (not Caribbean, Central American, Cuban, Mexican, Puerto Rican, or South American) and Mexican women had the highest rate of use and dependence with alcohol, and these two groups and Puerto Rican women had the highest rate of illicit drug, marijuana, and cocaine use. Mora (2002) recommends that treatment with this population focus on issues of empowerment and regaining their culture. Language barriers need to be considered to make sure they understand the information they are receiving at all levels of treatment, and possible immigration issues need to be considered.

Asian and Pacific Islander women include women from China, Japan, the Philippines, Korea, Southeast Asia, and the Pacific Islands. There is limited data on their alcohol use, but of the data that exist, use appears to be more moderate (Kitano & Louie, 2002). The authors also report that the "flush" tendency as a reaction to alcohol does not have enough research support to say they are different biologically or explain the variation in use patterns in this group. These women use drugs (pot, hash, THC, cocaine, crack, heroin, methamphetamine, barbiturates) less than all other races and less than males in their racial group. Few seek treatment; there appears to be a lack of information, denial, language barriers, lack of family support, possible financial problems, or other related immigration issues (deportation), the cultural component of "loss of face" (shame to family), and belief in fatalism. If a woman does seek treatment, it is often because of legal or family pressure. Treatment needs to reduce stigma, be nurturing, involve the family, have a harm reduction approach, reduce language barriers, respect the family hierarchy, assess for trauma in recent immigrants, and teach what therapy is.

This knowledge of the impact of alcohol/drugs on women can be used in the assessment process. The Addiction Severity Index (ASI) discussed in Chapter 3 has been modified for use with women. The counselor needs to make sure that a thorough physical examination is done, as well as an assessment that involves the use of prescription drugs, the usage pattern, and the consequences experienced (Pape, 1993). Assessment of dual diagnosis is also important. For example, Dixit and Crum (2000) found women who are depressed have a higher chance of developing a drinking problem. Also, women appear to have higher anxiety and depression, and these problems may occur before addiction (Alcoholism & Drug Abuse Weekly, 2002). The counselor needs to be aware of the higher susceptibility of women to alcohol addiction, the tendency for women to begin using due to a specific circumstance, and the possible impact of ethnicity on the use process. In addition, this information can be used during the treatment and aftercare process to educate the woman about her addiction.

Treatment and Aftercare

McClellan (2011) provides an excellent overview of alcoholism treatment for women in the United States. Four themes emerged in the review. First, female alcoholics are viewed as "sicker" than male alcoholics. Second, the views on maternity and sexuality impact how alcoholism in women is understood. Third, any drinking by a woman can be considered a problem, thereby making a definition of alcoholism difficult. Fourth, although it may be complicated to use research and treatment models developed for males, historically, at times, the emphasis on gender differences has excluded women from care and increased stigma.

Although fewer women than men enter treatment, their outcomes are similar to men's

(Brady & Back, 2008). This is impressive given the unique and additional barriers faced by women. Van Wormer and Davis (2008) call it a "double whammy" when a woman is addicted and female. The specific, unique *barriers to treatment access* that women may face include:

Hidden usage: Higher levels of guilt and shame about their addictions may result in women hiding their usage thereby reducing the identification of a problem by others (physicians, legal system employees, employee assistance counselors, etc.). In counseling, women may present other problems as their issues rather than their chemical usage which may need to be addressed as well as their substance abuse.

Economic: They may have low-paying jobs with limited flexibility that may hamper their access to treatment (Harvard Medical School Special Report, 2008a) as well as a lack of insurance (Straussner & Brown, 2002).

Intimate partner-related barriers: They may have substance-abusing partners that are unsupportive of treatment (Bright et al., 2011; Straussner & Brown, 2002). They may fear of being abused by or losing a partner for entering treatment (Straussner & Brown, 2002). Women who enter treatment have a greater likelihood of losing their relationships (Greenfield & Grella, 2009).

Child-related barriers: They may lack child-care resources (Harvard Medical School Special Report, 2008a; McMahon, Winkel, Suchman, & Luthar, 2002; Pape, 1993) or fear of losing their children (Harvard Medical School Special Report, 2008a; Straussner & Brown, 2002). Substance-abusing women risk being viewed as less fit to be mothers (Greenfield & Grella, 2009).

There are also *inherent treatment barriers* inhibiting the treatment process that include:

Absence of adequate dual diagnosis treatment responses: Additional disorders (mood, anxiety, eating) that need to be treated along with the substance abuse in order to recover are frequently present but often not addressed (Harvard Medical School Special Report, 2008a). Especially PTSD and eating disorders need to be addressed in this population (Zweben, 2009).

Male-oriented treatment models: Traditional male-oriented treatment models may not fit a woman's needs (Straussner & Brown, 2002). Women who are in treatment may not respond well to traditional high-confrontation addiction treatment programs because of low self-esteem.

Limited services: There may be a lack of comprehensive services (Straussner & Brown, 2002).

There are treatment models and approaches that can be especially beneficial in response to the above-mentioned barriers. Even if the reality is that the counselor does not have access to such programs/approaches, a counselor with a sensitivity to these barriers and a willingness to create a "patchwork" treatment plan adapted to the client's needs, can significantly assist the female addict in her recovery process.

Some of the potential programs/approaches with regard to the above mentioned areas include:

Dual diagnosis: Substance abuse treatment that does integrate trauma and mental health issues may be core to more effective treatment for women (Gatz et al., 2005). One such approach (Hien, Litt, Cohen, Miele, & Campbell, 2009) is outlined in the book *Trauma Services for Women in Substance Abuse Treatment: An Integrated Approach*, which is referenced at the end of this chapter.

Treatment models: Van Wormer and Davis (2008) state that political and economic issues are imbedded in a woman's addiction and recovery process. Greaves and Poole (2008) advocate a "gender responsive approach" in treatment. This approach, that addresses social and economic issues that reflect the experiences and roles of women, can be a validating experience for women.

Recovery for women appears better when women attend women-only programs (Alcoholism & Drug Abuse Weekly, 2002); van der Walde et al., 2002). Women-only programs, activities, and role models are important to female clients (Zweben, 2009). When services are especially matched to women's needs, it enhances their staying in treatment and reducing their substance use after treatment (Marsh, Cao, & Shin, 2009).

Because of the importance of relationships to a woman's life, the alcohol/drug usage of other individuals important to her must be assessed during treatment. Women need to change self and relationships (partners/friends/children) as well as their relationship with substances (Grant, 2008). This approach in combination with social support may substantially assist her recovery (Hunter, Jason, & Keys, 2012). Treatment also needs to include the involvement of partners and children (Zweben, 2009).

Comprehensive services: There may be practical problems as well as common issues related to family of origin, current family, and history of experiences of violence (Pape, 1993; van der Walde et al., 2002). Therefore, she needs a thorough assessment (physical abuse, sexual abuse, legal problems, physical problems, psychiatric problems, family usage of alcohol/drugs, etc.), opportunities for needed services (child care, couples or family therapy, medications, safe housing, etc.), and education (parenting skills, self-esteem building, sexism, etc.). In addition to a thorough assessment and a holistic treatment plan, all women in treatment should receive reproductive information, including how she and significant others think and feel about different forms of contraception and the impact of alcohol and drug use on the fetus (Mitchell, 1993). For the pregnant client, services should include health care and survival-related issues (e.g., housing, psychosocial problems, parenting/family skills). These services need to be available both during and after addiction treatment (Mitchell, 1993).

Women also need to look at their career and educational goals, because they may need to make more money than they are currently earning, or they may want to find a more fulfilling career. Kelly, Blacksin, and Mason (2001) found that women who had personal and social resources such as education, employment skills and history, fewer children, decreased involvement with child protective services, and less chaos (i.e., homelessness, dual diagnosis, child protective services involvement, domestic violence) were more likely to complete treatment. Therefore, it is crucial that women know of and have access to personal and social resources in the community in order to feel empowered (Hunter et al., 2012).

In general, a counselor who has good interpersonal skills and has an empathic rather than a problem-solving focus will facilitate the therapeutic relationship with an addicted woman (van der Walde et al., 2002). The authors also advocate the use of individual, family, and group therapy with a focus on education, outreach, and coordination of resources. Through education of the addictive process, the counselor can help a woman forgive herself for the harm she has done to herself and others and possibly help her find spiritual resources to assist her in this process (van der Walde et al., 2002).

Zilberman, Tavares, Blume, and el-Guebaly (2002) make eight recommendations for women in addiction treatment:

1. Widespread screening in different settings (e.g., health, correctional, social welfare) using instruments such as the TWEAK (as discussed in Chapter 3)

2. Thorough medical evaluation

3. Thorough psychiatric evaluation

4. Evaluation of prescription medication use

5. Careful assessment of substance-use problems in their significant others, history of physical/sexual abuse, and assessment of children's needs

6. Perinatal services

7. Self-help group links that fit their needs

8. Adapting treatment to fit their phase of life

Women who are pregnant add another dimension to the issues related to women and addiction. Women who are pregnant and abusing alcohol and drugs may experience even more ostracism than women in general. Pregnant women typically reduce alcohol and illicit drug use (Terplan, McNama, & Chisolm, 2012). The 2011 National Survey on Drug Use and Health found that

pregnant women (ages 15 to 44) used substantially less than nonpregnant women in their age group and that 9.4% reported current alcohol use, 2.6% reported binge drinking, and 0.4% reported heavy drinking. Binge drinking has decreased from combined totals of 2010 and 2011 in comparison with 2009 and 2010. Clark, Dee, Bale, and Martin (2001) report that 15% to 19% of women use alcohol when pregnant and 5% use illegal drugs.

More is known about the impact of alcohol on the fetus than illegal drugs on pregnant women (Center for Substance Abuse Treatment [CSAT], 1994). In a summary of the research, two major themes emerge: 1% to 3% of U.S. children are impacted by alcohol and 130,000 women drink at levels that increase FASD children (Truong, Reifsnider, Mayorga, & Spitler, 2013).

In an update on alcohol birth defect diagnoses, Warren and Foudin (2001) state that the Institute of Medicine (IOM) of the National Academy of Sciences reviewed major research in the fetal alcohol field that included a recommendation of revised terminology. Fetal alcohol spectrum disorders (FASD) is an umbrella term that is not a diagnostic category, but rather describes the effects connected to prenatal alcohol exposure. The term *fetal alcohol syndrome* was retained with two categories (confirmed maternal alcohol exposure and without confirmed maternal alcohol exposure) that include facial abnormalities, growth retardation, and neurodevelopmental abnormalities of the central nervous system (CNS). In fetal alcohol syndrome (FAS), the child may have low birth weight as well as physical, cognitive, or behavioral limitations (SAMHSA, 2013), with deficits in motor/language skills and problems with hyperactivity and irritability (Clark et al., 2001; Harvard Medical School Special Report, 2008a).

Three categories were added where FAS criteria were not met. In the past, the term *fetal alcohol effects* (FAE) was used. However, because of a lack of agreement as to the criteria of this diagnosis, three additional terms were added. A category called *partial FAS with confirmed maternal alcohol exposure* includes some FAS facial pattern and, with growth retardation, CNS neurodevelopmental abnormalities or complex abnormalities of a behavioral or cognitive nature that could not be explained by genetics or environment. The other two categories are *alcohol-related birth defects* (ARBD), which has confirmed maternal alcohol exposure and one or more congenital defects, and *alcohol-related neurodevelopmental disorder* (ARND), which also contains confirmed maternal alcohol exposure, CNS neurodevelopmental abnormalities, and/or a complex pattern of behavioral or cognitive deficits. Yet, the authors report that while every woman who drinks during pregnancy will give birth to a child who meets the criteria on one of these five categories, it appears that the risk is increased when a high number of drinks are consumed at once, resulting in a high blood alcohol concentration.

There is no safe level of drinking while pregnant—any alcohol can hurt the fetus (Harvard Medical School Special Report, 2008a). This is because alcohol goes through the placenta to the fetus, and it breaks down more slowly in the fetus, so the blood alcohol level can be high for a longer time (Harvard Medical School Special Report, 2008a). When a woman thinks of consuming alcohol when pregnant, she needs to remember there is no safe amount, no safe time, and no safe kind of alcohol.

Four of the neonatal effects of drugs are:

1. Heroin usage may result in low birth weight, sexually transmitted diseases, abstinence syndrome (the child experiences withdrawal symptoms that accompany abstinence from the drug), subacute withdrawal, an increase in sudden infant death syndrome (SIDS; Mitchell, 1993), spontaneous abortion, prematurity, irritability, attachment problems (Clark et al., 2001), and sometimes no effects (SAMHSA, 1993).

2. Cocaine usage may result in lower birth weight, smaller head circumference, premature birth,

central nervous system dysfunction (e.g., tremors), an increase in SIDS (Mitchell, 1993), cardiorespiratory problems, motor problems, death (Clark et al., 2001), and sometimes no effects (SAMHSA, 1993).

3. Sedative/hypnotics during pregnancy may result in toxicity, withdrawal, and morphologic and/or behavioral teratogenicity (L. J. Miller, 1995).

4. Marijuana may result in lower birth weight and body length (SAMHSA, 1993).

Pregnant women who use alcohol/drugs may be unaware of the impact on the fetus, or they may be addicted and cannot stop using (Geller, 1991). Pregnancy itself can be a barrier to treatment, because treatment programs may not want to accept these women because of liability concerns, or a barrier because of state laws that give criminal consequences to these women for using when pregnant (van der Walde et al., 2002). These consequences include: (1) removal of baby at birth based on positive drug testing (no trial or hearing) and (2) mandatory drug treatment (I. M. Young, 1994). Such a punishing approach to women legally is a blend of sexist, and when present, racist attitudes (I. M. Young, 1994). These four discriminatory attitudes show when it is known (I. M. Young, 1994):

1. It is difficult to determine whether birth problems result from drug use or related causes of poverty, depression, or poor prenatal care.

2. The degree of harm caused by alcohol and drug use varies among babies.

3. The rage is passionate toward this population.

4. No one uses with the intent to become addicted; in fact, the addictive process says the addict cannot use willpower to stop using.

Pregnant women using drugs are more likely to need treatment than nonpregnant women using drugs, but they are not more likely to get it—therefore, more treatment is needed for this population (Terplan et al., 2012). Kruk and Banga (2011) describe the pregnant addicts' dilemma: she may be motivated to sober up, but out of fear of losing her child (children), she may not seek treatment. Regarding *specific barriers*, these include lack of child care, insurance, money, and transportation; fear that their children will be removed from them as well as fear of homelessness if they admit to an addiction; and problems with depression, denial, and shame about their addiction (Hayes, 1997; Zweben, 2009). They also experience numerous barriers structurally and socially that include education, employment, childcare, and housing; barriers that can impact their treatment attendance (Terplan et al., 2012).

In addition to helping clients obtain access to resources that address these needs, clients need vocational and educational assistance, pediatric follow-up, and case management services (SAMHSA, 1993). Integrated programs (substance abuse treatment that includes on-site pregnancy, parenting, child-related services) may help encourage women's participation in prenatal care (Milligan et al., 2011) as well as child development (Nichols et al., 2012). Counseling needs to be offered in individual, group, and family formats. SAMHSA's tip manual, *Pregnant Substance-Using Women*, provides helpful suggestions in working with this population.

While generally more treatment needs to be available to this population, Kruk and Banga (2011) make six specific treatment recommendations for the pregnant addict:

1. The treatment model needs to focus on the woman, harm reduction, and value her connection with her children that includes not being separated from them in treatment.

2. There needs to be an awareness of and flexibility to changing needs of the woman before and after the child's birth.

3. An examination of her needs based on their social context (not just substance abuse) needs to be done.

4. Gender-specific programs are needed so she can get support around her guilt and shame.

5. Services need to be culturally sensitive (including traditional healing).

6. If children do need to be removed, trauma support services need to be provided to the mother.

Counselors working with this population need to be able to give women information about the consequences of the alcohol/drugs on the fetus in a firm, clear, but nonjudgmental manner. This is a health problem that includes prenatal care, obstetrical care, child care, and empowerment (I. M. Young, 1994). It may enhance counseling to approach the pregnant addict with this type of thinking: "If she feels judged by me, she may not return to treatment and the chances of helping both her and her unborn child are eliminated." (See Case Study 10.1.)

CASE STUDY 10.1

Debbie is a 28-year-old Caucasian female who is single and lives alone with her 3-year-old daughter. She is the sole supporter of her child. Her parents do not have any contact with her because of her drug usage (she has stolen money from them and lied to them), and the father of her child is in prison for drug dealing. Debbie has not had any contact with him since the birth of her daughter. She is a flight attendant and has contacted you, an employee assistance counselor, for assistance after her last binge of alcohol and cocaine. She became frightened because after coming off her 3-day binge, she realized she had no money left from her paycheck and did not know how she was going to pay her bills. She has low self-esteem, in part because of her involvement with the father of her child. During their involvement, she was a prostitute for him in order to obtain her drugs. Debbie quit being a prostitute when she became pregnant, but she still runs into individuals who know her from those days.

1. What lifestyle or value differences might make it difficult for you to work with Debbie?
2. What types of behavior would you need to show Debbie in order to develop a therapeutic environment?
3. What interventions might you need to take with Debbie's child? How might such interventions harm the therapeutic relationship?
4. What are possible issues underlying Debbie's drug addiction that need to be addressed in counseling?
5. How would you best approach obtaining information about possible underlying issues?

EXERCISE 10.1

Imagine that you are counseling an addicted, pregnant woman who belongs to an ethnic group different from your own. Answer these five questions:

1. What values about pregnancy would you bring to the counseling relationship?
2. What would make it difficult for you to work with her if she relapsed when pregnant?
3. What ethnic biases may arise for you in working with her?
4. How would you approach your differences in ethnicity to build a bridge? Specifically, what general treatment approaches do you think would be most beneficial?
5. How would you handle your biases that arise in response to the above questions so the best interests of the client are served?

Race/Ethnicity

With regard to substance abuse with and dependence on alcohol and illicit drugs in specific populations, the 2012a National Household Survey on Drug Use and Health found highest to lowest use as follows: American Indians or Alaska Natives (AI/ANs) (16.8%); Native Hawaiians or other Pacific Islanders (10.6%); Hispanics (8.7%); Whites (8.2%); African Americans (7.2%); Asians (3.3%).

In terms of alcohol use, the same survey found Whites used at the rate of 56.8%, 44.7% for AI/ANs, 42.5% for Hispanics, 42.1% for Blacks, and 40.0% for Asians. The findings for specific population illicit drug use in individuals 12 or older showed the lowest rate in Asians (3.8%), 8.4% for Hispanics, 8.7% for whites, 10.0% for Blacks, 11.0% for Native Hawaiians or Other Pacific Islanders, and 13.4% for AI/ANs. In terms of illicit drug use, African Americans have less substance abuse and dependence than some groups (Native Hawaiians or other Pacific Islanders; AI/ANs), but more than Asian Americans, Hispanics, and Whites. However, due to their illicit drug use, they are incarcerated at a higher rate than their population representation (van Wormer & Davis, 2008).

These rates show that substance use is a concern across different racial/ethnic groups. However, in the following presentation of studies done with different racial/ethnic groups, the reader is cautioned to recognize the specific limitations of each study to avoid generalizations and stereotypes. Prior to a discussion of various racial/ethnic groups, some general comments about counseling with regard to race follow.

Earlier in this chapter, there was general discussion of multicultural approaches. D. W. Sue and Sue (2013) provide an excellent summary of working with specific ethnic groups at the end of their chapters in a section entitled "Implications for Clinical Practice." As with all general suggestions made regarding working with a specific population, these implications can be an excellent starting point as well as a checkpoint guide for the counselor if they are held tentatively and practiced with the *cultural humility* discussed earlier in this chapter.

Some specific suggestions addressing racial/ethnic issues in therapy are presented now. Cardemil and Battle (2003) report that open talk about race and ethnicity in counseling will add a multicultural aspect to counseling, enhance the therapeutic alliance, and improve treatment outcome. They provide six suggestions:

1. Do not make assumptions about the client or the client's family members regarding race/ethnicity.

2. Realize the client may be different from other racial/ethnic group members in terms of racial identity development and acculturation.

3. Examine how differences between client and counselor on racial/ethnic factors might impact counseling (mental health and illness definitions, relating to family and community, communication styles).

4. Realize how power, privilege, and racist dynamics may impact how counselor and client relate.

5. Take risks with clients to discuss race.

6. Be open to learning about race and ethnicity.

African Americans

African Americans are a heterogeneous group, and there are limitations on the scientific drug abuse research with this population (John, Brown, & Primm, 1997). Substance abuse has a harmful impact on African Americans (Wicker & Brodie, 2004), and African Americans have low recovery rates after treatment completion that is not explained in the research ("Special Populations," 2002). Substance use in African Americans appears connected to value conflicts with the dominant culture (Harvey, 1985) and as a way to cope with the stresses of daily living (Gary, 1986; Harvey, 1985; Richardson & Williams, 1990). They are also targeted specifically by advertising (van Wormer & Davis, 2008). Alcohol abuse is negatively correlated with life span of this population (F. Brown & Tooley, 1989). For example, approximately twice as many African Americans die of cirrhosis of the liver as Caucasians (Herd, 1985). They are more likely to die from cirrhotic liver, alcohol/drug-related homicide, or alcohol-related crashes (Center on Alcohol Marketing & Youth [CAMI], 2006). They are also arrested at a higher rate for substance-related offenses and are more likely to enter treatment through the legal system (Polcin & Beattie, 2007). In a review of the literature, Achara-Abrahams et al. (2013) state they are less likely to pursue treatment and less likely to complete it.

Neville and Walters 2004 report that racism impacts African Americans educationally, financially, politically, and in terms of health-care access and quality. Snowden (2012) summarizes that mental health care far often occurs in emergency rooms and psychiatric hospitals and African

Americans are overrepresented in both emergency rooms and inpatient services.

Many live in poverty and experience violence, racism, poor housing, and few positive role models due to the middle-class African Americans moving to the suburbs (Wright, 2001). They have a lower life expectancy (than Whites) and have a higher death rate by AIDS and homicide than any other ethnic group (Hines & Boyd-Franklin, 2005). In 2006, in the United States, they comprised almost half of the new HIV infections (Centers for Disease Control and Prevention, 2011).

An important finding in recent studies (Chartier, Hesselbrock, & Hesselbrock, 2013; Lo & Cheng, 2012) is that increased education inhibited substance-use disorders in the African-American population. This finding may have important implications for the involvement of educational opportunities with regard to substance abuse prevention, treatment, and aftercare.

Assessment The CSAT (1999) cautions counselors to be aware that African Americans may be sensitive to being asked personal information because of experiences with social systems such as welfare, particularly as trust is being developed. Presenting problems may be a byproduct of "the social, political, economic, and historical forces that have had such significant impact on individuals, families, and communities" (Achara-Abrahams et al., 2013, p. 267). The assessment process needs to take into account the impact of cultural oppression and historical trauma on the client's use. This does not mean that the counselor negates the presence of abuse and addiction, but in the assessment process, sensitively gathers information leading potentially to a treatment process that considers the entire person, which includes their environmental context.

Bell (2002) states that the counselor's ethnicity may have an impact on the counseling relationship. Yet, regardless of the counselor's race, the counselor needs to focus on empathic skills that connect with hearing the needs of the client and the client's worldview in order to develop trust (CSAT, 1999). With African Americans, this means examining how slavery and institutional racism has affected and currently affects their lives and to know that socially, economically, politically, and culturally, the issues African Americans face interact. The cultural context has also shaped the client's view of substance abuse (E. M. Wright, 2001). Wright recommends using the person's full name and title and asking for personal information privately.

A racial identity model may help the counselor in multicultural counseling. Helms' (1995) model, with five identity stages, is reviewed here:

1. *Conformity.* Internalizing White middle-class values, seeing Whites as good and race as not important.

2. *Dissonance.* Exploring what it means personally to be Black.

3. *Immersion/emersion.* Immersing themselves in their Blackness and becoming more flexible in their racial perspective with a shift to the opposite of conformity (White is bad).

4. *Internalization.* Defining themselves internally regarding race and other identities of a social nature.

5. *Internalization commitment.* Stage 4 with a multicultural perspective. Placing a client within this framework may assist in the assessment process.

As to assessment, Bell (1990) states that African Americans tend to enter treatment later in the addiction process because of higher emotional pain tolerance, which is a result of experiencing racism; an awareness of the failures of treatment experiences; fewer treatment resources; and lack of clarity about appropriate alcohol and drug use. Bell elaborates that later entry often means African Americans are court-referred, have more problems because of their addiction, require more expensive treatment, and are less likely to be successful.

Bell (2002) summarizes the difficulty of addressing alcohol and drug addiction with this population by presenting the complicating factors of health care, crime, family stability (single-parent households, teen pregnancy, child abuse, spousal violence), employment and income, education, and housing. Some particular distinctions he makes are in three areas:

1. *Crime.* While in the White world addicts use crime to support a drug habit, crime may also be viewed as a form of employment (increase in money, status) by the African-American client before even becoming addicted. Also, African-American families may struggle with denial about the addiction as other families do, but there may be an additional component that their finances may improve by a family member being involved in criminal activities.

2. *Poverty.* Because of poverty, there may be credit problem issues (e.g., obtaining credit). Also, the author describes those in poverty as having less "margin for error" emotionally and financially.

3. *Single mothers.* These mothers who are young and poor (in both financial and educational arenas) may be susceptible to drug use because of overwhelming responsibility, sense of hopelessness, easy drug access, and high pressure to use.

These factors and characteristics mean that in addition to the counselor's looking at a client's cultural identity as a part of treatment, the counselor also needs to be sensitive for how treatment and recovery can be complicated by such factors and characteristics. For each client, the counselor needs to assess health care and housing needs, involvement in and impact of crime, family stability, and employment/income/education levels, and address these issues in treatment and aftercare in a culturally sensitive treatment plan and relapse prevention plan.

Treatment and Aftercare Overall counseling strategies are provided by D. W. Sue and Sue (2013). These include: discussing working with someone of a different ethnicity (if this is the case); clarifying their values and preferences; determining how counseling can be useful to them (especially if they are involuntary); assessing their positive assets; defining goals and ways to achieve them; developing an egalitarian relationship and working collaboratively; analyzing their racial identity and family structure; and examining external factors related to the presenting problem.

Van Wormer and Davis (2008) state that this population may face treatment barriers such as biased diagnostic tools, racist counselors, not enough treatment opportunities (or irrelevant treatment), and transference-countertransference issues related to White culture. During the treatment process, it is critical for the counselor to discuss race and culture with the African-American client (Bell, 1990). The related issues must be acknowledged, experienced, and worked through as a part of counseling. These issues can be understood more fully by knowing the level of acculturation of the client (Bell, 1990).

Bell (2002) reports there are four major groupings of African Americans: acculturated, bicultural, culturally immersed, and traditional unacculturated. He states: (a) these groupings are fluid because of how the African American needs to be flexible to survive; (b) the counselor needs to help the client determine the group to which the client belongs; and (c) the White counselor needs to expose himself or herself to African-American experiences to learn about the cultures and being in a minority. Bell describes the four groupings and their related intervention and treatment recommendations as:

1. *Acculturated* (10% to 15% of population): This group tends to "live" outside of the African-American community in the "White world," is typically well educated, and is good at interacting with Whites. The intervention recommendation is to help them see how their chemical use may hurt their standing in the

White world. Treatment may be impacted by the client being manipulative to a White counselor by offering acceptance and the Black client having a need to be viewed as credible by being accepted by Whites.

2. *Bicultural* (30% to 40%): This group can operate in both the African-American and White worlds, does not feel accepted in either, and tends to separate these worlds. Treatment issues can include acting acculturated while in treatment and then having difficulty applying the concepts to their bicultural world and needing to express their struggles in treatment with being bicultural.

3. *Culturally immersed* (three groups):

   a. *Culturally immersed conformists* (CICs; 10% to 15%): This group uses the White world to survive and the African-American world to meet personal needs. In treatment, they may use humor (such as "the dozens"), which is "a shame-based form of humor based on physical appearance and ridicule of family members" (p. 57) in a defensive manner, so the counselor needs to address it but not overreact to it. They also need to learn to have fun and to examine their involvement with African Americans involved in illegal actions, particularly those that are drug-related.

   b. *Culturally immersed Afrocentrics* (CIAs; 15% to 20%): This group is described as the "black intelligentsia" (p. 58), who are bright, educated, and employed in places such as academic settings and have their personal needs met in the African-American world. They view addiction as a result of racism, and in treatment they may challenge the counselor in power plays around the political theme of racism.

   c. *Culturally immersed deviants* (CIDs; 15% to 20%): This group does not interact much with Whites, are likely to be involved with crime, and may be the most "fear-inducing"

to Whites. They have both survival and personal needs met in the Black world. Treatment needs to be longer and more intensive while culturally relevant because of their views on everybody and every system being involved in a hustle and their tendency to have limited coping skills and community support.

4. *Traditional unacculturated* (10% to 15%). This group tends to be Christian, older, and Southern and, like other groups, meets survival needs in the White world and personal needs in the Black world. They want to hold on to their cultural identity.

Even though there has been an increase in awareness, current treatment practice has not reflected more culturally sensitive treatment because of "a flood of competing needs in an atmosphere that holds few resources to meet them (Achara-Abrahams et al., 2013, p. 268). The authors advocate a recovery management (RM) treatment approach that addresses the whole person in a comprehensive manner and specifically outline helpful treatment interventions. This model involves a spirit of hope and empowerment as well as an involvement of the community for the client.

One such involvement of the community may be the church and spirituality or religion that historically have been important for African Americans (Hudson, 1986). Spirituality has helped sustain them in the oppression of slavery and racism (Mohatt et al., 2007). This community can serve as a support system for their recovery (Dembo, Burgos, Babst, Schmeidler, & Le Grand, 1978). The counselor needs to keep in mind some possible limitations however. First, the client may not have had positive experiences with the church, so this may not be a resource for them. Second, the church may view addiction as a sin (Bell, 1990; Gordon, 1994). The counselor, then, needs to assess the comfort of each African American with that person's sense of spirituality, and if that sense of spirituality involves a church, it is necessary to find out how that church views addiction in order to determine the level of support it can provide.

Also, effective treatment and aftercare will assist the African-American client in developing some support for recovery within the African-American community, which may or may not include the church. Achara-Abrahams et al. (2013) describe the use of cultural heritage groups that helped clients learn how to live in mainstream culture while holding on to their ethnicity with a sense of pride in their heritage. Neville and Walters (2004) report that social support networks for the client (church, family, community) can help foster resilience. Drawing on informal resources, such as a tendency to communal rearing of children, the Black church can help with the development of a recovery support network (CSAT, 1999). Bowser and Bilal (2001) also recommend examining the client's spiritual explanation of addiction and the client's use of drug-related ritualized music and dance to enhance treatment effectiveness. Finally, CSAT (1999) makes the following treatment recommendations in working with this population. They recommend that treatment address nine areas:

1. Case management services.
2. Child-care services.
3. On-site 12-step programs.
4. Use of ethnically appropriate assessment.
5. Installation of a food program.
6. Involvement of other counselors (professional, paraprofessional, alternative).
7. Skill-building groups.
8. Development of social/recreational interests.
9. Employment of ethnic staff. (See Case Study 10.2.)

CASE STUDY 10.2

Chris is a 45-year-old African-American male who has never been in treatment for alcohol or drug addiction. He has always lived at home with his mother and relies on her and odd handyman jobs to support himself. Chris began developing a drinking and drug problem when he returned from the service at age 20. Since that time, he has not had a steady job or girlfriend.

His mother has been his biggest enabler, because she feels sorry for what the war did to her son, and she has never been able to set consistent consequences for him. His father died when Chris was an adolescent, and he is an only child. In the past few years, he has become increasingly violent when drunk or high, and his mother has been more frightened about being left alone with him. Recently, she confided her fears to a woman in her church, who shared her story about helping her son sober up. After their conversation, Chris's mother decided to call the police when he became violent again. She did and Chris was taken to detox.

1. What differences are there between you and Chris that might make it difficult for you to trust each other?
2. What might you do to bridge such differences?
3. What stereotypes might you hold of Chris and his mother that could interfere with hearing his story?

4. What issues may underlie Chris's alcohol and drug addiction, and how might you find out about them?

5. What facts do you need to know about this client's use history and its consequences in order to be helpful to him? How might you approach obtaining such sensitive information, taking into account the differences you share?

Asian Americans and Pacific Islanders

CSAT (1999) summarizes this group as including Asian Americans, Asian Indians, Vietnamese, Cambodians, Laotians, Hmong, and Thai. Asian Americans have been called a "model minority" since the mid-1960s because of overall success in academic and financial areas (Kim, 2004; Lo & Cheng, 2012). CSAT defines Pacific Islanders as Hawaiians, Vietnamese, Samoans, Chamorros, Tongans, Thai, and Burmese. They vary racially, ethnically, culturally, sociodemographically (i.e., education, income), and in migratory history. In terms of migration, they may have come to reunify with family, because of high education and skills, or as war refugees; and they vary on how long they have lived in the United States.

In terms of general mental health counseling, Sue, Cheng, Saad, and Chu (2012) provide an overview of the information available with this population that can be useful to the counselor. First, this population does not typically seek out/receive needed services. Second, this low usage may be due to "personal reluctance, misunderstanding of its value, or cultural inappropriateness of services" (p. 541). Third, suicide appears to be higher in older women in this population, while PTSD is higher in Southeast Asian refugees. Fourth, in the conclusion section of their article, specific recommendations made that can be translated to the counseling process include: (1) assessment needs to be expanded (sensitivity to cultural variations in how symptoms are expressed as well as awareness of disorders that are culture-bound), (2) the impact of stigma, shame, and emotional inhibition on disclosure needs to be examined, and (3) strategies to reduce treatment barriers need to be implemented. Since these recommendations are not clear cut in terms of specific applications,

counselors can be sensitive to these issues as they work with Asian Americans in counseling and particularly as to how these issues may evidence themselves in substance abuse counseling.

Typically, Asian Americans have one of the lowest alcohol use rates of ethnic minorities (Rebach, 1992; SAMHSA, 2012a). The National Survey on Drug Use and Health (NSDUH) (SAMHSA, 2012b) found they had the lowest alcohol use and substance dependency/abuse. However, the more acculturated they become, the more their use reflects that of the dominant culture (Sue, 1987). Also, in a study done with college students, those students who feel excluded from both cultures may drink to cope with their negative feelings, resulting in higher alcohol consequences rates (Pedersen, Hsu, Neighbors, Lee, & Larimer, 2013).

This population may experience a flushing response when drinking alcohol (i.e., skin color changes, as well as warmth and tingling sensations; Rebach, 1992), yet about 60% do not have the genetic variation that results in facial flushing, tachycardia, hypotension, or nausea (Kim, 2004). Sensitivity to alcohol and cultural values regarding its use may explain their lower overall use of alcohol and incidence of alcoholism (Ho, 1994).

CSAT (1999) discusses three roadblocks to understanding substance abuse and treatment with this population: (1) tendency to use at low rates, (2) tendency to be left out of epidemiological studies, and (3) each subgroup varying in drugs abused and how they abuse them. However, as with other minority groups, value conflicts with the mainstream culture seem related to substance use (Yee & Thu, 1987). For example, poorer Asian Americans showed a stronger link between discrimination and substance abuse in one recent study (Lo & Cheng, 2012). There are some known consequences, such as substance abuse and AIDS being related, as well as substance abuse and crime.

In addition, treatment admissions increased 37% between 1994 and 1999 for this group, with 19% being for stimulant abuse (5% typical in treatment) and the average age being younger (Drug and Alcohol Services Information System, 2002). Note, however, in a recent study, while researchers found methamphetamine to be a significant problem with this population, they did not find any differences regarding needs, experiences, or outcomes related to treatment in comparison with other racial/ethnic groups (Evans, Pierce, Li, Rawson, & Hser, 2012).

Assessment, Treatment, and Aftercare Again, overall counseling strategies are provided by D. W. Sue and Sue (2013). Some of these overlap with working with the African-American population: being aware of working with someone of a different ethnicity (if this is the case); assessing their positive assets; defining goals and ways to achieve them; and analyzing their racial identity and family structure. Some unique factors in working with this population require: (a) keeping in mind their collectivistic, hierarchical, and patriarchal orientation that may impact counseling interventions chosen; (b) considering the level and impact of acculturation as it influences problem definition and generational struggles; (c) being aware of possible somatic complaints, a preference for immediate problem resolution, an openness to problem-focused, time-limited approaches, and a sharing of strategies the counselor has personally used in the past for problem solving. Mohatt et al. (2007) describe three common values: avoidance of bringing shame to the family, the central social unit; being a part of a social hierarchy with respect to elders and social rank; and restraint personally and emotionally.

Specifically with substance abuse, CSAT (1999) states that substance abuse is not readily discussed in these families because of shame for both the person and the family. If it is acknowledged, typically, the assistance is sought through family, friends, and community networks before reaching out to the outside world. When assistance is asked for, it is common for it to be asked for in a manner that assumes the person can be quickly fixed.

An example of working with one subgroup of this population follows. Asian Americans typically do not enter treatment (Sakai, Ho, Shore, Risk, & Price, 2005: D. Sue, 1987). They tend to view alcoholism as a private problem (Goebert & Nishimura, 2011). If they do enter treatment, they may enter it late in their addiction because of shame-related issues, such as admitting a loss of control over their use, putting themselves before their family, and admitting that the family could not take care of the problem (Westermeyer, 1997). They may be concerned with "losing face" in the community (van Wormer & Davis, 2008).

Some of the traditional Asian values are to obey your parents and take care of the family (D. Sue & Sue, 1995). These values may run counter to the dominant culture value and create conflict for the Asian-American client. Typically, there is an emphasis on education and emotional restraint (D. Sue & Sue, 1995). Because Asian Americans tend to view counseling as bringing shame to their families, those who come in for counseling tend to be more disturbed and more likely to talk about somatic rather than emotional problems (D. Sue & Sue, 1987).

The counselor needs to arrange the assessment, treatment, and aftercare with an awareness of the traditionalism of the client and/or the significant others in the client's life. Asian-American clients may come to counseling with more severe problems, have more difficulty with expressing emotion openly, and may have a greater sense of shame, particularly concerning their families. D. Sue and Sue (1995) recommend a subtle, less confrontive counseling approach for both individual and group counseling. As to aftercare, it may be important to assess the individuals and systems that will be supportive to the recovery of the Asian American. For example, the client may have a difficult time speaking about concerns in a group setting, particularly when strong, direct confrontation may be used. The counselor working with an Asian-American client in this group setting may want to make a point of processing the group experience with the client initially to determine the fit of the group with the client's need and comfort level.

The counselor working with this population needs to (CSAT, 1999):

- Be aware of possible language barriers.

- Have agency staff that is culturally competent (can speak the language and understand the worldview of the client).

- Be aware of racial, ethnic, and cultural differences for each client.

- Be sensitive to differences in education, income, and migratory history for the client.

- Be aware of different levels of acculturation.

- Be aware of possible limited effectiveness of typical Western models of addiction treatment (i.e., group counseling, 12-step groups) with this population because of cultural differences.

- Collaborate with community leaders throughout the treatment continuum. (See Case Study 10.3.)

Hispanic Americans

Hispanics, which include individuals of Mexican, Puerto Rican, Spanish, Central and South American, Dominican Republic, and Cuban descent, are the fastest-growing racial minority in the United States (Eden & Aguilar, 1989; U.S. Census Bureau, 2009). The terminology can be confusing in this area. The following definitions are based on the U.S. Census Bureau that views race and ethnicity as separate entities (collects information on race and ethnicity in separate categories) and asks respondents to state the race they identify with the most. These definitions are provided in the event the reader wants to use them in clarifying the results of substance use and abuse within reported categories.

In terms of the *ethnic* category, the U.S. Census Bureau sorts out those who see their ancestry as being in Spain or Hispanic America (Hispanic and Latino Americans) and those who do not (Non-Hispanic Americans). Hispanic is considered an ethnic rather than racial category. Regarding race, White Americans are a racial category where people who live in the United States see themselves as originating from European, Middle Eastern, or North African countries. This group consists of White Hispanics (identifies as racially

CASE STUDY 10.3

Frank is a 30-year-old Asian American who teaches at a university in the United States. He moved here from China to attend school as an undergraduate and remained in the country through completing his degrees until he obtained a doctorate in business. He decided to become a U.S. citizen and teach at a research university. He has an American Caucasian wife and one child who is 2 years old. Frank graduated with his doctorate and began teaching 2 years ago.

During his doctoral training, he began to feel more stress than he could handle. Because he was viewed as such a success to his family, he did not want to tell them, including his wife, of his problems. The stress was affecting his ability to sleep and concentrate. He began taking muscle relaxers and minor tranquilizers, which he obtained from a physician friend. Frank believes he experiences a lot of racism, predominantly from Caucasian males in his department. He is afraid that the racism will keep him from being reappointed to his teaching position next year. Recently, his friend told him that he would not be able to continue writing prescriptions for him, because he is afraid that Frank is becoming addicted.

> He gave Frank your name as a counselor for him to see. Frank is in your office for the first time to obtain help for his stress.
>
> 1. What will Frank notice about your office when he enters the room? Will it be an atmosphere that is open and inviting?
> 2. What cultural assumptions might you make about Frank in terms of the information just given?
> 3. How would you invite Frank to discuss his concerns with you?
> 4. What cultural differences might you anticipate that would make counseling a difficult process between the two of you?
> 5. How would you invite Frank to discuss his drug usage with you?

White with Hispanic descent) and non-Hispanic Whites (those without Hispanophone ancestry). Those labeled Black Hispanics are from the Caribbean, the Dominican Republic, or Cuba).

CSAT (1999) provides a summary of variations among this group. First, they vary in where they live in the United States. Second, they vary in terms of income. Overall, this group is substantially impacted by poverty, but it is not necessarily related to unemployment. Third, they vary in why they have migrated to the United States: They may be political refugees or simply people from various occupations who want either a better life or to be connected with family and use either legal or illegal means to achieve this desire. The highest number of undocumented individuals in the United States come from Mexico (Moya & Shedlin, 2008). Fourth, they vary on how long they have been in the United States and how assimilated they are. Keep in mind that most of the research that has been gathered on this population has occurred in specific states (Texas, Arizona, New York, California, Florida) while many of the undocumented Hispanics are in rural areas of the United States (Valentine-Barrow, Adcock, & Jenkins, 2011).

Again, overall counseling strategies are provided by D. W. Sue and Sue (2013). Some of these overlap with working with the African-American and Asian American populations: assessing their positive assets; defining goals and ways to achieve them (as well as expectations and negative consequences); and analyzing their racial identity and family structure. As with the Asian American population approaches, the counselor needs to consider the acculturation level in terms of: (1) the client and the family members, (2) information about counseling and roles as well as confidentiality, and (3) the impact of it on the problem. Again, as with the Asian American population, there is a tendency for a collectivistic, hierarchical, patriarchal orientation and an openness to solution-focused, time-limited approaches. Some unique factors in working with this population require: (1) an awareness of possible language barriers that may require a translator (e.g., the client does not speak fluent English while it is the only fluent language the counselor speaks), (2) the influence of spiritual/religious beliefs on the perception of the problem, (3) possible problems in receiving external supports for basic needs, and (4) the concept of *personalismo* where the counselor is treated like a close friend, a family member, once there is trust in the relationship.

A counselor working with a Hispanic American needs to be sensitive to the variations in location, income, migration reasons, and length of time in the United States as well as degree of assimilation. Such cultural and individual sensitivity can facilitate the welfare of the client by improved assessment, treatment, and aftercare. For example, (a) historically, Mexican and Central/South American communities used alcohol as a way to come together culturally (Madsen & Madsen, 1969), and they used drugs in their religious ceremonies, which may facilitate a cultural tolerance toward the use of alcohol/drugs (Eden & Aguilar, 1989), and (b) machismo, the behavior of Hispanic men, may be viewed as including the use of alcohol (Eden & Aguilar, 1989) and difficult for the male to admit to having a problem (Alvarez & Ruiz, 2001).

NIAAA (2013) summarizes what is known about drinking alcohol in this population—the U.S. Census Bureau definitions given previously may assist with the understanding of these findings. First, Hispanics are less likely to drink alcohol than non-Hispanic Whites, but if they do drink they consume more alcohol than them. Second, in general, beer is the substance of preference. Third, those born in the United States, who have relaxed attitudes about drinking (Puerto Ricans and Mexican Americans), are: more likely to drink, drink heavily, and have alcohol-related problems. Fourth, those most likely to receive DUIs are Mexican American men and women and South/Central American men. Fifth, Hispanic men generally have high rates of liver disease.

Substance abuse has been explained in the research as stress resulting from issues of "acculturation, poverty, discrimination, and racism" (CSAT, 1999, p. 15). Drug use disorders (DUD) increase with acculturation (Blanco et al., 2013). Immigrants may underestimate the stressors they face, particularly socioeconomic disadvantages, that may increase their vulnerability to substance abuse (Moya & Shedlin, 2008). Poverty results in fewer life buffers and resources, and increased vulnerability for imprisonment and discrimination (Alvarez & Ruiz, 2001). As they become more educated, they show a weaker link between discrimination and substance abuse (Lo & Cheng, 2012). They are the most under-educated ethnic group in the United States (van Wormer & Davis, 2008). Hispanic Americans have higher mortality than non-Hispanic Whites due to diabetes, HIV/AIDS, and liver cirrhosis that may be related to substance use and abuse (Buka, 2002). CSAT (1999) summarized health-related consequences of use in this population as:

(a) the highest rates of AIDS related to injection drug use, (b) large number of homicide deaths related to substance abuse, and (c) high incarceration due to drug-related actions.

Assessment G. W. Lawson, Ellis, and Rivers (1984) suggest that three areas be examined for risk: sociocultural, psychological, and physiological. An elaboration of these three areas is provided by Eden and Aguilar (1989). Sociocultural risk factors include using alcohol to connect with others experiencing difficulties and stresses in adapting to U.S. culture, and having problems becoming or staying employed. The psychological risk factors involve self-esteem, a sense of personal control, isolation as connected to acculturation difficulties, and less frequent use of counseling services. Physiological risk factors, such as genetic predisposition, may be exacerbated by the sociocultural stressors they experience. Because of the frequency of alcohol use, it is important in the evaluation to ask the Hispanic client exactly how much is being used (Rebach, 1992). Direct confrontation needs to be avoided so the honor and dignity of the client is not threatened (van Wormer & Davis, 2008), but reviewing the facts of the client's use can be an effective assessment intervention (Alvarez & Ruiz, 2001).

Treatment and Aftercare Treatment of Hispanics needs to include bilingual/bicultural professional staff so that the cultural needs of the clients are better met (Rothe & Ruiz, 2001; Ruiz & Langrod, 1997). Eden and Aguilar (1989) suggest that treatment take into account the frequent use of alcohol in the Hispanic community, the power of women in the Hispanic community, and the possibility that being alcoholic may elicit a sense of failure and guilt, which may result in a shame that delays the addressing of the addiction problem (Rebach, 1992). Treatment that is less confrontive, but stresses areas such as family support, may be a better fit for the Hispanic client (Arrendondo, Weddige, Justice, & Fitz, 1987). Aftercare that draws on other sober Hispanic individuals, the importance of being sober to take care of the family, and an understanding of the process of addiction may reduce the relapse potential of the Hispanic client.

Three specific treatment recommendations for counselors are (CSAT, 1999):

1. Determine what the community and individual want to be called. *Hispanic*, the federal classification for this heterogeneous group, is preferred by some, whereas *Latino* is preferred by others, and other groups may have their own specific term, such as *Chicanos* for Mexican Americans. A sensitivity to using the preferred term can facilitate trust with both the individual client and the ethnic community—an important aspect with this population that views trust as a core value.

2. Be aware of and address barriers that include language (e.g., lack of bicultural staff), financial (limited financial resources for treatment due to lack of insurance), cultural (treatment programs tending to use confrontation techniques and a tendency to separate the person from his or her family), geographical, immigration status, acculturation level, and service integration.

3. Include positive role models and a cultural network (e.g., extended family, folk healers, religious institutions, neighborhood groups). (See Case Study 10.4.)

American Indians/Alaska Natives (AI/AN)

The federal government recognizes approximately 400 tribes in the United States; each has its own culture, and there can be differences within a tribe (CSAT, 1999). As a result, generalizations about this population need to be made with these cultural differences in mind.

Overall counseling strategies follow (D. W. Sue & Sue, 2013). Some of these overlap with working with the African-American, Asian American, and Hispanic populations: defining goals and ways to achieve them (especially with how change may impact family and community), and analyzing their racial identity (including tribal affiliation) and family structure. As with the Asian American and Hispanic population approaches, the counselor needs to consider the acculturation level in terms of the client and the family members, and the impact of it on the problem—particularly with oppression and local tribal or reservation issues. Like with the Hispanic population, the counselor needs to explore the incorporation of spiritual/religious beliefs (particularly regarding treatment strategies that include mind, body, and spirit), and possible client problems in receiving external supports for basic needs. A unique factor in working with this population requires use of a listening style that is unhurried and client-centered.

CASE STUDY 10.4

Jose is a 56-year-old Hispanic male who has been arrested for a DUI. This is his first arrest, and you are the DUI assessor who has been appointed to evaluate him. You have been told that Jose has been in the United States for about six months and that his English is fair, but in case of translation difficulties, an interpreter is present. When you enter the room with the interpreter, Jose makes eye contact with the interpreter, but not with you. In answer to your questions, Jose seems friendly, but brief.

1. How would you help Jose feel more comfortable in the session?

2. How would you use the interpreter to facilitate the session discussion?

3. What kinds of approaches would you take to facilitate Jose's answering your questions about his drinking?

4. Are there any other individuals you may need to contact about Jose's drinking? If so, who might they be and how might you contact them?

Overall, SAMHSA (2012b) reports 14.8% need alcohol treatment and 6% need drug treatment. In a summary of research findings, suicide rates, accidental deaths, liver disease, diabetes, and comorbid conditions are elevated with the AI/AN population (Reickmann et al., 2012). The authors also state that there is an interaction between alcohol and drug use with the problems of mental health, abuse, trauma (i.e., PTSD, intimate partner violence, violence, racism), unemployment, poverty, and cultural displacement.

Substance abuse problems vary across tribes (CSAT, 1999). There is limited data on substance use with this population (Reickmann et al., 2012). Research on American Indians is difficult to do because of problems in obtaining representative samples and variation in the research in terms of quality and generalizability (Akins, Mosher, Rotolo, & Griffin, 2003). Also, reservations are sovereign nations and often rural (Reickmann et al., 2012). Furthermore, about 650,000 of these 1 million American Indians live on or near a reservation (M. J. Anderson & Ellis, 1995), with a majority of AI/ANs living in urban areas (Spear, Crevecoeur-MacPhail, Denering, Dickerson, & Brecht, 2013). The difference in being on or off the reservation may have an impact on the types of stresses experienced. For example, there is higher alcohol use among urban American Indians (T. J. Young, 1988) and higher alcohol and drug use for those who live on reservations (Beauvais, Oetting, & Edwards, 1985). Other use findings are: (a) alcohol is the drug of choice (CSAT, 1999); (b) there is more use in younger people than any other age group (Beauvais et al., 1985); (c) there is little if any gender difference in use (Akins et al., 2003); and (d) high inhalant use typically precedes the use of other substances (Akins et al., 2003).

Differences in drinking are impacted by different cultural guidelines about the tolerance of deviance, socioeconomics, acculturation level, and the traditional cultural values, language, and lifestyle (van Wormer & Davis, 2008). CSAT (1999) reports that alcohol impacts this population in terms of cancer, diabetes, heart disease, injuries, and death. In a comparison of American Indians with the general population, May (1986) found higher death rates, more deaths caused by cirrhosis of the liver, and more incidents of suicide and homicide. T. J. Young (1988) reports that 75% of the deaths in this ethnic population are related to alcohol. May (1996) found that more than one-third of the deaths were due to cirrhosis and alcoholism. Alcohol is the number-one cause of arrests (CSAT, 1999). There has been a growing concern in recent years with methamphetamine and prescription opiate use on reservations (Radin, Banta-Green, Thomas, Kutz, & Donovan, 2011); their research found alcohol and prescription opiate use were still significant concerns, with methamphetamine being a concern in some communities.

Akins et al. (2003) state that the conflicting findings of substance use patterns are also present in theories that explain the use of substances in this population. The authors break the theoretical arguments into three groups: (1) genetic (they negate this theory by saying there is no evidence to suggest enhanced reactivity to alcohol), (2) cultural (the loss of culture due to colonialism contributes to substance abuse), and (3) social and economic (high unemployment and poverty and inferior education leading to dropping out of school could be related to substance abuse). Clearly, the impact of culture, society, and the economy needs to be addressed by the counselor in working with this population. One example of cultural explanation is *historical trauma*. This term means there has been wounding (emotional, psychological) that has a cumulative effect that comes from collective trauma (Maria Yellow Horse Brave Heart, 2007, as cited in van Wormer & Davis, 2008).

Assessment In the assessment process, it may be important to determine the acculturation level of the AI/AN client and his or her comfort with being acculturated. The problem assessment needs to include the family, extended family, and tribal community as well as the individual's assessment (D. W. Sue & Sue, 2013). There are many value conflicts between the dominant Caucasian culture and AI/AN ways. For example, success of the individual and competitiveness may be commonly valued in the dominant culture, but not the American Indian culture (Rebach, 1992). Clinics may lack cultural sensitivity/awareness (Larios, Wright, Jernstrom, Lebron, & Sorensen, 2011). Also, alcohol use may be involved in trying to cope with the stresses of being oppressed, which affects American Indians' income and day-to-day living (Beauvais & LaBoueff, 1985). In addition, alcohol may be used by some to self-medicate a dual disorder, especially if they live in an area (rural or ghetto) where psychiatric help may not be accessible (Westermeyer & Peake, 1983). These factors need to be taken into account when assessing the abuse problem of the AI/AN. Other factors include disclosing information after trust is established (which may take longer), lack of access to culturally sensitive treatment due to lack of funding and representative staff (especially in urban areas), and agency understanding (CSAT, 1999).

Treatment and Aftercare Frequently, American Indians enter treatment at a chronic stage of addiction without family or job resources (Westermeyer, 1997). Flores (1986) reports that differences in values between treatment staff and American Indian clients may result in mutual stereotyping and increased dropout rates. For example, traditional cultural practices or spiritual ceremonies may not be a part of treatment programs that typically focus on Western medicine (Larios et al., 2011). Treatment centers may find themselves in a bind with evidence-based approaches, a part of Western medicine techniques, being required by funding sources while there may not be enough evidence to trust their effectiveness and a mistrust in the AI/AN population with regard to these approaches (Larios et al., 2011). A common response in AI/AN communities that the culture (identity, orientation, practice) is considered treatment (Gone, 2012). M. J. Anderson and Ellis (1995) recommend that treatment counselors look for the reinforcements for drinking that exist within the individual and the culture. Both family and culture can have a significant impact on the drinking behaviors of American Indians (T. S. Weisner, Weibel-Orlando, &

Long, 1984). Communities that are strong, hopeful, and emphasize responsibility and focus can be a valuable resource for recovering individuals (Radin et al., 2011). In a study of urban AI/ANs, recovery social support and lack of a difficult living situation were predictors of posttreatment abstinence (Spear et al., 2013).

Treatment and aftercare need to fit with the values of this population. No single approach fits all AI/AN groups, as some clients may respond more to traditional healing while others to mainstream approaches (Sutton & Broken Nose, 2005). Typically, these values include a present-time focus, a harmony within and outside self, and a priority of group needs over individual needs (A. Hill, 1989). The counselor needs to examine meaningful value systems and support systems for the AI/AN who wants to remain sober. CSAT (1999) makes five specific recommendations for culturally sensitive treatment with the American Indian population:

1. Programs need to involve staff from the client's tribe as well as community members such as a healer.

2. Counselors need to be aware that comfort with disclosure may vary, and confrontation may be minimally effective if at all.

3. Family and community members need to be involved.

4. Links with other community resources need to be provided.

5. Traditional approaches may need to be used, including:

   - *Talking circle/talk stick.* Each person shares when it is his or her turn to talk in the circle or when he or she holds the stick.

   - *Sweat lodge.* Each person becomes closer to the Creator and others by participating in a sweat within a domed structure.

   - *Right path of life.* These include the Good Way (adapted 12-step format), the Peyote Road (blend of Christian/Indian beliefs with use of Peyote as a sacrament), the Red Road (the difference between being drunk and sober), and the Sacred Circle (one chooses to be drug free or use).

Specific recommendations for the Alaska Native are described by CSAT (1999). Seven groups that have their own language and culture comprise the Alaska Native (Alaska Athabaskans, Tlingit, Haida, Tsimsian, Aleut, Inupiat, and Yup'ik, previously called "Eskimo"). This group typically binge drinks, and counselors need to (a) use situational role modeling rather than confrontation, and (b) consider mobile treatment because of geographical isolation. Treatment that is positive, strength-based, and focuses on wellness can be especially effective with this population (Radin et al., 2011). Finally, culturally specific treatments that may be helpful are those such as cultural/spiritual camp immersion experiences, mindfulness and meditation, and the inclusion of traditional healers, and ceremonial life (Mohatt et al., 2007). (See Case Study 10.5.)

CASE STUDY 10.5

Tom is a 35-year-old Native American who was raised on a reservation until he was 6 years old and was then raised by a Caucasian foster family off the reservation and in another state until he completed high school. He returned to his reservation when he was age 18. Both of his birth parents were alcoholic, and his father died 10 years ago of alcoholism. Tom has a 6-year-old son by his ex-wife. He is currently on probation for a fight in a bar, where he almost killed another Native American man who said negative things about his wife at the time. He was in prison for the crime, was on probation, relapsed from his recovery program, had another fight in a bar, and returned to prison. Tom is currently on probation again, living at a halfway house, and involved in a local self-help program. He has told the staff he is most comfortable talking with other Native Americans from his tribe.

1. What potential counseling problems do you anticipate between yourself and Tom and why?
2. How would you approach Tom in terms of inviting him to trust you?
3. How would you handle a communication problem with Tom when you felt a "glass wall" appear?
4. What issues do you believe Tom may need to address in his recovery, and how would you facilitate these discussions?

EXERCISE 10.2

Look over the descriptions of each of the racial groups discussed in this section. Then answer three questions:

1. Which group of individuals would you anticipate being more comfortable to work with on substance abuse concerns? Why?
2. Which group would be more of a stretch for you to work with on substance abuse concerns? Why?
3. Now compare your reasons for the different comfort levels in working with these populations.

Sexual Orientation (Gay, Lesbian, Bisexual, and Transgender [GLBT])

Cabaj (1997) describes sexual orientation as based on desire rather than sexual behavior that may or may not be connected to sexual orientation. *Homosexuality* means that the sexual interest in another person is toward the person of the same sex, whereas in *bisexuality* that interest is toward people of both sexes. Sexual orientation ranges from same-sex attraction at one end of the spectrum to opposite-sex attraction at the other end (SAMHSA, 2003). SAMHSA provides some definitions of terms necessary for discussion of counseling this population. *Sexual behavior* (activity) does not define the person as GLBT, and *sexual identity* is how a person looks at his or her own desires and expressions. *Gender roles* are the behaviors a culture considers to be masculine or feminine. *Gender identity* is separate from gender role and is related to an individual's sense of being male or female. *Transgender* people follow gender roles of the opposite sex or identify with the gender of the opposite sex. They may be attracted to either or both males or females, and the term is usually used for people who are getting ready to have a sexual reassignment.

Schulman (2013) provides an update on the current acronym trend. Particularly popular on college campuses, at the current time, is a more inclusive, broader acronym: LGBTQIA. The acronym seems to stand for different words depending on who is being asked what it means. "Q" can stand for "questioning" or "queer"; "I" is for "Intersex" (one's anatomy is neither simply male or female); "A" is for "Ally" or "Asexual" (no sexual attraction). The American Counseling Association (ACA) division, the Association for Lesbian, Gay, Bisexual, and Transgender Issues in Counseling (ALGBTIC), currently uses the acronym LGBQQIA in its counseling competencies. Their use of the acronym follows: **L**esbian, **G**ay, **B**isexual, **Q**ueer, **Q**uestioning, **I**ntersex, and **A**lly individuals. More information on these competencies can be accessed at http://www.algbtic.org/images/stories/ALGBTIC_Comps_for_Counseling_LGBQQIA_Individuals_Final.pdf.

Their document does not discuss transgender, but refers the reader to the *ACA Competencies for Counseling with Transgender Clients* (ACA, 2009).

The acronym the author has chosen to use in this section is GLBT. When other acronyms are used in this chapter, it is because that specific acronym has been used by the author being referenced.

Although sexual orientation does not cause addiction, we live in a culture where GLBT individuals experience discrimination. Greater than two thirds of LGB adults reported at least one type of discrimination (sexual orientation, race, and gender) (McCabe, Bostwick, Hughes, West, & Boyd, 2010). This discrimination may be heightened for adolescents in both their family and peer groups, as well as GLBT individuals who are of an ethnic minority (Condit, Kitaji, Drabble, & Trocki, 2011) or immigrant status (Senreich & Vairo, 2004). Also, in one study, LGB participants with a diagnosis for at least one alcohol/drug use disorder reported a greater likelihood for the experience of heterosexism and internalized homophobia than those who did not have that type of diagnosis (Weber, 2008).

Focusing in on the gay/lesbian population, Heyward (1992) underscores the oppression and injustice experienced by gays and lesbians. T. S. Weinberg (1994) reports that in response to the oppression these individuals experience, friends may play important roles in their lives, thereby resulting in their drinking the way their friends drink. Cabaj (1997) states that high degrees of substance abuse with gay men and lesbians can be understood by their sexual orientation, coming-out process, and homophobia, which is probably the most influential. Cabaj (2008) makes three major points:

1. Development of a gay/lesbian identity and the coming-out process is complex and continues through one's entire life.

2. Identity development is shaped by the discrimination experienced in one's world.

3. Substance use can provide relief from the homophobia and allow the presence of the "forbidden" behavior and social comfort.

Cabaj (1997) states there is no firm agreement about the amount or incidence of drug use in this population. While there is a lack of empirical national data, some researchers state that approximately one third of gays and lesbians in the United States abuse alcohol (Saghir, Robins, Walbran, & Gentry, 1970; van Wormer & Davis, 2008; M. S. Weinberg & Williams, 1974). Stall and Wiley (1988) found that only 19% of their sample of gay men were frequent, heavy drinkers, only some of whom were dependent. There may also be cultural aspects specific to this population that may contribute to the development/maintenance of substance abuse issues and guide how prevention and treatment interventions may need to be designed (Chaney & Brubaker, 2012).

Although there may be a range in the estimated number of alcoholics in this population, drinking is often a component in the socializing of gay men in terms of gay bars and parties (gay clubs are also a location for alcohol and drug use [Burroughs, 2003), and this same process of role modeling/socializing may operate with the lesbian and bisexual populations (van Wormer & Davis, 2008; T. S. Weinberg, 1994). In a summary of the research findings with lesbians, van Wormer and Davis (2008) state that alcohol use may be high with this population because: (a) the older community members, who are role models, may tend to drink heavily and use marijuana; (b) the combination of specific factors (lifestyle stress due to being viewed as deviant, relationship strain due to no public role models, and internalized homophobia) may encourage use; (c) the fewer lesbians caring for children may provide more freedom for them to party; and (d) advertising encourages use. Bisexuals often stand alone because they are not accepted into either heterosexual or gay/lesbian groups (van Wormer & Davis, 2008). This alienation, not belonging to either orientation, may lead to substance abuse (Senreich & Vairo, 2004).

Assessment

In the assessment process, the counselor needs to be sensitive to both internal and external homophobia experienced by the client (Senreich & Vairo, 2004). This sensitivity can be expressed by obtaining historical as well as current information about both the client's view of being GLBT and that of others in his or her life.

The counselor can develop relationships with GLBT groups, examine forms, procedures, and language that exclude heterosexist bias, and have a question on sexual behavior, attraction, or orientation.

One of the main concerns for the counselor is countertransference issues with a client's sexual orientation. In 1973, the American Psychiatric Association stated that homosexuality, by itself, cannot be considered a psychiatric disorder (Finnegan & McNally, 1987). As a result, counselors do not have the professional support to view homosexuality or bisexuality as a psychiatric illness. Counselors also need to be careful about assuming that problems presented are a result of orientation and at the same time be aware that mental health problems may come from discrimination and oppression factors (D. W. Sue & Sue, 2013). Yet, due to heterosexism and homophobia, some counselors tend to operate in that manner with their homosexual and bisexual clients. Heterosexism, the belief that heterosexuality is better, results in homophobia, negative stereotypes and feelings toward gays and lesbians. Counselors need to examine their views of heterosexuality and the impact of those views on their LGBT clients as well as privilege (heterosexual and gender—self-perception of gender that matches the sex assigned by birth) (D. W. Sue & Sue, 2013).

Each counselor working with an addicted GLBT individual needs to examine his or her own reactions and biases toward that person's sexual orientation. Negative biases can be addressed in counseling, with colleagues, and/or a supervisor. Each client, regardless of sexual orientation, has a right to be treated with respect. If counselors truly believe they cannot work with addicted GLBT clients, the agency should be informed of the limitation so that such clients are assigned to counselors who are more comfortable working with them. If the counselor works alone, this limitation should be made clear to others who refer clients.

Internalized heterosexism (IH) needs to be discussed here. This term describes the internalization of conscious or unconscious negative attitudes. Brubaker, Garrett, and Dew (2009) found that the 20-plus-year theory of IH increasing anxiety, depression, and low self-esteem that leads to alcohol and drug use as a coping mechanism has little support. Rather, they make specific suggestions for the assessment process with regard to IH that the clinician may find helpful. These include assessing the client's:

• Personal acceptance

• LGB community acceptance

• Identity disclosure

• Readiness to change in relation to IH

• Spiritual strengths

• Lifespan changes and their relationship with IH (e.g., lack of legalized marriage)

Such a holistic assessment with the inclusion of the relationship of IH in the unique configuration of the client's life story can broaden and deepen the assessment process as it relates to substance use.

Treatment and Aftercare
D. W. Sue and Sue (2013) provide specific counseling strategies in working with this population. These include: CBT techniques, coping skills and assertiveness training, using social supports, and having positive, affirming identity messages.

Substance abuse treatment for the GLBT population, even though it is very important, is not addressed in research and clinical literature as deemed by its importance (Anderson, 2009). This is especially true with the transgender population whose issues are quite different from GLB clients. For example, transgender clients may need help in "making name changes, referrals to medical professionals for hormone or surgical options, and the name and location of support groups" (Bess & Stabb, 2009, as cited in D. W. Sue & Sue, 2013, p. 485). Also, in one qualitative study, transgender individuals stated treatment center staff needed more education and sensitivity to their issues (Senreich, 2011). Overall, professionals need to have access to the knowledge that does exist regarding the work with the GLBT population in treatment settings so they can best meet the needs of the client.

Sexual orientation issues need to be integrated into the treatment recovery plan. Generally, the counselor needs to focus on issues related to substance abuse recovery, homophobia, and acceptance of one's sexual orientation (Cabaj, 2008). However, rather than assuming what these issues are, the counselor needs to work with the client to determine these concerns. Initially, each client needs to be asked about sexual orientation in a relaxed manner as part of the normal treatment procedure (Finnegan & McNally, 1987). For those clients who are GLBT, some concerns may be considered typical. Cabaj (1997), for example, recommends that counselors consider the following aspects of each individual in development of a treatment plan: life stage, coming-out process, support available, current and past relationships with significant others and family, comfort with sexuality, and issues related to career, finances, and health.

The coming-out process is a series of steps taken over time where the client acknowledges his or her difference, pulls that difference into self-view, possibly acts on feelings, and then decides whom to inform about his or her sexual orientation (Cabaj, 1997). The counselor needs to determine the client's comfort with his or her sexual identity and respect that (SAMHSA, 2003). Cass (1979) described the stages of the coming-out process as identity confusion, comparison, tolerance, acceptance, pride, and identity synthesis. Savin-Williams (2001) has an excellent text on how families negotiate the coming-out process. Without the GLBT client's own acceptance of his or her sexual orientation, relapse may occur. Also, the counselor needs to be aware that increased alcohol/drug usage or relapse may be related to verbal and/or physical attacks by others because of the client's sexual orientation.

SAMHSA (2003) describes clinical issues as:

- GLBT:

  a. Each person's circumstances and experiences need to be explored.

  b. They have legal prohibitions against their behavior.

  c. They have experienced discrimination.

  d. They may have internalized homophobia.

  e. Gay men may return to a social life that involves partying (either when single or when a part of a couple raising children).

  f. They may be victims of violence and hate crimes.

- Lesbians:

  a. There are fewer who abstain from alcohol.

  b. There are higher rates of alcohol problems.

  c. Women's bars provide opportunities for socializing and support.

  d. They may "pass" as heterosexual and find this stressful.

  e. They may find coming out stressful.

  f. They may experience stress related to trauma.

- Gays:

  a. The "gay ghetto" is where gay bars are.

  b. HIV/AIDS is a part of their lives.

  c. Sex and intimacy might not be linked for some individuals.

  d. Some gay men may be effeminate, which can be looked down on in the gay community and increase their sense of shame.

- Bisexual:

  a. This may be seen as a sexual orientation, not necessarily behavioral.

  b. They may experience bias from providers because they are bisexual.

  c. They may feel alienated from both the heterosexual and lesbian/gay communities.

- Transgender:

  a. There are high rates of substance abuse.

  b. "Societal and internalized transphobia, violence, discrimination, family problems, isolation, lack of educational and job opportunities, lack of access to health care, and client's low self-esteem" (p. xix) can be issues.

  c. Bad experiences with health care providers may make them distrustful.

  d. Hormone therapy, while standard, may impact mood; street hormones may be risky; and testosterone injections may be relapse triggers.

  e. There may be issues in the use of restrooms and sleeping arrangements.

- Youth:

  a. They use for the same reasons other young people use, but they also may feel more isolated because of a need to hide their sexual identity, and they may use drugs to deal with shame, deny feelings, or cope with violence.

  b. They are usually aware of their sexual feelings around age 10, have sexual experiences between ages 13 and 15, and identify about age 15 or 16.

  c. They are at a high risk for being victims of violence.

344 CHAPTER 10 CULTURALLY SENSITIVE ADDICTION COUNSELING

Gays, lesbians, and bisexual men and women report experiences with discrimination and harassment in chemical dependency treatment centers (Eliason, 1996). Detox and treatment centers may not know much about the GLBT population, not discuss sexual orientation, or even know their client's sexual orientation (Hellman, Stanton, Lee, & Tytun, 1989). J. Hall (1994) states that there are three barriers in addiction treatment for lesbians: (1) distrust in terms of feeling that sexuality issues are not understood or that they are discriminated against, (2) incongruence between the client's and the provider's views of the problem and treatment, and (3) provider styles are not helpful (e.g., paternalistic and confrontational). When these individuals enter into recovery from addiction, their sexual orientation must be addressed, without prejudice, as a part of their recovery. Treatment needs to be GLBT affirmative, where the client feels welcomed (Senreich & Vairo, 2004) and at least *gay sensitive* if not *gay affirming* (the gay identity is accepted as a part of recovery) (Cabaj, 2008).

With ethnic minority GLBT clients and bisexual clients, counselors may need to emphasize strengthening the identity of the individual given the specific additional discrimination they may experience (Senreich & Vairo, 2004). One organization, the Pride Institute, that focuses on mental health and addictions treatment for GLBT clients began in 1986 (Amico & Neisen, 1997) and has centers in Florida and Minnesota. One study found that GLBT program components helped gay and bisexual men in treatment (Senreich, 2010b).

Some clients might use "gaydar" to determine whether a counselor is open to working with gays and lesbians. *Gaydar* is a term some gays and lesbians use to describe their internal radar or sense as to whether someone is open to gays and lesbians. The counselor can demonstrate an openness by being relaxed when discussing sexual orientation, answering questions about his or her sexual orientation (if appropriate and comfortable for the counselor), and speaking an inclusive language that does not assume sexual orientation. An example of inclusive language is a counselor talking with a client about intimate relationships and using a word such as *partner* rather than *boyfriend* or *girlfriend*.

Another concern of clients is not being able to go to gay bars to socialize. Gay bars serve a purpose broader than that of heterosexual bars. They are one of the few places in society that a client can safely assume that the others in the bar are gay or lesbian and can comfortably make connections with others (Finnegan & McNally, 1987). Therefore, a common counselor recommendation to avoid bars may not be possible for this population. However, counselors need to avoid the extreme of either prohibiting them or minimizing their danger to the client's recovery (Senreich & Vairo, 2004). It is more helpful if the counselor strikes a balanced perspective. For example, Finnegan and McNally suggest that clients who go to bars do so with other recovering gays, lesbians, and bisexuals after attending a recovery meeting. In whatever way the GLBT client attends these bars, it needs to be done in a self-protective manner that does not encourage relapse. The client may be encouraged to go to a bar only when not out of balance physically or emotionally or only at times when feeling less vulnerable to the influence of others. In addition, it may be helpful for the client to scrutinize his or her motives for going to the bar and determine whether those needs can be met somewhere else. There is a realistic vulnerability for lesbians and gays, as evidenced in an Australian study, for increased drug use in these settings, particularly with club drugs (Lea, 2013). Cabaj (2008) states that additional social outlets for gay men and lesbians are private homes, clubs, gay-travel parties, circuit parties (alcohol and other drugs—ecstasy, GHB, poppers—are dominant), and seeking sexual partners over the Internet. Counselors need to talk with clients about their past involvement in these social outlets and how they anticipate being involved in them in their recovery.

Typically, treatment for addiction involves a client's partner or family members. There is recent evidence, in one study, that involvement of a significant other, for at least one session, for LGBT clients had a positive impact on completion, satisfaction, feeling support from their counselor, and abstinence (Senreich, 2010a). The counselor needs to determine from the client whether his or her partner and/or family wants to be involved in treatment. It is possible that they may want to be involved but do not want sexual orientation addressed in a group of predominantly heterosexuals. The counselor can work with the client to determine whether group treatment is appropriate or whether individual or family counseling in combination with the provision of educational literature on addiction recovery and sexual orientation is more appropriate. Whatever the treatment modality, the counselor needs to be sure that clients are being treated with respect. This approach would be respectful of the reality in which clients and their partners and families live.

For those counselors working with lesbian, gay, and bisexual (LGB) youth, there needs to be an awareness that they are at a higher risk for depression and suicide attempts as well as alcohol and drug use (Huebner, 2013). They experience stress that includes school bullying, community discrimination, and friends rejection of them, and this stress can be exacerbated by negative family responses to their sexuality (Huebner, 2013). Counselors, then, need to be sensitive to the family's reaction to the sexuality of the client and how this may impact the client. For counselors able to make interventions with the family as a part of the client's treatment, Huebner (2013) provides information on three resources for parents: Parents, Families, and Friends of Lesbians and Gays (PFLAG) (a national nonprofit organization in the United States); the Family Acceptance Project (FAP) (a San Francisco State University initiative developing evidence-based resources for families of ethnic, social, and religious diversity); and *Lead with Love* (a film-based family intervention that can be viewed online at www.leadwithlovefilm.com).

Lesbians often have some different issues that need to be addressed in treatment. Typically, they have less income, are more likely to be older when they come out, have children, have their substance abuse ignored because they are female, experience bisexuality in terms of feelings or behavior, and are more likely to be in long-term relationships (Cabaj, 1997). Therefore, treatment with lesbians needs to focus on relationship-oriented issues such as parenting and domestic violence. Bobbe (2002) suggests that counselors focus on sobriety first and then address issues such as shame and internalized homophobia. The author also suggests that stress management tools such as relaxation, meditation, and spiritual development be taught to clients as well as counselors using expressive therapies to help their clients connect with a higher self. Specific treatment centers that are affirming to lesbians are the Pride Institute (Florida and Minnesota locations) and the Gables Recovery Home (Minnesota).

For sexual minority women (lesbians, bisexual women, same-sex experiences/attractions), there are higher substance use disorder rates (compared to heterosexual women), the same or higher help-seeking rates (compared to heterosexual women), and different issues in treatment as compared with sexual minority men and heterosexual women (Drabble & Eliason, 2012). Particular stressors, in one qualitative study, included: family (family's initial response to sexual orientation, alcoholism history, and abuse/criticism), relationships (partner use, coping with endings), trauma/violence, discrimination (homophobia, racism, sexual assault, other trauma) (Condit et al., 2011). In this study, the authors also found that effective coping resources included supportive family, friends, and community. With this population, treatment is enhanced when clients are: (a) welcomed as a part of the treatment community, (b) have a trauma component, (c) involve GLBT responsive agencies, and (d) assist in links with community resources/social networks specific to this population (Drabble & Eliason, 2012).

In an analysis of the 2004–2005 National Epidemiologic Survey on Alcohol and Related Conditions findings, McCabe et al. (2010) found substance abuse was almost 4 times that in the GLB population who reported all three types of discrimination (sexual orientation, race, gender) than those who did not. Therefore, counselors need to be sensitive to the interactive impact of multiple discrimination on the recovery process of their clients. The author and colleagues (McCabe, West, Hughes, & Boyd, 2013) also found that sexual minorities (especially women): (a) had a greater likelihood of substance use disorders over their lives and began drinking earlier, (b) more extensive family history of substance abuse, and (c) used treatment less extensively.

When counselors refer GLBT clients to self-help groups in the community, they need to be aware that discrimination exists in such groups as well as in the general population. It may be helpful if the counselor has contacts in the GLBT community and in recovery and/or self-help groups in that community. GLBT-friendly self-help groups may assist the client in becoming and remaining abstinent (Senreich & Vairo, 2004). Recovering GLBT individuals can help clients adjust to the recovery process at times when the counselor may be inaccessible or in ways the counselor cannot assist the client (e.g., attending a self-help group with the client). Remember, too, that some homosexual clients may be hesitant to go to AA or Narcotics Anonymous (NA) because they may connect these groups to religion, and often these clients have been ostracized by religions for their homosexuality (Cabaj, 1997). At the same time, there is evidence that these groups can provide social support, coping mechanisms, and enhance clients' perceptions of their strengths (Callicott, 2012).

If there is a self-help group in the community for GLBT individuals, the counselor needs to remember to ask the client about the meeting experience. As with heterosexual meetings, the health of the group can vary a great deal. As with any individual in recovery, the client may find someone to date at a self-help meeting, but that is not the intent of the meeting. The client may need to be reminded that the reason for attending meetings is to work on sobriety.

If there are no GLBT self-help groups, the counselor needs to discuss with the client the possibility of experiencing discriminatory reactions if the client discloses being GLBT. Some recovering clients never let group members know their sexual orientation and can live with that comfortably; they are comfortable using terms such as *partner* and avoiding terms such as *he* or *she* when discussing intimate relationships. If clients are not comfortable with that approach and want to disclose their sexual orientation, they need to be reminded that some self-help group members may be very discriminatory, and there may be ostracism in the group after disclosure of sexual orientation. Another caution of self-help groups concerns sponsorship or mentorship. Some groups, such as 12-step groups, encourage the individual to choose a sponsor or mentor of the same gender. This advice is generally thought to discourage "13 stepping" (someone sober for a while being sexual with someone who is new in recovery). However, for GLBT clients, this advice does not necessarily work. Clients may be better advised to choose a sponsor or mentor to whom they can relate without a lot of sexual energy between them. This may be someone of the same sex or someone of the opposite sex.

Not all addicted clients have issues about sexual orientation, but the therapist working with addicted clients needs to have an awareness that such issues are present for GLBT clients. There are additional issues that may need to be explored and addressed in the treatment and aftercare process. One of the unfortunate realities for the GLBT population is violence. There may need to be open discussions regarding hate crimes and violence that have been and may be directed at them as well as an assessment of domestic violence in their intimate relationship. Additionally, young gay and lesbian clients may have more of a risk of suicidal thinking and behavior. Aging gay men and lesbians may feel more isolated and disconnected and may have few social supports if they become a gay widow.

Brubaker et al. (2009) provide a helpful overview of clinical interventions with regard to a counselor working with a client on internalized heterosexism. Their main caution is that the counselor develop a sensitive timing on the addressing of these issues. Specifically they suggest:

- Do not push sexual identity development.

- Anticipate sexual identity disclosure impact on recovery with the client.

- Do not perpetuate bisexism or transsexism.

- With couples, examine the impact of IH on the relationship as well as the couple's ability to reach out for support.

Overall, the counselor needs to work with this clientele in a respectful, honest manner with an ongoing awareness of the discrimination toward this population. A welcoming, supportive, humane approach by the counselor and the agency can be especially healing for this population that often experiences discrimination and ostracism. (See Case Study 10.6.)

Disability

The disabled population is the largest minority group in the United States (Disability Funders Network, 2012; Olkin, 1999); approximately 1 in 5 Americans, or 54 million, live with at least one disability (Centers for Disease Control, 2009) (Disability Funders Network, 2012), and it is one of the fastest-growing U.S. minority groups (Kemp & Mallinckrodt, 1996). *Disability* means that an individual is limited in functioning (physical, mental, and/or emotional) because of an impairment that affects his or her life performance activities (Albrecht, 1992). The disabled person, especially one who has *acquired* the disability in living, may have to change how they view self, deal with pain, and cope with daily living as it relates to their schedule and employment. This shift in independence requires an adjustment time that may be impacted by the severity of the disability

CASE STUDY 10.6

Sandra has just entered addiction treatment for the first time. She is in an outpatient setting with a mixed group of male and female clients. When she talks with you about her significant other, she always uses the word *partner*, and when she talks about her struggles in the group setting, she emphasizes that everyone in the group is married and most have children. She says after her first few sessions that she does not know whether she will be able to stay sober, because much of her social life is around her friends who understand her and support her, but they often socialize together in a bar setting or in a social context where alcohol and marijuana are readily available. You believe that Sandra may be a lesbian.

1. How would you bring up sexual orientation with Sandra?
2. If she is a lesbian, how would you approach her social life in terms of relapse prevention?
3. If she is lesbian, how would you help her cope in the group treatment setting and in individual counseling with you?

EXERCISE 10.3

Take a few moments to reflect on three questions:

1. Of the GLBT clients, which group would be the most difficult for you to counsel?
2. What values, experiences, and beliefs might make it difficult for you to work with that clientele?
3. How would you address these possible countertransference issues?

(NIAAA, 2005). Also, people with severe disabilities can never entirely live on their own (Mackelprang & Salsgiver, 1999), and the more visible the disability, the more negatively the disabled person is viewed by others (Olkin & Howson, 1994). This population also experiences potential discrimination in numerous areas (housing, education, health care, employment, leisure) (Mackelprang & Salsgiver, 1999). The difficulties that come from living with the changes accompanying a disability may be fertile ground for substance abuse. In this author's experience, the more visible the disability, the more it impacts the awareness and actions of others in response to the disability whether that is negative or positive.

There is a lack of research on alcohol and drug use (NIAAA, 2005; Tyas & Rush, 1993) and on alcohol and drug abuse treatment with the disabled population (Glow, 1989). Yet, it is estimated that 15% to 30% of those who are disabled abuse alcohol and drugs (Nelipovich & Buss, 1991), which is twice as high as the general population (Rehabilitation Research and Training Center on Drugs and Disability, 1996). Substance abuse is a serious issue for people with disabilities (Bachman, Drainoni, & Tobias, 2004). The substance abuse among the disabled may have an impact on rehabilitation through behavioral or cognitive changes or medical problems, and may affect vocational rehabilitation (Heinemann, 1997).

In 1990, the Americans with Disabilities Act became a law to provide equal access to community services, yet Atkinson and Hackett (2004) report that disabled people report discrimination "in the form of social, educational, economic, and environmental discrimination, and abuse" (p. 47). Although it has been recommended by some that the disabled population be treated within a typical alcohol and drug treatment program, this approach would require treatment programs to look at the specific disability and then what the individual with that disability requires (Glow, 1989). Unfortunately, many treatment programs would prefer to not serve the disabled population (Tyas & Rush, 1993). Both sets of disciplines (rehabilitation, substance abuse) may feel inadequate in addressing these dual issues because of

a lack of training in the other area (Heinemann, 1993) and a lack of system flexibility to address both problems and the interaction between them. Treatment providers (organization, individual) may not accommodate for the disability, resulting in unequal service (Mackelprang & Salsgiver, 1999), and justify this inflexibility by a lack of funding (Leigh, Powers, Vash, & Nettles, 2004). Issues with accessibility (technology, communication devices, interpreters, telephones, restrooms and therapy offices, and chair ramps) are often present (Leigh et al., 2004). Therefore, the person who has both problems may not get the help they need (Heinemann, 1993; Ogborne & Smart, 1995). Counselors need to examine themselves for negative attitudes, biases, or beliefs that can impact client care.

In terms of the individual counselor, Glow (1989) recommends that the counselor focus not on the disability, but on the alcohol/drug problems while keeping the disability in mind. Olkin (1999) recommends eight guidelines for disability etiquette for counselors that include:

1. Not staring.

2. Not assuming the client needs help.

3. Knowing who the client is (especially if someone is with them, so roles in the session are understood from the beginning).

4. Stating when you do not understand a person who has a speaking impairment.

5. Avoiding being overly cautious with words (e.g., being hesitant to say "see" to a blind person).

6. Not touching assistive devices without permission.

7. Being aware of how disability may shift nonverbal cues.

8. Being aware of room temperature, because there might be heightened temperature sensitivity.

Regarding both individual and organizational approaches, SAMHSA (2002b) provides seven guidelines on overcoming barriers and providing treatment to clients who have both substance abuse and physical and/or cognitive disabilities that include:

1. Examining barriers to treatment (attitudes, discriminatory practices, communication, architectural).

2. Asking all clients whether they need accommodation.

3. Looking at issues with transportation, employment, social isolation, and physical abuse by providing for additional services and acting as advocates.

4. Making treatment plans flexible and varying the length of counseling sessions.

5. Referring to a disability service professional for an assessment if a disability diagnosis is suspected.

6. Providing a medical assessment of all medications (prescribed, over-the-counter) taken by the client, with one medical professional monitoring the medications being taken.

7. Hiring people with disabilities to work at the agency.

Also, family counseling needs to be included in the treatment plan. This counseling work needs to be done within the context of the disability, because family members may have enabling behaviors that are in response to the unique aspects of the disability as well as any unresolved issues they have in their own adjustment to the disability.

Future research and continuing education for practitioners are needed to improve service in the substance area with this population (Smedema & Ebener, 2010). For example, there appears to be a complicated relationship between the factors of disability adaptation, substance use disorder, and quality of life (Ebener & Smedema, 2011). Three disabled populations—the deaf and hard of hearing, the blind and visually impaired, and the physically injured—are discussed in this section.

Deaf and Hard of Hearing

Alcohol abuse is the same or greater with this population, but it is difficult to determine exact numbers and causality due to the population being viewed as not having a high incidence of substance abuse and barriers that are both cultural and language based (Guthmann & Graham, 2004). Also, both inpatient and outpatient programs in the United States have been decreasing in the past few years due to problems with funding, staff (specialized), and census (low) (Guthmann & Sternfield, 2013). Therefore, providers of treatment need to be creative in finding ways to counsel this population, especially since evidence-based treatments have not been adapted to them (Guthmann & Sternfield, 2013).

Excellent information on the alcohol/drug abuse treatment of this population has emerged from the Minnesota Chemical Dependency Program for Deaf and Hard of Hearing Individuals, located in the Fairview University Medical Center in Minneapolis, Minnesota. The program has a clinical manual and a best practices manual, which are described in the Suggested Readings section at the end of this chapter. They have noted six main barriers to treatment and recovery for this population (1994):

1. *Recognition of a problem.* There is a general lack of awareness of the problem and a stigma about having such a problem. This population does not have access to the dangers of use. For example, television may not have captioned announcements, and school prevention information may not be accommodated to this population (Guthmann & Blozis, 2001).

2. *Confidentiality.* There is a close communication network among individuals who are deaf. This may impact people who want to examine their problems with alcohol/drugs. The existence of a communication grapevine may cause deaf people to worry that information about them may cause a loss of status in the community (Guthmann & Blozis, 2001). For example, this population may be concerned

that an interpreter may not respect the confidentiality of the counseling process and will share information with individuals in their deaf community.

3. *Lack of resources.* Resources for information and services on alcohol and drug addiction are not often accessible to individuals who are deaf or hard of hearing. Resources that can overcome barriers include counselors fluent in American Sign Language (ASL), assistive listening devices, TV decoders, and teletypewriter (TTY; Guthmann & Blozis, 2001).

4. *Enabling.* Alcohol and drug use behaviors may be excused by family members and friends as a result of the disability; therefore, they may continually rescue these individuals from the consequences of their behavior. Because of a desire to present a positive image, the deaf and hard-of-hearing community may not acknowledge problems of alcohol and drug use (Guthmann & Blozis, 2001).

5. *Funding concerns.* People who are deaf or hard of hearing often must travel a significant distance to receive assistance from staff who are specially trained. In addition, interpreters are costly (as well as difficult to find) for 12-step programs (Guthmann & Blozis, 2001).

6. *Lack of support in recovery.* It is often difficult for people who are deaf or hard of hearing to receive support for their recovery, due to both the small numbers of individuals in their local deaf or hard-of-hearing community and the even smaller number who are in a recovery process. In addition, Guthmann and Blozis (2001) state that family members and friends of the person may not see the problem or do not confront the addicted person, thereby enabling the problem to continue.

Assessment Guthmann and Graham (2004) state that the assessment of substance abuse with this population is generally ineffectively done. Yet, assessment of this population is similar to that with other addicted populations. Physical, work,

school, social, legal, financial, emotional, and spiritual aspects of the person's life that show a pattern of alcohol/drug-related problems warrant a thorough assessment. In the assessment process, it is important to remember that about 75% of Americans who are deaf use ASL as their preferred mode of communication (Vernon, 1990). The individual completing the addiction assessment with this population needs to be fluent in ASL or use a qualified interpreter to ensure accurate communication. Often the assessment instruments used have a strong reliance on the ability to read written English (Guthmann & Sternfield, 2013). SAMHSA (2002b) encourages that questionnaires and forms be interpreted into sign language, because paper-and-pencil information gathering depends on the reading ability of the client, which can vary a great deal in the deaf population. One such instrument, the Substance Abuse Screener in American Sign Language (SAS_ASL), where a 42-item version was used in a study, showed promising reliability and validity screening with this population; this instrument can be administered electronically (Guthmann, Lazowski, Moore, Heinemann, & Embree, 2012).

The assessor also needs to be aware that alcohol/drug abuse education is not equivalent to that provided to the hearing population (Rendon, 1992). Because of the deaf community's lack of general education on addiction, the assessor may need to avoid commonly used addiction slang terms (e.g., blackouts). Rather, the assessor may communicate better by using descriptions of behavior, such as, "Have you ever had a period of time when you were drinking that you cannot remember what you said or did?" Also, it is important when assessing an individual who is deaf or hard of hearing to look at the individual when speaking, even when an interpreter is present, so the client has an option to read the counselor's lips and see facial expressions (SAMHSA, 2002b). Finally, cultural considerations need to be taken into account by the counselor. For example, storytelling, a part of deaf culture where information is packaged in a manner that makes conceptual sense, may make an evaluation a slower process with this population (Guthmann & Sternfield, 2013).

Treatment and Aftercare In a summary of the research on this population, Guthmann and Graham (2004) state that there are obstacles to treatment, such as knowledge and experience in working with this population, as well as attempts to adapt substance abuse treatment designed for the nondisabled to this population. They warn that such obstacles may end up hurting this population as they seek treatment. There are also problems that arise in the translation of concepts to American Sign Language (ASL); these concepts are included in the 12-step program, cognitive-behavioral therapy, and relapse prevention (Glickman, 2009).

Access to treatment can be enhanced for this population through telecommunication devices (TDD), presence of sign language use (qualified interpreters as well as counselors), collaboration with vocational rehabilitation personnel, and contact with the deaf community (outreach, community organizations, etc.; McCrone, 1982). In treatment, it is recommended that time be spent addressing defenses, educating and discussing feelings, attending a special focus group on deaf issues, working with the 12 steps of AA, addressing self-esteem issues, and involving families (Guthmann, Swan, & Gendreau, 1994). In addition to an overall treatment evaluation of the individual, it is also recommended that treatment involve an assessment of communication skills; education of chemical dependency, coping skills, and decision-making skills; and the need for occupational and recreational therapy (Guthmann, 1994). One treatment barrier is long-distance travel, which is often required for treatment services because of the low amount of substance abuse in this population; such travel makes treatment expensive, and funding sources may not recognize the needs of this group (Guthmann & Blozis, 2001).

A model treatment program in this area is the Minnesota Chemical Dependency Program for Deaf and Hard-of-Hearing individuals. Guthmann

and Sandberg (2003) describe it as a "culturally affirmative" program. They provide treatment in three phases: (1) evaluation/assessment (including a communication assessment to determine needs and preferred communication and assessment of use that involves client drawing to reduce communication barriers), (2) primary treatment (including information and involvement of the 12 steps of AA and NA, family week, education/support, behavior contracts, and treatment probation contract), and (3) aftercare/extended care (networking locally and nationally and relapse prevention). Overall, this program offers individual and group therapy, education groups on spirituality, grief, gender, 12-step access, and recreational therapy as well as assessment and aftercare.

Creative treatment strategies that reflect an adaptation to this population include: *storytelling* (narrative therapy) expressed in activities such as the Feelings Collage, the Life Lines Project, People, Places, and Things, *visual metaphors* (narrative therapy), *activities beyond discussion* such as role-plays and drawings, and *use of technology* (language-accessible substance abuse material adaptations such as pictoral tools; video phone; online web-cam meetings, etc.) (Guthmann & Sternfield, 2013). An overview of specific suggestions in applying these strategies to this population is provided in an excellent summary by Guthmann and Sternfield (2013).

Note that the most common forms of communication are person-to-person and the Internet, with deaf individuals commonly using text messaging, e-mail, video phones, etc. (Guthmann & Sternfield, 2013). In the future, the use of technology can help with treatment, support, professional training, and assessment development (Titus & Guthmann, 2010). An example of such forward movement is the "Deaf Off Drugs and Alcohol" (DODA), an e-therapy program out of Wright State University in Ohio that is funded by CSAT (Embree, 2012). This program is providing various forms of technology to facilitate treatment (web-based 12-step meetings, "teleconferencing software, videophones, email, text messaging, voice mail, and Internet hosted pages on mainstream social networking sites" (Guthmann & Sternfield, 2013, p. 250).

Finally, while aftercare planning is important in working with this population, Guthmann and Sternfield (2013) report counselors can feel as though they are putting together a jigsaw puzzle as they attempt to create an aftercare plan due to limited resources. Vocational rehabilitation counselors or other professionals providing services to people who are deaf or hard of hearing may be able to provide information about resources in the client's community. This individual may be able to help the client advocate for self and educate the community of recovery about what is needed to assist the individual (Sandberg, 1994). Guthmann and Blozis (2001) make 10 recommendations:

1. Have a positive relationship between abstinence and employment by including vocational rehabilitation.

2. Provide education of job-seeking and retention skills.

3. Have a consistent national policy of state vocational rehabilitation general requirements and abstinence/sobriety requirements.

4. Establish training programs for professionals who work with this population.

5. Have a substance abuse hotline for deaf and hard-of-hearing individuals.

6. Educate family/friends about substance abuse.

7. Have better access to self-help groups.

8. Make aftercare information more available.

9. Find additional sources of funding.

10. Have more research done with this population.

Blind and Visually Impaired

Too much isolation, time, and lack of employment are risk factors for substance abuse in this population (Nelipovich & Buss, 1989). Glass (1980) reported two kinds of blind and visually impaired drinkers: the client who drank before acquiring the disability (Type A) and the client who drank after the disability occurred (Type B). Glass states that the Type A client uses drinking as a main coping mechanism and requires substance abuse treatment. The Type B client may be able to stop using alcohol if the underlying stressors are examined in combination with skills to assist the person in coping with the disability. Continuing to use Glass's categorization system, the Type A client needs psychological or psychiatric help to assist with life problems that existed before the disability. This treatment has a skills training component to assist the individual in coping more effectively with problems (Glass, 1980–1981). The Type B client needs to learn skills to be able to be more independent. Either abstinence or controlled drinking may be recommended for this individual.

Because substance abuse and blindness in combination can complicate service delivery to this population, counselors need to be aware of specific issues that arise with this population in order to best meet the needs of the client (Davis, Koch, McKee, & Nelipovich, 2009). SAMHSA (2002b) makes specific treatment recommendations, including paths should be clear, and large-letter and Braille signs should be placed at all signs and elevator buttons. SAMHSA also suggests that intake forms be available in Braille, large print, audiocassette, or assistance by a sighted person depending on the client's choice; clients who are both deaf and blind need a tactile interpreter throughout the counseling process. Any reading materials given to this population will require more time.

Physically Injured

"Alcohol is a major risk factor for virtually all categories of intentional and unintentional injuries" (Degutis, Fiellin, & D'Onofrio, 2009). Individuals with these types of physical problems may self-medicate their pain as well as use drugs to cope with their feelings of anxiety and depression. Screening for problems with alcohol and drugs as well as careful assessment and appropriate referrals are a necessary part of general treatment for individuals with these conditions (Heinemann, 1997). Individuals working in emergency rooms could use the CAGE, TWEAK, or AUDIT, broad substance abuse screening instruments that are discussed in Chapter 3. Bombardier and Turner (2010) also add the use of the AUDIT-C, Rapid Alcohol Problems Screen (RAPS), SMAST, and SASSI as well as practical screening, assessment, and treatment approaches.

Two such injuries, traumatic brain injuries (TBI) and spinal cord injuries (SCI), are discussed here. There is a prevalence of substance use in these populations and such usage can diminish or complicate the recovery process from these injuries (Bombardier & Turner, 2010). Note that there is evidence that persons with disabilities (PWDs) are denied services by substance abuse treatment centers at extremely high rates due to physical barriers (West, Graham, & Cifu, 2009).

TBI is "a blow to the head or a penetrating head injury that disrupts brain function" (Morkides, 2009, p. 40), are one of the major causes of disability, and half of those injuries are caused by motor vehicle accidents, many of which involve the presence of alcohol (Heinemann, 1997; McCombs & Moore, 2002). The injury may range from mild to severe and has sometimes been called the *silent* epidemic (Morkides, 2009). Also, research shows that a person with alcohol/drug problems tends to have TBI complications that are more frequent and more severe (Degutis et al., 2009) and, therefore, are more difficult to treat (Bogner, 2013).

Difficulties with cognition, memory, sensory/ motor, and attention/concentration may be present (Bogner, 2013; Morkides, 2009). Cognitive deficits can be viewed as treatment resistance, so assessment of the presence of a TBI needs to be done as soon as possible with treatment focusing on psychological and behavioral interventions (Bogner, 2013). Counselors need to help clients take in their situation, and a professional team effort is needed to address all of the issues that may be present (Morkides,

2009). For example, individuals with a substance use disorder and severe mental illness showed, in one study, a high rate of TBI where those clients with a TBI started using substances earlier and had poorer functioning—this complexity calls for a more thorough assessment process than simply the presence or absence of a TBI (Corrigan & Deutschle, 2008). Three critical factors need to be considered by the counselor in the overall assessment of the substance abusing client: the injury severity, the client's age at the time of injury, and repeated injury (Corrigan, Bogner, & Holloman, 2012).

If someone has cognitive impairments, SAMHSA (2002b) recommends:

- Asking simple questions.

- Repeating questions.

- Having clients repeat what is said.

- Holding concrete discussions.

- Asking clients to provide specific examples of a general concept being discussed.

- Using verbal and nonverbal cues to enhance treatment (e.g., touch a leg while giving a simple instruction).

- Using expressive therapy or role playing.

Another disability, spinal cord injury (SCI), is damage to the spinal cord that impacts mobility and feeling loss and can result in problems with bladder/bowel, sex, breathing, and chronic pain (National Spinal Cord Injury Association [NSCIA], 2009). There are 7,800 spinal cord injuries in the United States each year (National Spinal Cord Injury Association, 2009). This injury is often related to the use of alcohol and drugs, which means that clinicians need to be aware of how alcohol/drugs can affect these clients medically and in terms of rehabilitation and independence.

SAMHSA (2002b) recommends that counselors make sure wheelchairs can fit in spaces and under surfaces, with the counselor no higher than the client, have frequent breaks in the session, and monitor when the client appears to be tired.

In general, in counseling disabled individuals, D. W. Sue and Sue (2013) recommend the following:

- Examine one's own reactions to disabilities.

- Be aware of prejudice and discrimination they face that may be multiplied for clients who belong to different minority groups.

- Assess and involve family members and social supports.

- Be sensitive to environmental factors. (See Case Study 10.7.)

Age

Adolescents

Bukstein (1995) notes that adolescence is marred by physical, cognitive, and social changes resulting in four typical developmental behaviors that can encourage substance use, such as striving to be more independent, being experimental, being involved with peers, and desiring to be an adult. Winters (2001) states that substance-abusing adolescents may be delayed in their development. There is currently an emphasis on genetic and other biological vulnerabilities in addressing the concerns of adolescent substance use, abuse, and dependence. As a result, some comments need to be made about adolescent brain development.

CASE STUDY 10.7

Brenda is a 32-year-old Caucasian woman who is deaf. She has been referred to you for an evaluation because she was found passed out in her apartment by her landlady. The landlady contacted 911, and Brenda was taken to the emergency room. While being detoxed in the hospital, the attending physician referred her for an alcohol/drug evaluation. A qualified interpreter is available for the evaluation.

1. What would you need to talk with the interpreter about before conducting the evaluation?
2. How would you approach Brenda to facilitate her communicating with you?
3. What types of questions would you ask of Brenda to facilitate her trust in you?
4. What would you do if Brenda refused to talk with you about her personal history, including her drug use?

EXERCISE 10.4

Expanding on Exercise 8.4, attend an open (anyone can attend) or closed (only addicted individuals can attend) self-help group meeting. As you are going to the meeting, entering the meeting area, in the meeting, and leaving the meeting, be aware of barriers you would experience in each of these areas if you were deaf, blind, or had cognitive limitations or physical impairments. Then imagine what resources you would need to access and overcome these barriers.

Adolescents appear to be hardwired for risk-taking behaviors such as alcohol and drug use, because they have a more developed limbic system than a prefrontal system (Volkow & Li, 2005). Therefore, they appear to be more vulnerable than adults to substance abuse and addiction (Volkow & Li, 2005). This is based on the view of addiction as a medical disease that has physiological and molecular changes (Volkow & Li, 2005). Giedd (2004) summarizes the state of the adolescent brain. There are dynamic brain anatomy changes throughout adolescence. Particularly the area for controlling impulses (dorsal lateral prefrontal cortex), which is one of the last brain regions to occur; it does not reach adult dimensions until a person is in their early 20s. This means there are limits as to how much an adolescent can reason, make decisions, and control impulses, while there is an enhanced drive to take risks. This is a powerful vulnerability when combined with the high need for peer acceptance (Nagy, 2010).

Adolescents may drink and use for many reasons, then. NIDA (January 2006) specifies six aspects:

1. Brain development into the 20s encouraging a propensity to take risks.

2. Expectancies about alcohol having a positive effect.

3. Heightened sensitivity and tolerance to alcohol. (They can consume larger amounts before they experience any negative consequences, e.g., drowsiness, and still receive the positive aspects of alcohol use, e.g., social ease.)

4. Personality characteristics (conduct problems) and psychiatric comorbidity (depressed, withdrawn, anxious).

5. Hereditary factors.

6. Environmental factors (parents, peers, media).

These six factors carry over into young adulthood and college drinking. NIDA (April 2006) reports that people tend to drink their heaviest in their late teens and early to mid-20s, and these young adults tend to binge drink. In addition to the six factors listed previously, adolescents are also influenced by *gender* (men drink more than women), *race* (Whites, Native Americans, Hispanics, African Americans, and Asian Americans, in that order, drink most heavily), *college attendance* (college students drink more when they do drink, but they appear to mature out more quickly), *employment* (there is a decrease in amount, but an increase in current use if employed after high school), *military service* (those in the service drink more), and *marriage and parenting* (this decreases use).

While these six factors are basically noted here, the reader is encouraged to take in how one or a number of these factors may significantly impact the individual client regarding his/her substance use. For example, Hardy and Qureshi (2012) underscore the deep sociocultural impact of racial oppression that feeds into acting out behaviors, self-destructive behaviors of urban African Americans as a result of feeling devalued, dehumanized, and rageful. Substance use can help "kill" the pain that is experienced emotionally and psychologically. These factors, then, need to be taken into account through the assessment and treatment process. The authors provide some specific examples of interventions that can be used to address the impact of the oppression experienced by the adolescents.

Assessment Alcohol and other drug use is a critical health problem with adolescents (Winters, Fahnhorst, Botzet, & Stinchfield, 2009). The 2012 National Household Survey on Drug Use and Health found a decline from 2002 to 2011 in the percentage of substance dependence or abuse: 8.9% to 6.9% in the 12-to-17-year-old category and 21.7% to 18.7% in the 18-to-25-year-old category. A decline, in these same years, was also shown with alcohol dependence and abuse: 5.9% to 3.8% (12 to 17 years old) and 17.7% to 14.4% (18 to 25 years old). It is important to remember that alcohol is an illegal drug with this population.

Yule and Prince (2012) make some important notations regarding the use of substances by adolescents:

- Alcohol, marijuana, and cigarettes are the most frequently used substances.

- Alcohol is the most common substance used with a prevalence of binge drinking in 23% of the population (2010).

- There has been an increase in marijuana use in the last three years.

- Substance use increases with age.

- There are specific risk factors associated with use: "use before age 14, family history of substance use disorders, comorbid psychiatric illness, exposure to parental and peer use, and poor academic performance" (p. 175).

- Usually their use begins with alcohol and cigarettes.

However, many counselors do not have the skills necessary to accurately screen and assess this population (R. C. Schwartz & Smith, 2003). Also, assessing adolescents in terms of their chemical use history is difficult for several reasons. First, there is often a shorter use history on which an assessment is based. Second, adolescents may be acting out family system issues or psychiatric problems through their chemical use. Yet, accuracy in the assessment of adolescent chemical usage is important because of the end results of the two extremes (Doweiko, 1990): (1) adolescents may be overly diagnosed as addicted due to the fears of their parents and/or the greed of institutions, and (2) adolescents may be underdiagnosed, resulting in suicide (Crumley, 1990) or physical problems. Therefore, the counselor who conducts a formal assessment resulting in a diagnosis needs training and supervision of assessments by a qualified addiction professional who has knowledge, skills, and experience in this area. A counselor who does not have this training can still do an assessment, but it would be prudent to limit the results of the assessment to a referral to an addiction professional who is certified/licensed to accurately diagnose the client.

While some counselors have jobs in the addiction counseling field where they automatically complete an assessment to determine whether the client is addicted, other professionals work in settings where a broad screening for possible use problems is needed. In the latter situation, the counselor needs to have a screening process for assessing the adolescent population. R. C. Schwartz and Smith (2003) recommend the use of a screening process as part of an interview, which is easy, quick, broad, and can be applied to different clients. The authors recommend that the screening focus on the presence of use and severity as well as psychological problems and conditions at home and school. They recommend the client be the primary source of information and the parents/guardian be secondary. (Some screening instruments for this population are discussed in Chapter 3. The GAIN, which assesses substance use disorders and problems according to the *DSM-IV-TR*, is the primary screener/assessment tool being currently used by clinicians. Information about the instrument can be obtained from www.chestnut.org/LI/gain/GAIN_QxQ/.)

The authors recommend that a screening be done when several of the following risk factors exist: "poor child/parent relationships, low self-esteem, depression, low academic motivation, absence of religion or spirituality, high excitement-oriented behavior, peer substance abuse, and early cigarette use" (p. 25). Winters (2001) reminds us that risk and protective factors are the same for this group: personal adjustments and the environments of peer, home, and community. Once there is a positive screening for substance abuse, a formal assessment needs to be done. Again, the addiction professional needs to consider the context of his or her job and qualifications to do this type of assessment. This author recommends that counselors who do assessments of adolescents do so with caution because of the difficulty of accurately assessing this population.

Margolis (1995) reports six characteristics that specifically pertain to working with this population in terms of chemical usage:

1. Problem behaviors are indicators of drug abuse.

2. The addiction cycle is more rapid in this population than in the adult population.

3. Adolescents often use more than one drug.

4. Adolescents often have stronger denial.

5. Adolescents tend to have strong enabling systems.

6. Drug use developmental delays are common.

Specific criteria can be examined for indications of dependency. First, the counselor needs to examine the consequences of chemical usage in terms of legal, social, educational, and vocational problems. In particular, if there has been a marked change in appearance, emotional expression, social group, or grades, there is legitimate cause for concern. Also, if the adolescent shows a preoccupation with usage and loss of control or using at inappropriate times, there may be a problem with alcohol/drugs.

The assessing counselor needs to be aware of any history of physical or sexual abuse that may be leading the adolescent to using chemicals to cope with the trauma. Also, the counselor needs to assess the family system to determine whether the adolescent seems to be acting out family struggles. In addition, the counselor needs to assess the adolescent for psychiatric problems that may be leading to alcohol/drug abuse.

SAMHSA (1999c) summarizes the purpose of the assessment is to identify: a need for treatment, the severity of use, the consequences of use, possible family involvement, strengths of the client, and possible other problems. A written report summarizing severity, contributing factors, plans (corrective, interim), referral recommendations, and coordination of services should also be completed. R. C. Schwartz and Smith (2003) recommend the following components for a formal assessment that are generally discussed in Chapter 3: a structured clinical interview, information from parents and significant others (school, work, etc.), behavioral observations, test instruments, and review of medical/psychiatric records. As to the substance use focus, the authors recommend examination of their history of use, the degree of involvement, reasons for use, contributing factors to use, treatment history, others' reactions to their use, and consequences of use (recreation, environment, legal, mental health, sexual, education, home, family history).

There are two main types of inventories: self-report and interview. When using an instrument, the clinician needs to remember it is only part of the picture. Instruments are developed, administered, and interpreted by humans and given to humans, which means there is always some degree of error. The results of a screening instrument need to be reflected in other areas of the adolescent's life to ensure that the client is appropriately diagnosed based on a pattern of behavior rather than just one source. This caution against using only one source of information applies to all components of the formal assessment as recommended by R. C. Schwartz and Smith (2003).

It may be difficult to engage the adolescent in the treatment process because of a distrust for authority (i.e., the assessing counselor may be viewed as another adult authority) and a tendency to be brought in for an assessment involuntarily by parents, school personnel, or legal system employees. It is important for the counselor to know state laws governing confidentiality of adolescent use and treatment. Schwartz and Smith (2003) summarize legal issues related to adolescent substance abuse. Federal regulations need to be adhered to above state and local regulations. Federal regulations ensure confidentiality through restrictions on communication about the client. SAMHSA (1999c) highlights these restrictions:

1. No information can be given (including that to parents) that identifies a potential problem with substance abuse, except:

   a. If written consent is given by the adolescent, and in some states parental consent is also required.

   b. If the parents need to be contacted because the director of the program believes the adolescent is not rational to make a consent decision, is seeking services (but has not accepted them), or disclosure is needed to protect the adolescent's well-being or life.

   c. The adolescent cannot be identified as a substance abuser.

   d. The practitioner needs to report abuse or neglect due to state laws.

   e. There is a need to have a medical condition treated that is threatening the health of the adolescent.

   f. There is a need to confer with outside agencies that are typically used, such as a laboratory that tests for drugs.

   g. Allowance needs to be made to facilitate internal communications between qualified staff.

   h. Information needs to be accessible to researchers, auditors, and evaluators who are qualified and have the program's approval to obtain the information.

SAMHSA (1999c) states that these federal laws often conflict with state duty-to-warn laws and recommends four options for counselors who are presented with a client who might harm him or herself or others: (1) obtain a special (federally sanctioned) court order authorizing disclosure; (2) make a disclosure that does not identify the adolescent who has threatened to harm himself or herself or another individual as a client; (3) make a limited report to medical personnel in order to receive medical intervention; or (4) obtain written informed consent from the adolescent to disclose mutually agreed-upon information (p. 31).

Some counselors report finding it helpful to tell the parents at the beginning of an interview that the counselor will not give the specifics of the adolescent's use, but they will tell them their diagnosis, recommendations, and general level of concern about the adolescent's use. Doing so in the adolescent's presence may increase the adolescent's degree of trust in the counselor and facilitate disclosure of the chemical history. In addition, interviewing the parents about the concern for the adolescent in the presence of the adolescent may facilitate the trust and an atmosphere of openness, so it does not seem to the adolescent that the adults are talking behind the adolescent's back. Winters (2001) reminds us that adolescents may exaggerate their use, and their parents may have limits as to knowledge of the specifics of the child's use. Finally, obtaining information from any additional adults is helpful. In particular, school counselors and teachers can be excellent resources for the assessing counselor when the adolescent is in school. If the adolescent is employed or in legal trouble, the authorities involved with these systems may be helpful.

Some specific drugs that need to be included in the assessment process are drugs that are currently popular in this age group. This includes a variety of drugs discussed below. While these drugs may vary in terms of current popularity and name (as well as what is known about their impact), the assessing counselor needs to make sure to include these drugs in the assessment process because many adolescents are exposed to them by the time they come in for an assessment. Two terms that may be a useful reference for the reader are: *designer drugs* (an informal term that is used to describe psychoactive drugs discovered through research on existing drugs) and *club drugs* (a heterogeneous psychoactive drug group used by young people in various social settings such as bars, nightclubs, concerts, parties, etc.). Only the club drugs are described here because of their usage by adolescents and young adults in social settings. More information on club drugs can be obtained at NIDA's website: http://www.drugabuse.gov/drugs-abuse/club-drugs

Two club drugs are:

1. *MDMA* (ecstasy in pill form, "Molly"—slang term for *molecular*—is the pure crystalline powder form of MDMA that usually comes in capsules). MDMA produces effects that are similar to methamphetamine and mescaline (energy, euphoria, warm feelings toward others, sensory and time distortions) and has similar physical effects to cocaine/amphetamines. http://www.drugabuse.gov/publications/drugfacts/mdma-ecstasy-or-molly

2. *GHB* (a central nervous system depressant; *Rohypnol* (a benzodiazepine); and *Ketamine* (a dissociative anesthetic commonly used in veterinary medicine)). The first two are odorless, colorless, and tasteless and often combine with alcohol or another beverage and have been used to commit sexual assaults because they sedate and incapacitate people. GHB has also been used by body builders. The third, Ketamine, distorts visual/auditory perceptions and results in a feeling of detachment. http://www.drugabuse.gov/publications/drugfacts/club-drugs-ghb-ketamine-rohypnol

There are also *emerging trends* that appear in adolescent use.

- *Bath salts* are a drug family that has at least one synthetic chemical related to cathinone that is an amphetamine-like substance found in the Khat plant that results in euphoria, increased sociability/sex drive, but can also result in cardiac and psychiatric symptoms resulting in emergency room visits. They have high abuse and addiction potential and are sold in drug paraphernalia stores or online under different names. http://www.drugabuse.gov/publications/drugfacts/synthetic-cathinones-bath-salts

- Prescription strength *cough syrup* (codeine, a central nervous system depressant, and promethazine, an antihistamine) is mixed with alcohol or other beverages (http://www.drugabuse.gov/drugs-abuse/emerging-trends).

- *K-2* ("Spice") consists of various herbal mixtures that are described as safe and legal alternatives to marijuana that provides similar effects. They can be bought at head shops, gas stations, on the Internet. They consist of active ingredients that are synthetic (designer) and they have a high abuse potential. It is illegal to sell, buy, or possess them because the Drug Enforcement Administration (DEA) has designated five of the active chemicals as Schedule I controlled substances. They are popular among young people because they are easily accessible, marketed as natural, and are not easily detected in standard drug tests (http://www.drugabuse.gov/publications/drugfacts/spice-synthetic-marijuana, 2012).

Other drugs often used by adolescents that might be missed during an assessment, but need to be included are heroin, prescription drugs, and inhalants.

- *Heroin* has held steady in terms of use from 2007 to 2012 (http://www.drugabuse.gov/publications/drugfacts/high-school-youth-trends). Regarding heroin and opiate-related drugs, medication assisted treatment may benefit this population (Kellogg et al., 2006), however, there has been little research done with this population (Smith, 2011). An additional caution is due to the impact of these medications on the developing brain of the adolescent.

- *Prescription drugs* is a growing problem in the United States and is a leading cause of death/disability with this population (Smith, 2011). Nonmedical prescription drug use (NMPDU) means using the drug without a prescription or for the feeling/experience the drug brings and this usage has resulted in increasing emergency room visits (Ford & Watkins, 2012). Friends, siblings, and parents are common sources of these medications for adolescents and young adults and they are used to treat sleep, pain, and concentration problems as well as used recreationally (Ford & Watkins, 2012).

- *Inhalants.* Of the three types of inhalant users described by Beauvais and Oetting (1987), two involve adolescents: young inhalant users (ages 12 and 13) and polydrug users (mid- to late adolescence). The first group does not use inhalants extensively or have severe physical problems, whereas the second group tends to use them moderately to severely. Inaba and Cohen (1993) report that 12- to 17-year-olds are most likely to use inhalants, and N. S. Miller and Gold (1990) report that the most common usage occurs between ages 10 and 15. Children seem most likely to be introduced to inhalants by their peers and are encouraged to stop their usage when, later in adolescence, their peers view it as "kid stuff " (G. A. Miller & Peele, 1995).

Inhalants provide a quick high with little hangover effects, although intense use within a brief period of time may result in a headache (Sharp & Rosenberg, 1997). G. A. Miller and Peele (1995) report that inhalant abuse is prolific and dangerous because inhalants are legal, cheap, and accessible; children typically do not understand their vulnerability to the dangers of inhalants, which can cause death, even at first usage. Although some signs of inhalant abuse are similar to the previously listed consequences of chemical use, there are other signs specific to the use of inhalants. Assessing counselors need to be aware of (1) chemical odors, paint stains, and cold symptoms (G. A. Miller & Peele, 1995); (2) nausea, headaches, memory loss, and inability to concentrate (D. D. Davis, 1993); and (3) empty spray cans, plastic bags, and school supplies at home (L. Davis & Baker, 1990).

A 2012 NIDA publication on inhalant abuse that provides an excellent overview on inhalant abuse and has numerous informational links can be located at: http://www.drugabuse.gov/publications/research-reports/inhalant-abuse

Treatment and Aftercare Since 1993, the number of adolescents admitted to publicly funded treatment programs has increased 60%, and that has resulted in more research being done with this population in terms of treatment (Gangi & Darling, 2012).

In examining the specific issues of this age group as related to treatment and aftercare, a model of recovery development can frame treatment and aftercare approaches. G. R. Ross (1994) reviews and elaborates on Dr. Forest Richeson's four recovery dimensions. The first plateau is *admitting*. In this dimension, the adolescent has reached a place of admitting to an alcohol/drug problem. In the second plateau, *submitting*, the adolescent asks for assistance in addressing his or her alcohol/drug problem. During the third dimension, *committing*, the adolescent begins to take action steps to go along with the new beliefs the client has about alcohol/drug usage. In the fourth stage, *transmitting*, the adolescent realizes that to maintain recovery, he or she must consistently work on habit changes.

Liddle et al. (2001) state that adolescent substance abuse is an important national public health concern. Parents and families appear to be important as an "antidrug" that can be utilized during prevention, treatment, and aftercare (Schlauch, Levitt, Connell, & Kaufman, 2013; Spas, Ramsey, Paiva, & Stein, 2012).

Liddle et al. (2001) state that because abuse develops from different paths that may cross over, the interventions need to reflect these complicated pathways' intersection. Additionally, adolescents are using even younger, so when they enter treatment, they may be lacking more developmentally. Early use is a reliable predictor of both abuse and dependence (Li, Hewett, & Grant, 2007). Adolescent treatment needs to be different from adult treatment because adolescents have: (1) trouble anticipating consequences; (2) different developmental issues, values, beliefs, and environments (peers); (3) lower tolerance; and (4) the impact of substance use on their development (SAMHSA, 1999c). Because of these differences between adolescents and adults, SAMHSA (1999c) makes five treatment recommendations:

1. Consider "gender, ethnicity, disability state, stage of readiness to change and cultural background" (p. xvii).

2. Be aware of possible developmental delays (cognitive, social-emotional) due to use, and examine the impact on their lives (personal, social, school).

3. Involve the family of origin in treatment if possible.

4. Have them go to adolescent treatment unless accessibility mandates their going to adult programs, and then use them with sensitive vigilance.

5. Use motivational strategies to engage them in treatment, because often they have been forced to attend.

Motivational interviewing (MI) is discussed in Chapter 9. There is limited research on using MI with an adolescent population, but it does demonstrate effectiveness as a strategy to enhance engagement and support (Nagy, 2010). For example, in The Cannabis Youth Treatment (CYT) study, five sessions of MI (combined with cognitive-behavioral therapy) showed equal effectiveness as long-term interventions (Dennis et al., 2004). CYT was designed to look at the effectiveness of five interventions: motivational enhancement therapy (MET), cognitive-behavioral therapy (CBT), family support network (FSN), adolescent community reinforcement approach (ACRA), or multidimensional family therapy (MDFT) (Dennis et al., 2004). All five CYT interventions showed significant treatment improvements in terms of days of abstinence and percentage of adolescents in recovery 12 months after random assignments to groups.

Nagy (2010) states that developmental issues of adolescence (identity formation, independence,

acceptance, connection) appear to be a good match with MI because of its inherently brief, focused, and yet personal intervention style. Adolescents typically are not ready to change, rebel against labels, may be defensive, and yet they respond to validation, collaboration, positive reinforcement, choices, and positive relations. In their study, Fitzpatrick and Irannejad (2008) found a relationship between adolescents' (ages 14 to 18) readiness to change and a working alliance with a counselor, especially regarding goal and task collaboration.

Effective treatment with adolescents involves a team approach made up of the different environments in which the adolescent is involved: school and/or employment, family, and peers. Meyers and McLellan (2005) state that the service delivery system for adolescents is a complex environment that can inhibit service access or confuse coordination of services across the different systems involved. Community agents in the educational, legal, religious, and medical systems can be a powerful source of support for adolescents; therefore, access and coordination are critical for the adolescent. Outreach and case management have been shown to improve the retention of at-risk youth, but this can be difficult to implement (Simmons et al., 2008). Nonetheless, the counselor needs to assess the environmental risk factors for relapse since adolescents seem especially sensitive to these components (Gangi & Darling, 2012).

Relapse occurs at high rates in the first few months following treatment (Gangi & Darling, 2012). Adolescents need to find a support group with individuals of similar age who can serve as role models for staying sober. For some adolescents (severe alcohol/drug use in combination with low social support) self-help groups in combination with aftercare may be especially helpful in their first few months after treatment (Gangi & Darling, 2012). Active aftercare that includes in-person and phone contact has been shown to be helpful in relapse prevention (Burleson, Kaminer, & Burke, 2012).

They also need to learn some aspects of adulthood in treatment (e.g., being responsible, setting limits on themselves) as well as aspects of childhood (e.g., allowing themselves to play). Sensation-seeking and impulsivity, that have been shown to positively impact substance misuse (Battista, Pencer, McGonnell, Durdle, & Stewart, 2013), need to be addressed in treatment. During treatment, the counselor needs to continuously assess psychiatric and family problems that may have been masked by the chemical usage.

Regarding psychiatric problems that may be masked by the adolescent's chemical usage, there is a significant overlap between substance misuse and mental health problems supporting the argument for treatment programs that address both areas simultaneously (Battista et al., 2013; Norberg, Battisti, Copeland, Hermens, & Hickie, 2012; Winstanley, Steinwachs, Stitzer, & Fishman, 2012). Some specific comments need to be made. Programs that have both mental health and substance abuse treatments that are delivered by multidisciplinary teams can be especially beneficial to the adolescent. Those teams can, as discussed in Chapter 4 on dual diagnosis, watch for the sensitive interaction between both areas of concern so that one area is treated while "neglecting" the impact of the other area on the adolescent's recovery. At the very least, there needs to be access to a reliable psychiatric resource as a consultant in the treatment of the adolescent.

If the diagnosis of chemical dependency is given to an adolescent, the family system is usually examined in terms of a medical model (physiological) or a psychosocial model (parenting), which have been respectively labeled "structure" and "process" (environmental supports), with the family containing both (Cook, 2001). Collaboration between parents and professionals improves treatment and recovery outcomes for adolescents (Hornberger & Smith, 2011).

Some specific components that need to be considered with families of adolescents are (SAMHSA, 1999c): (a) help them learn problem-solving skills (decrease conflict, increase communication), and (b) teach them how to raise teenagers through parenting skills (monitoring behavior, setting limits, having consequences;

positive and negative for behavior), engaging emotionally in a positive way, participating in activities away from home. They also stress the importance of being aware of cultural differences when working with a family. Chapter 5 discusses family therapy in general.

Greater parental use of treatment services has been shown to increase adolescent self-disclosure and reduction of substance use (Bertrand et al., 2013). The treatment focus is to change how the family interacts and improve relationships to decrease substance use (Waldron, Brody, & Slesnick, 2001). These authors recommend that the counselor engage the family in treatment through forming a therapeutic alliance, enhancing their motivation (reframe and examine the interdependence of behavior), and assessing family functioning (what needs to change and how to help that happen). They also recommend individual sessions in addition to family sessions to learn (a) antecedents and consequences of use, (b) how to cope with urges to use, and (c) skills of communication, problem solving, substance refusing, dealing with anger and negative moods, and developing social networks.

Family-based treatments that seem to show the greatest evidence-based effectiveness include (a) multidimensional family therapy (*MDFT*) (Liddle, 2010; Liddle, Rodriguez, Dakof, Kanzki, & Marvel, 2005), (b) brief strategic family therapy (*BSFT*) (Szapocznik, Hervis, & Schwartz, 2003), (c) multisystemic therapy (*MST*) (Randall, Henggeler, Cunningham, Rowland, & Swenson, 2001), and (d) adolescent community reinforcement approach (*CRA*) (Meyers & Miller, 2001). Jaffe, Attala, and Simeonova (2009) summarize these four therapies.

MDFT contains multiple system assessments and interventions of the family and the psychosocial environment. *BSFT* is a manualized therapy structural-strategic approach. It was originally developed for behavior-problem (drug use, sexual risk, delinquency) young people in Hispanic families, but appears to be useful with various racial/ethnic groups in the United States (Szapocznik, Schwartz, Muir, & Brown, 2012; Szapocznik,

Zarate, Duff, & Muir, 2013). *MST* combines family therapy with interventions in the systems that involve the individual, school, peer group, and community. It encourages each family member to be responsible and tries to help each member develop a capacity to manage his or her own problems. Counselors work with the adolescent and the family at home, school, and in the peer group. *CRA* was originally developed for adults. Here the client's life is rearranged so there are more rewards for abstinence than drinking. Behavior is closely monitored through such checks as urine screens, and rewards are given for negative urines (contingency management). There are behavioral and cognitive-behavioral protocols as well as contingency management.

Often substance-abusing adolescents are referred by the juvenile justice system (Szapocznik et al., 2012). Additional programs that have been advocated by the juvenile justice system that need to be mentioned here are *Seeking Safety* (see Chapter 5 for a general description of the trauma-related therapy of the *Seeking Safety* program) and *Seven Challenges*.

The application of the Seeking Safety program to adolescents ages 12 to 17 who have a history of trauma and/or substance abuse is emerging and on a 5-point scale, where 1 means "Well Supported by Research Evidence," the California Evidence-Based Clearinghouse for Child Welfare rates the application of the Seeking Safety program to adolescents at a "3" ("Promising Research Evidence"). More information on the program can be accessed from: http://www.cebc4cw.org/program/seeking-safety-for-adolescents/

The Seven Challenges program is described by SAMHSA's National Registry of Evidence-based Programs and Practices at the following link: http://www.nrepp.samhsa.gov/ViewIntervention.aspx?id=159

Their introduction to this program is as follows:

The Seven Challenges
The Seven Challenges is designed to treat adolescents with drug and other behavioral problems. Rather than using prestructured sessions, counselors and clients identify the most important issues at the moment and discuss these issues while the counselor seamlessly integrates a set of concepts called the seven challenges into the conversation. The challenges include (1) talking honestly about themselves and about alcohol and other drugs; (2) looking at what they like about alcohol and other drugs and why they are using them; (3) looking at the impact of drugs and alcohol on their lives; (4) looking at their responsibility and the responsibility of others for their problems; (5) thinking about where they are headed, where they want to go, and what they want to accomplish; (6) making thoughtful decisions about their lives and their use of alcohol and other drugs; and (7) following through on those decisions. These concepts are woven into counseling to help youth make decisions and follow through on them. Skills training, problem solving, and sometimes family participation are integrated into sessions that address drug problems, co-occurring problems, and life skills deficits. The Seven Challenges reader, a book of experiences told from the perspective of adolescents who have been successful in overcoming problems, is used by clients to generate ideas and inspiration related to their own lives. In addition to participating in counseling sessions, youth write in a set of nine Seven Challenges Journals, and counselors and youth engage in a written process called cooperative journaling. The program is flexible and can be implemented in an array of settings, including inpatient, outpatient, home-based, juvenile justice, day treatment, and school. The number, length, and frequency of sessions depend on the setting. Counselors with various levels of experience in working with mental health and substance abuse problems are trained in program implementation.
(http://www.nrepp.samhsa.gov/ViewIntervention. aspx?id=159)

Overall, the treatment counselor for the adolescent needs to have an awareness of rebelliousness and power struggles as well as the common developmental issues present at this stage. SAMHSA (1999c) recommends that adolescent treatment programs have these areas:

orientation to treatment, daily scheduled activities, peer monitoring, conflict resolution, client contracts (e.g., behavioral contracts), schooling, and vocational training. They also recommend that a treatment plan include: (a) addressing overall problems in "client and family, including substance use, psychosocial, medical, sexual, reproductive, and possible psychiatric disorders" (p. xx); (b) developing attainable goals with reasonable objectives and appropriate interventions including awareness of substance abuse consequences; (c) involving strengths of both client and family; and (d) involving educational, legal, and other agencies involved with the adolescent.

Also, while most interventions are group-based in treatment, there is research emerging that adolescents learn deviance by interacting with peers who are deviant (Dodge, Dishion, & Lansford, 2006). This is an important aspect to take into account if one is doing group counseling with adolescents. Aftercare for adolescent treatment is similar to treatment for addicts in general in that it involves applying the treatment goals to the posttreatment environment. To assist the adolescent in staying sober, it is important to involve the family, school, and/or work environment, and other systems in relapse prevention as well as assist the adolescent in understanding his or her own soft spots with regard to relapse. Wood, Drolet, Fetro, Synovitz, and Wood (2002) make six specific suggestions to schools to assist in recovery:

1. Have a collaborative relationship with local treatment centers.

2. Include school health professionals to serve on treatment boards and treatment staff to be involved in school substance abuse prevention.

3. Give space to treatment staff to meet at the school.

4. Provide information on health education related to drug use.

5. Have necessary medical information available on drug-related issues.

6. Work closely with treatment staff on treatment plans.

For treatment counselors, they recommend:

• Have a collaborative relationship with the schools.

• Refer to education records and follow guidance counselor suggestions.

• Find out school services available and involve teachers and counselors.

• Inform school personnel of medical information.

An example of another system is a church or social group in the community. It is helpful to the adolescent to have an aftercare plan of recovery and to remain in contact with the primary treatment source (Schonberg, 1993). Yule and Prince (2012) recommend that schools use Motivational Interviewing to engage students and coordinate their efforts to assist the students through consultation with the providers of their treatment. (See Case Study 10.8.)

CASE STUDY 10.8

Samantha is a 16-year-old female who has been referred to her school counselor for an alcohol/drug assessment. She was caught smoking marijuana on school grounds during morning classes the previous week. She has a C average and has never seen a school counselor before. Samantha is the oldest of five children, and her parents are influential in the local community. On entering the counseling session, she tells you that she has no interest in seeing a counselor, and you better be careful because her dad is a "big deal around here and he wouldn't want anybody messing with me."

1. How would you establish a trusting, respectful atmosphere with Samantha?

2. What about Samantha's behavior might you find offensive, and how would you handle that?

3. What would you need to know about confidentiality limitations with regard to this client, the school, and her parents? How would you communicate those limitations to Samantha?

4. How would you approach Samantha's implicit threats about her being carefully handled by you in terms of her father, the school administration, and liability issues?

EXERCISE 10.5

Find a colleague and discuss the general concerns you have with working with adolescents. Make sure to include in this discussion any previous experiences you have had working with adolescents (positive, negative) as well as your general attitude about working with them. Second, discuss how you anticipate working with this population in your practice in terms of type of contact (assessment, treatment, aftercare) and percentage of your client population. Finally, combine your concerns/attitude toward them with the reality of your clinical work with them by answering this question: How would I approach counseling these clients and their significant others so they feel welcomed and have a sense of hope?

The Elderly

The elderly are defined here as individuals over age 65. They make up about 12% of the population in the United States and are the fastest-growing age group (APA, 2010; Benshoff, Harrawood, & Koch, 2003; van Wormer & Davis, 2008). There is anticipation that clinicians will have increased chances of working with this population (Blow & Barry, 2009: Farkas, 2004) and that addiction treatment may be increasingly needed for this group. Legal and illegal drug use is an increasing problem with older adults, with increasing prescription drug use as a concern: one out of four use psychoactive medicine drugs with abuse potential (Simoni-Wastila & Yang, 2012).

Because of the tendency to not see substance abuse in this group, it has been called an invisible epidemic (Levin & Kruger, 2000, p. 1) or a hidden epidemic in terms of alcohol, illicit drug, and prescription medication (Shafer, 2004). Historically, alcohol and drug problems have not been addressed very often in the elderly population because of low problem rate estimations (K. Graham et al., 1995). Graham and colleagues indicate that this problem has received more focus in the past decade as a result of awareness that surveys may not accurately assess the problem level; evidence that alcohol and drug problems may differ for this group; knowledge that the human body has diminished capacity to process drugs with age, so it takes less for the elderly to experience the effects of alcohol/drugs; statistics showing the elderly have the highest prescription drug use; and requests from health-care clinicians on how to work effectively with this population. Goldberg (2008) adds that there are limits also due to a lack of diagnostic criteria and screening instruments, as well as treatments that have not been designed especially for elderly clients. Four barriers in assessing and treating addiction with this population are ageism, lack of awareness, clinical behavior, and comorbidity (SAMHSA, 1998c). Overall, throughout the process of assessment and treatment, the counselor needs to be sensitive to aging factors (cognitive, physical, emotional) (Simoni-Wastila & Yang, 2012) and use nonconfrontational, supportive, cognitive-behavioral therapy (Goldberg, 2008).

Some general suggestions (D. W. Sue & Sue, 2013) made regarding working with this population include:

- Being aware of own aging attitudes.

- Showing respect and encouraging autonomy (attention, language, treatment as an, seriousness about concerns).

- Having sensitivity for various issues and influences (developmental, racial/ethnic, cultural).

- Forming collaborations with caregivers.

- Assessing support systems and establishing them if necessary.

Assessment Alcohol use that is harmful (especially in combination with certain comorbidities/medication use) impacts about 10% of the elderly and is related with higher mortality within this population (Barnes et al., 2010). Because throughout the United States the elderly report at-risk and binge drinking, counselors working with this population need to assess for binge drinking and their use of other substances (Blazer & Wu, 2009).

However, we are limited in our knowledge of at-risk drinking categories within this population as well as demographics of this population (Barnes et al., 2010). For example, there is a limited knowledge base that clinicians can use to assess safe and harmful drinking with this population (Crome, Li, Rao, & Wu, 2012). This limited knowledge base is in part due to metabolic biological changes (i.e., less lean body mass and water resulting in higher blood alcohol content),

medications, and comorbid illness, (Crome et al., 2012). As a result, clinicians may want to recommend that the elderly: drink no more than one U.S. Standard Drink (14 g of alcohol) daily (with 3.6 a day being considered harmful), drink slowly (due to low absorption rates), and maybe not drink and drive at all (Crome et al., 2012). Also, there is a need to develop valid instruments that assess for alcohol use disorders specifically among the elderly (Malet, Brousse, & Llorca, 2009; Simoni-Wastila & Yang, 2012). Finally, there are specific issues within this population, such as end-of-life, that impact assessment and treatment (Bushfield & Deford, 2010). Although addiction is a concern, then, with this population, it is easy to overlook or misdiagnose alcohol and drug use in this population (Blow & Barry, 2009; Farkas, 2004).

Alcoholism and addiction among the elderly may be missed because of stereotypes of older people and/or because of uncertainty about how to treat the problem, the lack of hopefulness about treatment effectiveness, and discrimination about the elderly (Foster, 1995). Physicians may have difficulty with diagnosis, because the aging process may present similar symptoms (Blake, 1990). Warning signs of substance abuse that can be mistaken for aging problems are "tremors, unsteadiness, constipation, depression, malnutrition, fatigue, drowsiness, memory loss, falling, and anxiety" (Reid & Kampfe, 2000, p. 12). Significant others may not intervene because of feelings such as shame and guilt (E. Peluso & Peluso, 1989; Vandeputte, 1989). In addition, older alcoholics tend to be hidden (G. L. Duckworth & Rosenblatt, 1976); that is, consequences related to alcohol/drug abuse may not be present due to more limited social functioning and no or limited employment (Abrams & Alexopoulos, 1987). Many elderly people may not drive, thus limiting the chances of obtaining a legal consequence, and the elderly themselves may view a problem with alcohol as moral (Benshoff et al., 2003); they also may be more likely to use at home than in public (van Wormer & Davis, 2008).

Although causal factors for alcoholism in this population have been difficult to determine (K. Graham et al., 1995), A. Lawson (1989) reports some common risks: stresses that accompany the aging process, loss, bereavement, depression, isolation, retirement, and sex-related issues. Also, problems with depression, loneliness, and social support appear to precipitate drinking (Schonfeld & Dupree, 1991). They may use drugs more for relief of pain than recreational use, and unresolved grief may result in increased substance use (van Wormer & Davis, 2008). The vulnerability theory of aging may assist in understanding the vulnerability to substance abuse in this population. *Vulnerability theory* states that there is a greater sense of deprivation relative to losses and more psychological stress (Elmore, Brown, & Cook, 2009).

To assess addiction in the elderly, a classification system is helpful. Zimberg (1978) offers one kind of classification system for older alcoholics: late-onset alcoholics and early-onset alcoholics. *Late-onset alcoholics*, about one-third of elderly alcoholics, are defined as those elderly who develop drinking problems later in life and may be using in response to stresses common to aging. They may have a stronger social network and no previous treatment for addiction (Brennan & Moos, 1996). *Early-onset alcoholics*, about two-thirds of elderly alcoholics (Kinney, 2006), are those who either continued a chronic problem of drinking all of their adult lives or developed a more chronic problem as they aged. The early-onset alcoholic may also be using because of stresses and problems related to aging, and he or she may have more medical problems resulting from alcohol. The National Institute on Aging (2002) now labels these cases as situational or chronic, and they may be about two-thirds of the elderly (Rigler, 2000). Atkinson, Turner, Kofoed, and Tolson (1985) added a third category of *intermittent*, where the person had a substance abuse problem earlier in life, he or she recovered, and it reemerged later in life. This group looks like the late-onset group (Farkas, 2004).

Gambert (1997) recommends using red flags such as daily use of alcohol, times of drinking-related amnesia, refusal to stop using alcohol after warnings, physical problems related to usage, as well as changes in cognitive capacity and physical problems (anemia, liver abnormalities, frequent falls, seizures, etc.). Also, because the elderly often use medication for physical problems and experience depression and anxiety, their risk for addiction with prescribed medication is high (Gambert, 1997). They take 25% to 30% of drugs prescribed (Ondus, Hujer, Mann, & Mion, 1999), while they make up less than 13% of the population (van Wormer & Davis, 2008), and they are at higher risk for inappropriate use of these medications (Blow & Barry, 2009).

Regarding depression, when it co-occurs with substance use, these two can exacerbate each other because the alcohol fuels the depression that fuels the alcohol use (Blow & Barry, 2009). Regarding anxiety, generalized anxiety disorder (constant, debilitating worry often about typical events) is one of the most common problems for people over age 60, and they are often prescribed medication for it (Harvard Mental Health Letter, 2009). The problem here is three-fold: (1) drugs may not be the best choice of treatment for anxiety because of their side effects that are felt more keenly in this population (Harvard Mental Health Letter, 2009); (2) one of the common treatments used for this disorder is the benzodiazepines (Valium, Xanax); and (3) addiction to this group of medications is common in the elderly (van Wormer & Davis, 2008). In addition, they may also misuse over-the-counter drugs (Reid & Kampfe, 2000).

Another sign of substance abuse can be the extensive usage of commonly misused prescription medications by the elderly: sedative-hypnotics, antianxiety medications, and analgesics (Gambert, 1997). They may also pair their use, such as alcohol, with an accessible activity such as gambling, where they can experience excitement and avoid boredom (van Wormer & Davis, 2008). Techniques to improve assessment accuracy are suggested by Reid and Kampfe (2000): (1) ask first about physical conditions and then the drug taken for that condition, and (2) ask the client to show the medications being taken in each room of the house. The latter approach is sometimes called the "brown bag" approach (Blow & Barry, 2009). Reid and Kampfe (2000) also recommend that the client consult with the pharmacist or physician about interactive effects.

Specific instruments such as the CAGE, the MAST, the MAST-G (Geriatric version), the SMAST-G (shortened geriatric version), and the AUDIT (as well as the AUDIT-C which is the elderly specific modification), as discussed in Chapter 3, have been used with this population.

Colleran and Jay (2002) make five specific suggestions on how to approach an elderly person about his or her alcohol/drug usage:

1. Have realistic expectations.

2. Approach the person when sober and free of distractions, with plenty of time for discussion and a private meeting place that is away from his or her home.

3. Approach it as a general get-together rather than one that is drug focused.

4. Have someone else involved that the individual likes or respects.

5. Work at enhancing communication by addressing the person's fears, using words that do not involve stigma or blame, be gentle, stay recent on two or three examples of his or her behavior, make "I" statements, watch body language, do not force issues, take action right away if there is an opportunity, and consider involving doctors and using a crisis situation that arises.

Treatment and Aftercare Blow and Barry (2009) state that only recently is specific information on treatment and intervention with this population being dispersed. SAMHSA (1998b) describes treatment barriers with this population as transportation, limited social network, limited time, lack of expertise, and financial limitations.

Therefore, the addiction counselor may need to be more involved in organizing social service networks to provide services for elderly individuals.

Benshoff et al. (2003) caution that there are three barriers to treatment for the elderly: not individualized, not accessible, and too much self-help group reliance where the elderly may not fit in or their hearing problems and/or mobility issues may raise difficulties for them. The authors suggest that before making a referral to a treatment facility, the counselor should be assured that the facility can meet the needs of this age group. Even though the elderly may be as likely to recover from addiction as younger clients, treatment designed to meet the specific needs of the elderly may enhance their chances at recovery (Gambert, 1997). Rathbone-McCuan and Bland (1975) suggest that treatment center on three areas: the symptoms of their drinking problems, their health problems, and their social problems. Adequate treatment requires knowledge about both addiction and the aging process (K. Graham et al., 1995). As to their chemical usage, the elderly may require a longer withdrawal and a more structured environment while they are involved in treatment (Dunlop, Manghelli, & Tolson, 1989). It may be helpful to use the least intensive approaches first (Simoni-Wastila et al., 2012).

Elderly patients require a thorough medical exam (including neurological testing), as well as a psychiatric exam in terms of the impact of the chemical usage on their bodies and the aging process on their bodies. Their treatment program also needs to be based on and adapted to a comprehensive assessment, and social and emotional problems may need to be assessed to determine any causal problems underlying the chemical usage. This population needs to develop a social network that is sensitive to the needs of the elderly and that provides adequate recovery role models. Attendance at self-help meetings such as AA may be one way to reduce social isolation (Clay, 1996). However, even though this is the most common approach to treatment, and large-print literature is available through some self-help groups, the elderly may feel intimidated or stigmatized by such a referral experience (Farkas, 2004). Therefore, the counselor making such a referral needs to follow the guidelines for self-help group referrals outlined in Chapter 8 so the match between the client is the best possible.

Treatment approaches such as motivational interviewing (Chapter 9) and relapse prevention (Chapter 7) may be especially helpful with this population. SAMHSA also recommends general treatment approaches: cognitive-behavioral, group, individual, medical/psychiatric, marriage and family, and case management/community outreach.

Because U.S. culture seems biased against older people, it is helpful for the elderly to have the option of counseling to work on struggles they have with ageism and the losses that go along with old age. Their children, church, and other community agencies may provide them with a sense of meaningfulness about their lives, which can facilitate their recovery. A. Lawson (1989) recommends that treatment be accessible to the elderly in places they naturally attend and in their homes. Beechem (2002) recommends that counselors be aware of their own ageism, countertransference, avoidance, and denial and expressing sympathy rather than empathy. In addition, G. Corey and Corey (1992) recommend that the counselor have a respect for the elderly, a history of positive experiences with them, and knowledge of the age-related needs. (See Case Study 10.9.)

CASE STUDY 10.9

Evelyn is a 78-year-old woman who lives alone in her own home. She was referred to a community counselor for drug/alcohol assessment because her Meals-on-Wheels delivery people and her home health aide noticed that she seemed to be "out of it" when they would try to talk with her, and they noticed that she had several prescription medications on her dining room table as well as beer in the refrigerator. You have gone to her home to evaluate her, and you notice the home is quite messy. Evelyn begins to cry shortly after you introduce yourself and ask whether she has any close family or friends in the area. She seems unable to stop crying.

1. How would you help Evelyn begin to trust you with information about herself?
2. Would a messy home make it difficult to do an assessment of Evelyn's usage?
3. What stereotypes of the elderly do you hold that might make it difficult to hear Evelyn's life story, including her alcohol/drug history?
4. If an intervention on her usage is necessary, what factors would make it difficult for you to intervene in Evelyn's life?

EXERCISE 10.6

Repeat Exercise 10.5 with this population. Find a colleague and discuss the general concerns you have with working with the elderly. Make sure to include in this discussion any previous experiences you have had working with the elderly (positive, negative) as well as your general attitude about working with them. Second, discuss how you anticipate working with this population in your practice in terms of type of contact (assessment, treatment, aftercare) and percentage of your client population. Finally, combine your concerns/attitude toward them with the reality of your clinical work with them by answering this question: How would I approach counseling these clients and their significant others so they feel welcomed and have a sense of hope?

OVERALL SUBSTANCE USE/ABUSE EXPLORATION MULTICULTURAL EXERCISES

EXERCISE 10.7

In a dyad with someone you do not know well, explore the following areas by interviewing one another on any or all of these eight topic areas: the story of your name, your family of origin experience (i.e., holiday celebrations, fun activities, ancestors coming to this country), your educational story, your employment history, your religious history, your greatest success story, your experiences in being different from others, and your strengths in working with individuals different from you. Discuss these areas within the context of substance use (i.e., how the use of substances impacted your education, employment, etc.). This is an exercise that can also be used in counseling sessions (individual, couple/family, group).

EXERCISE 10.8

Develop a multicultural competence action plan for yourself with regard to substance abuse counseling. Begin by listing three struggles/issues you have in this area; for example, limited substance abuse training and/or limited exposure to different cultures. Then make a list of three barriers you have experienced (or anticipate experiencing) with regard to trying to enhance your multicultural competence in the area of substance abuse counseling. Finally, develop possible intervention strategies in response to these struggles/issues that address how you plan to work around the barriers to your professional development.

EXERCISE 10.9

Use an experiential tool to facilitate a discussion with clients about diversity in recovery. For example, use hula hoops to represent diversity: different sizes, colors, inner substances (water, no water, things that jingle, etc.), and types (arm hoops, different sized hoops on various body parts). Describe the overall representations of hoops in terms of diversity with clients and then ask them to apply it to their recovery process. Another example is talking about how each person in recovery may be different from others in terms of "size, color, inner substances, type," but while all hoops have their unique way of being, they are all hoops. This counseling approach can be applied to any experiential form that involves a category that can be separated into different parts (musical instruments, automobile parts, tools, etc.).

SUMMARY

This chapter surveys special multicultural issues that can emerge in addiction counseling in assessment, treatment, and aftercare: gender, race/ethnicity, sexual orientation, disability, and age (adolescents, elderly). Every counselor needs to be able to bridge differences with clients in order to develop treatment rapport. Awareness of how these different areas may affect assessment, treatment, and aftercare with these populations can help the counselor be sensitive to their issues and thereby facilitate the development of a personalized recovery plan that fits the client.

QUESTIONS

1. What is multicultural counseling?

2. What are four environmental aspects to consider when working with someone from a different culture?

3. What role does dialogue play in multicultural counseling?

4. How can a counselor create a dialogue-friendly atmosphere?

5. What are some barriers women face in treatment?

6. What are some cultural considerations that may affect treatment for African Americans? Asian Americans and Pacific Islanders?

Hispanic Americans? American Indians/ Alaska Natives?

7. How can sexual orientation influence treatment and recovery?

8. What are six main barriers to treatment for the clients who are hard of hearing or deaf?

9. What considerations need to be considered in working with the blind/visually impaired? The physically injured?

10. What components are needed for effective treatment for adolescents?

11. How do stereotypes affect the assessment of the elderly in terms of addiction?

READINGS/RESOURCES/WEBSITES

SUGGESTED READINGS

General Multicultural

Kelly, V. A., & Juhnke, G. A. (2005). *Critical incidents in addictions counseling*. Alexandria, VA: American Counseling Association.

This case-focused book has 18 chapters. Each chapter has a case that focuses on addiction followed by a response to the incident and questions from an addictions professional. There is a chapter on each of these areas: gender, race/ethnicity, sexual orientation, disability, and age (adolescents, elderly).

Gender
Professional

Brady, K. T., Back, S. E., & Greenfield, S. F. (2009). *Women & addiction*. New York, NY: Guilford Press.

This book has seven sections (overview, biological issues, co-occurring psychiatric disorders, treatment outcome, specific substances, special populations, and social policy issues) and 30 chapters.

Center for Substance Abuse Treatment (CSAT). (1994). *Practical approaches in the treatment of women who abuse alcohol and other drugs* (DHHS Publication No. 94–3006). Rockville, MD: Author.

This 275-page publication provides general information on addiction in women as well as specific suggestions for assessment, treatment, and aftercare issues.

Hien, D., Litt, L. C., Cohen, L. R., Miele, G. M., & Campbell, A. (2009). *Trauma services for women in substance abuse treatment*. Washington, DC: American Psychological Association.

This book has three sections: the relationship between trauma and substance abuse; the impact of trauma on functioning; and strategies for implementation.

Personal

Miller, B. (2005). *The woman's book of resilience: 12 qualities to cultivate*. York Beach, ME: Conari Press.

This book has 12 chapters (vulnerability, connection, personal management, meeting of needs, recognition of gifts/talents, limit setting, resentment/forgiveness, use of humor, adaptive responses, endurance of suffering, finding meaning, balancing self- and other-dependence) with stories and exercises throughout the text to encourage the reader to develop resilient qualities.

U.S. Department of Health and Human Services, Office on Women's Health. (n.d.). *Women's mental health: What it means to you.*

This 16-page pamphlet speaks generally with regard to mental health issues for women. It has a helpful two-page reference guide at the end. It can be downloaded atwww.womenshealth.gov

Ethnicity

Bell, P. (2002). *Chemical dependency and the African-American* (2nd ed.). Center City, MN: Hazelden.

This 141-page book provides an overview of the issues facing African Americans regarding addic-

tion recovery. It provides specific suggestions for counselors working with this population. It contains three sections on assessment tools (client, personal, school-climate) that a counselor may find helpful in facilitating discussions.

Chin, J. L. (Ed.) (2000). *Relationships among Asian American women*. Washington, DC: American Psychological Association.

This 251-page book has 12 chapters divided into four sections (diversity, adaptive relationships, biculturalism, and paradigms) that are useful in understanding the relationship dynamics with regard to gender and ethnicity.

Lee, L. C., & Zane, N. W. S. (Eds.). (1998). *Handbook of Asian American psychology*. Washington, DC: American Psychological Association.

This 587-page text has 17 chapters divided into two sections (life course development, social and personal adjustment)—one chapter specifically focuses on addictive behaviors.

Rastogi, M., & Wieling, E. (Eds.). (2005). *Voices of color: First-person accounts of ethnic minority therapists*. Thousand Oaks, CA: Sage.

This 389-page book divides 19 stories into three sections (therapists, classroom, interventions/approaches) where authors discuss their experiences as ethnic minority therapists.

Substance Abuse and Mental Health Services Administration (SAMHSA). (2000). *Cultural competence standards*. Rockville, MD: Author.

This 68-page booklet describes the standards for four underserved/underrepresented racial/ethnic groups in an easy-to-read, understandable format.

Sexual Orientation

Barret, B., & Logan, C. (2002). *Counseling gay men and lesbians*. Pacific Grove, CA: Brooks/Cole.

This book is a general counseling book for working with the GLBT population. It include chapters on identity development, couples counseling, youth, spiritual, parenting, and health issues.

Cabaj, R. J. (1997). Gays, lesbians, & bisexuals. In J. H. Lowinson, P. Ruiz, R. B. Millman, & J. G. Langrod (Eds.), *Substance abuse: A comprehensive textbook* (3rd ed., pp. 725–733). Baltimore, MD: Williams & Wilkins.

This chapter provides a succinct summary of issues facing the GLBT population in relation to substance abuse.

Finnegan, D. G., & McNally, E. B. (1987). *Dual identities: Counseling chemically dependent gay men and lesbians*. Center City, MN: Hazelden.

This book provides general information on treating the gay/lesbian population in addiction treatment.

Savin-Williams, R. C. (2001). *Mom, Dad. I'm gay*. Washington, DC: American Psychological Association.

This book has nine chapters that discuss GLBT concerns within the context of the family. Especially helpful are the chapters that examine the relationship between different family members (e.g., daughters and fathers).

Substance Abuse and Mental Health Services Administration (SAMHSA). (2003). *A provider's introduction to substance abuse treatment for lesbian, gay, bisexual, and transgender individuals*. Rockville, MD: Author.

This publication is an excellent resource for working with the GLBT population in terms of substance abuse treatment. It is divided into three main sections: an overview, a clinician's guide (the coming-out process; health issues; and clinical issues with lesbians, gay males, bisexuals, transgender individuals, youth, and families), and a program administrator's guide.

Disability
Professional

Minnesota Chemical Dependency Program for Deaf and Hard of Hearing Individuals. (1994). *Best practices manual for providing substance abuse services to deaf, hard of hearing, late-deafened and deaf-blind persons*. Minneapolis, MN: Author.

This manual provides information and suggestions on assessment, intervention, treatment, and aftercare for working with this population. Additionally, there are term definitions and information on communication and technology in working with this population.

Minnesota Chemical Dependency Program for Deaf and Hard of Hearing Individuals. (1994). *Clinical approaches: A model for treating chemically dependent deaf and hearing impaired individuals*. Minneapolis, MN: Author.

This 170-page manual provides three sections that cover evaluation, treatment, and aftercare. Exercises are provided that can be used with clients.

National Institute on Alcohol Abuse and Alcoholism (NIAAA). (2005). *Module 101: Disabilities and alcohol use disorders*. Available at http://pubs.niaaa.nih.gov/publications/Social/Module10IDisabilities/Module10I.html.

This module is designed to provide information on alcohol use disorders to individuals with disabilities.

Substance Abuse and Mental Health Services Administration (SAMHSA). (1998). *Substance abuse disorder treatment for people with physical and cognitive disabilities*. Rockville, MD: Author.

This 156-page publication examines treatment issues, screening issues, treatment planning, service delivery, community links and case management, and organizational commitment. It has appendixes of bibliography, information, referral, and alcohol and drug problems as related to the American Disabilities Act.

Personal

National Library Service for the Blind and Physically Handicapped. (1993). *How can I do this when I can't see what I am doing?* Washington, DC: U.S. Government Printing Office.

This short booklet is written for the individual who has a visual disability and wants to learn other ways to process information. It has six sections: everyday living skills, use of computers, personal management systems, jobs, leisure, and one's support system for blindness.

Age
Professional
Adolescents

Burrow-Sanchez, J. J., & Hawken, L. S. (2007). *Helping students overcome substance abuse*. New York, NY: Guilford Press.

This book is geared to school mental health professionals who deal with adolescent substance abuse. It has seven chapters (overview, development/maintenance of abuse, drug categories and screening, prevention programming, individual interventions, group interventions, and consultation/referral). It has several worksheets throughout the text that can be used in counseling.

Essau, C. A. (Ed.). (2008). *Adolescent addiction: Epidemiology, assessment, and treatment*. Boston, MA: Elsevier.

This book is divided into three sections. In Part 1, general factors and assessment are discussed. In Part 2, specific addictions (alcohol, cannabis, tobacco, eating, gambling, Internet, and sexual) are presented. Part 3 looks at comorbidity and social/political issues.

Nagy, P. (2010). Motivational Interviewing. In M. Dulcan (Ed.), *Dulcan's textbook of child and adolescent psychiatry* (pp. 915–924) Arlington, VA: American Psychiatric Press.

This book chapter provides an overview of the application of MI techniques in an adolescent population.

Substance Abuse and Mental Health Services Administration (SAMHSA). (1999). *Screening and assessing adolescents for substance use disorders*. Rockville, MD: Author.

This manual provides a helpful overview of screening and assessment with this population. Screening, assessment, and legal issues as well as working with the juvenile justice system are discussed. Specific instruments are presented.

Substance Abuse and Mental Health Services Administration (SAMHSA). (2001). *Motivational enhancement therapy and cognitive behavioral therapy for adolescent cannabis users: 5 sessions*. CYT cannabis youth treatment series, Volume 1. Rockville, MD: Author.

This manual describes the application of MET and CBT with an adolescent population.

Walters, S. T., & Baer, J. S. (2006). *Talking with college students about alcohol*. New York, NY: Guilford Press.

This book has eight chapters (overview, responses, assessment, interaction style, brief individual interventions, extended individual interventions, group interventions, and service integration/training). It has worksheets and techniques spread throughout the text that the counselor can use in counseling.

Professional
Elderly

Colleran, C., & Jay, D. (2002). *Aging and addiction*. Center City, MN: Hazelden.

This 211-page book provides helpful suggestions on addressing addiction in the elderly. It has six sections (family, disease, how to help, treatment, recovery issues, resources). The section on resources has some especially helpful information.

Mehrotra, C. M., & Wagner, L. S. (2009). *Aging and diversity* (2nd ed.). New York, NY: Routledge/Taylor.

This 426-page text has nine chapters that examine the relationship between aging and various aspects of diversity (ethnicity, culture, gender, sexual orientation, social class, urban/rural).

Moody, H. R. (2010). *Aging: Concepts and controversies* (6th ed.). Los Angeles, CA: Pine Forge Press.

This 503-page textbook is divided into three basic concepts (life course, aging/health care/society, social/economic) that consist of 11 controversies. There is a useful appendix on aging Internet resources.

Substance Abuse and Mental Health Services Administration (SAMHSA). (1998). *Substance abuse among older adults*. Rockville, MD: Author.

This 173-page manual provides an excellent overview on the issues of substance abuse providing general information, specifics on assessment, treatment, legal/ethical concerns, and assessment tools.

Substance Abuse and Mental Health Services Administration (SAMHSA). (2005). *Substance abuse relapse prevention for older adults: a group treatment approach* (DHHS Publication No. (SMA)05-4053). Rockville, MD: Author.

This manual provides information on the application of a relapse prevention approach within a group context (cognitive-behavioral, self-management). Although designed for outpatient settings, it can be applied to other settings.

Personal
Elderly

Hazelden. (1996). *How to talk to an older person who has a problem with alcohol or medications*. Center City, MN: Author.

This pamphlet is helpful for individuals who want to approach the topic of a possible substance abuse problem with an elderly person.

National Institute on Alcohol Abuse and Alcoholism (NIAAA). (2008). *Older adults and alcohol: You can get help* (NIH Publication No. 08-7350). Rockville, MD: Author.

This pamphlet provides general information about aging and alcohol, how to obtain help, and sections on questions/answers, significant others, encouragement, and contact information.

RESOURCES

PDF Documents
Gender

NIAAA (niaaa.nih.gov): *Alcohol: A Women's Health Issue*

NIAAA (niaaa.nih.gov): *Fetal Alcohol Exposure*

SAMHSA/CSAT (samhsa.org): *Substance Abuse Treatment: Addressing the Specific Needs for Women* (TIP 51)

SAMHSA (samhsa.org): *Using Matrix with Women Clients*

Sexual Orientation

SAMHSA (samhsa.org): *Top Health Issues for LGBT Populations Information and Resource Kit*

Disability

SAMHSA (samhsa.org): *Substance Use Disorders in People with Physical and Sensory Disabilities*

SAMHSA/CSAT (samhsa.org): *Substance Use Disorder Treatment for People with Physical and Cognitive Disabilities* (TIP 29)

Age–Adolescent

NIAAA (niaaa.nih.gov): *Alcohol Screening and Brief Intervention for Youth: A Practitioner's Guide*

Age–Elderly

NIAAA (niaaa.nih.gov): *Older Adults and Alcohol*

SAMHSA/CSAT (samhsa.org): *Substance Abuse among Older Adults* (TIP 26)

Support Groups

Although these populations are not specified in Chapter 8, see Chapter 8 for information on 12-step groups and alternatives to 12-step groups.

Videos

Huebner, D. M., & Mackenzie, J. (2011). *Lead with love* [Online Video]. Can be viewed online at www.leadwithlovefilm.com

This is a 35-minute documentary that responds to the question: "What do I do if my child is gay?" It follows four families and includes interviews with professional helpers that provide answers and guidelines to parents of lesbian, gay, and bisexual children.

Mystic Fire Video (Producer). (1991). *Circle of recovery* [Video]. Can be accessed through WorldCat.org http://www.worldcat.org/title/circle-of-recovery/oclc/24867131

This hour-long video portrays seven African-American men who have weekly meetings to help each other live with being addicts.

New Day Films (Producer). (1996). Stories of change [VHS]. Available from www.newday.com

This 58-minute film tells the stories of four women who have struggles with alcoholism/drug abuse, racism, sexism, and classism.

WEBSITES

General

NIAAA, "Brochures and Fact Sheets" page
http://www.niaaa.nih.gov/publications/bro-chures-and-fact-sheets

This website provides general information about alcohol use with various populations.

Gender

National Advocates for Pregnant Women
www.advocatesforpregnantwomen.org

The website for National Advocates for Pregnant Women is in Spanish as well as English. It has publications, events, and a blog.

National Women's Health Resource Center
www.healthywomen.org

This website for the National Women's Health Resource Center has health topics, centers, and publications/resources.

Ethnicity

American Indian Health Resources
www.ldb.org/vl/geo/america/indi_hn.htm

Alternative websites:
http://americanindianhealth.nlm.nih.gov/

These websites provide information on Indian health resources. The first one has four main areas (health topics, people and traditions, programs and services, research and data).

National Society for Hispanic Professionals,
http://network.nshp.org/

This website has numerous components that include groups, blogs, jobs, events, and videos.

National Association for Advancement of Colored People
www.naacp.org

This website provides information on the civil rights of African Americans and minority group members. It has general information as well as a legal section and a blog.

NIAAA, "Diversity and Health Disparities"
http://www.niaaa.nih.gov/alcohol-health/special-populations-co-occurring-disorders/diversity-health-disparities

This website offers summaries on the health of different racial/ethnic minority populations.

Sexual Orientation

National Association of Lesbian and Gay Addiction Professionals and their Allies
www.nalgap.org

The website for this group, National Association of Lesbian and Gay Addiction Professionals and their Allies, has a section on services, resources, and news/articles.

Parents, Families, and Friends of Lesbians and Gays (PFLAG)
www.pflag.org

The PFLAG website has information for families and friends, gays/lesbians/bisexuals, and transgender individuals.

Pride Institute
www.pride-institute.com

This website has information on substance abuse treatment for GLBT individuals. There is general information, admissions information, and locations of their treatment centers.

Southern Poverty Law Center
www.splcenter.org

This website has information about U.S. hate groups, has a newsletter, and files lawsuits against hate groups. It also publishes the magazine *Teaching Tolerance* and has free resources for teachers. In addition, it has a blog.

Disability

American Disability Association
www.adanet.org

The website for the American Disability Association has general information on issues related to disabilities including statistics.

American Psychological Association Disability Issues Office
http://www.apa.org/pi/disability/about/index.aspx

This website for the American Psychological Association's Disability Issues Office has articles, journals, and legislative links about disability and advice on improving clinician skills in working with this population.

Deaf Digest
http://deafdigest.com/mid-week-news/20130703/

This online publication describes itself as providing "America's Unique Deaf Stories."

Minnesota Chemical Dependency Program for Deaf and Hard of Hearing Individuals
www.mncddeaf.org

This website for the Minnesota Chemical Dependency Program for Deaf and Hard of Hearing Individuals provides information on referrals as well as articles, newsletters, trainings/presentations, program materials, and employment opportunities.

National Spinal Cord Injury Association (NSCIA)
www.sci-info-pages.com/factsheets.html

The National Spinal Cord Injury Association (NSCIA) website has books/resources, statistics, and information on choosing a facility and starting a support/discussion group.

National Library Service for the Blind and Physically Handicapped (NLS)
http://www.loc.gov/nls/

The website for the National Library Service for the Blind and Physically Handicapped (NLS) has information on Braille transcription/proofreading courses, a catalogue, finding a library, and an FAQ section.

Brain Injury Association of America
www.biausa.org

This is the website for the Brain Injury Association of America. It has information for individuals, families, and professionals who have been impacted by TBI. They provide general information as well as information about events, legislation, and research. They also have a bookstore, a directory of providers, and information on professional training and education.

Substance Abuse Resources and Disability Issues (SARDI) Program
www.med.wright.edu/citar/sardi/

The website for the Substance Abuse Resources and Disability Issues (SARDI) Program assists people who have both disability and behavioral health issues. They have research, intervention, and training programs. They also provide general information on these issues.

Age
Adolescents

NIAAA, "Adolescent Development and Alcohol Use" Video Presentation and Slide Show (@30 minutes)
https://webmeeting.nih.gov/p95927495/?launcher=false&fcsContent=true&pbMode=normal

Elderly

American Psychological Association Office on Aging
www.apa.org/pi/aging

This website has general information (research, interventions), publications, and referral information about the elderly.

Eldercare Locator
www.eldercare.gov

This service provides information on resources available to the elderly person.

CHAPTER 11

CHRONIC PAIN ASSESSMENT AND TREATMENT

PERSONAL REFLECTIONS

The overlap of pain and addiction is a very complex and important topic. Because many individuals experience pain that may trigger an urge to use drugs, initial use of a drug, or a relapse, these overlapping areas need to be explored in counseling addicted individuals. This overlap may be tempting to avoid because of the complications of treatment, the involvement of numerous professionals, the concern of balancing the welfare of the client while avoiding enabling, and so forth. If we as professionals can become overwhelmed with the numerous factors (funding limitations, limitations on our area of expertise, limited and/or fragmented resources available, etc.), imagine how overwhelmed our clients who are caught in this overlap feel. Therefore, we need to make a commitment to address this complicated area in order to better assist our clients to find their way into recovery and maintain a healthy recovery.

Also, we need to remember the idiosyncratic nature of pain for each addicted individual. While we may understand the physical aspect of the addiction to the drug, we can underestimate or not comprehend the psychological addiction to the drug that is unique for that individual. Additionally, we need to be aware that individuals may become exposed to one form of pain management, i.e. drugs, and become fixated on this avenue as *the* avenue of pain management, unable or unwilling to examine other options. The "quick fix" aspect of cultural dynamics can be a contributing, reinforcing factor to this individual tendency causing clients to take medicine or have surgery as a "one shot" attempt to eradicate the pain. As counselors, then, we need to carefully listen to the client's story of the psychological addiction to drugs and work with them on that perspective as well as invite and reinforce their exploration of other options. There is a self-help group adage when one does not know *how* to do something that serves as a guide: be *honest, open,* and *willing.* As we enter this area in counseling with our clients, we need to be honest, open, and willing to address the overlapping issues of pain and addiction in order to provide the client with the most humane, respectful treatment possible.

OBJECTIVES

1. To understand the general concepts and issues as they relate to the overlapping areas of pain and substance abuse.
2. To develop a general counseling approach (assessment and treatment) to pain management when working with substance-abusing clients.
3. To learn techniques that can be used with substance-abusing clients who live with pain management issues.

This chapter provides some basic information about the overlapping areas of pain and substance abuse. The intent is to provide the counselor with exposure to the general overlapping area of substance abuse and pain management with specific approaches and techniques to explore chronic pain in the substance-abusing client.

The decade of 2000 to 2010 has been labeled the *Decade of Pain* in the United States because of its dominance in health care delivery and professional education (Lasch, 2002). "[Pain] is the most common reason for medication appointments, nearly 40 million visits annually, and costs this country over $100 billion each year in health care and lost productivity" (NIH, 2003, p. 1). Chronic pain is common in Americans: about 35% experience chronic pain (Shurman, Sack, Shurman, Schnierow, & Gabriel, 2006)—one out of three persons (Jamison & Edwards, 2012), and 10% report having pain that has lasted more than year (Centers for Disease Control and Prevention, National Center for Health Statistics, 2006). Chronic pain impacts the health of Americans in debilitating ways physically, socially, and emotionally (Green, Baker, Sato, Washington, & Smith, 2003).

Merskey and Bogduk (1994) define pain as "An unpleasant sensory and emotional experience associated with actual or potential tissue damage, or described in terms of such damage" (p. 210). Benedict (2008) defines *chronic nonmalignant pain* as a non-cancer-related pain that persists more than 6 months and is classified as *nociceptive* or *neuropathic*. *Nociceptive* is thought of as musculoskeletal pain that is treated with anti-inflammatory medication until healing stops and the pain is gone, whereas *neuropathic* is the result of irritable or damaged nerves that exist even after healing has occurred. *Breakthrough*, *episodic*, and *transient* pain are used to describe flare-ups of pain that occur beyond the basic chronic pain experienced (Brown, 2005). *Breakthrough pain* (rapid change in pain signaling in a short period of time) is usually treated with opioids for pain management. Due to the frequency of chronic pain conditions and the frequent treatment of these conditions

with opioids because they are helpful in treating pain (Compton & Denisco, 2008), there is a risk of opioid misuse.

Opiate medication is often used in chronic pain treatment (Pohl & Smith, 2012). Chapter 1 touches on the prevalence of prescription drug use in America: (a) in 2011, the number of Americans aged 12 or older, who were current nonmedical users of pain relievers, was 4.5 million or 1.7 percent (SAMHSA, 2012b); (b) in 2010, every American could be medicated on prescribed painkiller medication for a month—while they were prescribed for medical reasons, they were misused or abused by others (CDC, 2013); (c) in the past 20 years there has been a tripling of prescription painkiller overdoses (opioid or narcotic) (SAMSHA, 2010, 2011); (d) abuse/misuse of them has doubled emergency room visits (SAMSHA, 2010); and (e) they are used by both teens and adults to experience a "high" or for other nonmedical reasons (SAMSHA, 2011). In a summary of the literature, Bannwarth (2012) states that Americans are consuming 80% of the global opioid supply while only being 4.6% of the world population—this medical use trend impacts opioid *availability* (the greater number of prescriptions has resulted in their availability in homes) and has resulted in a "*prescription opioid crisis*" that can negatively impact pain treatment.

Benedict (2008) states that pain management has become a high priority in the U.S. health-care system. In 2001, the U.S. Drug Enforcement Agency joined pain management groups in issuing a joint statement that professionals share a responsibility to make prescription pain medication available to people in need of it and be responsible to keep drugs from becoming an avenue for harm or abuse. The Federation of State Medical Boards in 2004 developed a policy that said not treating, under- and overtreating, and use of treatments that are ineffective is considered inappropriate. The U.S. Congress designated the years 2001 to 2010 as the "Decade of Pain Control and Research" (Gatchel, 2005, p. 12). Yet, as Brown (2005) states, pain is "under-treated, untreated or improperly treated" (p. 46). In America its treatment has historically been nonexistent or incorrect (Lasch, 2002).

Hojsted and Sjogren's (2007) review of the literature shows that addiction ranged from 0% to 50% in chronic, nonmalignant pain patients. It is highly probable, then, that counselors will address the complicated, crossover issues of chronic pain and substance abuse as they work with their clients through the assessment, treatment, and aftercare process (Markowitz, Francis, & Gonzales-Nolas, 2010). Although aftercare guidelines are not specifically separated out in this chapter, the treatment approaches can readily be translated to the treatment in the aftercare process as long as the counselor assists the client in adapting the strategies to the changed format of aftercare. Clients may develop an addiction to the pain medication without a previous addiction being present; they may have developed an addiction to the pain medication in addition to a previous alcohol/drug addiction; or they may experience the pain medication as a trigger to a relapse to their original drug of choice. As Compton (1999) states, "the presence of one may affect the expression of the other" (p. 430).

These crossover areas can become quite complicated and overwhelming to the individual counselor and agency in several ways. For example, if welfare of the client is the rudder in the counseling profession, *how does a counselor focus on the welfare of the client* (in terms of substance abuse recovery) when the client has pain being treated with opiates and yet the counselor works out of an abstinence-based recovery system (professional orientation, recovering community, agency philosophy)? In a second example, *how does the counselor address these overlapping issues* that may involve numerous professionals without an interagency team at the agency/in the community that focuses on pain management? Or if there is such a pain management team, is it sensitive to substance abuse issues? If there is a substance abuse treatment team, is that team sensitive to pain management issues? In a final example of the complicated overlap of these issues, *how can the counselor avoid*

being overwhelmed when the counselor: (1) may have difficulties reading the literature on pain management because of the technical medical language; (2) is aware of the propensity of addicted clients to "con" others for drugs; and (3) knows there is a fine line between enabling the client to use pain management drugs for "highs" and indirectly harming the client by not recognizing the pain the client is experiencing?

One example of a counselor and client journey in this complicated situation is outlined in an article by Mallow (2008) that presents the counselor's and client's stories of their experiences. Some recovering individuals, as evidenced in this story, may need to take pain medication for extended lengths of time while attending self-help groups that promote abstinence. Even short-term use of mood altering medication can create cognitive-dissonance in recovering addicted clients. These issues need to be carefully addressed in the counseling process so the counselor is assisting the client in developing a reasonable approach to the complicated situation of the client feeling caught between the extremes of total abstinence and a full-blown relapse.

Compton (1999) states that there are basically two challenges in working with this population: provision of pain relief to the client, who has currently or in the past a history with addiction, and assessing for addiction in pain patients who are on maintenance therapy with opioid analgesics. Because this book is written from the substance abuse perspective, the focus of this chapter is on the first challenge presented by Compton: the client with a substance-abusing history who is also struggling with chronic pain. The reader may find it beneficial to view this from the perspective of a co-occurring disorder, as addressed in Chapter 4, as well as the "dance" of addressing trauma issues and addiction as outlined in Chapter 6—these chapters can be used in concert with this chapter.

Some specific suggestions to the reader about the complicated, potentially overwhelming topic of pain management in recovery need to be made here. First, the influence of pain on the client's recovery process may require that traditional treatment approaches require modification in order to best serve the client's welfare. The experience of pain and/or pain medication can change a person. When we are in pain, we tend to develop a self-centered focus and experience fears and anxiety in relation to the pain. Counselors need to keep these tendencies in mind and assist clients in managing their fear and anxiety. Second, the individual counselor reading this text is encouraged to work with the information in a manner that best fits his or her setting. That may require some adaptation of approaches and techniques presented that fit both the counselor's setting and client population. Third, the counselor needs to explore the pain management resources in his or her professional community that are available for consultation and must possibly become creative in integrating these areas into a network addressing these concerns. Fourth, the counselor can find the balance between enabling addiction and ignoring pain management issues through consultation with experts (especially addiction medicine specialists) and establishment of a philosophical approach and a practical approach to working with clients who have both substance abuse and pain management issues. This latter area requires the counselor to be sensitive to countertransference issues that may arise with regard to pain management. For example, there is some evidence that medical staff may have impressions about pain intensity that varies based on characteristics of patients, such as ethnicity (Ernst, 2000), as well as negatively stereotype addicts (Liberto & Fornili, 2013); such evidence supports the hypothesis that counselors, too, may project their schema regarding pain and its management on clients.

There are many ways countertransference can enter into the counseling process of assessment, treatment, and aftercare. For example, a counselor may have a specific way of handling pain him/herself (i.e., chiropractic treatment) and advocate that way as an alternative method for a client; or the counselor may believe addicted clients need to "tough it out" and advocate abstinence without grasping the medical reality of the client's pain.

These are only some examples of how the counselor may be biased by countertransference in the assessment and treatment process of pain management in addicted clients. These examples elucidate the importance of exploring one's personal and professional experiences with pain and pain management. The exercises at the end of this chapter are included in the hope of facilitating that process in the reader.

DEFINITION OF PAIN

Pain is both personal and unique (Compton, Gallagher, & Mardini, 2009); it is both emotional and sensory (Jamison & Edwards, 2012). Therefore, each person defines his or her own pain. There is a myth researchers call the "Patient Uniformity Myth" that underestimates how complex the experience of pain is by negating individual differences in "pain perception, understanding, and ability to cope with pain" (Frey, 2007, p. 2). Pain is complex in that its experience in each person is impacted by previous experiences, behaviors they have learned, and the context of the situation (Brown, 2005). A client's status in various areas (mental health, socioeconomic, biomedical, and diagnostic) has an impact on the experience of pain (Turk & Gatchel, 2002). Also, the origin and severity of the chronic pain varies (Rosenblatt & Mekhail, 2005). Or, as Jarret (2011) so aptly summarizes the experience of pain: "The sensitivity and tolerance people show toward pain varies predictably according to several factors, including gender, ethnicity, personality, and culture all interacting, overlapping, and playing out in the tissues and synapses of the body" (p. 416). Therefore, the general client pain population is heterogeneous in nature, so it is difficult to develop a clear, standard, theoretical model for working with this population (Meredith, Ownsworth, & Strong, 2008).

In defining, assessing, and treating pain management issues in the substance-abusing client, counselors need to remember that the counselor cannot experience the pain of the client but needs to trust the self-report of the individual. Years ago, Engel (1959) stated that persistent or chronic pain patients not responding to treatment had difficult developmental years (e.g., trauma), resulting in *psychogenic pain*. More current views on pain management suggest it is outdated to view pain dichotomously as able to be verified or, if it cannot be verified, as the result of the client's psychological problems (Brown, 2005). Instead of asking the client to provide proof of the pain, the counselor needs to sensitively approach the issue *with* the client, viewing the experience of pain from his or her perspective. Because psychological and social issues complicate pain sufferers' lives, the "puzzle of pain" can be difficult to sort out in the counseling process (Jamison & Edwards, 2012). Therefore, counselors may need to: (1) be sensitive to different contributing factors, (2) be open to presenting a variety of pain management approaches, and (3) continue to recalibrate the effectiveness of approaches on the pain, especially as they are applied to activities of daily living.

Specifically with substance-abusing clients, Compton (1999) recommends that clinicians examine their negative biases about addiction and set them aside in order to provide the client with the best treatment. The professional needs to accept the self-report of pain by the substance-abusing client as with any client (Compton, 1999).

ISSUES OF LIVING SOBER WITH CHRONIC PAIN

Chronic pain (ongoing, without resolution) impacts every part of a person's life (Frey, 2007). In general, a vicious cycle can begin with the pain, which results in tension that causes the person to be less active, and then result in more tension, which results in more pain (Brown, 2005).

Chronic pain almost always disrupts sleep and mood (Schramm, 2007). Regarding *sleep*, the pain causes sleep disruption, which causes lower tolerance for pain and less stamina in addressing the pain, thereby resulting in less energy and increased tiredness. In addition to lowering the pain threshold, sleep disruption decreases the amount of REM sleep, which impacts mood. As the pain threshold decreases then, there is an increase in sleep disturbance and a negative impact on mood. (Note that in women, there is the need to watch for menopausal impact, menstrual cycle changes, and postpartum changes in mood.) However, when the person attempts to catch up on their sleep, their sleep is interrupted again by the pain, which continues to stimulate the negative impact on pain threshold and mood. (Note that mood disruption can be treated through antidepressants and therapy, and sleep dysfunction can be addressed by establishing a consistent schedule and routine, as well as counseling and relaxation methods [Schramm, 2007]).

In terms of *mood*, emotional states (i.e., anger, anxiety) can trigger or increase chronic pain (Compton et al., 2009; Jacobsen, Moldrup, Christrup, Sjogren, & Hansen, 2010). Depression, anxiety, avoidant behavior (i.e., avoiding activities that cause pain, tense muscles, or use protective movements/postures), and PTSD symptoms can emerge from pain (Brown, 2005).

Other aspects can contribute to the experience of pain. Personality traits (external locus of control, catastrophizing tendencies) can also negatively impact pain control (Compton et al., 2009). Somatoform disorders, personality disorders, and adjustment disorders may also be present whether they are related or not to the pain syndrome (Ziegler, 2005). The presence of a mental health disorder *and* pain can complicate treatment, because both need to be treated at the same time or the result could be treatment failure (Compton et al., 2009).

Addressing the pain in substance-abusing clients requires a multimodal approach because of this interaction between biomedical, psychological, and sociocultural aspects related to the individual (Brown, 2005). Addicted individuals may have problems with sleep, mood, problem personality traits (external locus of control, catastrophizing), somatoform disorders, personality

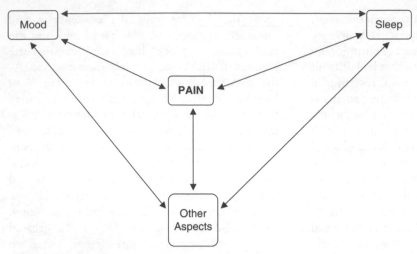

Figure 11.1 The Interactive Cycle of Chronic Pain.

disorders, and/or adjustment disorders that are exacerbated by pain and/or recovery from their addiction. For example, higher-risk patients for opioid misuse may experience more subjective pain and be more difficult to treat (Jamison, Link, & Marceau, 2009) and opioid addicts, in addition to these two factors, may also have higher opioid tolerance, be involved in illicit substance use, and have cross-tolerance to opioid pain medications (Eyler, 2013). As outlined in Figure 11.1, *The Interactive Cycle of Chronic Pain*, different factors that interact with the pain may be present or absent depending on the individual client and his/her experience of the pain.

A multidisciplinary approach for pain management is important when there is a pain-proneness in the client (Grzesniak, 2003); the recovering addict, especially early in recovery, may show a pain-proneness. Also, the recovering addict may have a dual diagnosis or intoxication/withdrawal effects, and "the interpersonal conflicts, role adjustments, and social support losses that characterize the social context of addiction can worsen the experience of pain, making the individual less able to manage or cope with discomfort" (Compton et al., 2009, p. 1285). Finally, the chaotic lifestyle that is a part of the addiction (Compton et al., 2009) may carry over into the

early recovery of the addicted person, making pain management *sober* a difficult task. These complicating factors encourage the counselor's collaboration with other professionals, a pain management team, and/or addiction medicine specialists.

In the face of so many confounding issues for recovery, it is critical to set up a trusting therapeutic relationship where the issues of recovery, as they relate to the pain experience, are addressed with the substance-abusing client. Thornton (2003) recommends that the counselor assume the substance-abusing client *does* experience pain and that *the client is the expert on his or her pain*. This will invite a trusting relationship with the client. The counselor needs to keep in mind, though, that the substance-abusing client may show the following four tendencies regarding pain that can cause problems in recovery (Thornton, 2003):

1. Having a negative global perception of pain ("Pain is always bad").

2. Lacking any sense of tolerable pain.

3. Believing pain is a purely physiological phenomenon negating any reason to have a counselor.

4. Excessively relying on narcotics for pain management.

While the counselor needs to be sensitive to the client's perception of pain, the counselor also needs to address these problem tendencies of the client during the therapy process. SAMHSA's (2011) Tip 54, *Managing Chronic Pain in Adults with or in Recovery from Substance Use Disorders*, provides an excellent overview of pain issues as they arise in the assessment and treatment process with substance abusers. A description of this publication is given in the resource section at the end of this chapter.

ASSESSMENT AND TREATMENT

Accurate and appropriate assessment and treatment of pain require a consideration of cultural influences on pain. This section begins with a discussion of cultural influences to encourage the reader to incorporate this perspective in the assessment and treatment process.

Cultural Influences

Prior to discussion of specific assessment and treatment of chronic pain and substance abuse, a review of cultural influences on pain needs to be presented. This material is included to encourage sensitivity to the influence of the client's culture on the experience and management of pain. As stated by Jarrett (2011): "The sensitivity and tolerance people show towards pain varies predictably according to several factors, including gender, ethnicity, personality, and culture, all interacting, overlapping and playing out in the tissues and synapses of the body" (p. 416). A client's culture can influence the ways their body experiences pain and the way their brain responds to it (Jarrett, 2011). The following overview of the impact of culture on the pain experience is based on the writing of Lasch (2002).

The expression and treatment of pain is rooted in social and cultural factors; pain involves emotional reactions to the pain as well as the sense of pain. Culture can impact client: beliefs about the pain condition, behavior in response to the pain, treatment-seeking approaches, treatment expectations, response to treatment interventions, and family and practitioner responses to the client's pain.

Cultural background may impact client coping strategies. Clients may seek out traditional healers and remedies first and then continue use of them during Western medicine treatment. The counselor, then, needs to ask the client about other sources of help (past and present) and show respect for the client's culture, traditional healers, and remedies.

Culture also impacts client language regarding pain. For example, immigrants may not speak English or not speak it well, thereby increasing the difficulties of pain assessment and management. Also, words used to describe the pain may be used differently depending on one's culture. Finally, there may be interethnic differences in reporting emotional responses to pain and its interference with daily functioning.

When exploring the impact of culture on a client's pain experience, the counselor needs to be careful to avoid stereotyping the client because of the differences between and within cultures regarding pain. While age, gender, SES, and acculturation may mediate the interaction between ethnic background and pain interaction, more research is needed to clarify inconsistent or new research findings. Jarrett (2011) adds to Lasch's writing (2002) that while the danger in this type of research is that it can promote stereotypes, it can also be used to improve quality of life. Lasch (2002) warns that it is difficult when reviewing research findings on race to determine if racial differences are due to experiences of pain and pain behavior or the staff's perception and treatment of pain. Therefore, it is imperative that the counselor collect information about the pain *within the individual's unique impact of his/her culture on the pain experience*.

Overall suggestions made by Lasch (2002) to physical therapists can be included by counselors involved in the assessment and treatment of pain. These include:

- Developing a culturally sensitive relationship.

- Being aware of communication and care access issues.

- If needed, choosing an appropriate interpreter (i.e., not a family member).

- Being sensitive to religious beliefs that may impact client dress, sexuality, privacy as they relate to the assessment and treatment process (this may be heightened by counselor and client gender differences).

- Working with different time orientations.

- Considering the influencing factors of age, race, gender, and occupational status.

Assessment

Assessment of the pain condition requires a theoretical framework. The *gate control theory* (Melzack & Wall, 1965), introduced in 1965, presented the interaction of the psychosocial and physiological aspects of pain. However, this theory was unable to explain various chronic pain problems (i.e., phantom limb pain) (Melzack, 1996). Currently, the acceptable model of pain is the *biopsychosocial model* (Frey, 2007; Lasch, 2002). This model is similar to the biopsychosocial model of addiction in that it looks at the interaction of biological, psychological, and social factors as they influence one's perception of pain. Substance abuse factors that need to be considered in pain management, such as tolerance and physical dependence, are discussed in Chapter 3.

Chronic pain does not stand alone in that it typically involves other symptoms and functioning problems, and it requires an assessment that is complex and comprehensive (Portenoy, Lussier, Kirsh, & Passik, 2005). The longer the pain experience, the more complexity involved (Compton et al., 2009). An example of how complicated an assessment can be in the areas of substance abuse and pain management follows. Some clients who struggle with pain may appear to be dependent when they are not. *Pseudo-addiction* (Kouyanou, Pither, & Wessely, 1997) is

present in the client who shows drug-seeking behavior (e.g., "hoarding prescribed medication"), but who, once receiving the required dosage to control the pain, complies with the medical regime and stops the drug-seeking behavior (Benedict, 2008). Yet, this tendency needs to be monitored because it can indicate the early stages of addiction. With *chronic pain clients who may be substance abusing*, a common presenting concern is tolerance for the medication that shows in increased dose or early refills of the prescription (Ziegler, 2005).

Whether addicted or not, the client may have a psychiatric disorder that has not been diagnosed previously, thereby contributing to the dysfunctional behavior (increased tolerance, early refills). The behavior also needs to be assessed for the possibility that the client is selling or distributing the drugs to others.

Ziegler (2005) states that assessments must be done with *pain management clients on possible substance abuse issues* and on *substance abusers regarding their pain management*. If the counselor does suspect that there is a substance abuse problem, the assessment instruments discussed in Chapter 3 of this book can be used for the assessment process. Additional reliable and valid instruments specific to pain management through opioids include the: Screener and Opioid Assessment for Patients with Pain–Revised (SOAPP-R), Current Opioid Misuse Measure (COMM), Opioid Risk Tool (ORT), DIRE (diagnosis, intractability, risk, efficacy), and Pain Assessment and Documentation Tool (Jamison & Edwards, 2012).

With *substance abusers with chronic pain*, Ziegler recommends an assessment be done of the person's physical and emotional health as well as their recovery. There is also the recommendation that a pain management plan is developed without opioids or sedatives. All forms of nonpharmaceutical approaches to pain management need to be explored. These include:

- Change in positions

- Cold packs

- Warm packs

- Massage

- Music

- Relaxation

- Rest

- Emotional support

- Aromatherapy

- Prayer or spiritual care

- Breathing exercises

- Visualization

- Walking or exercise

- Changes in lighting (this may be especially important for clients with head injuries who require reduced sensory stimulation)

- Changes in temperature (this simply means the body needs to be comfortable)

When exploring alternative options, a few notations need to be made. First, we cannot assume if a client says, "I have tried that" that they have experienced the alternative pain management method in a quality manner or they have been exhaustive in their use of this option. We need to elaborate on the statement in order to determine if the alternative has been adequately explored. If opioids are required, then the suggestion is for a structured plan to be developed as well as a written agreement regarding the treatment use of opioids. Second, it is important to assist clients in choosing an alternative that they are willing to explore given their personal preferences and experiences with pain management. For example, one might not like needles (therefore, avoid acupuncture) or one might not like to be touched (therefore, avoid massage). Also, although it is important to respect client limits, it is also important to encourage the client to stretch themselves in the exploration of options.

Regarding an overall assessment approach, Jamison and Edwards (2012) outline specific factors that need to be considered when assessing pain. One factor is that pain cannot be measured objectively, but must be anchored in what the client says and

does in response to the experience of pain requiring different measures of pain and psychosocial functioning. Another is to avoid assuming that the cause of pain is psychological when we know that quality of life is impacted by chronic pain (employment, memory, sleep, sexual functioning, social functioning, activities of daily living, energy, family roles, finances, lifestyle). Therefore, psychological assessments need to be holistic examining senses, affect, cognitions, and behaviors of the client.

According to the authors (Jamison & Edwards, 2012), the *sensory* component can be examined through understanding the location, severity, and temporal qualities of the pain. One example of this is Schramm's 11 assessment questions (2007):

1. When did the pain start?

2. How severe is the pain?

3. Where is the pain located?

4. Does it involve the jaw or ears?

5. Does it radiate to other parts of the body?

6. Is it worse when you touch the area?

7. Is it worse after physical exertion?

8. Is it better after you use medications?

9. Is it better after you use ice or heat?

10. Is it better after you rest?

11. How high is its predictability?

We can also ask simple questions such as: Is your pain ever at a zero level (totally absent)? When is your pain the worst? What is average pain for you? What times of day do you experience pain? How do you live with the pain you experience? Any questions that encourage the client to elaborate on the pain experience can be beneficial to the assessment process.

Affect, cognitions, and behaviors of the client also need to be evaluated (Jamison & Edwards, 2012). Regarding the *affective* component, the counselor needs to examine fears and depression because of their impact on the experience and reaction to pain. *Cognitive patterns* may enhance or maintain the pain as well as impact the coping behaviors of the client. In terms of *behaviors*, observe nonverbal behaviors in different settings, listen to self-reports of activities, and gather information on family, ethnic, and cultural aspects of the client with regard to pain and pain management. The authors provide an excellent overview of instruments in each of these areas that can be used in the assessment process.

A specific instrument to assess the client's readiness to develop a chronic pain self-management approach is the Pain Stages of Change Questionnaire (PSOCQ; Kerns, Rosenberg, Jamison, Caudill, & Haythornewalte, 1997). The instrument is based on the Transtheoretical Model of Behavior Change that is discussed at length in Chapter 9 of this book. The PSOCQ is a 30-item, self-report questionnaire that uses a 5-point Likert-type scale that ranges from "strongly disagree" to "strongly agree." Clients in the later stages of the model are viewed as more responsive to self-management approaches present in multidisciplinary pain programs. It has adequate internal consistency and test-retest reliability for four of the scales, therefore, counselors may find an instrument such as this one as *tentatively* helpful in clarifying the client's readiness to change with regard to pain management until further research is done on the reliability and validity of the instrument.

Finally, in the ongoing assessment of the overlap between substance abuse and pain management,

Grinstead (2007) points out 15 red flags the counselor can watch for with a substance-abusing client:

1. Having a positive urine screen.

2. Taking too much of a drug.

3. Developing a relationship with a drug.

4. Missing appointments until a refill is needed.

5. Displaying hyperdefensiveness.

6. Saying "Only this drug will work."

7. Showing a lack of engagement in the therapeutic process.

8. Not saying "*take* my drug," but "*eat* my drug."

9. Needing more of the drug.

10. Calling emergency rooms (ER) for narcotic shots.

11. Shopping for doctors.

12. Writing his or her own prescriptions.

13. Coaching a relative on symptoms to provide a doctor during a visit.

14. Saying "Yeah, but . . . " to alternative programs.

15. Getting medications from the Internet.

Again, these concerns can be addressed as a part of the recovery issues of the addicted individual. (See Case Study 11.1.)

CASE STUDY 11.1

Adrian is a 55-year-old woman who has come to see you as a counselor because she was reportedly referred by her physician. She has come to your office without any medical records and simply stated that her doctor was uncomfortable renewing her prescription for her pain medication.

Where would you begin in the assessment process with Adrian? Take into consideration the following factors: (1) Would you continue the interview with such incomplete information? (2) If so, what would you focus on in the session? (3) If not, what would you require for her to begin to work with you, and what would you focus on in the session? (4) What assessment information would you want to gather from Adrian? (in terms of major areas) and (5) How would you explain your approach to her?

Substance Abuse Treatment Approaches and Techniques

The danger with treatment of the substance abusing population is that they may be undertreated because of addiction biases of the professional, as well as concerns that the addicted individual is trying to con them (Compton, 1999). The result of such biases may be a negative relationship that invites anger and manipulation from the client (Compton, 1999). Also, clients who have problems with substance abuse have an increased risk of not receiving adequate pain management because of factors such as inadequate training regarding the overlap of these two areas, concern about enabling the addiction, prejudice within American society against addicts, and, for the prescribers, concern about the sanctions they may receive from regulatory boards (Savage, 1998). Finally, we need to keep in mind that when we are in severe pain, we may go to the place of being willing to do *anything* to get out of the pain. Such an attitude can result in clients being vulnerable to "snake oil" remedies and/or chronic consumers to even reliable medical practices that may be limited in their effectiveness with regard to the client's specific pain experience. As counselors, we need to advocate for our clients when they are experiencing such vulnerability as well as assist them in exploring numerous approaches to pain management with qualified, experienced pain management professionals.

General Strategies

Some general counseling strategies incorporating these different components are as follows. Jamison and Edwards (2012) highlight a number of treatment interventions that can be applied to the substance abusing population. These treatments include: cognitive-behavioral therapy, individual/group/family therapy, and relaxation training. In *cognitive-behavioral therapy*, the counselor helps the client view their problem as manageable and treatment (requiring their active participation) as able to help them, in addition to developing more functional thinking patterns. *Individual and group therapy* can help them manage their emotions and assist them with problem-solving strategies; *family therapy* can provide education to family members as well as sharing opportunities, improved communication, and ways to be supportive. *Relaxation training* (diaphragmatic breathing, progressive muscle relaxation, guided imagery, hypnosis, biofeedback) can help with pain and anxiety reduction and an enhanced sense of self-control.

In terms of counseling strategies specific to the substance abusing population, Thornton (2003) suggests that the counselor needs to:

- Join with the patient and validate her pain.
- Help the patient recognize the ineffectiveness of narcotics in treating chronic pain.
- Develop a more realistic perception of intensity of pain.
- Link pain with emotions/stress.
- Develop a contract to *manage* pain.
- Develop a plan to decrease pain medication.
- Use the *Gold Technique*: have them chart pain every hour on a scale of 1 to 10 of intensity (10 = highest), and based on this information, help them determine a tolerable level of pain ("I don't want it to be this awful").

Whether working within a system or as a part of one's private practice, a counselor needs to have in place a process for handling pain management in substance-abusing clients. As Fishbain (2006) states, because there is a medicolegal risk in working in this area, documentation is an important prevention strategy for malpractice claims. In terms of general treatment suggestions for the counselor in this context, Grinstead (2007) recommends that counselors:

- Document everything.
- Have policies and procedures in place.
- Have justification for each decision made.

Benedict (2008) proposes the shared-risk model (Shurman, Sack, Shurman, Schnierow, & Gabriel, 2006). This model includes five main areas: (1) consulting with a pain specialist, (2) advocating for clients and providing educational support (inclusion of family members), (3) documenting (e.g., signed narcotic contracts, informed consent, ongoing treatment notes), (4) taking precautions that involve screening for substance abuse, and (5) managing risk (e.g., reduction of risk for harm in the use of opiates).

Relapse–Prevention Strategies

Relapse is always possible for addicted clients in general as well as with chronic pain clients who are receiving opioid treatment and it needs to be recognized and managed when it occurs (Compton, 2011). Compton (2011) makes specific, overall suggestions on preventing relapse with this population. First, a thorough recovery and relapse history is needed. Second, triggering situations, as outlined in the Marlatt model of Chapter 7, need to be assessed. Third, the possible presence of psychiatric disorders needs to be determined. Fourth, addiction treatment is required. Fifth, medication needs to be highly structured and monitored. With regard to recognizing relapse, the author encourages the close monitoring of the treatment contract and with managing the relapse, the author suggests intervention that may include a relapse contract and a review of the relapse together.

Grinstead (2007) suggests that counselors look at *pain as a high-risk situation* for the client and help clients be aware of pain level rising ("Don't chase the pain"). Regarding relapse prevention, Grinstead (2007) suggests that counselors:

- Do an intervention plan.

- Look at future high-risk situations.

- Examine if there was a time in the past where one "blew it."

- Diagram the situation.

- Develop general strategies for when a client may be blindsided by a high-risk situation.

Specific Treatment Techniques

Many of the techniques discussed in this section have been translated from general mental health counseling techniques to an application to issues of pain and/or substance abuse. All of these can be built into an overall treatment plan. Also, these techniques can be used in the counseling session to explore the pain experience.

Exercises can be used that explore different aspects of the pain experience—pain level, stress, medication management, nonpharmacological approaches, denial, beliefs about medication—and can be useful in counseling the substance-abusing, pain management client. Many of these exercises are included in the resource texts mentioned at the end of this chapter. These exercises can be adapted from being verbal to being experiential (e.g., drawing) in the event that it is easier for the client to access and express that information in that context rather than verbally.

In terms of current reactions to the client's pain and messages about how it should be handled, it may be helpful to focus on those individuals and systems that convey messages of hope. Once these individuals and systems are identified, the counselor can assist the client in building those individuals and systems in to his or her life with an intentionality.

The following nine techniques can be used in treatment plans and in pain management counseling session interventions with a client who has substance abuse issues:

1. *Charting.* Client charts the times of the day when the pain seems the hardest using a cognitive-behavioral log that records the Date, Situation, Feeling, Pain Level, Automatic Thoughts, and Responding Thoughts.

2. *History of pain.* Client writes a history of his or her pain and both successful and unsuccessful coping strategies for the pain.

3. *Naming the pain.* Client names the different kinds of pain experienced. For example, "Tsunami pain," "Good pain," "Low-grade pain." Note that the client may already have names for the different types and levels of pain. Also ask the client to describe how he or she handles each type to tap into different adaptive strategies used.

4. *Visual analogue scale.* The client draws out a visual diagram of the pain on a continuum with no pain at one end and the worst pain experienced at the other end. This diagram can be in pictures or words or both.

5. *Questions.* Client explores *general* questions (verbally, experientially), such as:

   • Who was I before the pain impacted my life?

   • Who am I now that the pain has impacted my life?

   • Who do I want to be?

   • How have I changed in response to the change of pain in my life?

   • How have others changed in response to the pain?

   • How has my life changed in response to the pain?

   • How do I see my future with this pain?

      Client explores *recovery-related* questions (verbally, experientially), such as:

   • How has the pain impacted my addiction recovery?

   • What are the additional struggles I experience in recovery now that I have pain?

   • What seems to help the pain other than drugs? (people, activities, beliefs, etc.)

      Client explores *sensory-related* questions to determine how using the senses (seeing, hearing, touching, tasting, and smelling) can lead the body into a pain-free or pain-reduced state.

   • How might I use my senses to guide my body into a sense of safety, into a sense of hope?

   • How might I generally do this in my life?

   • How can I do this today?

6. *Family genogram.* Client creates a family genogram about pain. This genogram can contain historical family messages about pain and how to handle it in general as well as messages specifically sent to the client. In addition, it can contain current family reactions to the client's pain and messages about how it should be handled.

7. *Cultural genogram.* This one is similar to the family genogram except that it examines the client's culture(s) with which he or she identifies regarding messages about the pain and how to address it. It can also examine how these messages are conflicting or complimentary in terms of the different cultures the client experiences in daily living. This exercise may include the cultures with which the client does not identify, yet cultures with which he or she interacts.

8. *Social network system sociogram.* Client creates a sociogram about messages they have received and are receiving about the pain and pain management from the social network. This sociogram can contain historical messages about pain and how to handle it in general as well as messages specifically sent to the client. In addition, it can contain current reactions to the client's pain and messages about how it should be handled.

9. *Medical system sociogram.* Client creates a sociogram about messages being received about the pain and pain management from the medical network. This sociogram includes all of the helping professionals (including the receptionists, etc.) who are encountered in the treatment of the pain condition. This sociogram can contain historical messages about pain that have been received from this medical professional or clinic as well as from individuals in those roles in the past. It can also include messages received on how to handle the pain. (See Case Study 11.2.)

CASE STUDY 11.2

Joshua is a 25-year-old methamphetamine addict. He has been in recovery from meth-amphetamine addiction for 1 month. He is a part of your outpatient chemical dependency treatment program. You are concerned, as his counselor, about his use of pain medication (opiates) for lower back pain connected with an on-the-job construction accident he had 2 years ago. He reports that his use of methamphetamines came after his accident, because he had friends who manufactured the drug and suggested he try it to forget about his pain. Because he has been sober for the past month, you are concerned about his opiate use as a part of his pain management regimen. He told you in today's session that his doctor recently (in the past few weeks) began prescribing Oxycontin for him because of his self-reports of increased pain. You know his doctor and his reputation to overprescribe pain management drugs; you have heard these reports from other addiction counselors as well as clients in treatment.

1. What is the first course of action you will take in this situation and why?
2. Would you approach Joshua's doctor about his behavior? If so, how would you approach him? How does confidentiality constrain your behavior?
3. How would you confront Joshua about his behavior in the situation?
4. What treatment approaches would you use in your work with Joshua?
5. What are some exercises you might use in your work with him to help him clarify his awareness of how he handles pain?
6. What might be some pain management approaches you would suggest for him?
7. Do you need to make a referral for pain management for him and if so, who would you make the referral to based on information you receive from him on treatment he had after the accident (type of treatment, length, effectiveness, etc.)?

Guidelines for Pain Medication Use in Recovery

The Addiction-Free Pain Management (APM) system developed by Grinstead and Gorski is one theoretical orientation that can be used in treating the substance-abusing client. Some of their materials that can be useful for the counselor and the client are listed at the end of this chapter. APM focuses on managing chronic pain without addiction to pain medication, and thereby the client does not experience negative consequences that accompany the addiction (Grinstead, 2002). The emphasis in APM is on *addiction-free*. The authors explain the distinction between being addicted and being dependent. The client may be physically dependent on the medication, but may still take it according to prescription. The medication is used to relieve pain, but not to become high. The materials developed by the authors assist both the counselor and the client in making these important, yet difficult clarifications of prescription drug use medication.

Self-Help Group Support

One of the issues in living with chronic pain is having ongoing support for the struggles. Recovering addicts may feel comfortable processing their pain management with their normal self-help group members and meetings. Ziegler (2005) recommends they obtain increased support from this resource for acute pain, but for chronic pain experiences, more is involved as addressed under the assessment section of this chapter. It may help substance-abusing clients to attend self-help groups that are specifically focused on the overlap between substance abuse and pain management. Two self-help groups that the client may find helpful are Chronic Pain Anonymous and Pills Anonymous. The contact information for these groups is listed at the end of this chapter.

Chronic Pain Anonymous (CPA) is a group of individuals who live with physical disease and chronic pain. They are anchored in the 12 steps of Alcoholics Anonymous. The only changes they make to the 12 steps is that they substitute the word "pain" for alcohol in the first step, and in the 12th step they use the word "others" rather than "alcoholics." They consider themselves a spiritual fellowship, but not a religious one.

Pills Anonymous is very similar. This group is also anchored in the 12 steps, and the only changes made to the steps is in Step 1, where they use the phrase "prescription drugs" rather than "alcohol." They focus on abstinence from all mood-altering substances, including pills and medications that have become an addiction for the individual.

Because of the specificity of focus in these groups, the counselor may be limited in referring clients to them because of their location (e.g., a small town). However, the client may be able to access them via the Internet or through informational literature the counselor can provide to the client. (See Case Study 11.3.)

CASE STUDY 11.3

Alfred is a 50-year-old man who had been sober for 12 years before having a severe motorcycle accident this past year. He rear-ended a car when it stopped abruptly on the freeway without warning or cause (the brake lights did not work on the car and the driver was intoxicated). As a result, he was hospitalized for a month and had to have numerous surgeries for broken bones (pelvis, arm, leg). The pain was reportedly incredible, and he took the opiates prescribed to him for pain management in his recovery. He is comfortable with having taken the drugs for the few months he felt he needed them to cope and worked closely with his AA sponsor on the intake of the medication.

Now he is coming to you for counseling because he has heard that you are knowledgeable about addiction and he believes you can help him. The problem he presents to you is that he has had strong urges to use alcohol and drugs to cope with the residual, chronic pain he has from the accident and to cope psychologically with the limits it has placed on him: he lost his job as a factory worker and is on permanent disability. He says he has trouble sleeping at night and finds, much to his embarrassment, that he tears up easily when he is upset (he did not have these problems before the accident).

1. How would you make an assessment of his pain management?

2. What techniques might you use as a part of the assessment process?

3. What exercises would you use to help him learn about his reaction to pain?

4. What would be the components of a relapse-prevention plan you would develop with him?

5. How might you collaborate with and educate people in his recovery circle about his pain management struggles?

SUMMARY

This chapter presents the reader with general concepts and issues regarding pain and substance abuse that include a definition of pain. General counseling approaches to pain management issues in substance-abusing clients is explored through issues of living with pain sober and assessment and treatment sections. Techniques (general, relapse prevention, specific examples) that can be used in treatment plans and/or counseling sessions are provided, as well as discussion of pain medication use and self-help groups in the recovery process.

QUESTIONS

1. What did I learn about my general reaction to pain and substance abuse that could appear as countertransference in working with my clients about pain?

2. What is my philosophy about the use of drugs in relation to pain management?

3. What are specific types of pain management techniques I am comfortable using with clients?

EXERCISES

Exercise 11.1

Recall a time that you had the most severe physical injury you have ever experienced. Work with another person in a dyad in response to these four statements:

1. The hardest part of my recovery from this injury was. . . .

2. I did/did not use alcohol/drugs to cope with this physical pain because. . . .

3. The injury impacted my sense of safety in the world by. . . .

4. Methods I used to cope with the pain in my recovery (outside of alcohol/drugs) were. . . .

Exercise 11.2

Think of a time when you used alcohol and/or drugs to help you cope with physical and/or emotional pain in a situation. Record your responses to these five statements:

1. The alcohol/drugs helped me cope by. . . .

2. Other people were/were not concerned about my usage because. . . .

3. I was/was not concerned about my usage because. . . .

4. I think the situation(s) where I am most vulnerable to substance abuse with regard to pain management is (are). . . .

5. The alternative (to alcohol/drug use) pain management strategies for me are. . . .

Exercise 11.3

Use the following five questions to guide discussions on special challenges associated with this population. Work into the discussions how colleagues, supervisors, mentors, a team of professionals, and/or addiction medicine specialists may be helpful in addressing these challenging issues.

1. How would I handle the situation where doctors cut individuals off their pain medications

once they have become addicted and do not provide further assistance?

2. How would I assist my clients, who attend self-help support groups, deal with group reactions to their use of pain medication and/or their struggles with pain issues and how to address them in recovery?

3. How would I work with clients' significant others and/or family members who administer the pain medication so they do so with an educated approach and balanced involvement?

4. If I am working with a client without medical consultation, should I work to suppress the urge to advise clients to stop taking medication they may be abusing and if so, how will I do that? How soon and in what way would I seek medical consultation in working with this population?

5. How will I collaborate with other professionals on these complicated issues? With a team of professionals? With addiction medicine specialists?

READINGS, RESOURCES, WEBSITES

SUGGESTED READINGS

Alcoholics Anonymous World Services. (2011). *The A. A. member—Medications and other drugs*. New York, NY: Author.

This 22-page pamphlet reflects the opinions of physicians in AA, stories of AA members' drug experiences and those who need medication, and a listing of the 12 steps and 12 traditions of AA as well as the 12 concepts for world service.

Garland, E. L. (2013). *Mindfulness-oriented recovery enhancement: For addiction, stress, and pain*. Washington, DC: NASW Press.

This book presents mindfulness-oriented recovery enhancement (MORE) that is a combination of mindfulness techniques with cognitive therapy and positive psychology principles. It has three sections (concepts, treatment manual, research) divided into 14 chapters. The treatment manual has 10 sessions and the text provides nine client handouts.

Grinstead, S. F. (2006). *Addiction-free pain management: Relapse prevention counseling workbook*. Herald House/Independence Press: Independence, MO.

This 96-page booklet provides helpful exercises in addressing relapse-prevention issues with a client

Grinstead, S. F., & Gorski, T. T. (2002). *Addiction-free pain management professional guide*. Independence, MO: Herald House/Independence Press.

The 204-page book is written for the professional who is working with individuals on pain management. It has 10 chapters that explain the addiction pain syndrome, the Addiction-Free Pain Management System (APM), how to build a therapeutic relationship, how to identify and assess pain and substance abuse/dependence, the impact of drugs on the client, early treatment approaches, holistic treatments, reciprocal relapse prevention, the TFUAR (thinking, feelings, urges, actions, and reactions [relationships]) process, and measuring treatment effectiveness. It provides information and exercises that can be used by the professional.

Jamison, R. N., & Edwards, R. R. (2012). Integrating pain management in clinical practice. *Journal of Clinical Psychology in Medical Settings, 19*, 49–64. doi: 10.1007/s10880–012–9295–2

This article provides a comprehensive overview of a holistic assessment process and specifically provides information on approaches and instruments that can be used to assess clients in terms of sensory, affective, cognitive, and behavioral aspects regarding opioid use.

National Association for Alcoholism and Drug Abuse Counselors (NAADAC). (2007). *Pharmacotherapy: Integrating new tools into practice*. Alexandria, VA: Author. http://www.naadac.org/education/home-study-courses

This 154-page manual is divided into seven sections. Section 1 focuses on pharmacotherapies and myths, Section 2 on fitting pharmacotherapies into treatment,

Section 3 on FDA-approved pharmacotherapies, and Section 4 on program review. Sections 5, 6, and 7 are appendices, glossary, and reference sections.

National Institute of Drug Abuse (NIDA). *Facts about prescription drug abuse*. Washington, DC: Author. http://www.drugabuse.gov

This document lists facts about the abuse of prescription drugs.

Substance Abuse and Mental Health Services Administration. (2011b). *Managing chronic pain in adults with or in recovery from substance use disorders*, Technical Assistance Publication (TIP 54) Series (DHHS Publication No.). Rockville, MD: Author. http://www.samhsa.gov

This publication provides an overview of pain issues: general, assessment, pain management, addiction risk management with opioid treatment clients, and education/treatment.

RESOURCES

Grinstead, S. F. (2002). Addiction-free pain management recovery guide: *Managing pain and medication in recovery*. Independence, MO: Herald House/Independence Press.

This 204-page book provides a combination of information and exercises that can easily be used by the reader. It has 10 chapters that focus on empowerment, the addiction pain syndrome, the Addiction-Free Pain Management System (APM), learning to live with pain, beginning the APM process, the impact of medication, holistic treatment, reciprocal relapse prevention, recovery planning, and measuring treatment effectiveness.

Grinstead, S. F. (2007). Addiction-free pain management: APM Modules One: *Understanding and evaluating your chronic pain symptoms*. Independence, MO: Herald House/Independence Press. http://www.addiction-free.com/publications.html

Grinstead, S. F. (2007). Addiction-free pain management: APM Modules Two: *Examining your potential medication management problems*. Independence, MO: Herald House/Independence Press. http://www.addiction-free.com/publications.html

Grinstead, S. F. (2007). Addiction-free pain management: APM Modules Three: *Understanding and developing effective pain management*. Independence, MO: Herald House/Independence Press. http://www.addiction-free.com/publications.html

These three short (11- to 12-page) booklets provide simple exercises that can be used with a client to facilitate an awareness of his or her experience with pain.

Grinstead, S. F., Gorski, T. T., & Messier, J. C. (2002). *Denial management counseling for effective pain management: Practical exercises for motivating people in chronic pain toward more effective pain management*. Independence, MO: Herald House/Independence Press. http://www.addiction-free.com/publications.html

This 99-page workbook provides nine core exercises that focus on denial in general and specifically, denial as it relates to denial management principles, personal denial patterns, managing denial, stopping denial (when thinking about problems, pain history, medication use, deciding what action to take), and evaluating denial management skills. It has two useful appendices: the pain management medication agreement and treatment plan.

Seppala, M. D., & Martin, D. P. (2005). *Pain-free living for drug-free people*. Center City, MN: Hazelden.

This 216-page book is easy to read. It is designed for the recovering individual who is open to learning about living pain-free. It has a disease model/12-step orientation. It is divided into eight chapters that define pain, types of pain, the treatment of addiction, pain medications, complementary pain medicine, ways to cope with pain, control pain within the context of relapse, and opioid use in relation to pain. It has six appendices: definitions, common pain medications, journal writing, guidelines for taking addictive medications, resources for traditional and complementary medicine, and the 12 steps of Alcoholics Anonymous.

Turk, D. C., & Winter, F. (2006). *The pain survival guide*. Washington, DC: American Psychological Association.

The 203-page book has 10 chapters (lessons). These chapters include becoming one's own expert on pain, activity, relaxation, ways to address fatigue, relationship management, behavior change, thoughts and feelings change, increasing self-confidence, organizing a framework of pain management, and dealing with maintenance of a recovery program and setback issues. Each chapter has helpful activities that can be used by the reader.

WEBSITES

Organizations

The American Chronic Pain Association
www.theacpa.org
The ACPA
P.O. Box 850
Rocklin, CA 95677
(800) 533-3231
E-mail: ACPA@theacpa.org

This organization offers "peer support and education in pain management skills to people in pain, family and friends, and health care professionals."

American Society of Addiction Medicine
4601 North Park Avenue, Suite 101
Chevy Chase, MD 20815
www.asam.org

This group focuses on the education of physicians, health care providers, and the public. It also has an emphasis on research and prevention with the commitment to viewing addiction medicine as a specialty.

Herald House/Independence Press
P.O. Box 390
Independence, MO 64051-0390
(800) 767-8181
E-mail: sales@relapse.org
www.relapse.org

This publishing house has numerous pamphlets and books, some of which are referenced in the Suggested Readings section of this chapter, related to pain management from the Addiction-Free Pain Management System (APM) perspective.

NAADAC—The Association for Addiction Professionals (founded in 1972 as the National Association of Alcoholism and Drug Abuse Counselors)
(800) 548-0497
www.naadac.org

Their book, *Pharmacotherapy: Integrating New Tools Into Practice*, as referenced in the Suggested Readings section of this chapter, is an excellent summary of different drugs used in treatment.

Support Groups

Chronic Pain Anonymous (CPA)
www.chronicpainanonymous.org

This organization is based on the 12 steps of Alcoholics Anonymous. Its focus is on helping people recover from the emotional and spiritual difficulties related to chronic pain and illness. The website provides a list of meetings, member stories, resources, etc.

Pills Anonymous (PA)
c/o CFR 2740 Grant Street
Concord, CA 94520
www.pillsanonymous.net

This group, based on the 12 steps of Alcoholics Anonymous, addresses mood-altering substances (including pills and medications) that have become an addiction for the individual. The website is designed mainly for individuals who live in the San Francisco Bay area.

CHAPTER 12

INCORPORATING SPIRITUALITY INTO ADDICTION COUNSELING

OBJECTIVES

1. To learn the historical incorporation of spirituality and addiction counseling.
2. To be aware of some of the barriers and bridges to the incorporation of spirituality in addiction counseling.
3. To develop some counseling strategies that facilitate the incorporation of spirituality in addiction counseling.

The field of addiction counseling may be, both historically and currently, one of the counseling fields most open to the incorporation of spirituality and counseling. Because the influential roots of the field include the self-help group of AA, the

chapter opens with an in-depth discussion of the spiritual philosophy of AA. This discussion is a result of the tremendous impact AA has had (and in some cases still has) on both formal and informal treatment of addiction. The chapter

THE HISTORY OF INCORPORATING SPIRITUALITY INTO ADDICTION COUNSELING

evolves into a discussion of how counselors of any theoretical and philosophical orientation may explore the dimension of spirituality within the addicted population they counsel. This chapter's focus on spirituality is anchored in its broad definition presented in the personal reflection section: *"What keeps our spirit alive?"*

Frequently a discussion on spirituality begins with a definition of it that distinguishes it from religion. There are many views on this distinction. One example is Kelly's (1995) that describes spirituality as a connection with the universe that is personal while religion consists of a creed, institution, and rituals (Kelly, 1995). However the counselor makes this distinction, it is an important one to make because the area of spirituality may be a critical recovery resource for the addicted client that may or may not involve religion. For example, we may need to sensitively explore this area where their religious experiences are a "mixed bag" of healing and pain.

A more specific definition of spirituality may assist in its incorporation into counseling. The term *spirituality* is derived from the Latin word *spiritus* (breath of life). The definition of spirituality used in this chapter comes from the 1996 Summit on Spirituality sponsored by the American Counseling Association's (ACA) division of the Association of Spiritual, Ethical, and Religious Values in Counseling (ASERVIC):

> Spirit may be defined as the animating life force, represented by such images as breath, wind, vigor, and courage. Spirituality is the drawing out and infusion of spirit in one's life. It is experienced as an active and passive process. Spirituality is also defined as a capacity and tendency that is innate and unique to all persons. This spiritual tendency moves the individual toward knowledge, love, meaning, peace, hope, transcendence, connectedness, compassion, wellness, and wholeness. Spirituality includes one's capacity for creativity, growth, and the development of a value system. Spirituality encompasses a variety of phenomena, including experiences, beliefs, and practices. Spirituality is approached from a variety of perspectives, including psychospiritual,

religious, and transpersonal. While spirituality is usually expressed through culture, it both precedes and transcends culture.
>
> (*Position Paper, n.d., para. 3*)

[Note: Specific competencies for addressing spiritual and religious issues in counseling were developed by a group of 16 counselor educators and practitioners in 2008 and approved by the ASERVIC Board of Directors in 2009.]

This chapter examines four areas related to the incorporation of spiritual perspectives in the addiction counseling field: (1) the history; (2) barriers and bridges; (3) spiritual identity development; and (4) counseling resources and techniques.

THE HISTORY OF INCORPORATING SPIRITUALITY INTO ADDICTION COUNSELING

The condition of alcoholism/addiction, in the beginning, appears to have been viewed from a spiritual/religious perspective: An addicted person had something wrong with him- or herself morally. The alcoholic was seen as a degenerate who was morally weak (Keller, 1976) and lacking in willpower (Chapman, 1996). The exceptions to this moral perspective of alcoholism were espoused by Benjamin Rush and Thomas Trotter, who wrote about alcoholism as a disease before the 19th century (O'Dwyer, 1993).

If one approached treatment from this moral perspective, it was inevitably viewed as ineffective. A moral defect is incurable; therefore, the alcoholic was typically punished (McHugh, Beckman, & Frieze, 1979). Yet treatment of addiction was also paired with spirituality/religion. Courtenay Baylor began therapy in 1913 with addicts through Boston's Emmanuel Church Clinic, where he had received treatment for addiction (White, 1999). When Alcoholics Anonymous (AA) began in 1935, they presented a view of alcoholism as an allergic reaction; addiction was physical (allergy, craving). They surmised that the addict was sick and could not be blamed for the addiction, so recovery required abstinence and a spiritual experience.

Jellinek later developed the disease model of alcoholism, complementary to this perspective, through his alcoholism research and the development of the Yale School of Alcohol Studies in 1942 (Bowman & Jellinek, 1941; Gragg, 1995; Jellinek, 1960). In 1956 the American Medical Association determined that alcoholism was a disease (Marlatt, 1985). These shifts in perspective, from a moral model to a physically based model of addiction, created more respect for the addict, enhanced diagnosis and treatment of addiction (e.g., abstinence was seen as necessary [Chapman, 1996]), and provided a framework from which to view the addiction. Overall, it moved the view of alcoholism away from the moral perspective (Chapman, 1996).

The disease model of addiction is more of a medical model, because it is based in the physiology of a genetic predisposition to alcoholism and an allergic reaction. However, as discussed in Chapter 1, there is a shift from the typical medical model because the addict is considered responsible for future behavior, and spiritual help is viewed as a necessary component in the recovery process. In this model, alcoholism is defined as progressive and having specific symptoms; its hallmarks are loss of control over drinking and disease progression.

The disease model is frequently paired with the self-help group of Alcoholics Anonymous (AA). This may be evidenced in a formal treatment program based on the disease model that within its programming involves the philosophy of AA or within a counselor's referrals to clients to attend AA as a part of their treatment. Many recovering individuals attend 12-step groups in addition to or in replacement of counseling or formal treatment (Knack, 2009). Therefore, the spiritual philosophy/orientation of AA has become intricately interwoven with addiction treatment. Because of this incredible influence on treatment, the spiritual perspective of AA is further explored here.

AA partially agrees with the disease model by seeing: (a) alcoholism as an illness that is physically, mentally, and spiritually based, and (b) believing that the addict is not responsible for the addiction development, but is responsible for one's future regarding the addiction once it has developed (McHugh et al., 1979). From this perspective, the addict need not feel guilty about the addiction, and, as a way to overcome any guilt, is encouraged to be involved in the community (Gragg, 1995). In AA, spirituality is looked at in relation to self, others, and a Higher Power (Brown, Peterson, & Cunningham, 1988).

AA is a movement that came about because of people's spiritual needs (Galanter, 2009). Addiction is viewed as a result of a spiritual flaw where alcohol/drugs are used as a response to the spiritual search (Doweiko, 2009). This may be most aptly described by the character Eugene from Tom Wolfe's novel *Look Homeward, Angel*. After becoming intoxicated for the first time, Eugene said: "In all the earth there was no other like him, no other fitted to be so sublimely and magnificently drunken. . . . Why, when it was possible to buy God in a bottle, and drink him off, and become a God oneself, were not men forever drunken?" (Wolfe, 1947, p. 525). A spiritual experience is at the core of recovery in AA, based on the belief that the alcoholic drinks in response to an unresolved need to live and grow spiritually (W. R. Miller & Kurtz, 1994).

The AA solution for addiction, then, is spiritually based: One admits powerlessness over alcohol, admits to wrongs committed to others, and is open to assistance from a Higher Power (McHugh et al., 1979). Spiritual issues examined in recovery are related to being connected, having a purpose, and having healthy relationships with others (Chapman, 1996). Recovery involves a belief in a Higher Power, something bigger than oneself (Carroll, 2009). Recovery is a spiritual process where the addict finds a unity of spirit that was not possible to find chemically (Doweiko, 2009). "Many recovering individuals point to their spiritual lives as being central to their sobriety" (Cashwell, Clarke, & Graves, 2009, p. 37). In fact,

Morgan (2009) summarizes that addiction, as well as trauma, may create opportunities in terms of spiritual development out of the person's wounds.

As a result of the spiritual cornerstone of its philosophy, AA has been described as a spiritual model that guides living based on both abstinence of the client and the client's development of character (W. R. Miller & Kurtz, 1994). Fowler (1993) reports that AA involvement can lead to changes in one's faith ("the dynamic human process of finding and creating meaning in one's life," p. 113), meaning changes in values, power images, and core story(s) that guide one's life consciously or unconsciously. Fowler (1993) also describes AA as providing a spiritual discipline that includes acceptance and accountability, honesty, liberation through bondage admission, self-responsibility, texts offering models of recovery that include a spiritual philosophy, and peer sponsors practicing "tough-enough love" (p. 132).

This view of addiction is frequently incorporated into what may be viewed as the traditional way of treating addiction: the Minnesota Model, where AA's 12 steps are combined with professional services by counselors in addiction recovery (O'Dwyer, 1993). The disease model/Minnesota Model was very popular in the 1960s and 1970s and is still used today to treat the addict from a holistic perspective of the body, mind, and spirit (Goodman & Levy, 2003). This holistic perspective of addiction runs through current addiction treatment models that tend to be biopsychosocial: Biological, psychological, and social aspects are considered in the cause, treatment, and recovery from addiction. Causality of addiction is complicated (DiClemente, 2003), and all three aspects (biological, psychological, and social) are seen as interacting and impacting one another (Lawson, Lawson, & Rivers, 2001). The spiritual component has sometimes been added to these three aspects resulting in the development of biopsychosocial-spiritual models.

In summary, then, the spiritual perspective has been inherent in the view and treatment of addiction from its origin to the present day. It began with the view that it was a moral condition with treatment being viewed as incurable and the addict needing to be punished. Initial addiction treatment in the early 1900s was in the Christian church. From the 1930s on, the birth and evolution of AA, based on a Judeo-Christian philosophy, further encouraged the incorporation of spirituality into the addiction treatment approaches. The introduction of the disease model in the 1940s and the AMA acknowledgement of it as a disease encouraged the movement from the moral model into a more respectful and enhanced addiction assessment and treatment model. Beginning in the 1960s, the fusion of AA's 12 steps into the formal treatment of addiction (disease model/Minnesota Model) cemented the spiritual component as a part of the treatment for addiction. Although this form of treatment is still often considered to be the traditional form, other forms of treatment for addiction have evolved that may or may not include the spiritual component as a critical part of an addiction treatment depending on the philosophical orientation of the treatment program. When the spiritual component is present as a part of treatment, it is not necessarily based in the AA model. Nonetheless, because the foundation of addiction treatment has the spiritual component present in its history, there is an openness to discussing this dimension with addicted clients as a part of their treatment. The remainder of this chapter will present a more general discussion of the spiritual component as a part of addiction counseling.

INCORPORATION BARRIERS AND BRIDGES

A prelude to this section on incorporation barriers and bridges is a brief discussion on ethical issues in relation to spirituality. In Chapter 13, ethical principles guiding the behavior of counselors in order to enhance client welfare are discussed more extensively.

Ethical issues regarding the general incorporation of spirituality and counseling are addressed in G. Miller's (2003) chapter on ethical issues. The counselor needs to consider issues as they relate to:

- Informed consent
- Determination of secular or religious counseling
- Development of a spiritual identity
- Avoidance or minimization of dual or multiple relationships with clients
- Collaboration with clients' religious leaders
- Respect for clients' religious or spiritual values
- Boundaries of the counselor's work settings
- Counselor's area of competence

Each counselor will need to examine these issues as they relate to his or her own theoretical orientation, job, employment context, and so forth. While we may be hesitant to address spiritual concerns as a part of counseling because we may view it as practicing outside of our area of competence, we can explore this area with our clients if we frame it from a holistic perspective and consult with spiritual and religious professionals as needed. Addressing relevant spiritual issues for our clients in an appropriate manner is needed (Rao, 2005). The growing interest and openness in exploring spiritually with clients is evidenced in three areas discussed in this chapter (spirituality, religion and prayer, and meditation) being complementary or alternative medicine (CAM) modalities that are used by a diverse group of medical and health-care systems (Barnett & Shale, 2013).

It may be helpful to metaphorically view this exploration of spirituality as involving a "spiritual integration toolbox" (Cox, 2013). The counselor uses the tools appropriately by having: a distinction between religion and spirituality, awareness of ethical and legal issues as they relate to assessment/diagnosis/treatment, and an understanding of potential harm if counselor values are imposed on clients (Cox, 2013).

Counselor Barriers

Because addiction counseling may need to include a spiritual component to assist the client in obtaining and maintaining abstinence, the counselor needs to understand the power of countertransference as it relates to spirituality (Kersting, 2003). For example, a counselor who has a negative view of Christianity may recoil when working with an addicted client who "finds Jesus" in his recovery process. This counselor, unaware and/or uncaring about the intensity of her reaction to the client's views, may not be able to fairly assess how these religious views may be helping the client's recovery process as well as hindering it. In an opposite scenario, a client who is closed to the possible advantages of a spiritual aspect in recovery and who is being counseled by a strongly Christian counselor may feel unfairly pressured to include a spiritual perspective—possibly even a religious one—in the addiction recovery.

Therefore, every counselor needs to examine him or herself for the potential of personal barriers of countertransference that may unintentionally inhibit a client's recovery process. G. Miller (2003) provides three guidelines for counselors to reduce this risk:

1. Look at personal and professional experiences with religion that are extreme in both positive and negative directions. *Example*: The counselor may have been raised a certain religion that has been very helpful to him or her in daily living. He or she cannot understand why clients do not find religion or spirituality helpful and necessary in living and "pushes" the exploration of the spiritual component in treatment.

2. Watch for different or similar religious backgrounds with clients. *Example*: A counselor of the same spiritual or religious persuasion as his or her client may make assumptions that their views of spirituality are the same.

3. Examine any personal projections with regard to existential issues. *Example*: A counselor who

does not have any spiritual or religious beliefs may not understand why and how his/her client of a specific spiritual or religious orientation struggles with concerns about death connected to their beliefs.

The counselor may also have countertransference issues in response to self-help groups in general (12-step groups or alternatives to 12-step groups) and specifically for how they involve the spirituality component in recovery. This countertransference can be based on positive or negative stereotypes of these self-help groups. It can operate on a continuum where at one end the counselor is pushing attendance or a type of group too strongly or not encouraging them at all. These same guidelines for countertransference reactions to religion can be applied to addiction self-help groups by replacing the wording "religion" and "religious background" with "self-help groups" and "self-help background," respectively.

An examination of one's own spiritual views and development encourages awareness of countertransference issues. Awareness of countertransference issues can reduce or eliminate their impact on the counseling, thereby enhancing the welfare of the client because the counselor can accurately assess the strengths and weaknesses of the client's spiritual dimension. Assessment of spirituality helps us understand our clients' worldviews, show respect for these views, include possible interventions, determine unresolved concerns, and find beliefs that may be hurtful or helpful to the client (Richards, Bartz, & O'Grady, 2009). Examination of one's spiritual views and development can be done informally or formally (counseling, supervision, or consultation).

With enhanced awareness of one's own spirituality, the counselor can have a more balanced approach in working with the client's spirituality. The counselor, *with* the client, can more accurately:

- Assess the client's experiences with religion and spirituality from the past, present, and future.

- Examine how becoming sober impacts how the client looks at his or her religious/spiritual life.

- Determine if a spiritual/religious perspective may assist the client in becoming and staying sober.

Client Barriers

Clients enter addiction counseling with a *general range of barriers* to the exploration of spirituality. At one end of the continuum all they want to do is discuss spirituality and at the other they do not want to discuss it at all. The counselor may want to begin a discussion about spirituality with an exploration of what it means to the client and how it might be beneficial to the client's recovery. Early in the process the counselor may want to assist the client in finding a distinction between religion and spirituality. This distinction may help create a space where there can be discussions of experiences the client has had in the past and currently. For example, a lesbian client may have been rejected by her church when she came out of the closet and has wounds from this experience that cause her to be hesitant about involving any spiritual component in her recovery. Distinguishing between religion and spirituality may allow such a client to feel safe and explore spiritual resources that may be a benefit to her recovery.

Counselors need to be sensitive to the idiosyncratic reactions of clients and explore this area as it enhances client welfare. The counselor can invite, but not force, the exploration of an area that has the potential to be emotionally explosive and painful for the client. A simple question such as "Do you live by a creed?" may gently invite a discussion on spirituality. Or a broad exploration can be based on themes such as: awareness of the sacred, providence, faith, gratitude, repentance, connection, and vocation (Pruyser, 1976 as summarized in W. R. Miller, Forcehimes, & Zweben, 2011).

As counselors enter into this area with addicted clients, it is important to remember that they tend to operate in extremes. Therefore, the counselor can focus the discussion, exploration, and implementation of spirituality in recovery by helping the client find and maintain a balanced lifestyle perspective on spirituality. Specific counseling techniques addressed at the end of this chapter may assist the client in exploring this area of self.

An example of one barrier sometimes used by clients in recovery has been termed *spiritual bypass* (Cashwell et al., 2009). This barrier means that the client is avoiding upsetting emotions and necessary counseling work by working on the issue only spiritually. Spiritual bypass has been called "false transcendence," "denial of the shadow side," "assumed spiritual persona" (Cashwell et al., 2009). The clients do not view themselves as responsible for their problems or the resolution of them (Cashwell et al., 2009). The counselor needs to be aware of the possible presence of this in the client's recovery and assist the client in preventing or responding to its presence. Specific examples of spiritual bypass and counselor responses in terms of the 12-step recovery philosophy are provided by Cashwell et al. (2009). Appendix B in Chapter 8 explores the concept of emotional sobriety which is related to spiritual bypass. At the end of this appendix is an exercise on spiritual bypass that can be used by counselors.

Other client barriers may be specific ones in relation to *self-help groups*. First, clients may not be open to the spiritual dimension of recovery, or they may have had negative experiences in the past with self-help groups' perspectives on spirituality and recovery. One of the criticisms of AA is its basis in Christianity (e.g., the Oxford Group; Judge, 1994), and some clients struggle with the spiritual terminology and concepts used in the 12 steps and at meetings. For example, clients may struggle with deep shame and guilt issues, making it difficult for them to conceive of a loving God who can forgive them. They may also struggle with how some individual groups open or close meetings with prayers, such as the Serenity Prayer or the Lord's Prayer. Counselors can minimize these issues by encouraging a broader definition of spirituality (e.g., "God, *as we understood Him*") and by talking with clients about how they may respond to prayers that they hear in meetings (e.g., practicing the adage "Take what you like and leave the rest"). This has been called, by some authors, a *negotiated spirituality* where the client "constructs" his or her Higher Power and draws on spiritual resources in addition to the 12-step philosophy (Dossett, 2013).

Second, clients may take stories of recovery that they read, hear in meetings, or hear from their sponsors as a rigid, absolute formula of recovery. Counselors can encourage clients to try on ideas they hear, but also to be thoughtful about applying these ideas to their own lives. The client may want to follow the action through, cognitively anticipating consequences of application to his or her own life through cognitive rehearsals.

Third, clients may become too dependent on the support of groups, specific recovering individuals, or a sponsor. Such attachments can result in almost a cult-like mentality or behavior that is too highly self-regulated. Again the counselor can help the client learn to find a more balanced perspective of the recovery process through session discussions. The counselor, by being aware of his or her own countertransference regarding spirituality and self-help groups, provides the client with neutral ground on which to discuss problems and serve as a sounding board for issues throughout the recovery process, thereby assisting the client in developing a spiritual identity.

Client barriers to the component of spirituality in treatment need to be considered during the treatment process. These barriers need to be explored and re-explored through the treatment process of assessment, treatment, and aftercare.

Bridges

The strong history between spirituality and addiction counseling outlined above is based on common views of what causes addiction (moral weakness, spiritual malady) and methods of treating addiction. This overlapping history of spirituality and addiction counseling creates many bridges between the two areas. There is evidence that: (a) counselors who incorporate the spiritual development component (as a part of their counseling with addicted clients) may provide more comprehensive counseling (Weiss Ogden & Sias, 2011), (b) clients report an enhanced sense of spiritual well-being at the time of discharge (Morris, Johnson, Losier, Pierce, & Sridhar, 2013), and (c) clients find spirituality and religious faith to be helpful parts to a treatment program (Mason, Deane, Kelly, & Crowe, 2009).

In general, addicted clients may present issues that are very conducive to discussion of spirituality as it relates to their recovery. They may struggle with guilt and issues such as forgiveness and grief (van Wormer & Davis, 2008, 2013). They may need hope that they can recover (Ries et al., 2008). They may need to grieve their relationship with the drug(s) since they often describe the relationship as a love relationship (Liepman, Parran, Farkas, & Lagos-Saez, 2009). Existential issues around meaning of life, being unique and isolated, and death may be a part of the issues related to their addiction. The presentation of such issues invites an exploration of spirituality. For example, a sense of life purpose can be increased by spiritual awareness (O'Connell, 1999). Processing their feelings about such issues can lead to further exploration of their view of themselves, others, and the world that involves a spiritual component. Treatment programs that include a spiritual/religious component can positively impact a client's treatment (Unterrainer, Lewis, Collicut, & Fink, 2013).

Another bridge may be the need for clients to rely on self-help groups such as AA that focus on spirituality. AA can provide support (Flores, 1988), reduce isolation (Talbott, 1990), and guide regulation of self (Khantzian & Mack, 1994). This support, connectedness, and self-regulation can be viewed as a spiritual way of living that assists the client in finding ways to cope with life by transcending its struggles. AA can help clients develop a sense of powerlessness, experience acceptance, establish a relationship with a Higher Power, and find a way of living via first-person storytelling and a daily focus of recovery (Valverde & White-

Mair, 1999). Fowler (1993) states that the admission of powerlessness in AA encourages a person to move from a dichotomous (all-or-nothing) life approach to a realistic, responsible one: the experience of power out of powerlessness.

The emphasis on the spiritual aspect of recovery is evident in the guidelines for AA groups. The recovery program is tied to phrases of "spiritual experience" and "spiritual awakening" (Ries, Galanter, & Tonigan, 2008). Clients who work through the 12 steps of Alcoholics Anonymous will enhance their spiritual awakening, and following the spiritual principles of AA will result in abstinence that is maintained (Tonigan & Connors, 2008). For example, AA's 12 Traditions, which guide the AA fellowship, use spiritual wording: "one ultimate authority—a loving God as He may express Himself in our group conscience" (Tradition 2), and "Anonymity is the spiritual foundation of all our traditions" (Tradition 12). AA's 12 steps, which guide the addicted person's recovery based on an affinity with self, others, and a Higher Power, use:

- *Phrases* "Power greater than ourselves" (Step 2), "God, *as we understood Him*" (Step 3).

- *Words* "God" (Steps 3, 5, 6, and 11), "Him" (Steps 7 and 11).

- *Spiritually based wording* "moral inventory" (Step 4), "nature of wrongs" (Step 5), "amends" (Steps 8 and 9), "prayer and meditation" (Step 11), and "spiritual awakening" (Step 12).

Clients who attend AA may need to process their reactions to the spiritual views presented to them through such language or in the discussions they hear at meetings. In counseling sessions, experiences at meetings may naturally lead to therapeutic discussions focused on their spirituality. Clients may discuss examples of people's recovery from addiction involving spirituality. These written and oral stories from the AA cofounders and other addicts can serve as spiritual guides in the client's recovery. In addition, the counselor can fuse this perspective with an understanding of what is out of balance in the client's life and how treatment can assist the client in becoming more spiritually balanced. Broadening the concept of spirituality to include more than religion may facilitate the counselor in helping the client with AA's orientation to God or Higher Power.

Depending on the client's stage of recovery, spirituality issues may need to be addressed within that developmental context. Fowler (1993) describes these recovery stages. In the early recovery stage, the person begins to view self differently because of feedback from the AA group and sponsor and begins to find a personal relationship with a Higher Power. In ongoing recovery, the person uses others (sponsor, group, friends, therapist) in finding a third-person perspective, looks at beliefs and practices from a critical stance, and uses AA concepts explicitly rather than silently. The recovering person is realistic about his or her own limits, trusts a Higher Power, and cares for others in recovery. A sensitivity to the client's developmental stage can guide the counselor in how to incorporate the spiritual dimension into counseling.

SPIRITUAL IDENTITY DEVELOPMENT

Regarding the spiritual aspect of counseling, some factors may inhibit a counselor from including the spiritual dimension of counseling. First, the originator of counseling, Sigmund Freud, had a negative view of religion and the role it played in the client's life (Huguelet & Mohr, 2013; G. Miller, 2005). Freud saw the mature person as one who was able to abandon religion (Wulff, 1996) and face the world alone rather than depend on a god that he claimed consisted of neurotic childhood projections of the father (Rizzuto, 1998). Therefore, exposure to Freud's view of religion and spirituality may negatively impact a counselor's inclusion of this perspective in counseling simply by exclusion of this dimension in counseling. Second, in the past, counselors' formal education,

heavily based on Western values, typically did not necessarily include a spiritual component (Chapman, 1996). Third, counselors, like others, may possess limited information about religions other than the one in which they were raised (Eck, 2001). Finally, counselors in general are not as oriented toward religion as their clients (Worthington, 1989), which can result in a lack of understanding about the dynamics of religion in the client's life. To avoid automatically dismissing this area, counselors need to examine how they might assist clients in developing a spiritual identity.

Spirituality is an important aspect of the client (Bliss, 2009). Tisdell (2003) recommends looking at spiritual development as a spiral rather than a linear process. This means that people obtain new and different knowledge and meaning when returning to old experiences (G. Miller, 2005). In addition, spiritual development is fluid, because the past, present, and future interact (Tisdell, 2003). Life transitions and experiences in the present affect our thoughts, emotions, and behaviors both in the present and future. Finally, the view of spiritual development needs to be seen within the cultural context of the client.

This understanding of the client's spiritual development can facilitate the assessment of his or her spiritual identity. The assessment involves asking the client questions about how the spiritual realm provides a refuge, rituals that are healing, safe places of spirituality (e.g., location, rituals, other people), and spiritual community. G. Miller (2003) provides specific questions that can be used in counseling to help the counselor assess these aspects.

G. Miller (1999) provides three questions that help explore how to approach the development of a spiritual identity with a client:

1. How do we help people develop a spiritual identity?

2. Do we have a right and/or an obligation to help people develop a spiritual identity?

3. How does context impact application? (p. 501)

Spiritual identity development may have a unique twist in working with addicted clients. Typically, in the development of an addiction the client's drug(s) has become his or her Higher Power, as Thomas Wolfe (1947) described. That means the client has simply placed the drug at the focus of his or her life. When clients become sober, they face an existential vacuum of the meaninglessness and lack of focus in their life. All of a sudden, the client may have more time, energy, and/or money than before, merely because the addiction had previously been so consuming. Recovery can involve grief work where one lets go of the attachment to the drug (van Wormer & Davis, 2008, 2012) as well as other losses (Streifel & Servaty-Sieb, 2009). Spirituality may help the addicted client turn losses into growth thereby enhancing recovery (Streifel & Servaty-Sieb, 2009). A spiritual focus to recovery can assist the client in finding a balanced lifestyle that reduces the chance of relapse. Spirituality may help a person maintain recovery (Orzech, 2006).

As a part of recovery, then, the client may need to find spiritual nurturance in a refuge, in rituals, safe places, and/or a community that sustains his or her spirit (i.e., a replacement for the refuge, rituals, safe places, and community that housed and encouraged the drug addiction). This journey requires the use of specific counseling techniques and resources that can enhance the spiritual identity of the client, some of which are discussed later in this chapter.

Clients may also have *multicultural factors* that influence their spirituality and spiritual development. Van Wormer and Davis (2008, 2012) state that counselors need to include spirituality in counseling, because historically it has offered marginalized people great support. Because Chapter 10 extensively addresses multicultural concerns, only a few points will be made regarding some populations as they relate to spirituality.

Sheridan (2004) reports that *women* in residential treatment found nature healing. Treatment programs that increase spirituality may assist women in managing stress and PTSD stress symptoms (Arevalo, Prado, & Amaro, 2008). *Women*, *African Americans*, and *Native American Natives* may find spiritual beliefs a great resource to them in recovery (Douglas, Jimenez, Lin, & Frisman, 2008; van Wormer & Davis, 2008, 2012).

Gays and lesbians may struggle with AA because of exposure to homophobic aspects of religion that can limit their view of a Higher Power, but an encouragement of a broader view of spirituality (goodness, community, creator connection) can improve self-esteem and belonging (Davidson, 2000). Kus (1992) also recommends providing a distinction between spirituality and religion when working with this population. Encouragement of attendance at gay/lesbian 12-step meetings may be helpful, but such a recommendation needs to be discussed with the client to determine if the client is comfortable with such a referral (Senreich & Vairo, 2004). Two resources counselors may find helpful in working with this population, *Bulletproof Faith*; *Effects of Conservative Religion on Lesbian and Gay Clients and Practitioners: Practice Implications*, are reviewed in the resource section at the end of this chapter.

In terms of *age*, Perkinson (2008) states that addicted *adolescents* may struggle with surrender to a Higher Power and struggle more with spirituality in general. The recommendation made for working with this population is to use spiritual leaders who can facilitate trust and not intimidate them, as well as to use exercises such as meditation, which invites experiences with a Higher Power of their understanding. Van Wormer and Davis (2008, 2012) state that *elderly* clients may have spiritual issues related to their age as they face death (mortality, meaning of life); therefore, an exploration of their spirituality may be helpful to them.

A counselor needs to then consider unique aspects of the client that may significantly impact the incorporation of spirituality into their recovery process. Such consideration and sensitivity will be deeply appreciated by the client and enhance the therapeutic relationship.

COUNSELING RESOURCES AND TECHNIQUES

Exploration of self-help group resources and inclusion of specific counseling techniques may enhance the incorporation of the spiritual dimension in counseling. Select self-help group resources and counseling techniques are presented here.

Self-Help Group Resources

As discussed in Chapter 8, in order for a counselor to use 12-step groups as a support to counseling, the counselor needs to have an awareness of how these groups work. Understanding the philosophy of the groups provides the counselor a deeper insight into the 12-step orientation. Reading the group materials (core chapters from main texts, the story of someone in recovery from main texts, meditation books) and attending open meetings (groups that are open to the public) helps orient the counselor to the program. In addition, the counselor needs to assist the client in finding a successful match with self-help groups. Four questions that can assist in this process are:

1. What types of self-help groups are available where you live and/or work?

2. When you look at your life, where and how is it easiest to fit in meetings?

3. How comfortable are you with giving out your phone number to members of the self-help group?

4. How comfortable are you with being touched physically in a self-help group? (being hugged, holding hands)

Chapter 8 also provides guidelines for assessing a group's personality and health, and with regard to sponsorship (essentially a mentoring process of recovery where someone with more sobriety time serves as a personal guide), such as questions to ask a potential sponsor and guidelines for healthy sponsorship.

For those clients who are not comfortable with the 12-step spiritual perspective to recovery, the counselor may refer the client to other national, abstinence-based, self-help groups that are reviewed more extensively in Chapter 8. Two groups that include a spiritual aspect are Women for Sobriety (WFS) and Kasl's 16 Steps. A brief review of these groups follows.

Jean Kirkpatrick began WFS in 1976. It has an emphasis on both emotional and spiritual growth. Its philosophy combines cognitive-behavioral techniques, peer support, health promotion, and philosophies from various streams (Emerson, Thoreau, Unity Church) (Horvath, 1997). WFS was developed to help address struggles that are unique to women alcoholics, such as self-value, self-worth, guilt, shame, and stigma using a Thirteen Statement Program that is arranged in six levels of a New Life program. In 1994, it was expanded to Men for Sobriety (Horvath, 1997). WFS's 8th Statement highlights their spiritual dimension: "The fundamental object of life is emotional and spiritual growth." However, the emphasis on spirituality is not as strong as in the 12-step program, thus, this may be more appealing to some clients.

The 16 Steps was started by Charlotte Kasl. Her 1992 book, *Many Roads, One Journey: Moving Beyond the Twelve Steps*, summarized 7 years of her workshops, projects, and interviews. The 16 Steps focus on empowerment and discovery of the individual. The spiritual dimension is explicitly stated in Step 2: "We come to believe that God/the Goddess/Universe/Great Spirit/Higher Power awakens the healing wisdom within us when we open ourselves to that power." The wording of this step indicates the program's emphasis on different spiritual perspectives. Clients, then, may read and hear about different spiritual recovery models that could be healing for them.

There are three alternative national, abstinence-based programs that do not include a spiritual dimension to recovery. These three programs are Rational Recovery (RR), Secular Organization for Sobriety (SOS), and Self Management and Recovery Training (SMART). RR, based on Ellis's Rational Emotive Behavior Therapy, does not encourage group meetings, but does encourage use of a strategy labeled Addictive Voice Recognition Training (AVRT) (Rational Recovery, 1992). SOS looks at addiction as a cycle that includes physiological need, learned habit, and denial of need and habit. It follows six guidelines and has meetings that are open to an addict with any addiction problem, as well as his other family members and friends. SMART involves a cognitive-behavioral approach that is paired with Ellis' Rational Emotive Behavior Therapy. It incorporates a four-point program and advocates nine core ideas.

Techniques

G. Miller (2003) summarizes other spiritually based techniques that can be used in addiction counseling. These techniques are appropriate in individual or group counseling sessions as well as homework experiences outside of sessions. The techniques discussed in this chapter are by no means exhaustive; they are provided as a baseline from which a counselor may assist clients in exploring their spirituality in counseling. What is most critical is that the counselor uses these techniques with the welfare of the client at the foreground so that intervention choices are always based on the client's best interest: *What will assist the addicted client in staying sober?* Following the presentation of these specific techniques, a brief notation is made about group therapy within this context.

Bibliotherapy

Bibliotherapy can be a powerful spiritual self-exploration process. Therefore, the counselor needs to be careful about chosen readings and how these readings are presented to and processed with the client. G. Miller (2003) outlines specific bibliotherapy questions that can be used by the

counselor. The questions directed to the counselor consider the purpose of using the particular materials; how the materials might best be used; an assessment of the available materials; matching the client's reading ability, time availability, and values with the materials; and how the client may access these materials. The materials-based questions to the client are focused on the client's interest, time, money, and values. Once the materials have been read, the counselor needs to process the client's reaction: How did the client make meaning of the materials? These questions, outlined by G. Miller (2003), consider the client's thoughts and feelings about the materials, parts with which they agreed and/or disagreed, and how these materials integrate with the client's spiritual perspective.

In addiction recovery, clients can be exposed to many different sources of reading materials: national self-help group organizations' publications, self-help bookstore publications, significant individuals, and spiritual/religious groups. These can involve books of daily meditation, recovering addicts' stories (as written in the main texts of both 12-step and alternative 12-step programs), main texts of the group, and general spirituality books.

Clients often need assistance sorting through the available reading material. The counselor can assist the addicted client in determining which readings will sustain the client's spirit and fit with his or her values. This will vary for each client depending on his or her spiritual perspective. For example, one client may benefit by spending time each day reading the Bible while someone else may start each day reading a secular meditation book. It is often helpful to provide the client with an opportunity to discuss his or her reactions to the materials: What is the client's interpretation of what they are reading? The client may also need encouragement to incorporate the readings into daily life as a support for remaining sober. For example, the client who uses a daily meditation book may want to carry it with her and read it through the day at times when she feels upset or out of balance.

Mindfulness Exercises

Appel and Kim-Appel (2009) provide a review of the literature summarizing the application of this technique in counseling. The authors describe mindfulness as being: rooted in Buddhism, a component of other religions, and used in treatment programs without necessarily being connected to their original religious or cultural traditions—or what they call a "Western non-religious context" (p. 507). Mindfulness means that the client has a present moment, non-judgmental awareness with the intent to gain awareness of patterns (emotional, cognitive, interactions with others) in order to make conscious choices rather than automatic ones (Appel & Kim-Appel, 2009). This includes awareness and observation of one's sensory experiences.

One way mindfulness has been used in substance abuse counseling has been with urge coping and relapse prevention (Appel & Kim-Appel, 2009). The Marlatt's concept of "urge-surfing" discussed in Chapter 7 is an example of its application to relapse prevention. Appel and Kim-Appel (2009) provide a thorough overview of its application in the field.

Three books the counselor may find helpful in the application of mindfulness to an addicted population are: *The Mindfulness Workbook for Addiction*, *Mindfulness-Based Relapse Prevention for Addictive Behaviors: A Clinician's Guide*, and *Mindfulness-Oriented Recovery Enhancement: For Addiction, Stress, and Pain*. These books are discussed in the resource section at the end of this chapter.

Prayer and Meditation

Counselors may also encourage techniques such as prayer and meditation (Kus, 1995). Prayer is defined here as simply "talking" and meditation as "listening." Both meditation and prayer have been used in addiction treatment programs (Young, de Armas Delorenzi, & Cunningham, 2011). For the counselor to successfully help his or her client in this area, he or she must have a good handle on countertransference. The counselor needs to approach the topics of prayer and meditation within a trusting relationship and in a tentative manner. The counselor also needs to assist in fitting these approaches with the client's view of a Higher Power.

In terms of prayer, the counselor is essentially helping the client find a way to talk about concerns with or reach out for support to a Higher Power, especially when other supports are not immediately available. Discussion about the client's concept of a Higher Power and how to contact that Higher Power can assist an addict in staying sober. Determine the form of prayer as it fits within the client's views. For example, a client's Higher Power may be nature. Thus, prayer may be a nonverbal form of talking such as taking a walk or a hike. Van Wormer and Davis (2008, 2012) discuss how alcoholic clients can derive meaning and comfort from a sense of connection with nature. Other clients may have specific verbal prayers from their spiritual practice that assist them in staying in balance and feeling hopeful about living and staying sober.

The use of meditation needs to be approached with the same respectful sensitivity. This process involves finding out how a client listens. Depending on their personal history, quiet time may be very unsettling. First, it may be disturbing because the client relates quiet with previous negative experiences or traumas. In such a situation, quiet can result in the addicted person becoming very upset and wanting to "use." Second, quiet time may simply be uncomfortable because the addicted client is used to a lifestyle that is high intensity and crisis-driven. The client may not know what to do in quiet or simply find quiet boring. The counselor can help the client find a form of meditation that both calms and helps the client learn about self as well as process the client's reactions to these quiet moments.

The counselor often needs to approach this area in a gentle, paced fashion. For example, the counselor may encourage the client to sit alone quietly for 5 minutes a day and simply focus on breathing. Then, in session, the counselor can process the client's reactions to the experience.

Examples of other forms of meditation and guided imagery are discussed by G. Miller (2003). As with bibliotherapy, clients need to be prepared for these experiences and have an opportunity to process them with the counselor. Questions similar to those used with the bibliotherapy technique can be used regarding prayer and meditation: the purpose of prayer and meditation, how it might best be used, assessing means available, matching them with time availability and values, how the client may learn about them, and client questions focusing on interest, time, money, and values.

Spiritual Bypass/Emotional Sobriety Exercises

See Appendix 8.B in Chapter 8 for an explanation of these terms as well as exercises that can be used in exploring these spiritually related concepts with clients.

Spiritual/Religious Genogram

This exercise is similar to a family genogram. The goal is to look at spiritual/religious strengths, as well as weak spots, that exist in the family system. Some of its components can include: spiritual beliefs and religious affiliations (the meaning and importance of them within the family; the impact of them on marriage/parenting, rituals/celebrations, life/relationships); and unique aspects that are of importance to the client and their spiritual/religious experiences as they relate to their addiction recovery (dates, career, achievements, physical/mental problems, relationships, loss, etc.).

Spiritual/Religious Timeline

In this exercise, the client can note significant times, events/experiences, and people that were significant for them in their spiritual development. With addicted clients, it may also be enlightening to have them parallel this timeline with their use and recovery history, looking for potential recovery support resources. Finally, Dobmeier, Reiner, Casquarelli, and Fallon

(2013) state this spiritual timeline can be paired with a sexual orientation timeline that includes: "ages when an individual was first attracted to people of the opposite gender, same gender or both genders; realized that he or she was heterosexual, homosexual or bisexual; had his or her first sexual contact; had same-sex sexual contact and/or opposite-sex sexual contact; had an intimate relationship with persons of the opposite gender and/or same gender; and first told a family member about a romantic interest or relationship" (p. 50). The authors also state hate crimes and harassment experiences may be included. If it is not too overwhelming for the client, the counselor may suggest the inclusion of all three timelines (spiritual/religious, addiction use/recovery, sexual orientation) in order to explore the potential overlap of all three areas. The third timeline does not need to be limited to sexual orientation—it could focus on any multicultural aspect of the client that needs to be considered in their recovery process.

Group Exercises

Post, Cornish, Wade, and Tucker (2013) state that counselors need to consider exploring religion and spirituality within a group context because they: are a part of client diversity, may be helpful for clients, and may allow clients to work through issues related to this area that might be contributing to other problems. As discussed in Chapter 5, the group counselor needs to generally establish group rules. When discussing the sensitive area of spirituality, the parameters for discussion may need to be specifically stated and monitored in order to ensure the safety of the individual clients and the overall group.

Although each of the previous techniques can be applied to a group setting, G. Miller (2003, 2012) provides some additional exercises that can be used in helping addicted clients explore spirituality within a group. These techniques, as described in more detail in the texts, involve the use of recovery-related resources such as meditation books and the Serenity Prayer as well as experiential exercises involving music, etc. (See Case Studies 12.1 and 12.2.)

CASE STUDY 12.1

Your client is a 25-year-old ethnic minority individual who is attempting to become sober for the third time. The two recovery periods have been 1 to 3 months in length in the past year; relapses coincide with traditional Judeo-Christian religious holidays (i.e., Christmas, Easter). Your client struggles with feelings of isolation from his ethnic group because of his use: He specifically reports that a previous Christian church he attended called him a sinner because of his alcohol and drug use and told him he would not have a problem with alcohol and drugs if he only "got right with God." He does not feel like he belongs with AA either, because he struggles with the spiritual aspect of the program. He tells you he wants to stay sober, but he does not think there is much hope for him.

1. Upon hearing this description, are you aware of any possible countertransference issues that could arise based on the thoughts and feelings you have after hearing his story?
2. How would you approach such issues so they do not contaminate your counseling (i.e., consultation with colleagues, supervisors, mentors)?
3. What are indicators of possible spiritual/religious issues?
4. Where would you begin to explore any spiritual/religious issues he may be having in terms of his recovery?
5. How would you help him develop a community of support for his addiction recovery based on his spiritual issues?
6. Would his ethnicity be a contributing factor to how you would approach any issues with countertransference, spirituality/religion, or community support?

EXERCISE 12.1

Quiet yourself for a few minutes and then write any sentence, phrase, or question that comes to your mind when you think of spirituality. For the next 15 to 30 minutes, write a phrase that includes each word from the first sentence, phrase, or question you wrote. (For example, if you wrote a phrase that had four words, use each one of the four words in one phrase/sentence. Each word can be thought of as a kickoff to the new phrase/sentence. The word can be at the beginning, middle, or end of the phrase/sentence.) Stop when you want and share your writing with another person if you are comfortable about what you learned about yourself spiritually.

CASE STUDY 12.2

Your female, adolescent client is a trauma survivor (sexual abuse) who has "no time for this God stuff." She refuses to talk with you or anyone about her spiritual beliefs beyond that statement. All you know is that she becomes very agitated and angry whenever the topic arises in counseling sessions.

1. What would be your concerns about exploring her spirituality with her in counseling as it relates to her addiction? (Consider influencing factors such as your gender and age as well as bringing up a topic that elicits such a sense of mistrust.)
2. How would the history of her trauma influence your approach to her?
3. How would you begin an assessment of her spiritual beliefs?
4. What are some treatment techniques you might use to explore her spiritual views?
5. How would you balance exploration of her spirituality with developing and maintaining a trusting relationship with her?

EXERCISE 12.2

Develop ground rules for discussion of spirituality as it relates to addiction for different contexts of counseling (individual, couples, family, group). Focus the rules on simplicity and safety. The goals are to avoid judgment, encourage acceptance of current views and exploration of alternative views, and match the counseling context format to one's own theory of addiction counseling.

SUMMARY

This chapter discusses the historical merger of spirituality and addiction counseling, barriers and bridges to incorporation of spirituality into addiction counseling, development of client spiritual identity, and counseling resources and techniques. The overlap between spirituality and addiction counseling calls for continued exploration of the strengths and weaknesses of the use of spirituality in addiction counseling.

QUESTIONS

1. What is the history of the incorporation of spirituality in addiction counseling?

2. What are some barriers and bridges when incorporating spirituality in addiction counseling?

3. What are some strategies I feel comfortable using when working with addicted clients on their spiritual issues?

READINGS, RESOURCES, WEBSITES

SUGGESTED READINGS

General

Aten, J. D., & Leach, M. M. (Eds.). (2009). *Spirituality and the therapeutic process: A comprehensive resource from intake to termination*. Washington, DC: American Psychological Association.

This book contains 12 chapters, each of which addresses some aspect of the therapeutic process.

Cashwell, C. S., & Young, J. S. (2005). *Integrating spirituality and religion into counseling: A guide to competent practice*. Alexandria, VA: American Counseling Association.

This book has 10 chapters that generally look at integration, assessment, counselor awareness, lifespan development, cultural issues, therapy goals, and working within one's limits as a counselor.

Fukuyama, M. A., & Sevig, T. D. (1999). *Integrating spirituality into multicultural counseling*. Thousand Oaks, CA: Sage.

This book has nine chapters that examine worldviews, developmental models, expressions of spirituality, issues (content, process), and an integrative model.

Miller, G. (2003). *Incorporating spirituality in counseling and psychotherapy*. Hoboken, NJ: Wiley.

This textbook has eight chapters (introduction, historical development, western religions, eastern religions, theoretical integration with cultural implications, counseling focus integration, ethical issues, specific treatment techniques), all of which involve case studies and exercises that can be used by counselors for self-awareness or within the context of counseling.

Miller, L. J. (Ed.). (2012). *The Oxford handbook of psychology and spirituality*. New York, NY: Oxford University Press.

This book is divided into 10 sections and contains 39 chapters. It has one entire section focused on spiritual development, family, and culture.

Miller, W. R. (Ed.). (1999). *Integrating spirituality into treatment*. Washington, DC: American Psychological Association.

This book has 13 chapters divided into four sections: an overview, addressing spirituality in treatment, specific spiritual issues, and training.

Richards, P. S., & Bergin, A. E. (Eds.). (1997). *A spiritual strategy for counseling and psychotherapy*. Washington, DC: American Psychological Association.

This book has 13 chapters divided into four sections (overview, foundations, therapy process and methods, research/future). It has a short section in one of the chapters on AA.

Shafranske, E. P. (Ed.). (1996). *Religion and the clinical practice of psychology*. Washington, DC: American Psychological Association.

This book has four sections (an overview, clinical practice, psychotherapy with religious clients, afterword) consisting of 21 chapters. There is one chapter that specifically focuses on the 12-step program.

Sperry, L., & Shafranske, E. P. (Eds.). (2005). *Spirituality oriented psychotherapy*. Washington, DC: American Psychological Association.

This book has 15 chapters divided into three sections: theoretical foundations, contemporary approaches (related to specific theoretical frameworks), and commentary/critical analysis.

West, W. (2000). *Psychotherapy & spirituality: Crossing the line between therapy and religion*. Thousand Oaks, CA: Sage.

This book has nine chapters that discuss spirituality in terms of an overview, a part of therapy, issues related to the integration, and the general practice of spirituality in counseling.

Multicultural Factors

Chellew-Hodge, C. (2008). *Bulletproof faith: A spiritual survival guide for gay and lesbian Christians*. San Francisco, CA: Jossey-Bass.

This book, which has nine chapters, is specifically written for the gay/lesbian reader.

Hunter, S. (2010). *Effects of conservative religion on lesbian and gay clients and practitioners: Practice implications*. Washington, DC: NASW Press.

This book is divided into four sections: heterosexism and religion (three chapters); religious and sexual identity conflicts (two chapters); working through client conflict (three chapters); and working with heterosexist practitioners (two chapters). There is a chapter specifically on methods used to assist clients in reconciling their conflict between religion and sexuality.

Miller, G., Clark, C., & Choate, L. H. (2008). Women and spirituality. In L. H. Choate (Ed.), *Girls' and women's wellness* (pp. 221–240). Alexandria, VA: American Counseling Association.

This book chapter provides an overview of spirituality with women that includes discussion of related factors such as age and ethnicity.

Miller, L. J. (Ed.). (2012). *The Oxford handbook of psychology and spirituality*. New York, NY: Oxford University Press.

This book is divided into 10 sections and contains 39 chapters. It has one entire section focused on spiritual development, family, and culture.

Mindfulness

Bowen, S., Chawla, N., & Marlatt, G. A. (2011). *Mindfulness-based relapse prevention for addictive behaviors: A clinician's guide*. New York, NY: Guilford Press.

This book describes the mindfulness-based relapse prevention (MBRP) program that combines mindfulness meditation practices with relapse prevention. It has two parts: an overview and a facilitator's guide. The facilitator's guide describes each of the eight sessions that build on one another; it includes exercises and handouts.

Garland, E. L. (2013), *Mindfulness-oriented recovery enhancement: For addiction, stress, and pain*. Washington, DC: NASW Press.

This book presents mindfulness-oriented recovery enhancement (MORE) that is a combination of mindfulness techniques with cognitive therapy and positive psychology principles. It has three sections (concepts, treatment manual, research) divided into 14 chapters. The treatment manual has 10 sessions and the text provides nine client handouts.

Williams, R. E., & Kraft, M. A. (2012). *The mindfulness workbook for addiction*. Oakland, CA: New Harbinger.

This workbook has three sections (main concepts and skills, losses, and moving forward) divided into 10 chapters. It provides numerous exercises for each chapter.

Group Counseling

Miller, G. (2012). *Group exercises for addiction counseling*. Hoboken, NJ: Wiley.

This book has four sections: introduction, philosophy and practice of group work, group exercises, and resources. Group exercises are a compilation of "tried and true" group exercises used by experienced addiction treatment group counselors.

RESOURCES

Hazelden has numerous resources for exploration of spiritual views from a 12-step model:

Hazelden
P.O. Box 11
15251 Pleasant Valley Road
Center City, MN 55012-0011
E-mail: info@hazelden.org
www.hazeldon.org
(651) 213-4200; (800) 257-7810

The 12-step groups and 12-step alternative groups (Women for Sobriety, Kasl's 16 Steps) have materials that can be used in the exploration of spiritual views. See Chapter 8 for contact information on these different groups.

WEBSITES

American Association for Marriage and Family Therapy (AAMFT)
www.aamft.org

Information on spirituality as it relates to therapy can be searched for on this website.

American Counseling Association Division: Association for Spiritual, Ethical, and Religious Values in Counseling (ASERVIC)
www.aservic.org

As a division of the American Counseling Association, ASERVIC has resources of best practices (teaching modules, listserv, articles, and periodic conferences) to assist the counselor in integrating spirituality into their practice. There are also state affiliations of the national group.

American Psychological Association (APA) Division 36: Society for the Psychology of Religion and Spirituality
www.apa.org/about/division/div36.html

Society for the Psychology of Religion and Spirituality provides information and resources for the integration of spirituality into one's practice of psychology. The *Psychology of Religion and Spirituality* newsletter is published quarterly for its members.

National Association of Social Workers (NASW)
www.socialworkers.org

This website has information on spirituality as it relates to the profession.

CHAPTER 13

PERSONAL AND PROFESSIONAL DEVELOPMENT OF THE COUNSELOR

PERSONAL REFLECTIONS

In this chapter there is discussion of topics such as wounds and self-care that can be stimulated by experiences in working with addicts. Regarding wounds, ethical charges and legal charges can break the heart, the spirit, of counselors who are doing their best to work with difficult clients and their families in difficult situations during a tumultuous time in their lives. As I have said to counselors in such situations, we often feel alone when ethical or legal charges are made against us. In part, this is due to not sharing our current or past experiences with charges. As a result, we can end up feeling very isolated because we are not aware of others in the same situation. Also, in general, we cannot depend on others or systems to care for us, and often we only receive negative feedback on our behavior, not feedback that says we are doing well or that tells us to "Keep up the good work."

These professional realities emphasize why self-care and working with our own wounds is so critical in our profession. Self-care is critical if we are to survive the struggles we potentially face as a counselor *and* to be a healing force for our clients. We need to care for ourselves in a balanced, loving way so we can live through any struggles that occur both professionally and personally and so we can pass the self-compassion we experience on to our colleagues and our clients. We can role model self-care to them and gently invite them to care for themselves. We can share the suffering of the human experience as well as the joy and the comfort.

OBJECTIVES

1. To understand some core ethical dilemmas and general ways to approach them.
2. To learn guidelines for testifying in court.
3. To develop a perspective and approaches on working in difficult systems.
4. To understand general approaches to working with addicted individuals.
5. To develop a broad perspective on self-care.

Overall, counselors need to remember the importance of doing no harm to clients, yet it is also important to remember that harm can be done by inaction as well as action (Bissell & Royce, 1994). *Ethical principles* act as a rudder that guides the behavior of counselors; they are the principles that direct the moral- and value-based decisions that affect the counseling process. *Moral decisions* are the concrete decisions counselors make in a situation based on the values (beliefs, attitudes, and behaviors) that have important personal meaning to them. *Laws* are the formalized moral decisions of a culture. Ethical principles for counselors, then, are highly intertwined with the laws of culture; at the same time, because an action is legal does not mean that it is ethical (Bissell & Royce, 1994).

Washton and Zweben (2008) provide an example of an ethical dilemma that raises issues for the addiction counselor both ethically and legally. This is in the situation where clients may ask for a mental health diagnosis rather than a substance abuse one so reimbursement is enhanced. They suggest simply refusing such requests because of the seriousness of this falsification both ethically and legally. Counselors can protect themselves both ethically and legally in a threefold manner: documented consultation with colleagues, use of common therapy practices, and malpractice insurance (Werth, Welfel, & Benjamin, 2013).

Supervisors of addiction counselors, as well as agencies employing addiction counselors, should contact their respective professional organization (s), as well as their state addiction licensing or credentialing agencies, for copies of their ethical codes. Also, they would be well advised to have copies of federal and state laws and regulations pertinent to substance use as resources. Specifically those discussed in this section that pertain to duty to protect, confidentiality, child protective services, and/or impaired drivers may be useful (Werth et al., 2013). Finally, due to the significant impact of technology on counseling, counselors, supervisors, and agencies would be wise to consult the various professional organizations for guidelines on the interface of technology with the counseling practice especially as it relates to social media, counseling, and electronic records.

Some of the concerns with technology's impact on counseling are briefly addressed here. The communication forms presented are only a few of those that are available and that may pose ethical concerns for counselors. In order to prevent ethical dilemmas in relation to the following electronic forms of communication, the ethical concerns can be explored through contact with one's professional organizations as well as through dialogue with mentors, supervisors, and colleagues. Also, counselors may appropriately discuss these concerns with their clients through initial (informed consent) and ongoing counseling sessions.

E-mail, which began in 1971, has evolved into a commonly used communication form (Bradley, Hendricks, Lock, Whiting, & Parr, 2011). It expands and encourages communication, but issues with privacy, confidentiality, and professional relationships arise (Bradley & Hendricks, 2009; Bradley et al., 2011).

Sude (2013) provides an overview of ethical concerns and guidelines with the use of *text messaging* (TM), or *short message service* (SMS). This overview includes issues with confidentiality, documentation, competency of counselors, use appropriateness, and possible misinterpretations as well as boundary issues connected to dual relationships, counselor availability, and billing.

Facebook is a social outlet for many people and is used as a way to stay in contact with others both personally and professionally (Karas, 2013). While it has a privacy setting, some basic information is public unless one intentionally changes this information to being private (Karas, 2013). Specific recommendations for counselors using Facebook include: having awareness of the public nature of the medium (watch for unprofessional aspects in one's postings), setting boundaries openly with clients, and consulting with mental health and other professionals on concerns with its usage (Birky & Collins, 2011).

Twitter, which is more like a journal, involves posting comments ("tweets") on a person's page that their "followers" can read (Karas, 2013). Twitter can remain private, but the option to "retweet" allows the comment (the posting) to be sent beyond one's intended audience (Karas, 2013). A user can hashtag a word or a phrase without spaces; the hashtag is where a number sign (#) is put in front of the word/phrase that allows people to see who posted the picture. The hashtag allows the reader to access all the postings containing that word or phrase after the number sign. For example, if a hashtag was made that said, "#LookThisUp" and a search of this phrase using the Twitter search engine was done, every posting by any user that had "#LookThisUp" in their posting would appear. The same counselor recommendations made earlier for Facebook may be applied to this medium.

Instagram allows the uploading of pictures from a smartphone (a mobile phone that operates more like a computer than a feature phone—it has more computing capability and connectivity). Instagram, like Facebook and Twitter, is a form of personal disclosure. Therefore, the same ethical problems can arise with it as with the other two (Karas, 2013). For example, one can "follow" other people to see when they post pictures. The reader can "like" someone's picture and post comments to it. As with Facebook and Twitter, there is the option to make one's information private. However, a hashtag on the picture will link it to the other Instagram pictures that have the same hashtag (Karas, 2013). As a result, clients can find out personal information about their counselors through Google and social media sites. Karas (2013) recommends that counselors discuss these ethical considerations regarding Internet use and its potential impact on the counseling relationship.

E-therapy, online counseling, has five common ethical concerns that also need to be explored through informed consent. These five areas are: overall concerns about its use, possible misunderstandings, professional boundaries, confidentiality, and service interruption (Lee, 2010).

This chapter addresses general topic areas that impact the personal and professional development of the counselor. The areas explored are ethical issues, testifying in court, working in difficult systems, working with addicts, and self-care. As in other chapters, case studies and exercises are interspersed in the text to facilitate understanding of the material.

ETHICAL ISSUES

Ethical standards guide the behaviors of counselors by setting expectations for how they are to act professionally (Corey, 2013; Haley, 2008). Professional organizations promote ethical behavior primarily to protect the public (Gressard, 2008). Ethical dilemmas involve decisions about situations that are not explicitly prohibited or allowed by law (B. S. Anderson, 2008).

Ethical dilemmas for counselors are complex, multifaceted situations that resist a simplistic approach. To avoid ethical dilemmas, the counselor can use the following six guidelines (Hubert, 1996):

1. Inform the client of limitations on the counseling relationship before beginning counseling.

2. Always act in the best interest of the client.

3. Work within professional competency boundaries.

4. When needed, be able to explain the rationale for your professional decisions and behaviors.

5. Consult with other professionals about ethical dilemmas and consult with an attorney if necessary.

6. Stay current with professional and legal guidelines.

D. Smith (2003b) also advocates 10 guidelines for avoidance of ethical dilemmas:

1. Understanding the definition of a multiple relationship

2. Protecting confidentiality

3. Respecting autonomy

4. Knowing supervisory responsibilities

5. Identifying the client and your role with that client

6. Documenting

7. Practicing within areas of expertise

8. Knowing the difference between abandonment and termination

9. Basing professional opinions and evaluations on evidence

10. Being accurate in billing

D. Smith (2003a) also stresses the importance of being familiar with the ethics code, trusting your sense that the situation does not feel right, talking with colleagues, addressing issues with clients upfront, and looking at ethics in a deeper, investigative fashion.

A further complication for the addictions field is that it is multidimensional and multi-disciplinary, thereby requiring the professional to follow the ethical codes of their respective certification/licensure board as well as follow state/federal laws that may be in conflict with these codes (Haley, 2008). Although numerous ethical dilemmas can arise for counselors, three main ones for addiction counselors are explored in this section: confidentiality issues, dual relationship issues, and the crossover area between legal and ethical concerns.

B. S. Anderson (1996) discusses two other exceptions to privilege: duty to report and duty to warn. *Duty to report* means that the counselor has an ethical obligation to break confidentiality by contacting authorities when the client or a third person can be harmed. Counselors are mandated to report suspected child and adult abuse, so they are legally required to report suspected abuse to the authorities. *Duty to warn* means that the counselor needs to determine whether the client is seriously dangerous and, in some states, that the potential victim can be identified. Anderson suggests that counselors in this situation consult with a professional colleague or supervisor, make necessary referrals, possibly contact the police, and contact the potential victim. The counselor may also want to obtain a legal consultation. There is a possibility that civil commitment procedures for the client may need to be taken.

EXERCISE 13.1

Using Hubert's (1996) suggestions and D. Smith's (2003a, 2003b) guidelines, how do you avoid ethical dilemmas or how do you plan to avoid ethical dilemmas in the future?

Confidentiality

Some distinctions must be drawn between confidentiality and disclosure. *Confidentiality* means that the information obtained in a counseling session is not shared with others unless written permission has been given by the client. *Privileged communication* is legal protection for the benefit of the client in working with certain professionals under state law, which prohibits information being given without the client's consent. Therefore, while a counselor has a professional, ethical commitment to confidentiality, this commitment may or may not be held up under privileged communication laws in the state where the counselor works. For example, in North Carolina, the general statute would be that a judge may overrule privilege for "proper administration of justice."

Haley (2008) reminds us that these duties vary among states, so the counselor needs to know the requirements of the state in which he or she practices. Yet, it is important to remember that if state and federal guidelines conflict, the federal guidelines will take precedent (Myers & Salt, 2007). Excellent additional reading in the areas of confidentiality and privileged communication and exceptions to these areas are in the American Counseling Association (ACA)'s *ACA Legal Series*, volumes 6 and 8 (ACA, 1993), respectively. Also, for a specific focus on addiction, "Ethical and Legal Aspects of Confidentiality" (Brooks, 1997) covers a variety of external and internal disclosures related to areas such as medical, legal, and criminal; research, audit, and evaluation; child abuse and neglect; duty to warn; HIV and AIDS; and modern technology issues.

Confidentiality has been critical in the addictions field for three decades, because addicted clients face the risks of discrimination and arrest. In the 1970s, recognition was given that potential clients did not go to treatment for substance abuse because of stigma and fear of being prosecuted. Illegal activity and illegal drugs related to the substance abuse disorder were the concerns regarding prosecution. In the early 1970s, then, legislation was enacted for those individuals who received a diagnosis or treatment for substance abuse that gave them stricter confidentiality rights (U.S. Department of Health & Human Services, 2004). In the early 1970s, the statute on substance abuse treatment patient disclosure information was passed (42 USC 290dd-2 and 42 Code of Federal Regulations, Part 2; 42CFR) and was clarified in 1975 regulations ("Confidentiality of Alcohol and Drug Abuse Patient Records"), which were amended in 1987 and 1995 (Brooks, 1997). In the area of confidentiality and disclosure, the *42CFR, Part 2* (1987) promulgates the regulations applicable for all federally funded drug treatment programs. These federal regulations supersede less protective state laws (Brooks, 1997).

Because the client's involvement with an addiction treatment program states the client's diagnosis, the individual's presence or absence at the facility cannot be told without a signed release of information (Bissell & Royce, 1994); no identifying information can be given. All patient records are confidential. Programs cannot disclose patient information except in certain situations. These exceptions include a client's proper consent, a medical emergency, a court order, a crime committed against agency personnel or on the agency's premises, and research and/or auditing requests.

In 1996, the Health Insurance Portability and Accountability Act (HIPAA, Public Law 104–191), regarding confidentiality rules, was passed by Congress. It established privacy standards for health information that would identify an individual (Wilford, 2009). HIPAA protected client-identifying information, requiring the disclosure had to be limited to the minimally necessary information required for the disclosure's purpose (Haley, 2008). HIPAA began as a means to enhance health insurance access and restrain health care fraud, and eventually resulted in national standards designed to protect patient privacy and encourage health care information being exchanged electronically (Coombs, 2005). In 2000, the Department of Health & Human Services issued the Privacy Rule pursuant to the HIPAA of 1996 provisions that addressed health plans and health care providers (covered entities). The focus was to guarantee clients' confidentiality to facilitate the treatment process.

Proper consent means that the patient has been informed of the need for and the extent of the disclosure (Haley, 2008; Myers & Salt, 2007). Note that counselors need to tell clients, if the counselor is being supervised: who their supervisor is (along with their credentials) and what information may be shared with the supervisor, such as videotapes (Haley, 2008). Proper consent also requires that the consent form have the names of the program, disclosure recipient, and patient; the signature of the patient; the date of the signature; the right of the patient to revoke the disclosure; and written notification to the disclosure recipient of the prohibition to redisclose the information to another agency.

For example, a consent form for a client may use the following format:

The Rural Addictions Treatment Center in Alexandria, South Carolina (name of program), releases information specifically to the Rural Halfway House in Alexandria, South Carolina (disclosure recipient who cannot redisclose the information), regarding the treatment of Rod Hoop (patient), who has the right to revoke this disclosure at any point; the maximum HIPAA consent time is one year of the signed date (patient signature and date of signature is on the form).

Disclosure is allowed for the purposes of diagnosis, treatment, or rehabilitation; central registry, which prevents the client from being enrolled in more than one program concurrently; funding; employment; contacts with legal counsel, family, significant others, and the criminal justice system; and other situations where consent is given and no harm is anticipated to the patient or the relationship between the patient and the program.

Some communications are not viewed as disclosures as governed by *42CFR, Part 2* (1987). These include communications within a program or between a program and the agency that has administrative control over the program, the qualified service organization that provides services to the program, and communications that do not involve any patient-identifying information. Minors have basically the same rights as adults—they must be informed before disclosure occurs and be involved in and updated about decisions made (Remley, 1985). To have information released—even if the information is to be given to the parents—the minor has to sign the consent form (Brooks, 1997). Clark and Bizzell (2009) report that more than half of the states allow adolescents to have consent rights for screening, assessment, and treatment of an addictive disorder. If state law requires parental permission to treat the minor, a parent's signature is also necessary (Brooks, 1997). However, some states are considering legislation that will *not* allow adolescents the right to consent to treatment.

When counseling minors, issues regarding parents and schools often arise. Again, the counselor needs to focus on the welfare of the client (adolescent) in a decision based on the client's age and education, the client's relationship with parents or guardians, and the extent of potential for harm of disclosing or not disclosing (B. S. Anderson, 1996). As to schools, Salo and Shumate (1993) state that the parent or guardian should be consulted before releasing information to school personnel, because the parent or guardian technically owns the privacy rights of the adolescent. Anderson (1996) also suggests that school personnel be given only information they need to know within the context of the educational setting. Recommendations on the duty to warn and protect with minor students in the areas of self-injury, eating disorders, depression and suicidality, dating violence, and bullying is provided by Hays, Craigen, Knght, Healey, and Sikes (2009). (See Case Study 13.1.)

Clark and Bizzell (2009) make some suggestions for obtaining consent from older adults who are somewhere on the continuum between being clear about what consent means and having no understanding about the treatment. These suggestions include careful presentation of the information, awareness of the obstacles the client has in making the decision, involvement of family and/or close friends, and exploration of the possibility of guardianship.

CASE STUDY 13.1

Julian is a 16-year-old male who recently completed inpatient/outpatient addiction treatment and has come in for counseling on recovery issues. His parents have come with him to the first session and make some demands: (1) they want a weekly summary of what issues are discussed in counseling; (2) they want this summary to be specific and written; and (3) they want copies of the written summary to go to them and the principal of Julian's school. Julian appears quiet and sullen while his parents make their demands. Discuss how you would handle this situation in light of three questions:

1. What information would you need to have about Julian and his parents to make clinical decisions about confidentiality that are in Julian's best interests?

2. What limits would you set with his parents about information sent to them? To the school?

3. How would you structure sessions with Julian and his parents (e.g., who would be present)?

EXERCISE 13.2

In a small group, discuss experiences either you have had or that you have heard others have had with *duty to report* and *duty to warn*. With each of these real or imagined situations, answer three questions about the counseling:

1. How did I feel/what did I think when I realized I was in the situation?
2. How did I manage the stress of this situation?
3. If I could do it differently, how would I handle a similar situation now?

A counselor may be required to go to court because of a subpoena or a verbal or written order from a judge but may be prohibited from giving the court information about the client based on the regulations of the *42CFR, Part 2* (1987). A subpoena does not give the counselor the right to testify, but it can result in the counselor's being charged with contempt of court if it is ignored. This is an ethical dilemma in that the counselor has a responsibility to go to court, has limits on information that can be given in court, and faces contempt-of-court charges if not viewed as being compliant with the court's demands. The counselor has three options in this ethical dilemma. The counselor can testify, refuse to testify (and possibly face contempt of court charges), or explore some limited recourse strategies when receiving a subpoena or a court order. Three limited recourse strategies are appealing for privileged communication, testifying in the judge's chambers, or dialoguing with the client's lawyer (Herlihy & Sheeley, 1986). A dialogue with the client's lawyer may include exploring other options besides testifying in court, such as writing a court summary.

When a counselor receives a subpoena or a court order, it is wise to consult either a supervisor, the agency director, and/or a colleague experienced in legal matters to clarify what needs to be taken to court (self, documents), what needs to be released in court, and options for responding to the subpoena. Note that in some states a subpoena can be delivered by telephone from a sheriff. In such a case, the counselor needs to ask which party is serving the subpoena and obtain a copy of the subpoena later from either that attorney or the court. Finally, the counselor needs to request that the subpoenaing attorney be clear about the focus of the testimony and tell the counselor: (1) whether his or her testimony is expected to be damaging, (2) if he or she needs to be on call, (3) if he or she will be contacted if not called or the case is continued, and (4) what to bring to court. The counselor must be assertive about obtaining this information.

Addiction counselors who are following *42CFR, Part 2* (1987) regulations need to communicate the limitations of their disclosure to others in a respectful way. For example, when other professionals request information, a thoughtful explanation of the guidelines and resulting limitations of disclosure cooperation can communicate professional respect, which can facilitate ongoing collaboration.

Dual Relationships

A common source of ethical dilemmas in counseling practice is found in the area of dual relationships. Dual relationships are defined as the counselor and client having relationships additional to the counseling one or succeeding the counseling relationship; there is more than one professional role or a combination of professional and personal roles (Moleski & Kiselica, 2005). These multiple roles can be social-communal, sexual, business, professional, or familial (Zur, 2007). They cannot necessarily be avoided, are not necessarily exploitive or harmful, or clearly violate ethical codes resulting in variations among professionals (Heaton & Black, 2009). For example, dual relationships are impossible to avoid in rural communities or if practicing in a small-town clientele context in a larger community (being a gay therapist with GLBT clients) (Coombs, 2005).

Some dual relationship issues clearly need to be avoided, such as being sexual with current clients. However, professional organizations vary in ethical time frames allowed for sexual relationships with previous clients. The lack of consistency and clarity can include other types of dual relationships that involve touch, appointment times and locations, social interaction, self-disclosure, gifts, and rides (Robinson, 2006). Yet, because there are many different types and outcomes of these relationships, counselors are typically given less guidance in addressing these issues (Clipson, 2005). This lack of guidance can increase the danger that the counselor's judgment may result from conflicting emotion and personal need (Clipson, 2005).

This lack of clarity may be particularly present with addiction counselors who are in some type of recovery process that involves self-help groups. The counselor may be in recovery from addictions or be involved in a related organization such as Al-Anon. The 1994 membership data of the National Association of Alcoholism and Drug Abuse Counselors (NAADAC) showed that 58% of its members were recovering addicts (NAADAC Education and Research Foundation, 1995). Issues of dual relationships may emerge around self-help meeting attendance, sponsorship, or general recovery support. As Doyle (1997) points out, risks exist when client and counselor attend the same self-help group in terms of anonymity (for the counselor) and confidentiality (for the client). Although the counselor may have the best intentions, a dual relationship with a client can be very confusing and potentially damaging for the client. The counselor should ask himself or herself nine questions:

1. What are the different roles I have with this client?

2. Are these roles conflictual with one another or potentially confusing or damaging for my client?

3. What is the least number of roles I can feasibly have with this client?

4. What is the most important role I can have with my client?

5. Am I trying to have personal needs of my own met with my client?

6. Is there anyone else in the recovering community who can meet these needs with my client?

7. Is a referral to another addictions counselor necessary to clarify my role and responsibility to my client?

8. Should I consult with another professional about the roles I carry with my client?

9. Am I trying to treat someone with whom I have a strong personal relationship (or with one of their family members)?

Questions such as these may assist the counselor in clarifying the roles held with a client. A motto of "The fewer the roles, the better" may be a solid rule for a counselor to follow. In addition, a counselor may need to examine the general boundary setting around gift giving. Typically, the rule is to not accept gifts; however, some inexpensive, handmade gifts by clients may be appropriate to receive. Other colleagues or supervisors may be helpful in determining the extent of the dual relationship if they have a sensitivity to dual relationship issues. Doyle (1997) makes the following recommendations to addiction counselors: Examine applicable ethical codes and regulations, seek out experienced colleagues for advice, minimize potential dual relationships, carefully self-disclose your own personal recovery, and advocate within the profession the clarity of dual relationship issues. These relationships need to be evaluated regarding intimacy level, negative impact on therapy effectiveness, and a diminished sense of safety and comfort for the client.

An issue related to dual relationships is self-disclosure. How much do addiction counselors disclose about their own use history and/or the usage of significant others in their life as well as the consequences/impact of such usage on the counselor? Before examining the impact of disclosure specific to addiction issues, it may be helpful to examine counselor disclosure in general, because it can impact the therapeutic bond in a positive or negative way.

Freud displayed mixed messages about disclosure. While he disclosed information about his family, his feelings, and even gave gifts and financial support to his patients at times, he advocated an objective, detached, mirroring approach to clinicians because of a concern about client vulnerability (G. Miller, 2002). The benefit to this approach was the encouragement of transference and a focus on the client's problems (G. Miller, 2002). Yet, the inconsistency between his behavior and his recommendations to counselors suggests he did not believe that the mirroring approach had to be rigid and that a counselor needed to avoid all disclosure (Peterson, 2002).

Even when counselors do not intentionally reveal information about themselves, their nonverbal behavior, style, and method of answering questions or describing things reveal information about themselves (G. Miller, 2002). Heightened self-awareness can help the counselor be aware of unintentional self-disclosure. Intentional self-disclosure is examined here. Wells (1994) described four categories of self-disclosure: professional information (training, practice), personal information (experience, attitude, circumstances), personal reactions to clients (feelings), and admission of mistakes. The *content of the disclosure* as it relates to the different categories is a critical concern to take into account.

Theoretical orientation is another important concern because disclosure, in part, depends on the theoretical orientation of the counselor. Most of the writings on self-disclosure come from two divergent orientations: psychoanalytic and feminist (Peterson, 2002). While psychoanalysis prohibits disclosure (Peterson, 2002), feminist theory views it as maintaining an equal role and connection with the client (L. S. Brown & Walker, 1990). Many counselors find themselves in the middle area of these two extremes, attempting to determine how to be ethical and self-disclose.

Motivation to share information is a third concern. It is wrong to disclose information to meet your own needs, but appropriate to do so to enhance connection or show empathy (Peterson, 2002). Along with motivation, the counselor needs to consider the client "audience" for the disclosure in terms of personality traits and impact. Some client personality traits may not be conducive to counselor self-disclosure. These personality traits include poor boundaries, poor reality testing, focus on others, intimacy fears, self-absorption, and avoidance of intense emotions (Goldstein, 1994). Also, the counselor needs to be sensitive to the fact that the impact of a disclosure on a client cannot be predicted (Peterson, 2002).

The addiction counselor, then, needs to examine disclosure around usage and its consequences and impact on his or her personal life by examining disclosure content, theoretical orientation, and motivation. Because the ethical issues in this area are ambiguous and complex, the counselor can use ethical principles as a guide through this decision-making maze. Peterson (2002) presents five ethical principles that can serve as a guide for counselor disclosure: beneficence (beneficial to the client), nonmalfeasance (not harmful to the client), fidelity (trust), autonomy (independence), and justice (equal and fair treatment). The counselor can ask himself or herself five questions:

1. Would disclosing this information help my client? (beneficence)

2. Would disclosing this information not hurt my client? (nonmalfeasance)

3. Would disclosing this information facilitate client trust? (fidelity)

4. Would disclosing this information facilitate the client's informed choice to work with me? (autonomy)

5. Would I disclose this information to all of my clients in similar situations? (justice)

If a counselor can answer yes to these questions, then self-disclosure related to the addictions would seem relatively safe. Nonetheless, the counselor needs to consider the unique circumstances of each disclosure and think ahead about

Perhaps the best rudder in this confusion is a combination of the best interest of the client (Is the disclosure in the best interest of the client?) and whether this type of disclosure is a common practice. (Do I normally disclose this information, and is this information normally disclosed by other professionals working with this population?) In addition, G. Miller (2002) advocates disclosure that combines professionalism, warmth, flexibility, and technique in relation to the disclosure. (See Case Study 13.2.)

CASE STUDY 13.2

You have a client named Shelly who is the same age as you and is in a similar life situation as you in terms of partner, children, and living situation. Shelly is a recovering alcoholic. You have started to attend Al-Anon as a way of educating yourself about addiction, and as you attend, you discover some family issues that you had previously overlooked and been in denial about. You have attended one Al-Anon group for about 3 months, and you feel very comfortable talking with the members about your personal issues. After 3 months of being in the group and 2 weeks of counseling Shelly, she shows up at your Al-Anon group. Discuss your reactions to her presence with the following five questions as a guide:

1. How would you greet Shelly?
2. How would you interact with her in the group?
3. How would you change your sharing in the group?
4. Would you give up this group so Shelly could go to it, would you insist Shelly not join the group, or would you continue to attend even though she is there?
5. How would Shelly's presence at the meeting affect the focus of your next counseling session with her? Future sessions with her?

EXERCISE 13.3

Think of a client with whom you had or potentially had a dual relationship. (If you have not worked as a counselor, imagine yourself in such a situation.) In dialogue with another person, respond to the nine questions earlier in the chapter when thinking of that dual relationship.

how to respond to typical self-disclosures asked for by addicted clients, such as: Are you in addiction recovery? Are or were any members of your family chemically dependent? How has your or others' alcohol/drug usage negatively affected you? Do you work a recovery program?

Crossover Area Between Legal and Ethical Concerns

In some areas, ethics and the law cross over extensively. Two areas that may involve the addictions counselor are documentation (making progress notes) and consultation. Documenting requires a safe balance between giving the facts as reported and giving too much information on the client. Seven basic guidelines include:

1. Write in black ink so that copies can be made easily.

2. Write clearly (or have notes typed) so that it is easy to read the notes, thereby reducing misunderstandings of the notes.

3. Use a note-writing format approved by the agency.

4. Carefully choose words that place the emphasis on the self-report aspects of the information (e.g., "Client said," "Client stated, " "Client reported").

5. Write enough so critical information is captured, but not so much as to increase your liability.

6. Keep in mind who may be reading the chart notes, including the courts.

7. Remember: If it is not written down, it did not happen.

Regarding consultation, when in doubt of what action to take about a client, it is commonly good protection to consult with a colleague. The courts generally respect a professional who acted in good conscience, focused on the welfare of the client, adhered to commonly practiced therapy approaches, and consulted with a colleague. The consultation effort should also be charted.

Remley and Herlihy (2005) suggest some additional guidelines for avoiding problems legally and ethically. These include not suing clients for not paying fees, having accurate and thorough disclosure and informed consent statements, not guaranteeing therapy outcomes, monitoring self-disclosure, and monitoring counselor effectiveness.

Until a counselor or a colleague of a counselor is sued, the concern about legal matters may seem academic or overreactionary. Once a counselor has been sued or has watched a colleague be sued, the serious reality of the following ethical and legal principles cannot be ignored. The anxiety, frustration, confusion, and apprehension involved in a lawsuit—as well as the time, energy, and money it requires—can be overwhelming for the counselor. The following case study presents the legal reality of being sued. (See Case Study 13.3.)

CASE STUDY 13.3

You are an addictions counselor at a mental health agency. Your client is a single, 33-year-old female who comes for addiction treatment on her own. It is discovered during treatment for her addiction that she also struggles with depression. She sees a psychiatrist affiliated with the agency and is prescribed antidepressants. After 2 weeks of addictions and mental health treatment, she overdoses on the antidepressants and kills herself. Even though you have seen her weekly, you did not pick up any indicators of suicidal tendencies; however, you did not chart that she stated she was not suicidal. Also, you did not consult directly with the psychiatrist or a colleague when she was diagnosed as depressed. Your chart notes make it appear that you talked with her only about attending self-help meetings and that she reported being sober. One week after her suicide, the family contacts the director of your agency and states that they will be suing you for malpractice.

1. What mistakes did you make in working with this client?

2. What actions could you have taken to protect yourself better?

3. What is your best course of action now?

4. How will you cope with your fears about the lawsuit?

TESTIFYING IN COURT

Addictions counselors, as other counselors, must use ethical principles to guide their behavior (Swenson, 1993). However, for the counselor in a different setting (e.g., a courtroom), the ethical principles may be too vague to guide behavior (Swenson, 1993). This section discusses some basic tenets for courtroom testimony, common court involvements for addictions counselors, and how to increase their effectiveness.

First, the addictions counselor must qualify as an expert witness: having access to more than common knowledge in an area, demonstrating that knowledge, and using reliable information from the scientific (addictions) community (Haugaard & Reppucci, 1988; Swenson, 1993). Second, the addictions counselor must work closely with the attorney who is using the counselor's testimony (Bossin, 1992). Third, the addictions counselor needs to be aware of how differently counseling and the law look at issues in order to speak an understandable, ethical language in the courtroom. Fourth, documented consultation may include a review of ethical guidelines, contact with an attorney, and contact with an addictions counselor.

Stevens (2008) emphasizes that court can be unnerving for mental health professionals because of a sense of professional vulnerability where one feels one's competence is being challenged. The author encourages counselors to remember the court is concerned about our opinion: The counselor is an advocate for the objective data he/she has obtained—not an advocate for the client.

Three main areas of testimony involving the addictions counselor are the DUI (driving under the influence)/DWI (driving while impaired)/OUI (operating under the influence)/OWI (operating while intoxicated); the process of addiction; and custody hearings. Only a brief summary of the first area is provided here because it is rare that counselors are asked to testify in *DUI/DWI/OUI/OWI hearings* (the label used depends on the state's legislation on using alcohol/drugs and

driving). In this assessment testimony, the addictions counselor is generally being asked to testify whether or not the person is addicted. As Shaffer and Kauffman (1985) suggest, the counselor enhances the assessment by drawing from several sources (interviews with clients and their significant others; various measurements such as self-report, psychometric, and physiological; case histories, behavioral observations). The more thorough and broad the assessment, the more likely the counselor will be viewed as an expert and have his or her testimony taken seriously. It is also critical to know the assessment instruments typically used in the state in which the counselor is testifying.

When testifying about the *process of addiction*, two areas emerge: the development of addiction and the recovery from addiction. There are different theories as to the cause of addiction, as discussed more extensively in Chapter 1. McHugh, Beckman, and Frieze (1979) organized these theories into four models:

1. *Moral* theories view the alcoholic as a degenerate who is morally weak and should be treated with punishment.

2. *Psychological* models focus on psychodynamic issues (personal pathology caused by unconscious conflicts that must be changed), personality trait issues (personality traits that cause the problems must be changed), and behavior learning (alcohol and the environment reinforcers must be changed).

3. *Sociocultural* models view the alcoholic in a problem situation containing social forces and contexts that need to be addressed.

4. *Medical* models view the alcoholic as the patient and the cause of the addiction as a physiological dysfunction.

Also, more recent *biopsychosocial* models of addiction account for both biogenetic traits and psychosocial factors. The biopsychosocial model looks at how biological aspects impact psychological aspects, which in turn impact social aspects of a person in an ongoing and interactive manner.

There is no firm agreement in the field of addictions as to the cause of addiction and the one proven method of recovery. In some parts of the country, the disease model of addiction (Jellinek, 1960) is the most widely used and respected. This model, which fits under the medical model discussed in Chapter 1, views alcoholism as a disease with symptoms that are progressive. The two key elements in this model are loss of control over drinking and progression of the disease, which ends in death. Counselors typically using this model refer to a Jellinek symptomology sheet. It is important to remember, however, that although the disease model is popular in some parts of the country, in other areas of the country, other models—such as the harm reduction model (Sorge, 1991), which encourages reduction of harm to self and others resulting from drug use—are more widely used. The harm-reduction model, as discussed at length in Chapter 5, focuses more on decreasing problems connected to using alcohol and drugs than on the amount of alcohol and drugs used. The focus is pragmatic in its discussion of harm being done to the individual and the society.

The best approach for the addiction counselor is to determine a model he or she is most comfortable using in the assessment and treatment process, a model that his or her organization recommends, and a model used by the state in which the counselor is testifying. Despite the theoretical disagreements in the field of addictions, the counselor can provide testimony on specific behaviors, a history of drinking/using-related consequences (i.e., drinking on the job, unable to quit drinking), and reports by significant others. Probably the most common model now used is the biopsychosocial model, because it is complex in its view of cause, maintenance, and cessation of the active addictive process.

Maintenance of the recovery process is also a type of testimony for the addiction counselor. This classification of testimony involves areas such as general relapse concerns, drug testing,

and support group attendance. The counselor may need to educate the court as to the danger of relapse. G. A. Marlatt and Gordon (1985) and Prochaska, DiClemente, and Norcross (1992) do an excellent job of describing the difficulties in making a behavior change and would be a good reference for the addictions counselor. Court testimony that focuses on behavioral indicators of recovery maintenance (no legal problems, apparent attendance at self-help groups, contact with addictions counselor, etc.) is more beneficial than testimony that focuses on the individual client's motivations or intentions to remain drug free (G. Miller & Kaplan, 1996).

Drug testing is one avenue for determining whether the client is free from the use of drugs. Inaba and Cohen (1989) describe approximately two dozen drug-testing methods involving samples of urine, blood, saliva, hair, and tissue. The authors also caution that no method is absolutely accurate because of problems that can occur with the technology, handling, or manipulation of the samples. If the counselor testifies about drug testing, it is important for the counselor to know the quality of the laboratory working with the specimens, the strengths and limitations of the type of drug testings used, as well as the informed consent of the client being tested (G. Miller & Kaplan, 1996).

Courts have frequently referred clients with drug/alcohol problems to attend support groups. Often, courts ask clients to have attendance slips signed by the group leader to acknowledge that they went to the meeting. The counselor needs to keep in mind that these slips can be easily forged by clients (only the first name and last initial are required for the signature) and that some groups, particularly 12-step groups, do not want to sign them because they believe it violates their group traditions. Finally, clients have often been referred to Alcoholics Anonymous (AA) by the courts; however, due to an increase in different types of self-help groups (see Chapter 8) and concerns about religious freedom (Trimpey, 1989), counselors may need to provide clients with alternative self-help group information as well as 12-step group information. Counselors must remember that the ease of forgery, group resistance to signing attendance slips, and the right to choose a self-help group that fits their values may shape the clients' behaviors toward recovery and limit the soundness of counselor testimony.

Child custody testimony may arise for the addiction counselor when one or both parents are actively using alcohol/drugs or in the recovery process. Once again, the capacity to inform the court about the addiction and recovery process is important. The additional information that the counselor needs to incorporate at this stage is that which specifically addresses child custody. Bossin (1992) recommends that counselors (a) evaluate the family to determine the child's best interest, (b) demonstrate psychological deficiency in one parent and mental health in the other, and (c) educate the court about the psychological problems. The addiction counselor needs to use these guidelines within the context of addictions and probably in conjunction with another mental health professional making the child custody assessment. Poirier (1991) encourages counselors to do very thorough evaluations in order to predict future behavior, and other authors (Howell, 1990; Remley & Miranti, 1991) encourage breadth and depth to the evaluations to improve the quality of evaluations. As stated previously, the counselor needs to acknowledge the limits to predicting parental behavior and use multiple data-gathering methods to make such predictions.

G. Miller and Kaplan (1996) offer these four suggestions for expert testimony:

1. On receiving a subpoena or verbal order, either testify, risk contempt of court by refusing to testify, or explore limited recourse strategies (appeal for privileged communication, testify in camera [chambers], or cooperate with the client's lawyer).

2. When testifying about a diagnosis of substance abuse/dependency, be thorough and use psychometric assessment instruments approved by the state in which testimony is made.

3. When testifying about drug test results, know the strengths and limitations of the drug-testing method used.

4. In response to questions about a client's potential relapse, respond by commenting on behavioral indicators of abstinence.

When child custody is involved in a substance abuse case, make sure a thorough evaluation is done and know the limits of being able to predict relapse in a recovering individual.

G. Miller and Kaplan (1996) provide 16 general guidelines for court testimony:

1. Watch other individuals testify.

2. Find out what the court expects from the testimony.

3. Be knowledgeable of current professional literature on the relevant mental health topic(s).

4. Obtain informed consent from the client.

5. Talk with the attorney representing the counselor prior to the court appearance.

6. Prepare testimony with the representing attorney and/or an experienced colleague.

7. Dress professionally for the court appearance.

8. Look confident in court, but do not appear overprepared.

9. Relax while testifying.

10. Listen carefully to the attorneys and the judge when on the stand; then take time to formulate a clear response.

11. Do not take notes to the stand.

12. Take a contact sheet with general dates and descriptions to the stand.

13. Provide testimony based on therapeutic knowledge:

- Characteristics observed in the client.

- Conversations with the client and significant others.

14. Admit not knowing an answer.

15. Be brief at cross-examination.

16. Avoid arguments with opposing counsel. (p. 28)

Additional guidelines include:

- Avoiding use of technical terminology (Brodsky & Robey, 1972; Loftus, 1991)

- Directing comments to the jury and judge (Brodsky & Robey, 1972)

- Being aware there is not a guarantee of witness immunity; therefore, the counselor may be held liable for testimony given (Binder, 2002). Note, however, that generally there is witness immunity.

- Remembering the importance of being objective, not being drawn to the advocate role (Gaughwin, 2004)

The counselor needs to listen carefully to questions; ask for questions to be repeated or rephrased if necessary; make answers honest, verbal, and direct; and address answers to the judge, explaining them if necessary. In general, be prepared for the unexpected and do not take challenges personally. (See Case Study 13.4.)

CASE STUDY 13.4

Julianna has been subpoenaed to court by the client's attorney to testify about her addicted client, who is facing a child custody battle. Her client is a heroin addict in her 30s who had previously lost custody of her three older children to the Department of Social Services. Her ex-husband, father of the youngest child, filed for child custody when her client entered drug addiction treatment. Julianna has never testified in court and is panicked over receiving her first subpoena.

1. What would you suggest she do first and why?

2. Based on your knowledge and experience, how would you suggest she prepare for testimony?

3. What suggestions for self-care would you make to her as she goes through the process of working with the legal system?

EXERCISE 13.4

With a colleague, discuss the following four items (If you have no experience in working with the legal system, complete these sentences within an imaginary context.):

1. My most positive experience with the legal system was . . . .

2. My most difficult experience with the legal system was . . . .

3. The place I feel most inadequate or vulnerable with the legal system is . . . .

4. A strategy I would like to develop to make myself stronger with regard to the legal system is . . . .

WORKING IN DIFFICULT SYSTEMS

To work effectively with others who are difficult (agency personnel, other professionals, clients), it is helpful for the counselor to have a framework and a decision-making process. The wounded healer framework and a discussion on whether to stay in the system are presented here.

Wounded Healer Theoretical Framework

Remen, May, Young, and Berland (1985) present the polarized relationship between being wounded and being healed. Often, this view, when applied to counselors, holds the expectation that the counselor is and will be immune to psychological, spiritual, and emotional vulnerabilities. Remen and colleagues, Jourard (1971), and Frankl (1963) describe the wounded healer more along a continuum than a dichotomy, where the wounded healer bridges the worlds of wellness and illness: "Rather than concealing their wounds, shamanic healers often display them as marks of the authenticity of their skills" (Remen et al., 1985, p. 84). This section is an expansion of the article by G. Miller, Wagner, Britton, and Gridley (1998).

The counselor who is able to transcend painful, tragic life experiences can bridge the mental illness and mental health worlds, bringing compassion to the therapeutic relationship (Hollis, 1989; Holmes, 1991; G. D. Miller & Baldwin, 1987). There is a power in drawing from one's personal pain—one's own sense of suffering in the world (Bein, 2008). Clients and counselors share the vulnerability, and the healed wounds of the counselor guide the counselor's choices, empathy, and provides the counselor with stamina to do therapy (Mander, 2007). One example of this bridging between mental illness and mental health worlds is addiction counseling, where counselors who are recovering addicts or who have lived in addicted systems have learned from and transcended their pain, thereby becoming wounded healers. However, untreated wounds can be destructive to counselors' lives and the lives of their clients

(A. Miller, 1981). It is important, then, for counselors to understand their own wounds so that they can do more effective work with their clients.

In this framework, the individual *counselor's history of emotional pain* is the first area addressed. These areas can be considered vulnerabilities. Because of different life experiences, these vulnerabilities vary in frequency and depth for each counselor. They may emerge most readily in counseling with countertransference issues—when the counselor projects his or her own issues onto the client. For example, an addicted female client may be difficult for a counselor to work with in therapy because she reminds the counselor of his or her addicted mother. The client may then unknowingly elicit critical, defensive, self-protective attitudes, comments, and behaviors from the counselor, simply by the interaction. These projections can also occur with coworkers, supervisors, or administrators with whom the counselor has difficulty working at the agency.

The second level of the framework is at the *system entry level*. Two concepts important to discuss before system entry discussion are chance encounters and empty self. Bandura (1982) defines a *chance encounter* as "an unintended meeting of persons unfamiliar with each other" (p. 748), which has an impact on a person's life because of liking the other person or obtaining satisfaction from the other person. The vulnerability of the individual to such encounters is enhanced by the loss of internal behavior guides and potential social rewards. Cushman (1990) discusses this vulnerability in a cultural sense: An individual has an *empty self* because of a lack of family, community, and tradition. In this experience of emptiness, a person may be vulnerable to addictive tendencies and having systems define who he or she is and what he or she does. Chance encounters with individuals and an empty sense of self can be powerfully healing or crippling experiences for the unprepared counselor: The counselor can learn from and transcend the pain or become lost in it.

When entering a system, three aspects are operating: power differential, losses, and discrepancy.

On entering the system, those with the least power will be new and lower-status individuals. As a counselor becomes more involved in the mental health system, the counselor becomes more aware of the amount of power and influence he or she holds in the system. Also affecting the influence of the system on the individual is the amount of losses experienced. Any change involves both gains and losses. The types and extremes of losses experienced in joining a new agency depend on the individual counselor. Greater losses result in greater uprootedness and vulnerability to the influence of the system. The impaired counselor may reflect the malfunctions of the work system (Stadler, Willing, Eberhage, & Ward, 1988).

Finally, the greater the discrepancy between the counselor's expectations of the job and the reality of the job, the greater the cognitive dissonance experienced by the counselor. Forsyth (1983) reports that individuals who invest in a group with high costs will emphasize the rewards, minimize the costs, and become more favorable to the group. Minimizing the costs of being involved in a system may make the counselor more vulnerable to being abused by the system: The denial about the abuse may keep the counselor from protecting himself or herself. The greater the discrepancy between the expectations and the reality of working in a mental health system, the more potential for abuse to the counselor by the system. A counselor may be abused by a system in many ways. For example, the counselor may be given the least desired on-call schedule, be asked to take on additional responsibilities without adequate compensation, and/or be harassed openly or subtly by other staff members. By contrast, counselors who are aware of manipulations they experienced as a child will be better able to protect themselves, because they are less likely to idealize others or the system, to feel helpless, or to allow themselves to be manipulated.

It is at the third level, *continuance in the system*, that critical incidents occur for the counselor. Because environments, like people, have personalities, they can affect an individual's potential, initiative, and coping (Insel & Moos, 1974). The

struggle with being at a particular mental health agency may hinge on the match between the agency's values and the individual's values. A counselor who is new to a mental health system may neglect his or her own self-care to impress others, and veterans of the mental health system may feel dethroned by the new counselor. The *critical incident* is a painful, transitional point that combines vulnerabilities and current authority figure interactions. The system authority response to a critical incident can have an impact on future interactions of the counselor within the system and the individual's feelings toward the system.

Following a critical incident, there will be a critical authority response or a compassionate authority response. The occurrence of and ramifications of the incident are blamed on the counselor in a *critical authority response*, resulting in more pain for the counselor and possibly an increase in isolation, vulnerability, self-neglect, and competitiveness within the counselor and among other counselors at the agency. In a *compassionate authority response*, the painful incident is compassionately discussed with the counselor, resulting in a reduction of pain and an increase of trust. In this response, the issue of "who started it" is not relevant; it is more important that the counselor be heard and the issue addressed. The latter response recognizes that the counselor may be responding to behavior settings in the environment (Barker & Wright, 1955)—that is, a system environment that encourages certain behaviors in individuals. In such a case, the counselor is not behaving solely out of individual characteristics, but is being shaped by the system to act in a certain manner. The latter response encourages a compassionate dialogue between the counselor and the system.

Recognition of Problems: Leaving versus Staying

The counselor needs to be able to recognize critical incidents at his or her agency and develop a strategy for approaching such problems.

Generally, such an approach involves recognition of the difficult encounter (critical incident), use of coping strategies that include stress management, and a decision to stay at or leave the agency.

Most counselors will not have difficulty recognizing the critical incident for them at an agency. As described previously, it is an incident that is uncomfortable and emotionally painful for the counselor. It is during such incidents that the counselor may reexamine his or her commitment to the field of counseling, particularly to this agency. Probably the best indicator of a critical incident is when the counselor experiences intense emotions about a work-related incident. These critical incidents may underscore an unknown or known difference in values between the counselor and the agency. The incident may also highlight the degree of the match and/or mismatch between the counselor and the agency.

While the incident itself may be difficult for the counselor, it may be even more difficult if the authority response is critical in nature. The counselor may ask himself or herself: Can I continue to do the type of counseling I value and remain at this agency? Can I survive personally in such an environment? There are a number of avenues the counselor can explore in the process of addressing these questions.

Because both individual and situational factors are related to the impact of stress on a person's health (Levi, 1990), the counselor may want to obtain a therapist to determine how much of the struggle is the counselor's and how much is the agency's. If a counselor chooses this approach, it is wise to select a therapist the counselor does not know personally or professionally. Another approach to self-reflection is to obtain a supervisor with whom the counselor can process the difficulties of the system. This supervisor would preferably be someone outside the agency who is either familiar with the dynamics of the agency or willing to learn about the dynamics. The danger of talking with only colleagues in the system is that the counselor may not be encouraged to examine thoroughly his or her own involvement in the process.

The process of determining whether to stay or leave involves self-care. The counselor needs to determine whether there is a need to stay in the system and, if so, how to survive within the difficulties of the system. Although it is preferable to operate in healthy systems, creating support groups may enhance the counselor's ability to cope with the stresses of the system. French and Raven (1959) discuss the importance of referent power with groups: When individuals identify with a group, their behavior will be consistent with that group. If a counselor has a referent group outside of the mental health system, the counselor may be able to use the referent group as an anchor, a way of surviving the upheaval of being involved in the abusive system. The referent group may provide the counselor with a model of behavior that is self-respectful, as well as provide support to the counselor during times of critical incidents.

Common stress management strategies include individual and organizational reactions (Cherniss & Dantzig, 1986). Individual techniques include relaxation (yoga, biofeedback, meditation, relaxation training, etc.) and cognitive-behavioral approaches (addressing irrational thoughts; Lazarus & Folkman, 1984). Organizational approaches such as changing jobs, providing supervision, and building in problem-solving processes may also be helpful. Although the counselor cannot rely on the agency to provide stress management strategies, the counselor can develop a support system that assists in the self-care of the counselor. R. R. Ross, Altmaier, and Russell (1989) found among doctoral-level counseling center staff that although higher job stress was associated with higher burnout, support from supervisors and colleagues was related to lower burnout. In addition, the counselor may attempt to have an impact on the system by respectfully educating influential individuals within the organization about the importance of creating a community of wellness. Witmer and Young (1996) suggest the following components be present in a wellness community: compassion, commitment, leadership, involvement, creative problem solving and conflict resolution, communication, and autonomy. (See Case Study 13.5.)

CASE STUDY 13.5

Jason is a 24-year-old addictions counselor who recently graduated from a master's program. He is single, lives alone, and has few close friends. He has little contact with his parents or siblings. Although he is not in recovery himself, he grew up in a very physically and emotionally violent family. He has never been in therapy to examine any of the issues stemming from his chaotic childhood. He is heterosexual and has come across a woman at his workplace who is a few years older than he, divorced, "pleasingly flirtatious" with him, and quick to anger. She is his clinical supervisor, and she wears low-cut tops that show her cleavage in supervision sessions, making a point to lean over when asking him to take on additional work responsibilities. When he began his job 3 months ago, he was very excited about it being his first job and making more money than he ever had in his life. However, he has recently realized that he is very tired after his long days at work, is finding himself resentful of his supervisor asking him to take on extra responsibilities and extra hours at the agency, and is irritable with his clients when they ask him for assistance. He has recently wondered whether he should stay in his job. When he brought his concerns to his supervisor recently, she became very angry and highly confrontational. She told him he was lucky to find a job right after graduating, and he should simply accept his job responsibilities without question. Jason left the meeting quite shaken. He had a difficult time sleeping the next week and focusing on his clinical work with his clients.

1. What is Jason's history of emotional pain that may make him vulnerable to system abuse?
2. How does his relationship with his supervisor fit the criteria of a chance encounter?
3. How does his life fit Cushman's model of an empty self?
4. Is he being abused at his workplace, and if so, how?
5. What was his supervisor's critical authority response?
6. How did his supervisor's response impact him and possibly trigger his "soft spots"?
7. Would you recommend that he stay or leave? Whichever option you choose for him, what specific suggestions would you have for him on the path chosen?

EXERCISE 13.5

Recall two work settings that represent the extremes (positive, negative) of your work experience in terms of matches between yourself and the work environment. For each setting (and doing only one setting at a time), jot brief answers to the following seven questions:

1. Was there a *chance encounter* with a person who had a powerful impact on my personal/professional development? If so, was I experiencing an empty-self state where I was particularly vulnerable to that chance encounter?

2. When I was new in that system, how much *power* did I have, what *losses* did I experience when taking the job, and what were the *discrepancies* between what I expected and what the job really was like?

3. What is my main professional value, and how did this match with the main value of my employer?

4. What is an example of a *critical authority* experience I had at the workplace?

5. What is an example of a *compassionate authority* experience I had at the workplace?

6. Was I abused in that work system, and if so, how?

7. Did I decide to stay or leave in response to my experiences, and what were the contributing factors in my decision?

WORKING WITH ADDICTS

Agencies can assist in the work with addicted clients by having nondiscriminatory policies for counselors regarding their treatment at the agency. Recovering counselors are often scrutinized and supervised at higher standards, may be looked over for promotions because of assumptions about their recovery, and may be viewed suspiciously if they have mood changes or performance problems (Substance Abuse and Mental Health Services Administration [SAMHSA], 2010). To prevent discriminatory treatment, agencies need to have clear, consistent standards, determine if alcohol/drug use can impair job performance, consider impact on the community in terms of treatment and agency perception, and use intervention protocols if relapse occurs (SAMHSA, 2010).

Working with clients who are addicted means the counselor needs to do some self-examination. Four areas of necessary self-examination are one's own use history, one's limits in working with this population, danger spots, and supports.

Examination of Own Use History

Addicts can be a difficult group of clients to counsel. They may be very challenging and rebellious with authority figures, such as counselors, and they may have a difficult time changing their habits and behaviors. They can be trying for any counselor, even one who has no negative history with an alcoholic/addict.

For the counselor who grew up in a home with an alcoholic parent, sibling, or relative, or who has a spouse or child who is addicted, working with addicts and alcoholics can be even more difficult. Although the chemicals used and the type of relationship may differ, the dynamics and the pain of the relationship are the same. Counselors may find themselves trying to reason with clients in the same manner they tried to reason with the addicted significant other in their lives. They may feel the same feelings of frustration and helplessness. For this type of counselor, the addict/alcoholic holds the promise for uncomfortable countertransference, which may affect the professional abilities of the counselor.

There are a number of ways in which the counselor may address such unresolved issues. First, a counselor wanting to work with addicted individuals will need to have a clear understanding of his or her current and past drug usage. This process may require an assessment from an addictions specialist. At the very least, the counselor needs to be sure no chemical abuse is presently occurring that would interfere with his or her professional abilities. A counselor who does determine that there is an addictions problem, be it through personal or professional assessment, needs to obtain treatment for the addiction as any addicted individual needs. This treatment could be through a formalized addictions program, through therapy with an addictions specialist, and/or through a self-help group. Some counselors, who are not addicted to drugs, do use illegal drugs recreationally/

socially. Counselors who do this need to be aware of the risk they run professionally and personally if they are caught with such a substance. For example, a counselor who periodically smokes marijuana may see no harm in it; however, if this counselor is arrested for purchasing or using marijuana, he or she may face negative consequences both personally and professionally. Even if a counselor does not use illegal drugs, he or she needs to be prepared for running into clients in social gatherings where there is alcohol use (e.g., a bar).

The counselor who does not have an addiction problem, but has lived with or currently lives with someone who does, may also want to join a self-help organization. Groups such as Al-Anon, Nar-Anon, and SOS were discussed in Chapters 5 and 8. The questions used in Chapter 8 to assist a counselor in helping a client find a good match with a self-help group can also be used by counselors who need a self-help group to cope with their own or a loved one's addiction. Some special concerns arise, however, when a counselor joins a self-help group.

When members of self-help groups find out that a counselor is in the group, the members may be tempted to try to obtain free counseling from the counselor. They may also have difficulty imagining counselors having problems and, as a result, not respect the counselor for joining the group or not take the counselor's issues as seriously as those of other group members. Although anonymity is encouraged in different self-help groups, a member might accidentally let others know that the counselor has joined the group. Such a break of anonymity may have an impact on the counselor's professional life. Therefore, a counselor joining a self-help group needs to answer four specific questions:

1. In what type of group am I comfortable letting members know I am a counselor?

2. What type of negative impact might I experience professionally if the self-help group

members were to let others in the community know that I have joined the group?

3. What types of limits must I put on the sharing I do in the group, given my profession?

4. How will I set limits on the time I will listen to others, and how can I make sure that my own needs are being met?

Some counselors cope with this situation by attending meetings away from the area in which they live or work. Other counselors attend meetings specifically designed for professionals or professional counselors, or they may attend meetings and talk only in general ways about concerns they have in their lives. Also, some counselors choose not to attend meetings but spend time reading the literature from the self-help organizations to obtain support. There is a fine line between running from your own issues and making yourself vulnerable professionally. Although surgeons are never expected to have the objectivity to operate on themselves, counselors are often expected by laypeople not to have any personal problems if they are "good" counselors.

A third approach to addressing your own issues is to obtain therapy to address these unresolved issues. Therapy will be most beneficial if the counselor chosen as the therapist is knowledgeable in addictions counseling. The chosen therapist can understand some of the difficulties inherent in working with addicted individuals and can perceive how these interactions have an impact on the counselor-as-client with regard to the counselor's personal history.

Self-help group attendance, self-help group literature, and therapy can be used in whatever mix-and-match fashion that seems most beneficial to the counselor and that counselor's situation. Certain factors, such as living in a small town, may influence the treatment selected by the counselor. Yet, even if a counselor does not live in a small town, the small-townness of the addiction recovery world may still have an impact on the counselor. As with any client, counselors in the client role must be respected for the values they hold.

Knowledge of Own Limitations

Counselors who work with addicts need to be aware of their own limitations as they apply to the use of chemicals/drugs, soft spots for the counselor, and danger spots for counselors who are in recovery and those who are not. Sometimes, it almost seems assumed that the counselor needs to be addicted to work with addicts effectively. However, both addicted and nonaddicted counselors have issues they need to address in the counseling context with the addicted individual. The face of the issue may change, but the existence of the issue does not.

Both addicted and nonaddicted counselors must look at their own chemical usage. Addicted counselors need to remain chemically free, and nonaddicted counselors need to determine whether they want to use. Three questions must be addressed by the nonaddicted counselor:

1. Should I give up the use of mood-altering substances in order to work with addicted clients?

2. Can I understand the addictive issues with mood-altering substances if I continue to use them?

3. If I continue to use mood-altering substances, how will I respond in situations where I meet addicted clients and I am under the influence of the substances?

These types of questions need to be addressed by the counselor who is planning to work with addicted clients. At the very least, nonaddicted counselors may need to work on changing a habit or addiction that they have struggled with in order to understand and have compassion for the addicted client's struggle with change. Addicted clients will frequently ask nonaddicted counselors how they can counsel them when they are not addicted. Counselors need to be prepared to answer such a question based on limits they have set on their own chemical usage and habits they have tried to change. Many addicted clients

will be satisfied with a thoughtful, genuine answer by a nonaddicted counselor.

Both addicted and nonaddicted counselors will have soft spots in certain areas that will make them less comfortable in working with clients on their issues. It is important for the counselor to know these limitations and then work within them. For example, a counselor may work more effectively with same-gender clients if the alcoholic/addict in his or her background was the opposite gender or may work more effectively with certain types of addicts (based on their drug of choice) or with addicts from a certain socioeconomic status level. A counselor may want to reduce these limitations by dealing with personal countertransference issues in his or her own therapy, or the counselor may simply state that he or she is unable to work with that population due to personal values or life experiences. If the counselor works at a mental health agency, these limitations must be stated from the start so that any intake process will take the counselor's preferences into account. If the counselor works privately, it is helpful to state these limitations in a manner most respectful to clients and to let possible referral sources know of these limitations. Experiences in working with different addicted individuals with good supervision and self-examination of their own issues can allow counselors to stretch themselves yet learn the limitations that are not negotiable.

Danger Spots (Addicted Counselors)

Addicted counselors have some areas they need to be aware of in their work with addicted clients. It is often assumed that addicted counselors have some time in their own recovery process before they begin counseling others. This minimum is often established by addictions counselor certification or licensure boards and is typically in the range of 1 to 2 years. Kinney (2006) also raises the point that people enter the addiction counseling field and then realize they may have a substance abuse problem. In this situation, the recommendation is to carefully evaluate and monitor the situation, which may require the counselor taking a leave of absence (Kinney, 2006).

Because of their addiction, these counselors may experience a relapse while they are practicing as counselors. There are a number of potential relapse risks for the recovering counselor. Some of these are: their original motivation for coming in to the field; loss of self-help groups once they work in the field; becoming overly involved with their clients or their work; and identifying too strongly with clients (Doukas & Cullen, 2010). Recovering counselors who relapse need to be aware that the relapse may have a significant impact on clients (negative feelings) and that the relapse needs to be addressed in a straightforward manner with clients after such an approach is discussed with supervisors and experienced colleagues (Kinney, 2006). Ethical and client implications of a relapse need to be carefully explored (Haley, 2008).

When a relapse occurs, it is best for the counselor to be evaluated by someone who works outside the system or organization for whom the counselor works. Another option is to contact the state certification or licensure board and determine its process for ethically handling such a situation. If the counselor is certified or licensed in the state, he or she must inform the board of the relapse and follow the board's recommendations. If the counselor works with addicted individuals in some capacity, but is not licensed, the organization for whom he or she works will determine the best way to address the situation. For example, in larger organizations, the counselor could be transferred to a no-patient-contact job (Bissell & Royce, 1994). However, whatever the situation, when an addicted person relapses, it is best to consult with someone outside of the organization to be sure that the addicted employee will not be enabled by the organization.

Another common issue for addicted counselors centers on the actual treatment of addicts. Recovering addicted counselors may be tempted to treat clients in the same manner in which they were treated. This may be especially true for the counselor who views a client (and the client's usage) as very similar to himself or herself. Recovering addicted counselors need to remember that each client is an individual and each recovery path is unique. The most important concern is to assist the client in becoming sober; the path to obtaining that goal may be less important. In addition, the counselor needs to avoid the temptation of competing with the client as to who had the worse addiction problem or what is sometimes called being "junkie of the year."

A final issue for recovering addicted counselors may be attendance at self-help groups. They will need to determine how comfortable they are being at meetings with their clients and how to handle such dual relationships. This crossover may be more common in small towns or with certain populations that have a small-town atmosphere due to being an oppressed group (e.g., gays and lesbians) or a small group in terms of numbers (e.g., deaf individuals). A counselor may need to consider attending the same meetings, but being cautious of what he or she discusses, or attend meetings specifically for professional counselors. Kinney (2006) describes these people as having two hats and recommends "working one's own program," having clear boundaries (e.g., not talking about work at meetings), and avoiding superiority feelings with colleagues (e.g., the recovering counselor knows more than other counselors because he or she is in recovery). (See Case Study 13.6.)

CASE STUDY 13.6

Jake is a recovering addict who has worked as a licensed addictions counselor in a small town for 8 years. He was sober 10 years, until a relapse a month ago following the sudden death of his mother. Jake is well respected in the local community and at the treatment center where he works. He has not told anyone (including his sponsor and his NA group) of his relapse with cocaine. He is afraid he will lose his job, his wife, and his reputation if he speaks of his relapse. Many of his former clients attend the same self-help groups he attends.

1. If Jake came to you as a colleague for advice, what recommendations would you make about action he should take?

2. What are your professional responsibilities as a counselor if you are aware that Jake has relapsed?

3. What action would you take professionally and personally to be of assistance to Jake?

EXERCISE 13.6

This exercise is for addiction counselors who are in addiction recovery. Answer the following self-reflection questions and, if comfortable, discuss with a trusted individual.

1. Relapse prevention:

   a. Do I feel strong in my recovery?

   b. If not, what are some areas that I need to address to bring myself more into balance?

2. Recovery formula:

   a. What is my own personal formula for recovery (i.e., type and frequency of self-help meetings, type and frequency of contact with sponsor, readings)?

   b. What are the core components, the most important aspects of this recovery formula for me?

3. Countertransference:

   a. What parts of my own recovery formula might I think are so important (e.g., attending self-help meetings) that I may insist my clients take part in those same activities in order to stay sober?

   b. How might I provide a check and balance in my counseling to avoid such projections?

4. Dual relationships:

   a. How might I handle possible dual relationships when my recovery path crosses with my clients?

   b. Specifically, with whom would I feel comfortable and safe discussing such issues?

Danger Spots (Nonaddicted Counselors)

Nonaddicted counselors may have some issues particular to their work with addicted clients, such as difficulty understanding the struggles clients experience in making a behavior change. As stated previously, it may help with their compassion for addicts if these counselors attempt to change a habit with which they struggle. These counselors may want to obtain supervision and/or therapy to address unresolved issues they have with addicts they have known, which promotes countertransference. This countertransference may be overly critical, enabling, or fluctuate between the extremes, depending on the clients with whom these counselors work.

A second problem can be the bias held against nonaddicts working in the addictions field. When a nonaddicted counselor is attempting to understand recovery-related issues and struggles, it may be best to approach clients in a manner that encourages dialogue. A nonaddicted counselor who acknowledges his or her own ignorance about addiction is more likely to be educated by both clients and addicted counselors about the recovery concerns. If nonaddicted counselors seek self-help group assistance, they will likely run into struggles similar to those of addicted counselors. Thus, they will need to be prepared to address these same concerns.

A third possible problem is nonaddicted counselors examining their personal usage of alcohol and drugs. By thoughtfully approaching what and where to use alcohol and drugs in their personal lives, the counselor can anticipate and possibly prevent both negative consequences and awkward social situations. (See Case Study 13.7.)

CASE STUDY 13.7

Ruth is a new addictions counselor who just began facilitating a DUI group at her work. She is not a recovering addict, but she is the daughter of an alcoholic. Her childhood was very traumatic for her in terms of physical, psychological, and emotional abuse from her alcoholic father. She has had some short-term therapy for these issues and felt relatively resolved about them for the past year. She has been facilitating the group for a couple of months and overall has enjoyed the challenges. Recently, a member came into the group who looks, acts, and talks like her father. Although she has been very comfortable with group members in the past, when this group member speaks or even sits quietly in the group, she experiences a range of emotions: fear, anger, and hurt. Ruth is confused and overwhelmed with the intensity of her feelings. She is afraid to talk with her supervisor or colleagues about her reactions to this member, because she is concerned that they will view her as unprofessional. She has rationalized that it is okay to not say anything to anyone because the DUI group is just about over, she never had another client who elicited such a reaction from her, and she is sure it will not be an issue in the future.

1. If you believe that Ruth's course of action is wrong, what specifically is she doing wrong?

2. If you could intervene in the situation with Ruth, what action would you take?

3. If possible, what advice would you give Ruth about actions she needs to take for both herself and the welfare of her client?

EXERCISE 13.7

Answer the following self-reflection questions, and, if comfortable, discuss with a trusted individual.

1. Habit change:
   a. What is a habit with which I struggle?

    b. Am I willing to abstain from this habit for 2 weeks? If so, what supports would I need to place in my life for such a shift to happen?

    c. What thoughts and feelings arise when I even think of making such a habit change?

2. Painful experiences with addicts:

    a. Who are the addicts I have known in my life personally who have been most hurtful to me?

    b. Who are the addicts I have known professionally who have been most hurtful to me?

    c. What are three common ways these two groups of individuals have been hurtful to me?

    d. How might these hurts surface as I work with clients who are addicted?

    e. How would I handle my intense emotions if they are triggered by a client?

3. Professional collaboration:

    a. Who is an addiction professional I trust and with whom I can process questions about the addictive process?

    b. If I do not know someone like that, who might I approach to develop such a contact?

    c. If I do not have someone in mind, how might I set up my work life to enhance collaboration with that individual?

4. Professional discrimination:

    a. Have I experienced discrimination by others (professionals, clients) because I am not in addiction recovery?

    b. If so, what were some of the most stinging or frustrating experiences?

    c. How might I handle such discrimination in the future?

Same Support

The issue of attending the same support group has been discussed previously for both addicted and nonaddicted counselors. Another related issue is having a mentor or sponsor in a self-help group who also served as a mentor or sponsor to a client. Sometimes this situation occurs by accident, and sometimes it is due to small-town meetings or minority population meetings. The sponsor in this situation may be the critical component. The sponsor needs to make sure that he or she has good boundaries regarding the confidence of the sponsee. The counselor needs to reinforce these boundaries in the counseling session by limiting conversations about the sponsor as much as possible or providing minimal self-disclosure with the client. It may be easiest for all concerned if the counselor obtains a different sponsor while working with the client on therapy issues.

SELF-CARE

The increasing and ever-changing financial and clinical aspects to mental health work can place a significant amount of stress on counselors (Acker, 2011). In such a climate of change, self-care is critical for counselors. Sowa, May, and Niles (1994) underscore the importance of self-care for counselors by reporting studies that demonstrate a negative correlation between burnout and coping strategies/self-care: The more coping strategies, the less burnout. Burnout has been defined as consisting of three dimensions: exhaustion (emotional), depersonalization, and a lowering of personal accomplishment perceptions (Gallavan & Newman, 2013). Burnout has also been called *compassion fatigue* and *vicarious trauma* (Warren, Morgan, Morris, & Morris, 2010) as well as secondary traumatic stress disorder (James,

2008) and negative countertransference (Greene, Kane, Christ, Lynch, & Corrigan, 2006).

If a counselor does not develop effective coping strategies, he or she may leave the field of counseling (Cherniss, 1991) or continue to practice counseling when impaired (Emerson & Markos, 1996). However, counselors are rarely taught about self-care in their academic preparation, yet they work in a demanding field that consistently exposes them to the dysfunctional behavior of humans that can be discouraging, disheartening, and stressful. We are trained to care for others and tend to overlook our own needs (O'Halloran & Linton, 2000). Our altruism can work against us as we become caught in superhuman heroic actions and view ourselves as invulnerable to stress as well as impairment (Shallcross, 2013a). We tend to see people at their worst and hear their worst struggles—we hear difficult stories (Shallcross, 2013a). This stress can result in professional or personal problems for the counselor (Hendricks, Bradley, Brogan, & Brogan, 2009).

To prevent relapse or dysfunctional behavior in the counselor, each counselor must develop an individualized approach as well as a commitment to self-care. This means self-care needs to be a lifestyle where we learn to manage stress, make healthy decisions, and incorporate behaviors that invite a balanced lifestyle on a daily basis (Shallcross, 2013a). Additionally, counselors may need to turn to supervisors, peers, and in-service trainings as interventions to prevent burnout (Acker, 2011). We need to protect ourselves against burnout by focusing on our own needs even though our lives are complex and demanding (Skovhold, 2012; Williams, Richardson, Moore, Gambrel, & Keeling, 2010). For addiction counselors who are in recovery, the negative impact of relapse can be reduced through systemic intervention as early as possible through policies that address and treat it rather than disguise it or punish it with immediate termination (Jones, Sells, and Rehfuss, 2009).

The attempt in this section is to avoid "shoulding" the reader or providing a pat formula for self-care. Rather the reader is encouraged to develop a self-care practice that is humane, self-respectful, and realistic; a self-care practice that is flexible and fits one's life and values personally and professionally. We hold an ideal of self-care as a guide, but practice it with flexibility that reflects self-compassion.

Guidelines to Realistic Self-Care

The counseling field may reinforce behaviors that are not self-care oriented. For example, in some agencies, the highly respected counselor is one who may have difficulty setting limits in giving to others, perhaps too idealistic and dedicated (Emerson & Markos, 1996). This counselor may be willing to fill in whenever someone is needed, will work overtime without pay, or will drop his or her schedule to meet the needs of others. Although this counselor may be appreciated and valued, if he or she does not practice self-care, this individual will likely burn out on the job. Furthermore, Gladding (1991) reports that counselors may abuse themselves by acting in dysfunctional ways on the job and by not setting necessary boundaries between themselves and their clients or colleagues. Wearing yourself out at a job appears related to negative perceptions about yourself, your job, and your clients (Cummings & Nall, 1983).

One way to prevent job burnout is to examine your counseling philosophy. Some self-help phrases such as "Progress, not perfection" and "Be responsible for the effort, not the outcome" may help counselors realize the limits of what they can do. "Progress, not perfection" means that the counselor may not be perfect either professionally or personally but that the counselor does not need to give up on improvement simply because perfection is not attainable. Examining yourself with too critical of an eye can result in a sense of being discouraged and overwhelmed by your flaws and limitations, where you may simply give up on self-improvement. The "Progress, not perfection" philosophy encourages the counselor to continue to try to make improvements on him- or herself no matter how minuscule they may seem. Such a balanced perspective may help the counselor continue to feel encouraged about his or her work. For example, a counselor may need to carefully choose workshops and trainings where both accurate, challenging professional perspectives are presented and opportunities are provided for the counselor to catch his or her breath personally (e.g., getting a break from work by relaxing while learning). Such an experience can rejuvenate the counselor both professionally and personally.

The second adage, "Be responsible for the effort, not the outcome," can also assist the counselor in maintaining a balanced perspective. A counselor is responsible only for making the best effort he or she can. This does not mean that the client will be able to stay sober, nor does it mean that others may not hold the counselor accountable for his or her counseling efforts. This philosophy, though, may help the counselor realize that there are limits on what can be provided to the client. Counselors are metaphorically standing in a river and need to work with whom or what floats their way on the river: Some objects may be missed, some may be able to be worked with for only a short time, and some may stay until they are more in balance.

Focusing on a responsibility to make the best effort possible can help the counselor remember what he or she is in control of, where the counselor can have an impact, and realistically let go of what cannot be impacted. Self-care is both individual and in relation to others (Domar & Dreher, 2000). Counselors need to renew themselves and nurture their own happiness (Willer, 2009). We need to nourish ourselves physically, emotionally, and spiritually. We cannot nourish our clients if we do not nurture ourselves (Hood & Ersever, 2009).

It is critical that we practice self-care while we care for others. G. Miller (2002), in discussing her response to mental health work as a 9/11 disaster mental health counselor with the American Red Cross, reports that self-care, caring for

ourselves and others, provides us with hope and meaning to face the world. Wellness strategies that include the physical, emotional, social, spiritual, and intellectual components are encouraged for disaster mental health counselors, as well as counselors in general, to facilitate resilience and client welfare (Lambert & Lawson, 2013). Self-care has an important influence on therapy (Norcross & Barnett, 2008a; Warren et al., 2010); therefore, counselors have an ethical and moral responsibility to be committed to self-care. The areas for self-care include mind, body, emotions, and spirit.

In terms of the *mind*, counselors are often aware of the need for challenges and positive thinking to encourage themselves. There is also a need to be aware of leisure activities where we lose ourselves in manners that are not harmful to ourselves. Domar and Dreher (2000) state we typically lose leisure and creative time when we are stressed. Losing ourselves requires a sense of timelessness and playfulness where we forget our problems. *Flow* is an activity that involves "skills, concentration, and perseverance—an activity where one can become lost" (Csikszentmihalyi, 1999, p. 825) while being challenged. Nothing else matters during our experience of engagement in an enjoyable activity where we experience harmony and self-integration. The enjoyment involves both novelty and accomplishment. We are happy, then, because of *how* an activity is done rather than *what* is done. G. Miller (2001) states that counselors can become caught in a professional flow by being lost in the skillful process of counseling. Domar and Dreher (2000) state that the experience of flow reduces our anxiety, allows us to witness negative thoughts, and helps us connect with our creativity.

In terms of the *body*, counselors are also aware of the need for eating, sleeping, and exercising correctly. Counselors need to learn to listen to their bodies, because their bodies will not lie: The body will not say it is relaxed when it feels stress. The self-help acronym of HALT may help the counselor here. This acronym is meant as a temperature gauge for self: Am I **H**ungry, **A**ngry,

Lonely, or Tired? By doing this simple check, counselors can target an area that needs to be addressed, take a break, and bring themselves back into balance. Yet taking breaks also requires an ease. For example, a counselor who works intensely and then heads off for an intense vacation or attempts to hurriedly shift to a relaxation mode may find himself or herself with an experience like the bends (decompression sickness). Taking a break from the stress may require the counselor to gradually prepare for the relaxation. Again, a counselor taking a vacation may want to schedule a day both before and after the vacation to help prepare for the exit and the reentry into the professional world.

Exercise is also a critical component of self-care. In a review of the literature, Lehmann and Herkenham (2012) report that physical exercise and psychosocial activities enhance resilience in humans by improving cognitive functioning and reducing maladaptive behaviors when under stress. It has also been shown to increase self-esteem, energy, and physical health and decrease stress, anxiety, depression, fatigue, and aging (Milkman & Sunderwirth, 2010). It has been called, "The Magic Bullet" (Milkman & Sunderwirth, 2010). It is important to find exercise that fits one's lifestyle, one's personal and professional lives, and be a form of exercise that one enjoys (Milkman & Sunderwirth, 2010).

Counselors also need to respond to their *psychological needs* by giving themselves room to be away from work and take part in thinking activities that focus on self (journal writing, own therapy), enjoyable activities (reading for pleasure, the arts, reexperiences with pleasurable books, movies), and allowance for being human (crying, expressing anger, experiencing pleasure, playing).

Counselors are also aware of the need to express thoughts and feelings in "I" statements and to respond to their *emotional* needs. G. Miller (2002) states that counselors need to be aware of their social supports and be with people who see them as people, not in the role of being a counselor.

Possibly the area that counselors are least familiar with is the *spirit*. This area does not necessarily mean religious, but it is the basis for answering the questions: What keeps my spirit alive? What makes me glad to be alive, interested in living, and want to face the day? It is this area, these interests, that must be incorporated into the lives of therapists to keep them alive and healthy. What is it that provides meaning, purpose, hope, and enjoyment in life? In the spiritual dimension, the counselor needs to find activities and people who rejuvenate his or her sense of life and hope. For some, this may be nature; for others, it may be hearing a doctrine that inspires them to be the best they can be and accept who they are. The senses exercise (Exercise 13.8) may especially help the counselor, because it does not involve logic, but rather the experience of feeling cared for.

One block to self-care for counselors seems to be the illusion that self-care takes another chunk of time from the counselor—that it requires a lot of time, energy, or money. Such a perspective can result in the counselor becoming so overwhelmed that it seems like too much to care for himself or herself. The approach to self-care being advocated here is self-care on the run. Most counselors have very demanding work schedules and personal lives. They need to learn to practice self-care in spurts as time and opportunity allow (rather than wait for a significant period of time off work) or make a simple shift to set off a chain reaction in their life. In small, regular ways, the counselor must fuse his or her life with activities that keep the spirit alive and nurture the interest in work. For example, during a stressful workday, a counselor may need to find brief breaks and do something enjoyable, such as take a short walk, listen to some music, talk with a friend, or simply wear comfortable clothes.

One way to do this self-care is to examine your typical work schedule. Exercise 13.9 addresses this area. Organizing his or her work schedule can help the counselor manage stress more easily and build in a structure that supports self-care, or at least the counselor can diagnose sources of stress that may be more difficult to address than others. For example, a counselor may need to shift from one professional role to another numerous times in a day (supervisor, counselor, employee), and on those days when role shifts are numerous or significant, the counselor may need to practice even more self-care. By becoming aware of the stress and responding to it as quickly as possible, the counselor can reduce the impact of long-term stress and handle the current situation as best as possible.

Yet self-care requires that counselors do it within the context of their life. For example, at a counselor training, a participant said to this author, "I'm just too tired to practice self-care right now." What we discussed was how this counselor needed to practice self-care in the current context of her life by easing off her expectations of herself and not allowing herself to add some type of self-improvement component to her life, but rather respect her state of being tired.

There may also be times that the counselor can more easily and readily practice self-care than others and times that the counselor needs to take a longer break to catch his or her breath. The point is that the counselor needs to be self-aware and attempt to find a realistic, self-respectful way to care for self. The self-care exercise through the senses (Exercise 13.8) may assist the counselor in developing a self-care approach. As stated previously, our bodies cannot lie, and we can use our senses to help us find ways to respond to ourselves in a caring manner. Finally, there may be other times that are extremely stressful in a counselor's life. The American Psychological Association's (APA; 2001) pamphlet on resilience for practitioners in response to the September 11, 2001, attack on America suggests greater self-monitoring during such times. Specifically emphasized is the nurturing of our bodies, responding to the awareness of our stress points, focusing on our relationships, attending to our spiritual needs, and being involved in activities to balance work. Such factors facilitate resilience in the individual.

Resilience is ordinary, not magical (Masten, 2001), and it helps us cope with life's difficulties and adversities such as outlined in the wounded healer framework. There are five main resiliency concepts: (1) resilience can be learned (people can learn to bounce back); (2) development of resilience is a personal, unique process; (3) difficult times can happen even if a person is resilient; (4) resilience is not an extraordinary part of a person; and (5) resilience requires time and effort because it is an ongoing process (Masten, 2001). These five concepts are expressed in the 10 ways to build resilience (discussed in Chapter 9) are published in the brochure of the American Psychological Association (Discovery Health Channel & APA, 2002) as a part of their packet, *Aftermath: The Road to Resilience.* These 10 factors, which can be used as guidelines for counselors as well as with clients, are:

1. Making connections
2. Avoiding seeing crises as insurmountable
3. Accepting change as a part of living
4. Moving toward one's goals
5. Taking decisive actions
6. Looking for self-discovery opportunities
7. Nurturing a positive view of self
8. Keeping things in perspective
9. Maintaining a hopeful outlook
10. Taking care of self

It is also important for the counselor to practice ongoing self-compassion and forgiveness. The counselor must learn to aim for his or her best, both personally and professionally, and then let it go. Although these may sound like lofty goals, the counselor also needs to prepare for a sense of failure and/or helplessness. Compassion in general moves us as people to respond to the suffering of others. Self-compassion is the same approach to one's own suffering: "one is kind and understanding toward oneself when failure, inadequacy, or misfortune is experienced" (Neff, 2008, p. 95). Pain, imperfection is experienced by all humans. We can respond to our own suffering in a balanced way, avoiding extremes of suppressing/denying or exaggerating/dramatizing (Neff, 2008).

In this perspective, all people, including ourselves, deserve compassion. Neff (2008) describes self-compassion as being composed of three factors: self-kindness; recognition of a common humanity (pain, imperfection, mortality, vulnerability are experienced by everyone); and mindfulness (being aware of our negative emotions in response to our own suffering; not letting them control us, but also not ignoring the pain). It has also been defined by experienced counselors as: being gentle with self, being mindful, being aware we are all in this together, speaking our truth, having spiritual awareness, and having professional ethics (Patsiopoulos & Buchanan, 2011). To experience self-compassion, we need to be aware of our pain and have a balanced, humane, and kind response to ourselves and our reactions to our suffering. Self-compassion can facilitate the process of self-forgiveness when at times we need to forgive ourselves for our mistakes. Smedes (1984) presents a forgiveness model of four states: hurt, hate, heal, and coming together. The focus of the stages is as their labels imply and will be explored here.

Counselors may feel wronged by their clients, their clients' families, the organization for which they work, or their own powerlessness in helping their clients. They may need to practice forgiveness with others as well as themselves in order to continue working as counselors. In the *hurt stage*, the counselor needs to feel the hurt and the wrong that has occurred. In the *hate stage*, the counselor needs to allow himself or herself to experience the hatred and the urge for revenge to right the wrong. In the *heal stage*, the counselor begins to feel free of the hurt and hatred and look at the wrongdoer in a different light. Finally, in the *coming together stage*, the counselor begins to invite the other into his or her life. In terms of self, counselors can experience a similar process. They may hurt when recognizing their failure, hate self for making such a failure, heal by beginning to integrate the judging self with the failure self, and come together by integrating the failure into the fabric of their life.

Whether this process is other- or self-focused (or both), this process cannot be hurried, nor, as Smedes (1984) suggests, can stages be skipped. Therapists must learn to acknowledge and learn from their own mistakes and forgive themselves for their humanness, even though others may continue to hold them accountable for their behavior. The counselor must work at the practice of forgiveness to retain or regain a balanced perspective on self, others, and life. This overall perspective is captured in Saakvitne's (2002) RICH (Respect, Information, Connection, Hope) guidelines to reduce stress. *Respect* means that the counselor knows his or her own limits, needs, and experience. *Information* means understanding therapy risks, being self-aware, and knowing your own work. *Connection* means being connected to self, others, and community. *Hope* means to have, give/receive, and live it.

Importance of Commitment to Self-Care

Frequently, in working with addicted clients, counselors talk with them about taking care of their own needs. These words will appear more meaningful and have more basis if the clients can look to the therapists to see how the therapists take care of themselves. If counselors do not set limits or care for their bodies, minds, emotions, and spirits, their words may look empty for their clients. G. Miller (2001) states that self-examination and self-care commitment can reduce suffering and increase happiness in the counselor, thereby providing a role model for clients, as well as having a contagion effect on them and assisting the counselor in operating from a place of balance. The exercises at the end of this section are designed to facilitate counselor awareness.

It is important for the counselor to personalize and individualize a self-care plan. What is self-care for one individual may not be self-care for another. Also, what is self-care at one point in a person's life is not necessarily the best self-care at another point. A counselor may find it helpful to discuss how to practice a self-care plan with someone who knows him or her well both personally and professionally. For instance, a counselor may want to have more physical exercise in his or her life but need to look at the type and frequency of the exercise program so it is not another burden. Also, the counselor needs to approach self-care with a balanced perspective so it does not become a rigid formula at odds with a flexible, reasonable self-care approach. As Domar and Dreher (2000) state, be aware, gentle, flexible, and focus on desire when developing a self-care plan. O'Halloran and Linton (2000) provide a description of self-care resources for counselors in terms of social, emotional, cognitive, physical, spiritual, and vocational aspects.

In general, counselors can examine their work life from an overall self-care perspective by asking five questions such as:

1. Where do I spend time physically at work, and is that space comfortable for me physically, emotionally, psychologically, spiritually?

2. Do I take time to eat a meal, and if I do, is it without interruption?

3. Do I visit (in person, phone, e-mail) with people I like with whom I work?

4. Do I leave work to do something to break up the routine (walk, receive a massage, shop)?

5. Can meetings be held in a different location that still invite professional behavior but are more relaxing?

Families, loved ones, employers, and clients cannot be expected to know or respond to all of the demands put on therapists. In fact, loved ones may knowingly or unknowingly add to the stress of the counselor by their reasonable or unreasonable requests to have their own wants and needs met. Employers may focus on absenteeism and productivity rather than the job stress (Weir, 2013). Exercise 13.9 explores some of the issues related to role conflicts of the counselor that may contribute to stress. A commitment to self-care is critical if counselors plan to stay alive professionally and personally. Self-nurturance is a lifelong commitment (Domar & Dreher, 2000; Shallcross, 2013a). (See Case Study 13.8.)

CASE STUDY 13.8

Clyde is an addictions counselor at a local mental health center and has worked in the field for the past 15 years. He has been married, for the second time, for the past 5 years. Clyde has worked a 12-step recovery program for 17 years. At work, he believes he is increasingly asked to do more with less and feels frustrated with how he is asked to know more about the field of addictions (working with specific issues of sexual abuse and domestic violence) and working with special populations (women and racial minorities). Clyde is also upset that his agency may be having cutbacks, which will mean more responsibility for him. In particular, the new director of his agency called Clyde into her office and yelled at him for being "too independent " on the job and compared him with recent graduates working at the agency, whom she views as more open to teamwork and new ideas. Since that incident, he has spoken very little to others at work except to say that he feels burned out and overwhelmed by stress. He has lost interest in activities he used to enjoy, such as car racing and watching sports.

1. What type of authority response did Clyde experience, and how did it affect him?
2. What recommendations would you make to Clyde about staying or leaving the agency? The field of counseling?
3. What recommendations would you make to him about self-care?

EXERCISE 13.8

Choose someone with whom you feel comfortable for this exercise. Then briefly answer each of the three items under the five main headings being discussed:

1. Hearing
   - One of my favorite *sounds* is:
   - My strongest positive memory of this *sound* is:
   - I promise you I will include this *sound* in my life by:
2. Touching
   - One of my favorite *things to touch* is:
   - My strongest positive memory of this *body experience* is:
   - I promise you I will include this *body experience* more in my life by:
3. Seeing
   - One of my favorite *sights* is:
   - My strongest positive memory of this *sight* is:
   - I promise you I will include this *sight* more in my life by:
4. Smelling
   - One of my favorite *smells* is:
   - My strongest positive memory of this *smell* is:
   - I promise you I will include this *smell* in my life by:
5. Tasting
   - One of my favorite *tastes* is:
   - My strongest positive memory of this *taste* is:
   - I promise you I will include this *taste* more in my life by:

EXERCISE 13.9

Draw one circle per life role as though your life roles were a part of a solar system. Choose 7 to 10 major life roles. Place those roles most important to you in the center and those of increasingly less importance away from the center. Then talk with another person to complete these five sentences:

1. I have drawn my role system this way because I value . . . .
2. My roles that complement each other in terms of time, energy, and money are . . . .
3. My roles that work against each other in terms of time, energy, and money are . . . .
4. The roles that typically help my self-care are . . . .
5. The roles that typically block my self-care are . . . .

Now redraw your role system as you would like to have it appear. Discuss with another person what blocks you from having the role system this way.

EXERCISE 13.10

Draw out a typical workweek schedule for yourself generally describing your activities (clients, meetings, lunches, etc.). Circle those activities that are breaks you take for relaxation or pleasure. Then list at least three major sources of general stress and one major *daily* source of stress. Finally, recall one particularly stressful month this past year and make a list of common themes of stress during that month.

Now compare your lists of stress (general, daily, monthly) and look for at least three common stressors among them. Keep a list of these stressors along with a list of relaxation or pleasure activities at your workplace. During a high-stress time, diagnose and treat your stress. If possible, spend time with someone who knows you well personally and professionally to discuss your lists and how you might be able to make healthy changes for yourself.

SUMMARY

This chapter highlights significant personal and professional issues in the arenas of ethics, law, agency, working with addicts, and self-care. Counselors are encouraged to stay current with these issues by joining professional organizations; reading current theoretical research articles in journals and books; attending workshops, courses, and conventions; and working closely with other colleagues in the field of addictions counseling. Given the current, rapid changes in the mental health service delivery system, a counselor needs to work within a network of other professionals in order to be both self-protective and appropriately concerned with the client's welfare. All counselors need to be concerned with these personal and professional issues in order to provide the highest quality of addictions counseling possible.

QUESTIONS

1. What are some common ethical dilemmas facing addiction counselors?

2. How can a counselor avoid ethical dilemmas?

3. What questions can counselors ask themselves to clarify their relationships with clients?

4. What are some basic documentation guidelines?

5. What are common court involvements for addiction counselors?

6. What are some general guidelines for testifying in court? Specific guidelines for substance abuse cases?

7. What are the components of a wounded healer theoretical framework?

8. What process can a counselor use to decide whether to stay or leave an agency?

9. What are some ways for counselors to address their own issues?

10. What are danger spots for addicted counselors? Nonaddicted counselors?

11. What are some guidelines for realistic counselor self-care?

READINGS/RESOURCES/WEBSITES

SUGGESTED READINGS

Ethical/Legal

Anderson, B. S. (2008). *The counselor and the law* (5th ed.). Alexandria, VA: American Counseling Association.

This book provides an overview of the legal aspects of counseling.

Berton, J. D. (2014). *Ethics for addiction professionals*. Hoboken, NJ: Wiley.

This book has 19 chapters divided into four sections on protecting the client, clinical information, clinician, and community.

Bissell, L. C., & Royce, J. E. (1994). *Ethics for addiction professionals* (2nd ed). Center City, MN: Hazelden.

This 97-page book has seven chapters that look at ethics in regard to the worker, competence, patient rights, exploitation, economics/funds/fictions, and public relations.

Brooks, M. K. (1997). Ethical and legal aspects of confidentiality. In J. H. Lowinson, P. Ruiz, R. B.

Millman, & J. G. Langrod (Eds.), *Substance abuse: A comprehensive textbook* (3rd ed., pp. 884–899). Baltimore, MD: Williams & Wilkins.

This chapter provides an overview of confidentiality issues as they relate to the ethical and legal realms.

Geppert, C. M. A., & Roberts, L. W. (2008). *The book of ethics: Expert guidance for professionals who treat addiction*. Center City, MN: Hazelden.

This book (173 pages) has nine chapters that cover ethical issues as they relate to pertinent areas in the addiction counseling field: treatment foundations, the therapeutic relationship, harm reduction, co-occurring disorders, cultural/spiritual dimensions, forensic issues, women, children/adolescents, and chronic pain.

Remley, T. P. (Ed). (1993). *ACA legal series* (Vols. 1–12). Alexandria, VA: American Counseling Association.

This series covers a number of legal issues counselors typically face. Particularly relevant to issues discussed in this chapter are volumes 6 (Confidentiality and Privileged Communication) and 8 (The Danger-to-Self-or-Others Exception to Confidentiality).

Taleff, M. J. (2008). *Critical thinking for addiction professionals*. New York, NY: Springer.

This book (160 pages) is divided into two sections: overview of critical thinking and how it applies to the addictions field (Part 1) and how fallacies of thinking interfere with decisions made regarding the addictions field. In the second part there is a short chapter on ethics.

Taleff, M. J. (2010). *Advanced ethics for addiction professionals*. New York, NY: Springer.

This book is divided into two parts: a foundation of ethics (4 chapters) and theories/applications (10 chapters).

Self-Care

Domar, A. D., & Dreher, H. (2000). *Self-nurture: Learning to care for yourself as effectively as you care for everyone else*. New York, NY: Viking.

This 306-page book is written from a cognitive-behavioral perspective that provides numerous helpful exercises on self-care.

Germer, C. K. (2009). *The mindful path to self-compassion*. New York, NY: Guilford Press.

This book is divided into three parts: discovering self-compassion, practicing loving-kindness, and customizing self-compassion. It has numerous exercises throughout the book as well as one of three appendices that focuses specifically on exercises.

Neff, K. D. (2008). Self-compassion: Moving beyond the pitfalls of a separate self-concept. In H. A. Wayment & J. J. Bauer (Eds.), *Transcending self-interest: Psychological explorations of the quiet ego* (pp. 95–105). Washington, DC: American Psychological Association.

This chapter discusses the concept of self-compassion in terms of self-kindness, common humanity, and mindfulness.

O'Halloran, T. M., & Linton, J. M. (2000). Stress on the job: Self-care resources for counselors. *Journal of Mental Health Counseling, 22*, 354–364.

This article provides an excellent list and description of self-care resources for counselors in the following areas: social, emotional, cognitive, physical, spiritual, and vocational.

WEBSITES

Ethics

The following four websites provide general information about the organizations as well as information about ethics for their members:

American Association for Marriage and Family Therapy (AAMFT)
www.aamft.org

American Counseling Association (ACA)
www.counseling.org

American Psychological Association (APA)
www.apa.org

National Association of Social Workers (NASW)
www.socialworkers.org

The following website has information on confidentiality and ethics:

HIPAA Standards for Privacy of Individual Identifiable Health Information
www.hhs.gov/ocr/privacy/

Legal

The Legal Action Center (LAC)
http://lac.org/index.php/lac/lacs_mission

This law and policy nonprofit organization is the only one of its kind in the United States. The LAC works to fight discrimination of individuals who have histories of addiction, HIV/AIDS, or criminal records.

CHAPTER 14

OBTAINING ADDICTION PROFESSIONAL CREDENTIALS

OBJECTIVES

1. To understand the different types of credentials.
2. To learn the different stages of the credentialing process.
3. To learn some helpful strategies to assist in the credentialing process.

Addiction credentialing boards evolved for two reasons (Morgen, Miller, & Stretch, 2012). One was to professionalize the field (mandated supervised practice hours and education requirements) and the second was to grandparent seasoned addiction counselors into the field. During the development of the addiction counseling field in the United States, various credentialing processes emerged. Currently, the overall United States credentialing process is a checkered, chaotic system because of the variation of standards (G. Miller, Scarborough, Clark, Leonard, & Keziah, 2010). In one state there may be additional requirements for credentials with different boards or variation in requirements for different levels of credentials within the same board. The variability can lead

to problems such as competing boards within a state or a feeling of discrimination between addiction professionals in the state due to different amounts of formal educational degrees.

If you are seeking formal addiction counseling education, entering the field of addiction counseling, or changing your credential because of relocation to another state, you may become confused and overwhelmed as you seek and obtain information on the credentialing process. It is best to determine the most widely recognized credential in the state in which you want to live and practice as an addiction professional and then follow those requirements.

A board in each state, then, varies in the type and amount of credential requirements, and each state varies in the number of organizations offering an addiction credential. Some states require that one must be credentialed. Because states vary on the type of addiction counseling credential available, three terms need to be defined to assist the reader in understanding the credential of his or her state: certification, licensure, and credentialing.

1. *Certification*, which is often voluntary, is established by professional groups monitoring the professional behavior of its counselors (Henderson, 2005).

2. *Licensure* means that counselors cannot practice or identify themselves professionally without having passed required exams and meeting certain criteria (Henderson, 2005).

3. *Credentialing* is a process handled by boards and some may be at the state level.

Certification and licensure as an addiction professional means that a minimum level of competence has been established that sets a standard for qualified professionals.

Kinney (2003) points out some possible variations of state certification types, requirements, testing, and recertification:

- Certification types:
  - Administrative/supervisory certification and clinical certification
  - Distinction between experienced and neophyte counselors
- Requirements:
  - Amount of experience, education/training, and supervision
  - Time requirements and exchange of work experience for education
  - Type of clinical competency, education, and special requirements (e.g., length of recovery)
- Testing:
  - Written examination

- Interview
- Clinical work evidence (portfolio, case presentation, videotape of session)
- Recertification:
  - Time required
  - Educational/training requirements

[Note that some boards may require ongoing supervision as well.]

With regard to credentialing, almost all states have at least a similar component for minimum basic standards; the widest variations in the standards tend to lie more in the higher standards. A summary of credentialing standards for substance abuse counselors and prevention professionals is provided by the Substance Abuse and Mental Health Services Administration (SAMHSA, 2005). The minimal requirements for most states are as follows:

- Level I
  - Work experience
  - Volunteer experience
  - High school diploma/GED
  - Sometimes an associate's degree
  - Education/training/classes
  - Supervision
  - Ethics
  - Exam—written and/or oral
  - Recertification
- Level II and Level III
  - Work experience
  - Work experience with a bachelor's degree
  - Work experience with a master's degree
  - Education/training/classes

- Supervision

- Exam—written and/or oral

- Ethics

- Recertification

Because of the variety and changing nature of the credentialing process, becoming a credentialed substance abuse professional can appear to be an overwhelming or daunting task. The Technical Assistance Publication Series (TAPS) Manual 21, *Addiction Counseling Competencies: The Knowledge, Skills, and Attitudes of Professional Practice*, published by the U.S. Department of Health and Human Services, Substance Abuse and Mental Health Services Administration (SAMHSA, 2008), provides an overview of the required addiction counseling competencies with training guidelines. An overview of the current state of credentialing standards for U.S. addiction counselors is provided by G. Miller et al. (2010). Also note that in June 2013 the International Certification & Reciprocity Consortium/Alcohol and Other Drug Abuse (IC&RC) and the Association for Addiction Professionals (NAADAC) began ongoing discussions with national credentialing boards regarding national credentials for addiction counselors. (Note that NAADAC, the Association for Addiction Professionals, was formerly called the National Association for Alcoholism and Drug Abuse Counselors [NAADAC].)

Depending on your professional and/or personal circumstances, the credentialing process can be demanding in terms of time, energy, and money. It can also seem to be unappreciated by some individuals or organizations, because the process requires the professional to spend personal time, energy, and money on the credentialing process.

So why do it? In order to navigate the complexities of addiction treatment, a counselor must have a certain level of professionalism. Increasingly, a simple, grassroots fashion of counseling is becoming less acceptable. In addition, an addictions counselor must be able to work with organizations outside of the field (i.e., managed care groups, insurance companies), many of which require credentials for reimbursement. Finally, the process of credentialing forces the professional to expand, organize, and clarify his or her knowledge about the addiction counseling field, and employers are increasingly requiring it of their practitioners.

SELF-CARE ON THE JOURNEY

Because of the importance of obtaining credentials to practice and because the demands to acquire credentials are high, it is critical for the professional to practice self-care on the journey. Although this chapter addresses concepts similar to those discussed at length in Chapter 13, issues of self-care are discussed here to fit the context of the credentialing process.

Gathering Information

A critical first step is to determine the type of credential you will find most helpful. You should determine the type and number of credentials that you need to work in your chosen area or state. For example, a practicing, licensed psychologist may pursue the American Psychological Association's (APA) Certificate of Proficiency in the Treatment of Alcohol and Other Psychoactive Substance Use Disorders, because this national credential is all that is needed to work with addicted clients in that geographic area. By comparison, a recent graduate from a Master's program in counseling, who anticipates working full time with alcoholics and drug addicts as an addiction counselor, may choose to obtain a board or state credential that is typically chosen or required in that state to work in that type of job.

What is important is to thoughtfully consider the type of work you want to do in the addictions field and then determine the credential that can best help you reach your goal. Such thoughtful planning can prevent the professional from obtaining unnecessary credentials and instead, invest time, money, and energy into those credentials that have the most bearing and weight. As one mentor commented about the numerous credentials available: "At some point in time, you have to decide when you get off the merry-go-round."

Four questions you can use in this self-examination process are:

1. What type of work do I want to do with addicted individuals?

Once you narrow the options of appropriate credentials, you can contact the various organizations to obtain application packets. Narrowing the options also reduces cost, because some of the application packets require a fee. When you receive the packets, it may be beneficial to review them with your mentor to make a final determination of which credential(s) to pursue. Carefully read the information you receive and clarify any confusion with the credentialing board directly rather than relying on the information provided by others. The credentialing board will provide the most accurate, up-to-date information about the standards you need to meet to receive the credential. (See Case Study 14.1.)

CASE STUDY 14.1

Jane is an experienced therapist who is licensed in her mental health specialty. She is finding herself working more with addicted clients and their loved ones. She has decided she wants to become credentialed in this area of expertise and has come to you for advice. Answer the following questions based on your limited knowledge of her situation:

1. What additional information would you need to know about her to provide her with adequate advice?
2. Where would you suggest she begin the process of credentialing?
3. What questions would you have for her in terms of the commitment of her personal resources (time, energy, money)?

2. How much of my work life do I want to spend focused on this population?

3. In the state in which I live, which credential is most respected or required by the addiction counseling field as it relates to my behavioral health care specialty (i.e., psychology, social work, counseling, or marriage and family counseling)?

4. How important is this credential to me in terms of committing my time, energy, and money in pursuit of it?

Personal Reactions

If you are seeking credentialing, you must first work with your own reactions to the process. A combination of negative thoughts and feelings that can slow down, block, or stop the process of seeking credentialing is common. It is helpful to determine what thoughts and feelings may inhibit the process. Exercise 14.1 can help clarify potential or existing roadblocks.

This exercise may require repetition throughout the process, especially if unexpected barriers appear. For example, you may have an unexpected

> **EXERCISE 14.1**
>
> Divide a piece of paper into three columns labeled First Thoughts, Feelings, and Responding Thoughts. Under First Thoughts, write any negative thoughts you have about the credentialing process, such as "I can't do this" or "This is too complicated and overwhelming for me." In the Feelings column, write corresponding feelings to those thoughts such as "Fear" or "Anger."
>
> Once you have exhausted all of the thoughts and corresponding feelings that come to mind, quickly write in the third column under Responding Thoughts ways you might counter them mentally. For example, if you have written, "I can't do this" and the emotion "Fear," a possible responding thought would be, "I can do one small step of contacting the credentialing board and obtaining an application packet."
>
> The critical component of this exercise is to allow yourself to freely express negative thoughts and feelings (no matter how ridiculous they may sound) and then work creatively to poke holes in the negativity of the thoughts and feelings by developing responding thoughts. If the Responding Thoughts section is difficult, you may want to brainstorm this section with a trusted loved one or colleague.

personal crisis, or you may fail the exam. Such a barrier may cause you to reexamine pursuing the credential. That is the time to pause the process and self-reflect on your decision to become credentialed and, if necessary, either stop the process temporarily (formally or informally) or explore another option for addressing the barrier. Before stopping the process, you need to determine whether there is another way to achieve your goal—another way to bounce back from the discouragement. Keep in mind also that employers may not allow any flexibility at the agency for failing the exam, so you may want to wait to take the exam until you have done everything you and your supervisor believe you need to do to prepare for it.

One aspect of a self-care plan may be to find a buddy, coach, or mentor for the journey. This person could be your supervisor who has experience with the credentialing process or another addiction professional who has gone through the credentialing process. This person can be especially helpful to you because (1) his or her knowing you can result in suggestions that better fit you and your life context, and (2) this person is a safe person to whom to turn if an unexpected barrier occurs. Choose someone with whom you can be extremely honest and whom you trust deeply. If you are new to the

field of addiction counseling, it may be difficult to determine who could serve in that role. In that case, ask an experienced addiction professional for suggestions on individuals who could be approached as mentors.

General Suggestions

You may be able to reduce the stress of the process by looking at its different components and developing a schedule and time frame for achieving the various stages. This may require you to reduce or restructure your professional and personal commitments at different points in the process. It is also important to examine the different stages in terms of stress levels. For example, if you do not take standardized tests well, you may want to accelerate your self-care strategies for that component of the process.

The following general self-care checklist based on Chapter 13 can be used by the professional:

- Memorize helpful adages to use when you feel discouraged or overwhelmed:

  - "Progress not perfection."

  - "Be responsible for the effort, not the outcome."

- "Do one step at a time."
- Attend to your mind, body, emotions, and spirit.
  - *Mind:* Regularly take part in *flow* activities— leisure activities—especially at high-stress points.
  - *Body:* Use the HALT acronym as a checkpoint throughout the process: "Am I Hungry, Angry, Lonely, or Tired?" Exercise as a way to reduce stress.
  - *Emotions:* Allow expression of emotions about the process and spend time with supportive people who believe in you and what you are doing.
  - *Spirit:* Spend time with people and in activities that are encouraging and hopeful about continuing in the process.
- Practice self-forgiveness and other forgiveness if a failure or negative experience occurs in the process.

Overall, it may be most important for you to keep in mind why you are pursuing this credential and maintain contact with other individuals who understand this and support you. In addition, you need to recognize when it is important to reach out for help from others. For example, if you struggle with writing, you may become fearful about the writing process of the credential. Recognize this as a place of vulnerability and ask for assistance from people who can help you in this area by providing editing services or feedback on a writing sample.

Finally, you need to work with the credentialing organization from a stance of mutual respect. Approach the organization in a respectful, cooperative manner, but document all aspects of the process in anticipation of any later problems by keeping copies of all correspondence and materials sent to the organization and having hard-copy (or e-mail) agreements made with the organization, especially if there is a modification of standards to fit your unique situation. (See Case Study 14.2.)

CASE STUDY 14.2

Monica is a graduate student in the human services profession. She has a moderate interest in working in the substance abuse field, but she is unaware of what the credentialing process is in her state. As a result, she does not know if it will benefit her professionally to seek the credential after graduation, as well as if she should take classes on it during her training.

1. Where would you suggest she begin to learn about the field to help her determine if she wants to work in it?
2. What avenues outside of the university might she pursue for information about credentials available?
3. What suggestions for self-care would you suggest she practice on her journey?

SUPERVISION

Choosing a supervisor for the credentialing process may be different from the selection process of a mentor described earlier because of a shift of purpose. In some states and for some credentialing organizations, not only is a supervisor required for the process but also only specific types of supervisors are acceptable. For example,

EXERCISE 14.2

Imagine you are in the process of becoming credentialed or licensed in your state as a substance abuse professional. Then answer these three questions on self-care:

1. How do I plan to practice self-care on this journey?
2. What kind of mentor do I want to support me through the process?
3. Who do I know who might be willing to mentor me on the journey?

some states have a specific addiction credential for supervisors. To determine the type of addiction credential you want to obtain, find out whether there is a specific requirement for supervisors, because arranging and maintaining this relationship may require additional time, money, and energy. Also, check with your state organization, with which you seek your credential, about who is considered an appropriate supervisor so supervision hours accrued will count, if allowed, toward the credential. Finally, if you are planning to obtain more than one credential, you may want to determine if the supervisor can meet the criteria for all the credentials.

If you need or want a supervisor for the credentialing process, be aware of some specific aspects of supervision. Both sides need to be aware of their responsibilities, expectations, boundaries (e.g., possible dual relationships), administrative tasks, and ways to resolve conflict, as well as the logistics, goals, methods, and feedback/evaluation components of supervision. Suggestions for finding an appropriate supervisor include:

- Determine whether the supervisor meets the criteria for supervision by the credentialing body.

- Approach the individual to see whether he or she is willing to be your supervisor and to learn enough about the individual to determine whether it is a good match:

1. Clarify the theoretical perspective on addiction counseling (it's not necessary to have a perfect agreement, but mutual respect is needed).

2. Determine the pragmatics of supervision structure (time involvement, cost, commitment to entire process).

3. Specify the expectations of supervision (e.g., format such as taping, charting).

4. Develop expectations of the evaluation process (mutual feedback on the supervision process).

5. Determine whether the supervisor has knowledge of credentialing requirements.

For the supervision to work best, you need to feel safe discussing different areas and issues, and the supervisor needs to be qualified to conduct the supervision. The supervisor plays a critical role in shaping your future. For you to develop professionally, the supervisor needs to help you examine personal issues as they arise in relation to clients. Although the supervisor is not acting as a counselor, the supervisor does have a responsibility to assist you in finding your areas of weakness and making suggestions on how to address them so they are not harmful to clients. The supervisor also needs to assist you in developing a minimum competency of skills and be able to express that competency to the credentialing organization. The supervisor needs to be both critical and supportive. You may want to suggest that your supervisor use evaluation materials as referenced in the Suggested

CASE STUDY 14.3

John has decided on the type of addiction credential he wants to receive, and he has determined that he is willing to make the commitment to obtain the credential. He decides that he wants you to be his supervisor, because he likes and trusts you, and you meet the credentialing organization's criteria for a supervisor. Answer three questions within this context:

1. What would you need to know from John before you agree to be his supervisor?
2. What action(s) would you take to make the supervision process as beneficial as possible for both of you?
3. How would you monitor the quality of the supervision for both of you?

EXERCISE 14.3

Imagine that you are in the process of finding a supervisor. Write down all the characteristics you would like in an ideal supervisor. With this in mind, fuse these characteristics with three questions:

1. What are the qualifications required for a supervisor in my state?
2. Who would I feel comfortable asking to supervise me?
3. How do I plan to approach this individual?

Readings section at the end of this chapter (Addiction Technology Transfer Center, 2011). Powell's (1993) book on supervision is considered a classic in the addiction counseling field. Both supervisors and supervisees may find it a helpful reference. Appendix 14A is a sample supervision form that may be useful to supervisors and supervisees.

In making the best use of your supervision, the following five suggestions may be helpful (Patel & Wendler, 2007):

1. Be open to feedback.

2. Resist letting your fears about competency hold you back.

3. Use audio/videotapes.

4. Make sure to talk about the area you are hesitant to discuss.

5. Give yourself permission to disagree with your supervisor. (See Case Study 14.3.)

CREDENTIALING

The addictions field credentialing organizations recommended in this text are those that are member boards with the IC&RC. The IC&RC is a nonprofit, voluntary membership organization that is made up of certifying agencies that credential alcohol and drug abuse counselors, clinical supervisors, and specialists in prevention. Its intention is to protect the public by having credentialing programs and minimum standards for reciprocity with regard to credentialing. It has 76 member boards in 24 countries. IC&RC does not independently credential anybody; individual boards credential counselors. IC&RC recognizes one agency per credential per jurisdiction, and a jurisdiction may say that they have exclusive rights to the IC&RC tests.

The IC&RC offers reciprocal credentials: Alcohol and Drug Counselor (ADC), Advanced Alcohol and Drug Counselor (AADC), Clinical

Supervisor (CS), Prevention Specialist (PS), Certified Criminal Justice Addictions Professional (CCJP), Certified Prevention Specialist (CPS), Certified Co-Occurring Disorders Professional (CCDP), Certified Co-Occurring Disorders Professional Diplomate (CCDPD), and Peer Recovery (PR). Minimum standards for each credential can be found at the IC&RC website (www.internationalcredentialing.org).

This chapter addresses the first two credentials: ADC and AADC. The IC&RC is committed to public protection by the establishment of credentialing programs requiring that minimal standards of competency be met. Reciprocity and general information can be obtained by contacting the IC&RC at their website (www.internationalcredentialing.org).

Kinney (2003) reports that state credentialing organizations, in general, require a written test, an interview, and evidence of clinical work in the form of a portfolio, case presentation, or videotape. Because this chapter focuses on IC&RC requirements for two of the credentials (ADC, AADC), the following section describes the written test that is based on the 12 core functions. The 12 core functions section is followed by a section on the case presentation method. Although these two IC&RC credentials no longer require an oral exam component, some state boards may still require an oral exam that is based on the 12 core functions.

Written Exam

Both the ADC and AADC credential require written exams. In preparation for both exams, the IC&RC recommends *Getting Ready to Test: A Review and Preparation Manual for Drug and Alcohol Credentialing Exams* (7th ed.). The book, which is described in the resource section at the end of this chapter, can be ordered online (www.readytotest.com/ICRCOrderSite.html). The book can be used in preparation for the IC&RC exams as well as the NAADAC exam. [Note that NAADAC, the Association for Addiction Professionals, was formerly called the National Association for Alcoholism and Drug Abuse Counselors (NAADAC).]

The IC&RC *Study Guide* (2002) provides helpful examination tips. This guide encourages the following in preparation for the multiple-choice question exam:

- Follow your preferred learning style (i.e., reading, using notecards, etc.).
- Study the domains being tested.
- Review the tasks in the study guide for each domain, determine areas that are strengths and weaknesses, and prioritize study times accordingly.
- Set up a schedule for exam preparation and collect resource materials.
- Pace yourself through activities such as study sessions and collegial consultations.
- Use the sample exams in the study guide.
- Follow the philosophy of "Relax-Prepare-Relax-Perform" (p. 7).

The authors also recommend five specific test-taking strategies:

1. Do your best (no penalty for guessing).
2. Remember that your initial response to a question is usually the best answer.
3. Answer questions in order.
4. Choose the best answer.
5. Read all answers carefully before choosing one.

12 Core Functions

Each core function has global criteria to assist in the evaluation of minimal competence for the counselor. These 12 core functions and global criteria are (IC&RC, 1998) as follows[1]:

[1]Reprinted with permission.

I. **Screening:** The process by which the client is determined appropriate and eligible for admission to a particular program.

Global Criteria

1. Evaluate psychological, social, and physiological signs and symptoms of alcohol and other drug use and abuse.

2. Determine the client's appropriateness for admission or referral.

3. Determine the client's eligibility for admission or referral.

4. Identify any coexisting conditions (medical, psychiatric, physical, etc.) that indicate need for additional professional assessment and/or services.

5. Adhere to applicable laws, regulations, and agency policies governing alcohol and other drug abuse services. (p. 15)

II. **Intake:** The administrative and initial assessment procedures for admission to a program.

Global Criteria

6. Complete required documents for admission to the program.

7. Complete required documents for program eligibility and appropriateness.

8. Obtain appropriately signed consents when soliciting from or providing information to outside sources to protect client confidentiality and rights. (p. 16)

III. **Orientation:** Describing to the client the following: general nature and goals of the program; rules governing client conduct and infractions that can lead to disciplinary action or discharge from the program; in a nonresidential program, the hours during which services are available; treatment costs to be borne by the client, if any; and client rights.

Global Criteria

9. Provide an overview to the client by describing program goals and objectives for client care.

10. Provide an overview to the client by describing program rules, and client obligations and rights.

11. Provide an overview to the client of program operations. (p. 17)

IV. **Assessment:** The procedures by which a counselor/program identifies and evaluates an individual's strengths, weaknesses, problems, and needs for the development of a treatment plan.

Global Criteria

12. Gather relevant history from the client, including but not limited to alcohol and other drug abuse, using appropriate interview techniques.

13. Identify methods and procedures for obtaining corroborative information from significant secondary sources regarding clients' alcohol and other drug abuse and psychosocial history.

14. Identify appropriate assessment tools.

15. Explain to the client the rationale for the use of assessment techniques in order to facilitate understanding.

16. Develop a diagnostic evaluation of the client's substance abuse and any coexisting conditions based on the results of all assessments in order to provide an integrated approach to treatment planning based on the client's strengths, weaknesses, and identified problems and needs. (pp. 17–18)

V. **Treatment Planning:** Process by which the counselor and the client identify and rank problems needing resolution; establish agreed-upon immediate and long-term goals; and decide upon a treatment process and the resources to be utilized.

Global Criteria

17. Explain assessment results to client in an understandable manner.

18. Identify and rank problems based on individual client needs in the written treatment plan.

19. Formulate agreed-upon immediate and long-term goals using behavioral terms in the written treatment plan.

20. Identify the treatment methods and resources to be utilized as appropriate for the individual client. (pp. 18–19)

VI. **Counseling** (Individual, Group, and Significant Others): The utilization of special skills to assist individuals, families, or groups in achieving objectives through exploration of a problem and its ramifications; examination of attitudes and feelings; consideration of alternative solutions; and decision making.

Global Criteria

21. Select the counseling theory(ies) that apply(ies).

22. Apply technique(s) to assist the client, group, and/or family in exploring problems and ramifications.

23. Apply technique(s) to assist the client, group, and/or family in examining the client's behavior, attitudes, and/or feelings, if appropriate, in the treatment setting.

24. Individualize counseling in accordance with cultural, gender, and lifestyle differences.

25. Interact with the client in an appropriate therapeutic manner.

26. Elicit solutions and decisions from the client.

27. Implement the treatment plan. (p. 19)

VII. **Case Management:** Activities that bring services, agencies, resources, or people together within a planned framework of action toward the achievement of established goals. It may involve liaison activities and collateral contacts.

Global Criteria

28. Coordinate services for client care.

29. Explain the rationale of case management activities to the client. (p. 20)

VIII. **Crisis Intervention:** Those services that respond to an alcohol and/or other drug abuser's needs during acute emotional and/or physical distress.

Global Criteria

30. Recognize the elements of the client crisis.

31. Implement an immediate course of action appropriate to the crisis.

32. Enhance overall treatment by utilizing crisis events. (p. 21)

IX. **Client Education:** Provision of information to individuals and groups concerning alcohol and other drug abuse and the available services and resources.

Global Criteria

33. Present relevant alcohol and other drug use/abuse information to the client through formal and/or informal processes.

34. Present information about available alcohol and other drug services and resources. (p. 21)

X. **Referral:** Identifying the needs of a client that cannot be met by the counselor or agency and assisting the client to utilize the support systems and community resources available.

Global Criteria

35. Identify need(s) and/or problem(s) that the agency and/or counselor cannot meet.

36. Explain the rationale for the referral to the client.

37. Match client needs and/or problems to appropriate resources.

38. Adhere to applicable laws, regulations, and agency policies governing procedures related to the protection of the client's confidentiality.

39. Assist the client in utilizing the available support systems and community resources. (p. 22)

XI. **Report and Record Keeping:** Charting the results of the assessment and treatment plan, writing reports, progress notes, discharge summaries, and other client-related data.

Global Criteria

40. Prepare reports and relevant records integrating available information to facilitate the continuum of care.

41. Chart pertinent ongoing information pertaining to the client.

42. Utilize relevant information from written documents for client care. (p. 22)

XII. **Consultation with Other Professionals in Regard to Client Treatment Services:** Relating with in-house staff or outside professionals to assure comprehensive, quality care for the client.

Global Criteria

43. Recognize issues that are beyond the counselor's base of knowledge and/or skill.

44. Consult with appropriate resources to ensure the provision of effective treatment services.

45. Adhere to applicable laws, regulations, and agency policies governing the disclosure of client-identifying data.

46. Explain the rationale for the consultation to the client, if appropriate. (p. 23)

Case Presentation

Presenting a case requires the submission of a case study to the credentialing organization. While the IC&RC no longer requires an oral presentation and many states no longer require an oral exam, some states still do, which is why this information is included here.

The supervisor should assist you in choosing a case that you know very well and one that represents your typical client/counselor approach. The typical counseling approach includes the choice of a theory and specific techniques. Exercise 14.2 in this chapter may assist you in this process. It is recommended that you use standard counseling theories as outlined in Chapter 2. While it may be tempting to use an unusual or new theory in the presentation of a case, the time allowed for case presentation is limited, and there is little time to explain alternative theories, thereby increasing the chance that the evaluators would not understand your unique theoretical approach. The supervisor also may need to assist you by critiquing the write-up of the case and the demonstration of competence in the 12 core functions as they apply to the case. If a core function was not addressed in the case, the supervisor can assist you in providing an example from another case where you addressed the core function.

Herdman (2001) makes four specific suggestions in preparation for the case presentation method:

1. Ask colleagues for critiques.

2. Practice being tape-recorded under the time constrictions.

3. Provide examples throughout the presentation.

4. Make comments clearly and in an orderly fashion to facilitate examiner comprehension.

It may also help to practice the case presentation in front of three people (or at least one) who do not provide eye contact or feedback during the entire presentation. This experience may assist you in the actual case presentation, because evaluators are trained to *listen* to the case presentation rather than be distracted visually (through eye contact or visual images of the professional), and they are trained to not give feedback to the case presenter.

In addition, it is helpful to develop strategies for time management and anxiety management before, during, and after the exam. You are responsible for the management of the time (making sure each core function is covered and telling the examiners when you have completed your answer) as well as your management of personal anxiety. The time and anxiety management strategies will be idiosyncratic. For example, if you tend to be more verbal when presenting, you may need to pare down comments for the presentation. Perhaps you will find it less stressful to stay in a hotel near the examination site the night before the case presentation. However, these strategies may not work well for someone who tends to speak concisely and finds that staying in a hotel heightens stress. If you examine how to use time efficiently in the presentation process, along with examining how to reduce stress, the chances of doing your best are enhanced. These considerations will also help you after the exam. As well as practicing self-care before the exam, it is also important to practice it once the exam is finished.

SUMMARY

This chapter is an overview of the credentialing process for an addictions professional. The guidelines provided for test taking and case presentation can be translated for use with any written or oral exam you might need to take in the addictions field. If you work hard, care well for yourself on the journey, and persist in the process, you can obtain your addiction counseling credential.

QUESTIONS

1. What are some helpful components to build into a self-care plan for the credentialing process?

2. What are some questions a counselor may use to determine which credential to seek?

3. What are some general self-care suggestions made in this chapter?

4. What are some specific suggestions for evaluating a potential supervisor?

5. What are two IC&RC credentials discussed in this chapter?

6. What are some suggestions for preparing for the written exam?

7. What are the 12 Core Functions and related global criteria?

8. What are some suggestions for preparing for the oral exam?

READINGS/RESOURCES/WEBSITES

SUGGESTED READINGS

Addiction Technology Transfer Center Network. (2011). *Performance assessment rubrics for the addiction counseling competencies.* Retrieved from www.attcnetwork.org/userfiles/file/NorthwestFrontier/Final%20ATTC%20Rubrics%20Assessment.pdf

This provides rubrics for transdisciplinary foundations (understanding addiction, treatment knowledge, application to practice, professional readiness), professional practice dimension rubrics (clinical evaluation, treatment planning, service coordination, counseling, client/family/community education, professional and ethical responsibilities), and a performance rating summary sheet that those seeking the credential and their supervisors may find helpful.

Boylan, J. C., & Scott, J. (2008). *Practicum and internship* (4th ed.). New York, NY: Routledge.

This textbook and resource guide for students and their supervisors covers theoretical and practical aspects of practicum and internship from site selection to site evaluation. Forms are included in the book as well as on an accompanying CD.

Coombs, R. H. (Ed.). (2005). *Addiction counseling review: Preparing for comprehensive certification and licensing examination.* Mahwah, NJ: Erlbaum.

This 648-page book has six main sections: addiction basics, individuals/families/drugs, common client problems, counseling theories and skills, treatment resources, and career issues. It is a thorough overview of topics typically covered in examinations for substance abuse–related credentials.

Herdman, J. (2008). *Global criteria: The 12 core functions of the substance abuse counselor* (5th ed.). Lincoln, NE: Author. www.johnherdman.com

This book provides an overview of the 12 core functions and their corresponding global criteria in accordance with IC&RC Standards and the Case Presentation Method (CPM). It also provides helpful assignments at the end of each chapter to assist the reader in applying the information.

International Certification and Reciprocity Consortium. (2012). *Getting ready to test: A review and preparation manual for drug and alcohol credentialing exams* (7th ed.). www.readytotest.com/ICRCOrderSite.html

This self-guided 734-page comprehensive manual provides an overview of information required for drug and alcohol written examinations. It can be used in preparation for either the IC&RC or NAADAC written exams. It includes a 150-question written exam sample. It includes four sections: basic addiction information, core functions, specialty information, and the testing process. There is also information on IC&RC's computer-based testing (CBT).

Kiser, P. M. (2012). *The human service internship: Getting the most from your experience* (3rd ed.). Belmont, CA: Brooks/Cole.

This 384-page book presents information that can be used by students from the start through the end of their internship. It is designed to assist students in analyzing their internship experiences and situations. Material is presented in this workbook-formatted text that facilitates self-assessment.

Substance Abuse and Mental Health Services Administration. (2008). *Addiction counseling competencies: The knowledge, skills, and attitudes of professional practice* (TAP 21, DHHS Publication No. SMA 13–4171). Rockville, MD: Author.

This 224-page manual covers the basic competencies required of an addictions counselor.

WEBSITES

International Certification & Reciprocity Consortium (IC&RC)
www.internationalcredentialing.org

This website provides a broad range of information in terms of credentialing, boards, testing, reciprocity, resources, etc..

APPENDIX 14A

Sample Supervision Documentation

Employee Name: _____

Credential for Supervision: _____

Date of Supervision: _____

Duration of Supervision: _____

Type of Supervision:

Individual ☐   Group ☐   Clinical ☐ SA ☐

Please check topic(s) below which were discussed in supervision with brief summary of discussion at bottom of the page. Clinical and SA 12 core functions. ☑

☐ Accuracy of assessment and referral skills

☐ Appropriateness of the treatment selected relative to specific needs of each client

☐ Treatment effectiveness as reflected by progress toward goals

☐ The provision of feedback that enhances the skills of direct service personnel

☐ Clinical documentation issues identified through ongoing compliance review

☐ Cultural competency issues

☐ High-risk cases reviewed

☐ Outpatient commitment cases reviewed

☐ Caseload review for clients appropriate for groups

☐ Productivity Action Plan discussed or developed

☐ Screening

☐ Intake

☐ Assessment

☐ Orientation

☐ Treatment Planning

☐ Counseling

☐ Case Management

☐ Crisis Intervention

☐ Client Education

☐ Referral

☐ Reports and Record Keeping

☐ Consultation

Supervision Summary: _____

_____

_____

_____

Signature and Credentials of Supervisor

_____

Clinical Supervisor

Signature and Credentials of Supervisee

_____

REFERENCES

Aase, D. M., Jason, L. A., & Robinson, W. L. (2008). 12-step participation among dually-diagnosed individuals: A review of individual and contextual factors. *Clinical Psychology Review, 28*, 1235–1348.

Abrams, R. C., & Alexopoulos, G. (1987). Substance abuse in the elderly: Alcohol and prescription drugs. *Hospital and Community Psychiatry, 38*, 1285–1288.

Achara-Abrahams, I., Evans, A. C., Ortiz, J., Villegas, D. L., O'Dell, J., & Hawkins, O. (2013). Recovery management and African Americans: A report from the field. *Alcoholism Treatment Quarterly, 30*, 263–292. doi: 10.1080/07347324.2012.691049

Acierno, R., Coffey, S. F., & Resnick, H. S. (2003). Introduction to the special issue: Interpersonal violence and substance use problems. *Addictive Behaviors, 28*, 1529–1532.

Acker, G. M. (2011). Burnout among mental health care providers. *Journal of Social Work, 12*, 475–490. doi: 10.1177/1468017310392418

Adams, D. C., & McCormick, A. J. (1982). Men unlearning violence: A group approach based on the collective model. In M. Roy (Ed.), *The abusive partner* (pp. 170–197). New York, NY: Van Nostrand Reinhold.

Adams, J. B., & Madson, M. B. (2006). Reflection and outlook for the future of addictions treatment and training: An interview with William R. Miller. *Journal of Teaching in the Addictions, 5*, 95–109.

Adams, J. Q., & Welsch, J. R. (2007). Multiculturalism: The manifest destiny of the U.S.A.: An interview with Ronald Takaki. *Multicultural Perspectives, 11*, 227–231.

Adamson, S. J., & Sellman, J. D. (2003). A prototype screening instrument for cannabis use disorders: The cannabis use disorders identification test (CUDIT) in an alcohol dependent clinical sample. *Drug Alcohol Review, 22*, 309–315.

Adamson, S. J., Kay-Lambkin, F. J., Baker, A. L., Lewin, T. J., Thornton, L., Kelly, B. J., & Sellman, J. D. (2010). An improved brief measure of cannabis misuse: The cannabis use disorders identification test-revised (CUDIT-R). *Drug and Alcohol Dependence, 110*, 137–143.

Addiction Technology Transfer Center (Northwest Frontier). (2001). *Performance assessment rubrics for the addiction counseling competencies*. Retrieved from www.attcnetwork.org/regcenters/index_northwest-frontier.asp

Addictions Foundation of Manitoba. (2000, June). *A biopsychosocial model of addiction*. Retrieved from Afm.mb.ca/AFM/PDF/BPS-FINAL.pdf

ADE Incorporated. (1988). *Juvenile Automated Substance Abuse Evaluation (JASAE)* Clarkston, MI: Author.

ADE Incorporated. (1991). *Substance Abuse Life Circumstances Evaluation (SALCE)* Clarkston, MI: Author.

Afful, S. E., Strickland, J. R., Cottler, L., & Bierut, L. J. (2010). Exposure to trauma: A comparison of cocaine-dependent cases and a community-matched sample. *Drug and Alcohol Dependence, 112*, 46–53.

Akins, S., Mosher, C., Rotolo, T., & Griffin, R. (2003, Winter). Patterns and correlates of substance use among American Indians in Washington state. *Journal of Drug Issues, 33*, 45–72.

Albrecht, G. L. (1992). *The disability business: Rehabilitation in America*. Newbury Park, CA: Sage.

Alcoholics Anonymous. (1939). *Alcoholics Anonymous*. New York, NY: Author.

Alcoholics Anonymous. (1990). *Hope: Alcoholics Anonymous* [Videotape]. (Available from Alcoholics Anonymous World Services, Inc., P.O. Box 459, Grand Central Station, New York, NY 10163.)

Alcoholics Anonymous (2005). *The A.A. group: Where it all begins*. New York, NY: Author.

Alcoholics Anonymous World Services. (1953). *Twelve steps and twelve traditions*. New York, NY: Author.

Alcoholics Anonymous World Services (1976). *Alcoholics Anonymous* (3rd ed.). New York, NY: Author.

Alcoholics Anonymous World Services (2001). *Alcoholics Anonymous* (4th ed.). New York, NY: Author.

Alcoholism & Drug Abuse Weekly. (2002). Recovery rates better for women in gender-specific programs. *Alcoholism & Drug Abuse Weekly 7*(4), 3–4.

Alcoholism & Drug Abuse Weekly. (2011). AAP recommends pediatricians use SBIRT for all adolescent patients . . . Screening for Substance Use, Brief Intervention and/or Referral to Treatment (SBIRT). *Alcoholism & Drug Abuse Weekly, 23*(43), 1–3.

Alelrod, S. R., Perepletchikova, F., Holtzman, K., & Sinha, R. (2011). Emotion regulation and substance use frequency in women with substance dependence and borderline personality disorder receiving dialectical behavior therapy. *American Journal of Drug and Alcohol Abuse, 37*, 37–42.

Alim, T. N., Lawson, W. B., Feder, A., Iacoviello, B. M., Saxena, S., Bailey, C. R., . . . Neumeister, A. (2012). Resilience to meet the challenge of addiction. *Alcohol Research Current Reviews, 34*, 506–515.

Alvarez, L. R., & Ruiz, P. (2001). Substance abuse in the Mexican American population. In S. L. A. Straussner (Ed.), *Ethnocultural factors in substance abuse treatment* (pp. 111–136). New York, NY: Guilford Press.

Alvidrez, J. (1999). Ethnic variations in mental health attitudes and service use among low-income African American, Latina, and European American young women. *Community Mental Health Journal, 35*, 515–530.

Amchin, J., & Polan, H. J. (1986). A longitudinal account of staff adaptation to AIDS patients on a psychiatric unit. *Hospital and Community Psychiatry, 37*, 1235–1238.

American Counseling Association (1993). *ACA Legal Series* (Vols. 6 & 8). Alexandria, VA: Author.

American Counseling Association (2009). *Competencies for counseling with transgender clients*. Retrieved from http://www.counseling.org/docs/competencies/algbtic_competencies.pdf?sfvrsn=3

American Psychiatric Association. (2013). *Diagnostic and statistical manual of mental disorders* (5th ed.). Arlington, VA: American Psychiatric Publishing.

American Psychological Association. (1996). *Hope training manual*. Washington, DC: Author.

American Psychological Association (Producer). (1997). *Cognitive-behavioral relapse prevention for addictions: With G. Alan Marlatt, PhD* [APA Psychotherapy Videotape Series II]. [Motion Picture]. (Available from the American Psychological Association, 750 First Street, N.E., Washington, DC: 20002-4242.)

American Psychological Association. (2001, October). *Tapping your resilience in the wake of terrorism: Pointers for practitioners*. Washington, DC: Author.

American Psychological Association. (2006). *Report of the APA task force on socioeconomic status*. Washington, DC: Author.

American Psychological Association (2010, January). *Psychology and aging: Psychologists make a significant contribution*. Retrieved from http://www.apa.org/pi/aging/resources/guides/psychology-and-aging.aspx

American Society of Addiction Medicine. (1996). *Patient placement criteria for the treatment of substance-related disorders* (2nd ed.) Chevy Chase, MD: Author.

American Society of Addiction Medicine. (2013). *The ASAM criteria—Treatment criteria for addictive, substance-related, and co-occurring conditions* (4th ed.). Carson City, NV: Change Companies.

Americans with Disabilities Act of 1990 Pub. L. No. 101–336, §2, 104 Stat. 328 (1991).

Amico, J. M., & Neisen, J. (1997, May/June). Sharing the secret: The need for gay-specific treatment. *Counselor*, 12–15.

Amodeo, M., & Jones, L. K. (1997). Viewing alcohol and other drug use cross culturally: A cultural framework for clinical practice. *Families in Society: Journal of Contemporary Human Services, 78*, 240–253.

Amodia, D. S., Cano, C., & Eliason, M. J. (2005). An integral approach to substance abuse. *Journal of Psychoactive Drugs, 37*, 363–371.

Anderson, B. S. (1996). *The counselor and the law* (4th ed.). Alexandria, VA: American Counseling Association.

Anderson, B. S. (2008). *The counselor and the law* (5th ed.). Alexandria, VA: American Counseling Association.

Anderson, M. J., & Ellis, R. (1995). On the reservation. In N. A. Vacc, S. B. DeVaney, & J. Wittmer (Eds.), *Experiencing and counseling multicultural and diverse populations* (pp. 179–198). Bristol, PA: Accelerated Development.

Anderson, S. C. (2009). *Substance use disorders in lesbian, gay, bisexual, and transgender clients: Assessment and treatment*. New York, NY: Columbia University Press.

Anderson, T. (2008). *Neither villain nor victim: Empowerment and agency among women substance abusers*. New Brunswick, NJ: Rutgers University Press.

Añez, L. M., Silva, M. A., Paris, M., & Bedregal, L. E. (2008). Engaging Latinos through the integration of cultural values and motivational interviewing principles. *Professional Psychology: Research & Practice*, *39*, 153–159.

Angove, R., & Fothergill, A. (2003). Women and alcohol: Misrepresented and misunderstood. *Journal of Psychiatric Mental Health Nursing*, *10*, 213–219.

Annis, H. M., Graham, J. M., & Davis, C. S. (1988). *Inventory of drinking situations: User's guide*. Toronto, Ontario, Canada: Addiction Research Foundation of Ontario.

APA Task Force on Evidence-Based Practice. (2006). Evidence-based practice in psychology. *American Psychologist*, *61*, 271–285.

Appel, J., & Kim-Appel, D. (2009). Mindfulness: Implications for substance abuse and addiction. *International Journal of Mental Health and Addiction*, *7*, 506–512. doi: 10.1007/s11469-009-9199-z

Arevalo, S., Prado, G., & Amaro, H. (2008). Spirituality, sense of coherence, and coping responses in women receiving treatment for alcohol and drug addiction. *Evaluation and Program Planning*, *31*, 113–123. doi: 10.1016/j.evalprogplan.2007.05.009

Arkowitz, H., Westra, H. A., Miller, W. R., & Rollnick, S. (2008). *Motivational interviewing in the treatment of psychological problems*. New York, NY: Guilford Press.

Armsworth, M. W. (1989). Therapy of incest survivors: Abuse or support. *Child Abuse and Neglect*, *13*, 549–562.

Arrendondo, R., Weddige, R. L., Justice, C. L., & Fitz, J. (1987). Alcoholism in Mexican Americans: Intervention and treatment. *Hospital and Community Psychiatry*, *38*, 180–183.

Arseneault, L., Ladouceur, R., & Vitaro, F. (2001). Gambling and consumption of psychotropic drugs: Prevalence, coexistence and consequences, *Canadian Psychology*, *42*, 173–184.

Atkinson, D. R., & Hackett, G. (2004). *Counseling diverse populations* (3rd ed.). Boston, MA: McGraw-Hill.

Atkinson, D. R., Morten, G., & Sue, D. W. (1993). *Counseling American minorities: A crosscultural perspective* (4th ed.). Madison, WI: Brown & Benchmark.

Atkinson, R. M., Turner, J. A., Kofoed, L. L., & Tolson, R. L. (1985). Early versus late onset alcoholism in older persons: Preliminary findings. *Alcoholism: Clinical and Experimental Research*, *9*, 513–515.

Austad, C. S., & Berman, W. H. (1991). Managed health care and the evolution of psychotherapy. In C. S. Austad & W. H. Berman (Eds.), *Psychotherapy in managed health care* (pp. 3–18). Washington, DC: American Psychological Association.

Austin, J., McKellar, J. D., & Moos, R. (2011). The influence of co-occurring Axis I disorders on treatment utilization and outcome in homeless patients with substance use disorders. *Addictive Behaviors*, *36*, 941–944.

Azar, B. (2011). Positive psychology advances, with growing pains. *APA Monitor*, *42*, 32.

Babor, T. F., & Higgins Biddle, J. (2002). *AUDIT: The alcohol use disorders identification test: Guidelines for use in primary care* (2nd ed.). Geneva, Switzerland: World Health Organization.

Bachman, S. S., Drainoni, M-L., & Tobias, C. (2004). Medicaid managed care, substance abuse treatment, and people with disabilities: Review of the literature. *Health and Social Work*, *29*, 189.

Back, S. E., Waldrop, A. E., Brady, K. T., & Hien, D. (2006). Evidence-based time-limited treatment of co-occurring substance-use disorders and civilian-related posttraumatic stress disorder. *Brief Treatment and Crisis Intervention*, *6*, 283–294.

Bagoien, G., Bjorngaard, J. H., Ostensen, C., Reitan, S. K., Romundstad, P., & Morken, G. (2013). The effects of motivational interviewing on patients with comorbid substance use admitted to a psychiatric emergency unit—A randomized controlled trial with two year follow up. *BioMedCentral Psychiatry*, *13*, 1–10.

Balthip, Q., Boddy, J., Kong-In, W., & Nilmanat, K. (2011). Supportive relationships: Creating meaning and purpose in life for persons living with HIV/AIDS. *Counseling and Spirituality*, *30*, 37–55.

Bandura, A. (1977). Self-efficacy: Toward a unifying theory of behavioral change. *Psychological Review*, *84*, 191–215.

Bandura, A. (1982). The psychology of chance encounters and life paths. *American Psychologist*, *33*, 334–358.

Bannwarth, B. (2012). Will abuse-deterrent formulations of opioid analgesics be successful in achieving their purpose? *Drugs*, *72*, 1713–1723.

Barker, R. G., & Wright, H. F. (1955). *Midwest and its children: The psychological ecology of an American town*. New York, NY: Harper & Row.

Barnes, A. J., Moore, A. A., Xu, H., Ang, A., Tallen, L., Mirkin, M., & Ettner, S. L. (2010). Prevalence and correlates of at-risk drinking among older adults: The project SHARE study. *Journal of General Internal Medicine, 25,* 840–846.

Barnett, E., Sussman, S., Smith, C., Rohrbach, L. A., & Spruijt-Metz, D. (2012). Motivational interviewing for adolescent substance use: A review of the literature. *Addictive Behaviors, 37,* 1325–1334.

Barnett, J. E., & Shale, A. J. (April, 2013). Alternative techniques. *APA Monitor,* 48–56.

Barnett, O. W., & Planeaux, P. S. (1989, January) A hostility-guilt assessment of counseled and uncounseled batterers. Paper presented at the Responses to Family Violence Research Conference, Purdue University, Lafayette, IN.

Barrett, R., & Logan, C. (2002). *Counseling gay men and lesbians: A practice primer.* Pacific Grove, CA: Brooks/Cole.

Barry, H., III. (1974). Psychological factors in alcoholism. In B. Kissin & H. Begleiter (Eds.), *The biology of alcoholism: Vol. 3. Clinical pathology* (pp. 53–108). New York, NY: Plenum Press.

Bartlett, J. G. (1993). *The Johns Hopkins Hospital guide to medical care of patients with HIV infection* (3rd ed.). Baltimore, MD: Williams & Wilkins.

Bass, E., & Davis, L. (1988). *The courage to heal: A guide for women survivors of child sexual abuse.* New York, NY: Harper & Row.

Batki, S. L., & Nathan, K. I. (2008). HIV/AIDS and hepatitis C. In M. Galanter & H. D. Kleber (Eds.), *Substance abuse treatment* (4th ed., pp. 581–593). Washington, DC: American Psychiatric Publishing.

Battista, S. R., Pencer, A., McGonnell, M., Durdle, H., & Stewart, S. H. (2013). Relations of personality to substance use problems and mental health disorder symptoms in two clinical samples of adolescents. *International Journal of Mental Health and Addiction, 11,* 1557–1874.

Beauvais, F., & LaBoueff, S. (1985). Drug and alcohol abuse intervention in American Indian communities. *International Journal of the Addictions, 20,* 139–171.

Beauvais, F., & Oetting, E. R. (1987). Toward a clear definition of inhalant abuse. *International Journal of the Addictions, 22,* 779–784.

Beauvais, F., Oetting, E. R., & Edwards, R. W. (1985). Trends in drug use of Indian adolescents living on reservations. *American Journal of Drug and Alcohol Abuse, 11,* 209–229.

Beck, A. T. (1976). *Cognitive therapy and the emotional disorders.* New York, NY: International Universities Press.

Bednar, S. G. (2003, June). Substance abuse and woman abuse: A proposal for integrated treatment. *Federal Probation, 67,* 52–57.

Beechem, M. (2002). *Elderly alcoholism: Intervention strategies.* Springfield, IL: Thomas.

Behavior Data Systems. (1987). *Driver Risk Inventory.* Phoenix, AZ: Author.

Bein, A. (2008). *The zen of helping: Spiritual principles for mindful and open-hearted practice.* Hoboken, NJ: Wiley.

Bell, P. (1990). *Chemical dependency and the African-American* [Brochure]. Center City, MN: Hazelden.

Bell, P. (2002). *Chemical dependency and the African-American* (2nd ed.). Center City, MN: Hazelden.

Benedict, D. G. (2008, September). Walking the tightrope: Chronic pain and substance abuse. *Journal for Nurse Practitioners, 4,* 604–609.

Bennett, L., & Lawson, M. (1994, May). Barriers to cooperation between domestic-violence and substance-abuse programs. *Families in Society: Journal of Contemporary Human Services,* 277–286.

Benowitz, M. (1986). How homophobia affects lesbians' response to violence in lesbian relationships. In K. Lobel (Ed.), *Naming the violence: Speaking out about lesbian battering* (pp. 198–201). Seattle, WA: Seal Press.

Benshoff, J. J., Harrawood, L. K., & Koch, D. S. (2003). Substance abuse and the elderly: Unique issues and concerns. *Journal of Rehabilitation, 69,* 43–48.

Benson, A. L., & Eisenach, D. A. (2013). Stopping overshopping: An approach to the treatment of compulsive-buying disorder. *Journal of Groups in Addiction & Recovery* (Vol. 8, pp. 3–24).

Berg, I. K. (1995). Solution-focused brief therapy with substance abusers. In A. M. Washton (Ed.), *Psychotherapy and substance abuse: A practitioner's handbook* (pp. 223–242). New York, NY: Guilford Press.

Berg, I. K. (2000). Building solutions with mandated clients [Workshop handout]. Milwaukee, WI: Brief Focused Therapy Center.

Berg, I. K., & Miller, S. D. (1992). *Working with the problem drinker: A solution-focused approach.* New York, NY: Norton.

Berman, A. H., Forsberg, L., Durbeej, N., Kaellmen, H., & Hermansson, U. (2010). Single-session motivation interviewing for drug detoxification inpatients: Effects on self-efficacy, stages of change and substance abuse. *Substance Use and Misuse, 45,* 384–402.

Berry, J. W. (2002). Conceptual approaches to acculturation. In K. M. Chun, P. B. Organista, & G. Marin (Eds.), *Acculturation: Advances in theory, measurement, and applied research* (pp. 17–37). Washington, DC: American Psychological Association.

Bersoff, D. N. (1976). Therapists as protectors and policemen: New roles as a result of Tarasoff. *Professional Psychology, 7,* 267–273.

Bertrand, K., Richer, I., Brunelle, N., Beaudoin, I., Lemieux, A., & Menard, J.-M. (2013). Substance abuse treatment for adolescents: How are family factors related to substance use change? *Journal of Psychoactive Drugs, 45,* 28–38.

Bess, J. A., & Stabb, S. D. (2009). The experiences of transgendered persons in psychotherapy: Voices and recommendations. *Journal of Mental Health Counseling, 31,* 264–282.

Bickelhaupt, E. (1986). Psychosocial aspects of AIDS. *Kansas Medicine, 87,* 66–83.

Biegel, D. E., Kola, L. A., Ronis, R. J., & Kruszynski, R. (2013). Evidence-based treatment for adults with co-occurring mental and substance use disorders: Current practice and future directions. In J. Rosenberg & S. Rosenberg (Eds.), *Community mental health: Challenges for the 21st century* (2nd ed., pp. 215–237). New York, NY: Routledge/ Taylor & Francis.

Bill W., AA Grapevine, January 1958 as referenced in Berger, A. (2010). *12 smart things to do when the booze and drugs are gone.* Center City, MN: Hazelden.

Biller, R., & Rice, S. (1990). Experiencing multiple loss of persons with AIDS: Grief and bereavement issues. *Health and Social Work, 15,* 283–290.

Binder, R. (2002, November). Liability for the psychiatrist expert witness. *American Journal of Psychiatry, 159,* 1819–1825.

Birky, I., & Collins, W. (2011). Facebook: Maintaining ethical practice in the cyberspace age. *Journal of College Student Psychotherapy, 25,* 193–203. doi: 10.1080/87568225.2011.581922

Bissell, L. C., & Royce, J. E. (1994). *Ethics for addiction professionals.* Center City, MN: Hazelden.

Black, D. W., Monihan, P., Schlosser, S., & Repertinger, S. (2001). Compulsive buying severity: An analysis of Compulsive Buying Scale results in 44 subjects. *Journal of Nervous and Mental Disorders, 189,* 123–126.

Blake, R. (1990). Mental health counseling and older problem drinkers. *Journal of Mental Health Counseling, 12,* 354–367.

Blanco, C., Morcillo, C., Alegria, M., Dedios, M. C., Fernandez-Navarro, P., Regincos, R., & Wang, S. (2013). Acculturation and drug use disorders among Hispanics in the U.S. *Journal of Psychiatric Research, 47,* 226–232.

Blazer, D. G., & Wu, L.-T. (2009). The epidemiology of at-risk and binge drinking among middle-aged and elderly community adults: National Survey on Drug Use and Health. *American Journal of Psychiatry, 166,* 1162–1169.

Bliss, D. L. (2009). Ethnic differences in spirituality in a sample of men and women in diverse substance abuse treatment settings: Implications for practitioners. *Journal of Ethnicity in Substance Abuse, 8,* 413–430. doi: 10.1080/15332640903327583

Bloom, B. L. (1997). *Planned short-term psychotherapy: A clinical handbook* (2nd ed.). Boston, MA: Allyn & Bacon.

Blow, F. C., & Barry, K. L. (2009). Treatment of older adults. In R. K. Ries, D. A. Fiellin, S. C. Miller, & R. Saitz (Eds.), *Principles of addiction medicine* (4th ed., pp. 479–492). Philadelphia, PA: Wolters Kluwer.

Blow, F. C., Brower, K. J., Schulenberg, J. E., Demo-Dananberg, L. M., Young, J. P., & Beresford, T. P. (1992). The Michigan alcoholism screening test—Geriatric version (MAST-G): A new elderly-specific screening instrument. *Alcoholism: Clinical and Experimental Research, 16,* 372.

Blume, A. W. (2005). *Treating drug problems.* Hoboken, NJ: Wiley.

Blume, A. W., & Garcia de la Cruz, B. (2005). Relapse prevention among diverse populations. In G. A. Marlatt & D. M. Donovan (Eds.), *Relapse prevention* (2nd ed., pp. 45–64). New York, NY: Guilford Press.

Blume, E. S. (1990). *Secret survivors: Uncovering incest and its aftereffects in women.* New York, NY: Wiley.

Blume, S. B. (1997). Women: Clinical aspects. In J. H. Lowinson, P. Ruiz, R. B. Millman, & J. G. Langrod (Eds.), *Substance abuse: A comprehensive textbook* (3rd ed., pp. 645–654). Baltimore, MD: Williams & Wilkins.

Bobbe, J. (2002). Treatment with lesbian alcoholics: Healing shame and internalized homophobia for ongoing sobriety. *Health and Social Work, 27,* 218–222.

Boden, M. T., Kimerling, R., Jacobs-Lentz, J., Bowman, D., Weaver, C., Carney, D., . . . Trafton, J. A. (2011). Seeking safety treatment for male veterans with a substance use disorder and post-traumatic stress disorder symptomology. *Addiction, 107,* 578–586. doi: 10.1111/j.13600443.2011.03658.x

Bogat, G. A., Garcia, A. M., & Levendosky, A. A. (2013). Assessment and psychotherapy with women experiencing intimate partner violence: Integrating research and practice. *Psychodynamic Psychiatry, 41,* 189–217.

Bogenschutz, M. P., Geppert, C. M. A., & George, J. (2006). The role of twelve-step approaches in dual diagnosis treatment and recovery. *American Journal on Addictions, 15,* 50–60.

Bogner, J. (2013). Substance use disorders. In D. B. Arciniegas & N. D. Zasler (Eds.), *Management of adults with traumatic brain injury.* Arlington, VA: American Psychiatric Publishing.

Bolier, L., Haverman, M., Westerhof, G. J., Riper, H., Smit, F., & Bohlmeijer, E. (2013) Positive psychology interventions: A meta-analysis of randomized controlled studies. *BMC Public Health, 13,* 119–139.

Bombardier, C. H., & Turner, A. P. (2010). Alcohol and other drug use in traumatic disability. In R. G. Frank, M. Rosenthal, & B. Caplan (Eds.), *Handbook of rehabilitation psychology* (2nd ed., pp. 241–258). Washington, DC: American Psychological Association.

Bossin, P. G. (1992). How to handle custody cases. *Trial, 28,* 24–26, 28.

Bowen, M. (1978). *Family therapy in clinical practice.* New York, NY: Aronson.

Bowen, S., Witkiewitz, K., Dillworth, T. M., Chawla, N., Simpson, T. L., Ostafin, B. D., . . . Marlatt, G. A. (2006). Mindfulness meditation and substance use in an incarcerated population. *Psychology of Addictive Behaviors, 20,* 343–347.

Bowman, K., & Jellinek, E. M. (1941). Alcohol addiction and its treatment. *Quarterly Journal of Studies on Alcohol, 2,* 18–176.

Bowser, B. P., & Bilal, R. (2001). Drug treatment effectiveness: African-American culture in recovery. *Journal of Psychoactive Drugs, 33,* 391–402.

Bradley, A. M. (1988). Keep coming back. *Alcohol Health and Research World, 15,* 194–199.

Bradley, L. J., & Hendricks, B. (2009). E-mail and ethical issues. *Family Journal: Counseling and Therapy for Couples and Families, 17,* 267–271. doi: 10.1177/1066480709338293

Bradley, L. J., Hendricks, B., Lock, R., Whiting, P. P., & Parr, G. (2011). E-mail communication: Issues for mental health counselors. *Journal of Mental Health Counseling, 33,* 67–79.

Brady, K. J. (2001). Exposure therapy in the treatment of PTSD among cocaine-dependent individuals: Preliminary findings. *Journal of Substance Abuse Treatment, 21,* 47–54.

Brady, K. T., & Back, S. E. (2008). Women and addiction. In M. Galanter & H. D. Kleber (Eds.), *Substance abuse treatment* (4th ed., pp. 555–564). Washington, DC: American Psychiatric Publishing.

Brandon, T. H., Vidrine, J. I., & Litvin, E. B. (2007). Relapse and relapse prevention. *Annual Review of Clinical Psychology, 3,* 257–284.

Bratter, T. E. (1985). Special clinical psychotherapeutic concerns for alcoholic and drug addicted individuals. In T. E. Bratter & G. G. Forrest (Eds.), *Alcoholism and substance abuse strategies for clinical intervention* (pp. 523–574). New York, NY: Free Press.

Bray, J. H., Kowalchuk, A., Waters, V., Laufman, L., & Shilling, E. H. (2012). Baylor SBIRT medical residency training program: Model description and initial evaluation. *Substance Abuse, 33,* 231–240.

Brekke, J. S. (1987, June). Detecting wife and child abuse in clinical settings. *Social Casework: Journal of Contemporary Social Work,* 332–338.

Brennan, P. L., & Moos, R. H. (1996). Late-life drinking behavior. *Alcohol Health and Research World, 20,* 197–205.

Briere, J. (1989). *Therapy for adults molested as children: Beyond survival.* New York, NY: Springer.

Briere, J., & Scott, C. (2006). *Principles of trauma therapy.* Thousand Oaks, CA: Sage.

Bright, C. L., Osborne, V. A., & Greif, G. L. (2011). One dozen considerations when working with women in substance abuse groups. *Journal of Psychoactive Drugs, 43,* 64–68.

Bright, C. L., Ward, S. K., & Negi, N. J. (2011). "The chain has to be broken": A qualitative investigation of the experiences of young women following juvenile court involvement. *Feminist Criminology, 6,* 32–53.

Bristow-Braitman, A. (1995). Addiction recovery: 12-Step programs and cognitive behavioral psychology. *Journal of Counseling and Development, 73,* 414–418.

Brodsky, S., & Robey, A. (1972, March). On becoming an expert witness: Issues of orientation and effectiveness. *Professional Psychology, 3,* 173–176.

Brooke, S. L. (2007). *The use of creative therapies with sexual abuse survivors.* Springfield, IL: Thomas.

Brooks, M. K. (1997). Ethical and legal aspects of confidentiality. In J. H. Lowinson, P. Ruiz, R. B.

Millman, & J. G. Langrod (Eds.), *Substance abuse: A comprehensive textbook* (3rd ed., pp. 884–899). Baltimore, MD: Williams & Wilkins.

Brown, F., & Tooley, J. (1989). Alcoholism in the black community. In G. W. Lawson & A. W. Lawson (Eds.), *Alcoholism and substance abuse in special populations* (pp. 115–130). Rockville, MD: Aspen Press.

Brown, G. R., & Anderson, B. (1991). Psychiatric morbidity in adult inpatients with childhood histories of sexual and physical abuse. *American Journal of Psychiatry, 148,* 55–61.

Brown, H. P., Peterson, J. H., & Cunningham, O. (1988). Rationale and theoretical basis for a behavioral/cognitive approach to spirituality. *Alcohol Treatment Quarterly, 5,* 47–59.

Brown, K. S. (2005, Fall). The neurophysiology of pain. *Register Report,* 46–53.

Brown, L. S., & Walker, L. E. (1990). Feminist therapy perspectives on self-disclosure. In G. Stricker & M. Fisher (Eds.), *Self-disclosure in the therapeutic relationship* (pp. 135–156). New York, NY: Plenum Press.

Brown, R. (2011). Drug court effectiveness: A matched cohort study in the Dane County drug treatment court. *Journal of Offender Rehabilitation, 50,* 191–201.

Brown, R. L., Leonard, T., Saunders, L. A., & Papasouliotis, O. (2001). A two-item conjoint screen for alcohol and other drug problems. *Journal of the American Board of Family Practice, 14,* 95–106.

Brown, S., & Brown, D. R. (2001). *A biography of Mrs. Marty Mann: The first lady of Alcoholics Anonymous.* Center City, MN: Hazelden.

Brown University Digest of Addiction Theory and Application (2009, June). Therapy-directed strategy increases AA involvement among outpatients. *Brown University Digest of Addiction Theory and Application, 28*(1), 6–7.

Brubaker, M. D., Garrett, M. T., & Dew, B. J. (2009). Examining the relationship between internalized heterosexism and substance abuse among lesbian, gay, and bisexual individuals: A critical review. *Journal of LGBT Issues in Counseling, 3,* 62–89. doi: 10.1080/15538600902754494

Bruckner, D. F., & Johnson, P. E. (1987). Treatment for adult male victims of childhood sexual abuse. *Social Casework: Journal of Contemporary Social Work, 68,* 81–87.

Buchanan, L. P., & Buchanan, W. L. (1992). Eating disorders: Bulimia and anorexia. In L. L'Abate, J. E. Farrar, & D. A. Serritella (Eds.), *Handbook of differential treatments for addictions* (pp. 165–188). Boston, MA: Allyn & Bacon.

Buck, T., & Sales, A. (2000). *Related addictive disorders* (ERIC Document Reproduction Service No. ED440345).

Buelow, G. D., & Buelow, S. A. (1998). *Psychotherapy in chemical dependence treatment: A practical and integrative approach.* Pacific Grove, CA: Brooks/Cole.

Buka, S. (2002). Disparities in health status and substance use: Ethnicity and socioeconomic factors. *Public Health Reports, 117,* 118–125.

Bukstein, O. G. (1995). *Adolescent substance abuse.* New York, NY: Wiley.

Burbules, N. C. (1993). *Dialogue in teaching.* New York, NY: Teachers College Press.

Bureau of Justice Statistics (FBJ). (2004). *National crime victimization survey, criminal victimization, 2003.* Retrieved from http://www.ojp.usdoj.gov/bjs/pub/pdf/cv03.pdf#search=22%National%20Crime%

Bureau of Justice Statistics (FBJ). (2005). *Family violence statistics, 2004.* Retrieved from http://www.ojp.usdoj.gov/bjs/pub/pdf/cv03.pdf#search=22%National%20Crime%

Burke, M. T., & Miller, G. A. (1996). Using the spiritual perspective in counseling persons with HIV/AIDS: An integrative approach. *Counseling and Values, 40,* 185–195.

Burleson, J. A., Kaminer, Y., & Burke, R. H. (2012). Twelve-month follow-up of aftercare for adolescents with alcohol use. *Journal of Substance Abuse Treatment, 42,* 78–86.

Burnett, R., Porter, E., & Stallings, K. (2011). Treatment options for individuals with dual diagnosis. *Journal of Human Behavior in the Social Environment, 21,* 849–857.

Burroughs, A. (2003). *Dry: A memoir.* New York, NY: St. Martin's Press.

Burton, D. L. (1998, November). Integrating care for dually diagnosed: Making it happen. *Alcoholism & Drug Abuse Weekly, 10,* 5.

Bushfield, S. Y., & Deford, B. (2010). *End-of-life care and addiction: A family systems approach.* New York, NY: Springer.

Cabaj, R. J. (1997). Gays, lesbians, & bisexuals. In J. H. Lowinson, P. Ruiz, R. B. Millman, & J. G. Langrod (Eds.), *Substance abuse: A comprehensive textbook* (3rd ed., pp. 725–733). Baltimore, MD: Williams & Wilkins.

Cabaj, R. P. (2008). Gay men and lesbians. In M. Galanter & H. D. Kleber (Eds.), *Substance abuse treatment* (4th ed., pp. 623–638). Washington, DC: American Psychiatric Press.

Cahill, A. J. (2001). *Rethinking rape*. Ithaca, NY: Cornell Press.

Callicott, Q. (2012). Exploring strengths of gay men in 12-step recovery. *Journal of Gay & Lesbian Social Services: Issues in Practice, Policy, & Research, 24,* 396–416.

Cameron, S., & turtle-song, I. (2002). Learning to write case notes using the SOAP format. *Journal of Counseling and Development, 80,* 286–292.

Caprara, G. V., & Cervone, D. (2003). A conception of personality for a psychology of human strengths: Personality as an agentic, self-regulating system. In L. G. Aspinwall & U. M. Staudinger (Eds.), *A psychology of human strengths: Fundamental questions and future directions for a positive psychology* (pp. 61–74). Washington, DC: American Psychological Association.

Capuzzi, D., & Gross, D. R. (1992). *Introduction to group counseling*. Denver, CO: Love.

Capuzzi, D., & Stauffer, M. D. (Eds.). (2008). *Foundations of addictions counseling*. Boston, MA: Allyn & Bacon.

Cardemil, E. V., & Battle, C. L. (2003). Guess who's coming to therapy? Getting comfortable with conversations about race and ethnicity in psychotherapy. *Professional Psychology: Research and Practice, 34,* 278–286.

Carnes, P. (1995, October). Sexual addiction. Paper presented at the National Dual Disorder Conference, Las Vegas, NV.

Carroll, K. M. (2009). Twelve step facilitation approaches. In R. K. Ries, D. A. Fiellin, S. C. Miller, & R. Saitz (Eds.), *Principles of addiction medicine* (4th ed., pp. 869–873). Philadelphia, PA: Wolters Kluwer.

Carver, C. S., & Scheier, M. F. (2003). Three human strengths. In L. G. Aspinwall & U. M. Staudinger (Eds.), *A psychology of human strengths: Fundamental questions and future directions for a positive psychology* (pp. 87–102). Washington, DC: American Psychological Association.

Cashwell, C. S., Clarke, P. B., & Graves, E. G. (2009). Step by step: Avoiding spiritual bypass in 12-step work. *Journal of Addictions & Offender Counseling, 30,* 37–48.

Cass, V. C. (1979). Homosexual identity formation: A theoretical model. *Journal of Homosexuality, 4,* 219–235.

Center for Substance Abuse Treatment. (1994). *Practical approaches in the treatment of women who abuse alcohol and other drugs* (DHHS Publication No. SMA 94–3006). Rockville, MD: Author.

Center for Substance Abuse Treatment. (1999). *Cultural issues in substance abuse treatment* (DHHS Publication No. SMA 99–3278) Rockville, MD: Author.

Center on Alcohol Marketing and Youth (CAMI). (2006, June). *African-American youth and alcohol advertising*. Retrieved from http://camy.org/factsheets

Centers for Disease Control and Prevention. (1989). *AIDS surveillance/epidemiology* [Slide presentation]. Atlanta, GA: Author.

Centers for Disease Control and Prevention, National Center for Health Statistics. (2006). *Health, United States, 2006 with chartbook on trends in the health of Americans*. Hyattsville, MD: National Center for Health Statistics. Retrieved from http://www.cdc.gov/nchs/data/hus/hus06.pdf

Centers for Disease Control and Prevention. (2007). *HIV/AIDS surveillance report*. Atlanta, GA. Retrieved from www.cd.cgov/hiv/topics/surveillance/basic.htm#hivest

Centers for Disease Control and Prevention. (2009). *General statistics on Americans with disabilities*. Retrieved from http://www.cdc.gov/Features/ParalysisResource/

Centers for Disease Control and Prevention. (2011). Focus Area/Prescription Drug Overdose/Injury Center. *Saving lives and protecting people: Preventing prescription painkiller overdoses*. http://www.cdc.gov/injury/about/focus-rx.html

Centers for Disease Control and Prevention. (2011). National Center for HIV/AIDS, Hepatitis, STD, and TB prevention. Division of HIV/AIDS Prevention. *HIV among African Americans*. Retrieved from http://www.cdc.gov/hiv/topics/aa/pdf/aa.pdf

Centers for Disease Control and Prevention. (2013a). *HIV in the United States: At a glance*. http://www.cdc.gov/hiv/statistics/basics/ataglance.html

Centers for Disease Control and Prevention. (2013b). *HIV among women*. http://www.cdc.gov/hiv/pdf/risk_women.pdf

Chambless, D. L., & Ollendick, T. H. (2001). Change in psychotherapy: A plea for no more "nonspecific" and false dichotomies. *Clinical Psychology: Science and Practice*, 12, 198–201.

Chaney, M. P., & Brubaker, M. D. (2012). Addiction in LGBTQ communities: Influences, treatment, and prevention. *Journal of LGBT Issues in Counseling*, 6, 234–236.

Chapman, R. J. (1996). Spirituality in the treatment of alcoholism: A worldview approach. *Counseling and Values*, 41, 39–50.

Chariyeva, Z., Golin, C. E., Earp, J. A., Maman, S., Suchindran, C., & Zimmer, C. (2013). The role of self-efficacy and motivation to explain the effect of motivational interviewing time on changes in risky sexual behavior among people living with HIV: A mediation analysis. *AIDS and Behavior*, 17, 813–823.

Chartier, K. G., Hesselbrock, M. N., & Hesselbrock, V. M. (2013). Ethnicity and gender comparisons of health consequences in adults with alcohol dependence. *Substance Use & Misues*, 48, 200–210.

Cherniss, C. (1991). Career commitment in human service professionals: A biographical study. *Human Relations*, 44, 419–437.

Cherniss, C., & Dantzig, S. A. (1986). Preventing and managing job-related stress. In R. Kilburg, P. E. Nathan, & R. W. Thoreson (Eds.), *Professionals in distress: Issues, syndromes, and solutions in psychology* (pp. 255–273). Washington, DC: American Psychological Association.

Cheung, Y. W. (2000). Substance abuse and developments in harm reduction. *Canadian Medical Association Journal*, 162, 1690–1697.

Cho, C., & Cassidy, D. F. (1994). Parallel processes for workers and their clients in chronic bereavement resulting from HIV. *Death Studies*, 18, 273–292.

Christopher, J. (1988). *How to stay sober: Recovery without religion*. Buffalo, NY: Prometheus Books.

Christopher, J. (1992). *SOS sobriety*. Buffalo, NY: Prometheus Books.

Christopher, J. (1997). Secular organizations for sobriety. In J. H. Lowinson, P. Ruiz, R. B. Millman, & J. G. Langrod (Eds.), *Substance abuse: A comprehensive textbook* (3rd ed., pp. 396–399). Baltimore, MD: Williams & Wilkins.

Chung, R. C.-Y., & Bemak, F. (2002). The relationship of culture and empathy in cross-cultural counseling. *Journal of Counseling and Development*, 80, 154–159.

Ciarrocchi, J. W. (2012). Positive psychology and spirituality: A virtue-informed approach to well-being. In L. J. Miller (Ed.), *The Oxford handbook of psychology and spirituality* (pp. 425–436). New York, NY: Oxford University Press.

Clark, H. W., & Bizzell, A. C. (2009). Ethical issues in addiction practice. In R. K. Ries, D. A. Fiellin, S. C. Miller, & R. Saitz (Eds.), *Principles of addiction medicine* (4th ed., pp. 1485–1490). Philadelphia, PA: Wolters Kluwer.

Clark, K. A., Dee, D. L., Bale, P. L., & Martin, S. L. (2001). Treatment compliance among prenatal care patients with substance abuse problems. *American Journal of Drug and Alcohol Abuse*, 27, 121–136.

Clay, R. (1996, December). Older alcoholics isolated, yet in need of treatment. *APA Monitor*, 38.

Clinician's Research Digest. (2013, September). Cultural humility of therapists is associated with stronger working alliance and better psychotherapy outcomes. *Clinician's Research Digest*, p. 5. Washington, DC: American Psychological Association.

Clipson, C. R. (2005). Misuse of psychologist influence: Multiple relationships. In S. F. Bucky, J. E. Callan, & G. Stricker (Eds.), *Ethical and legal issues for mental health professionals: A comprehensive handbook of principles and standards* (pp. 169–203). Binghampton, NY: Haworth.

Cohen, L. R., Field, C., Campbell, A. N. C., & Hien, D. A. (2013). Intimate partner violence outcomes in women with PTSD and substance use: A secondary analysis of NIDA Clinical Trials Network "Women and Trauma" Multi-site Study. *Addictive Behaviors*, 38, 2325–2332.

Cohn, A. M., Hagman, B. T., Graff, F. S., & Noel, N. E. (2011). Modeling the severity of drinking consequences in first-year college women: An item response theory analysis of the Rutgers Alcohol Problem Index. *Journal of Studies on Alcohol and Drugs*, 72, 981–990.

Coker, A. L., Smith, P. H., McKeown, R. E., & King, M. J. (2000). Frequency and correlates of intimate partner violence by type: Physical, sexual, and psychological battering. *American Journal of Public Health*, 90, 553–559.

Colleran, C., & Jay, D. (2002). *Aging and addiction*. Center City, MN: Hazelden.

Collins, G. (1993). Reconstructing codependency using self-in-relation theory: A feminist perspective. *Social Work*, 38, 470–476.

Compton, P. (1999). Substance abuse. In M. McCaffery & C. Pasero (Eds.), *Pain: Clinical manual* (pp. 429–466). St. Louis, MO: Mosby.

Compton, P. (2011). Treating chronic pain with prescription opioids in the substance abuser: Relapse prevention and management. *Journal of Addictions Nursing*, *22*, 39–45. doi: 10.3109/10884602.2010.545092

Compton, P., Gallagher, R. M., & Mardini, I. A. (2009). The neurophysiology of pain and interfaces with addiction. In R. K. Ries, D.A. Fiellin, S. C. Miller, & R. Saitz (Eds.), *Principles of addiction medicine* (4th ed., pp. 1277–1295). Philadelphia, PA: Wolters Kluwer.

Compton, W. M., & Denisco, R. (2008). Prescription drug use. In M. Galanter & H. D. Kleber (Eds.), *Textbook of substance abuse treatment* (4th ed., pp. 595–607). Washington, DC: American Psychiatric Publishing.

Conant, M., Hardy, D., Sernatinger, J., Spicer, D., & Levy, J. A. (1986). Condoms prevent transmission of AIDS-associated retrovirus. *Journal of the American Medical Association*, *255*, 1706.

Condit, M., Kitaji, K., Drabble, L., & Trocki, K. (2011). Sexual-minority women and alcohol: Intersections between drinking, relational contexts, stress, and coping. *Journal of Gay & Lesbian Social Services: The Quarterly Journal of Community & Clinical Practice*, *23*, 351–375.

Connors, G. J., DiClemente, C. C., Velasquez, M. M., & Donovan, D. M. (2013). *Substance abuse treatment and the stages of change*. (2nd ed.). New York, NY: Guilford Press.

Connors, G. J., Donovan, D. M., & DiClemente, C. C. (2001). *Substance abuse treatment and the stages of change*. New York, NY: Guilford Press.

Connors, G. J., & Tarbox, A. R. (1985). Michigan alcoholism screening test. In D. J. Keyer & R. C. Sweetland (Eds.), *Test critiques* (Vol. 3, pp. 439–446). Kansas City, MO: Westport.

Cook, L. S. (2001). Adolescent addiction and delinquency in the family system. *Issues in Mental Health Nursing*, *22*, 151–157.

Coombs, R. H. (Ed.). (2005). *Addiction counseling review: Preparing for comprehensive, certification and licensing examination*. Mahwah, NJ: Erlbaum.

Coombs, R. H., & Howatt, W. A. (2005). *The addiction counselor's desk reference*. Hoboken, NJ: Wiley.

Corey, G. (1995). *Theory and practice of group counseling* (4th ed.). Pacific Grove, CA: Brooks/Cole.

Corey, G. (2004a). *Theory and practice of group counseling* (6th ed.). Belmont, CA: Brooks/Cole.

Corey, G. (2004b). *Theory and practice of group counseling: Student manual* (6th ed.). Belmont, CA: Brooks/Cole.

Corey, G. (2012). *Theory and practice of counseling and psychotherapy* (8th ed.). Belmont, CA: Brooks/Cole.

Corey, G. (2013). *Theories and practice of counseling and psychotherapy* (9th ed.). Belmont, CA: Brooks/Cole.

Corey, G., & Corey, M. S. (1992). *Groups: Process and practice* (4th ed.). Pacific Grove, CA: Brooks/Cole.

Corey, G., Corey, M. S., & Callanan, P. (1998). *Issues and ethics in the helping professions*. Pacific Grove, CA: Brooks/Cole.

Cormier, S., & Cormier, B. (1998). *Interviewing strategies for helpers* (4th ed.). Pacific Grove, CA: Brooks/Cole.

Corrigan, J. D., Bogner, J., & Holloman, C. (2012). Lifetime history of traumatic brain injury among persons with substance use disorders. *Brain Injury*, *26*, 139–150.

Corrigan, J. D., & Deutschle, J. J. (2008). The presence and impact of traumatic brain injury among clients in treatment for co-occurring mental illness and substance abuse. *Brain Inury*, *22*, 223–231.

Cosci, F., & Fava, G. A. (2010). New clinical strategies of assessment of comordity associated with substance use disorders. *Clinical Psychology Review*, *31*, 418–427.

Cosden, M. (2008, Summer). Research on drug courts. *Addictions Newsletter*, *15*, 11–12.

Countering domestic violence. (2004, April). *Harvard Mental Health Letter*, *20*, 1–5.

Courbasson, C. M., Nishikawa, Y., & Shapira, L. B. (2011). Mindfulness-action based cognitive behavioral therapy for concurrent binge eating disorder and substance use disorders. *Eating Disorders*, *19*, 17–33. doi: 10.1080/10640266.2011.533603

Cox, M. J. (2013). Taking the lock off the Spiritual Integration Toolbox. *Counseling Today*, *56*, 52–56.

CRAFFT. Retrieved from http://www.slp3d2.com/rwj_1027

Craig, E. (2007). Tao psychotherapy: Introducing a new approach to humanistic practice. *Humanistic Psychologist*, *35*, 109–133.

Craig, L. (2012). Motivational interviewing. *Corrections Today, April/May 2012*, 88–90.

Crome, I., Li, T.-K., Rao, R., & Wu, L.-T. (2012). Alcohol limits in older people. *Addiction*, *107*, 1541–1543.

Cross, T. L., Bazron, B. J., Dennis, K. W., & Isaacs, M. R. (1989). *Towards a culturally competent system of* care: *A monograph on effective services for minority children who are severely emotionally disturbed.* Washington, DC: Georgetown University Child Development Center, Child and Adolescent Service System Program Technical Assistance Center.

Crumley, F. E. (1990). Substance abuse and adolescent suicidal behavior. *Journal of the American Medical Association, 263,* 3051–3056.

Csikszentmihalyi, M. (1990). *Flow.* New York, NY: Harper.

Csikszentmihalyi, M. (1999). If we are so rich, why aren't we happy? *American Psychologist, 54,* 821–827.

Csikszentmihalyi, M. (2008). *Flow* (2nd ed.). New York, NY: Harper Perennial.

Cummings, O. W., & Nall, R. L. (1983). Relationships of leadership style and burnout to counselors' perceptions of their jobs, themselves, and their clients. *Counselor Education and Supervision, 22,* 227–234.

Cushman, P. (1990). Why the self is empty. *American Psychologist, 45,* 599–611. http://www.cdc.gov/hiv/pdf/statistics_basics_factsheet.pdf

Dadich, A. (2010). Expanding our understanding of self-help support groups for substance use issues. *Journal of Drug Education, 40,* 189–202.

Dahlbeck, D. T., & Lease, S. H. (2010). Career issues and concerns for persons living with HIV/AIDS. *Career Development Quarterly, 58,* 359–368.

Daire, A. P., Jacobson, L., & Carlson, R. G. (2012). Emotional stocks and bonds: A metaphorical model for conceptualizing and treating codependency and other forms of emotional overinvesting. *American Journal of Psychotherapy, 66,* 259–279.

Daley, D. (1995, October). *Relapse prevention with dual disorder patients.* Paper presented at the National Dual Disorder Conference, Las Vegas, NV.

Daley, D. C., & Marlatt, G. A. (1997). Relapse prevention. In J. H. Lowinson, P. Ruiz, R. B. Millman, & J. G. Langrod (Eds.), *Substance abuse: A comprehensive textbook* (3rd ed., pp. 458–467). Baltimore, MD: Williams & Wilkins.

Daley, D. C., & Marlatt, G. A. (2006a). *Overcoming your alcohol or drug problem: Effective recovery strategies* (Therapist guide, 2nd ed.). New York, NY: Oxford University Press.

Daley, D. C., & Marlatt, G. A. (2006b). *Overcoming your alcohol or drug problem: Effective recovery strategies* (Workbook, 2nd ed.). New York, NY: Oxford University Press.

Daley, D. C., & Zuckoff, A. (1999). *Improving treatment compliance: Counseling & systems strategies for substance abuse & dual disorders.* Center City, MN: Hazelden.

Daly, G. (1996). *Homeless: Policies, strategies, and lives on the street.* New York, NY: Routledge.

Danielson, C. K., Amstadter, A. B., Dangelmaier, R. E., Resnick, H. S., Saunders, B. E., & Kilpatrick, D. G. (2009). Does typography of substance abuse and dependence differ as a function of exposure to child maltreatment? *Journal of Child & Adolescent Substance Abuse, 18,* 323–342.

Davanloo, H. (1980). A method of short-term dynamic psychotherapy. In H. Davanloo (Ed.), *Short-term dynamic psychotherapy* (pp. 75–91). Northvale, NJ: Aronson.

Davidson, M. G. (2000). Religion and spirituality. In R. M. Perez, K. A. DeBord, & J. Bieschke (Eds.), *Handbook of counseling and psychotherapy with lesbian, gay, and bisexual clients* (pp. 409–433). Washington, DC: American Psychological Association.

Davis, D. D. (1993). Inhalants: Know the facts. *Next Step: Step One, 6,* 7.

Davis, D. J. (1990). Prevention issues in developing programs. In R. C. Engs (Ed.), *Women: Alcohol and other drugs* (pp. 71–77). Dubuque, IA: Kendall/Hunt.

Davis, L. (Discussion Guide Writer), & Baker, S. (Ed.). (1990). *Inhalant abuse: Kids in danger/Adults in the dark* [Film]. (Available from Media Projects, Inc., 5215 Homer Street, Dallas, TX 75206.)

Davis, L. L., Pilkinton, P., Wisniewski, S. R., Trivedi, M. H., Gaynes, B. N., Howland, R. H., . . . Rush, A. J. (2012). Effect of concurrent substance use disorder on the effectiveness of single and combination antidepressant medications for the treatment of major depression: An exploratory analysis of a single-blind randomized trial. *Depression and Anxiety, 29,* 111–122.

Davis, S. J., Koch, D. S., McKee, M. F., & Nelipovich, M. (2009). AODA training experiences of blindness and visual impairment professionals. *Journal of Teaching in the Addictions, 8,* 42–50.

Davis, T. A., & Ancis, J. (2012). Look to the relationship: A review of African American women substance users' poor treatment retention and working alliance development. *Substance Use & Misuse, 47,* 662–672.

Day-Vines, N. L., Wood, S. M., Grothaus, T., Craigen, L., Holman, A., Dotson-Blake, K., & Douglas, M. J. (2007). Broaching the subjects of race, ethnicity, and culture in the counseling process. *Journal of Counseling & Development, 85,* 401–409.

DeAngelis, T. (2013, November). Fresh ideas for combating HIV/AIDS. *Monitor on Psychology, 44,* 28–32.

De Biaze Vilela, F. A., Jungerman, F. S., Laranjeira, R., & Callaghan, R. (2009). The transtheoretical model and substance dependence: Theoretical and practical aspects. *Revista Brasileira de Psiquiatria, 31,* 362–36.

Deci, E. L., & Ryan, R. M. (2008). Hedonia, eudaimonia, and well-being: An introduction. *Journal of Happiness Studies, 9,* 1–11.

Degutis, L. C., Fiellin, D. A., & D'Onofrio, G. (2009). Traumatic injuries related to alcohol and other drug use. In R. K. Ries, D. A. Fiellin, S. C. Miller, & R. Saitz (Eds.), *Principles of addiction medicine* (4th ed., pp. 1091–1098). Philadelphia, PA: Wolters Kluwer.

DeJong, W. (1994). Relapse prevention: An emerging technology for promoting long-term drug abstinence. *International Journal of the Addictions, 29,* 681–705.

DelGiudice, M. J., & Kutinsky, J. (2007). Applying motivational interviewing to the treatment of sexual compulsivity and addiction. *Sexual Addiction & Compulsivity, 14,* 303–319.

Dembo, R., Burgos, W., Babst, D. U., Schmeidler, J., & LeGrand, L. E. (1978). Neighborhood relationships and drug involvement among inner city junior high school youths: Implications for drug education and prevention programming. *Journal of Drug Education, 8,* 231–252.

Denning, P. (2005). Harm reduction tools and programs. In R. H. Coombs (Ed.), *Addiction counseling review* (pp. 487–509). Mahwah, NJ: Erlbaum.

Dennis, M., Godley, S. H., Diamond, G., Babor, T., Liddle, H., Kaminer, Y., . . . Tims, F. M. (2004). The cannabis youth treatment (CYT) study: Main findings from two randomized trials. *Journal of Substance Abuse Treatment, 27,* 197–213.

de Shazer, S. (1985). *Keys to solution in brief therapy.* New York, NY: Norton.

Diaz, N., Green, D., & Horton, E. G. (2009). Predictors of depressive symptoms among inpatient substance abusers. *International Journal of Mental Health and Addiction, 7,* 347–356.

DiClemente, C. C. (2003). *Addiction and change.* New York, NY: Guilford Press.

DiClemente, C. C., Garay, M., & Gemmell, L. (2008). Motivational enhancement. In M. Galanter & H. D. Kleber (Eds.), *Substance abuse treatment* (4th ed., pp. 361–371). Washington, DC: American Psychiatric Publishing.

DiClemente, C. C., Prochaska, J. O., Fairhurst, S. K., Velicer, W. F., Velasquez, M. M., & Rossi, J. S. (1991). The process of smoking cessation: An analysis of precontemplation, contemplation, and preparation stages of change. *Journal of Consulting and Clinical Psychology, 59,* 295–304.

Dimeff, L. A., Comtois, K. A., & Linehan, M. M. (2003). Co-occurring addictive and borderline personality disorders. In R. K. Ries, D. A. Fiellin, S. C. Miller, & R. Saitz (Eds.), *Principles of addiction medicine* (3rd ed., pp. 1227–1238). Chevy Chase, MD: American Society of Addiction Medicine.

Dimeff, L. A., Comtois, K. A., & Linehan, M. M. (2009). Co-occurring addiction and borderline personality disorder. In R. K. Ries, D. A. Fiellin, S. C. Miller, & R. Saitz (Eds.), *Principles of addiction medicine* (4th ed., pp. 1227–1237). Philadelphia, PA: Wolters Kluwer.

Dimeff, L. A., & Linehan, M. M. (2008). Dialectical behavior therapy for substance abusers. *Addiction Science & Clinical Practice, 4,* 39–47.

Dimeff, L. A., & Marlatt, G. A. (1998). Preventing relapse and maintaining change in addictive behaviors. *Clinical Psychology: Science and Practice, 5,* 513–525.

Dimock, P. T. (1988). Adult males sexually abused as children: Characteristics and implications for treatment. *Journal of Interpersonal Violence, 3,* 203–221.

Director, L. (1995). Dual diagnosis: Outpatient treatment of substance abusers with coexisting psychiatric disorders. In A. M. Washton (Ed.), *Psychotherapy and substance abuse: A practitioner's handbook* (pp. 375–393). New York, NY: Guilford Press.

Disability Funders Network. (2012). Retrieved from http://www.disabilityfunders.org/disability-stats-and-facts

Discovery Health Channel & American Psychological Association. (2002). *Aftermath: The road to resilience* [Packet]. Washington, DC: American Psychological Association.

Dixit, A. R., & Crum, R. M. (2000). Prospective study of depression and the risk of heavy alcohol use in women. *American Journal of Psychiatry, 157,* 751–758.

Dobmeier, R. A., Reiner, S. M., Casquarelli, E. J., & Fallon, K. M. (2013). Overcoming the schism between spiritual identity and sexual orientation. *Counseling Today, 55*, 48–52.

Dobson, D., & Dobson, K. S. (2009). *Evidence-based practice of cognitive-behavioral therapy.* New York, NY: Guilford Press.

Dobson, K. S., & Dozois, D. (2001). Historical and philosophical bases of the cognitive-behavioral therapies. In K. S. Dobson (Ed.), *Handbook of cognitive-behavioral therapies* (2nd ed., pp. 3–39). New York, NY: Guilford Press.

Dodge, K., Dishion, T. J., & Lansford, J. (Eds.). (2006). *Deviant peer influences in programs for youth problems and solutions.* New York, NY: Guilford Press.

Do mainstream treatment, harm reduction mix? (2001, January 29). *Alcoholism & Drug Abuse Weekly, 13,* 1–4.

Domar, A. D., & Dreher, H. (2000). *Self-nurture.* New York, NY: Viking.

D'Onofrio, G., Fiellin, D. A., Pantalon, M. V., Chawarski, M. C., Owens, P. H., Degutis, L. C., . . . O'Connor, P. G. (2012). A brief intervention reduces hazardous and harmful drinking in emergency department patients. *Annals of Emergency Medicine, 60,* 181–192.

Doran, N., Hohman, M., & Koutsenok, I. (2011). Motivational interviewing training outcomes for juvenile correctional staff in California. *Journal of Psychoactive Drugs, 43,* 19–26.

Dossett, W. (2013). Addiction, spirituality and 12-step programmes. *International Social Work, 56,* 369–383. doi: 10.1177/0020872813475689

Douglas, A. N., Jimenez, S., Lin, H. J., & Frisman, L. K. (2008). Ethnic differences in the effects of spiritual well-being on long-term psychological and behavioral outcomes within a sample of homeless women. *Cultural Diversity and Ethnic Minority Psychology, 14,* 344–352. doi: 10.1037/1099-9809. 14.4.344

Doukas, N., & Cullen, J. (2010). Recovered addicts working in the addiction field: Pitfalls to substance abuse relapse. *Drugs: Education, Prevention and Policy, 17,* 216–231. doi: 10.3109/09687630802378864

Doweiko, H. F. (1990). *Concepts of chemical dependency* (2nd ed.). Pacific Grove, CA: Brooks/Cole.

Doweiko, H. F. (1996). *Concepts of chemical dependency* (3rd ed.). Pacific Grove, CA: Brooks/Cole.

Doweiko, H. F. (2002). *Concepts of chemical dependency* (5th ed.). Pacific Grove, CA: Brooks/Cole.

Doweiko, H. F. (2009). *Concepts of chemical dependency* (7th ed.). Belmont, CA: Brooks/Cole.

Downs, W. R., Capshew, T., & Rindels, B. (2004). Relationships between adult men's alcohol problems and their childhood experiences of parental violence and psychological aggression. *Journal of Studies on Alcohol, 65,* 336–345.

Downs, W. R., & Harrison, L. (1998). Childhood maltreatment and the risk of substance abuse problems in later life. *Health and School Care in the Community, 6,* 35–36.

Doyle, K. (1997). Substance abuse counselors in recovery: Implications for the ethical issue of dual relationships. *Journal of Counseling and Development, 75,* 428–432.

Drabble, L., & Eliason, M. J. (2012). Substance use disorders treatment for sexual minority women. *Journal of LGBT Issues in Counseling, 6,* 274–292.

Drake, R. E., & Green, A. I. (2013). The challenge of heterogeneity and complexity in dual diagnosis. *Journal of Dual Diagnosis, 9,* 105–106.

Drug and Alcohol Services Information System (2002, August 16). Asian and Pacific Islanders in substance abuse treatment: 1999. In the *DASIS Report.* Rockville, MD: SAMHSA. Retrieved from www.oas. samhsa.gov/2K2/AsiansallTx/AsiansallTx.htm

Drumm, R., Popescu, M., Cooper, L., Trecartin, S., Sifert, M., Foster, T., & Kilcher, C. (2013). "God just brought me through it": Spiritual coping strategies for resilience among intimate partner violence survivors. *Clinical Social Work Journal.* doi: 10/1007/ s10615–013–0449-y.

D'Sylva, F., Graffam, J., Hardcastel, L., & Shinkfield, A. J. (2012). Analysis of the stages of change model of drug and alcohol treatment readiness among prisoners. *International Journal of Offender Therapy and Comparative Criminology, 56,* 265–280.

Dual diagnosis: Part I. (2003a, August). *Harvard Mental Health Letter, 20,* 1–3.

Dual diagnosis: Part II. (2003b, September). *Harvard Mental Health Letter, 20,* 1–5.

Duckworth, G. L., & Rosenblatt, A. (1976). Helping the elderly alcoholic. *Social Casework: Journal of Contemporary Social Work, 57,* 291–301.

Duckworth, J., & Anderson, W. (1986). *MMPI interpretation manual for counselors and clinicians* (3rd ed.). Muncie, IN: Accelerated Development.

Dunlop, J., Manghelli, D., & Tolson, R. (1989). Senior alcohol and drug coalition statement of treatment philosophy for the elderly. *Professional Counselor, 4,* 39–42.

Durham, J., & Hatcher, B. (1984). Reducing psychological complications for the critically ill AIDS patient. *Dimensions of Critical Care Nursing, 3,* 300–306.

Ebener, D. J., & Smedema, S. M. (2011). Physical disability and substance use disorders: A convergence of adaptation and recovery. *Rehabilitation Counseling Bulletin, 54,* 131–141.

Eberle, P. (1982). Alcohol abusers and non-users: A discriminant analysis of differences between two subgroups of batterers. *Journal of Health and Social Behavior, 23,* 260–271.

Eck, D. (2001). *A new religious America.* San Francisco, CA: Harper.

Edelson, J. L., & Tolman, R. M. (1992). *Intervention for men who batter: An ecological approach.* Newbury Park, CA: Sage.

Eden, S. L., & Aguilar, R. J. (1989). The Hispanic chemically dependent client: Considerations for diagnosis and treatment. In G. W. Lawson & A. W. Lawson (Eds.), *Alcoholism and substance abuse in special populations* (pp. 205–222). Rockville, MD: Aspen Press.

Edmond, T., Bowland, S., & Yu, M. (2013). Use of mental health services by survivors of intimate partner violence. *Social Work in Mental Health, 11,* 34–54.

Edward, K.-L., & Robins, A. (2012). Dual diagnosis, as described by those who experience the disorder: Using the Internet as a source of data. *International Journal of Mental Health Nursing, 21,* 550–559.

Edwards, C. L., Johnson, S., & Feliu, M. (2003, November/December). Diversity and cultural competence: Part 2. Issues of practical conceptualization and implementation. *North Carolina Psychologist, 55, 1,* 13.

Edwards, K. M., Dixon, K. J., Gidycz, C. A., & Desai, A. D. (2013). Family-of-origin violence and college men's reports of intimate partner violence perpetration in adolescence and young adulthood: The role of maladaptive interpersonal patterns. *Psychology of Men & Masculinity.* Advance online publication. doi: 10/1037a0033031

Eisenberg, N., & Wang, V. O. (2003). Toward a positive psychology: Social developmental and cultural contributions. In L. G. Aspinwall & U. M. Staudinger (Eds.), *A psychology of human strengths: Fundamental questions and future directions for a positive psychology* (pp. 61–74). Washington, DC: American Psychological Association.

el-Guebaly, N. (2008). Cross-cultural aspects of addiction. In M. Galanter & H. D. Kleber (Eds.), *Substance abuse treatment* (4th ed., pp. 45–52). Washington, DC: American Psychiatric.

Eliason, M. J. (1996). *Who cares?: Institutional barriers to health care for lesbian, gay, and bisexual persons.* New York, NY: National League for Nursing.

Ellis, A. (1962). *Reason and emotion in psychotherapy.* New York, NY: Stuart.

Ellis, A. (1992). Brief therapy: The rational-emotive approach. In S. H. Budman, M. F. Hoyt, & S. Friedman (Eds.), *The first session in brief therapy* (pp. 36–58). New York, NY: Guilford Press.

Elmore, D. L., Brown, L. M., & Cook, J. M. (2009, August). International perspectives on addressing the needs of older adults during disasters. Presentation at the annual meeting of the American Psychological Association, Toronto, Canada.

Embree, J. A. (2012). Prevalence of suicide attempts in a deaf population with co-occurring substance use disorder. *Journal of Addiction Medicine, 6,* 258–272.

Emerson, S., & Markos, P. A. (1996). Signs and symptoms of the impaired counselor. *Journal of Humanistic Education and Development, 34,* 108–117.

Engel, G. L. (1959). Psychogenic pain and the pain-prone patient. *American Journal of Medicine, 26,* 899–918.

Erford, B. T. (2013). *Assessment for counselors* (2nd ed.). Belmont, CA: Brooks/Cole Cengage.

Erickson, P. G. (1999). The three phases of harm reduction: An examination of emerging concepts, methodologies, and critiques. *Substance Use and Misuse, 34,* 1–7.

Ernst, G. (2000). The myth of the "Mediterranean Syndrome": Do immigrants feel different pain? *Ethnicity & Health, 5,* 121–126.

Evans, E., Pierce, J., Li, L., Rawson, R., & Hser, Y. (2012). More alike than different: Health needs, services utilization, and outcomes of Asian American and Pacific Islaneer (AAPI) populations treated for substance use disorders. *Journal of Ethnicity in Substance Abuse, 11,* 318–338.

Evans, K., & Sullivan, J. M. (2001). *Dual diagnosis: Counseling the mentally ill substance abuser* (2nd ed.). New York, NY: Guilford Press.

Evans, K., & Sullivan, M. (1991a). *Understanding depression and addiction* [Brochure]. Center City, MN: Hazelden.

Evans, K., & Sullivan, M. (1991b). *Understanding major anxiety disorders and addiction* [Brochure]. Center City, MN: Hazelden.

Evans, K., & Sullivan, M. (1991c). *Understanding post-traumatic stress disorder and addiction* [Brochure]. Center City, MN: Hazelden.

Evans, K., & Sullivan, M. (1995, October). PTSD and the adolescent dual disorder patient. Paper presented at the National Dual Disorder Conference, Las Vegas, NV.

Evans, S., & Schaefer, S. (1987). Incest and chemically dependent women: Treatment implications. *Journal of Chemical Dependency Treatment, 1*, 141–173.

Ewing, J. A. (1984). Detecting alcoholism: The CAGE questionnaire. *Journal of the American Medical Association, 252*, 1905–1907.

Eyler, E. C. H. (2013). Chronic and acute pain and pain management for patients in methadone maintenance treatment. *American Journal on Addictions, 22*, 75–83. doi: 10.1111.u.1521-0391.2013.00308.

Fagan, R. W. (1986). The use of volunteer sponsors in the rehabilitation of skid-row alcoholics. *Journal of Drug Issues, 16*, 321–337.

Fals-Stewart, W., & Lam, W. K. K. (2008). Brief behavioral couples therapy for drug abuse: A randomized clinical trial examining clinical efficacy and cost-effectiveness. *Families, Systems, & Health, 26*, 377–392.

Farkas, K. J. (2004). Substance abuse problems among older adults. In S. L. A. Straussner (Ed.), *Clinical work with substance-abusing clients* (2nd ed., pp. 330–346). New York, NY: Guilford Press.

Faupel, C. E., Horowitz, A. M., & Weaver, G. S. (2004). *The sociology of American drug use.* Boston, MA: McGraw-Hill.

Fayne, M. (1993). Recognizing dual diagnosis patients in various clinical settings. In J. Solomon, S. Zimberg, & E. Shollar (Eds.), *Dual diagnosis: Evaluation, treatment, training, and program development* (pp. 39–53). New York, NY: Plenum Press.

Federal Register. Part II. Department of Health and Human Services, 42 C.F.R. Part 2 Vol. *52* (June 1987) (No. 110, 2179621814). Washington, DC: Author.

Feldstein, S. W., & Ginsburg, J. I. D. (2006). Motivational interviewing with dually diagnosed adolescents in juvenile justice settings. *Brief Treatment and Crisis Intervention, 6*(3), 218–233.

Ferraro, K. J. (1993). Cops, courts, and woman battering. In P. B. Bart & E. G. Moran (Eds.), *Violence against women: The bloody footprints* (pp. 165–176). London, England: Sage.

Fields, R. (1995). *Drugs in perspective* (2nd ed.). Madison, WI: Brown & Benchmark.

Fields, R., & Vandenbelt, R. (1992a). *Understanding mood disorders and addiction* [Brochure]. Center City, MN: Hazelden.

Fields, R., & Vandenbelt, R. (1992b). *Understanding personality problems and addiction* [Brochure]. Center City, MN: Hazelden.

Finkelhor, D. (1986). *A sourcebook on child sexual abuse.* Beverly Hills, CA: Sage.

Finley, J. R. (2004). *Integrating the 12 steps into addiction therapy.* Hoboken, NJ: Wiley.

Finnegan, D. G., & McNally, E. B. (1987). *Dual identities: Counseling chemically dependent gay men and lesbians.* Center City, MN: Hazelden.

Finnell, D. S. (2003). Addiction services: Use of the transtheoretical model for individuals with co-occuring disorders. *Community Mental Health Journal, 39*, 3–15.

First, M. B., & Gladis, M. M. (1993). Diagnosis and differential diagnosis of psychiatric and substance use disorders. In J. Solomon, S. Zimberg, & E. Shollar (Eds.), *Dual diagnosis: Evaluation, treatment, training, and program development* (pp. 23–37). New York, NY: Plenum Press.

Fishbain, D. A. (2006). Chronic pain and addiction. In M. V. Boswell and B. E. Cole (Eds.), *Weiner's pain management: A practical guide for clinicians* (7th ed., pp. 117–139). London, England: Informa Healthcare.

Fisher, G. L., & Harrison, T. C. (1997). *Substance abuse: Information for school counselors, social workers, therapists, and counselors.* Boston, MA: Allyn & Bacon.

Fisher, N. L., & Pina, A. (2013). An overview of the literature on female-perpetrated adult male sexual victimization. *Aggression and Violent Behavior, 18*, 54–61.

Fiske, S. T., & Taylor, S. E. (1983). *Social cognition.* Reading, MA: Addison-Wesley.

Fitzpatrick, M. R., & Irannejad, S. (2008). Adolescent readiness for change and the working alliance in counseling. *Journal of Counseling & Development, 86*, 438–445.

Fleming, M. F. (2003). Screening for at-risk, problem, and dependent alcohol use. In R. K. Hester & W. R. Miller (Eds.), *Handbook of alcoholism treatment approaches: Effective alternatives* (3rd ed., pp. 64–77). Boston, MA: Allyn & Bacon.

Flores, P. J. (1986). Alcoholism treatment and the relationship of Native American cultural values to recovery. *International Journal of the Addictions, 20,* 1707–1726.

Flores, P. J. (1988). Alcoholics Anonymous: A phenomenological and existential perspective. *Alcoholism Treatment Quarterly, 5,* 73–94.

Fong, T. W., Reid, R. C., & Parhami, I. (2012). Behavioral addictions: Where to draw the lines? *Psychiatric Clinics of North America, 35,* 279–296.

Ford, J. A., & Watkins, W. C. (2012). Adolescent nonmedical prescription drug use. *Prevention Researcher, 19,* 3–6.

Ford, J. D., Russo, E. M., & Mallon, S. D. (2007). Integrating treatment of posttraumatic stress disorder and substance use disorder. *Journal of Counseling & Development, 85,* 475–489.

Forrest, L. U. (2004). Approaches to counseling and psychotherapy with women. In D. R. Atkinson & G. Hackett (Eds.), *Counseling diverse populations* (3rd ed., pp. 308–322). Boston, MA: McGraw-Hill.

Forsyth, D. R. (1983). *An introduction to group dynamics.* Monterey, CA: Brooks/Cole.

Foster, S. (1995, November). Alcoholism: A growing and hidden epidemic among the elderly. *Counseling Today,* 19–26.

Fowler, J. W. (1993). Alcoholics Anonymous and faith development. In B. S. McCrady & W. R. Miller (Eds.), *Research on Alcoholics Anonymous* (pp. 113–135). New Brunswick, NJ: Rutgers Center of Alcohol Studies.

Frank, P. B., & Golden, G. K. (1992). Blaming by naming: Battered women and the epidemic of codependence. *Social Work, 37,* 5–6.

Frankl, V. E. (1963). *Man's search for meaning.* New York, NY: Simon & Schuster.

Frazier, P., Harlow, T., Schauben, L., & Byrne, C. (1993, August). Predictors of postrape trauma. Paper presented at the 101st annual meeting of the American Psychological Association, Toronto, Ontario, Canada.

Freimuth, M. (2002). The unseen diagnosis: Substance use disorder. *Psychotherapy Bulletin, 37,* 26–30.

French, J., & Raven, B. (1959). The basis of social power. In D. D. Cartwright (Ed.), *Studies on social power* (pp. 150–167). Ann Arbor: University of Michigan, Institute for Social Research.

Frey, J. (2007). Motivational interviewing and behavioral compliance in chronic pain patients: A treatment outcome study. Unpublished doctoral dissertation. George Fox University of Newberg, OR.

Frezza, M., DiPodova, C., Pozzato, G., Terpin, M., Baraona, E., & Lieber, D. S. (1990). High blood alcohol levels in women. *New England Journal of Medicine, 322,* 95–99.

Friedman, H. L., & Robbins, B. D. (2012). The negative shadow cast by positive psychology: Contrasting views and implications of humanistic and positive psychology on resiliency. *Humanistic Psychologist, 40,* 87–102.

Friedman, S., & Fanger, M. T. (1991). *Expanding therapeutic possibilities: Getting results in brief psychotherapy.* Lexington, MA: Lexington Books.

Friere, P. (1989). *Pedagogy of the oppressed.* New York, NY: Continuum.

Galanter, M. (2007). Spirituality and recovery in 12-step programs: An empirical model. *Journal of Substance Abuse Treatment, 33,* 265–272.

Galanter, M. (2009). Network therapy. In R. K. Ries, D. A. Fiellin, S. A. Miller, & R. Saitz (Eds.), *Principles of addiction medicine* (4th ed., pp. 819–829). Philadelphia, PA: Wolters Kluwer.

Galanter, M. (2009). Spirituality in the recovery process. In R. K. Ries, D. A. Fiellin, S. C. Miller, & R. Saitz (Eds.), *Principles of addiction medicine* (4th ed., pp. 939–942). Philadelphia, PA: Wolters Kluwer.

Galanter, M., & Brook, D. (2001). Network therapy for addiction: Bringing family and peer support into office practice. *International Journal of Group Psychotherapy, 51,* 101–122.

Galanter, M., Egelko, S., & Edwards, H. (1993). Rational recovery: Alternative to AA for addiction? *American Journal of Drug and Alcohol Abuse, 19,* 499–510.

Gallavan, D. B., & Newman, J. L. (2013). Predictors of burnout among correctional mental health professionals. *Psychological Services, 10,* 115–122. doi: 10.1037/a0031341

Gambert, S. R. (1997). The elderly. In J. H. Lowinson, P. Ruiz, R. B. Millman, & J. G. Langrod (Eds.), *Substance abuse: A comprehensive textbook* (3rd ed., pp. 692–699). Baltimore, MD: Williams & Wilkins.

Gambrill, G. (2010). Evidence-based practice and policy: Choices ahead. In K. van Wormer & B. A. Thyer (Eds.), *Evidence-based practice in the field of substance abuse: A book of readings* (pp. 13–42). Los Angeles, CA: Sage.

Gangi, J., & Darling, C. A. (2012). Adolescent substance-use frequency following self-help group attendance and outpatient substance abuse treatment.

Journal of Child & Adolescent Substance Abuse, 21, 293–309.

Ganley, A. L., & Harris, L. (1978). *Domestic violence on trial* (pp. 155–173). New York, NY: Springer.

Garcia, F. D., & Thibaut, F. (2010). Sexual addictions. *American Journal of Drug and Alcohol Abuse, 36,* 254–260.

Gary, L. E. (1986). Drinking, homicide, and the Black male. *Journal of Black Studies, 17,* 15–31.

Gatchel, R. J. (2005). *Clinical essentials of pain management.* Washington, DC: American Psychiatric Association.

Gatz, M., Russell, L. A., Grady, J., Kram-Fernandez, D., Clark, C., & Marshall, B. (2005). Women's recollections of victimization, psychological problems, and substance use. *Journal of Community Psychology, 33,* 479–493.

Gaughwin, P. (2004, January). A consideration of the relationship between the rules of court and the code of ethics in forensic psychiatry. *Australian and New Zealand Journal of Psychiatry, 38,* 20–25.

Geller, A. (1991). The effects of drug use during pregnancy. In P. Roth (Ed.), *Alcohol and drugs are women's issues: Vol. 1. A review of the issues* (pp. 101–106). Metuchen, NJ: Scarecrow Press and Women's Action Alliance.

Gelso, C. J., & Woodhouse, S. (2003). Toward a positive psychotherapy: Focus on human strength. In W. B. Walsh (Ed.), *Counseling psychology and optimal human functioning* (pp. 171–197). Mahwah, NJ: Erlbaum.

Giannetti, V. J. (1993). Brief relapse prevention with substance abusers. In R. A. Wells & V. J. Giannetti (Eds.), *Casebook of the brief psychotherapies* (pp. 159–178). New York, NY: Plenum Press.

Gianoli, M. O., Serrita, J. J., O'Brien, E., & Ralevski, E. (2012). Treatment for comorbid borderline personality disorder and alcohol use disorders: A review of the evidence and future recommendations. *Experimental and Clinical Psychopharmacology, 20,* 333–344.

Giedd, J. N. (2004). Structural magnetic resonance imaging of the adolescent brain. In R. E. Dahl & L. Patia (Eds.), *Adolescent brain development: Vulnerabilities and opportunities* (pp. 77–85). New York, NY: Annals of the New York Academy of Sciences.

Gifford, P. D. (1991). A.A. and N.A. for adolescents. *Journal of Adolescent Chemical Dependency, 1,* 101–120.

Gilbert, M. J. (1991). Acculturation and changes in drinking patterns among Mexican American women: Implications for prevention. *Alcohol Health and Research World, 15,* 234–238.

Gillette, J. (2012, Spring). Prevent violence against young women. *Prevention & Recovery, 1,* 1.

Gilman, S. M., Galanter, M., & Dermatis, H. (2001). Methadone anonymous: A 12-step program for methadone maintained heroin addicts. *Substance Abuse, 22,* 247–256.

Gilmartin, P. (1994). *Rape, incest, and child sexual abuse: Consequences and recovery.* New York, NY: Garland Press.

Gladding, S. (1991). Counselor self-abuse. *Journal of Mental Health Counseling, 13,* 414–419.

Glaser, F. B., & Edmondson, T. D. (2000, August/September). Brief interventions for alcohol and drug problems. *Next Step: Step One,* 5.

Glass, E. J. (1980–1981). Problem drinking among the blind and visually impaired. *Alcohol Health and Research World, 5,* 26–30.

Glasser, W., & Wubbolding, R. E. (1995). Reality therapy. In R. Corsini & D. Wedding (Eds.), *Current psychotherapies* (5th ed., pp. 293–321). Itasca, IL: Peacock Press.

Glaze, L. E., & Bonczar, T. P. (2007). *Probation and parole in the United States, 2006.* Bureau of Justice Statistics Bulletin. NCJ Publication No. 221218. Washington, DC: Department of Justice.

Glickman, N. (2009). *Cognitive behavioral therapy for deaf and hearing individuals with language and learning challenges.* New York, NY: Routledge.

Glow, B. A. (1989). Alcoholism, drugs, and the disabled. In G. W. Lawson & A. W. Lawson (Eds.), *Alcoholism and substance abuse in special populations* (pp. 65–93). Rockville, MD: Aspen Press.

Goebert, D., & Nishimura, S. (2011). Comparison of substance abuse treatment utilization and preferences among Native Hawaiians, Asian Americans, and Euro Americans. *Journal of Substance Use, 16,* 161–170.

Gold, M. S. (1995, February). What can we learn from clinical research? Broadening the base of treatment options. Paper presented at the North Carolina Governors' Institute, Greensboro.

Goldberg, R. (2008, April). Substance abuse and the aging brain: Screening, diagnoses and treatment. *Brown University Geriatric Psychopharmacology Update, 12,* 3–6.

Golden, G. K., & Frank, P. B. (1994). When 50–50 isn't fair: The case against couple counseling in domestic abuse. *Social Work, 39,* 636–637.

Goldstein, E. G. (1994). Self-disclosure in treatment: What therapists do and don't talk about. *Clinical Social Work Journal, 22,* 417–433.

Goldstein, E. G. (2004). Substance abusers with borderline disorders. In S. L. A. Straussner (Ed.), *Clinical work with substance-abusing clients* (2nd ed., pp. 370–391). New York, NY: Guilford Press.

Gomberg, E., & Nirenberg, T. (1991). Commentary: Women and substance abuse. *Journal of Substance Abuse, 3,* 255–267.

Gondolf, E. (1992). Discussion of violence in psychiatric evaluations. *Journal of Interpersonal Violence, 7,* 334–349.

Gone, J. P. (2012). Indigenous traditional knowledge and substance abuse treatment outcomes: The problem of efficacy evaluation. *American Journal of Drug and Alcohol Abuse, 38,* 493–497.

Gonsiorek, J. C., Bera, W. H., & LeTourneau, D. (1994). *Male sexual abuse.* Thousand Oaks, CA: Sage.

Gonzales, A., Westerberg, V., Peterson, T. R., Moseley, A., Gryczynski, J., Mitchell, S. G., . . . Schwartz, R. P. (2012). Implementing a statewide screening, brief intervention, and referral to treatment (SBIRT) service in rural health settings: New Mexico SBIRT. *Substance Abuse, 33,* 114–123.

Goodman, A. (1997). Sexual addiction. In J. H. Lowinson, P. Ruiz, R. B. Millman, & J. G. Langrod (Eds.), *Substance abuse: A comprehensive textbook* (3rd ed., pp. 340–354). Baltimore, MD: Williams & Wilkins.

Goodman, M. S., & Fallon, B. C. (1995). *Pattern changing for abused women.* Thousand Oaks, CA: Sage.

Goodman, S., & Levy, S. J. (2003). *The biopsychosocial model revisited: A psychodynamic view of addiction.* Retrieved from www.rocklandpscych.com/biopsychosocial/htm

Gordon, J. U. (1994). African American perspective. In J. U. Gordon (Ed.), *Managing multiculturalism in substance abuse services* (pp. 45–71). Thousand Oaks, CA: Sage.

Gordon, S. M. (2003). *Relapse & recovery: Behavioral strategies for change.* Wernersville, PA: Caron.

Gorski, T. T. (1989a). *Passages through recovery: An action plan for preventing relapse.* Center City, MN: Hazelden.

Gorski, T. T. (1989b). *The relapse/recovery grid.* Center City, MN: Hazelden.

Gorski, T. T. (1990). The CENAPS model of relapse prevention: Basic principles and procedures. *Journal of Psychoactive Drugs, 22,* 125–133.

Gorski, T. T. (1992). *The staying sober workbook: A serious solution for the problem of relapse.* Independence, MO: Herald House/Independence Press.

Gorski, T. T. (1998). *Brief therapy for relapse prevention.* Homewood, IL: CENAPS.

Gorski, T. T. (2003). *Relapse prevention in the managed care environment.* Retrieved from www.tgorski.com.

Gorski, T. T., & Miller, M. (1986). *Staying sober: A guide for relapse prevention.* Independence, MO: Herald House/Independence Press.

Gorski, T. T., & Miller, M. (1988). *Mistaken beliefs about relapse.* Independence, MO: Herald House/Independence Press.

Gragg, D. M. (1995). Managed health care systems: Chemical dependency treatment. In C. S. Austad & W. H. Berman (Eds.), *Psychotherapy in managed health care* (pp. 202–219). Washington, DC: American Psychological Association.

Graham, J. R. (1990). *MMPI-2: Assessing personality and psychopathology.* New York, NY: Oxford University Press.

Graham, K., Saunders, S. J., Flower, M. C., Timney, C. B., White-Campbell, M., & Pietropaolo, A. Z. (1995). *Addictions treatment for older adults: Evaluation of an innovative client-centered approach.* New York, NY: Haworth Press.

Grant, G. (2008). *Charting women's journeys: From addiction to recovery.* Lanham, MD: Lexington Books.

Grant, G. (2011). *Using trauma-informed AOD treatment practices to improve outcomes for African American survivors of domestic violence.* Retrieved from http://www.adp.ca.gov/women/PDF/Trauma_Informed.pdf

Gray, M., & Littlefield, M. B. (2002). Black women and addictions. In S. L. A. Straussner & S. Brown (Eds.), *The handbook of addiction treatment for women: Theory and practice* (pp. 301–322). San Francisco, CA: Jossey-Bass.

Greanias, T., & Siegel, S. (2000). Dual diagnosis. In J. R. White & A. S. Freeman (Eds.), *Cognitive-behavioral group therapy for specific problems and populations* (pp. 149–173). Washington, DC: American Psychological Association.

Greaves, L., & Poole, N. (2008). Bringing sex and gender into women's substance use treatment programs. *Substance Use & Misuse, 43,* 1271–1273.

Green, C. R., Baker, T. A., Sato, Y., Washington, T. L., & Smith, E. M. (2003). Race and chronic pain: A comparative study of young black and white Americans presenting for management. *Journal of Pain, 4,* 176–183. doi: 10.1016/S1526-5900(02)65013-8

Greene, D., & Faltz, B. (1991). Chemical dependency and relapse in gay men with HIV infection: Issues and treatment. *Journal of Chemical Dependency Treatment, 4,* 79–90.

Greene, K., & Bogo, M. (2002). The different faces of intimate violence: Implications for assessment and treatment. *Journal of Marital and Family Therapy, 28,* 455–466.

Greene, P., Kane, D., Christ, G., Lynch, S., & Corrigan, M. (2006). *FDNY crisis counseling: Innovative responses to 9/11 firefighters, families, and communities.* Hoboken, NJ: Wiley.

Greenfield, S. F., & Grella, C. E. (2009). What is "women-focused" treatment for substance use disorders? *Psychiatric Services, 60,* 880–882.

Greenfield, S. F., & Hennessy, G. (2008). Assessment of the patient. In M. Galanter & H. D. Kleber (Eds.), *Substance abuse treatment* (4th ed., pp. 55–78). Washington, DC: American Psychiatric Publishing.

Greenstone, J. L., & Leviton, S. C. (1993). *Elements of crisis intervention.* Pacific Grove, CA: Brooks/Cole.

Gressard, C. F. (2010). Substance abuse counseling. In S. G. Niles & S. C. Nassar-McMillan (Eds.), *Developing your identity as a professional counselor: Standards, settings, and specialties.* Belmont, CA: Brooks/Cole.

Griffin, R. E. (1991). Assessing the drug involved client. *Families in Society: Journal of Contemporary Human Services, 72,* 87–94.

Griffiths, M. (2003). Internet gambling: Issues, concerns, and recommendations. *CyberPsychology & Behavior, 6,* 557–568.

Grinstead, S. F. (2002). *Addiction-free pain management.* Independence, MO: Herald House/Independent Press.

Grinstead, S. F. (2007, September). Addiction-free pain management. Workshop held at Appalachian State University, Boone, NC.

Gross, M. (1945). The relation of the pituitary gland to some symptoms of alcohol intoxication and chronic alcoholism. *Quarterly Journal of Studies on Alcohol, 6,* 25–35.

Grzesniac, R. C. (2003). Revisiting pain-prone personalities: Combining psychodynamics with the neurobiological sequelae of trauma. *American Journal of Pain Management, 13,* 6–15.

Guillem, E., Notides, C., Debray, M., Vorspan, F., Musa, C., Leroux, M., . . . Lepine, J-P. (2011). Psychometric properties of the cannabis use disorders identification test in French cannabis misusers. *Journal of Addictions Nursing, 22,* 214–223. doi: 10.3109/10884602.2011.616604

Guthmann, D. (1994, November). Counseling deaf and hard of hearing persons with substance abuse and/or mental health issues: Is cross cultural counseling possible? Paper presented at the meeting of the Innovative Partnerships in Recovery, Overland Park, KS.

Guthmann, D., & Blozis, S. A. (2001). Unique issues faced by deaf individuals entering substance abuse treatment and following discharge. *American Annals of the Deaf, 146,* 294–303.

Guthmann, D., & Graham, V. (2004). Substance abuse: A hidden problem within the deaf and hard of hearing communities. *Journal of Teaching in the Addictions, 3,* 49–64.

Guthmann, D., Lazowski, L. E., Moore, D., Heinemann, A. W., & Embree, J. (2012). Validation of the substance abuse screener in American Sign Language (SAS-ASL). *Rehabilitation Psychology, 57,* 140–148.

Guthmann, D., & Sandberg, K. A. (2003). Culturally affirmative substance abuse treatment for deaf people: Approaches, materials, and administrative considerations. In N. S. Glickman & S. Gulati (Eds.), *Mental health care of deaf people: A culturally affirmative approach* (pp. 261–303). Mahwah, NJ: Erlbaum.

Guthmann, D., & Sternfeld, C. (2013). Substance abuse treatment and recovery: Adaptations to best practices when working with culturally deaf persons. In N. S. Glickman (Ed.), *Counseling and psychotherapy: Investigating practice from scientific, historical, and cultural perspectives* (pp. 234–267). New York, NY: Routledge/Taylor & Francis.

Guthmann, D., Swan, K., & Gendreau, C. (1994, November). Placement, treatment, transition and ethical issues when serving chemically dependent deaf and hard-of-hearing clients. Paper presented at the meeting of the Innovative Partnerships in Recovery, Overland Park, KS.

Hagedorn, W. B., & Hirshhorn, M. A. (2009). When talking won't work: Implementing experiential group activities with addicted clients. *Journal for Specialists in Group Work, 34*(1), 43–67.

Haley, M. (2008). Professional issues. (2008). In D. Capuzzi & M. D. Stauffer (Eds.), *Foundations of addictions counseling* (pp. 46–75). Boston, MA: Allyn & Bacon.

Hall, B. A. (1994). Ways of maintaining hope in HIV disease. *Research in Nursing and Health*, *17*, 283–293.

Hall, J. (1994). Lesbians recovering from alcohol problems: An ethnographic study of health care experiences. *Nursing Research*, *43*, 238–244.

Hall, R. P., Kassees, J. M., & Hoffman, C. (1980). Treatment for survivors of incest. *Journal for Specialists in Group Work*, *11*, 85–92.

Hamilton, T., & Samples, P. (1994). *The twelve steps and dual disorders*. Center City, MN: Hazelden.

Hankin, A., Daugherty, M., Bethea, A., & Haley, L. (2013). The emergency department as a prevention site: A demographic analysis of substance use among ED patients. *Drug and Alcohol Dependence*, *130*, 230–233.

Hansen, M., Ganley, B., & Carlucci, C. (2008). Journeys from addiction to recovery. *Research and Theory for Nursing Practice*, *22*, 256–272.

Hanson, G. R. (2002). New insights into relapse. *NIDA Notes*, *17*(3), 3–4.

Hardy, K. V., & Qureshi, M. E. (2012). Devaluation, loss, and rage: A postscript to urban African American youth with substance abuse. *Alcoholism Treatment Quarterly*, *30*, 326–342.

Harris, A. H. S., Thoresen, C. E., & Lopez, S. J. (2007). Integrating positive psychology into counseling: Why and (when appropriate) how. *Journal of Counseling & Development*, *85*, 3–13.

Hart, C. L., & Ksir, C. (2012). *Drugs, society, and human behavior* (15th ed.). Boston, MA: McGraw-Hill.

Hart, K. E., & Sasso, T. (2011). Mapping the contours of contemporary positive psychology. *Canadian Psychology*, *52*, 82–92.

Hartston, H. (2012). The case for compulsive shopping as an addiction. *Journal of Psychoactive Drugs*, *44*, 64–67.

Harvard Medical School Special Report. (2008). *Alcohol use and abuse*. Boston, MA: Harvard Health Publications.

Harvard Medical School Special Report. (2008). *Overcoming addiction*. Boston, MA: Harvard Health Publications.

Harvard Mental Health Letter. (2003a, August). Dual diagnosis: Part I. *Harvard Mental Health Letter*, *20*, 1–3.

Harvard Mental Health Letter. (2003b, September). Dual diagnosis: Part II. *Harvard Mental Health Letter*, *20*, 1–5.

Harvard Mental Health Letter. (2008, May). Positive psychology in practice. *Harvard Mental Health Letter*, *24*, 1–3.

Harvard Mental Health Letter. (2008, July). Moving from one stage of addiction recovery to the next. *Harvard Mental Health Letter*, *25*, 6–7.

Harvard Mental Health Letter. (2009, September). Treating generalized anxiety disorder in the elderly. *Harvard Mental Health Letter*, *26*, 1–3.

Harvard Mental Health Letter. (2009, November). One question may screen for unhealthy alcohol use. *Harvard Mental Health Letter*, *26*, 7.

Harvey, W. B. (1985). Alcohol abuse and the Black community: A contemporary analysis. *Journal of Drug Issues*, *15*, 81–91.

Haseltine, F. P. (2000). Gender differences in addiction and recovery. *Journal of Women's Health and Gender-Based Medicine*, *9*, 579–583.

Haugaard, J. J., & Reppucci, N. D. (1988). *The sexual abuse of children*. San Francisco, CA: Jossey-Bass.

Hayes, L. L. (1997, June). Comprehensive services required when helping pregnant women overcome addiction. *Counseling Today*, *1*, 20.

Hayes, L. L. (1999, January). New technology helps spur rise in compulsive gambling. *Counseling Today*, 1.

Hays, D. G., Craigen, L. M., Knight, J., Healey, A., & Sikes, A. (2009). Duty to warn and protect against self-destructive behaviors and interpersonal violence. *Journal of School Counseling*, 7.

Hays, D. G., & Erford, B. T. (2014). *Developing multicultural counseling competence: A systems approach* (2nd ed.). Boston, MA: Pearson.

Hazelden. (1996). *How to talk to an older person who has a problem with alcohol or medications*. Center City, MN: Author.

Heather, N., Hoenekopp, J., & Smailes, D. (2009). Progressive stage transition does mean getting better: A further test of the transtheoretical model in recovery from alcohol problems. *Addiction*, *104*, 949–958.

Heather, N., & McCambridge, J. (2013). Post-treatment stage of change predicts 12-month outcome of treatment for alcohol problems. *Alcohol and Alcoholism*, *48*, 329–336.

Heaton, K. J., & Black, L. L. (2009). I knew you when: A case study of managing preexisting nonamorous relationships in counseling. *Family Journal, 17*, 134–138. doi: 10.1177/1066480709332854

Heinemann, A. W. (Ed.). (1993). *Substance abuse and physical disability*. New York, NY: Haworth Press.

Heinemann, A. W. (1997). Persons with disabilities. In J. H. Lowinson, P. Ruiz, R. B. Millman, & J. G. Langrod (Eds.), *Substance abuse: A comprehensive textbook* (3rd ed., pp. 716–725). Baltimore, MD: Williams & Wilkins.

Hellman, R. E., Stanton, M., Lee, J., & Tytun, A. (1989). Treatment of homosexual alcoholics in government-funded agencies: Provider training and attitudes. *Hospital Community Psychiatry, 40*, 1163–1168.

Helms, J. E. (1995). An update of Helms's white and people of color racial identity models. In J. G. Ponterotto, J. M. Cases, L. A. Suzuki, & C. M. Alexander (Eds.), *Handbook of multicultural counseling* (pp. 155–180). Thousand Oaks, CA: Sage.

Hendershot, C. S., Witkiewitz, K., George, W. H., & Marlatt, G. A. (2011). Relapse prevention for addictive behaviors. *Substance Abuse Treatment, Prevention, and Policy, 6*, 1–17.

Henderson, J. P. (2005). Professional examinations in alcohol and other drug abuse counseling. In R. H. Coombs (Ed.), *Addiction counseling review: Preparing for comprehensive certification and licensing examinations* (pp. 577–598). Mahwah, NJ: Erlbaum.

Hendricks, B., Bradley, L. J., Brogan, W. C., & Brogan, C. (2009). Shelly: A case study focusing on ethics and counselor wellness. *Family Journal: Counseling and Therapy for Couples and Families, 17*, 355–359. doi: 10.1177/1066480709348034

Henwood, B. G., Padgett, D. K., & Tiderington, E. (2013). Provider views of harm reduction versus abstinence policies within homeless services for dually diagnosed adults. *Journal of Behavioral Health Services & Research*. [PsycINFO Database Record [c] 2013 APA, all rights reserved].

Herd, D. (1985). Migration, cultural transformation, and the rise of Black liver cirrhosis. *British Journal of Addiction, 80*, 397–410.

Herdman, J. (2001). *Global criteria: The 12 core functions of the substance abuse counselor* (3rd ed.). Holmes Beach, FL: Learning.

Herek, G. M., & Glunt, E. K. (1988). An epidemic of stigma: Public reactions to AIDS. *American Psychologist, 43*, 886–891.

Herlihy, B., & Sheeley, V. L. (1986, April). Privileged communication: Legal status & ethical issues. Paper presented at the annual convention of the American Association for Counseling and Development, Los Angeles, CA.

Hernandez, V. R., & Mendoza, C. T. (2011). Shame resilience: A strategy for empowering women in treatment for substance abuse. *Journal of Social Work Practice in the Addictions, 11*, 375–393.

Hersey, P., & Blanchard, K. (1982). *Management of organizational behavior: Utilizing human resources* (4th ed.). Englewood Cliffs, NJ: Prentice-Hall.

Hester, R. K., & Bien, T. H. (1995). Brief treatment. In A. M. Washton (Ed.), *Psychotherapy and substance abuse: A practitioner's handbook* (pp. 204–222). New York, NY: Guilford Press.

Hester, R. K., & Miller, W. R. (2003). *Handbook of alcoholism treatment approaches* (3rd ed.). Boston, MA: Allyn & Bacon.

Heyward, C. (1992). Healing addiction and homophobia: Reflections on empowerment and liberation. In D. L. Weinstein (Ed.), *Lesbians and gay men: Chemical dependency treatment issues* (pp. 5–18). Binghamton, NY: Haworth Press.

Hien, D. A., Cohen, L. R., Miele, G. M., Litt, L. C., & Capstick, C. (2004). Promising treatments for women with comorbid PTSD and substance use disorders. *American Journal of Psychiatry, 161*, 1426–1432.

Hien, D., Litt, L. C., Cohen, L. R., Miele, G. M., & Campbell, A. (2009). *Trauma services for women in substance abuse treatment: An integrated approach*. Washington, DC: American Psychological Association.

Hill, A. (1989). Treatment and prevention of alcoholism in the Native American family. In G. W. Lawson & A. W. Lawson (Eds.), *Alcoholism and substance abuse in special populations* (pp. 247–272). Rockville, MD: Aspen Press.

Hines, D. A., & Malley-Morrison, K. M. (2005). *Family violence in the United States*. Thousand Oaks, CA: Sage.

Hines, P. M., & Boyd-Franklin, N. (2005). African American families. In M. McGoldrick, J. Giordano, & N. Garcia-Preto (Eds.), *Ethnicity and family therapy* (3rd ed., pp. 87–100). New York, NY: Guilford Press.

Hirschfield, J. (1990). *The twelve steps for everyone . . . who really wants them*. Center City, MN: Hazelden.

Ho, M. K. (1994). Asian American perspective. In J. U. Gordon (Ed.), *Managing multiculturalism in substance abuse services* (pp. 72–98). Thousand Oaks, CA: Sage.

Hodges, E. A., & Myers, J. E. (2010). Counseling adult women survivors of childhood sexual abuse: Benefits of a wellness approach. *Journal of Mental Health Counseling, 32,* 139–154.

Hodges, K. (1993). Domestic violence: A health crisis. *Health Watch, 54,* 213–216.

Hoff, L. A. (2009). *People in crisis: Clinical and diversity perspectives* (6th ed.). New York, NY: Routledge.

Hoff, L. A., Hallisey, B. J., & Hoff, M. (2009). *People in crisis: Clinical and diversity perspectives* (6th ed.). New York, NY: Routledge.

Hojsted, J., & Sjogren, P. (2007). Addiction to opioids in chronic pain patients: A literature review. *European Journal of Pain, 11,* 490–518.

Holbrook, J. (2011). Veterans' courts and criminal responsibility: A problem-solving history and approach to the liminality of combat trauma. In D. C. Kelly (Ed.), *Treating young veterans: Promoting resilience through practice and advocacy* (pp. 259–300). New York, NY: Springer.

Hollis, J. (1989). The wounded vision: The myth of the tragic flaw. *Quadrant, 22,* 25–36.

Holmes, C. (1991). The wounded healer. *Society for Psychoanalytic Psychotherapy Bulletin, 6,* 33–36.

Hood, R., & Ersever, H. (2009, June). Ethics. Workshop presented at the annual Al Greene Addictions Institute, Boone, NC.

Hood, R., & Miller, G. (1997). Maintaining compassion in an era of health care management technology. Proceedings of the Sixth International Counseling Conference. Beijing, China.

Hook, J. N., Davis, D. E., Owen, J., Worthington, E. L. Jr., & Utsey, S. O. (2013). Cultural humility: Measuring openness to culturally diverse clients. *Journal of Counseling Psychology, 60,* 353–366. Advance online publication. doi: 10.1037/a00032595

Hora, P. F., & Schma, W. G. (2009). Drug courts and the treatment of incarcerated populations. In R. K. Ries, D. A. Fiellin, S. C. Miller, & R. Saitz (Eds.), *Principles of addiction medicine* (4th ed., pp. 1513–1520). Philadelphia, PA: Wolters Kluwer.

Horn, J. L., Wanberg, K. W., & Foster, F. M. (1987). *Guide to the alcohol use inventory.* Minneapolis, MN: National Computer Systems.

Hornberger, S., & Smith, S. (2011). Family involvement in adolescent substance abuse treatment and recovery: What do we know? What lies ahead? *Children & Youth Services Review, 33,* S70–S76.

Horvath, A. T. (1997). Alternative support groups. In J. H. Lowinson, P. Ruiz, R. B. Millman, & J. G. Langrod (Eds.), *Substance abuse: A comprehensive textbook* (3rd ed., pp. 390–396). Baltimore, MD: Williams & Wilkins.

Howell, R. J. (1990). Professional standards of practice in child custody examinations. *Psychotherapy in Private Practice, 8,* 15–23.

Huber, C. H., & Backlund, B. A. (1992). *The twenty-minute counselor.* New York, NY: Continuum.

Huber, J. T. (1993). Death and AIDS: A review of the medico-legal literature. *Death Studies, 17,* 225–232.

Hubert, M. (1996, February). Guidelines for avoiding ethical pitfalls. *Counseling Today, 10,* 14.

Hudson, H. L. (1986). How and why Alcoholics Anonymous works for blacks. *Alcoholism Treatment Quarterly, 2,* 31–43.

Huebner, D. M. (2013). Leading with love: Interventions to support families of lesbian, gay, and bisexual adolescents. *Register Report, 39,* 8–13.

Huguelet, P., & Mohr, S. (2013, March 15). Religion, spirituality, and psychiatry. *Psychiatric Times,* 1–3.

Humphreys, K. (1993). Psychotherapy and the twelve step approach for substance abusers: The limits of integration. *Psychotherapy, 30,* 207–213.

Humphreys, K., & Rappaport, J. (1994). Researching self-help/mutual aid groups and organizations: Many roads, one journey. *Applied and Preventive Psychology, 3,* 217–231.

Hunter, B. A., Jason, L. A., & Keys, C. B. (2012). Factors of empowerment for women in recovery from substance abuse. *American Journal of Community Psychology, 51,* 91–102.

Hurley, D. L. (1991). Women, alcohol and incest: An analytical review. *Journal of Studies on Alcohol, 52,* 253–268.

Hwang, S. W., Tolomiczenko, G., Kouyoumdjian, F. G., & Garner, R. E. (2005). Interventions to improve the health of the homeless: A systematic review. *American Journal of Preventive Medicine, 29,* 311–319.

Hyman, S. M., Paliwal, P., Chaplin, T. M., Mazure, C. M., Rounsaville, B. J., & Sinha, R. (2008). Severity of childhood trauma is predictive of cocaine relapse outcomes in women but not men. *Drug and Alcohol Dependence, 92,* 208–216.

Inaba, D. S. (1995, November). Current advances in the medical management of dually diagnosed clients. Paper presented at the National Dual Diagnosis Conference, Las Vegas, NV.

Inaba, D. S., & Cohen, W. E. (1989). *Uppers, downers, all arounders*. Ashland, OR: CNS.

Inaba, D. S., & Cohen, W. E. (1993). *Uppers, downers, all arounders* (2nd ed.). Ashland, OR: CNS.

Inaba, D. S., & Cohen, W. E. (2000). *Uppers, downers, all arounders* (4th ed.). Ashland, OR: CNS.

Ingersoll, K. S., Wagner, C. C., & Gharib, S. (2002). *Motivational groups for community substance abuse programs*. Richmond, VA: Mid-Atlantic ATTC.

Insel, P. M., & Moos, R. H. (1974). Psychological environments: Expanding the scope of human ecology. *American Psychologist, 29*, 179–187.

International Certification and Reciprocity Consortium. (1998). *Study guide for case presentation method oral interview for alcohol and other drug abuse counselors*. Research Triangle Park, NC: Columbia Assessment Services.

International Certification and Reciprocity Consortium. (2002). *Study guide for international written examination for alcohol and other drug counselors*. Research Triangle Park, NC: Columbia Assessment Services.

Irvin, J. E., Bowers, C. A., Dunn, M. E., & Wang, M. C. (1999). Efficacy of relapse prevention: A meta-analytic review. *Journal of Consulting and Clinical Psychology, 67*, 563–570.

Isganaityte, G., & Cepukiene, V. (2012). The relationship between resilience and substance misuse among adolescents in foster care. *Special Education, 2*, 35–41.

Jackson-Cherry, L. W., & Erford, B. T. (2014). *Crisis assessment, intervention, and prevention*. Boston, MA: Pearson.

Jacobsen, R., Moldrup, C., Christrup, L., Sjogren, P., & Hansen, O. B. (2010). Psychological and behavioral predictors of pain management outcomes in patients with cancer. *Scandinavian Journal of Caring Sciences, 24*, 781–790. doi: 10.1111/j.1471-6712.2010.00776.x

Jacobson, N., & Gottman, J. (1998). *When men batter women: New insights into ending abusive relationships*. New York, NY: Simon & Schuster.

Jaffe, S. L, Attalla, A., & Simeonova, D. I. (2009). Adolescent treatment and relapse prevention. In R. K. Ries, D. A. Fiellin, S. C. Miller, & R. Saitz (Eds.), *Principles of addiction medicine* (4th ed., pp. 1249–1262). Philadelphia, PA: Wolters Kluwer.

James, D. J., & Glaze, L. E. (2006). *Mental health problems of prison and jail inmates*. Bureau of Justice Statistics Special Report. NCJ Publication No. 213600. Washington, DC: Department of Justice.

James, R. K. (2008). *Crisis intervention strategies*. Belmont, CA: Thomson Brooks/Cole.

James, R. K. (2008). *Crisis intervention strategies* (6th ed.). Belmont, CA: Thomson Brooks/Cole.

Jamison, R. N., Butler, S. F., Budman, S. H., Edwards, R. R., & Wasan, A. D. (2010). Gender differences in risk factors for aberrant prescription opioid use. *Journal of Pain, 11*, 312–320.

Jamison, R. N., & Edwards, R. R. (2012). Integrating pain management in clinical practice. *Journal of Clinical Psychology in Medical Settings, 19*, 49–64. doi: 10. 1007/s10880-012-9295-2.

Jamison, R. N., Link, C. L., & Marceau, L. D. (2009). Do pain patients at high risk for substance misuse experience more pain?: A longitudinal outcomes study. *Pain Medicine, 10*, 1085–1094. doi: 10.1111/j.1526-4637.2009.00679.x

Jarret, C. (2011). Ouch! The different ways people experience pain. *Psychologist, 24*, 416–420.

Jellinek, E. M. (1960). *The disease concept of alcoholism*. New Haven, CT: College and University Press.

Jensen, C. D., Cushing, C. C., Aylward, B. S., Craig, J. T., Sorell, D. M., & Steele, R. G. (2011). Effectiveness of motivational interviewing interventions for adolescent substance use behavior change: A meta-analytic review. *Journal of Consulting and Clinical Psychology, 79*, 433–440.

Jensen, E. (2009). *Teaching with poverty in mind*. Alexandria, VA: ASCD.

Jerrell, J. M., Wilson, J. L., & Hiller, D. C. (2000). Issues and outcomes in integrated treatment programs for dual disorders. *Journal of Behavioral Health Services and Research, 27*, 303–313.

Jewel, J. D., & Hupp, S. D. A. (2005). Examining the effects of fatal vision goggles on changing attitudes and behaviors related to drinking and driving. *Journal of Primary Prevention, 26*, 553–565.

Jewel, J. D., Hupp, S. D. A., & Segrist, D. J. (2008). Assessing DUI risk: Examination of the Behaviors & Attitudes Drinking & Driving Scale (BADDS). *Addictive Behaviors, 33*, 853–865.

John, S., Brown, L. S., & Primm, B. J. (1997). African Americans: Epidemiologic, prevention, and treatment issues. In J. H. Lowinson, P. Ruiz, R. B. Millman, & J. G. Langrod (Eds.), *Substance abuse: A comprehensive textbook* (3rd ed., pp. 699–705). Baltimore, MD: Williams & Wilkins.

Johnson, J. L. (2004). *Fundamentals of substance abuse practice*. Belmont, CA: Brooks/Cole.

Johnson, N., Dinsmore, J. A., & Hof, D. D. (2011). The relationship between college students' resilience level and type of alcohol use. *International Journal of Psychology: A Biopsychosocial Approach*, *8*, 67–82.

Johnson, N. L., & Johnson, D. M. (2013). Correlates of readiness to change in victims of intimate partner violence. *Journal of Aggression, Maltreatment & Trauma*, *22*, 127–144.

Johnson, P. N., & Chappel, J. N. (1994). Using AA and other 12-step programs more effectively. *Journal of Substance Abuse Treatment*, *11*, 137–142.

Johnson, P. N., & Phelps, G. L. (1991). Effectiveness in self-help groups: Alcoholics Anonymous as a prototype. *Family and Community Health*, *14*, 22–27.

Johnson, S. (1991). Recent research: Alcohol and women's bodies. In P. Roth (Ed.), *Alcohol and drugs are women's issues: Vol. 1. A review of the issues* (pp. 32–42). Metuchen, NJ: Scarecrow Press and Women's Action Alliance.

Jones, A., & Schechter, S. (1992). *When love goes wrong*. New York, NY: HarperCollins.

Jones, M. K., & Jones, B. M. (1984). Ethanol metabolism in women taking oral contraceptives. *Alcoholism: Clinical and Experimental Research*, *8*, 24–28.

Jones, T., Sells, J. N., & Rehfuss, M. (2009). How wounded the healers? The prevalence of relapse among addiction counselors in recovery from alcohol and other drugs. *Alcoholism Treatment Quarterly*, *27*, 389–408. doi: 10.1080/07347320903209863

Joseph, H., & Paone, D. (1997). The homeless. In J. H. Lowinson, P. Ruiz, R. B. Millman, & J. G. Langrod (Eds.), *Substance abuse: A comprehensive textbook* (3rd ed., pp. 733–743). Baltimore, MD: Williams & Wilkins.

Joseph, S., & Murphy, D. (2013). Person-centered approach, positive psychology, and relational helping: Building bridges. *Journal of Humanistic Psychology*, *53*, 26–51.

Jourard, S. M. (1971). *The transparent self*. New York, NY: Van Nostrand.

Judge, M. G. (1994). Recovery's next step. *Common Boundary*, *12*, 16–24.

Kafka, M. P. (2010). Hypersexual disorder: A proposed diagnosis for DSM-V. *Archives of Sexual Behavior*, *39*(2), 377–400.

Kain, C. D. (1996). *Positive: HIV affirmative counseling*. Alexandria, VA: American Counseling Association.

Kalichman, S.C. (1996). *Answering your questions about AIDS*. Washington, DC: American Psychological Association.

Kalichman, S. C. (1998). *Understanding AIDS: A guide for mental health professionals*. Washington, DC: American Psychological Association.

Kanel, K. (2007). *A guide to crisis intervention*. (3rd ed.). Belmont, CA: Thomson/Brooks Cole.

Karas, A. (2013). Ethics in psychotherapy: Ethical issues and social media. *Psychotherapy Bulletin*, *48*, 25–27.

Karim, R., & Chaudhri, P. (2012). Behavioral addictions: An overview. *Journal of Psychoactive Drugs*, *44*, 5–17.

Kaskutas, L. (1994). What do women get out of self-help? Their reasons for attending women for sobriety and Alcoholics Anonymous. *Journal of Substance Abuse Treatment*, *11*, 185–195.

Kasl, C. (2011). http://charlottekasl.com/16-step-program/

Kasl, C. D. (1990). The twelve step controversy. *Ms.*, *1*, 30–31.

Kasl, C. D. (1992). *Many roads, one journey: Moving beyond the 12 Steps*. New York, NY: Harper Perennial.

Kasl, C. D. (1995). *Yes, you can: A guide to empowerment groups*. Lolo, MT: Many Roads, One Journey.

Kasper, L. B., Hill, C. E., & Kivlighan, D. M. (2008). Therapist immediacy in brief psychotherapy: Case study I. *Psychotherapy Theory, Research, Practice, Training*, *45*, 281–297.

Kassing, L. R., & Prieto, L. R. (2003). The rape myth and blame-based beliefs of counselors-in-training toward male victims of rape. *Journal of Counseling and Development*, *81*, 455–462.

Kauffman, C. (2006). Positive psychology: The science at the heart of coaching. In D. R. Stober and A. M. Grant (Eds.), *Evidence-based coaching handbook: Putting best practices to work for your clients* (pp. 219–253). Hoboken, NJ: Wiley.

Kaufman, E. (1985). Family therapy in the treatment of alcoholism. In T. E. Bratter & G. G. Forrest (Eds.), *Alcoholism and substance abuse* (pp. 376–397). New York, NY: Free Press.

Kavanagh, D. J., Mueser, K. T., & Tidsskrift (2007). Current evidence on integrated treatment for serious mental disorder and substance misuse. *Tidsskrift for Norsk Psykologforening*, *44*, 618–637.

Kegeles, S. M., Coates, T. J., Christopher, T. A., & Lazarus, J. L. (1989). Perceptions of AIDS: The continuing saga of AIDS related stigma. *AIDS*, *3*, 253–258.

Keller, D. S. (2003). Exploration in the service of relapse prevention. In F. Rotgers, J. Morgenstern, & S. T. Walters (Eds.), *Treating substance abuse: Theory and technique* (2nd ed., pp. 82–111). New York, NY: Guilford Press.

Keller, M. (1976). The disease concept of alcoholism revisited. *Journal of Studies on Alcohol*, *11*, 1701.

Kelley, J. F. (2005, May/June). Seventy years of mutual-help for addiction. *Family Therapy Magazine*, *4*, 14–17.

Kellogg, S., Melia, D., Khuri, E., Lin, A., Ho, A., & Kreek, M. J. (2006). Adolescent and young adult heroin patients: Drug use and success in methadone maintenance treatment. *Journal of Addictive Diseases*, *25*, 15–25.

Kelly, E. W. (1995). *Spirituality and religion in counseling and psychotherapy: Diversity in theory and practice*. Alexandria, VA: American Counseling Association.

Kelly, J. F., & Yeterian, J. D. (2008). Mutual-help groups for dually diagnosed individuals: Rationale, description, and review of the evidence. *Journal of Groups in Addiction & Recovery*, *3*, 217–242.

Kelly, P. J., Blacksin, B., & Mason, E. (2001). Factors affecting substance abuse treatment completion for women. *Issues in Mental Health Nursing*, *22*, 287–304.

Kelly, T. M., Daley, D. C., & Douaihy, A. B. (2012). Treatment of substance abusing patients with comorbid psychiatric disorders. *Addictive Behaviors*, *37*, 11–24.

Kemp, N., & Mallinckrodt, B. (1996). Impact of professional training on case conceptualization of clients with a disability. *Professional Psychology: Research and Practice*, *27*, 378–385.

Kendall, C. S. (2004). Treatment of mental illness and comorbid substance abuse: Concepts for evidence-based practice. *Journal of Addictions Nursing*, *15*, 183–186.

Kerns, R. D., Rosenberg, R., Jamison, R. N., Caudill, M. A., & Haythornewalte, J. (1997). Readiness to adopt a self-management approach to chronic pain: The Pain Stages of Change Questionnaire (PSOCQQ), *Pain*, *72*, 227–224.

Kersting, K. (2003). Religion and spirituality in the treatment room. *Monitor*, *34*, 40.

Keyes, C. L. M., & Haidt, J. (2003). Introduction: Human flourishing—The study of that which makes life worthwhile. In C. L. M. Keyes & J. Haidt (Eds.), *Flourishing: Positive psychology and the life well-lived* (pp. 3–12). Washington, DC: American Psychological Association.

Khantzian, E. J., & Mack, J. E. (1994). How AA works and why it's important for clinicians to understand. *Journal of Substance Abuse Treatment*, *11*, 77–92.

Kia-Keating, M., Sorsoli, L., & Grossman, F. K. (2010). Relational challenges and recovery processes in male survivors of childhood sexual abuse. *Journal of Interpersonal Violence*, *25*, 666–683.

Kim, A. U. (2004). Asian Americans: A practical history and overview. In D. R. Atkinson & G. Hackett (Eds.), *Counseling diverse populations* (3rd ed., pp. 217–238). Boston, MA: McGraw-Hill.

King, M. B. (1989). Prejudice and AIDS: The views and experiences of people with HIV infection. *AIDS Care*, *1*, 137–143.

Kingsbury, S. J. (1997, April). What is solution-focused therapy? *Harvard Mental Health Letter*, 8.

Kinney, J. (2003). *Loosening the grip* (7th ed.). Boston, MA: McGraw-Hill.

Kinney, J. (2006). *Loosening the grip* (8th ed.). Boston, MA: McGraw-Hill.

Kirkpatrick, J. (1978). *Turnabout: Help for a new life*. New York, NY: Doubleday.

Kirkpatrick, J. (1990). *Stages of the "new life" program*. Quakertown, PA: Women for Sobriety.

Kitano, K. J., & Louie, L. J. (2002). Asian and Pacific Islander women and addiction. In S. L. A. Straussner & S. Brown (Eds.), *The handbook of addiction treatment for women: Theory and practice* (pp. 348–373). San Francisco, CA: Jossey-Bass.

Knack, W. A. (2009). Psychotherapy and Alcoholics Anonymous: An integrated approach. *Journal of Psychotherapy Integration*, *19*, 86–109.

Knapp, S. J., & VandeCreek, L. (1997). *Treating patients with memories of abuse: Legal risk management*. Washington, DC: American Psychological Association.

Knight, J. R., Sherritt, L., Shrier, L. A., Harris, S. K., & Chang, G. (2002). Validity of the CRAFFT substance abuse screening test among adolescent clinic patients. *Archives of Pediatrics & Adolescent Medicine*, *156*, 607–614.

Kobau, R., Seligman, M. E. P., Peterson, C., Diener, E., Zack, M. M., Chapman, D., & Thompson, W. (2011). Mental health promotion in public health: Perspectives and strategies from positive psychology. *American Journal of Public Health*, *101*, e1–e9.

Koegel, P., Burnam, M. A., & Baumohl, J. (1996). The causes of homelessness. In J. Baumohl (Ed.), *Homelessness in America* (pp. 24–33). Phoenix, AZ: Oryx.

Koester, K. A., Majorana, A., Morin, S. F., Rose, C. D., Shade, S., & Myers, J. J. (2012). People living with HIV are receptive to HIV prevention interventions in clinical settings: A qualitative evaluation. *AIDS Education and Prevention, 24*, 295–308.

Kogan, M. (2001). Where happiness lies. *Monitor on Psychology, 32*, 74–76.

Kohn, C. (Ed.). (2002, November 7). Important to recognize that addiction abuse in females is different. *Women's Health Weekly*, 8–9.

Kolar, K. (2011). Resilience: Revisiting the concept and its utility for social research. *International Journal of Mental Health and Addiction, 9*, 421–433.

Kor, A., Fogel, Y., Reid, R. C., & Potenza, M. N. (2013). Should hypersexual disorder be classified as an addiction? *Sexual Addiction & Compulsivity, 20*, 27–47.

Koss-Chioino, J. D., & Vargas, L. A. (1992). Through the cultural looking glass: A model for understanding culturally responsive psychotherapies. In L. A. Vargas & J. D. Koss-Chioino (Eds.), *Working with culture* (pp. 1–22). San Francisco, CA: Jossey-Bass.

Koss, M. P., & Shiang, J. (1994). Research on brief psychotherapy. In A. E. Bergin & S. L. Garfield (Eds.), *Handbook of psychotherapy and behavior change* (pp. 664–700). New York, NY: Wiley.

Kouyanou, K., Pither, C., & Wessely, S. (1997). Medication misuse, abuse and dependence in chronic pain patients. *Journal of Psychometric Research, 43*, 497–504.

Kranitz, L. S., Holt, L. J., & Cooney, N. L. (2009). Individualized problem assessment II: Assessing clients from a broader perspective. In P. M. Miller (Ed.), *Evidence-based addiction treatment* (pp. 139–155). New York, NY: Academic Press.

Krentzman, A. R. (2013). Review of the application of positive psychology to substance use, addiction, and recovery research. *Psychology of Addictive Behaviors, 27*, 151–165.

Krinsley, K. (2007). Seeking safety: Therapy for PTSD and substance abuse. Workshop at Mountain Area Health Education Center, Asheville, NC, November 5–6.

Kristjansson, K. (2010). Positive psychology, happiness, and virtue: The troublesome conceptual issues. *Review of General Psychology, 14*, 296–310.

Krug, R. S. (1989). Adult male report of childhood sexual abuse by mothers: Case descriptions, motivations and long-term consequences. *Child Abuse and Neglect, 13*, 111–119.

Kruk, E., & Banga, P. S. (2011). Engagement of substance-using pregnant women in addiction recovery. *Canadian Journal of Community Mental Health, 30*, 79–91.

Kuhn, C., Swartzwelder, S., & Wilson, W. (2008). *Buzzed*. (3rd ed.). New York, NY: Norton.

Kumpfer, K. L., Trunnell, E. P., & Whiteside, H. O. (2003). The biopsychosocial model: Application to the addictions field. In R. C. Engs (Ed.), *Controversies in the addictions field* (pp. 55–67). Dubuque, IA: Kendall-Hunt.

Kurtz, E. (1988). *A. A.: The story*. San Francisco, CA: Harper & Row.

Kus, R. J. (1992). Spirituality in everyday life: Experiences of gay men of Alcoholics Anonymous. In D. L. Weinstein (Ed.), *Lesbians and gay men: Chemical dependency treatment issues* (pp. 49–66). New York, NY: Haworth Press.

Kus, R. J. (1995). Prayer and meditation in addiction recovery. In R. J. Kus (Ed.), *Spirituality and chemical dependency* (pp. 101–115). Binghamton, NY: Haworth Press.

Lambert, S. F., & Lawson, G. (2013). Resilience of professional counselors following hurricanes Katrina and Rita. *Journal of Counseling and Development, 91*, 261–268.

Langender, L. (2013). Alcohol use among partner violent adults: Reviewing recent literature to inform intervention. *Aggression and Violent Behavior, 18*, 152–158.

Larimer, M. E., Dillworth, T. M., Neighbors, C., Lewis, M. A., Montoya, H. D., & Logan, D. E. (2012). Harm reduction for alcohol problems. In G. A. Marlatt, M. E. Larimer, & K. Witkiewitz (Eds.), *Harm reduction: Pragmatic strategies for managing high-risk behaviors* (2nd ed., pp. 63–106). New York, NY: Guilford Press.

Larimer, M. E., Palmer, R. S., & Marlatt, G. A. (1999). Relapse prevention: An overview of Marlatt's cognitive-behavioral model. *Alcohol Research and Health, 23*, 151–160.

Larios, S. E., Wright, S., Jernstrom, A., Lebron, D., & Sorensen, J. L. (2011). Evidence-based practices, attitudes, and beliefs in substance abuse treatment programs serving American Indians and Alaska

Natives: A qualitative study. *Journal of Psychoactive Drugs*, *43*, 355–359.

Larm, P., Hodgins, S., Tengstroem, A., & Larsson, A. (2010). Trajectories of resilience over 25 years of individuals who as adolescents consulted for substance misuse and a matched comparison group. *Addiction*, *105*, 1216–1225.

Lasch, K. E. (2002). Sociocultural considerations in chronic pain and its management. In H. Wittink & T. H. Michel (Eds.), *Chronic pain management for physical therapists* (2nd ed., pp. 23–35). Boston, MA: Butterworth-Heinemann.

Lawson, A. (1989). Substance abuse problems of the elderly: Considerations for treatment and prevention. In G. W. Lawson & A. W. Lawson (Eds.), *Alcoholism and substance abuse in special populations* (pp. 95–113). Rockville, MD: Aspen Press.

Lawson, G. W., Ellis, D. C., & Rivers, P. C. (1984). *Essentials of chemical dependency counseling*. Rockville, MD: Aspen Press.

Lawson, G. W., Lawson, A. W., & Rivers, P. C. (2001). *Essentials of chemical dependency counseling* (3rd ed.). Gaithersburg, MD: Aspen Press.

Lazarus, R. S., & Folkman, S. (1984). *Stress, appraisal, and coping*. New York, NY: Springer.

Le, C., Ingvarson, E. P., & Page, R. C. (1995). Alcoholics Anonymous and the counseling profession: Philosophies in conflict. *Journal of Counseling and Development*, *73*, 603–609.

Lea, T. (2013). Alcohol and club drug use among same-sex attracted young people: Associations with frequenting the lesbian and gay scene and other bars and nightclubs. *Substance Use & Misuse*, *48*, 129–136.

Leadbeater, B., Dodgen, D., & Solarz, A. (2005). The resilience revolution: A paradigm shift for research and policy? In R. D. Peters, B. Leadbeater, & R. J. McMahon (Eds.), *Resilience in children, families, and communities: Linking context to practice and policy* (pp. 47–61). New York, NY: Kluwer Academic/Plenum.

Lee, C. C. (2003, Fall). Counseling in a changing world. *Chi Sigma Iota Exemplar*, 1–3, 6, 7.

Lee, J. H., Nam, S. K., Kim, A.-R., Kim, B., Lee, M. Y., & Lee, S. M. (2013). Resilience: A meta-analytic approach. *Journal of Counseling & Development*, *91*, 269–279.

Lee, S. (2010). Contemporary issues of ethical e-therapy. *Journal of Ethics in Mental Health*, *5*, 1–4.

Leeder, E. (1988). Enmeshed in pain: Counseling the lesbian battering couple. *Women and Therapy*, *7*, 81–99.

Leffingwell, T. R., Hendrix, B., & Mignogna, M., & Mignogna, J. (2008, Spring). Ten things to love about drug courts. *Addictions Newsletter*, *15*, 11–12.

Lehmann, M. L., & Herkenham, M. (2012). Environmental enrichment confers stress resiliency to social defeat through an infra-limbic cortex-dependent neuroanatomical pathway. *Journal of Neuroscience*, *31*, 6159–6173.

Leigh, G. (1985). Psychosocial factors in the etiology of substance abuse. In T. E. Bratter & G. G. Forrest (Eds.), *Alcoholism and substance abuse: Strategies for clinical intervention* (pp. 3–48). New York, NY: Free Press.

Leigh, I. W., Powers, L., Vash, C., & Nettles, R. (2004). Survey of psychological services to clients with disabilities: The need for awareness. *Rehabilitation Psychology*, *49*(1), 48–54.

Leming, M. R., & Dickinson, G. E. (1998). The grieving process. In M. R. Lemming and G. E. Dickinson (Eds.), *Dying, death, and bereavement* (pp. 476–487). Fort Worth, TX: Holt, Rinehart, & Winston.

Levi, L. (1990). Occupational stress: Spice of life or kiss of death? *American Psychologist*, *45*, 1142–1145.

Levin, S. M., & Kruger, J. (Eds.). (2000). *Substance abuse among older adults: A guide for social service providers*. Rockville, MD: SAMHSA.

Levinthal, C. F. (1996). *Drugs, behavior, and modern society*. Boston, MA: Allyn & Bacon.

Levy, A. J., & Brekke, J. S. (1990). Spouse battering and chemical dependency: Dynamics, treatment, and service delivery. In R. T. Potter-Efron & P. S. Potter-Efron (Eds.), *Aggression, family violence and chemical dependency* (pp. 81–97). New York, NY: Haworth Press.

Lewis, J. A., Dana, R. Q., & Blevins, G. A. (1994). *Substance abuse counseling: An individualized approach* (2nd ed.). Pacific Grove, CA: Brooks/Cole.

Li, T., Hewett, B. G., & Grant, T. F. (2007). Is there a future for quantifying drinking in the diagnosis, treatment, and prevention of alcohol use disorders? *Alcohol and Alcoholism*, *42*, 1183–1192.

Liberto, L. A., & Fornili, K. S. (2013). Managing pain in opioid-dependent patients in general hospital settings. *MEDSURG Nursing*, *22*, 33–37.

Liddle, H. A. (2010). Multidimensional family therapy: A science-based treatment system. *Australian & New Zealand Journal of Family Therapy, 31,* 133–148.

Liddle, H. A., Dakof, G. A., Parker, K., Diamond, G. S., Barrett, K., & Tejeda, M. (2001). Multidimensional family therapy for adolescent drug abuse: Results of a randomized clinical trial. *American Journal of Drug and Alcohol Abuse, 27,* 651–688.

Liddle, H. A., Rodriguez, R. A., Dakof, G. A., Kanzki, E., & Marvel, F. A. (2005). Multidimensional family therapy: A science-based treatment for adolescent drug abuse. In J. L. Lebow (Ed.), *Handbook of clinical family therapy* (pp. 128–163). Hoboken, NJ: Wiley.

Liepman, M. R., Parran, T. V, Farkas, K. J., & Lagos-Saez, M. (2009). Family involvement in addiction, treatment and recovery. In R. K. Ries, D. A. Fiellin, S. C. Miller, & R. Saitz (Eds.), *Principles of addiction medicine* (4th ed., pp. 857–867). Philadelphia, PA: Wolters Kluwer.

Light, L. S., McCoy, T. P., Thompson, M. P., Spitler, H. D., Sutfin, E. L., & Rhodes, S. D. (2011). Modeling the Rutgers Alcohol Problem Index (RAPI): A comparison of statistical methods. *Addiction Research and Theory, 19,* 510–518.

Lile, B. (2003). Twelve step programs: An update. *Addictive Disorders & Their Treatment, 2,* 19–24.

Linehan, M. M. (1993). *Skills training manual for borderline personality disorder.* New York, NY: Guilford Press.

Lisak, D., & Miller, P. M. (2003). Childhood trauma, posttraumatic stress disorder, substance abuse and violence. In P. Ouimette & P. J. Brown (Eds.), *Trauma and substance abuse* (pp. 73–88). Washington, DC: American Psychological Association.

Littell, J. H., & Girvin, H. (2002). Stages of change: A critique. *Behavior Modification, 26,* 223–273.

Littleton, H., & Breitkopf, C. R. (2006). Coping with the experience of rape. *Psychology of Women Quarterly, 30,* 106–116.

Littrell, J. (2000, June). Should the expression of emotional memories be a goal of therapy? *Harvard Mental Health Letter, 16,* 8.

Littrell, J. M. (1998). *Brief counseling in action.* New York, NY: Norton.

Liu, T., & Potenza, M. N. (2007). Problematic Internet use: Clinical implications. *CNS Spectrums, 12*(6), 453–466.

Lo, C.C., & Cheng, T.C. (2012). Discrimination's role in minority groups' rates of substance-use disorder. *American Journal on Addictions, 21,* 150–156.

Loftus, E. (1991, October). Resolving legal questions with psychological data. *American Psychologist, 46,* 1046–1048.

Loosen, P. T., Dew, B. W., & Prange, A. (1990). Long-term predictors of outcome in abstinent alcoholic men. *American Journal of Psychiatry, 147,* 1662–1666.

Lopez, S. R., Grover, K. P., Holland, D., Johnson, M. J., Kain, C. D., Kanel, K., . . . Rhyne, M. C. (1989). Development of culturally sensitive psychotherapists. *Professional Psychology: Research and Practice, 20,* 369–376.

Lundholm, L., Haggard, U., Moeller, J., Hallqvist, J., & Thiblin, I. (2013). The triggering effect of alcohol and illicit drugs on violent crime in a remand prison population: A case crossover study. *Drug and Alcohol Dependence, 129,* 110–115. doi: 10.1016/j.drugalcdep.2012.09.019

MacDonald, J. M. (1995). *Rape: Controversial issues.* Springfield, IL: Thomas.

MacDonald, K., Lambie, I., & Simmonds, L. (1995). *Counseling for sexual abuse: A therapist's guide to working with adults, children, and families.* Melbourne, Australia: Oxford University Press.

Mackay, P. W., Donovan, D. M., & Marlatt, G. A. (1991). Cognitive and behavioral approaches to alcohol abuse. In R. J. Frances & S. I. Miller (Eds.), *Clinical textbook of addictive disorders* (pp. 452–481). New York, NY: Guilford Press.

Mackay, P. W., & Marlatt, G. A. (1990–1991). Maintaining sobriety: Stopping is starting. *International Journal of the Addictions, 25,* 1257–1276.

Mackelprang, R., & Salsgiver, R. (1999). *Disability: A diversity model approach to human service practice.* Pacific Grove, CA: Brooks/Cole.

Mackrill, T., Elklit, A., & Lindgarrd, H. (2012). Treatment-seeking young adults from families with alcohol problems: What have they been through? What state are they in? *Counselling & Psychotherapy Research, 12,* 276–286.

Macy, R. J., & Goodbourn, M. (2012). Promoting successful collaborations between domestic violence and substance abuse treatment service sectors: A review of the literature. *Trauma, Violence, & Abuse, 13,* 234–251.

Madsen, W., & Madsen, C. (1969). The cultural structure of Mexican drinking behavior. *Quarterly Journal of Studies on Alcohol, 30,* 701–718.

Magnusson, A., Lundholm, C., Goransson, M., Copeland, W., Heilig, M., & Pederssen, N. L. (2012).

Familial influence and childhood trauma in female alcoholism. *Psychological Medicine, 42*, 381–389.

Malet, L., Brousse, G., & Llorca, P.-M. (2009). CAGE unsound for alcohol misuse in seniors. *International Journal of Geriatric Psychiatry, 24*, 434–435.

Mallow, A. (2008). Who wants to be a martyr? A recovering client's experience with pain medication. *Journal of Social Work Practice in the Addictions, 8*, 557–560. doi: 10.1080/15332560802323899

Mander, G. (2007). *Diversity, discipline and devotion in psychoanalytic psychotherapy: Clinical and training perspectives*. London, England: Karnac Books.

Mannion, L. (1991). Codependency: A case of inflation. *Employee Assistance Quarterly, 7*, 67–81.

Margolis, R. D. (1995). Adolescent chemical dependence: Assessment, treatment, and management. *Psychotherapy, 32*, 172–179.

Margolis, R. D., & Zweben, J. E. (1998). *Treating patients with alcohol and other drug problems: An integrated approach*. Washington, DC: American Psychological Association.

Margolis, R. D., & Zweben, J. E. (2011). Assessment of substance abuse and dependence. In R. D. Margolis & J. E. Zweben (Ed.), *Treating patients with alcohol and other drug problems: An integrated approach* (2nd ed., pp. 59–81). Washington, DC: American Psychological Association.

Marijuana Anonymous. (2001). *Life with hope*. Van Nuys, CA: Author.

Markowitz, J. D., Francis, E. M., & Gonzales-Nolas, C. (2010). Substance abuse treatment program for the addicted individual early in recovery: A current controversy. *Journal of Psychoactive Drugs, 42*, 193–198.

Markowitz, R. (1993). Dynamics and treatment issues with children of drug and alcohol abusers. In S. L. A. Straussner (Ed.), *Clinical work with substance-abusing clients* (pp. 214–229). New York, NY: Guilford Press.

Marlatt, A. (2000, October 7). Changing addictive behaviors. Presentation at 2000 NC Psychological Association/Foundation Fall Continuing Education Conference, Raleigh, NC.

Marlatt, G. A. (1985a). Cognitive factors in the relapse process. In G. A. Marlatt & J. R. Gordon (Eds.), *Relapse prevention: Maintenance strategies in the treatment of addictive behaviors* (pp. 128–200). New York, NY: Guilford Press.

Marlatt, G. A. (1985b). Relapse prevention: Theoretical rationale and overview of the model. In G. A.

Marlatt & J. R. Gordon (Eds.), *Relapse prevention: Maintenance strategies in the treatment of addictive behaviors* (pp. 3–70). New York, NY: Guilford Press.

Marlatt, G. A. (2000, October 7). *Changing addictive behaviors*. Presentation at 2000 NC Psychological Association/Foundation Fall Continuing Education Conference, Raleigh, NC.

Marlatt, G. A., Bowen, S. W., & Witkiewitz, K. (2009). Relapse prevention: Evidence base and future directions. In P. M. Miller (Ed.), *Evidence-based addiction treatment* (pp. 215–232). New York, NY: Academic Press.

Marlatt, G. A., & Donovan, D. M. (Ed.). (2005). *Relapse prevention: Maintenance strategies in the treatment of addictive behaviors*. New York, NY: Guilford Press.

Marlatt, G. A., & Fromme, K. (1988). Metaphors for addiction. In S. Peele (Ed.), *Visions of addiction* (pp. 1–23). Lexington, MA: Lexington Books.

Marlatt, G. A., & George, W. H. (1984). Relapse prevention: Introduction and overview of the model. *British Journal of Addiction, 79*, 261–273.

Marlatt, G. A., & Gordon, J. R. (1985). *Relapse prevention: A self-control strategy for the maintenance of behavior change*. New York, NY: Guilford Press.

Marlatt, G. A., & Kristeller, J. (1999). Mindfulness and meditation. In W. R. Miller (Ed.), *Integrating spirituality in treatment: Resources for practitioners* (pp. 67–84). Washington, DC: American Psychological Association.

Marlatt, G. A., Parks, G. A., & Witkiewitz, K. (2002). *Clinical guidelines for implementing relapse prevention therapy*. Retrieved from http://www.bhrm.org/guidelines/RPT%20guideline.pdf

Marlatt, G. A., & Witkiewitz, K. (2005). Relapse prevention for alcohol and drug problems. In G. A. Marlatt & D. M. Donovan (Eds.), *Relapse prevention* (2nd ed., pp. 1–44). New York, NY: Guilford Press.

Marra, T. (2004). *Depressed and anxious*. Oakland, CA: New Harbinger.

Marsh, J. C., Cao, D., & Shin, H-C. (2009). Closing the need-service gap: Gender differences in matching services to client needs in comprehensive substance abuse treatment. *Social Work Research, 33*, 183–192.

Martin, P. R., Weinberg, B. A., & Bealer, B. K. (2007). *Healing addiction*. Hoboken, NJ: Wiley.

Mason, S. J., Deane, F. P., Kelly, P. J., & Crowe, T. P. (2009). Do spirituality and religiosity help in the management of cravings in substance abuse treatment? *Substance Use and Misuse, 44,* 1926–1940. doi: 10.3109/10826080802486723

Masten, A. S. (2001). Ordinary magic: Resilience processes in development. *American Psychologist, 56,* 227–238.

Mathias, R. (2003, June). Joint treatment of PTSD and cocaine abuse may reduce severity of both disorders. *NIDA Notes, 18*(1), 6, 14.

Mattson, M. E., & Fuller, R. K. (1997, June). Reply from NIAAA. *Epikrisis, 8,* 2.

May, P. A. (1986). Alcohol and drug misuse prevention programs for American Indians: Needs and opportunities. *Journal of Studies on Alcohol, 47,* 187–195.

May, P. A. (1996). Overview of alcohol abuse epidemiology for American Indian populations. In G. D. Sandefur, R. R. Rindfuss, & B. Cohen (Eds.), *Changing numbers, changing needs: American Indian demography and public health* (pp. 235–261). Washington, DC: National Academies Press.

McCabe, S. E., Bostwick, W. B., Hughes, T. L., West, B. T., & Boyd, C. J. (2010). The relationship between discrimination and substance use disorders among lesbian, gay, and bisexual adults in the United States (2013). *American Journal of Public Health, 100,* 1946–1952.

McCabe, S. E., West, B. T., Hughes, T. L., & Boyd, C. J. (2013). Sexual orientation and substance abuse treatment utilization in the United States: Results from a national survey. *Journal of Substance Abuse Treatment, 44,* 4–12.

McClellan, M. (2011). Historical perspectives on alcoholism treatment for women in the United States, 1870–1990. *Alcoholism Treatment Quarterly, 29,* 332–356.

McClelland, D. (1975). *Power: The inner experience.* New York, NY: Irvington.

McCombs, K., & Moore, D. (2002). *Substance abuse prevention and intervention for students with disabilities: A call to educators.* Arlington, VA: ERIC Clearinghouse on Disabilities and Gifted Education (ERIC Document Reproduction Service No. ED469441).

McConnaughy, E. A., DiClemente, C. C., Prochaska, J. O., & Velicer, W. F. (1989). Stages of change in psychotherapy: A follow-up report. *Psychotherapy, 26,* 494–503.

McConnaughy, E. A., Prochaska, J. O., & Velicer, W. F. (1983). Stages of change in psychotherapy: Measurement and sample profiles. *Psychotherapy: Theory, Research and Practice, 20,* 368–375.

McCrady, B. S., Epstein, E. E., & Sell, R. D. (2003). Theoretical bases of family approaches to substance abuse treatment. In F. Rotgers, J. Morgenstern, & S. T. Walters (Eds.), *Treating substance abuse: Theory and technique* (2nd ed., pp. 112–139). New York, NY: Guilford Press.

McCrone, W. P. (1982). Serving the deaf substance abuser. *Journal of Psychoactive Drugs, 14,* 199–203.

McDonell, J. R. (1993). Judgments of personal responsibility for HIV infection: An attributional analysis. *Social Work, 38,* 403–410.

McFadden, J. (1999). Historical approaches in transcultural counseling. In J. McFadden (Ed.), *Transcultural counseling* (2nd ed., pp. 3–22). Alexandria, VA: American Counseling Association.

McGovern, M. P., Lambert-Harris, C., Acquilano, S., Xie, H., Alterman, A. I., & Weiss, R. D. (2009). A cognitive behavioral therapy for co-occurring substance use and posttraumatic stress disorders. *Addictive Behaviors, 34,* 892–897.

McHugh, M., Beckman, L., & Frieze, I. H. (1979). Analyzing alcoholism. In I. H. Frieze, D. Bar-Tal, & J. S. Carroll (Eds.), *New approaches to social problems* (pp. 168–208). San Francisco, CA: Jossey-Bass.

McIntyre, J. R. (1993). Family treatment of substance abuse. In S. L. A. Straussner (Ed.), *Clinical work with substance-abusing clients* (pp. 171–195). New York, NY: Guilford Press.

McIntyre, J. R. (2004). Family treatment of substance abuse. In S. L. A. Straussner (Ed.), *Clinical work with substance-abusing clients* (2nd ed., pp. 237–263). New York, NY: Guilford Press.

McLellan, A. T. (2008). Evolution in addiction treatment concepts and methods. In M. Galanter & H. D. Kleber (Eds.), *Substance abuse treatment* (4th ed., pp. 93–108). Washington, DC: American Psychiatric Publishing.

McLellan, A. T., Luborsky, L., O'Brien, C. P., & Woody, G. E. (1980). An improved evaluation instrument for substance abuse patients: The addiction severity index. *Journal of Nervous and Mental Diseases, 168,* 26–33.

McMahon, T. J., Winkel, J. D., Suchman, N. E., & Luthar, S. S. (2002). Drug dependence, parenting responsibilities and treatment history: Why doesn't Mom go for help? *Drug and Alcohol Dependence, 65,* 105–114.

McMullin, D., & White, J. W. (2006). Long-term effects of labeling a rape experience. *Psychology of Women Quarterly, 30,* 96–105.

McMullin, R. E. (2000). *The new handbook of cognitive therapy techniques*. New York, NY: Norton.

Melzack, R. (1996). Gate control theory: On the evolution of pain concepts. *Pain Forum, 5,* 128–138.

Melzack, R., & Wall, P. D. (1965). Pain mechanisms: A new theory. *Science, 150,* 971–979.

Meredith, P., Ownsworth, T., & Strong, J. (2008). A review of the evidence linking adult attachment theory and chronic pain: Presenting a conceptual model. *Clinical Psychology Review, 28,* 407–429.

Mericle, A. A., Martin, C., Carise, D., & Love, M. (2012). Identifying need for mental health services in substance abuse clients. *Journal of Dual Diagnosis, 8,* 218–228.

Merskey, H., & Bogduk, N. (Eds.). (1994). *Classification of chronic pain: Descriptions of chronic pain syndromes and definitions of pain terms* (2nd ed.). Seattle, WA: IASP Press.

Messman-Moore, T. L., Ward, R. M., & Brown, A. L. (2009). Substance use and PTSD symptoms impact the likelihood of rape and revictimization in college women. *Journal of Interpersonal Violence, 24,* 499–521.

Meyers, K., & McLellan, A. T. (2005). The American treatment system for adolescent substance abuse: Formidable challenges, fundamental revisions, and mechanisms for improvements. In D. L. Evans, E. B. Foa, R. E. Gur, H. Hendin, C. P. O'Brien, M. E. P. Seligman, & T. Walsh (Eds.), *Treating and preventing adolescent mental health disorders: What we know and what we don't know: A research agenda for improving the mental health of our youth* (pp. 561–578). New York, NY: Oxford University Press.

Meyers, R. J., & Miller, W. R. (Ed.). (2001). *A community reinforcement approach to addiction treatment.* New York, NY: Cambridge University Press.

Milkman, H. B., & Sunderwirth, S. G. (2010). *Craving for ecstasy and natural highs: A positive approach to mood alteration.* Los Angeles, CA: Sage.

Miller, A. (1981). *The drama of the gifted child.* New York, NY: Basic Books.

Miller, G. (1997). Sexual abuse and domestic violence counseling: Working together. *Epikrisis, 8,* 2.

Miller, G. (1999). The development of the spiritual focus in counseling and counselor education. *Journal of Counseling and Development, 77,* 498–501.

Miller, G. (2001). Finding happiness for ourselves and our clients. *Journal of Counseling and Development, 79,* 382–384.

Miller, G. (2002). Maintaining hope in the face of evil. *Journal of Counseling and Development, 80,* 503–506.

Miller, G. (2003). *Incorporating spirituality in counseling and psychotherapy.* Hoboken, NJ: Wiley.

Miller, G. (2005). Religious/spiritual life span development. In C. S. Cashwell & J. S. Young, *Integrating spiritual and religious values in counseling: A guide to competent practice* (pp. 105–122). Alexandria, VA: American Counseling Association.

Miller, G., Clark, C., & Herman, J. (2007). Domestic violence in a rural setting. *Journal of Rural Mental Health, 31,* 28–42.

Miller, G., & Kaplan, B. (1996). Testifying in court. *Psychotherapist in Private Practice, 15,* 15–32.

Miller, G., Kirkley, D., & Willis, M. (1995, January). Blending two worlds: Supporting group functions within an addictions' framework. Paper presented at the meeting of the Third National Conference of the Association for Specialists in Group Work, Athens, GA.

Miller, G., Scarborough, J., Clark, C., Leonard, J. C., & Keziah, T. (2010). The need for national credentialing standards for addiction counselors. *Journal of Addictions & Offender Counseling, 30,* 50–57.

Miller, G., Wagner, A. U., Britton, T., & Gridley, B. (1998). A framework for understanding the wounding of healers. *Counseling and Values, 42,* 124–132.

Miller, G. A. (1985). *The substance abuse subtle screening inventory manual.* Spencer, IN: Spencer Evening World.

Miller, G. A. (2012a). *Fundamentals of crisis counseling.* Hoboken, NJ: Wiley.

Miller, G. A. (2012b). *Group exercises for addiction counseling.* Hoboken, NJ: Wiley.

Miller, G. A., & Peele, T. (1995). Inhalant abuse: An overview. *Focus on Later Childhood/Early Adolescence, 8,* 1–3.

Miller, G. A., Sack, T., & Simmons, K. (1994). Sexual abuse and alcohol: Women survivors [Summary]. Proceedings of the Fourth International Counseling Conference. Vancouver, British Columbia, Canada.

Miller, G. D., & Baldwin, D. C. (1987). Implications of the wounded-healer paradigm for the use of the self in therapy. *Journal of Psychotherapy and the Family, 3,* 139–151.

Miller, J. B. (1976). *Toward a new psychology of women.* Boston, MA: Beacon Press.

Miller, J. B. (1986). *Toward a new psychology of women* (2nd ed.). Boston, MA: Beacon Press.

Miller, L. J. (1995, October). Addiction in women. Paper presented at the National Dual Disorder Conference, Las Vegas, NV.

Miller, M., Gorski, T. T., & Miller, D. K. (1982). *Learning to live again.* Independence, MO: Independence Press.

Miller, N. S., & Gold, M. S. (1990). Organic solvents and aerosols: An overview of abuse and dependence. *Annals of Clinical Psychiatry, 2,* 85–92.

Miller, P. M. (Ed.). (2008). *Evidence-based addiction treatment.* Burlington, MA: Academic Press.

Miller, W. R. (2004, August). Motivational interviewing. Workshop presented at the meeting of the American Psychological Association, Toronto, Canada.

Miller, W. R., Forcehimes, A. A., & Zweben, A. (2011). *Treating addiction: A guide for professionals.* New York, NY: Guilford Press.

Miller, W. R., & Harris, R. J. (2000). A simple scale of Gorski's warning signs for relapse. *Journal of Studies on Alcohol, 61,* 759–765.

Miller, W. R., & Kurtz, E. (1994). Models of alcoholism used in treatment: Contrasting AA and other perspectives with which it is often confused. *Journal of Studies on Alcohol, 55,* 19–166.

Miller, W. R., & Rollnick, S. (1991). *Motivational interviewing: Preparing people to change addictive behavior.* New York, NY: Guilford Press.

Miller, W. R., & Rollnick, S. (2002). *Motivational interviewing* (2nd ed.). New York, NY: Guilford Press.

Miller, W. R., & Rollnick, S. (2009). Ten things that motivational interviewing is not. *Behavioral and Cognitive Psychotherapy, 37,* 129–140.

Miller, W. R., & Rollnick, S. (2013). *Motivational Interviewing* (3rd ed.). New York, NY: Guilford Press.

Miller, W. R., & Rose, G. S. (2009). Toward a theory of motivational interviewing. *American Psychologist, 64,* 527–537.

Miller, W. R., & Sanchez, V. C. (1994). Motivating young adults for treatment and lifestyle change. In G. Howard (Ed.), *Issues in alcohol use and misuse by young adults* (pp. 55–81). Notre Dame, IN: University of Notre Dame Press.

Miller, W. R., & Tonigan, J. S. (1996). Assessing drinkers' motivations for change: The Stages of Change Readiness and Treatment Eagerness Scale (SOCRATES). *Psychology of Addictive Behaviors, 10,* 81–89.

Miller, W. R., Westerberg, V. S., Harris, R. J., & Tonigan, J. S. (1996). What predicts relapse? Prospective testing of antecedent models. *Addiction, 91* (Suppl.): S155–S172.

Milligan, K., Niccols, A., Sword, W., Thabane, L., Henderson, J., & Smith, A. (2011). Birth outcomes for infants born to women participating in integrated substance abuse treatment programs: A meta-analytic review. *Addiction Research & Theory, 19,* 542–555.

Minnesota Chemical Dependency Program for Deaf and Hard of Hearing Individuals. (1994, November). Barriers to treatment and recovery. Handout presented at the meeting of the Innovative Partnerships in Recovery, Overland Park, KS.

Minnesota Coalition for Battered Women. (1992). *Safety first: A guide for counselors and advocates.* St. Paul, MN: Author.

Mitchell, J. L. (1993). *Pregnant, substance-abusing women* (DHHS Publication No. SMA 93–1998). Rockville, MD: U.S. Department of Health and Human Services.

Mitchell, O., Wilson, D. B., Eggers, A., & MacKenzie, D. L. (2012). Assessing the effectiveness of drug courts on recidivism: A meta-analytic review of traditional and non-traditional drug courts. *Journal of Criminal Justice, 40,* 60–71.

Mohatt, G. V., Allen, J., & Thomas, L. R. (2007). Drug and alcohol abuse in cross-cultural counseling. In P. B. Pedersen, J. G. Draguns, W. J. Lonner, & J. E. Trimble (Eds.), *Counseling across cultures* (6th ed., pp. 395–413). Thousand Oaks, CA: Sage.

Moleski, S. M., & Kiselica, M. S. (2005). Dual relationships: A continuum ranging from the destructive to the therapeutic. *Journal of Counseling and Development, 83,* 3–11.

Mondragon, D., Kirkman-Liff, B., & Schneller, E. S. (1991). Hostility to people with AIDS: Risk perception and demographic factors. *Society of Science and Medicine, 32,* 1137–1142.

Monti, P. M., & Operario, D. (2009, May). Alcohol use, sex-risk behaviors, and HIV. *The Brown University Digest of Addiction Theory and Application, 28,* 8.

Mook, D. G. (1987). *Motivation: The organization of action.* New York, NY: Norton.

Mora, J. (2002). Latinas in cultural transition: Addiction, treatment, and recovery. In S. L. A. Straussner & S. Brown (Eds.), *The handbook of addiction treatment for women: Theory and practice* (pp. 323–347). San Francisco, CA: Jossey-Bass.

Morgan, O. J. (2009). Thoughts on the interaction of trauma, addiction, and spirituality. *Journal of Addictions & Offender Counseling, 30,* 5–15.

Morgen, K., Miller, G., & Stretch, L. (2012). Addiction counseling licensure issues for licensed professional counselors. *Professional Counselor: Research and Practice, 2,* 58–65.

Morgenstern, J., Kuerbis, A., Amrhein, P., Hail, L., Lynch, K., & McKay, J. R. (2012). Motivational interviewing: A pilot test of active ingredients and mechanisms of change. *Psychology of Addictive Behaviors, 26,* 859–869.

Morkides, C. (2009, October). A silent epidemic. *Counseling Today, 52,* 40–42.

Morojele, N. K., Saban, A., & Seedat, S. (2012). Clinical presentations and diagnostic issues in dual diagnosis disorders. *Current Opinion in Psychiatry, 25,* 181–186.

Morris, D. N., Johnson, A., Losier, A., Pierce, M., & Sridhar, V. (2013). Spirituality and substance abuse recovery. *Occupational Therapy in Mental Health, 29,* 78–84. doi: 10.1080/0164212X.2013.761112

Moya, E. M., & Shedlin, M. G. (2008) Policies and laws affecting Mexican-origin immigrant access and utilization of substance abuse treatment: Obstacles to recovery and immigrant health. *Substance Use & Misuse, 43,* 1747–1769.

Moyers, T.B. (Producer). (1998). *Motivational interviewing: Professional training videotape series* (A–F) [Videotapes]. Available from www.motivationalinterviewing.org

Moyers, T. B., & Houck, J. (2011). Combining motivational interviewing with cognitive-behavior treatments for substance abuse: Lessons from the COMBINE research project. *Cognitive and Behavioral Practice, 18,* 38–45.

Moyers, T. B., Martin, T., Christopher, P. J., Houck, J. M., Tonigan, J. S., & Amrhein, P. A. (2007). Client language as a mediator of motivational interviewing efficacy: Where is the evidence? *Alcoholism: Clinical and Experimental Research, 31,* 40s–47s.

Moyers, W. C. (2012). *Now what? An insider's guide to addiction and recovery.* Center City, MN: Hazelden.

Moynihan, R., Christ, G., & Silver, L. G. (1988). AIDS and terminal illness. *Social Casework, 69,* 380–387.

Mueser, K. T., Gottlieb, J. D., Cather, C., Glynn, S. M., Zarate, R., Smith, M. F., . . . Wolfe, R. (2012). Antisocial personality disorder in people with co-occurring severe mental illness and substance use disorders: Clinical, functional, and family relationship correlates. *Psychosis and Personality Disorder, 4,* 52–62.

Mueser, K. T., Noordsy, D. L., Drake, R. E., & Fox, L. (2003). *Integrated treatment for dual disorders.* New York, NY: Guilford Press.

Murphy, C. (1995). Scapegroup. *Atlantic Monthly, 275,* 22–24.

Myer, R. A., Peterson, S. E., & Stoffel-Rosales, M. (1991). Co-dependency: An examination of underlying assumptions. *Journal of Mental Health Counseling, 13,* 449–458.

Myers, P. L., & Salt, N. R. (2007). *Becoming an addictions counselor: A comprehensive text* (2nd ed.). Sudbury, MA: Jones & Bartlett.

Nace, E. P. (1992). Emerging concepts in dual diagnosis. *Counselor, 10,* 10–13.

Nace, E. P. (1997). Alcoholics anonymous. In J. H. Lowinson, P. Ruiz, R. B. Millman, & J. G. Langrod (Eds.), *Substance abuse: A comprehensive textbook* (3rd ed., pp. 383–390). Baltimore, MD: Williams & Wilkins.

Nagy, P. (2010). Motivational interviewing. In M. Dulcan (Ed.), *Dulcan's textbook of child and adolescent psychiatry* (pp. 915–924) Arlington, VA: American Psychiatric Press.

Najavits, L. M. (2002). *Seeking safety: A treatment manual for PTSD and substance abuse.* New York, NY: Guilford Press.

Najavits, L. M. (2007). Seeking safety: An evidence-based model for substance abuse and trauma/PTSD. In K. A. Witkiewitz & G. A. Marlatt (Eds.), *Therapist guide to evidence based relapse prevention: Practical resources for the mental health professional* (pp. 141–167). San Diego, CA: Elsevier Press.

Najavits, L. M., Weiss, R. D., & Shaw, S. R. (1997). The link between substance abuse and post-traumatic stress disorder in women. *American Journal of Addiction, 6,* 273–283.

Narcotics Anonymous. (1982). *Narcotics Anonymous.* Sun Valley, CA: CARENA.

Narcotics Anonymous. (1998). *Narcotics Anonymous.* Van Nuys, CA: Author.

National Association of Alcoholism and Drug Abuse Counselors Education and Research Foundation. (1995). *Income and compensation study of alcohol and drug counseling professionals.* Arlington, VA: Author.

National Association of Drug Court Professionals. (2008). *The facts: Facts on drug courts.* Retrieved from www.nadcp.org/docs/FACTS_final.pdf

National Association of Social Workers. (2006, February). *NASW practice snapshot: The mental health recovery model.* Retrieved from http://www.socialworkers.org/practice/behavioral_health/0206snapshot.asp

National Coalition Against Domestic Violence. (n.d.). *Fact sheet.* Washington, DC: Author.

National Institute on Aging. (2002). Age page: Aging and alcoholism. Retrieved from www.nia.nih.gov/health/agepages/alcohol.html

National Institute on Alcohol Abuse and Alcoholism. (1994, January). Alcohol and minorities. *Alcohol Alert, 23.* Rockville, MD: Author.

National Institute on Alcohol Abuse and Alcoholism. (1995a). *Assessing alcohol problems: A guide for clinicians and researchers* (NIH Publication No. 95–3745). Rockville, MD: Author.

National Institute on Alcohol Abuse and Alcoholism. (1995b). *Twelve step facilitation therapy manual: A clinical research guide for therapists treating individuals with alcohol abuse and dependence: Vol. 1.* Project MATCH monograph series (NIH Publication No. 95–3722).

National Institute on Alcohol Abuse and Alcoholism. (1997, April). Patient-treatment matching. *Alcohol Alert, 36,* 1–4.

National Institute on Alcohol Abuse and Alcoholism. (1999, April). Brief intervention for alcohol problems. *Alcohol Alert, 43,* 1–4.

National Institute on Alcohol Abuse and Alcoholism. (2000). Alcohol and women: An overview. In *Tenth special report to congress on alcohol* (pp. 253–257). Rockville, MD: Author.

National Institute on Alcohol Abuse and Alcoholism. (2005, July). Brief interventions. *Alcohol Alert, 66,* 1–7.

National Institute on Alcohol Abuse and Alcoholism. (2005). *Module 101: Disabilities and alcohol use disorders.* Retrieved from http://pubs.niaaa.nih.gov/publications/Social/Module10Idisabilities/Module10I.html

National Institute on Alcohol Abuse and Alcoholism. (2013, July). *Alcohol and the Hispanic community.* Retrieved from http://pubs.niaaa.nih.gov/publications/HispanicFact/hispanicFact.pdf

National Institute on Drug Abuse. (1994a). *Recovery training and self help: Relapse prevention and aftercare for drug addicts* (NIH Publication No. 94–3521). Rockville, MD: Author.

National Institute on Drug Abuse. (1994b). *Relapse prevention* (NIH Publication No. 94–3845). Rockville, MD: Author.

National Institute on Drug Abuse. (1999). *Principles of drug addiction treatment* (NIH Publication No. 00–4180). Rockville, MD: Author.

National Institute on Drug Abuse. (2002). Gender matters in drug abuse. *NIDA Notes, 13,* 59–60.

National Institute on Drug Abuse. (2003a). *Family therapy. Addiction alternatives.* Retrieved from www.aa2.org/philosophy/brieffamily.htm

National Institute on Drug Abuse. (2003b, October). Multiculturalism at least as effective as cultural specificity in test of prevention program. *NIDA Notes, 18,* 8–10.

National Institute on Drug Abuse. (2006). *Stress and substance abuse.* Community Drug Alert Bulletin. Rockville, MD: Author.

National Institute on Drug Abuse. (2006, March). *HIV/AIDS.* Research Report Series (NIH Pub. 06–5750). Rockville, MD: Author.

National Institute on Drug Abuse. (2006, July). *Treatment for drug abusers in the criminal justice system* (NIDA InfoFacts). Rockville, MD: Author.

National Institute on Drug Abuse. (2008). *Comorbidity: Addiction and other mental illnesses.* Research Report Series. Rockville, MD: Author.

National Institute on Drug Abuse. (2008). High-risk drug offenders do better with close judicial supervision. *NIDA Notes, 22,* 9–10. Rockville, MD: Author.

National Institute on Drug Abuse. (2010, September). *Comorbidity: Addiction and other mental illnesses.* (NIH Publication No. 10–5771). Rockville, MD: Author.

National Institute on Drug Abuse. (2011, September). *Comorbidity: Addiction and other mental disorders.* (NIDA InfoFacts). Rockville, MD: Author.

National Institute on Drug Abuse. (2011, November). AAP recommends pediatricians use SBIRT for all adolescent patients. *Alcoholism Drug Abuse Weekly, 43,* 1–3.

National Institute on Drug Abuse. (2012, July). *Drug abuse and HIV* (NIH Pub. 12–5760). Rockville, MD: Author.

National Institute on Drug Abuse. (2012, July). *Inhalant abuse.* (NIH Pub. 10–3818). Rockville, MD: Author.

National Institute on Drug Abuse. (2012, December). *Principles of drug addiction treatment* (3rd ed.; NIH Publication No. 12–4180). Rockville, MD: Author.

National Institutes of Health. (1993). *Recovery training and self-help: Relapse prevention and aftercare for drug addicts* (NIH Publication No.93-3521). Rockville, MD: National Institute on Drug Abuse.

National Institutes of Health. (2003). *Biobehavioral pain research*. Retrieved from http://grants2.nih.gov/grants/guide/pa-files/PA-03-152.html

National Spinal Cord Injury Association (NSCIA). (2009). National Spinal Cord Injury Association resource center fact sheets. Retrieved from http://www.sci-info-pages.com/factsheets.html

National Task Force on Juvenile Sexual Offending. (1988). A statement of philosophy for management and treatment of sex offenders: Preliminary report. *Juvenile and Family Court Journal, 39*, 2.

National Woman Abuse Prevention Project. (1989). *Understanding domestic violence*. Washington, DC: Author.

Neal, D. J., Corbin, W. R., & Fromme, K. (2006). Measurement of alcohol-related consequences among high school and college students: Application of item response models to the Rutgers alcohol problem index. *Psychological Assessment, 18*, 402–414.

Neff, K. D. (2008). Self-compassion: Moving beyond the pitfalls of a separate self-concept. In H. A. Wayment & J. J. Bauer, *Transcending self-interest* (pp. 95–105). Washington, DC: American Psychological Association.

Neimeyer, G. J. (2013, August). *APA Workshop 181: Understanding the DSM-5: Problems and prospects in the diagnostic revisions*. Honolulu, HI: American Psychological Association.

Neimeyer, R. A., & Wogrin, C. (2008). Complicated bereavement: A meaning-oriented approach. *Illness, Crisis, & Loss, 16*, 1–20.

Nelipovich, M., & Buss, E. (1989). Alcohol abuse and persons who are blind. *Alcohol Health Research World, 13*, 128–131.

Nelipovich, M., & Buss, E. (1991). Investigating alcohol abuse among persons who are blind. *Journal of Visual Impairment and Blindness, 85*, 343–345.

Neville, H. A., & Walters, J. M. (2004). Contextualizing Black Americans' health. In D. R. Atkinson & G. Hackett (Eds.), *Counseling diverse populations* (3rd ed., pp. 83–103). Boston, MA: McGraw-Hill.

Newmark, D. (1984). Review of a support group for patients with AIDS. *Topics in Clinical Nursing, 6*, 38–44.

Nichols, A., Milligan, K., Smith, A., Sword, W., Thabane, L., & Henderson, J. (2012). Integrated programs for mothers with substance abuse issues and their children: A systematic review of studies reporting on child outcomes. *Child Abuse & Neglect, 36*, 308–322.

Nichols, S. (1985). Psychosocial reactions of persons with the Acquired Immunodeficiency Syndrome. *Annals of Internal Medicine, 103*, 765–767.

N. J. (1992). *Understanding bipolar disorder and addiction* [Brochure]. Center City, MN: Hazelden.

Norberg, M. M., Battisti, R. A., Copeland, J., Hermens, D. F., & Hickie, I. B. (2012). Two sides of the same coin: Cannabis dependence and mental health problems in help-seeking adolescent and young adult outpatients. *International Journal of Mental Health & Addiction, 10*, 818–828.

Norcross, J. C. (2003, August). Integrating self-help into psychotherapy: A revolution in mental health practice [Invited address]. Rosalee G. Weiss Lecture on Psychotherapy at the American Psychological Association, Toronto, Ontario, Canada.

Norcross, J. C., & Barnett, J. E. (2008). Self-care as an ethical imperative. *Register Report, 34*, 20–27.

Norcross, J. C., Hogan, T. P., & Koocher, G. P. (2008a). Evidence-based practice in psychology. *Register Report, 34*, 10–15.

Norcross, J. C., Hogan, T. P., & Koocher, G. P. (2008b). *Clinician's guide to evidence-based practices: Mental health and the addictions*. New York, NY: Oxford University Press.

North Carolina Bar Association. (1995). *Domestic violence and the law: A practical guide for survivors*. Raleigh, NC: Author.

North Carolina Coalition Against Domestic Violence. (1995). *Project Esperanza: A guide to working with battered Latinas*. Raleigh, NC: Author.

Nowinski, J., Baker, S., & Carroll, K. (1995). *Twelve step facilitation therapy manual*. Rockville, MD: National Institute on Alcohol Abuse and Alcoholism.

Nuckols, C. C., (1995, October). Working with the angry/violent patient. Paper presented at the National Dual Disorder Conference, Las Vegas, NV.

Nugent, F. A. (1994). *An introduction to the profession of counseling* (2nd ed.). New York, NY: Macmillan.

Nussbaum, A. M. (2013). *The pocket guide to the DSM-5 diagnostic exam* (5th ed.). Washington, DC: Author.

Oakeshott, M. (1991). *Rationalism in politics and other essays*. Indianapolis, IN: Liberty Press.

Oakley, B. (2012). *Pathological altruism*. New York, NY: Oxford University Press.

Oakley, D., & Dennis, D. L. (1996). Responding to the needs of the homeless people with alcohol, drug, and/or mental disorders. In J. Baumohl (Ed.), *Homelessness in America* (pp. 179–186). Phoenix, AZ: Oryx.

O'Brien, M. C., Reboussin, B., Veach, L. J., & Miller, P. R. (2012). *Robert Wood Johnson Grant #65032: The Teachable Moment Study* [Unpublished research report].

O'Connell, D. F. (1999, December 13). Spirituality's importance in recovery cannot be denied. *Alcoholism & Drug Abuse Weekly, 11,* 5.

O'Dwyer, P. (1993). Alcoholism treatment facilities. In S. L. A. Straussner (Ed.), *Clinical work with substance-abusing clients* (pp. 119–134). New York, NY: Guilford Press.

Oegel, K., & Coskun, S. (2011). Cognitive behavioral therapy-based brief intervention for volatile substance misusers during adolescence: A follow-up study. *Substance Use and Misuse, 46,* 128–133.

O'Farrell, T. J., Murphy, M., Alter, J., & Fals-Stewart, W. (2008). Brief family treatment intervention to promote continuing care among alcohol-dependent patients in inpatient detoxification: A randomized pilot study. *SAT Journal of Substance Abuse Treatment, 34*(3), 363–369.

Ogborne, A. C., & Smart, R. G. (1995). People with physical disabilities admitted to a residential addiction treatment program. *American Journal of Drug & Alcohol Abuse, 21,* 137–145.

O'Halloran, T. M., & Linton, J. M. (2000). Stress on the job: Self-care resources for counselors. *Journal of Mental Health Counseling, 22,* 354–364.

Olkin, R. (1999). *What every therapist should know about disability*. New York, NY: Guilford Press.

Olkin, R. (1999). *What psychotherapists should know about disability*. New York, NY: Guilford Press.

Olkin, R., & Howson, L. (1994). Attitudes toward and images of physical disability. *Journal of Social Behavior and Personality, 9,* 81–96.

Olson, P. E. (1990). The sexual abuse of boys: A study of the long-term psychological effects. In M. Hunter (Ed.), *The sexually abused male: Vol. 1. Prevalence, impact and treatment* (pp. 137–152). Lexington, MA: Lexington Books.

Ondus, K. A., Hujer, M. E., Mann, A. E., & Mion, L. C. (1999). Substance abuse and the hospitalized elderly. *Orthopedic Nursing, 18,* 27–36.

Orlin, L., & Davis, J. (1993). Assessment and intervention with drug and alcohol abusers in psychiatric settings. In S. L. A. Straussner (Ed.), *Clinical work with substance-abusing clients* (pp. 50–68). New York, NY: Guilford Press.

Orrok, B. (1992). Diverse presentations of substance abuse and post-traumatic stress disorder in incest survivors. In S. Shapiro & G. Dominiak (Eds.), *Sexual trauma and psychopathology* (pp. 113–142). New York, NY: Lexington Books.

Orzech, D. (2006, March/April). Soul survivors. *Social Work Today,* 36–39.

Osborn, C. J. (2001). Brief interventions in the treatment of alcohol use disorders: Definition and overview. *Journal of Addictions and Offender Counseling, 21,* 76–84.

Osten, K. A., & Switzer, R. (2014). *Integrating 12-steps and psychotherapy: Helping clients find sobriety and recovery*. Los Angeles, CA: Sage.

Padgett, D. K., Stanhope, V., Henwood, B. F., & Stefancic, A. (2011). Substance use outcomes among homeless clients with serious mental illness: Comparing housing first with treatment first programs. *Community Mental Health Journal, 47,* 227–232.

Paliwal, P., Hyman, S. M., & Sinha, R. (2008). Craving predicts time to cocaine relapse: Further validation of the now and brief versions of the cocaine craving questionnaire. *Drug and Alcohol Dependence, 93,* 252–259.

Palmieri, C. D., & Accordino, M. P. (2004). Dual diagnosis: Effective treatment and barriers to recovery. *Journal of Applied Rehabilitation Counseling, 35,* 35–41.

Pape, P. A. (1993). Issues in assessment and intervention with alcohol- and drug-abusing women. In S. L. A. Straussner (Ed.), *Clinical work with substance-abusing clients* (pp. 251–269). New York, NY: Guilford Press.

Paris, J. (2013). *The intelligent clinician's guide to the DSM-5*. New York, NY: Oxford University Press.

Parrot, A. (1991a). Institutional response: How can acquaintance rape be prevented? In A. Parrot & L. Bechhofer (Eds.), *Acquaintance rape: The hidden crime* (pp. 355–367). New York, NY: Wiley.

Parrot, A. (1991b). Recommendations for college policies and procedures to deal with acquaintance rape.

In A. Parrot & L. Bechhofer (Eds.), *Acquaintance rape: The hidden crime* (pp. 368–380). New York, NY: Wiley.

Parry, C. D., Blank, M. B., & Pithey, A. L. (2007). Responding to the threat of HIV among persons with mental illness and substance abuse. *Current Opinion in Psychiatry, 20,* 235–241.

Parry, M. (2012, November). The neighborhood effect. *Chronicle Review,* pp. B6–B10.

Patel, A. B., & Wendler, A. (2007, Spring). Making the most of clinical supervision. *Addictions Newsletter, 14,* 8–9.

Patsiopoulos, A. T., & Buchanan, M. J. (2011). The practice of self-compassion in counseling: A narrative inquiry. *Professional psychology: Research and Practice, 42,* 301–307. doi: 10.1037/a0024482

Patterson, D. A., & Buckingham, S. L. (2010). Does motivational interviewing stages of change increase treatment retention among person who are alcohol and other drug dependent and HIV infected? *Journal of HIV/AIDS & Social Services, 9,* 45–57.

Patterson, J., Williams, L., Grauf-Grounds, C., & Chamow, L. (2009). *Essential skills in family therapy* (2nd ed.). New York, NY: Guilford Press.

Patterson, W. M., Dohn, H. H., Bird, J., & Patterson, G. A. (1983). Evaluation of suicidal patients: The SAD PERSONS Scale. *Psychosomatics, 24,* 343–349.

Pedersen, R. R., Hsu, S. H., Neighbors, C., Lee, C. M., & Larimer M. E. (2013). The relationship between collective self-esteem, acculturation, and alcohol-related consequences among Asian American young adults. *Journal of Ethnicity in Substance Abuse, 12,* 51–67.

Pedulla, B. M., & Pedulla, M. A. (2001). Sharing the wealth: A model for brief mental health volunteer work in developing countries. *Professional Psychology: Research and Practice, 32,* 402–406.

Peled, E., & Sacks, Il. (2008). The self-perception of women who live with an alcoholic partner: Dialoging with deviance, strength, and self-fulfillment. *Family Relations: An Interdisciplinary Journal of Applied Family Studies, 57,* 390–403.

Peluso, E., & Peluso, L. S. (1989). Alcohol and the elderly. *Professional Counselor, 4,* 44–46.

Pence, E., & Paymar, M. (1993). *Education groups for men who batter: The Duluth model.* New York, NY: Springer.

Perkinson, R. R. (1997). *Chemical dependency counseling: A practical guide.* Thousand Oaks, CA: Sage.

Perkinson, R. R. (2004). *Treating alcoholism.* Hoboken, NJ: Wiley.

Perkinson, R. R. (2008). *Chemical dependency counseling: A practical guide* (3rd ed.). Los Angeles, CA: Sage.

Peterman, L. M., & Dixon, C. G. (2003). Domestic violence between same-sex partners: Implications for counseling. *Journal of Counseling and Development, 8,* 40–47.

Peterson, C., Park, N., & Seligman, M. E. P. (2005). Assessment of character strengths. In G. P. Koocher, J. C. Norcross, & S. S. Hill (Eds.), *Psychologists' desk reference* (2nd ed., pp. 93–98). New York, NY: Oxford University Press.

Peterson, Z. (2002). More than a mirror: The ethics of therapist self-disclosure. *Psychotherapy: Theory, Research, Practice and Training, 39,* 21–31.

Petry, N. M. (2002). A comparison of young, middle-aged, and older adult treatment-seeking pathological gamblers. *Gerontologist, 42,* 92–99.

Phillips, J. C., Webel, A., Rose, C. D., Corless, I. B., Sullivan, K. M., Voss, J., . . . Holzemer, W. L. (2013). Associations between the legal context of HIV, perceived social capital, and HIV antiretroviral adherence in North America. *BMC Public Health, 13,* 1–16.

Phillips, K. T., Stein, M. D., Anderson, B. J., & Corsi, K. F. (2012). Skin and needle hygiene intervention for injection drug users: Results from a randomized, controlled Stage I pilot trial. *Journal of Substance Abuse Treatment, 43,* 313–321.

Pilowsky, D. J., & Wu, L.-T. (2013). Screening instruments for substance use and brief interventions targeting adolescents in primary care: A literature review. *Addictive Behaviors, 38,* 2146–2153.

Pipal, J. E. (1995). Managed care: Is it the corpse in the living room? An exposé. *Psychotherapy, 32,* 39–40.

Pohl, M., & Smith, L. (2012). Chronic pain and addiction: Challenging co-occurring disorders. *Journal of Psychoactive Drugs, 44,* 119–124. doi: 10.1080/02791072.2012.684621

Poirier, J. G. (1991). Disputed custody and concerns of parental violence. *Psychotherapy in Private Practice, 9,* 7–23.

Pokorny, A. D., Miller, B. A., & Kaplan, H. B. (1972). The brief MAST: A shortened version of the Michigan alcoholism screening test. *American Journal of Psychiatry, 129,* 342–345.

Polcin, D. L., & Beattie, M. (2007). Relationship and institutional pressure to enter treatment: Differences by demographics, problem severity, and motivation. *Journal of Studies on Alcohol and Drugs*, *68*, 428–436.

Pope, R. L., Reynolds, A. L., & Mueller, J. A. (2004). *Multicultural competence in student affairs*. Hoboken, NJ: Wiley.

Portenoy, R. K., Lussier, D., Kirsh, K. L., & Passik, S. D. (2005). Pain and addiction. In R. J. Frances, S. I. Miller, & A. H. Mack (Eds.), *Clinical textbook of addictive disorders* (3rd ed., pp. 367–395). New York, NY: Guilford Press.

Post, B. C., Cornish, M. A., Wade, N. G., & Tucker, J. R. (2013). Religion and spirituality in group counseling: Beliefs and practices of university counseling center counselors. *Journal for Specialists in Group Work*, *38*, 264–284.

Post, R. (1996, Winter). Once a taboo topic, relapse prevention is a frontline issue. *Hazelden Voice*, *1*, 1–2.

Potter-Efron, R. T. (1989). *Shame, guilt and alcoholism: Treatment issues in clinical practice*. New York, NY: Haworth Press.

Powell, D. J. (1993). *Clinical supervision in alcohol and drug abuse counseling*. New York, NY: Lexington.

Powell, T., & Perron, B. E. (2010). Self-help groups and mental health/substance use agencies: The benefits of organizational exchange. *substance Use & Misuse*, *45*, 315–329.

Preston, J. (1998). *Integrative brief therapy*. San Luis Obispo, CA: Impact.

Prince, D. W., & Hoppe, M. H. (2000). *Communicating across cultures*. Greensboro, NC: Center for Creative Leadership.

Problem gambling. (2004, March). *Harvard Mental Health Letter*, *20*, 1–4.

Prochaska, J. O. (2012). Individual dynamics of addiction: Common pathways to change. In H. J. Shaffer (Ed.), *APA addiction syndrome handbook: Vol. 1. Foundations, influences, and expressions of addiction* (pp. 103–118). doi: 10.1037/13751–005

Prochaska, J. O., & DiClemente, C. C. (1992). Stages of change in the modification of problem behaviors. In M. Hersen, R. M. Eisler, & P. M. Miller (Eds.), *Progress in behavior modification* (Vol. 28, pp. 183–218). Sycamore, IL: Sycamore.

Prochaska, J. O., DiClemente, C. C., & Norcross, J. C. (1992). In search of how people change. *American Psychologist*, *47*, 1102–1114.

Prochaska, J. O., & Norcross, J. C. (2001). Stages of change. *Psychotherapy: Theory, Research, Practice, Training*, *38*, 443–448.

Prochaska, J. O., & Norcross, J. C. (2002). Stages of change. In J. C. Norcross (Ed.), *Psychotherapy relationships that work: Therapist contributions and responsiveness to patients* (pp. 303–313). New York, NY: Oxford University Press.

Quigley, L. A., & Marlatt, G. A. (1999). Relapse prevention: Maintenance of change after initial treatment. In B. S. McCrady & E. E. Epstein (Eds.), *Addictions: A comprehensive guidebook* (pp. 370–384). New York, NY: Oxford University Press.

Racey, R. C., Zhang, W., Brandson, E. K., Fernandes, K. A., Tzemis, D., Harrigan, P. R., . . . Hogg, R. S. (2010). HIV antiviral drug resistance: Patient comprehension. *AIDS Care*, *22*, 816–826.

Radin, S. M., Banta-Green, C. J., Thomas, L. R., Kutz, S. H., & Donovan, D. M. (2011). Substance use, treatment admissions, and recovery trends in diverse Washington State tribal communities. *American Journal of Drug and Alcohol Abuse*, *38*, 511–517.

Raistrick, D. (2007). Motivation and barriers to change. In G. Tober & D. Raistrick (Eds.), *Motivational dialogue* (pp. 16–33). New York, NY: Routledge.

Ramey, L. (1998). The use of gestalt interventions in the treatment of the resistant alcohol dependent client. *Journal of Mental Health Counseling*, *20*, 202–215.

Randall, J., Henggeler, S. W., Cunningham, P. B., Rowland, M., & Swenson, C. (2001). Adapting multisystemic therapy to treat adolescent substance abuse more effectively. *Cognitive and Behavioral Practice*, *8*, 359–366.

Rao, M. S. (2005). Spirituality in psychiatry. *Psychiatry*, *2*, 20–22.

Rao, U. (2006). Links between depression and substance abuse in adolescents: Neurobiological mechanisms. *American Journal of Preventive Medicine*, *31*, S161–S174.

Rathbone-McCuan, E., & Bland, J. (1975). A treatment typology for the elderly alcohol abuser. *Journal of the American Geriatrics Society*, *23*, 553–557.

Ratican, K. L. (1992). Sexual abuse survivors: Identifying symptoms and special treatment considerations. *Journal of Counseling and Development*, *71*, 33–38.

Rational Recovery. (1992). *Self-empowered recovery from substance dependency*. Lotus, CA: Author.

Raven, B. H., & Kruglanski, A. W. (1975). Conflict and power. In D. G. Swingle (Ed.), *The structure of conflict* (pp. 177–219). New York, NY: Academic Press.

Rawson, R. A., Obert, J. L., McCann, M. J., & Marinelli-Casey, P. (1993). Relapse prevention strategies in outpatient substance abuse treatment. *Psychology of Addictive Behaviors, 7,* 85–95.

Ray, O., & Ksir, C. (2004). *Drugs, society, and human behavior* (10th ed.). New York, NY: McGraw-Hill.

Rebach, H. (1992). *Ethnic and multicultural drug abuse: Perspectives on current research.* New York, NY: Haworth Press.

Rehabilitation Research and Training Center on Drugs and Disability. (1996). *Substance abuse, disability, and vocational rehabilitation.* Dayton, OH: Author.

Reichenberg, L. W. (2014). *DSM-5 essentials.* Hoboken, NJ: Wiley.

Reickmann, T., McCarty, D., Kovas, A., Spicer, P., Bray, J., Gilbert, S., & Mercer, M. (2012). American Indians with substance used disorders: Treatment needs and comorbid conditions. *American Journal of Drug and Alcohol Abuse, 38,* 498–504.

Reid, C., & Kampfe, C. (2000). *Multicultural issues* (ERIC Document Reproduction Service No. ED440351).

Reif, S. S., Whetten, K., Wilson, E. R., McAllaster, C., Pence, B. W., Legrand, S., & Gong, W. (2012). HIV/AIDS in the southern USA: A disproportionate epidemic. *AIDS Care.* Electronic publication. *Informa Healthcare* NLM ID: 8915313 Publication Model: Printing Electronic Cited Medium: Internet ISSN: 1360–0451 [Electronic] Linking ISSN: 09540121 NLM ISO Abbreviation: AIDS Care.

Remen, N., May, R., Young, D., & Berland, W. (1985). The wounded healer. *Saybrook Review, 5,* 84–93.

Remley, T. P. Jr. (1985). The law and ethical practices in elementary and middle schools. *Elementary School Guidance and Counseling, 19,* 181–189.

Remley, T. P., & Herlighy, B. (2005). *Ethical, legal, and professional issues in counseling* (2nd ed.). Upper Saddle River, NJ: Merrill Prentice Hall.

Remley, T. P., & Miranti, J. G. (1991). Child custody evaluator: A new role for mental health counselors. *Journal of Mental Health Counseling, 13,* 334–342.

Rempel, M., Green, M., & Kralstein, D. (2012). The impact of drug courts on crime and incarceration: Findings from a multi-site quasi-experimental design. *Journal of Experimental Criminology, 8,* 165–192.

Rendon, V. (1992). Deaf culture and alcohol and substance abuse. *Journal of Substance Abuse Treatment, 9,* 103–110.

Richards, P. S., Bartz, J. D., & O'Grady, K. A. (2009). Assessing religion and spirituality in counseling: Some reflections and recommendations. *Counseling and Values, 54,* 65–79.

Richardson, T. M., & Williams, B. A. (1990). *African-Americans in treatment: Dealing with cultural differences* [Brochure]. Center City, MN: Hazelden.

Ries, R. K. (1993). The dually diagnosed patient with psychotic symptoms. *Journal of Addictive Diseases, 12,* 103–122.

Ries, R. K., Galanter, M., & Tonigan, J. S. (2008). Twelve step facilitation: An adaptation for psychiatric practitioners and patients. In M. Galanter & H. D. Kleber (Eds.), *Textbook of substance abuse treatment* (3rd ed., pp. 373–386). Washington, DC: American Psychiatric Publishing.

Ries, R. K., Galanter, M., Tonigan, J. S., & Ziegler, P. P. (2011). Twelve step facilitation for dually diagnosed patients. In M. Galanter and H. D. Kleber (Eds.), *Psychotherapy for the treatment of substance abuse* (4th ed., pp. 299–327). Washington, DC: American Psychiatric Publishing.

Rigler, S. K. (2000). Alcoholism in the elderly. *American Family Physician, 61,* 1710–1716.

Rinella, V. J., & Dubin, W. R. (1988). The hidden victims of AIDS: Health care workers and families. *Psychiatric Hospital, 19,* 115–120.

Riordan, R. J., & Walsh, L. (1994). Guidelines for professional referral to Alcoholics Anonymous and other twelve step groups. *Journal of Counseling and Development, 72,* 351–355.

Ritvo, J. I., & Causey, H. L. (2008). Community-based treatment. In M. Galanter & H. D. Kleber (Eds.), *Substance abuse treatment* (4th ed., pp. 477–490). Washington, DC: American Psychiatric Publishing.

Rizvi, S. L., Steffel, L. M., & Carson-Wong, A. (2013). An overview of dialectical behavior therapy for professional psychologists. *Professional Psychology: Research and Practice, 44,* 73–80.

Rizzuto, A. M. (1998). *Why did Freud reject God?* New Haven, CT: Yale University Press.

Robbins, B. D. (2008). What is the good life? Positive psychology and the renaissance of humanistic psychology. *Humanistic Psychologist, 36,* 96–112.

Roberts, S. (2004, Winter). Dual diagnosis: Substance abuse and mental illness don't mix. *Schizophrenia Digest,* 30–36.

Robertson, N. (1988, February 21). The changing world of Alcoholics Anonymous. *New York Times Magazine, 40,* 42–44, 47, 92.

Robinson, G. E. (2003, December). Current concepts in domestic violence. *Primary Psychiatry, 10,* 48–52.

Robinson, G. E. (2006). Supervision of boundary issues. In J. H. Gold (Ed.), *Psychotherapy supervision and consultation in clinical practice* (pp. 83–106). Lanham, MD: Aronson.

Rogan, A. (1985, Winter). Domestic violence and alcohol: Barriers to cooperation. *Alcohol Health and Research World, 9,* 22–27.

Rogers, C. R. (1951). *Client-centered therapy.* Boston, MA: Houghton Mifflin.

Rogers, C. R. (1987). The underlying theory: Drawn from experiences with individuals and groups. *Counseling and Values, 32,* 38–45.

Rollins, J. (2013, May). The dawn of a new DSM. *Counseling Today,* 42–50.

Rollnick, S., Heather, N., Gold, R., & Hall, W. (1992). Development of a short "readiness to change" questionnaire for use in brief, opportunistic interventions among excessive drinkers. *British Journal of Addiction, 87,* 743–754.

Ronel, N., Gueta, K., Abramsohn, Y., Caspi, N., & Adelson, M. (2011). Can a 12-step program work in a methadone maintenance treatment? *International Journal of Offender Therapy and Comparative Criminology, 55,* 1135–1153.

Root, M. P. (1989). Treatment failures: The role of sexual victimization in women's addictive behavior. *American Journal of Orthopsychiatry, 59,* 542–549.

Rorty, M., & Yager, J. (1996). Speculations on the role of childhood abuse in the development of eating disorders among women. In M. F. Schwartz & L. Cohn (Eds.), *Sexual abuse and eating disorders* (pp. 23–35). New York, NY: Brunner/Mazel.

Rosen, C. S., Ouimette, P. C., Sheikh, J. I., Gregg, J. A., & Moos, R. H. (2002). Physical and sexual abuse history and addiction treatment outcomes. *Journal of Studies on Alcohol, 63,* 683–687.

Rosenblatt, A. B., & Mekhail, N. A. (2005). Management of pain in addicted/illicit and legal substance abusing patients. *Pain and Addiction, 5,* 2–10.

Ross, G. R. (1994). *Treating adolescent substance abuse: Understanding the fundamental elements.* Boston, MA: Allyn & Bacon.

Ross, R. R., Altmaier, E. M., & Russell, D. W. (1989). Job stress, social support, and burnout among counseling center staff. *Journal of Counseling Psychology, 36,* 464–470.

Ross, S. (2008). The mentally ill substance abuser. In M. Galanter & H. D. Kleber (Eds.), *Substance abuse treatment* (4th ed., pp. 537–554). Washington, DC: American Psychiatric Publishing.

Rotgers, F. (2003). Cognitive-behavioral theories of substance abuse. In F. Rotgers, J. Morgenstern, & S. T. Walters (Eds.), *Treating substance abuse: Theory and technique* (2nd ed., pp. 166–216). New York, NY: Guilford Press.

Roth, J. (2013). Inclusive group facilitation strategies for all abilities. *Counseling Today, 56,* 53–57.

Rothe, E., & Ruiz, P. (2001). Substance abuse among Cuban Americans. In L. A. Straussner (Ed.), *Ethnocultural factors in substance abuse treatment* (pp. 97–100). New York, NY: Guilford Press.

Rothschild, B. (2000). *The body remembers.* New York, NY: Norton.

Rowe, C. R. (2012). Family therapy for drug abuse: Review and updates 2003–2010. *Journal of Marital and Family Therapy, 38,* 59–81.

Rubin, E. (2003). Integration of theory, research, and practice: A clinician's perspective. In F. Rotgers, J. Morgenstern, & S. T. Walters (Eds.), *Treating substance abuse: Theory and technique* (2nd ed., pp. 343–363). New York, NY: Guilford Press.

Ruiz, P., & Langrod, J. G. (1997). Hispanic Americans. In J. H. Lowinson, P. Ruiz, R. B. Millman, & J. G. Langrod (Eds.), *Substance abuse: A comprehensive textbook* (3rd ed., pp. 705–711). Baltimore, MD: Williams & Wilkins.

Rumpf, H.-J., Wohlert, T., Freyer-Adam, J., Grothues, J. B., & Bischof, G. (2013). Screening questionnaires for problem drinking in adolescents: Performance of AUDIT, AUDIT-C, CRAGGT and POSIT. *European Addiction Research, 19,* 121–127.

Russell, D. E. H., & Bolen, R. M. (2000). *The epidemic of rape and child sexual abuse in the United States.* Thousand Oaks, CA: Sage.

Russell, M., Martier, S. S., & Sokol, R. J. (1991). Screening for pregnancy risk-drinking: TWEAKING the tests. *Alcoholism: Clinical and Experimental Research, 15,* 368.

Russell, S. A., & Wilsnack, S. (1991). Adult survivors of childhood sexual abuse: Substance abuse and other consequences. In P. Roth (Ed.), *Alcohol and drugs are women's issues: Vol. 1. A review of the issues* (pp. 61–70). Metuchen, NJ: Scarecrow Press and Women's Action Alliance.

Ryan, R. M., Huta, V., & Deci, E. L. (2008). Living well: A self-determination theory perspective on eudaimonia. *Journal of Happiness Studies, 9,* 139–170.

Ryff, C. D., & Singer, B. (2003). Flourishing under fire: Resilience as a prototype of challenged thriving. In C. L. M. Keyes & J. Haidt (Eds.), *Flourishing: Positive psychology and the life well-lived*. Washington, DC: American Psychological Association.

Saag, M. S. (1992). AIDS testing: Now and in the future. In M. A. Sande & P. A. Volberding (Eds.), *The medical management of AIDS* (4th ed., pp. 65–88). Philadelphia, PA: Saunders.

Saakvitne, K. W. (2002). How to avoid the occupational hazards of being a psychotherapist. In L. VandeCreek & T. L. Jackson (Eds.), *Innovations in clinical practice: A source book* (pp. 325–341). Sarasota, FL: Professional Resource Press.

Saarnio, P. (2011). Therapist's preference on motivational interviewing and its relationship to interpersonal functioning and personality traits. *Counseling Psychology Quarterly, 24*, 171–180.

Sachs, K. (1996). Surviving managed care through integrity. *Psychotherapy Bulletin, 31*, 39–40.

Safren, S. A., O'Cleirigh, C. M., Bullis, J. R., Otto, M. W., Stein, M. D., & Pollack, M. H. (2012). Cognitive behavioral therapy for adherence and depression (CBT-AD) in HIV-infected injection drug users: A randomized controlled trial. *Journal of Consulting and Clinical Psychology, 80*, 404–415.

Saghir, M. T., Robins, E., Walbran, B., & Gentry, K. E. (1970). Homosexuality: III. Psychiatric disorders and disability in the male homosexual. *American Journal of Psychiatry, 126*, 1079–1086.

Sakai, J., Ho, P., Shore, J., Risk, N., & Price, R. (2005). Asians in the United States: Substance dependence and use of substance-dependence treatment. *Journal of Substance Abuse Treatment, 29*, 75–84.

Saladin, M. E., Back, S. E., & Payne, R. A. (2009). Posttraumatic stress disorder and substance use disorder comorbidity. In R. K. Ries, D. A. Fiellin, S. C. Miller, & R. Saitz (Eds.), *Principles of addiction medicine* (4th ed., pp. 1249–1262). Philadelphia, PA: Wolters Kluwer.

Salo, M. M., & Shumate, S. G. (1993). *Counseling minor clients* (ACA Legal Series Vol. 9) Alexandria, VA: American Counseling Association.

Sandberg, G. G., & Marlatt, G. A. (1991). Relapse prevention. In R. I. Shader (Ed.), *Clinical manual of chemical dependence* (pp. 377–399). Washington, DC: American Psychiatric Association.

Sandberg, K. A. (1994, November). Rehabilitation and substance abuse treatment working together to serve deaf clients. Paper presented at the meeting of Innovative Partnerships in Recovery, Overland Park, KS.

Sandberg, K. M., Richards, T. E., & Erford, B. T. (2013). *Assessing common mental health and addiction issues with free-access instrument*. New York, NY: Routledge.

Sandovai, J., Scott, A. N., & Padilla, I. (2009). Crisis counseling: An overview. *Psychology in the Schools, 46*, 246–256.

Sannibale, C., Teesson, M., Creamer, M., Stharthan, T., Bryant, R. A., Sutherland, K., . . . Peek-O'Leary, M. (2013). Randomized controlled trial of cognitive behaviour therapy for comorbid posttraumatic stress disorder and alcohol use disorders. *British Journal of Addiction, 108*, 1397–1410.

Sartor, C. E., Waldron, M., Duncan, A. E., Grant, J. D., McCutcheon, V. V., Nelson, E. C., . . . Heath, A. C. (2013). Childhood sexual abuse and early substance use in adolescent girls: The role of familial influences. *Addiction, 108*, 993–1000.

Sattler, J. M. (1992). *Assessment of children* (3rd ed.). San Diego, CA: Author.

Saunders, J. B., Aasland, O. G., Babor, T. F., de la Fuente, J. R., & Grant, M. (1993). Development of the Alcohol Use Disorders Identification Test (AUDIT): WHO collaborative project on early detection of persons with harmful alcohol consumption—II. *Addiction, 88*, 791–804.

Savage, S. R. (1998). Principles of pain treatment in the addicted patient. In A. W. Graham, T. K. Schultz, & B. B. Wilford (Eds.), *Principles of addiction medicine* (2nd ed., pp. 919–944). Chevy Chase, MD: American Society of Addiction Medicine.

Savin-Williams, R. C. (2001). *Mom, dad. I'm gay*. Washington, DC: American Psychological Association.

Schechter, N. E., & Barnett, J. E. (2010). Psychotherapy and the suicidal client: A brief introduction. *Psychotherapy Bulletin, 45*, 11–15.

Scheffler, S. (2004). Substance abuse in homeless persons. In S. L. A. Straussner (Ed.), *Clinical work with substance-abusing clients* (2nd ed., pp. 423–442). New York, NY: Guilford Press.

Schenker, M. D. (2009). *A clinician's guide to 12-step recovery: Integrating 12-step programs into psychotherapy*. New York, NY: Norton.

Schlauch, R. C., Levitt, A., Connell, C. M., & Kaufman, J. S. (2013). The moderating effect of family involvement on substance use risk factors in adolescents with severe emotional and behavioral challenges. *Addictive Behaviors, 38*, 2333–2342.

Schneider, J. P. (2005). Coexisting disorders. In R. H. Coombs (Ed.), *Addiction counseling review* (pp. 293–316). Mahwah, NJ: Erlbaum.

Schneider, K. (2011). Toward a humanistic positive psychology: Why can't we just get along? *Existential Analysis*, *22*, 32–38.

Schneier, F. R., Foose, T. E., Hasin, D. S., Heimberg, R. G., Liu, S.-M., Grant, B. F., & Blanco, C. (2010). Social anxiety disorder and alcohol use disorder comorbidity in the National Epidemiologic Survey on Alcohol and Related Conditions. *Psychological Medicine*, *40*, 977–988. doi: 10.1017/S0033291709991231

Schonberg, S. K. (1993). *Guidelines for the treatment of alcohol- and other drug-abusing adolescents* (DHHS Publication No. SMA 93–3059). Rockville, MD: U.S. Department of Health and Human Services.

Schonfeld, L., & Dupree, L. W. (1991). Antecedents of drinking for early and late onset elderly alcohol abusers. *Journal of Studies on Alcohol*, *52*, 587–592.

Schramm, D. (2007, July). Chronic pain workshop. Workshop in Johnson City, TN.

Schulman, M. (2013, January 9). Generation LGBTQIA. *New York Times*. http://www.nytimes.com/2013/01/10/fashion/generation-lgbtqia.html?pagewanted=all&_r=0

Schulz, J. E., Williams, V., & Galligan, J. E. (2009). Twelve step programs in recovery. In R. K. Ries, D. A. Fiellin, S. C. Miller, & R. Saitz (Ed.), *Principles of addiction medicine* (4th ed., pp. 911–922). Philadelphia, PA: Wolters Kluwer.

Schutt, R. K., & Garrett, G. R. (1988). Social background, residential experiences and health problems of the homeless. *Psychosocial Rehabilitation Journal*, *12*, 67–70.

Schutt, R. K., & Garrett, G. R. (1992). *Responding to the homeless: Policy and practice*. New York, NY: Plenum Press.

Schwartz, M. F., & Cohn, L. (1996). Introduction: Eating disorders and sexual trauma. In M. F. Schwartz & L. Cohn (Eds.), *Sexual abuse and eating disorders* (pp. ix–xii). New York, NY: Brunner/Mazel.

Schwartz, R. C., & Smith, S. D. (2003). Screening and assessing adolescent substance abuse: A primer for counselors. *Journal of Addictions and Offender Counseling*, *24*, 23–34.

Schwarz, B. (1995). The diversity myth: America's leading export. *Atlantic Monthly*, *275*, 57–67.

Scott, D. (1983). Alcohol and food abuse: Some comparisons. *British Medical Journal*, *3*, 301.

Scott, M. (1995, October). Practical approach to dual diagnosis. Paper presented at the National Dual Disorder Conference, Las Vegas, NV.

Seligman, M. E. P. (2002). *Authentic happiness*. New York, NY: Free Press.

Seligman, M. E. P. (2002). Opening Remarks to the Summit. 2002 Positive Psychology Summit: First International Positive Psychology Summit. Washington, DC: Gallup.

Seligman, M. E. P. (2011). *Flourish*. New York, NY: Free Press.

Seligman, M. E. P., & Csikszentmihalyi, M. (2000). Positive psychology: An introduction. *American Psychologist*, *55*, 5–14.

Seligman, M. E. P., Steen, T. A., Park, N., & Peterson, C. (2005). Positive psychology progress: Empirical validation of interventions. *American Psychologist*, *60*, 410–421.

Selzer, M. L. (1971). The Michigan alcohol screening test: The quest for a new diagnostic instrument. *American Journal of Psychiatry*, *127*, 1653–1658.

Selzer, M. L. (1985). Michigan alcoholism screening test. In D. J. Keyser & R. C. Sweetland (Eds.), *Test critiques* (Vol. 3, pp. 439–446). Kansas City, MO: Test Corporation of America.

Selzer, M. L., Vinokur, A., & vanRooijen, L. (1975). A self-administered short Michigan alcoholism screening test (SMAST). *Journal of Studies on Alcohol*, *36*, 117–126.

Senay, E. C. (1997). Diagnostic interview and mental status examination. In J. H. Lowinson, P. Ruiz, R. B. Millman, & J. G. Langrod (Eds.), *Substance abuse: A comprehensive textbook* (3rd ed., pp. 364–369). Baltimore, MD: Williams & Wilkins.

Senreich, E. (2010a). Inviting the significant other of LGBT clients in substance abuse treatment programs: Frequency and impact. *Contemporary Family Therapy: An International Journal*, *32*, 427–433.

Senreich, E. (2010b). Are specialized LGBT program components helpful for gay and bisexual men in substance abuse treatment? *Substance Use & Misuse*, *45*, 1077–1096.

Senreich, E. (2011). The substance abuse treatment experiences of a small sample of transgender clients. *Journal of Social Work Practice in the Addictions*, *11*, 295–299.

Senreich, E., & Vairo, E. (2004). Treatment of gay, lesbian, and bisexual substance abusers. In S. L. A.

Straussner (Ed.), *Clinical work with substance-abusing clients* (2nd ed., pp. 392–422). New York, NY: Guilford Press.

Shafer, K.C. (2004). Trauma and the substance-abusing older adult: Innovative questions for accurate assessment. *Journal of Loss and Trauma: International Perspectives on Stress & Coping, 9,* 345–358.

Shaffer, H. J. (1997). Psychology of stage change. In J. H. Lowinson, P. Ruiz, R. B. Millman, & J. G. Langrod (Eds.), *Substance abuse: A comprehensive textbook* (3rd ed., pp. 100–106). Baltimore, MD: Williams & Wilkins.

Shaffer, H. J., & Kauffman, J. (1985). The clinical assessment and diagnosis of addiction. In T. E. Bratter & G. G. Forrest (Eds.), *Alcoholism and substance abuse: Strategies for intervention* (pp. 225–258). New York, NY: Free Press.

Shah, N. G., Galai, N., Celentano, D. D., Vlahov, D., & Strathdee, S. A. (2006). Longitudinal predictors of injection cessation and subsequent relapse among a cohort of injection drug users in Baltimore, MD, 1988–2000. *Drug and Alcohol Dependence, 83,* 147–156.

Shallcross, L. (2009). Rewriting the "rules" of grief. *Counseling Today, 52,* 28–33.

Shallcross, L. (2013a). Who's taking care of Superman? *Counseling Today, 55,* 42–46.

Shallcross, L. (2013b). Multicultural competence: A continual pursuit. *Counseling Today, 56,* 31–43.

Sharp, C. W., & Rosenberg, N. L. (1997). Inhalants. In J. H. Lowinson, P. Ruiz, R. B. Millman, & J. G. Langrod (Eds.), *Substance abuse: A comprehensive textbook* (3rd ed., pp. 246–264). Baltimore, MD: Williams & Wilkins.

Shaw, B. F., Ritvo, P., & Irvine, J. (2005). *Addiction and recovery for dummies.* Hoboken, NJ: Wiley.

Shea, S. C. (2002). *The practical art of suicide assessment: A guide for mental health professionals and substance abuse counselors.* Hoboken, NJ: Wiley.

Sheridan, M. (2004). Earth as source of spirit. *Spirituality and Social Work Forum, 10,* 14–15.

Shollar, E. (1993). The long-term treatment of the dually diagnosed. In J. Solomon, S. Zimberg, & E. Shollar (Eds.), *Dual diagnosis: Evaluation, treatment, training, and program development* (pp. 77–104). New York, NY: Plenum Press.

Sholomskas, D. E., & Carroll, K. M. (2006). One small step for manuals: Computer-assisted training in twelve-step facilitation. *Journal of Studies on Alcohol, 67,* 939–945.

Shoptaw, S. J. (2009). Sexual addiction. In R. K. Ries, D. A. Fiellin, S. C. Miller, & R. Saitz (Eds.), *Principles of addiction medicine* (4th ed., pp. 519–530). Philadelphia, PA: Wolters Kluwer.

Shulman, G. D. (1997, May). The ASAM patient placement criteria—2: Making it work. *Epikrisis, 8,* 2.

Shumway, S. T., Bradshaw, S. D., Harris, K. S., & Baker, A. K. (2013). Important factors of early addiction recovery and inpatient treatment. *Alcoholism Treatment Quarterly, 31,* 3–24.

Shurman, J., Sack, J., Shurman, G., Schnierow, B., & Gabriel, C. (2006). Share the risk model. *Practical Pain Management, 6,* 10–18.

Siegel, D. J. (2009). Mindful awareness, mindsight, and neural integration. *Humanistic Psychologist, 37,* 137–158.

Simmons, R., Ungemack, J., Sussman, J., Adorno, S., Black, K., Tirnady, R., . . . Anderson, R. (2008). Bringing adolescents into substance abuse treatment through community outreach and engagement: The Hartford youth project. *Journal of Psychoactive Drugs, 40,* 41–54.

Simoni-Wastila, L., & Strickler, G. (2004). Risk factors associated with problem use of prescription drugs. *American Journal of Public Health, 94,* 266–268.

Simoni-Wastila, S., & Yang, H.-W., K. (2012). Drug abuse and addiction in elderly. In J. C. Verster, K. Brady, M. Galanter, and P. Conrod (Eds.), *Drug abuse and addiction in medical illness: Causes, consequences, and treatment.* (pp. 455–465). New York, NY: Springer.

Sinha, R. (2011). New findings on biological factors predicting addiction relapse vulnerability. *Current Psychiatric Reports, 13,* 398–405.

Sinha, R., & Schottenfeld, R. (2001). The role of comorbidity in relapse and recovery. In F. M. Tims, C. G. Leukefeld, & J. J. Platt (Eds.), *Relapse and recovery in addictions* (pp. 172–207). New Haven, CT: Yale University Press.

Skovhold, T. M. (2012). The counselor's resilient self. *Turkish Psychological Counseling and Guidance Journal, 4,* 137–146.

Slaikeu, K. A. (1990). *Crisis intervention: A handbook for practice and research* (2nd ed.). Boston, MA: Allyn & Bacon.

Smedema, S. M., & Ebener, D. (2010). Substance abuse and psychosocial adaptation to physical disability: Analysis of the literature and future directions. *Disability and Rehabilitation: An International, Multidisciplinary Journal, 32,* 1311–1319.

Smedes, L. B. (1984). *Forgive and forget: Healing the hurts we don't deserve*. San Francisco, CA: Harper & Row.

Smith, D. (2003a). In an ethical bind? *Monitor on Psychology, 34*, 61.

Smith, D. (2003b). 10 ways practitioners can avoid frequent ethical pitfalls. *Monitor on Psychology, 34*, 50–55.

Smith, D. E. (2011). Editor's note: Integration of pharmacotherapy and psychosocial treatment in opiate-addicted youth. *Journal of Psychoactive Drugs, 43*, 175–179.

Smith, D. E., & Seymour, R. B. (2001). *Clinician's guide to substance abuse*. New York, NY: McGraw-Hill Professional.

Smith, J. E., & Meyers, R. J. (2004). *Motivating substance abusers to enter treatment: Working with family members*. New York, NY: Guilford Press.

Smith, P. H., Earp, J. A., & DeVillis, R. (1995). Measuring battering: Development of the Women's Experience with Battering (WEB) Scale. *Women's Health: Research on Gender, Behavior, and Policy, 4*, 273–288.

Smith, R. C., Fortin, A. H., Dwamena, F., & Frankel, R. M. (2013). An evidence-based patient-centered method makes the biopsychosocial model scientific. *Patient Education and Counseling, 91*, 265–270.

Smock, S. A., Trepper, T. S., Wetchler, J. L., McCollum, E. E., Ray, R., & Pierce, K. (2008). Solution-focused group therapy for level 1 substance abusers. *Journal of Marital and Family Therapy, 34*, 107–120.

Snowden, L. R. (2012). Health and mental health policies' role in better understanding and closing African American-White American disparities in treatment access and quality of care. *American Psychologist, 67*, 524–531.

Snyder, C. R., Berg, C., & Thompson, L. Y. (2003, June). Introducing clinicians to hope and positive psychology. *Clinician's Research Digest, Supplemental Bulletin, 28*.

Sokol, R. J., Martier, S. S., & Ager, J. W. (1989). The T-ACE questions: Practical prenatal detection of risk drinking. *American Journal of Obstetrics and Gynecology, 160*, 863–870.

Solomon, J. (1993). Management of acute problems in the dual diagnosis patient. In J. Solomon, S. Zimberg, & E. Shollar (Eds.), *Dual diagnosis: Evaluation, treatment, training, and program development* (pp. 57–76). New York, NY: Plenum Press.

Sorbell, L. (2009, August). Motivational interviewing: Common currency among health and mental health care practitioners for treating risky problem behaviors. Paper session presented at the meeting of the American Psychological Association, Toronto, Canada

Sorge, R. (1991, Winter). Harm reduction: A new approach to drug services. *Health/Policy Advisory Center Bulletin*, 22–27.

Sowa, C. J., May, K. M., & Niles, S. G. (1994). Occupational stress within the counseling profession: Implication for counselor training. *Counselor Education, 34*, 19–29.

Spas, J., Ramsey, S., Paiva, A. L., & Stein, L. A. R. (2012). All might have won, but not all have the prize: Optimal treatment for substance abuse among adolescents with conduct problems. *Substance Abuse: Research & Treatment, 6*, 141–155.

Spear, S. E., Crevecoeur-MacPhail, D., Denering, L., Dickerson, D., & Brecht, M.-L. (2013, March 13). Determinants of successful treatment outcomes among a sample of urban American Indians/Alaska Natives: The role of social environments. *Journal of Behavioral Health Services & Research*. Berlin, Germany: Springer.

Special populations: Race may impact treatment efficacy, clients' sobriety. (2002, June). *Brown University Digest of Addiction Theory and Application*, 4–5.

Spelman, E. V. (1988). *Inessential woman: Problems of exclusion in feminist thought*. Boston, MA: Beacon Press.

Springer, E. (1991). Effective AIDS prevention with active drug users: The harm reduction model. *Journal of Chemical Dependency Treatment, 4*, 141–157.

St. Clair, M. (2000). *Object relations and self-psychology* (3rd ed.). Belmont, CA: Wadsworth.

Stadler, H. A., Willing, K. L., Eberhage, M. G., & Ward, W. H. (1988). Impairment: Implications for the counseling profession. *Journal of Counseling and Development, 66*, 258–260.

Stahler, G. J. (1995). Social interventions for homeless substance abusers: Evaluating treatment outcomes. In G. J. Stahler & B. Stimmel (Eds.), *The effectiveness of social interventions for homeless substance abusers* (pp. xiii–xxiv). Binghamton, NY: Haworth Press.

Stahler, G. J., & Stimmel, B. (1995). *The effectiveness of social interventions for homeless substance abusers*. Binghamton, NY: Haworth Press.

Staiger, P. K., Thomas, A. C., Ricciardelli, L. A., McCabe, M. P., Cross, W., & Young, G. (2011).

Improving services for individuals with a dual diagnosis: A qualitative study reporting on the views of service users. *Addiction Research & Theory, 19,* 47–55.

Stall, R., & Wiley, J. (1988). A comparison of alcohol and drug use patterns of homosexual and heterosexual men: The San Francisco men's health study. *Drug and Alcohol Dependence, 22,* 63–73.

Stanton, M. D., & Heath, A. W. (1997). Family and marital therapy. In J. H. Lowinson, P. Ruiz, R. B. Millman, & J. G. Langrod (Eds.), *Substance abuse: A comprehensive textbook* (3rd ed., pp. 448–454). Baltimore, MD: Williams & Wilkins.

Staudinger, U. M., Marsiske, M., & Baltes, P. B. (1995). Resilience and reserve capacity in later adulthood: Potentials and limits of development across the life span. In D. Cicchetti & D. J. Cohen (Eds.), *Developmental psychopathology, Vol. 2: Risk, disorder, and adaptation* (pp. 801–847). New York, NY: Wiley.

Stauffer, M. D., Capuzzi, D., & Tanigoshi, H. (2008). Assessment: An overview. In D. Capuzzi & M. D. Stauffer (Eds.), *Foundations of addiction counseling* (pp. 76–100). Boston, MA: Pearson.

Ste-Marie, C., Gupta, R., & Derevensky, J. L. (2006). Anxiety and social stress related to adolescent gambling behavior and substance use. *Journal of Child and Adolescent Substance Abuse, 15,* 55–74.

Steenbarger, B. N. (1993). A multicontextual model of counseling: Bridging brevity and diversity. *Journal of Counseling and Development, 7,* 8–14.

Steigerwald, F., & Stone, D. (1999). Cognitive restructuring and the 12-step program of Alcoholics Anonymous. *Journal of Substance Abuse Treatment, 16,* 321–327.

Stevens, B. A. (2008). *Crossfire: How to survive giving expert evidence as a psychologist.* Bowen Hills, QLD, Australia: Australian Academic Press.

Stevens-Smith, P., & Smith, R. L. (1998). *Substance abuse counseling: Theory and practice.* Upper Saddle River, NJ: Prentice-Hall.

Stoff, D. M., Mitnick, L., & Kalichman, S. (2004). Research issues in the multiple diagnoses of HIV/ AIDS, mental illness and substance abuse. *AIDS Care, 16,* S1–S5.

Straus, M. A., Gelles, R. J., & Steinmetz, S. K. (1980). *Behind closed doors: Violence in the American family.* New York, NY: Anchor.

Straussner, S. L. A. (1985). Alcoholism in women: Current knowledge and implications for treatment. In D. Cook, S. L. A. Straussner, &

C. Fewell (Eds.), *Psychosocial issues in the treatment of alcoholism* (pp. 61–74). New York, NY: Haworth Press.

Straussner, S. L. A. (1993). Assessment and treatment of clients with alcohol and other drug abuse problems: An overview. In S. L. A. Straussner (Ed.), *Clinical work with substance-abusing clients* (pp. 3–30). New York, NY: Guilford Press.

Straussner, S. L. A. (2004). Assessment and treatment of clients with alcohol and other drug abuse problems: An overview. In S. L. A. Straussner (Ed.), *Clinical work with substance-abusing clients* (2nd ed., pp. 3–35). New York, NY: Guilford Press.

Straussner, S. L. A., & Brown, S. (Eds.). (2002). *The handbook of addiction treatment for women: Theory and practice.* San Francisco, CA: Jossey-Bass.

Streifel, C., & Servaty-Sieb, H. L. (2009). Recovering from alcohol and other drug dependency: Loss and spirituality in a 12-step context. *Alcoholism Treatment Quarterly, 27,* 184–198. doi: 10.1080/ 07347320902785558

Stroebe, M. S., Hansson, R. O., Stroebe, W., & Schut, H. (2001). Introduction: Concepts and issues in contemporary research on bereavement. In H. Schut (Ed.), *Handbook of bereavement research: Consequences, coping, and care* (pp. 3–22). Washington, DC: American Psychological Association.

Stuart, G. L., Moore, T. M., Elkins, S. R., O'Farrell, T. J., Temple, J. R., Ramsey, S. E., & Shorey, R. C. (2013). The temporal association between substance use and intimate partner violence among women arrested for domestic violence. *Journal of Consulting and Clinical Psychology, 81,* 681–690.

Sturza, M. L., & Campbell, R. (2005, December). An exploratory study of rape survivors' prescription drug use as a means of coping with sexual assault. *Psychology of Women Quarterly, 29,* 253– 263.

Substance Abuse and Mental Health Services Administration. (1993). *Pregnant substance-using women.* Treatment Improvement Protocol (TIP 2) Series (DHHS Publication No. SMA 93–1998). Rockville, MD: Author.

Substance Abuse and Mental Health Services Administration. (1994). *Assessment and treatment of patients with coexisting mental illness and alcohol and other drug abuse.* Treatment Improvement Protocol (TIP 9) Series (DHHS Publication No. SMA 94–2078). Rockville, MD: Author.

Substance Abuse and Mental Health Services Administration. (1995). *The role and current status of patient placement criteria in the treatment of substance use disorders.* Treatment Improvement Protocol (TIP 13) Series (DHHS Publication No. SMA 95–3021). Rockville, MD: Author.

Substance Abuse and Mental Health Services Administration. (1996). *Counselor's manual for relapse prevention with chemically dependent criminal offenders.* Technical Assistance Publication (TAP 19) Series (DHHS Publication No. SMA 96–3115). Rockville, MD: Author.

Substance Abuse and Mental Health Services Administration. (1997). *Substance abuse treatment and domestic violence.* Treatment Improvement Protocol (TIP 25) Series (DHHS Publication No. SMA 97–3163). Rockville, MD: Author.

Substance Abuse and Mental Health Services Administration. (1998a). *Prevalence of substance use among racial and ethnic groups in the United States* (DHHS Publication No. SMA 98–3202). Rockville, MD: Author.

Substance Abuse and Mental Health Services Administration. (1998b). *Substance abuse among older adults.* Treatment Improvement Protocol (TIP 26) Series (DHHS Publication No. SMA 98–3179). Rockville, MD: Author.

Substance Abuse and Mental Health Services Administration. (1999a). *Enhancing motivation for change in substance abuse treatment.* Treatment Improvement Protocol (TIP 35) Series (DHHS Publication No. SMA 99–3354). Rockville, MD: Author.

Substance Abuse and Mental Health Services Administration. (1999b). *Screening and assessing adolescents for substance use disorders.* Treatment Improvement Protocol (TIP 31) Series (DHHS Publication No. SMA 99–3282). Rockville, MD: Author.

Substance Abuse and Mental Health Services Administration. (2000a). *Cultural competence standards* (DHHS Publication No. SMA 00–3457). Rockville, MD: Author.

Substance Abuse and Mental Health Services Administration. (2000b). *Substance abuse treatment for persons with child abuse and neglect issues.* Treatment Improvement Protocol (TIP 36) Series (DHHS Publication No. SMA 00–3357). Rockville, MD: Author.

Substance Abuse and Mental Health Services Administration. (2000c). *Substance abuse treatment for persons with HIV/AIDS.* Treatment Improvement Protocol (TIP 37) Series (DHHS Publication No. SMA 00–3459). Rockville, MD: Author.

Substance Abuse and Mental Health Services Administration. (2002a, November). *Report to Congress on the prevention and treatment of co-occurring substance abuse disorders and mental disorders.* Rockville, MD: Author.

Substance Abuse and Mental Health Services Administration. (2002b). *Substance use disorder treatment for people with physical and cognitive disabilities.* Treatment Improvement Protocol (TIP 29) Series (DHHS Publication No. SMA 02–3744). Rockville, MD: Author.

Substance Abuse and Mental Health Services Administration. (2003). *A provider's introduction to substance abuse treatment for lesbian, gay, bisexual, and transgender individuals* (DHHS Publication No. SMA 03–3819). Rockville, MD: Author.

Substance Abuse and Mental Health Services Administration. (2005). *A national review of state alcohol and drug treatment programs and certification standards for substance abuse counselors and prevention professionals* (DHHS Publication No. SMA 05–3994). Rockville, MD: Author.

Substance Abuse and Mental Health Services Administration, Office of Applied Studies. (2005, August 19). *The DASIS Report: Hispanic substance abuse treatment admissions: 2003.* Retrieved from www.oas.samhsa.gov/2k5/HispanicTX/HispanicTx.htm

Substance Abuse and Mental Health Services Administration, Office of Applied Studies. (2006). *Results from the 2005 National Survey on drug use and health: National findings.* Retrieved from www.oas.samhsa.gov/NSDUH/2k5NSDUH/2k5results.htm

Substance Abuse and Mental Health Services Administration. (2007). *The epidemiology of co-occurring substance use and mental disorders.* Overview Paper 8 (DHHS Publication No. SMA 07–4308). Rockville, MD: Author.

Substance Abuse and Mental Health Services Administration. (2008). *Addiction counseling competencies: The knowledge, skills, and attitudes of professional practice. Technical Assistance Publication Series 21* (DHHS Publication No. SMA 98–3171). Rockville, MD: Author.

Substance Abuse and Mental Health Services Administration, Office of Applied Studies. (2008). *Results from the 2008 National Survey on Drug Use and*

Health: National findings. Retrieved from www.oas.samhsa.gov/NSDUH/2k8NSDUH/2k8results.htm

Substance Abuse and Mental Health Services Administration. (2010). *Alcohol and other drug problems among addiction professionals.* Center for Substance Abuse Treatment publication. Rockville, MD: Author.

Substance Abuse and Mental Health Services Administration. (2011a). *Managing chronic pain in adults with or in recovery from substance use disorders.* Technical Assistance Publication (TIP 54) Series (DHHS Publication No. SMA 13–4571). Rockville, MD: Author. Retrieved from http://www.kap.samhsa.gov

Substance Abuse and Mental Health Services Administration. (2011b). *Clients with substance use and eating disorders,* HHS Publication No. SMA 10–4617. Rockville, MD: Substance Abuse and Mental Health Services Administrations. Retrieved from http://www.kap.samhsa.gov

Substance Abuse and Mental Health Services Administration. (2012a). *Results from the 2010 National Survey on Drug Use and Health: Mental health findings* (NSDUH Scrics H-42, HHS Publication No. SMA 11–4667). Retrieved from http://www.samhsa.gov/data/nsduh/2k10MH_Findings/2k10MHResults.htm

Substance Abuse and Mental Health Services Administration. (2012b). *Results from the 2011 National Survey on Drug Use and Health: Summary of national findings,* NSDUH Series H-44, HHS Publication No. SMA 12–4713. Rockville, MD: Substance Abuse and Mental Health Services Administrations. Retrieved from http://www.samhsa.gov/data/NSDUH/2k11Results/NSDUHresults2011.htm# 3.1.4

Substance Abuse and Mental Health Services Administration. (2013). *Seven challenges intervention summary.* Retrieved from http://www.nrepp.samhsa.gov/ViewIntervention.aspx?id=159

Substance Abuse and Mental Health Services Administration. (2013a). *Fetal alcohol syndrome spectrum disorders.* Retrieved from http://www.fasdcenter.samhsa.gov/aboutUs/aboutFASD.aspx

Substance Abuse and Mental Health Services Administration. (2013, Winter). *Drug treatment courts offer hope for youth.* Retrieved from http://www.samhsa.gov/samhsaNewsLetter/Volume_21_Number_1/drug_treatment.aspx

Sude, M. E. (2013). Text messaging and private practice: Ethical challenges and guidelines for developing personal best practices. *Journal of Mental Health Counseling, 35,* 211–227.

Sue, D. (1987). Use and abuse of alcohol by Asian Americans. *Journal of Psychoactive Drugs, 19,* 57–66.

Sue, D., & Sue, D. M. (1995). Asian Americans. In N. A. Vacc, S. B. DeVaney, & J. Wittmer (Eds.), *Experiencing and counseling multicultural and diverse populations* (pp. 63–89). Bristol, PA: Accelerated Development.

Sue, D., & Sue, S. (1987). Cultural factors in the clinical assessment of Asian-Americans. *Journal of Clinical and Consulting Psychology, 55,* 479–487.

Sue, D. W., & Sue, D. (2013). *Counseling the culturally diverse: Theory and practice.* Hoboken, NJ: Wiley.

Sue, S., Cheng, J. K. Y, Saad, C. S., & Chu, J. P. (2012). Asian American mental health. *American Psychologist, 67,* 532–544.

Sulis, C. A. (2009). HIV, TB, and other infectious diseases related to alcohol and other drug use. In R. K. Ries, D. A. Fiellin, S. C. Miller, & R. Saitz (Eds.), *Principles of addiction medicine* (4th ed., pp. 1057–1076). Philadelphia, PA: Wolters Kluwer.

Sunich, M. F., & Juhnke, G. A. (1994, November) Substance abuse and suicide. *Amethyst Journal, 1,* 1–2.

Surry, J. (1985). *The "self-in-relation": A theory of women's development.* Work in progress (No. 13) Wellesley, MA: Stone Center Working Papers Series.

Sutton, C. T., & Broken Nose, M. A. (2005). American Indian families: An overview. In M. McGoldrick, J. Giordano, & N. Garcia-Preto (Eds.), *Ethnicity and family therapy* (pp. 43–54). New York, NY: Guilford Press.

Swenson, L. C. (1993). *Psychology and the law for the helping professions.* Pacific Grove, CA: Brooks/Cole.

Szapocznik, J., Hervis, O., & Schwartz, S. (2003). *Brief strategic family therapy for adolescent drug use. Therapy manuals for drug abuse: Manual 5* (National Institute on Drug Abuse, NIH Publication No. 03–4751). Retrieved from www.drugabuse.gov/txmanuals/bsft/BSFTIndex.html

Szapocznik, J., Schwartz, S. J., Muir, J. A., & Brown, C. H. (2012). Brief strategic family therapy: An intervention to reduce adolescent risk behavior. *Couple & Family Psychology, 1,* 134–145.

Szapocznik, J., & Williams, R. A. (2000). Brief strategic family therapy: Twenty-five years of interplay among theory, research and practice in adolescent behavior problems and drug abuse, *Clinical Child & Family Psychology Review, 3,* 117–134.

Szapocznik, J., Zarate, M., Duff, J., & Muir, J. (2013). Engaging drug using/problem behavior adolescents and their families in treatment. *Social Work in Public Health*, *28*, 206–223.

Szasz, T. (1994). *Cruel compassion: Psychiatric control of society's unwanted*. New York, NY: Wiley.

Talbott, G. D. (1990). Commentary on "Divine intervention and the treatment of chemical dependency." *Journal of Substance Abuse*, *2*, 46–47.

Talmon, M. (1990). *Single session therapy*. San Francisco, CA: Jossey-Bass.

Tatarsky, A., & Marlatt, G. A. (2010). State of the art in harm reduction psychotherapy: An emerging treatment for substance misuse. *Journal of Clinical Psychology*, *66*, 117–122.

Taylor, E. (2001). Positive psychology and humanistic psychology: A reply to Seligman. *Journal of Humanistic Psychology*, *41*, 13–29.

Tedeschi, R. G., & Calhoun, L. G. (1995). *Trauma and transformation: Growing in the aftermath of suffering*. Thousand Oaks, CA: Sage.

Terplan, M., McNamara, E. J., & Chisolm, M. S. (2012). Pregnant and non-pregnant women with substance use disorders: The gap between treatment need and receipt. *Journal of Addictive Diseases*, *31*, 342–349.

Testa, M., & Hoffman, J. (2012). Naturally occurring changes in women's drinking from high school to college and implications for sexual victimization. *Journal of Studies on Alcohol*, *73*, 26–33.

Testa, M., & Livingston, J. A. (2009). Alcohol consumption and women's vulnerability to sexual victimization: Can reducing women's drinking prevent rape? *Substance Use & Misuse*, *44*, 1349–1376.

Thiesse, J. (1984). Working with dual disability clients. *Grapevine*, 3–4.

Thomas, A. C., Staiger, P. K., & McCabe, M. (2012). Implementation and evaluation of brief depression and anxiety screening in clients contacting a drug and alcohol service. *Drug and Alcohol Review*, *31*, 303–310. doi: 10.1111/j.1465-3362.2011.00323.x

Thompson, J. K., Heinberg, L. J., Altabe, M., & Tantleff-Dunn, S. (1999). *Exacting beauty: Theory, assessment, and treatment of body image disturbance*. Washington, DC: American Psychological Association.

Thornton, J. (2003, October). Chronic pain and prescription drug addiction. Paper presented at a class on addiction counseling at Appalachian State University, Boone, NC.

Thurang, A., Fagerberg, I., Palmstierna, T., & Bengtsson, T. A. (2010). Women's experiences of caring when in treatment for alcohol dependency. *Scandinavian Journal of Caring Sciences*, *24*, 700–706.

Tiderington, E., Stanhhope, V., & Henwood, B. F. (2013). A qualitative analysis of case managers' use of harm reduction in practice. *Journal of Substance Abuse Treatment*, *44*, 71–77.

Timko, C., Cronkite, R. C., McKellar, J., Zemore, S., & Moos, R. H. (2013). Dually diagnosed patients' benefits of mutal-help groups and the role of social anxiety. *Journal of Substance Abuse Treatment*, *44*, 216–223. doi: dx.doi.org/10.1016/j.jsat.2012.05.007

Tisdell, E. J. (2003). *Exploring spirituality and culture in adult and higher education*. San Francisco, CA: Jossey-Bass.

Titus, J. C., & Guthmann, D. (2010). Addressing the black hole in substance abuse treatment for deaf and hard of hearing individuals: Technology to the rescue. *Journal of the American Deafness and Rehabilitation Association*, *43*, 92–100.

Tober, G., & Raistrick, D. (2007). What is motivational dialogue? In G. Tober and D. Raistrick (Eds.), *Motivational dialogue* (pp. 3–15). New York, NY: Routledge.

Tonigan, J. S., & Connors, G. J. (2008). Psychological mechanisms in Alcoholics Anonymous. In M. Galanter & H. D. Kleber (Eds.), *Textbook of substance abuse treatment* (4th ed., pp. 491–498). Washington, DC: American Psychiatric.

Travin, S. (1995). Compulsive sexual behaviors. *Psychiatric Clinics of North America*, *18*, 155–169.

Treatment of alcoholism: Part II. (1996). *Harvard Mental Health Letter*, *13*, 1–5.

Trimpey, J. (1989). *Rational recovery from alcoholism: The small book*. New York, NY: Delacorte.

Trimpey, J. (1996). *Rational recovery: The new cure for substance addiction*. New York, NY: Pocket Books.

Trimpey, J. (2013). *Rational recovery*. Retrieved from https://rational.org/index.php?id=94

Truong, K. D, Reifsnider, O. S., Mayorga, M. E., & Spitler, H. (2013). Estimated number of preterm births and low birth weight children born in the United States due to maternal binge drinking. *Maternal and Child Health Journal*, *17*, 677–688.

Turk, D. C., & Gatchel, R. J. (Eds.). (2002). *Psychological approaches to pain management: A practitioner's handbook* (2nd ed.). New York, NY: Guilford Press.

Turnell, G. (1989). *Complications in working with AIDS patients in group psychotherapy.* Paper presented at the 97th annual meeting of the American Psychological Association, New Orleans, LA.

Tuttle, A. (2011). Family systems and recovery from sexual violence and trauma. In T. Bryant-Davis (Ed.), *Surviving sexual violence: A guide to recovery and empowerment* (pp. 142–159). Lanham, MD: Rowman & Littlefield.

Tuunanen, M., Aalto, M., & Seppa, K. (2013). Mean-weekly alcohol questions are not recommended for clinical work. *Alcohol and Alcoholism*, *48*, 308–311.

Tyas, S., & Rush, B. (1993). The treatment of disabled persons with alcohol and drug problems: Results of a survey of addiction services. *Journal of Studies on Alcohol*, *54*, 275–282.

Uhler, A. S., & Parker, O. V. (2002). Treating women drug abusers: Action therapy and trauma assessment. *Science and Practice Perspectives*, *1*, 30–36.

Unterrainer, H. F., Lewis, A., Collicut, J., & Fink, A. (2013). Religious/spiritual well being, coping styles, and personality dimensions in people with substance use disorders. *International Journal for the Psychology of Religion*, *23*, 204–213.

Urquiza, A. J. (1993, August). *Adult male survivors of child sexual abuse: Issues in intimacy.* Paper presented at the 101st annual convention of the American Psychological Association, Toronto, Ontario, Canada.

U.S. Census Bureau. (2009, May). *Census Bureau estimates nearly half of children under age 5 are minorities.* Retrieved from http://www.census.gov/newsroom/releases/archives/population/cb09-75.html

U.S. Department of Health and Human Services, National Institutes of Health, National Institute on Alcohol Abuse and Alcoholism. (2006, December). *National Epidemiologic Survey on Alcohol and Related Conditions (NESARC)-Wave 2.* Retrieved from http://aspe.hhs.gov/hsp/06/catalog-AI-AN-NA/NESARC.htm

U.S. Department of Justice (2005). *Family violence statistics including statistics on strangers and acquaintances* (NCJ 207846). Washington, DC: Bureau of Justice Statistics.

Vacc, N. A., DeVaney, S. B., & Wittmer, J. (1995). Introduction. In N. A. Vacc, S. B. DeVaney, & J. Wittmer (Eds.), *Experiencing and counseling multicultural and diverse populations* (pp. 1–8). Bristol, PA: Accelerated Development.

Valencia, E. Y., & Johnson, V. (2008). Acculturation among Latino youth and the risk for substance use: Issues of definition and measurement. *Journal of Drug Issues*, *38*, 37–68.

Valentine-Barrow, M. D., Adcock, K. R., & Jenkins, K. Y. (2011). Substance abuse risk factors affecting the Hispanic population in the United States. *Journal of Human Behavior in the Social Environment*, *21*, 715–726, doi: 10.1080/10911359.2011.615684

Valverde, M., & White-Mair, K. (1999). "One day at a time"; and other slogans for everyday life: The ethical practices of Alcoholics Anonymous. *Sociology*, *33*, 393–403.

Van Buskirk, K. A., & Wetherell, J. L. (2013, August 11). Motivational interviewing with primary care populations: A systematic review and meta-analysis. *Journal of Behavioral Medicine.* Advance online publication.

Vandeputte, C. (1989). Why bother to treat older adults? The answer is compelling. *Professional Counselor*, *4*, 34–38.

Vanderlinden, J., & Vandereycken, W. (1996). Is sexual abuse a risk for developing an eating disorder? In M. F. Schwartz & L. Cohn (Eds.), *Sexual abuse and eating disorders* (pp. 17–22). New York, NY: Brunner/Mazel.

van der Walde, H., Urgenson, F. T., Weltz, S. H., & Hanna, F. J. (2002). Women and alcoholism: A biopsychosocial perspective and treatment approaches. *Journal of Counseling and Development*, *86*, 145–153.

Vannicelli, M. (1995). Group psychotherapy with substance abusers and family members. In A. M. Washton (Ed.), *Psychotherapy and substance abuse* (pp. 337–356). New York, NY: Guilford Press.

van Wormer, K. (1989). Co-dependency: Implications for women and therapy. *Women and Therapy*, *8*, 51–63.

van Wormer, K., & Davis, D. R. (2008). *Addiction treatment: A strengths perspective* (2nd ed.). Belmont, CA: Thomson.

van Wormer, K., & Davis, D. R. (2013). *Addiction treatment: A strengths perspective* (3rd ed.). Belmont, CA: Brooks/Cole.

van Wormer, K., & Thyer, B. A. (2010). Evidence-based practice in the area of substance abuse. In

K. van Wormer & B. A. Thyer (Eds.), *Evidence-based practice in the field of substance abuse: A book of readings.* (pp. 3–11). Los Angeles, CA: Sage.

Vastag, B. (2001). What's the connection? No easy answers for people with eating disorders and drug abuse. *Journal of the American Medical Association, 285,* 1006–1007.

Velasquez, M. M., Stephens, N. S., & Ingersoll, K. (2006). Motivational interviewing in groups. *Journal of Groups in Addiction & Recovery Journal of Groups in Addiction & Recovery, 1*(1), 27–50.

Vereby, K. G., & Buchan, B. J. (1997). Diagnostic laboratory: Screening for drug abuse. In J. H. Lowinson, P. Ruiz, R. B. Millman, & J. G. Langrod (Eds.), *Substance abuse: A comprehensive textbook* (3rd ed., pp. 369–377). Baltimore, MD: Williams & Wilkins.

Vernon, M. (1990). *The psychology of deafness.* Reading, MA: Addison-Wesley.

Vickerman, P., Martin, N., Turner, K., & Hickman, M. (2012). Can needle and syringe programmes and opiate substitution therapy achieve substantial reductions in hepatitis C virus prevalence? Model projections for different epidemic settings. *Addiction, 107,* 1984–1995.

Villagomez, R. E., Meyer, T. J., & Lin, M. M. (1995). Post-traumatic stress disorder among inner-city methadone maintenance patients. *Journal of Substance Abuse Treatment, 12,* 253–257.

Viney, L. L., Henry, R., Walker, B. M., & Crooks, L. (1989). The emotional reactions of HIV antibody positive men. *British Journal of Medical Psychology, 62,* 153–161.

Voeller, B., Coulson, A. H., Bernstein, G. S., & Nakamura, R. M. (1989). Mineral oil lubricants cause rapid deterioration of latex condoms. *Contraception, 39,* 95–102.

Volkow, N., & Li, T-K. (2005). The neuroscience of addiction. *Nature Neuroscience, 8,* 1429–1430.

Waehler, C. A. (2013). Curiousity and biculturalism as key therapeutic change activities. *Psychotherapy, 50,* 351–355.

Waldron, M. B., Brody, J. L., & Slesnick, N. (2001). Integrative behavioral and family therapy for adolescent substance abuse. In P. M. Monti, S. M. Colby, & T. A. O'Leary (Eds.), *Adolescents, alcohol, and substance abuse: Reaching teens through brief interventions* (pp. 216–243). New York, NY: Guilford Press.

Walker, L. (1979). *The battered woman.* New York, NY: Harper & Row.

Walker, L. (1980). *The battered woman* (2nd ed.). New York, NY: Harper & Row.

Walker, L. (1984). *The battered woman syndrome.* New York, NY: Springer.

Walker, T. (2013). Voices from the group: Violent women's experiences of intervention. *Journal of Family Violence, 28,* 419–426.

Wallace, J. (1985). Behavioral modification methods as adjuncts to psychotherapy. In S. Zimberg, J. Wallace, & S. Blume (Eds.), *Practical approaches to alcoholism psychotherapy* (pp. 109–129). New York, NY: Plenum Press.

Walters, G. D. (2002). Twelve reasons why we need to find alternatives to Alcoholics Anonymous. *Addictive Disorders & Their Treatment, 1,* 53–59.

Walters, S. T., & Rotgers, F. (Ed.). (2011). *Treating substance abuse: Theory and technique* (3rd ed.). New York, NY: Guilford Press.

Walters, S. T., Rotgers, F., Saunders, B., Wilkinson, C., & Towers, T. (2003). Theoretical perspectives on motivation and addictive behavior. In F. Rotgers, J. Morgenstern, & S. T. Walters (Eds.), *Treating substance abuse* (2nd ed.). New York, NY: Guilford Press.

Warren, J., Morgan, M. M., Morris, L. B., & Morris, T. M. (2010). Breathing words slowly: Creative writing and counselor self-care—the writing workout. *Journal of Creativity in Mental Health, 5,* 109–124. doi: 10.1080/15401383.2010.485074

Warren, K. R. & Foudin, L. L. (2001). Alcohol-related birth defects: The past, present, and future. *Alcohol Research and Health, 25,* 153–158.

Washton, A. M., & Stone-Washton, N. (1990). Abstinence and relapse in outpatient cocaine addicts. *Journal of Psychoactive Drugs, 22,* 135–147.

Washton, A. M., & Zweben, J. E. (2008). *Treating alcohol and drug problems in psychotherapy practice.* New York, NY: Guilford Press.

Waterman, A. S. (2013). The humanistic psychology–positive psychology divide: Contrasts in philosophical foundations. *American Psychologist, 68,* 124–133.

Watkins, T. R., Lewellen, A., & Barrett, M. C. (2001). *Dual diagnosis: An integrated approach to treatment.* Thousand Oaks, CA: Sage.

Weaver, J. D. (1995). *Disasters: Mental health interventions.* Sarasota, FL: Professional Resource Press.

Weber, G. N. (2008). Using to numb the pain: Substance use and abuse among lesbian, gay and bisexual individuals. *Journal of Mental Health Counseling, 30,* 31–48.

Wegscheider, S. (1981). *Another chance: Hope and health for the alcoholic family.* Palo Alto, CA: Science and Behavioral Books.

Weinberg, M. S., & Williams, C. J. (1974). *Male homosexuals: Their problems and adaptations.* New York, NY: Oxford University Press.

Weinberg, T. S. (1994). *Gay men, drinking and alcoholism.* Carbondale, IL: Southern Illinois University Press.

Weir, K. (2013). Work, stress, and health. *Monitor on Psychology, 44,* 40–43.

Weisner, T. S., Weibel-Orlando, J. C., & Long, J. (1984). "Serious drinking," "white man's drinking" and "teetotaling": Drinking levels and styles in an urban Indian population. *Journal of Studies on Alcohol, 45,* 237–249.

Weiss Ogden, K. R., & Sias, S. M. (2011). An integrative spiritual development model of supervision for substance abuse counselors-in-training. *Journal of Addictions & Offender Counseling, 32,* 84–96.

Wells, T. L. (1994). Therapist self-disclosure: Its effects on clients and the treatment relationship. *Smith College Studies in Social Work, 65,* 23–41.

Wenzel, H. G., & Dahl, A. A. (2009). Female pathological gamblers: A critical review of the clinical findings. *International Journal of Mental Health and Addiction, 7,* 190–202.

Werth, J. L., Welfel, E. R., & Benjamin, G. A. H. (2013, August). American Psychological Association Workshop: The duty to protect: Ethical, legal, and professional considerations. Honolulu, HI: American Psychological Association.

West, S. L., Graham, C. W., & Cifu, D. X. (2009). Rates of alcohol/other drug treatment denials to persons with physical disabilities: Accessibility concerns. *Alcoholism Treatment Quarterly, 27,* 305–316.

Westermeyer, J. (1997). Native Americans, Asians, and new immigrants. In J. H. Lowinson, P. Ruiz, R. B. Millman, & J. G. Langrod (Eds.), *Substance abuse: A comprehensive textbook* (3rd ed., pp. 712–716). Baltimore, MD: Williams & Wilkins.

Westermeyer, J. J. (2009). Cultural issues in addiction medicine. In R. K. Ries, D. A. Fiellin, S. C. Miller, & R. Saitz (Eds.), *Principles of addiction medicine* (4th ed., pp. 493–500). Philadelphia, PA: Wolters Kluwer.

Westermeyer, J., & Peake, E. (1983). A ten-year follow-up of alcoholic Native Americans in Minnesota. *American Journal of Psychiatry, 140,* 189–194.

Westra, H. A., Aviram, A., & Doell, F. K. (2011). Extending motivational interviewing to the treatment of major mental health problems: Current directions and evidence. *Canadian Journal of Psychiatry, 56,* 643–650.

Westra, H. A., & Aviram, A. (2013). Core skills in motivational interviewing. *Psychotherapy, 50,* 273–278.

Wheelis, J. (2009). Theory and practice of dialectical behavioral therapy. In G. O. Gabbard (Ed.), *Textbook of therapeutic treatments* (pp. 727–756). Arlington, VA: American Psychiatric Press.

Whipple, V. (1987). Counseling battered women from fundamentalist churches. *Journal of Marital and Family Therapy, 13,* 251–258.

White, E. (1994). *Chain, chain, change: For black women in abusive relationships.* Seattle, WA: Seal Press.

White, H. R., & Labouvie, E. W. (1989). Towards the assessment of adolescent problem drinking. *Journal of Studies on Alcohol, 50,* 30–37.

White, H. R., & Labouvie, E. W. (2000). Longitudinal trends in problem drinking as measured by the Rutgers alcohol problem index. *Alcoholism: Clinical and Experimental Research, 24,* 76A.

White, W. L. (1999, November/December). From calling to career: The birth of addiction counseling as a specialized role. *Counselor,* 9–12.

White, W. L., & Evans, A. C. (2013). Toward a core recovery-focused knowledge base for addiction professionals and recovery support specialists. Retrieved from www.williamwhitepapers.com

Whitfield, C. L. (1997). Co-dependence, addictions, and related disorders. In J. H. Lowinson, P. Ruiz, R. B. Millman, & J. G. Langrod (Eds.), *Substance abuse: A comprehensive textbook* (3rd ed., pp. 672–683). Baltimore, MD: Williams & Wilkins.

Whittinghill, D., Whittinghill, L. R., & Loesch, L. C. (2000). The benefits of a self-efficacy approach to substance abuse counseling in the era of managed care. *Journal of Addictions and Offender Counseling, 20,* 64–74.

Wicker, L. R., & Brodie, R. E. (2004). The physical and mental health needs of African Americans. In D. R. Atkinson & G. Hackett (Eds.), *Counseling diverse populations* (3rd ed., pp. 105–124). Boston, MA: McGraw-Hill.

Wicks, R. J., Fine, J. A., & Platt, J. J. (Eds.). (1978). *Crisis intervention: A practical clinical guide.* New York, NY: Slack.

Wilford, B. B. (2009). Consent and confidentiality in addiction practice. In R. K. Ries, D. Fiellin, S. C.

Miller, & R. Saitz (Eds.), *Principles of addiction medicine* (4th ed., pp. 1491–1498). Philadelphia, PA: Wolters Kluwer.

Willer, J. (2009). *The beginning psychotherapist's companion*. Lanham, MD: Rowman & Littlefield.

Williams, I. D., Richardson, T. A., Moore, D. D., Gambrel, L. E., & Keeling, M. L. (2010). Perspectives on self-care. *Journal of Creativity in Mental Health, 5*, 321–338. doi: 10.1080/15401383.2010.507700

Williams, R., & Gorski, T. T. (1997). *Relapse warning signs for African Americans: A culturally specific model*. Independence, MO: Herald House/Independence Press.

Wilsnack, S. C. (1973). Sex-role identity in female alcoholism. *Journal of Abnormal Psychology, 82*, 25–26.

Winstanley, E. L., Steinwachs, D. M., Stitzer, M. L., & Fishman, M. J. (2012). Adolescent substance abuse and mental health: Problem co-occurrence and access to services. *Journal of Child & Adolescent Substance Abuse, 21*, 310–322.

Winek, J. L. (2009). *Systemic family therapy: From theory to practice*. Thousand Oaks, CA: Sage.

Winters, K. C. (1991). *Personal experience screening questionnaire*. Los Angeles, CA: Western Psychological Services.

Winters, K. C. (2001). Assessing adolescent substance use problems and other areas of functioning: State of the art. In P. M. Monti, S. M. Colby, & T. A. O'Leary (Eds.), *Adolescents, alcohol, and substance abuse* (pp. 80–108). New York, NY: Guilford Press.

Winters, K. C., Fahnhorst, T., Botzet, A., & Stinchfield, R. (2009). Assessing adolescent substance use. In R. K. Ries, D. A. Fiellin, S. C. Miller, & R. Saitz (Eds.), *Principles of addiction medicine* (4th ed., pp. 1429–1443). Philadelphia, PA: Wolters Kluwer.

Witkiewitz, K., & Bowen, S. (2010). Depression, craving, and substance use following a randomized trial of mindfulness-based relapse prevention. *Journal of Consulting and Clinical Psychology, 78*, 362–374.

Witkiewitz, K., & Marlatt, G. A. (2004). Relapse prevention for alcohol and drug problems: That was Zen, this is Tao. *American Psychologist, 59*, 224–235.

Witkiewitz, K., & Marlatt, G. A. (2007). High-risk situations: Relapse as a dynamic process. In K. Witkiewitz & G. A. Marlatt (Eds.), *Practical resources for the mental health professional series: Therapist's guide to evidence-based relapse prevention* (pp. 19–33). San Diego, CA: Elsevier.

Witkiewitz, K., Marlatt, G. A., & Walker, D. (2005). Mindfulness-based relapse prevention for alcohol and substance use disorders. *Journal of Cognitive Psychotherapy, 19*, 211–218.

Witmer, J. M., & Young, M. E. (1996). Preventing counselor impairment: A wellness approach. *Journal of Humanistic Education and Development, 34*, 141–155.

Wolfe, T. (1947). *Look homeward, angel*. New York, NY: Scribner's.

Wood, R. J., Drolet, J. C., Fetro, J. V., Synovitz, L. B., & Wood, A. R. (2002). Residential adolescent substance abuse treatment: Recommendations for collaboration between school health and substance abuse treatment personnel. *Journal of School Health, 72*, 363–367.

Woodhead, E. L., Hindash, A. C., & Tinko, C. (2013). Diagnosis, mutual-help use, and outcomes: A naturalistic follow-up. *Journal of Dual Diagnosis, 9*, 158–164.

Woolfolk, R. L., & Wasserman, R. H. (2005). Count no one happy: Eudaimonia and positive psychology. *Journal of Theoretical and Philosophical Psychology, 25*, 81–90.

Worden, W. (2009). *Grief counseling & grief therapy: A handbook for the mental health practitioner* (4th ed.). New York, NY: Springer.

Worobey, M., Gemmel, M., Teuwen, D. E., Haselkorn, T., Kunstman, K., Bunce, M., . . . Wolinsky, S. M. (2008). Direct evidence of extensive diversity of HIV-1 in Kinshasa by 1960. *Nature, 455*, 661–665.

Worthington, E. L. (1989). Religious faith across the life span: Implications for counseling and research. *Counseling Psychologist, 17*, 555–612.

Wright, C. V., & Johnson, D. M. (2012). Encouraging legal help seeking for victims of intimate partner violence: The therapeutic effects of the civil protection order. *Journal of Traumatic Stress, 2*, 675–681.

Wright, E. M. (2001). Substance abuse in African American communities. In S. L. A. Straussner (Ed.), *Ethnocultural factors in substance abuse treatment* (pp. 31–51). New York, NY: Guilford Press.

Wright, J., & Popham, J. (1982). Alcohol and battering: The double bind. *Aegis, 36*, 53–59.

Wubbolding, R. E. (1991). *Understanding reality therapy*. New York, NY: Harper & Row.

Wubbolding, R. E. (1994). *Cycle of managing, supervising, counseling and coaching using reality therapy* (chart; Rev. 8). Cincinnati, OH: Center for Reality Therapy.

Wulff, D. M. (1996). The psychology of religion: An overview. In E. P. Shafranske (Ed.), *Religion and the clinical practice of psychology* (pp. 71–112). Washington, DC: American Psychological Association.

Yalom, I. D. (1985). *The theory and practice of group psychotherapy* (3rd ed.) New York, NY: Basic Books.

Yee, B. W. K., & Thu, N. D. (1987). Correlates of drug use and abuse among Indo-Chinese refugees: Mental health implications. *Journal of Psychoactive Drugs, 19*, 77–83.

Yip, S. W., & Potenza, M. N. (2009). Understanding "behavioral addictions" insights from research. In R. K. Ries, D. A. Fiellin, S. C. Miller, & R. Saitz (Eds.), *Principles of addiction medicine* (4th ed., pp. 45–61). Philadelphia, PA: Wolters Kluwer.

Young, E. B. (1995). The role of incest issues in relapse and recovery. In A. M. Washton (Ed.), *Psychotherapy and substance abuse: A practitioner's handbook* (pp. 451–469). New York, NY: Guilford Press.

Young, I. M. (1994). Punishment, treatment, empowerment: Three approaches to policy for pregnant addicts. *Feminist Studies, 94*, 33–48.

Young, K. S. (2011). CBT-IA: The first treatment model for Internet addiction. *Journal of Cognitive Psychotherapy, 25*, 304–312.

Young, M. E., de Armas Delorenzi, L., & Cunningham, L. (2011). Using meditation in addiction counseling. *Journal of Addictions & Offender Counseling, 32*, 58–71.

Young, T. J. (1988). Substance abuse among Native Americans. *Clinical Psychology Review, 8*, 125–138.

Yule, A. M., & Prince, J. B. (2012). Adolescent substance use disorders in the school setting. *Child and Adolescent Psychiatric Clinics of North America, 21*, 175–186.

Zahradnik, A., Otto, C., Crackau, B., Loehrmann, I., Bischof, G., John, U., & Rumpf, H. J. (2009). Randomized controlled trial of a brief intervention for problematic prescription drug use in non-treatment-seeking patients. *Addiction, 104*, 109–117.

Zaro, J. S., Barach, R., Nedelman, D. J., & Dreiblatt, I. S. (1996). *A guide for beginning psychotherapists.* New York, NY: Cambridge University Press.

Zaslav, P. (1993). The role of self-help groups in the treatment of the dual diagnosis patient. In J. Solomon, S. Zimberg, & E. Shollar (Eds.), *Dual diagnosis: Evaluation, treatment, training, and program development* (pp. 106–126). New York, NY: Plenum Press.

Zelvin, E. (1993). Treating the partners of substance abusers. In S. L. A. Straussner (Ed.), *Clinical work with substance-abusing clients* (pp. 196–213). New York, NY: Guilford Press.

Zgierska, A., Rabago, D., Chawla, N., Ushner, K., Koehler, R., & Marlatt, A. (2009). Mindfulness meditation for substance use disorders: A systematic review. *Substance Abuse, 30*, 266–294.

Zhu, T., Korber, B., Nahmias, A., Hooper, E., Sharp, P., & Ho, D. (1998). An African HIV-1 sequence from 1959 and implications for the origin of the epidemic. *Nature, 391*, 594–597.

Ziegler, P. P. (2005). Addiction and the treatment of pain. *Substance Use & Misuse, 40*, 1945–1954.

Zilberman, M. L. (2009). Substance abuse across the lifespan in women. In K. T. Brady, S. E. Back, & S. F. Greenfield (Eds.), *Women & addiction* (pp. 3–13). New York, NY: Guilford Press.

Zilberman, M. L., Tavares, H., Blume, S. B., & el-Guebaly, N. (2002). Towards best practices in the treatment of women with addictive disorders. *Addictive Disorders & Their Treatment, 1*, 39–46.

Zimberg, S. (1978). Psychosocial treatment of elderly alcoholics. In S. Zimberg, J. Wallace, & S. B. Blume (Eds.), *Practical approaches to alcoholism psychotherapy* (pp. 347–362). New York, NY: Plenum Press.

Zimberg, S. (1985). Principles of alcoholism psychotherapy. In S. Zimberg, J. Wallace, & S. B. Blume (Eds.), *Practical approaches to alcoholism psychotherapy* (pp. 3–21). New York, NY: Plenum Press.

Zimberg, S. (1993). Introduction and general concepts of dual diagnosis. In J. Solomon, S. Zimberg, & E. Shollar (Eds.), *Dual diagnosis: Evaluation, treatment, training, and program development* (pp. 3–21). New York, NY: Plenum Press.

Zimmerman, J., & Winek., J. L. (2013). *Group activities for families in recovery.* Los Angeles, CA: Sage.

Zolkoski, S. M. & Bullock, L. M. (2012). Resilience in children and youth: A review. *Children and Youth Services Review, 34*, 2295–2303.

Zuckerman, M. (2012). Psychological factors and addiction: Personality. In H. J. Shaffer, D. A. LaPlante, S. E. Nelson (Ed.), *APA addiction syndrome handbook: Vol. 1. Foundations, influences, and expressions of addiction* (pp. 175–194). Washington, DC: American Psychological Association.

Zur, O. (2007). Dual relationships. In O. Zur (Ed.), *Boundaries in psychotherapy: Ethical and clinical explorations* (pp. 21–46). Washington, DC: American Psychological Association.

Zweben, J. E. (1995, October). *Engaging dual disorder patients into treatment.* Paper presented at the National Dual Disorder Conference, Las Vegas, NV.

Zweben, J. E. (2009). Special issues in treatment: Women. In R. K. Ries, D. A. Fiellin, S. Miller, & R. Saitz (Eds.), *Principles of addiction medicine* (4th ed., pp. 465–477). Philadelphia, PA: Wolters Kluwer.

AUTHOR INDEX

SUBJECT INDEX

AA. *See* Alcoholics Anonymous
Abstinence:
  brief therapy motivation toward, 285
  co-occurring disorders and, 59, 60, 64, 67, 68, 69, 70, 72
  dialectical, 174–175
  drug court focus on, 180
  family therapy baseline of, 126
  harm reduction *vs.*, 91, 92–95, 131, 137, 155, 170, 171, 429
  medical/disease model of addiction on, 8, 92
  relapse as break in, prevention of (*see* Relapse prevention)
  self-help groups advocating, 70, 226–247, 393, 408–409 (*see also* Self-help groups)
  stages-of-change model on, 276–277
  withdrawal prior to (*see* Withdrawal)
Acculturation, 307, 328–329, 332, 334, 335, 336, 385
Addiction:
  assessment and diagnosis of (*see* Assessment and diagnosis)
  behavioral, 80–84, 87–88, 89, 90
  behavior-learning model of, 8, 428
  biopsychosocial model of, 9–10, 93, 401, 428–429
  chronic pain and, 291, 379–397
  co-occurring disorders with (*see* Co-occurring disorders)
  counseling for (*see* Addiction counseling and treatment)
  counselors' personal issues related to, 1, 18, 436–437
  cultural factors influencing (*see* Cultural factors)
  developmental factors influencing, 20, 202–203, 361
  disease model of, 3–4, 8–9, 399–401, 428–429
  enabling of (*see* Enabling behavior)
  environmental factors influencing, 7, 8, 59, 305–308
  gambling, 32, 76–77, 87, 88–90, 220
  genetic factors influencing, 9, 59
  harm reduction approach to, 91, 92–95, 131, 137, 155, 170, 171, 429
  HIV/AIDS co-occurring with, 92–93, 149–158, 184–185, 192–193, 327, 335
  homelessness co-occurring with, 59, 169–173, 194
  Internet/video game, 81–82
  interpersonal factors influencing (*see* Interpersonal factors)
  intimate partner violence co-occurring with, 158–169, 185–186, 189, 193, 217–218, 346
  intrapersonal factors influencing, 7–8
  medical model of, 8, 428–429
  models of, 3–4, 6–10, 93, 399–401, 428–429
  moral model of, 7, 399, 401, 428
  personality trait model of, 7–8
  prevalence of substance use and, 1–2, 91, 317, 322, 325–326, 331–332, 337, 341, 348, 355–356, 365, 380
  process of, 428–429
  psychodynamic model of, 7, 428
  research on, 3, 4 (*see also* Evidence-based practices)
  sexual, 82–83, 89, 90
  sexual issues associated with (*see* Sexual issues)

sociocultural model of, 8, 428
spiritual factors associated with (*see* Spiritual factors)
Addiction counseling and treatment:
  addiction research approach to, 3, 4
  adolescent community reinforcement approach to, 361, 362, 363
  assertiveness training as, 26
  assessment and diagnosis determining appropriate, 52–53 (*see also* Assessment and diagnosis)
  behavior therapy as, 25–26, 67, 291
  bibliotherapy as, 409
  brief therapy/interventions as, 43, 47, 98–99, 282, 284–290, 294, 296–297, 298, 299, 362–363
  case management as, 67, 156, 171, 361, 463
  case studies on (*see* Case studies)
  for chronic pain and addiction, 380–382, 386–387, 389–393, 397
  client resilience and, 267–269, 296, 300
  cognitive-behavioral therapy as, 16, 26–27, 67, 72, 73–74, 75, 77, 82, 176–177, 187, 190, 194, 202–208, 245, 287–288, 291–292, 361, 363, 389, 409, 434
  control theory/reality therapy as, 24–25
  coping skills training as, 67, 97–98, 127, 145, 203, 207–208, 210, 214, 269
  core treatment process, 91–137
  costs of and payment for, 2, 3, 4–6, 107, 284, 291
  counseling theories applied to, 13–30, 464
  counselors in (*see* Counselors)
  covert sensitization as, 77
  credentialing in (*see* Credentialing, certification, and licensing)
  crisis intervention as, 97–103, 132, 463
  cultural factors impacting, 214–215, 236, 242, 280, 289–290, 291–292, 301–378, 385, 407, 411, 415 (*see also* Culturally sensitive addiction counseling *for details*)
  dialectical behavior therapy as, 67, 72, 78, 173–175, 186–187, 189–190, 194, 291
  disease model of addiction influencing, 3–4, 8–9, 399–401, 428–429
  drug court as, 180–182, 187, 191–192, 194–195
  empty chair technique as, 24, 112, 123, 179, 209
  e-therapy as, 419
  evidence-based practices in, 290–292, 294–295, 297, 299, 363
  existential therapy as, 23–24
  family therapy as, 67, 123–130, 133–134, 137, 290, 322, 361, 362–363, 389
  Gestalt techniques of, 14, 23–24
  group therapy as, 67, 110–123, 132–133, 135–137, 165–166, 296, 322, 389, 411, 415
  guided imagery as, 209

535